The Correspondence of
Jonathan Swift

JONATHAN SWIFT

From the portrait by Jervas in the possession of Sir Harold Williams

The Correspondence of
Jonathan Swift

EDITED BY

HAROLD WILLIAMS

VOLUME I

1690–1713

OXFORD
AT THE CLARENDON PRESS

Oxford University Press, Amen House, London, E C.4

GLASGOW NEW YORK TORONTO MELBOURNE WELLINGTON
BOMBAY CALCUTTA MADRAS KARACHI LAHORE DACCA
CAPE TOWN SALISBURY NAIROBI IBADAN
KUALA LUMPUR HONG KONG

© *Oxford University Press 1963*

FIRST PUBLISHED 1963
REPRINTED, WITH CORRECTIONS, 1965

PRINTED IN GREAT BRITAIN

PREFACE

As the reader will find, on turning to the list provided in the Introduction, there are some sixteen collections of Swift's correspondence, in part or as a substantial whole, published between 1740 and 1935. The last complete edition, in six volumes, 1910–14, was the work of an outstanding Anglo-Irish scholar, Dr. F. Elrington Ball, who must always be held in the highest respect for the amount of information which he there made available for the student of Swift. I make no attempt to conceal my debt to him. The present edition is to some extent a reissue of Dr. Ball's. It differs mainly in the text, in which I have always printed from the autographs, wherever they are available, in libraries and in private hands both in this country and in the United States, and otherwise from early printed editions. Dr. Ball made no use of manuscripts in America, and only a limited use of those in private hands; he conventionalized the text of the letters whether of Swift or his correspondents and resigned the pointing to the printing-house. This edition follows the spelling and the punctuation of the originals as closely as possible. I have also been allowed to incorporate here both the text and the annotations of the Letters to Charles Ford, which were edited from the autographs in 1935 by David Nichol Smith. I have thus been able to bring together here a considerably larger number of letters than in any previous edition.

From the earliest item of the correspondence—the first published in this edition is Sir William Temple's recommendation of Swift to Southwell, 28 May 1690, written when Swift was about twenty-four years of age—until 20 October 1708, there survive forty-five letters in all covering approximately eighteen years. Thirty are by Swift and ten of these have survived in his autograph. Considering that at this time he was comparatively unknown, this may be accounted remarkable. The more important letters were those addressed to William King, Archbishop of Dublin.

In 1708 Swift began a practice of entering lists of correspondents (letters addressed to and received from) in small notebooks (Forster Collection Nos. 506, 507, 508, 509). Account Book 506 covers the period 1 November 1708–30 October 1709. Twenty-five letters of this correspondence have reached us, and of these eight only are Swift autographs. The total number of listed letters, to and from, in this period amounts to just over 220. Of this number nearly one-half are letters written by Swift. Thus for this single year a large proportion of the letters written by Swift are missing, and the missing letters include those written to persons of importance and interest: for example, to MD (Stella), Addison, and Sir Andrew Fountaine. Despite the fact that far more letters are listed than the surviving number it seems doubtful whether all the letters addressed or written during this period have been entered. Some are of questionable dates. Only fourteen letters are entered in Account Book No. 507. The list obviously makes no pretence at inclusiveness. Not one of the letters listed has come down to us unless possibly the letter from Archbishop King entered under 25 September 1710 may be that written in Dublin on the 16th and delayed in transit. The chief interest of the Account Books 508 and 509 are the letters to MD which constitute the *Journal to Stella*. MD's replies have disappeared.

In my Introduction I have listed the important libraries of England, Scotland, and Ireland, and the United States which I have consulted for textual sources of Swift's letters and the letters of his correspondents; and also of the private collections to which I am indebted. I wish here to make grateful acknowledgement to all those libraries and private owners who have generously allowed me to make use of the manuscripts in their possession.

I turn to others from whom I have sought guidance and information, and here I should like to name especially Professor D. Nichol Smith of Merton College, Oxford. Professor George Sherburn's edition of the Pope letters has proved invaluable. For advice and help I am also much indebted to Professor W. A. Jackson of Harvard University Library. Among those who have offered me private information are the late Dr. Francis Bourke of Dublin, Professor Irvin Ehrenpreis, Dr. Robert Halsband, Mr. John Hayward, and Dr. James Osborn. I am indebted to the staff of the Clarendon Press for their careful attention to a work beset with problems and difficulties while it was passing through the press.

HAROLD WILLIAMS

London, 1961

CONTENTS

APPENDIXES

Contents

LIST OF PLATES

VOLUME I

VOLUME II

VOLUME III

AUTOGRAPH SOURCES

FROM WHICH THE TEXT OF LETTERS
WHETHER WRITTEN BY SWIFT
OR HIS CORRESPONDENTS HAVE BEEN DRAWN

Institutions have furnished manuscripts of letters as follows:

The British Museum—Add. 4804-6, 39839.
The Public Record Office, London, State Papers.
The Victoria and Albert Museum—Forster Collection.
Royal College of Surgeons, London.
Trinity College, Dublin.
National Library of Ireland, Dublin.
King's Hospital, Dublin.
Public Library, Armagh.
National Library of Scotland, Edinburgh.
John Rylands Library, Manchester.
Harvard University Library, Cambridge, Mass.
Yale University Library, New Haven, Conn.
Pierpont Morgan Library, New York.
New York Public Library—Berg Collection.
Huntington Library, California.
Haverford College Library, Pennsylvania.
Wellesley College Library, Mass.
Historical Society of Pennsylvania.

Family Archives and private owners have furnished letters as follows:

Marquess of Bath, Longleat.
Duke of Marlborough, Blenheim.
Lord Bathurst, Cirencester Park.
Earl Stanhope, Chavering, Sevenoaks.
Lord Rothschild, Merton Hall, Cambridge
Major-General Sir Eustace Tickell, Wood End, Silvermere, Cobham, Surrey.
Colonel Stopford Sackville, Drayton House, Northants.
T. Cottrell-Dormer, Rousham.
A. Loftus Bryan.
Harold Williams.

Professor James Clifford, Columbia University, New York.

Carl H. Pforzheimer, New York.
Arthur A. Houghton, Jr., New York.
Dr. Dallas Pratt, New York.
Roger Barrett, Kenilworth, Illinois.

INTRODUCTION

I

UNLIKE Pope, who regarded his letters as an integral feature of his *Works*, Swift, despite the personal and political importance of his correspondence, exhibited no desire to see his letters in print.

By 1736-7 few letters passing between Pope and Swift had appeared in print. In 1736 Pope began to turn his energies continuously towards preparing an authentic edition of his letters, endeavouring to persuade Swift to return letters which he had addressed to him. It may be that an exaggerated view of Swift's ill health prompted him to active steps. Swift himself encouraged a belief that he had only nine years to live, that 'continual indisposition' was preparing him 'every season' for the grave. In April of this same year Pope professed alarm to Lord Orrery at the possibility of 'ill use' which Swift might make of his letters. The publication of a commendable edition of their united correspondence became a major preoccupation.

With Orrery working as his intermediary Pope received in July 1737 the letters which he had addressed to Swift. In the same month Orrery wrote to Swift 'your commands were obeyed long ago. Dr. King has his cargo, Mrs. Barber her conversation, and Mr. Pope his letters'. Three years later, about May–August 1740, Swift received 'a printed volume, without title-page, preface, or other introduction' containing a version of the correspondence between Pope, Gay, Bolingbroke, and himself. At the same time an unsigned letter was received from Pope stating that the volume was submitted for inspection and not to be published without his approval. To this volume, or collection of letters, Swift never gave his consent. The clandestine volume, which consisted of a collection of letters by Pope and Swift, was left at St. Patrick's Deanery by an unknown hand in May 1740. It was edited by Swift with names and notes plainly Irish in origin and handed to Faulkner, the Dublin bookseller and printer. In October Faulkner sent to Pope the first two sheets he had printed. In November Orrery sent to Pope, in nine packets, the broken-up clandestine volume from which Pope 'caused a copy to be taken' (Orrery to Pope, 17 Oct. 1740). In the middle of April Pope brought out his *Works in Prose* containing the letters under the pretence that they were printed from a Dublin edition. In June Faulkner published *Letters to and from Dr. J. Swift* in octavo and duodecimo. A complete history of the Swift–Pope letters in Dublin and London, and of Pope's double-dealing with Swift, under colour of unimpeachable friendship, would occupy much space and detailed study.

At an early stage, the booksellers and printers of the eighteenth century began to embody those letters of Swift's which they could collect in editions of the *Works*. As early as 1741 Faulkner, the Dublin printer, thus appeared in the field. In 1766 John Hawkesworth followed with volumes of letters collected as part of Swift's *Works* and published as part of an edition for the London trade. In 1767 came Deane Swift's *Letters written by the late Jonathan Swift D.D. . . . and Several of his Friends.* He found reason to describe Hawkesworth's edition as 'the vilest that ever was yet published' (*Lit. Illustr.* v. 376). In 1784 was published Thomas Sheridan's *Life of the Dean* and the *Works* in seventeen volumes. Although this edition gathered the *Works* into a better semblance of order Sheridan was far from displaying sound gifts as an editor. A real editorial advance was made by John Nichols's octavo edition of the *Works* in nineteen volumes, 1801. To his immense energy and industry all students of eighteenth-century literature, biography, and printing owe a large debt. In addition to other activities he busied himself with Swift for nearly fifty years. It was natural that Sir Walter Scott's edition of the *Works*, 1814, aggrieved him. He described it as 'somewhat similar' to his own and compiled by 'a neat shuffling of the cards'. In the advertisement of his first volume (*Memoirs of Swift*) Scott claimed that his edition contributed 'considerably upwards of a hundred original Letters, Essays, and Poems by Dean Swift which have not hitherto been printed with his works'. Among letters he admitted as a debt to the Rev. Edward Berwick the communication of letters in the Swift–Vanessa correspondence 'so long a desideratum in all editions of the author'. The last volume adds over thirty letters claimed as previously unpublished. Scott's editions of the *Works*, 1814 and 1824, make no pretence to patient research or the presentation of a faithfully accurate text.

In this connexion the elaborate annotation in 1872 of Pope's *Works*, by Elwin, viii. 366–524, may well be examined, and next, 1875, *Papers of a Critic* by Charles Wentworth Dilke. Later came Ball's Appendix, pp. 197–202, to the sixth volume of his edition of the *Swift Correspondence* which appeared in 1914. The note in

Teerink's volume, pp. 64–67, is useful. In *The Library*, Fourth Series, xix. 465–85, came 'The First Printing of the Letters of Pope and Swift' by Professor Maynard Mack; and in the same periodical, xxiv. 74–80, 1943, 'New Light on the First Printing of the Letters of Pope and Swift' by Professor Vinton A. Dearing. Lastly we come to the Introduction by Professor George Sherburn to his admirable and scholarly edition of Pope's *Correspondence*. The following table may be helpful:

Editions of Swift's Letters

1740 Letters Between Dr. Swift, Mr. Pope, &c. From the Year 1714 to 1736. Publish'd from a Copy Transmitted from Dublin. London: Printed for T. Cooper in the Year MDCCXLI.

> Sm. 8vo. This volume had no title-page. It was sent by Pope to Swift in May or June of 1740. See Teerink, *Bibliography*, No. 60. See also Professor Maynard Mack, *The Library*, xix. 465–85, and Professor V. A. Dearing, ibid. xxiv. 74–80.

1741 Letters to and from Dr. J. Swift, D.S.P.D. from the Year 1714 to 1738. To which are added, several notes and Translations not in the London Edition. Dublin: Printed by and for George Faulkner, MDCCXLI.

> 8vo. This is the first Dublin edition of the Pope–Swift letters. It was largely prepared before publication of the 1741 Knapton, Bathurst, and Dodsley edition.

1742 Under this date further volumes of the Works of Alexander Pope 'printed for T. Cooper' or Printed for R. Dodsley, and sold by T. Cooper appeared in London. Textually these are of no significance.

1745 Miscellanies. The Tenth Volume. By Dr. Swift, London. Printed for R. Dodsley in Pall-mall. M.DCC.XLV.

> Sm. 8vo. P. 57 Swift to Carteret, 3 July 1725; Swift to Mrs. Moore, 7 Dec. 1727; Pope to Sheridan, n.d.; Pope to Sheridan, 6 Sept.; Swift to Sheridan, thirty letters.

1746 Volume VIII of the Author's Works, Containing Directions to Servants. . . . Poems, Letters, and other Pieces . . . Dublin: Printed by and for George Faulkner. M.DCC.XLVI.

> 8vo. The Letters to and from Doctor Swift appear on pp. 356–451.

1765 The Works of Dr. Jonathan Swift, Dean of St. Patrick's, Dublin. Volume XVI. Collected and Revised By Deane

Swift Esq; . . . London: Printed by W. Johnston, in
Ludgate-Street. MDCCLXV.

Sm. 8vo. Letters to and from Several Persons. Pp. 145–221.
1710–1724.

1765 The Works of Dr. Jonathan Swift, Dean of St. Patrick's,
Dublin. Volume XVII. Collected and Revised by Deane
Swift Esq; . . . London; Printed for W. Johnston, in
Ludgate-Street, MDCCLXV.

Sm. 8vo: Letters to and from Several Persons. Pp. 1–109. 1724–1739.

1766 Letters, Written by Jonathan Swift, D.D. Dean of St.
Patrick's, Dublin, and his Friends. From the Year 1703
to 1740. Published from the Originals, with Notes Explanatory and historical, By John Hawkesworth, L.L.D.
MDCCLXVI.

Sm. 8vo. Vol. III contains an index.

1768 Letters Written by the Late Jonathan Swift, D.D. . . . and
Several of his Friends from the Year 1710 to 1742. Published
from the Originals; Collected and Revised By Deane Swift,
Esq. . . . MDCCLVIII, XXII, XXIII, XXIV.

1779 A Supplement to Dr. Swift's Works: . . . In Three Volumes.
Volume the First . . . London. Printed for John Nichols:
Sold by H. Payne, Pall Mall; And N. Conant, Fleet-Street.
MDCCLXXIX.

1801 The Works of the Rev. Jonathan Swift, D.D., Dean of St.
Patrick's, Dublin. . . . A New Edition, in Nineteen Volumes;
Corrected and Revised By John Nichols, F.S.A. Edinburgh
and Perth. . . London: 1801.

The Letters are contained in vols. XI–XIII. The *Journal to Stella*
appears in Volumes XIV and XV. Pp. 307–25 in the index which
appears in Vol. XIX presents a most useful reference guide to the
letters.

1814 The Works of Jonathan Swift, D.D. . . . Containing Addi-
tional Letters, Tracts, and Poems not hitherto Published:
With Notes and a Life of the Author, By Walter Scott, Esq.
. . . Edinburgh: 1814. 19 Vols.

In the Advertisement to his first volume (*Memoirs* of Swift), he
claimed, and with justification, to have contributed 'considerably
upwards of a hundred original Letters, Essays, and Poems by Dean
Swift, which have not hitherto been printed with his works'. The
Letters are contained in Vols. XVI–XIX.

1899 Unpublished Letters of Dean Swift. George Birkbeck Hill. London. 1899.

The Knightley-Chetwode–Swift Correspondence.

1910 The Correspondence of Jonathan Swift, D.D. Edited by
–14 F. Elrington Ball with an Introduction by The Very Rev. J. H. Bernard, D.D. Dean of St. Patrick's, London: G. Bell and Sons, Ltd. 6 Vols.

The content of these six volumes, running to over 1,300 letters, annotated with a knowledge and scholarship hitherto unattempted and indeed beyond the reach of any previous editor, placed this great work in a monumental position.

1921 Vanessa and her Correspondence with Jonathan Swift. The Letters edited for the First Time from the Originals. With an Introduction by A. Martin Freeman. Selwyn & Blount, London. 1921.

The manuscript is now in the British Museum, Add. 39839. The following inscription, in an eighteenth-century hand, appears on the first leaf: 'Original Letters of Dr. Jonathan Swift Dean of St. Patrick's, Dublin. to Mrs. Van Homrigh celebrated by him in his published Works under the name of Vanessa.

'With the foul copies of her Letters & Answers in her own hand Writing!'

1935 The Letters of Jonathan Swift to Charles Ford. Edited by David Nichol Smith . . . Oxford At the Clarendon Press. MCMXXXV.

The friendship of Swift and Charles Ford was to prove an unbroken circumstance of their lives; but only part of their correspondence had been published. Here for the first time all Swift's letters to Ford which have survived are printed from the autographs.

II

Swift's outstanding gift as a prose-stylist responds unfailingly whether he is occupied in direct narrative, in vivid account of present or past events, in the story of everyday affairs, in kindly observation, in humour, in ridicule, in irony, directed to a variety of correspondents, forty or fifty, counting those only with whom in course of time letters were frequently exchanged.

After his exile to Ireland by far the greatest number of his correspondents were London friends. Expectantly he awaited replies with news of the wider world from which he had been banished. Among the more notable of these friends were John

Barber, Arbuthnot, John Gay, Benjamin Motte, Pope, Prior, and Charles Ford—for the last-named, though Irish by birth, was to be accounted an English correspondent, for London had become definitely his home. To these, in another category, must be added the first and second Earls of Oxford, Bolingbroke, Lord Carteret, the Duke of Dorset, and the Earl of Orrery; and among women the Duchess of Ormonde, the Duchess of Queensberry, Lady Elizabeth Germain, Lady Masham, and Mrs. Howard, Later Countess of Suffolk.

Among Irish friends Swift could count but a few to whom he wrote with fair regularity. In earlier years a frequent interchange of letters passed with Dr. William King, Archbishop of Dublin. For King's letters we are dependent upon the Archbishop's secretarial copies in his official letter-books. These are preserved in the library of Trinity College, Dublin, not a few in a sadly injured state. At one time over sixty letters were preserved between Swift and Knightley Chetwode. These, buried in a chest under the floor of the family home, perished from damp. Fortunately transcripts had been made. The strict accuracy of these transcripts cannot, however, be accepted. More letters came and went from and to Sheridan, if all of these are to be accounted examples of correspondence. Among other Irish correspondents were Delany, Archdeacon Walls, John Worrall, Lord Castle-Durrow, and Robert Cope.

If we scan Swift's letters, to whomsoever written, to men and women in various stations of life, it is borne in upon us how naturally he adapts matter and phrasing to the station and character of those whom he addresses.

III

Where the editor has had the advantage of using autographs his aim has been to reproduce Swift's letters and those of his correspondents with exact care. This involves the preservation of variants in spelling, capitalization, and punctuation as between one correspondent and another; and, of course, between eighteenth-century and modern practice. Letter-writers differ in their habits and in the legibility of their hands. On the whole Swift is not difficult to read. He has certain peculiarities, habitually spelling 'onely' for 'only'; frequently concluding the third person singular in 'th'; of ending a sentence on a colon. Arbuthnot writes a shocking hand and points erratically. Bolingbroke might well be expected to show distinction in phrasing and pointing, but can hardly so claim. For Archbishop King's correspondence with Swift we are largely dependent on his letter-books, written in the hasty hand of a copyist or of the secretary to whom the letter was dictated. Many of these clerical transcripts are in a sadly injured state.

In general the editor has retained raised letters (M$^{rs.}$, L^d, &^{c}): 'y' for 'th' is normalized.

Bracketed words [ ] are such as do not appear in the original text but were either carelessly omitted by the writer of the letter or have been lost by injury to the paper.

Transcripts tend to exhibit carelessness. For example, Vanessa preserved copies of her letters to Swift in a hasty and scarcely legible scribble.

When no autographs or transcripts have been available the editor has had to rely on texts printed in printed books or periodicals and has reproduced them accordingly.

The letter-content of each volume appears in a tabulated list of six columns, showing the names of the correspondents, the date and place of writing, the source of the letter, original manuscript, transcript, or printed text, and the paged position in the volume.

A customary editorial habit of numbering letters from first to last has not been followed. The important reference to a letter is the date, not a numeral.

The source of each text is indicated at the left head of each letter. It has not been thought necessary to state the folio number of a letter where the source is a member of a direct sequence in a collection, as, for example, the volumes in the British Museum, Add. MSS. 4804–6. The indication 4804, 4805, and 4806 has been regarded as sufficient.

Doubtful or conjectural dates have been placed, with a question mark, between square brackets.

LIST OF LETTERS

VOLUME I

List of Letters

Correspondents	Date	Place	Original source	Printed source or transcript	Page
S. to Archbishop King	29 Mar. 1712	London		Faulkner 1762	292
S. to Archbishop King	20 May 1712	,,		Faulkner 1762	295
Archbishop King to S.	29 May 1712	Castlelaugh		T.C.D.Letter-Book	297
S. to Archbishop King	26 June 1712	Kensington		Faulkner 1762	299
Archbishop King to S.	23 July 1712	Dublin		T.C.D.Letter-Book	302
Archbishop King to S.	29 July 1712	,,		T.C.D.Letter-Book	302
S. to Esther Vanhomrigh	1 Aug. 1712	Windsor	B.M. Add. 39839		304
S. to John Hill	12 Aug. 1712	,,		Deane Swift 1765	305
S. to Esther Vanhomrigh	15 Aug. 1712	,,	B.M. Add. 39839		308
Esther Vanhomrigh to S.	1 Sept. 1712	London	B.M. Add. 39839		309
Esther Vanhomrigh to S.	2 Sept. 1712	,,	B.M. Add. 39839		310
S. to Esther Vanhomrigh	3 Sept. 1712	Windsor	B.M. Add. 39839		311
Countess of Orkney and Miss Ramsay to S.	15 Sept. 1712	Cliefden	B.M. Add. 4806		312
Countess of Orkney to S.	22 Sept. 1712	Windsor	B.M. Add. 4806		313
S. to Esther Vanhomrigh	28 Sept. 1712	,,	B.M. Add. 39839		313
S. to Archbishop King	21 Oct. 1712	London		Faulkner 1762	314
Duchess of Ormonde to S.	3 Nov. 1712	,,	B.M. Add. 4804		316
Archbishop King to S.	4 Nov. 1712	Dublin		T.C.D.Letter-Book	317
S. to Miss Alice Hill	Nov. 1712	London		Deane Swift 1765	318
Countess of Orkney to S.	21 Nov. 1712	,,	B.M. Add. 4804		319
S. to Countess of Orkney	21 Nov. 1712	,,		Deane Swift 1765	320
Countess of Orkney to S.	22 Nov. 1712	,,	B.M. Add. 4804		322
S. to E. of Dartmouth	13 Dec. 1712	,,		H.M.C. Report 11	322
Wm. Harrison to S.	16 Dec. 1712	Utrecht	B.M. Add. 4804		323
S. to Duchess of Ormonde	20 Dec. 1712	London		Deane Swift 1765	326
S. to Archbishop King	8 (or 3) Jan. 1713	,,		Faulkner 1762	327
S. to Duke of Argyle	20 Jan. 1713	,,		Deane Swift 1765	330
Archbishop King to S.	22 Jan. 1713	Dublin		T.C.D.Letter-Book	331
Robert Hunter to S.	Recd. 1 Mar. 1713	New York	B.M. Add. 4804		334

Correspondents	Date	Place	Original source	Printed source or transcript	Page
S. to Sir Andrew Fountaine	6 Mar. 1713	London	Morgan Library		336
S. to Archbishop King	28 Mar. 1713	,,		Faulkner 1762	337
Matthew Prior to S.	8 Apr. [o.s. 28 Mar.] 1713	Paris	B.M. Add. 4804		340
Earl Poulett to S.	29 Mar. 1713	London	B.M. Add. 4806		342
Archbishop King to S.	14 Apr. 1713	Dublin		T.C.D.Letter-Book	342
Dean Atterbury to S.	21 Apr. 1713	Chelsea	B.M. Add. 4804		344
S. to Archbishop King	30 Apr. 1713	London		Faulkner 1762	344
S. to Rev. William Diaper	30 Apr. 1713	,,		Forster	345
Provost Pratt and S. to Edward Southwell	5 May 1713	,,		Rothschild	346
S. to Joseph Addison	13 May 1713	,,		Deane Swift 1765	347
S. on Isaiah Parvisol	16 May 1713	,,	Journal to Stella		348
Archbishop King to S.	16 May 1713	Chester		T.C.D.Letter-Book	349
Richard Steele to S.	19 May 1713	London		Deane Swift 1765	351
Sir Thomas Hanmer to S.	19 May 1713	,,	B.M. Add. 4804		351
S. to Lord Harcourt	23 May 1713	,,		Deane Swift 1765	352
S. to Archbishop King	23 May 1713	,,		Faulkner 1762	353
S. to Richard Steele	23 May 1713	,,		Deane Swift 1765	354
Archbishop King to S.	25 May 1713	Bath		T.C.D.Letter-Book	356
Richard Steele to S.	26 May 1713	Bloomsbury		Deane Swift 1765	358
S. to Richard Steele	27 May 1713	London		Deane Swift 1765	359
S. to Esther Vanhomrigh	31 May 1713	Kensington	B.M. Add. 39839		360
Erasmus Lewis to S.	2 June 1713	Whitehall	B.M. Add. 4804		361
Rev. John Sharpe to S.	4 June 1713	London	B.M. Add. 4804		362
Robert Hunter to S. *Enclosure*	14 Mar. 1713	New York	B.M. Add. 4804		363
Esther Vanhomrigh to S.	6 June 1713	London	B.M. Add. 39839		364
S. to Mrs. Vanhomrigh	6 June 1713	Chester	B.M. Add. 39839		365
Fragment: S. to Charles Ford	7 June 1713	,,		Christie Catalogue	367
Esther Vanhomrigh to S.	23 June 1713	London	B.M. Add. 39839		367
Esther Vanhomrigh to S.	27(?) June 1713	,,	B.M. Add. 39839		369
S. to Joshua Dawson	29 June 1713	Trim	P.R.O. Dublin		370

List of Letters

Correspondents	Date	Place	Original source	Printed source or transcript	Page
S. to Archdeacon Walls	6 Mar. 1714	London	Rothschild		15
S. to Archdeacon Walls	27 Mar. 1714	,,	Rothschild		16
Lady Betty Butler to S.	19 Apr. 1714	London (?)	P.R.O. State Papers		17
Duchess of Ormonde to S.	24 Apr. 1714	Kensington or Richmond	B.M. Add. 4804		17
Rev. John Geree to S.	24 Apr. 1714	Letcombe Bassett	P.R.O. State Papers		18
S. to E. of Peterborough	18 May 1714	London		Deane Swift 1765	20
Chiverton Charlton to S.	22 May 1714	Richmond (?)	B.M. Add. 4804		23
S. to Esther Vanhomrigh	8 June 1714	Letcombe Bassett	B.M. Add. 49839		25
John Gay to S.	8 June 1714	London	B.M. Add. 4804		27
John Barber to S.	8 June 1714	,,	B.M. Add. 4804		29
S. to Archdeacon Walls	11 June 1714	Letcombe Bassett	Rothschild		30
S. to Charles Ford	12 June 1714	Letcombe Bassett	Rothschild		32
S. to John Gay	12 June 1714	Letcombe Bassett	Royal College of Surgeons		33
John Arbuthnot to S.	12 June 1714	London	B.M. Add. 4804		34
S. to John Arbuthnot	16 June 1714	Letcombe Bassett	Royal College of Surgeons		35
S. to Charles Ford	16 June 1714	Letcombe Bassett	Rothschild		37
Pope to S.	18 June 1714	London		Faulkner 1741	37
Thomas Harley to S.	19 June 1714	,,	B.M. Add. 4804		39
William Thomas to S.	22 June 1714	,,	B.M. Add. 4804		40
John Arbuthnot to S.	26 June 1714	Kensington	B.M. Add. 4804		41
S. to Charles Ford	1 July 1714	Letcombe Bassett	Rothschild		43
S. to E. of Oxford	3 July 1714	Letcombe Bassett	B.M. Portland MSS.		44
S. to John Arbuthnot	3 July 1714	Letcombe Bassett	Forster		46
S. to Archdeacon Walls	3 July 1714	Letcombe Bassett	Rothschild		48
Charles Ford to S.	6 July 1714	London	Rothschild		50
William Thomas to S.	6 July 1714	,,	B.M. Add. 4804		52
Erasmus Lewis to S.	6 July 1714	Whitehall	B.M. Add. 4804		53

Correspondents	Date	Place	Original source	Printed source or transcript	Page
John Barber to S.	6 July 1714	London	B.M. Add. 4804		55
S. to Esther Vanhomrigh	8 July 1714	Letcombe Bassett	B.M. Add. 39839		56
John Arbuthnot to S.	10 July 1714	Kensington	B.M. Add. 4804		57
Charles Ford to S.	10 July 1714	London	B.M. Add. 4804		58
Enclosure: John Barber to S. Bridges	[6 July]	[Lambeth Hill]	B.M. Add. 4804		60
S. to Charles Ford	11 July 1714	Letcombe Bassett	Rothschild		60
Viscount Bolingbroke to S.	13 July 1714	London	B.M. Add. 4804		61
S. to John Arbuthnot	13 July 1714	Letcombe Bassett	Morgan Library		62
Charles Ford to S.	15 July 1714	London		Deane Swift 1768	64
Charles Ford to S.	17 July 1714	,,		Deane Swift 1768	65
Erasmus Lewis to S.	17 July 1714	Whitehall	B.M. Add. 4804		67
Lord Harley to S.	17 July 1714	London (?)	B.M. Add. 4804		68
John Arbuthnot to S.	17 July 1714	London	B.M. Add. 4804		69
S. to Duke of Ormonde	17 July 1714	Letcombe Bassett		Deane Swift 1765	70
S. to Charles Ford	18 July 1714	Letcombe Bassett	Rothschild		71
Charles Ford to S.	20 July 1714	London	B.M. Add. 4804		73
S. to John Grigsby	20 July 1714	Letcombe Bassett		Forster copy	74
S. to John Arbuthnot	22 July 1714	Oxford	Royal College of Surgeons		75
Duke of Ormonde to S.	22 July 1714	Richmond?	B.M. Add. 4804		76
Erasmus Lewis to S.	22 July 1714	Whitehall	B.M. Add. 4804		76
Charles Ford to S.	22 July 1714	London	B.M. Add. 4804		77
Charles Ford to S.	24 July 1714	,,	B.M. Add. 4804		78
William Thomas to S.	24 July 1714	,,	Williams		79
Erasmus Lewis to S.	24 July 1714	Whitehall	B.M. Add. 4804		80
John Arbuthnot to S.	24 July 1714	London	B.M. Add. 4804		81
S. to John Arbuthnot	25 July 1714	Letcombe Bassett	Royal College of Surgeons		82
S. to Charles Ford	25 July 1714	Letcombe Bassett	Rothschild		83
S. to E. of Oxford	25 July 1714	Letcombe Bassett		Deane Swift 1765	84

Correspondents	Date	Place	Original source	Printed source or transcript	Page
S. to Bishop Atterbury	18 Apr. 1716	Dublin		Nichols 1801	197
Viscountess Bolingbroke to S.	5 May 1716	London		Deane Swift 1768	199
S. to Archdeacon Walls	6 May 1716	Trim	Rothschild		201
S. to Archdeacon Walls	15 May 1716	Martry	Rothschild		202
S. to Archdeacon Walls	6 June 1716	Gaulstown	Rothschild		203
S. to Archdeacon Walls	14 June 1716	,,	Rothschild		204
S. to Archbishop King	17 June 1716	,,		Nichols 1801	205
S. to Archdeacon Walls	18 June 1716	,,	Rothschild		207
Archbishop King to S.	20 June 1716	Dublin	Library, Armagh		210
Pope to S.	20 June 1716	London (?)		Faulkner 1741	210
Viscountess Bolingbroke to S.	4 Aug. 1716	London	B.M. Add. 4805		212
S. to Pope	30 Aug. 1716	Dublin		Faulkner 1741	213
Duchess of Ormonde to S.	14 Sept. 1716	Richmond (?)	B.M. Add. 4805		216
S. to Archdeacon Walls	4 Oct. 1716	Trim	Rothschild		217
Viscount Bolingbroke to S.	23 Oct. [o.s. 12] 1716	Paris	B.M. Add. 4805		218
Charles Ford to S.	23 Oct. [o.s. 12] 1716	,,	B.M. Add. 4805		220
S. to Archbishop King	13 Nov. 1716	Dublin		Faulkner 1762	221
Archbishop King to S.	22 Nov. 1716	London	Rothschild		223
S. to Archdeacon Walls	6 Dec. 1716	Trim	Rothschild		228
S. to Archdeacon Walls	13 Dec. 1716	,,	Rothschild		229
S. to Archdeacon Walls	16 Dec. 1716	,,	Rothschild		231
S. to Archdeacon Walls	17 Dec. 1716	,,	Rothschild		232
S. to Isaiah Parvisol	18 Dec. 1716	,,	Rothschild		233
S. to Archdeacon Walls	19 Dec. 1716	,,	Rothschild		233
S. to Archbishop King	22 Dec. 1716	,,	Library, Armagh		235
S. to Esther Vanhomrigh	(?) Dec. 1716	,,	B.M. Add. 39839		239
S. to Archdeacon Walls	23 Dec. 1716	,,	Rothschild		240
S. to Archdeacon Walls	27 Dec. 1716	,,	Rothschild		241
S. to Archdeacon Walls	30 Dec. 1716	,,	Rothschild		242
S. to Archdeacon Walls	3 Jan. 1717	Trim	Rothschild		243

Correspondents	Date	Place	Original source	Printed source or transcript	Page
S. to Archdeacon Walls	(?) Jan. 1717	—	Rothschild		244
S. to Archdeacon Walls	(?) Jan. 1717	—	Rothschild		244
Erasmus Lewis to S.	12 Jan. 1717	London	B.M. Add. 4805		245
Archbishop King to S.	12 Jan. 1717	,,		T.C.D.Letter-Book	247
S. to Archdeacon Walls	13 Jan. 1717	Trim	Rothschild		248
S. to Archdeacon Walls	24 Jan. 1717	,,	Rothschild		250
S. to Archdeacon Walls	27 Jan. 1717	,,	Rothschild		251
S. to Archbishop Walls	28 Jan. 1717	,,	Rothschild		252
S. to Archdeacon Walls	31 Jan. 1717	,,	Rothschild		252
S. to Archdeacon Walls	3 Feb. 1717	,,	Rothschild		253
S. to Archbishop King	2 Mar. 1717	Dublin		Faulkner 1762	255
Archbishop King to S.	2 Mar. 1717	London		T.C.D.Letter-Book	257
S. to Archbishop King	9 Mar. 1717	Dublin		Faulkner 1762	258
Archbishop King to S.	12 Mar. 1717	London		T.C.D. Letter-Book	260
Archbishop King to S.	21 Mar. 1717	,,		T.C.D.Letter-Book	261
S. to Archdeacon Walls	28 Mar. 1717	Trim	Rothschild		263
S. to Archdeacon Walls	30 Mar. 1717	,,	Rothschild		264
S. to Archbishop King	1 May 1717	Magheralin		Faulkner 1762	265
Archbishop King to S.	13 May 1717	Bath		T.C.D.Letter-Book	267
S. to Archdeacon Walls	19 May 1717	Magheralin	Rothschild		268
S. to Archdeacon Walls	23 May 1717	Trim	Rothschild		269
Erasmus Lewis to S.	15 June 1717	London	B.M. Add. 4805		270
Erasmus Lewis to S.	18 June 1717	,,	B.M. Add. 4805		272
Erasmus Lewis to S.	2 July 1717	,,	B.M. Add. 4805		273
S. to Robert Cope	9 July 1717	Dublin		Nichols 1779	274
S. to E. of Oxford	9 July 1717	,,	Longleat xiii		276
S. to Joseph Addison	9 July 1717	,,	Berg Collection, New York Public Library		276

Correspondents	Date	Place	Original source	Printed source or transcript	Page
Matthew Prior to S.	5 May 1719	London	B.M. Add. 4805		323
S. to Esther Vanhomrigh	12 May 1719	Trim	B.M. Add. 39839		324
S. to Bishop Evans	22 May 1719	Gaulstown		Nichols 1801	326
Matthew Prior to S.	8 Dec. 1719	Westminster	B.M. Add. 4805		328
S. to Charles Ford	8 Dec. 1719	Dublin	Morgan Library		329
S. to Viscount Bolingbroke	19 Dec. 1719	,,		Deane Swift 1765	331
Ether Vanhomrigh to S.	(?) 1720	(?) Dublin	B.M. Add. 39839		334
S. to Esther Vanhomrigh	(?) 1720	—	B.M. Add. 39839		335
S. to Matthew Prior	26 (?) Jan. 1720	Dublin	Longleat vii		336
S. to Edward Harley	9 Feb. 1720	,,	Brotherton Collection, Univ. of Leeds		338
S. to E. of Oxford	16 Feb. 1720	,,	B.M. Portland MSS.		340
S. to Matthew Prior	24 Mar. 1720	,,	Longleat vii		341
S. to Charles Ford	4 Apr. 1720	,,	Rothschild		341
Duchess of Ormonde to S.	18 Apr. 1720	—	B.M. Add. 4805		344
Matthew Prior to S.	4 May 1720	Westminster	B.M. Add. 4805		345
S. to Robert Cope	26 May 1720	Dublin		Nichols 1779	347
S. to Esther Vanhomrigh	(?) 13 or 20 July 1720	(?) Dublin	B.M. Add. 39839		349
Esther Vanhomrigh to S.	27 or 28 July 1720	Celbridge	B.M. Add. 39839		352
S. to Esther Vanhomrigh	4 Aug. 1720	(?) Dublin	B.M. Add. 39839		352
Esther Vanhomrigh to S.	(?) 8 Aug. 1720	Celbridge	B.M. Add. 39839		354
S. to Esther Vanhomrigh	12 Aug. 1720	(?) Dublin	B.M. Add. 39839		355
Esther Vanhomrigh to S.	(?) 14 Aug. 1720	Celbridge	B.M. Add. 39839		357
S. to Sir Thomas Hanmer	1 Oct. 1720	Dublin	Rothschild		357
S. to Esther Vanhomrigh	15 Oct. 1720	,,	B.M. Add. 39839		359
Sir Thomas Hanmer to S.	22 Oct. 1720	Mildenhall	B.M. Add. 4805		361
Esther Vanhomrigh to S.	(?) Nov. 1720	Celbridge	B.M. Add. 39839		362
Esther Vanhomrigh to S.	(?) Nov. 1720	,,	B.M. Add. 39839		362
Esther Vanhomrigh to S.	(?) Dec. 1720	,,	B.M. Add. 39839		363
S. to Charles Ford	15 Dec. 1720	Dublin	Rothschild		364

Correspondents	Date	Place	Original source	Printed source or transcript	Page
S. to Viscount Molesworth	(?) Dec. 1720	Dublin		H.M.C. Various Collections	365
S. to Pope	10 Jan. 1721	,,		Faulkner 1741	365
Sir Constantine Phipps to S.	14 Jan. 1721	London	B.M. Add. 4805		375
S. to Dean Mossom	14 Feb. 1721	Dublin	Hist. Society of Pennsylvania		376
S. to Esther Vanhomrigh	(?) 27 Feb. 1721	,,	B.M. Add. 39839		377
Matthew Prior to S.	28 Feb. 1721	Westminster	B.M. Add. 4805		378
S. to Charles Ford	15 Apr. 1721	Dublin	Rothschild		379
Matthew Prior to S.	25 Apr. 1721	Westminster		Hawkesworth 1766	382
S. to Knightley Chetwode	29 Apr. 1721	Dublin		Forster copy	384
S. to Stella	30 Apr. 1721	,,		Deane Swift 1768	385
S. to Knightley Chetwode	9 May 1721	,,		Forster copy	386
S. to Rev. Thomas Wallis	13 May 1721	,,		Duncombe	387
S. to Esther Vanhomrigh	1 June 1721	,,	B.M. Add. 39839		388
S. to Bishop Evans	5 June 1721	,,		Deane Swift 1765	388
S. to Knightley Chetwode	10 June 1721	,,		Forster copy	390
S. to Charles Ford	19 June 1721	,,	Rothschild		391
S. to Esther Vanhomrigh	5 July 1721	Gaulstown	B.M. Add. 39839		392
Esther Vanhomrigh to S.	July 1721	Celbridge	B.M. Add. 39839		393
Viscount Bolingbroke to S.	28 [o.s. 17] July 1721	—	B.M. Add. 4805		394
Duchess of Ormonde to S.	1 Sept. 1721	—	B.M. Add. 4805		400
S. to Knightley Chetwode	14 Sept. 1721	Gaulstown		Forster copy	401
S. to Rev. John Worrall	14 Sept. 1721	,,		Hawkesworth 1766	402
S. to Archbishop King	28 Sept. 1721	,,		Faulkner 1762	404
S. to Charles Ford	30 Sept. 1721	,,	Rothschild		407
S. to Rev. Daniel Jackson	6 Oct. 1721	Dublin		Nichols 1801	407
S. to Rev. Thomas Wallis	3 Nov. 1721	,,		Duncombe	409
S. to Knightley Chetwode	11 Nov. 1721	,,		Forster copy	410
S. to Knightley Chetwode	5 Dec. 1721	,,		Forster copy	410
Viscount Bolingbroke to S.	1 Jan. 1722 [o.s. 21 Dec. 1721]	Marcilly	B.M. Add. 4805		412
Adrian Drift to S.	25 Jan. 1722	Westminster	Portland MSS.		416

List of Letters

Correspondents	Date	Place	Original source	Printed source or transcript	Page
S. to Knightley Chetwode	30 Jan. 1722	Dublin		Forster copy	417
S. to Adrian Drift	3 Feb. 1722	,,	Portland MSS.		419
Adrian Drift to S.	15 Feb. 1722	London	Portland MSS.		420
S. to Knightley Chetwode	13 Mar. 1722	Dublin		Forster copy	421
S. to Rev. Daniel Jackson	26 [28?] Mar. 1722	,,	Arthur A. Houghton Jr.		423
Rev. Andrew Snape to S.	23 Apr. 1722	Windsor	B.M. Add. 4805		425
S. to Esther Vanhomrigh	1 June 1722	Clogher	B.M. Add. 39839		426
Esther Vanhomrigh to S.	June 1722	(?) Celbridge	B.M. Add. 39839		428
S. to Esther Vanhomrigh	13 July 1722	Loughgall	B.M. Add. 39839		429
S. to Charles Ford	22 July 1722	,,	Rothschild		430
S. to Esther Vanhomrigh	7 Aug. 1722	,,	B.M. Add. 39839		432
S. to Robert Cope	9 Oct. 1722	Dublin		Nichols 1779	434
S. to E. of Oxford	11 Oct. 1722	,,	B.M. Portland MSS. List I		437
John Gay to S.	22 Dec. 1722	London	B.M. Add. 4805		439
S. to Rev. Thomas Sheridan	22 Dec. 1722	Dublin		Dodsley *Miscellanies* 1745	440
S. to John Gay	8 Jan. 1723	,,		Longleat xiii, ff. 92–93	441
S. to the Duke of Grafton	24 Jan. 1723	,,		Hawkesworth 1766	444
John Gay to S.	3 Feb. 1723	London	B.M. Add. 4805		445
S. to Knightley Chetwode	12 Feb. 1723	Dublin		Forster copy	448
S. to Rev. Thomas Wallis	12 Feb. 1723	,,		Duncombe	449
S. to Archbishop King	22 Feb. 1723	,,		Faulkner 1762	450
S. to Knightley Chetwode	25 Feb. 1723	,,		Forster copy	451
Knightley Chetwode to S.	26 Feb. 1723	,,		Forster copy	451
S. to Robert Cope	11 May 1723	,,		Nichols 1779	452
S. to Knightley Chetwode	May 1723	,,		Forster copy	455
S. to Robert Cope	1 June 1723	,,		Nichols 1779	455
S. to Knightley Chetwode	2 June 1723	,,		Forster copy	457
Pope to Swift	Aug. 1723	—		Transcript at Cirencester	457
Viscount Bolingbroke to S.	Aug. 1723	La Source		Curll 1736	460

Correspondents	Date	Place	Original source	Printed source or transcript	Page
S. to Rev. Thomas Sheridan	3 Aug. 1723	Clonfert		Dodsley *Miscellanies* 1745	463
S. to Pope	20 Sept. 1723	Dublin		Longleat xiii	464
S. to Rev. Thomas Sheridan	12 Oct. 1723	Dublin		Nichols 1779	467
S. to E. of Oxford	6 Nov. 1723	Dublin		Portland MSS.	467
John Arbuthnot to S.	7 Nov. 1723	London	B.M. Add. 4805		469
Duchess of Ormonde to S.	9 Dec. 1723	—	B.M. Add. 4805		471
Viscount Bolingbroke to S.	25 [o.s. 14] Dec. 1723	—	B.M. Add. 4805		472
S. to Knightley Chetwode	Dec. 1723	Dublin		Forster copy	474
Archbishop King to S.	19 Dec. 1723	Dublin		No copy in T.C.D. Letter-Book	475

VOLUME III

Correspondents	Date	Place	Original source	Printed source or transcript	Page
S. to Knightley Chetwode	9 Jan. 1724	Dublin		Forster copy	1
S. to Knightley Chetwode	9 Jan. 1724	,,		Forster copy	1
S. to Knightley Chetwode	19 Jan. 1724	,,		Forster copy	2
S. to Charles Ford	19 Jan. 1724	,,	Rothschild		2
S. to Charles Ford	13 Feb. 1724	,,	Rothschild		5
Lady Masham to S.	Feb. 1724	Langley	B.M. Add. 4805		7
S. to Bishop Stearne	28 Feb. 1724	Dublin	Forster 543		8
S. to Charles Ford	2 Apr. 1724	,,	Rothschild		9
S. to Lord Carteret	28 Apr. 1724	,,		Deane Swift 1765	10
S. to Lord Carteret	9 June 1724	,,		Deane Swift 1765	13
S. to Charles Ford	16 June 1724	,,	Rothschild		14
Lord Carteret to S.	20 June 1724	London	B.M. Add. 4805		16
S. to Lord Carteret	9 July 1724	Dublin		Deane Swift 1765	17
S. to E. Oxford	9 July 1724	,,	Portland MSS.		18
S. to Thomas Tickell	11 July 1724	,,		Tickell Letter-Book No. 2	19
S. to Archbishop King	14 July 1724	,,		Faulkner 1762	20
S. to Knightley Chetwode	14 July 1724	,,		Forster copy	21
Archbishop King to S.	20 July 1724	Carlow		Ball's transcript	22
S. to Thomas Tickell	3 Aug. 1724	Dublin		Tickell Letter-Book No. 2	24
Lord Carteret to S.	4 Aug. 1724	London	B.M. Add. 4805		25
Viscount Bolingbroke to S.	12 [o.s. 1] Sept. 1724	—	B.M. Add. 4805		26

List of Letters

Correspondents	Date	Place	Original source	Printed source or transcript	Page
S. to Lord Carteret	4 Sept. 1724	Dublin	Rothschild		30
S. to Thomas Tickell	4 Sept. 1724	,,	Tickell Papers		33
George Rochfort to S.	9 Sept. 1724	,,		Deane Swift 1768	33
S. to Knightley Chetwode	Sept. 1724	,,		Forster copy	34
S. to Knightley Chetwode	Oct. 1724	,,		Forster copy	35
S. to Thomas Tickell	24 Oct. 1724	,,	Tickell Papers		37
E. of Oxford to S.	2 Nov. 1724	Wimpole	Portland MSS.		38
S. to E. of Oxford	27 Nov. 1724	Dublin	Longleat xiii		39
S. to Charles Ford	27 Nov. 1724	,,	Rothschild		41
S. to Knightley Chetwode	19 Dec. 1724	,,		Forster copy	43
S. to Charles Ford	29 Dec. 1724	,,	Rothschild		45
S. to Charles Ford	31 Dec. 1724	,,	Rothschild		45
S. to Thomas Staunton	5 Jan. 1725	,,	B.M. Add. 38671		47
S. to Knightley Chetwode	18 Jan. 1725	,,		Forster copy	48
S. to Knightley Chetwode	30 Jan. 1725	,,		Forster copy	49
S. to Knightley Chetwode	20 Feb. 1725	,,		Forster copy	50
S. to Charles Ford	1 Mar. 1725	,,	Rothschild		52
S. to Charles Ford	11 Mar. 1725	,,	Rothschild		52
S. to Mrs. Pratt	18 Mar. 1725	,,	Harvard College Library		53
S. to James Stopford	(?) Apr. 1725	,,		Forster copy	56
S. to Lord Carteret	17 Apr. 1725	,,	Tickell Papers		57
S. to Knightley Chetwode	(?) April 1725	,,		Forster copy	58
S. to Rev. Stafford Lightburne	22 Apr. 1725	Quilca		*Kilkenny Archaeological Society Journal*	59
S. to Knightley Chetwode	27 May 1725	,,		Forster copy	60
S. to Rev. James Stopford	19 June 1725	,,		Forster copy	62
S. to Rev. Thomas Sheridan	25 June 1725	,,		Dodsley *Miscellanies* 1745	63
S. to — Sheridan	26 June 1725	,,	Library, Armagh		65
S. to Rev. Thomas Sheridan	28 June 1725	,,		Dodsley *Miscellanies* 1745	66
S. to Rev. Thomas Sheridan	29 June 1725	,,	National Library, Dublin		68
S. to Lord Carteret	3 July 1725	,,		Dodsley *Miscellanies* 1745	70
S. to Archdeacon Walls	9 July 1725	,,	Rothschild		72

Correspondents	Date	Place	Original source	Printed source or transcript	Page
S. to Rev. John Worrall	9 July 1725	Quilca		Hawkesworth 1766	74
S. to Knightley Chetwode	19 July 1725	,,		Forster copy	75
S. to Thomas Tickell	19 July 1725	,,		Tickell Letter-Book No. 2	76
S. to Pope	19 July 1725	,,		Longleat xiii (Harleian transcript)	78
S. to — Sheridan	22 July 1725	,,	Library, Armagh		79
S. to Rev. Anthony Raymond	23 July 1725	,,		*Dublin Magazine* 1762	80
Viscount Bolingbroke to S.	24 July 1725	London	B.M. Add. 4805		81
E. of Oxford to S.	26 July 1725	London		Deane Swift 1768	83
S. to E. of Oxford	14 Aug. 1725	Quilca		Forster copy	84
S. to Charles Ford	14 Aug. 1725	,,	Rothschild		86
S. to Charles Ford	16 Aug. 1725	,,	Rothschild		88
S. to Charles Ford	27 Aug. 1725	,,	Rothschild		90
S. to Rev. John Worrall	27 Aug. 1725	,,		Hawkesworth 1766	90
E. of Oxford to S.	30 Aug. 1725	London		Deane Swift 1768	92
S. to Rev. John Worrall	31 Aug. 1725	Quilca		Hawkesworth 1766	92
S. to Rev. Thomas Sheridan	11 Sept. 1725	,,		Dodsley *Miscellanies* 1745	93
Pope to S.	14 Sept. 1725	(?)Twickenham		Faulkner 1741	95
S. to Thomas Tickell	18 Sept. 1725	Quilca		Tickell Letter-Book No. 2.	97
S. to Rev. Thomas Sheridan	19 Sept. 1725	,,		Dodsley *Miscellanies* 1745	99
S. to Rev. Thomas Sheridan	25 Sept. 1725	,,		Dodsley *Miscellanies* 1745	100
S. to Pope	29 Sept. 1725	,,		Longleat xiii (Harleian transcript)	102
S. to E. of Oxford	1 Oct. 1725	? Quilca		Forster copy	105
Pope to S.	15 Oct. 1725	Twickenham		Longleat xiii (Harleian transcript)	106
John Arbuthnot to S.	17 Oct. 1725	London	B.M. Add. 4805		109
E. of Oxford to S.	19 Oct. 1725	,,	Portland MSS.		111
S. to E. of Oxford	26 Oct. 1725	Dublin	Huntington Library		111
S. to Thomas Tickell	12 Nov. 1725	,,	Tickell Papers		112
S. to Rev. James Stopford	26 Nov. 1725	,,		Nichols 1801	113
S. to Pope	26 Nov. 1725	,,		Longleat xiii (Harleian transcript)	116
Pope and Bolingbroke to S.	14 Dec. 1725	(?)Twickenham		Longleat xiii (Harleian transcript)	119

Correspondents	Date	Place	Original source	Printed source or transcript	Page
S. to Viscount Palmerston	1 Jan. 1726	Dublin		Nichols 1801	122
Viscount Palmerston to S.	15 Jan. 1726	London		Nichols 1801	123
S. to Viscount Palmerston	29 Jan. 1726	Dublin		Nichols 1801	124
John Arbuthnot to S.	5 Apr. 1726	London	B.M. Add. 4805		127
S. to Thomas Tickell	16 Apr. 1726	,,	Tickell Papers		128
S. to Rev. John Worrall	16 Apr. 1726	,,		Hawkesworth 1766	129
S. to Knightley Chetwode	19 Apr. 1726	,,		Forster copy	129
E. of Peterborough to S.	23 Apr. 1726	Parsons Green	B.M. Add. 4806		131
S. to E. of Peterborough	28 Apr. 1726	London		Nichols 1779	131
Thomas Tickell to S.	10 May 1726	Dublin	Tickell Letter-Book No. 2		135
S. and Pope to E. of Oxford	3 July 1726	Twickenham	Portland MSS. Harley Papers		136
S. to Thomas Tickell	7 July 1726	London	Tickell Papers		137
S. to Rev. Thomas Sheridan	8 July 1726	,,		Dodsley *Miscellanies* 1745	138
S. to Rev. John Worrall	15 July 1726	Twickenham	B.M. Add. 4805		140
S. to E. of Oxford	15 July 1726	,,	Portland MSS. Harley Papers		142
S. to Rev. James Stopford	20 July 1726	,,		Nichols 1801	143
Viscount Bolingbroke to S., Pope, and Gay	23 July 1726	Oakley Park	B.M. Add. 4805		146
S. to Rev. Thomas Sheridan	27 July 1726	Twickenham		Dodsley *Miscellanies* 1745	147
S. to E. of Oxford	(?) July 1726	—	Portland MSS. Harley Papers		148
S. to Pope	1 Aug. 1726	London	Harvard Univ.		148
S. to Pope	4 Aug. 1726	Whitehall		Faulkner 1741	149
Duchess of Hamilton to S.	(?) 1726	—	B.M. Add. 4806		150
S. to Rev. James Stopford	6 Aug. 1726	London		Forster copy	150
S. to Rev. John Worrall	6 Aug. 1726	,,	B.M. Add. 4805		151

Correspondents	Date	Place	Original source	Printed source or transcript	Page
'Richard Sympson' to Benjamin Motte	8 Aug. 1726	London	Morgan Library		152
B. Motte to 'Richard Sympson'	11 Aug. 1726	,,	Morgan Library		154
'R. Sympson' to B. Motte	13 Aug. 1726	,,	—		155
S. to E. of Oxford	12 Aug. 1726	,,	Portland MSS. Harley Papers		155
S. to Rev. John Worrall	13 Aug. 1726	,,		Hawkesworth 1766	156
Pope to S.	22 Aug. 1726	Twickenham		Faulkner 1741	156
S. to Pope	Aug. 1726	Dublin		Faulkner 1741	158
Pope to S.	3 Sept. 1726	—		Faulkner 1741	160
William Pulteney to S.	3 Sept. 1726	London	B.M. Add. 4805		162
John Gay to S.	16 Sept. 1726	,,	B.M. Add. 4805		163
John Arbuthnot to S.	20 Sept. 1726	,,	B.M. Add. 4805		165
Viscount Bolingbroke to S.	22 Sept. 1726	,,	B.M. Add. 4805		167
John Gay to S.	Sept. 1726	(?) London	B.M. Add. 4805		168
S. to Rev. James Stopford	15 Oct. 1726	Dublin		Forster copy	169
S. to Pope and John Gay	15 Oct. 1726	,,		Longleat xiii Portland Papers	170
John Gay to S.	22 Oct. 1726	Whitehall	B.M. Add. 4805		174
S. to Mrs. Howard	Oct. 1726	Dublin	B.M. Add. 22625		176
S. to Knightley Chetwode	24 Oct. 1726	,,		Forster copy	177
John Arbuthnot to S.	5 Nov. 1726	London	B.M. Add. 4805		178
Pope to S.	16 Nov. 1726	,,		Faulkner 1741	180
John Gay to S.	17 Nov. 1726	,,		Faulkner 1741	182
Mrs. Howard to S.	17 Nov. 1726	,,	B.M. Add. 4805		184
S. to Mrs. Greenfield	23 Nov. 1726	Dublin		H.M.C. Report V. App., p. 296	186
S. to Mrs. Howard	27 Nov. 1726	,,	B.M. Add. 22625		187
S. to Pope	27 Nov. 1726	,,		Faulkner 1741	189
'Lemuel Gulliver' to Mrs. Howard	28 Nov. 1726	'Newark'	B.M. Add. 22625		190
E. of Peterborough to S.	29 Nov. 1726	(?) London	B.M. Add. 4805		191
S. to Pope	5 Dec. 1726	Dublin		Faulkner 1741	192
S. to ——	8 Dec. 1726	—	—	—	194
C. Ford to Benjamin Motte	3 Jan. 1727	Dublin	Forster 561		194
S. to Mrs. Howard	1 Feb. 1727	,,	B.M. Add. 22625		195

Correspondents	Date	Place	Original source	Printed source or transcript	Page
Viscountess Boling-broke to S.	1 Feb. 1727	Dawley	B.M. Add. 4805		197
S. to Knightley Chetwode	14 Feb. 1727	Dublin		Forster copy	198
Viscount Boling-broke to S.	17 Feb. 1727	London	B.M. Add. 4805		199
Pope to S.	(?) 17 Feb. 1727	Twickenham		Faulkner 1741	200
John Gay to S.	18 Feb. 1727	Whitehall	B.M. Add. 4805		202
'Prince of Lilliput' to 'Stella'	11 Mar. 1727	London		Deane Swift 1768	203
S. to Thomas Tickell	7 Apr. 1727	Dublin	Alfred Morrison Catalogue		204
S. to Rev. Thomas Wallis	8 Apr. 1727	,,		Duncombe 1772	205
'Richard Sympson' to Benjamin Motte	27 Apr. 1727	Twickenham	Morgan Library		206
S. to Rev. Thomas Sheridan	13 May 1727	London		Dodsley *Miscellanies* 1745	206
S. to E. of Oxford	13 May 1727	Whitehall	Portland MSS. Harley Papers		208
S. to E. of Oxford.	18 May 1727	Twickenham	Portland MSS. Harley Papers		209
S. to Archbishop. King	18 May 1727	,,		Deane Swift 1768	209
Viscount Boling-broke to S.	18 May 1727	Dawley	B.M. Add. 4805		211
Archbishop King to S.	3 June 1727	Dublin		T.C.D. Letter-Book	212
Viscount Boling-broke to S.	6 June 1727	Dawley	B.M. Add. 4805		212
Viscount Boling-broke to S.	11 June 1727	,,	B.M. Add. 4805		213
Voltaire to S.	16 June 1727	London	B.M. Add. 4805		214
Viscount Boling-broke to S.	17 June 1727	Twickenham	B.M. Add. 4805		215
Viscount Boling-broke to S.	(?) 20 June 1727	Cranford	B.M. Add. 4805		216
L'Abbé Des Fontaines to S.	4 July [o.s. 23 June] 1727	Paris	B.M. Add. 4805		217
S. to Rev. Thomas Sheridan	24 June 1727	London		Dodsley *Miscellanies* 1745	218
S. to Mrs. Howard	June 1727	(?) London	B.M. Add. 22625		220
S. to Rev. Thomas Sheridan	1 July 1727	Twickenham		Dodsley *Miscellanies* 1745	220
S. to Mrs. Howard	9 July 1727	,,	B.M. Add. 22625		223

Correspondents	Date	Place	Original source	Printed source or transcript	Page
Voltaire to S.	14 Dec. 1727	London	B.M. Add. 4805		256
S. to Benjamin Motte	28 Dec. 1727	Dublin	Forster No. 544		257
S. to Lord Carteret	18 Jan. 1728	Dublin		Deane Swift 1765	259
Pope to S.	(?) Jan. 1728	Twickenham		Longleat xiii (Harleian transcript)	260
S. to Benjamin Motte	Feb. 1728	Dublin	Forster No. 545		263
Bolingbroke and Pope to S.	Feb. 1728	Dawley		Faulkner 1741	264
John Gay to S.	15 Feb. 1728	London	B.M. Add. 4805		265
S. to John Gay	26 Feb. 1728	Dublin		Longleat xiii (Harleian transcript)	267
S. to Martha Blount	29 Feb. 1728	,,	B.M. Stowe MS. 755		268
Benj. Motte to Woodford	12 Mar. 1728	London	Morgan Library		270
John Gay to S.	20 Mar. 1728	(?) London	B.M. Add. 4805		271
Pope to S.	23 Mar. 1728	(?)Twickenham		Faulkner 1741	273
S. to John Gay	28 Mar. 1728	Dublin		Longleat xiii (Harleian transcript)	275
Lady Bolingbroke to S.	(?) 1728	Dawley	B.M. Add. 4806		278
Voltaire to S.	[Mar. 1728]	(?) London	B.M. Add. 4805		279
John Browne to S.	4 Apr. 1728	Dublin	Foster No. 562		280
Martha Blount to S.	7 May 1728	—		Deane Swift 1768	283
S. to Pope	10 May 1728	Dublin		Faulkner 1741	285
S. to E. of Oxford	11 May 1728	,,	Portland MSS.		286
John Gay to S.	16 May 1728	Bath	B.M. Add. 4805		287
S. to Pope	1 June 1728	Dublin		Faulkner 1741	288
Pope to S.	28 June 1728	Dawley		Faulkner 1741	290
John Gay to S.	6 July 1728	Bath	B.M. Add. 4805		291
S. to Pope	16 July 1728	Market Hill		Faulkner 1741	293
E. of Oxford to S.	27 July 1728	Down Hall		Longleat xiii (Harleian transcript)	294
S. to Rev. Thomas Sheridan	2 Aug. 1728	Market Hill		Dodsley *Miscellanies* 1745	295
S. to Rev. Thomas Sheridan	18 Sept. 1728	,,		Dodsley *Miscellanies* 1745	297
S. to Charles Ford	20 Sept. 1728	,,	Rothschild		298
S. to E. of Oxford	21 Sept. 1728	,,	Carl H. Pforz-heimer		299
S. to Rev. John Worrall	28 Sept. 1728	,,	B.M. Add. 4805		301

Correspondents	Date	Place	Original source	Printed source or transcript	Page
Viscount Boling-broke to S.	30 [o.s. 19] Aug. 1729	Aix-la-Chapelle	B.M. Add. 4805		347
Pope to S.	9 Oct. 1729	Twickenham		Faulkner 1741	351
Knightley Chetwode to S.	25 Oct. 1729	(?) Wood-brooke		Forster copy	352
S. to Viscount Bolingbroke	11 Oct. 1729	Dublin		Longleat xiii, f. 123	353
S. to Pope	31 Oct. 1729	,,		Faulkner 1741	355
John Gay to S.	9 Nov. 1729	Middleton Stoney	B.M. Add. 4806		356
Viscount Boling-broke to S.	19 Nov. 1729	(?) Dawley		Longleat xiii, f. 124	358
S. to John Gay	20 Nov. 1729	Dublin		Longleat xiii, ff. 125–6	359
Pope to S.	28 Nov. 1729	Twickenham		Faulkner 1741	362
S. to Robert Percival	11 Dec. 1729	Dublin	B.M. Add. 38671		365
S. to Robert Percival	3 Jan. 1730	,,	B.M. Add. 38671		366
S. to Pope	6 Feb. 1730	,,		Longleat xiii (Portland Papers)	369
S. to Knightley Chetwode	12 Feb. 1730	,,		Forster copy	370
Lord Bathurst to S.	12 Feb. 1730	(?) Ritchings	B.M. Add. 4805		371
S. to Pope	26 Feb. 1730	Dublin		Longleat xiii (Harleian transcript)	373
John Gay to S.	3 Mar. 1730	London	B.M. Add. 4805		376
Pope to S.	4 Mar. 1730	Twickenham		Faulkner 1741	377
E. of Oxford to S.	4 Mar. 1730	London		Longleat xiii (Harleian transcript)	378
S. to John Gay	19 Mar. 1730	Dublin		Longleat xiii (Harleian transcript)	379
S. to Viscount Bolingbroke	21 Mar. 1730	,,		Faulkner 1741	382
John Gay to S.	31 Mar. 1730	London	B.M. Add. 4805		384
Pope and Boling-broke to S.	9 Apr. 1730	Twickenham		Longleat xiii, ff. 134–5	386
S. to Lord Carteret	Apr. 1730	Dublin		Deane Swift 1765	389
S. to Lady Worsley	12 Apr. 1730	,,		Deane Swift 1765	391
S. to E. of Oxford	28 Apr. 1730	,,	B.M. Port-land Papers		392
S. to Pope	2 May 1730	,,		Longleat xiii (Har-leian transcript)	394
Pope to S.	c. 19 June 1730	Twickenham		Faulkner 1741	397
S. to Knightley Chetwode	24 June 1730	Dublin		Forster copy	398
Lord Bathurst to S.	30 June 1730	Cirencester	B.M. Add. 4805		400

Correspondents	Date	Place	Original source	Printed source or transcript	Page
John Gay to S.	4 July 1730	Amesbury	B.M. Add. 4805		402
E. of Oxford to S.	15 July 1730	London		Longleat xiii (Harleian transcript)	403
S. to E. of Oxford	28 Aug. 1730	Market Hill	B.M. Portland Papers		404
Lord Bathurst to S.	9 Sept. 1730	Cirencester	B.M. Add. 4806		406
Lady Elizabeth Germain to S.	19 Sept. 1730	London	B.M. Add. 4806		408
S. to Lord Bathurst	Oct. 1730	Dublin		Forster transcript	409
John Arbuthnot to S.	5 Nov. 1730	London	B.M. Add. 4806		413
Gay and Duchess of Queensberry to S.	8 Nov. 1730	Amesbury	B.M. Add. 4806		414
S. to John Gay	10 Nov. 1730	Dublin		Longleat xiii (Harleian transcript)	416
S. to E. of Chesterfield	10 Nov. 1730	,,		Deane Swift 1765	419
S. to John Gay and Duchess of Queensberry	19 Nov. 1730	,,		Longleat xiii (Harleian transcript)	420
S. to Mrs. Howard	21 Nov. 1730	,,	B.M. Add. 22625		422
S. to Mrs. Caesar	3 Dec. 1730	,,	T. Cottrell-Dormer		425
E. of Chesterfield to S.	15 Dec. [o.s. 4] 1730	Hague	B.M. Add. 4806		426
Gay and Duchess of Queensberry to S.	6 Dec. 1730	Amesbury	B.M. Add. 4806		427
Lady Elizabeth Germain to S.	24 Dec. 1730	(?) London	B.M. Add. 4806		429
S. to Mrs. Whiteway	28 Dec. 1730	Dublin		Deane Swift 1768	431
S. to E. of Chesterfield	5 Jan. 1731	,,		Deane Swift 1765	431
S. to Samuel Gerrard	6 Jan. 1731	,,		Scott 1814	433
S. to Pope	15 Jan. 1731	,,		Longleat (Portland Papers)	434
Viscount Bolingbroke to S.	(?) 17 Jan. 1731	Dawley		Faulkner 1741	437
William Pulteney to S.	9 Feb. 1731	London	B.M. Add. 4806		438
S. to Mrs. Barber	23 Feb. 1731	Dublin	Rothschild		439
Lady Elizabeth Germain to S.	23 Feb. 1731	London	B.M. Add. 4806		441
Knightley Chetwode to S.	Feb. 1731	Dublin		Forster copy	442
S. to Gay and Duchess of Queensberry	13 Mar. 1731	,,		Longleat xiii (Harleian transcript)	443
John Gay to S.	20 Mar. 1731	London	B.M. Add. 4806		446
Viscount Bolingbroke and Pope to S.	20 Mar. 1731	,,		Longleat xiii (Harleian transcript)	448

Correspondents	Date	Place	Original source	Printed source or transcript	Page
John Gay and Pope to S.	1 Dec. 1731	London		Faulkner 1741	508
S. to Mrs. Fenton	28 Dec. 1731	Dublin	W. R. Le Fanu		511

VOLUME IV

Correspondents	Date	Place	Original source	Printed source or transcript	Page
Lady Elizabeth Germain to S.	11 Jan. 1732	London	B.M. Add. 4806		1
John Gay to S.	18 Jan. 1732	,,	B.M. Add. 4806		2
S. to Rev. John Winder	19 Jan. 1732	Dublin	Rothschild		3
Lady Elizabeth Germain to S.	23 Feb. 1732	London	B.M. Add. 4806		5
Viscount Bolingbroke and Pope to S.	[Mar.] 1732	Dawley		Faulkner 1741	6
John Gay to S.	13 Mar. 1732	London	B.M. Add. 4806		8
S. to George Faulkner	29 Mar. 1732	Dublin		Faulkner 1762	10
S. to Lady Acheson	1 Apr. 1732	,,		Deane Swift 1768	11
Lady Acheson to S.	1 Apr. 1732	,,		Deane Swift 1768	12
S. to Duke of Dorset	20 Apr. 1732	,,	Stopford-Sackville MSS.		12
Knightley Chetwode to S.	Apr. 1732	,,		Forster copy	13
S. to John Gay	4 May 1732	,,		Longleat xiii (Harleian transcript)	14
Lady Elizabeth Germain to S.	13 May 1732	London	B.M. Add. 4806		17
S. to Rev. Thomas Sheridan	13 May 1732	Dublin		Hawkesworth	18
Rev. Thomas Sheridan to S.	15 May 1732	(?) Dublin		Hawkesworth	20
John Gay to S.	16 May 1732	London	B.M. Add. 4806		21
S. to Charles Ford	17 May 1732	Dublin	Morgan Library		23
S. to Rev. Henry Jenney	8 June 1732	,,		Barrett's *Essay* 1808	26
S. to Pope	12 June 1732	,,		Faulkner 1741	29
Lady Catherine Jones to S.	15 June 1732	(?) Chelsea	B.M. Add. 4806		32
S. to Dean Brandreth	30 June 1732	Dublin		Barrett's *Essay* 1808	33

Correspondents	Date	Place	Original source	Printed source or transcript	Page
S. to John Barber	3 Sept. 1735	Dublin	Huntington Library		380
S. to Pope	3 Sept. 1735	,,		Faulkner 1741	382
S. to Pope	3 Sept. 1735	,,		Portland transcript	383
Lady Elizabeth Germain to S.	4 Sept. 1735	Knole	B.M. Add. 4806		385
Lord Orrery to S.	8 Sept. 1735	Ballynort		Orrery Papers	387
S. to Rev. Thomas Sheridan	12 Sept. 1735	Dublin		Dodsley *Miscellanies* 1745	388
Lord Bathurst to S.	13 Sept. 1735	Cirencester		Deane Swift 1768	389
Rev. Thomas Sheridan to S.	17 Sept. 1735	Cavan		Deane Swift 1768	391
William King to S.	20 Sept. 1735	London		Deane Swift 1768	394
S. to Lord Orrery	25 Sept. 1735	Dublin	Morgan Library		395
S. to Rev. Thomas Sheridan	30 Sept. 1735	,,		Dodsley *Miscellanies* 1745	397
Pope to S.	Sept. 1735	Twickenham		Faulkner 1741	400
Benjamin Motte to S.	4 Oct. 1735	London		Deane Swift 1768	401
Lord Orrery to S.	Oct. 1735	Cork		Orrery Papers	401
Rev. Thomas Sheridan to S.	5 Oct. 1735	Cavan		Deane Swift 1768	403
S. to Lord Orrery	19 Oct. 1735	Dublin	Morgan Library		405
S. to E. of Oxford	21 Oct. 1735	,,	B.M. Portland MSS.		407
S. to Pope	21 Oct. 1735	,,		Faulkner 1741	408
S. to Lord Bathurst	21 Oct. 1735	,,		Forster transcript	409
S. to Benjamin Motte	25 Oct. 1735	,,	Morgan Library		410
S. to Rev. James King	27 Oct. 1735	,,	Rothschild		411
Rev. Christopher Donnellan to S.	31 Oct. 1735	Cloyne		Deane Swift 1768	412
S. to Benjamin Motte	1 Nov. 1735	Dublin	Lord Bathurst MS.		413
Mrs. Pendarves to S.	1 Nov. 1735	Fulham		Deane Swift 1768	414
S. and Sheridan to Mrs. Whiteway	8 Nov. 1735	Cavan		Deane Swift 1768	416
S. to John Rochfort	8 Nov. 1735	,,	B.M. Add. 38671		418
Mrs. Whiteway to S.	8 Nov. 1735	Dublin		Deane Swift 1768	419
—— to S.	9 Nov. 1735	Castletown		Deane Swift 1768	420
Lady Elizabeth Germain to S.	13 Nov. 1735	London	B.M. Add. 4806		421
Mrs. Sican to S.	15 Nov. 1735	Dublin		Deane Swift 1768	422
John Sican to S.	20 Oct. [o.s. 9] 1735	Paris		Deane Swift 1768	423
S. and Sheridan to Mrs. Whiteway	15 Nov. 1735	Cavan		Deane Swift 1768	426
Mrs. Whiteway to S. and Sheridan	15 Nov. 1735	Dublin		Deane Swift 1768	428
S. to Mrs. Whiteway	18 Nov. 1735	Cavan		Deane Swift 1768	430

List of Letters

Correspondents	Date	Place	Original source	Printed source or transcript	Page
Rev. Thomas Sheridan to Mrs. Whiteway	18 Nov. 1735	Cavan		Deane Swift 1768	431
S. and Sheridan to Mrs. Whiteway	22 Nov. 1735	,,		Deane Swift 1768	432
Mrs. Whiteway to S. and Sheridan	22 Nov. 1735	Dublin		Deane Swift 1768	433
William Pulteney to S.	22 Nov. 1735	Bath		Deane Swift 1768	435
Mrs. Whiteway to S.	25 Nov. 1735	Dublin		Deane Swift 1768	439
S. and Sheridan to Mrs. Whiteway	28 Nov. 1735	Cavan		Deane Swift 1768	440
Mrs. Whiteway to S.	29 Nov. 1735	Dublin		Deane Swift 1768	443
Mrs. Whiteway to S.	2 Dec. 1735	,,		Deane Swift 1768	444
S. to Mrs. Whiteway	6 Dec. 1735	Cavan		Deane Swift 1768	446
Pope to S.	Dec. 1735	Twickenham		Faulkner 1741	447
S. to Duke of Dorset	30 Dec. 1735	Dublin	Stopford-Sackville MSS.		448
Mrs. Pendarves to S.	7 Jan. 1736	Bath		Deane Swift 1768	451
S. to George Faulkner	8 Jan. 1736	Dublin		Faulkner 1762	452
Lord Orrery to S.	13 Jan. 1736	,,		Deane Swift 1768	453
S. to Lord Orrery	13 Jan. 1736	,,	Morgan Library		453
Rev. Thomas Sheridan to S.	17 Jan. 1736	Cavan		Deane Swift 1768	454
S. to Mrs. Pendarves	Jan. 1736	Dublin		Mrs. Delany's Correspondence	455
S. to Pope	7 Feb. 1736	,,		Faulkner 1741	457
Thomas Griffith to S.	8 Feb. 1736	,,	Forster No. 530		458
Lady Elizabeth Germain to S.	10 Feb. 1736	London	B.M. Add. 4806		459
S. to Mrs. Whiteway	18 Feb. 1736	Dublin		Deane Swift 1768	460
Bishop Hort to S.	23 Feb. 1736	(?) Kilmore		Deane Swift 1768	461
S. to Miss Harrison	23 Feb. 1736	Dublin		Deane Swift 1768	462
Rev. Thomas Sheridan to S.	23 Feb. 1736	Cavan		Deane Swift 1768	462
S. to Mrs. Whiteway	25 Feb. 1736	Dublin		Deane Swift 1768	463
Rev. Thomas Sheridan to S.	29 Feb. 1736	Cavan		Deane Swift 1768	464
S. to Rev. Thomas Sheridan	2 Mar. 1736	Dublin	W. R. Le Fanu		465
S. to Lord Orrery	9 Mar. 1736	,,	Morgan Library		467
S. to Charles Wogan	(?) Mar. 1736	,,		Deane Swift 1765	468
Thomas Carter to S.	15 Mar. 1736	,,		Deane Swift 1768	470
S. to an Unknown Lady	24 Mar. 1736	,,	Rothschild		470
Pope to S.	25 Mar. 1736	Twickenham		Faulkner 1741	471
Rev. Thomas Sheridan to S.	27 Mar. 1736	Cavan		Deane Swift 1768	473
Rev. Thomas Sheridan to S.	3 Apr. 1736	,,		Deane Swift 1768	473

List of Letters

Correspondents	Date	Place	Original source	Printed source or transcript	Page
Lady Howth to S.	6 Aug. 1736	Turlaghvan		Deane Swift 1768	521
Thomas Carte to S.	11 Aug. 1736	London		Deane Swift 1768	523
Sheridan to Mrs. Whiteway	14 Aug. 1736	Cavan		Deane Swift 1768	525
Pope to S.	17 Aug. 1736	Twickenham		Faulkner 1741	526
Mrs. Pendarves to S.	2 Sept. 1736	London	B.M. Add. 4806		527
S. to John Nichols	6 Sept. 1736	Dublin		Scott 1814	529
William King to Mrs. Whiteway	14 Sept. 1736	Edinburgh	Huntington Library		529
Rev. Thomas Sheridan to S.	15 Sept. 1736	Cavan		Deane Swift 1768	530
S. to Mrs. Pilkington	12 Oct. 1736	Dublin	Forster No. 532		532
S. to Duke of Dorset	14 Oct. 1736	,,	Stopford Sackville MSS.		533
S. to Rev. Patrick Delany	22 Oct. 1736	,,		*Blackwood's Magazine*	534
S. to William Richardson	23 Oct. 1736	,,	National Library of Scotland		534
S. to Sir John Stanley	30 Oct. 1736	,,		Nichols 1779	537
Lady Elizabeth Germain to S.	2 Nov. 1736	London	B.M. Add. 4806		538
Mrs. Barber to S.	3 Nov. 1736	Bath	B.M. Add. 4806		538
William King to Mrs. Whiteway	9 Nov. 1736	Paris		Deane Swift 1768	541
Rev. Thomas Sheridan to Mrs. Whiteway	21 Nov. 1736	—		Deane Swift 1768	543
Rev. William Dunkin to Mrs. Whiteway	30 Nov. 1736	Dublin		Deane Swift 1768	544
S. to Pope	2 Dec. 1736	,,		Longleat xiii (Harleian transcript)	545
Lord Castle-Durrow to S.	4 Dec. 1736	Castle Durrow	B.M. Add. 4806		547
William King to S.	7 Dec. 1736	London		Deane Swift 1768	550
S. to John Barber	8 Dec. 1736	Dublin		Scott 1814	551
William Pulteney to S.	21 Dec. 1736	London	B.M. Add. 4806		552
S. to Lord Castle-Durrow	24 Dec. 1736	Dublin	Morgan Library		554
Pope to S.	30 Dec. 1736	—		Faulkner 1741	557

VOLUME V

Correspondents	Date	Place	Original source	Printed source or transcript	Page
Lord Castle-Durrow to S.	11 Jan. 1737	Castle-Durrow	B.M. Add. 4806		1
S. to Lady Elizabeth Germain	29 Jan. 1737	Dublin	B.M. Add. 4806		2
S. to Pope	9 Feb. 1737	,,		Faulkner 1741	4
S. to John Temple	Feb. 1737	,,		Hawkesworth 1766	5
S. to William Pulteney	7 Mar. 1737	,,	B.M. Add. 4806		6
Lord Orrery to S.	15 Mar. 1737	Cork	B.M. Add. 4806		9
Lord Orrery to S.	18 Mar. 1737	,,	B.M. Add. 4806		10
Pope to Lord Orrery	4 Mar. 1737	(?) Twicken-ham	Morgan Library		11
William Richardson to S.	18 Mar. 1737	Coleraine	Forster No. 566		14
S. to —— Gibson	23 Mar. 1737	—		Berkeley's *Literary Relics* 1789	15
Pope to S.	23 Mar. 1737	Twickenham		Faulkner 1741	15
Lord Carteret to S.	24 Mar. 1737	London	B.M. Add. 4806		17
S. to John Barber	30 Mar. 1737	Dublin	Huntington Library		18
S. to Lord Orrery	31 Mar. 1737	,,	Morgan Library		21
Lord Orrery to S.	3 Apr. 1737	Cork		Deane Swift 1768	24
E. of Oxford to S.	7 Apr. 1737	London		Longleat xiii (Harleian transcript)	26
S. to Rev. Thomas Sheridan	9 Apr. 1737	(?) Quilca		Faulkner 1746	28
S. to Wm. Richardson	9 Apr. 1737	Dublin	Rothschild		31
S. to ——	15 Apr. 1737	,,	B.M. Egerton MS. 201		32
William Richardson to S.	17 Apr. 1737	Summerseat		Deane Swift 1768	33
S. to Mrs. Whiteway	16 and 22 Apr. 1737	Dublin	Huntington Library		34
S. to William Graham	26 Apr. 1737	,,		Scott 1814	36
S. to William Richardson	30 Apr. 1737	,,		Berkeley's *Literary Relics*	37
S. to John Rochfort	3 May 1737	,,	B.M. Add. 38671		39
Margaret Davys to S.	27 May 1737	—		Deane Swift 1768	40
S. to Pope	31 May 1737	Dublin		Faulkner 1741	41
S. to Rev. James Stopford	9 June 1737	,,		Forster transcript	43
S. to Lord Orrery	11 June 1737	,,	Morgan Library		43
Lord Orrery to S.	12 June 1737	,,	Harvard University		44
S. to E. of Oxford	14 June 1737	,,	B.M. Portland MSS.		45

Correspondents	Date	Place	Original source	Printed source or transcript	Page
S. to Miss Katharine Richardson	28 Jan. 1738	Dublin		Deane Swift 1768	87
S. and Mrs. Whiteway to Orrery	2 Feb. 1738	,,	Morgan Library		89
Andrew Ramsay to S.	20 Feb. [o.s. 9] 1738	Paris	B.M. Add. 4806		91
Lord Orrery to Mrs. Whiteway	14 Feb. 1738	Westminster		Deane Swift 1768	91
Miss Katharine Richardson to S.	23 Feb. 1738	Summerseat		Deane Swift 1768	92
Wm. King to Mrs. Whiteway	2 Mar. 1738	London	John Rylands Library		93
S. to George Faulkner	8 Mar. 1738	Dublin		Faulkner 1762	94
S. to John Barber	9 Mar. 1738	,,	Huntington Library		95
John Barber to S.	13 Mar. 1738	London		Deane Swift 1768	97
S. to John Nichols	14 Mar. 1738	Belcamp	B.M. Add. 12113		99
Wm. King to Deane Swift	15 Mar. 1738	Oxford		Deane Swift 1768	99
Lord Orrery to Faulkner	26 Mar. 1738	Westminster	Harvard Library		101
Lord Orrery to Mrs. Whiteway	26 Mar. 1738	,,	Harvard Library		101
S. to John Barber	31 Mar. 1738	Dublin	Huntington Library		102
S. to E. of Oxford	3 Apr. 1738	,,	Longleat xiii. 55		103
Erasmus Lewis to S.	8 Apr. 1738	London		Scott 1814	104
Alexander Macaulay to S.	13 Apr. 1738	Dublin		Deane Swift 1768	106
Wm. King to Deane Swift	28 Apr. 1738	Oxford		Deane Swift 1768	107
Miss Katharine Richardson to Mrs. Whiteway	6 May 1738	Belturbert		Deane Swift 1768	108
E. of Oxford to S.	30 May 1738	London	B.M. Portland MSS.		109
S. to Miss Margaret Hamilton	8 June 1738	Dublin		Nichols 1779	110
Lord Orrery to S.	13 June 1738	,,		Deane Swift 1768	111
Lord Orrery to S.	29 June 1738	—		Deane Swift 1768	111
S. to George Faulkner	13 July 1738	Dublin		Nichols 1779	112
William Richardson to S.	25 July 1738	London		Deane Swift 1768	113
John Barber to S.	27 July 1738	,,		Deane Swift 1768	114
Mrs. Whiteway to William Richardson	8 Aug. 1738	Dublin		Berkeley, *Literary Relics*	116
S. to John Barber	8 Aug. 1738	,,		Deane Swift 1765	117
S. to Pope and Bolingbroke	8 Aug. 1738	,,		Faulkner 1741	119
S. to George Faulkner	31 Aug. 1738	,,		Faulkner 1762	121

List of Letters

Correspondents	Date	Place	Original source	Printed source or transcript	Page
S. and Mrs. Whiteway to Wm. Richardson	16 Sept. 1738	Dublin	Rothschild	Berkeley, *Literary Relics*	121
Bishop Synge to S.	18 Sept. 1738	—		Deane Swift 1768	124
S. to Mrs. Whiteway	3 Oct. 1738	Dublin		Deane Swift 1768	125
Pope to S.	12 Oct. 1738	Twickenham		Deane Swift 1768	125
S. to Lord Orrery	21 Nov. 1738	Dublin	Morgan Library		127
S. to Mrs. Whiteway	27 Nov. 1738	,,		Deane Swift 1768	128
Miss Katharine Richardson to Mrs. Whiteway	29 Nov. 1738	Belturbert		Deane Swift 1768	128
Countess of Orrery to S.	4 Dec. 1738	Marston	B.M. Egerton MS. 201		129
William Richardson to S.	2 Jan. 1739	London		Deane Swift 1768	130
Lord Orrery to S.	2 Jan. 1739	Marston		Orrery Papers	131
William King to S.	5 Jan. 1739	Oxford		Deane Swift 1768	133
Deane Swift to S.	12 Jan. 1739	—		Deane Swift 1768	134
William King to S.	23 Jan. 1739	London		Deane Swift 1768	135
William King to Mrs. Whiteway	30 Jan. 1739	(?) Oxford		Deane Swift 1768	136
S. to John Barber	16 Feb. 1739	Dublin	Huntington Library		137
William King to Mrs. Whiteway	6 Mar. 1739	London		Deane Swift 1768	139
Mrs. Whiteway to Wm. Richardson	28 Mar. 1739	Dublin		Berkeley, *Literary Relics*	141
Wm. Richardson to Mrs. Whiteway	5 Apr. 1739	London		Deane Swift 1768	142
William Richardson to S.	10 Apr. 1739	,,		Deane Swift 1768	143
S. and Mrs. Whiteway to Wm. Richardson	17 Apr. 1739	Dublin	Rothschild		144
William Richardson to S.	17 Apr. 1739	London		Deane Swift 1768	146
S. to John Barber	19 Apr. 1739	Dublin	Huntington Library		146
Mrs. Whiteway to Wm. Richardson	19 Apr. 1739	,,		Berkeley, *Literary Relics*	147
S. to the Irish Society	19 Apr. 1739	,,		Deane Swift 1765	148
Rev. Wm. Dunkin to Mrs. Whiteway	25 Apr. 1739	—		Deane Swift 1768	149
S. to Pope	28 Apr. 1739	Dublin		Faulkner 1746	150
S. to Pope	10 May 1739	,,		Deane Swift 1765	151
George Lyttelton to S.	16 May 1739	London		Deane Swift 1768	152
Pope to S.	17 May 1739	,,	B.M. Add. 4806		152
Lord Orrery to S.	May 1739	—	James L. Clifford		15
S. to George Lyttelton	5 June 1739	Dublin		Deane Swift 1765	15
Mrs. Whiteway to Pope	June–July 1739	,,	Huntington Library		15

Correspondents	Date	Place	Original source	Printed source or transcript	Page
Mrs. Whiteway to Wm. Richardson	20 July 1739	Dublin		Berkeley, *Literary Relics*	160
George Lyttelton to S.	4 Aug. 1739	Worcestershire	B.M. Add. 4806		162
John Scott to S.	7 Sept. 1739	London		Deane Swift 1768	163
James Corbridge to S.	Sept. 1739	,,	Forster No. 568		165
Lord Orrery to S.	29 Sept. 1739	Caledon		Orrery Papers	168
S. to the E. of Arran	Autumn 1739		B.M. Add. 4806		169
S. to Rev. James King	(?) 1739	Dublin		Scott 1814	171
S. to George Faulkner	4 Dec. 1739	,,		Faulkner 1762	172
Rev. Robert Throp to S.	10 Dec. 1739	—		Deane Swift 1768	172
S. to Mrs. Whiteway	31 Dec. 1739	Dublin		Deane Swift 1768	173
S. to Mrs. Whiteway	1 Jan. 1740	,,		Deane Swift 1768	173
S. to ——	2 Jan. 1740	,,	A. Loftus Bryan		174
S. to ——	9 Jan. 1740	,,		Mrs. Pilkington's *Memoirs*	174
S. to Mrs. Whiteway	13 Jan. 1740	,,		Deane Swift 1768	175
S. to Mrs. Whiteway	18 Jan. 1740	,,		Deane Swift 1768	176
Lord Castle-Durrow to S.	2 Feb. 1740	,,	B.M. Add. 4806		177
S. to Mrs. Whiteway	3 Feb. 1740	,,		Deane Swift 1768	179
S. to Rev. James Stopford	17 Mar. 1740	,,		Forster transcript 555	179
Lady Orrery to Mrs. Whiteway	17 Mar. 1740	Caledon	James L. Clifford		180
Mrs. Whiteway to Wm. Richardson	25 Mar. 1740	Dublin		Berkeley, *Literary Relics*	181
Robert Nugent to Mrs. Whiteway	2 Apr. 1740	Bath		Deane Swift 1768	182
S. to Mrs. Whiteway	29 Apr. 1740	Dublin		Deane Swift 1768	183
Pope to S.	[? May 1740]	(?)Twickenham		Harvard University	184
Mrs. Whiteway and S. to Wm. Richardson	13 May 1740	Dublin	Dallas Pratt		185
Mrs. Whiteway to Pope	16 May 1740	,,		Deane Swift 1768	187
William Pulteney to S.	3 June 1740	London	B.M. Add. 4806		189
Pope to Mrs. Whiteway	18 June 1740	Twickenham		Deane Swift 1768	191
John Barber to Mrs. Whiteway	26 June 1740	London	Huntington Library		192
S. to Mrs. Whiteway	26 July 1740	Dublin		Deane Swift 1768	192
Mrs. Whiteway to Lord Orrery	7 Oct. 1740	,,		Elwin-Courthope	193
Lord Orrery to S.	8 Oct. 1740	Caledon		Elwin-Courthope	194
Lord Orrery to S.	17 Dec. 1740	,,	B.M. Add. 4806		195
Mrs. Whiteway to Lord Orrery	20 Dec. 1740	Dublin		Elwin-Courthope	195
Lord Orrery to Mrs. Whiteway	24 Dec. 1740	Caledon		Elwin-Courthope	196

List of Letters

Correspondents	Date	Place	Original source	Printed source or transcript	Page
Lady Orrery to Mrs. Whiteway	24 Dec. 1740	Caledon	Huntington Library		197
Mrs. Whiteway to Lord Orrery	30 Dec. 1740	Dublin	Huntington Library		198
Lord Orrery to Mrs. Whiteway	2 Jan. 1741	Caledon	Huntington Library		200
Lord Orrery to Mrs. Whiteway	10 Jan. 1741	,,		Elwin-Courthope	202
Orrery and Pope to S.	22 Mar. 1741	London	Huntington Library		203
S. to Eaton Stannard	8 June 1741	Dublin		Forster transcript 556	205
Lord Orrery to S.	7 July 1741	London		Deane Swift 1768	205
Mrs. Whiteway to Orrery	22 Nov. 1742	Dublin		Orrery, *Remarks*	207
Lord Orrery to Deane Swift	4 Dec. 1742	Marston		Deane Swift 1768	208
Deane Swift to Orrery	19 Dec. 1742	—		Orrery's amanuensis	209
Lady Orrery to Mrs. Whiteway	29 Dec. 1742	Marston	Rylands Library		212
Lady Orrery to Mrs. Whiteway	26 Mar. 1744	,,	Huntington Library		213
Deane Swift to Orrery	4 Apr. 1744	Dublin		Orrery, *Remarks*	214
Mrs. Whiteway to one of Swift's executors	22 Oct. 1745		Huntington Library		215

Forster No. 560

Sir William Temple to Sir Robert Southwell[1]

[Moor Park, 29 May 1690]

S[r],[2]

I was lately acquainted by Mr Hanbury[3] with the favour of your remembrance and enquiries after me and my family, by wch we are all obliged, and returne you all our wishes for your good health and good fortunes wch way soever you turne them. This afternoon I hear though by a common hand that you are going over into Ireland, Secretary of State for that kingdome,[4] upon wch I venture to make you the offer of a servant, in case you may have occasion for such a one as this bearer. He was borne and bred there (though of a good family in Herefordshire) was neer seven years in the Colledge of Dublyn, and ready to take his degree of Master of Arts, when he was forced away by the desertion of that Colledge upon the calamitys of the Country.[5] Since that time he has lived in my house, read to mee, writ for mee, and kept all accounts as farr as my small occa-

[1] The original was, at one time, in the possession of John Young, of Vanbrugh Fields, Blackheath. Now no. 560 in the Forster Collection.

[2] Swift entered Temple's service in the spring of 1689, probably accompanying him from Sheen to Moor Park. Alleged reasons of health prompted a return to Ireland about May 1690.

[3] His identity is in doubt although probability attaches to Ball's suggestion that he was William Hanbury, brother-in-law of Sir John Cotton (1679-1731), fourth baronet, descended from Sir Robert Cotton, the famous antiquary and collector. The Cottonian library passed into public use and for a brief period, 1706, Hanbury acted as keeper. There are letters from Hanbury to Harley and Humphrey Wanley in the British Museum.

[4] Sir Robert Southwell (1635-1702), son of the Robert who was active during the civil war on the King's side in Ireland. The son, appointed one of the clerks to the Privy Council, was knighted in 1665. He served as envoy extraordinary to Portugal, Brussels, and the Prince of Brandenburg. He accompanied William to Ireland, by whom he was appointed Secretary of State for that kingdom. Poor health, by which he was afflicted throughout life, hindered him from making for himself a more important figure in diplomacy.

[5] In Apr. 1689 Swift would have completed seven years' residence in Trinity College, Dublin, and then would have been eligible for his degree of Master of Arts. On 19 Feb. of that year the Board of the College, in view of the dangers attending those who remained, issued a permissive to all who so wished to leave 'for their better security' (Stubbs's *History of the University of Dublin*, p. 129). Barrett (*History of the Earlier Part of the Life of Swift*, p. 13) believes that Swift, with his cousin Thomas, left about 26 Jan. 1688-9.

sions required. He has latine and greeke some French, writes a very
good and current hand, is very honest and diligent, and has good
friends though they have for the present lost their fortunes in
Ireland and his whole family having been long known to mee[1]
obliged mee thus farr to take care of Him. If you please to accept
him into your service, either as a gentleman to wait on you, or as
Clarke to write under you, and either to use Him so if you like his
service, or upon any establishment of the Colledge to recommend
him to a fellowship there, which he has a just pretence to I shall
acknowledge it as a great obligation to mee as well as to him, and
endeavour to deserve it by the constancy of being alwaies, S[r] Your
most faithfull and humble servant
                                                            W. Temple.

Moor Parke[2] neer Farnham, May 29 1690.

Address: For S[r] Robert Southwell.
Endorsed: Moorgate 29 May 1690 | From S[r] W[m] Temple | for M[r] Hanbury

Leicester Museum transcript[3]

Swift to the Rev. John Kendall

S[r4]   Feb: 11th 1691–2.

   If any thing made me wonder at yr letter it was your almost
inviting me to do so in the beginning, wch indeed grew less upon

---

   [1] It has been frequently stated that Swift was received into Temple's household on account of a relationship between his mother and Lady Temple.
Temple's words, however, state explicitly that the Swift family had long been
known to him; and in his fragment of autobiography Swift states that 'he was
received by Sir William Temple, whose father had been a great friend to the
family' (Deane Swift, *Essay*, 1755, Appendix, p. 42).
   [2] In 1686 Temple moved into residence at Moor Park, formerly known by other
names, including Compton Hall and More House. He and Dorothy Osborne,
married in 1654, spent their honeymoon at Moor Park, near Rickmansworth, in
Hertfordshire, and it is believed, not without reason, that he renamed their
Surrey home in memory of early and happy days. In his essay *Upon the Gardens
of Epicurus; or, of Gardening*, dated 1685, he writes: 'The perfectest Figure of a
Garden I ever saw, either at Home or Abroad, was that of Moor Park in Hart-
fordshire, when I knew it about thirty Years ago.' During the seventeenth
century the property of Moor Park, Rickmansworth, passed through several
hands. See *Victoria County History. Hertford*, ii. 375 ff. For changes which have
taken place in Moor Park, Surrey, which now bears little resemblance to the
house of Swift's day, see op. cit., *Surrey*, ii. 581, 584, 591, 593.

                                              [*For notes 3, 4 see opposite.*]

knowing the occasion, since tis what I have heard from more than one in & about Leicester; and for the friendship between us, as I suppose yrs to be real, so I think it woud be proper to imagine mine, until you find any cause to believe it pretended: tho' I might have some quarrel at you in 3 or 4 lines, wch are very ill bestow'd in complimenting me: & as to that of my great prospects of making my fortune, on wch as your kindness only looks on the best side; and so my own cold temper, & unconfin'd humour, is much greater hindrance than any fear of that wch is the subject of yr letter.—I shall speak plainly to you, that the very ordinary observations I made with going Half a mile beyond the University, have taught me experience enough not to think of marriage, till I settle my fortune in the world, wch I am sure, will not be in some years, and even then my self I am so hard to please that I suppose I shall put it off to the other world ——How all this suits with my behaviour to the woman in hand,[1] you may easily imagine; when you know, that there is something in me which must be employ'd, & when I am alone, turns all, for want

[1] In a letter to John Worrall, 18 Jan. 1728–9, Swift makes mention of a certain Betty Jones of Leicestershire with whom his 'prudent mother' feared he might fall in love. Fortunately she married a Perkins, innkeeper in Loughborough. It may be supposed that 'the woman in hand' was not Betty Jones but another.

---

[3] The original of this letter cannot be traced. The text is printed from the transcript which reads as if it followed the original closely. It will be seen by the date of the next letter that Swift was writing to Kendall from Moor Park, whither, after about fourteen months in Ireland and a visit to his mother in Leicester, he had returned towards the end of 1691.

[4] Nichols in his *Hist. of Leicestershire*, ii. 669, says that the original of this letter was, at the end of the eighteenth century, in the possession of John Kendall of Thorpe Langton, a grandson of the clergyman to whom it was addressed, and that it was given by him to Charles Lloyd, the friend of Coleridge and Lamb. In 1851 Thomas Macaulay of Leicester gave what he believed to be the original letter to the Leicester Literary and Philosophical Society, which, in the same year, presented it to the Leicester Museum, where it has since remained (Catalogue no. 263/1854). At the same time, in an article headed 'Literary Curiosity. An Original Letter by Dean Swift' it was printed in *The Midland Counties Historical Collector*, vol. i, no. 4, pp. 62–63. From this periodical Ball transcribed his text. The transcript in the museum, long accepted as the original letter, has no claim to that distinction. The paper on which it is written, as the watermark shows, belongs to the latter half of the eighteenth century; and the script suggests the end of that century or the beginning of the next. The hand is not that of Swift; and the document has never passed through the post.

of practice, into speculation & thought; insomuch that in these seven weeks I have been here, I have writt, & burnt and writt again, upon almost all manner of subjects, more perhaps than any man in England. And this is it, wch a person of great Honour[1] in Ireland (who was pleas'd to stoop so low as to look into my mind) & us'd to tell me, that my mind was like a conjur'd spirit, that would do mischief if I would not give it employment,—'Tis this humor, that makes me so busy when I am in Company to turn all that way, and since it comonly ends in talk, whether it be love or Common Conversation it is all alike, This is so Common that I coud remember twenty women in my life to whom I have behavd my self just the same way, and I profess without any other Design than that of entertaining my self when I am very Idle, or when something goes amiss in my affairs. This I have always done as a man of the world when I had no design of any thing grave in it, & what I thought at worst a harmless Impertinence——But when ever I began to take sober resolutions, or (as now) of entring into the Church, I never found it woud be hard to putt off this kind of folly at the porch; besides perhaps in so general a Conversation among that sex, I might pretend a little to understand where I am, when I go to choose for a wife; and though the Cunningest Sharper of the Town may have a Cheat put upon him, yet it must be cleanlier carried on than this which you think I am going to Top upon my self; and truly if you knew how metaphysicall I am that way, you woud little fear I shoud venture on one who has given so much occasion to toungs; For tho' the people is a lying sort of a Beast (and I think in Leicester above all parts that I ever was in) yet they seldom talk without some glimpse of Reason, wch I declare, (so unpardonably jealous I am) to be a sufficient cause for me [not] to have any woman any farther than a bare acquaintance, except all things else were agreable, and that I had mathematicall Demonstration for the falsehood of the first wch if it be not impossible I am sure is very like it—among all the young gentlemen that I have known to have Ruind their selves by marrying (which I assure you is a great number) I have made this general Rule that they are either young, raw & ignorant Scholars, who for want of knowing company, believe every silk petticoat includes an angell, or else they have been a sort of honest young men,

---

[1] The 'person of great Honour' has on no plausible grounds been identified with Lord Berkeley; but there is no proof that Berkeley had ever been in Ireland before he came over in 1699 as a Lord Justice.

who perhaps are too literal in rather marrying than burning &
entail misery on them selves & posterity by an over acting modesty,
—I think I am very far excluded from listing under either of these
heads.—I confess I have known one or two men of sence enough,
who inclined to frolicks have marryed & Ruind themselves, out of a
maggot; But a thousand Household thoughts, wch always drive
matrimony out of my mind, whenever it chances to come there, will
I am sure fright me from that, Besides that I am naturaly temperate,
and never engaged in the contrary, which usually produces those
effects,—yr hints at particular Storys I do not understand; having
never heard them but just hinted, I thought it proper to give you
this, to shew how I thank you for your regard of me, & I hope my
Carriage will be so as my friends need not be ashamed of the name,
—I shoud not have behavd my self after the manner I did in Leicester
if I had not valued my own entertainment beyond the obloquy of a
parcel of very wretched fools which I solemnly pronounce the
inhabitants of Leicester to be, & so I content my self with Retaliation—I hope you will forgive this trouble & so with my service to
your good wife, I am good cousin your very friend and servant |
Jon: Swift.

Address: To the Revnd mr. John Kendall | Vicar of Thornton, to be left at | Mr
Birkheads over against the | Free School in Leicester.

The Athenian Gazette

Swift to the Athenian Society

Moor-park, Feb. 14. 1691.

Gentlemen,

Since every Body pretends to trouble you with their Follies, I
thought I might claim the Priviledge of an Englishman, and put in
my share among the rest. Being last year in Ireland (from whence
I returned about half a year ago), I heard only a loose talk of your
Society, and believed the design to be only some new Folly just
suitable to the Age, which God knows, I little expected ever to produce any thing extraordinary.[1] Since my being in England, having

[1] With his *Ode to the Athenian Society* and the accompanying prefatory
letter Swift saw himself in print for the first time. The letter and the poem
appeared in *The Supplement to the Fifth Volume of the Athenian Gazette*; . . .
London, Printed for John Dunton at the Raven in the Poultry, . . . (1691-2).
Sir William Temple appears to have been a contributor to the *Gazette*

still continued in the Countrey, and much out of Company; I had but little advantage of knowing any more, till about two Months ago, passing through Oxford, a very learned Gentleman there, first shew'd me two or three of your Volumes, and gave me his Account and Opinion of you; a while after I came to this place, upon a visit to [Sir William Temple] where I have been ever since, and have seen all the four Volumes with their Supplements, which answering my expectation. The perusal has produced, what you find inclosed.

As I have been somewhat inclined to this Folly, so I have seldom wanted some-body to flatter me in it. As for the Ode inclosed, I have sent it to a Person of very great Learning and Honour, and since to some others, the best of my Acquaintance, (to which I thought very proper to inure it for a greater light) and they have all been pleased to tell me, that they are sure it will not be unwelcome, and that I should beg the Honour of You to let it be Printed before Your next Volume (which I think, is soon to be published,) it being so usual before most Books of any great value among Poets, and before it's seeing the World, I submit it wholly to the Correction of your Pens.

I intreat, therefore, one of You would descend so far, as to write two or three lines to me of your Pleasure upon it. Which, as I cannot but expect from Gentlemen, who have so well shewn, upon so many occasions, that greatest Character of Scholars, in being favourable to the Ignorant, so, I am sure, nothing at present can more highly oblige me, or make me happier. I am,|(Gentlemen)| Your ever most Humble,|and most|admiring Servant.

Jonathan Swift.

Rothschild[1]

Swift to Thomas Swift

Moorpark.[2] May 3^d 1692.

I confess I hve been tedious in answering y^r letter, and I putt it up so carefully that I was half an hour looking for it just now, I had

(Dunton's *Life and Errors*, 1705, p. 261). In the same work (p. 260) Dunton refers to Swift as 'a Country Gentleman' who sent 'an ingenious Poem' to the fifth supplement of the *Athenian Mercury*. See, further, *Poems*, pp. 13–25.

[For notes 1, 2 see opposite.

no excuse but too much idleness, which is allways a sufficient one with me, and thô it would not pass well in the world, yet I am sure has the same effect on me as too much business has there. I beg your pardon for my false intelligence, I assure you news and reports are what I usually give perhaps but too little credit (if it be possible) to but hearing this from Mr Ash[1] who having been secretary in the Emperor's Court, and frequenting ours here very much, and bringing this news that day from thence, which agreeing with what I had from yr Mother[2] when I was in Oxford, I say all this deceivd me, and has given you this unsightly adventure, and it just now comes into my head, that I have writt a letter to Congratulate my Tutor upon the Kings giving him the Provostship of Dublin Colledge, which I read in a French news paper printed in Holland t'other day, and the Blockhead mistook his name and calld him (Chevalier George Ash) which is the Knight &c deceivd by his spelling his name St George,[3] but now if this be false news as well as the first it will be a just judgment on him for reporting at a venture. I remember when I usd the Court[4] above two years ago I heard very much that Complaint you make of Foreign—and I suppose Sr

[1] St. George Ashe (1658?–1718), who became a Fellow of Trinity College in 1679, was later Swift's tutor. During the rebellion he left the country, and became chaplain to Lord Paget, ambassador of William III at Vienna. Ashe was at Vienna from 1689 till the close of the year 1691. See letter from Ashe to James W. Imhoff, B.M. Add MS. 24927. He became Provost of Trinity in 1692; Bishop of Cloyne in 1695; of Clogher in 1697; and was thence translated to Derry 1716–17. He and Swift remained lifelong friends.

[2] Thomas Swift's father, Thomas, married a daughter of Sir William Davenant. The son, born in 1665, educated at Kilkenny and Dublin University, was thus a school and college companion of Jonathan.

[3] The name was spelled Saint George by Ashe's ancestors.—Ball.

[4] It is improbable that Swift had much converse with Court circles so early. Not till the following year was he commissioned by Temple to attempt to dissuade William III from his opposition to the bill for triennial Parliaments.

---

[1] This letter was first printed by Ball, i. 361–6, among supplemental letters it was then in the possession of Lieutenant More Molyneux McCowen of Losely Park, Surrey. Thence it passed to Mrs. More-Molyneux, Losely House; and in 1937 into Lord Rothschild's collection. The name of a former owner is written, under the original address, in what appears to be an eighteenth-century hand: 'Swift's lettr from Mrs Cathrals Papers.'

[2] It is clear that since Swift had been to Oxford in the previous December, and after he had returned to Moor Park, several letters had passed between his cousin Thomas Swift and himself.

John M.[1] is not Knave enough to thrive there, I believe he is still a Coll[2] and Governor of Chester. It makes me mad to hear you talk of making a Copy of verses next morning, which tho indeed they are not so correct as yr others are what I could not do under 2 or 3 days, nor does it enter into my head to make any thing of a sudden but what I find to be exceeding silly stuff except by great chance, I esteem the time of studying Poetry to be 2 hours in a morning, and that only when the humor sits, which I esteem for the flower of the whole Day, and truly I make bold to employ them that way and yet I seldom write above 2 Stanzas in a week I mean such as are to any Pindarick Ode, and yet I have known my self in so good a humor as to make 2 in a day, but it may be no more in a week after, and when all's done, I alter them a hundred times, and yet I do not believe my self to be a laborious dry writer, because if the fitt comes not immediatly I never heed it but think of something else, and besides, the Poem I writt to the Athen. Society was all ruff drawn in a week, and finishd in 2 days after, and yet it consists of 12 stanza[3] and some of them above thirty lines, all above 20, and yet it is so well thought of that the unknown Gentlemen printed it before one of their Books, and the Bookseller writes me word that another Gentleman has in a book calld the History of the Athen Society, quoted my Poem very Honorably[4] (as the fellow calld it) so that perhaps I was in a good humor all the week, or at least S[r] W[m] T[5] speaking to me so much in their Praise made me zealous for their cause, for really I take that to be a part of the Honesty of Poets that they can not write well except they think the subject deserves it. But that it self will not allways hold, for I have had an ode in hand these 5 months inscribed to my late L[d] of Canterbury D[r] Sancroft, a gentleman I admire at a degree more than I can express, putt into

---

[1] As the address of this letter shows, Thomas Swift was living with Sir John Morgan, second baronet, of Kinnersley in the county of Hereford. He may have been acting as tutor to his son. The first Sir John Morgan assisted Monk in the restoration of Charles II.
[2] Coll, i.e. Colonel.
[3] *Sic.*
[4] The other gentleman was Charles Gildon, who, in his *History of the Athenian Society*, 1691, quoted the last three lines of Swift's ode with approbation:

> How strange a Paradox is true,
> That Men, who liv'd and dy'd without a Name,
> Are the chief Heroes in the sacred List of Fame.

[5] Sir William Temple.

me partly by some experience of him, but more by an unhappy reverend Gentleman my L^d the Bishop of Ely with whom I usd to converse about 2 or 3 years ago, and very often upon that Subject, but I say, I cannot finish it for my life, and I have done nine stanzas and do not like half of them, nor am nigh finished, but there it lyes and I sometimes add to it, and would wish it were done to my desire, I would send it to my Bookseller and make him print it with my name and all, to show my respect and Gratitude to that excellent person, and to perform half a Promise I made His L^dship of Ely upon it[1]—I am not mistaken in my critick, for it is written To thee all conq—&c in that Poem, nor do I like yr mending it any better, therefore give it another wipe, and then it will be one of my Favorits. —I have a sort of vanity, or Foibless, I do not know what to call it, and which I would fain know if you partake of it, it is (not to be circumstantiall) that I am overfond of my own writings, I would not have the world think so for a million, but it is so, and I find when I writt what pleases me I am Cowley to my self[2] and can read it a hundred times over, I know 'tis a desperate weakness and has nothing to defend it but it's secrecy, and I know farther, that I am wholly in the wrong, but have the same pretence the Baboon had to praise her Children, and indeed I think the love in both is much alike, and their being our own ofspring is what makes me such a blockhead, I am just the same way to yours, and thô I resolve to be a severe critick, yet I can not but think I see a thousand beautyes, and no faults in what you take any pains about, for as to the rest I can easily distinguish when either of us have been idle. I am just so to all my acquaintance I mean in proportion to my love of them,

[1] For the *Ode to Sancroft* see *Poems*, pp. 33–42. The poem was first printed by John Nichols in 1789. At the time of writing this letter Swift had finished nine stanzas. As it stands with twelve stanzas the poem is still unfinished. Nichols, presumably copying from the manuscript, heads the poem: 'Written May 1689, at the desire of the late Lord Bishop of E——.' But three years later it was still in hand denying every effort. Furthermore, stanza iii refers to Sancroft's 'divinity of retreat', and xi to his 'exaltation of retreat'. Although Sancroft was suspended 1 Aug. 1689, and deprived 1 Feb. 1690, for refusing the oath of allegiance to William and Mary, he did not leave Lambeth until his ejectment, 23 June 1691. We may surmise that the poem was begun in 1689, at the request of Francis Turner, Bishop of Ely, also a non-juror, and abandoned incomplete in 1692.

[2] In his *Letter Concerning the Sacramental Test*, 1708 (*Prose Works*, ed. H. Davis, ii. 114), Swift quotes 'Mr. *Cowley*'s Love Verses', which, even at fifteen, he 'thought extraordinary'. For the greater part of his life a copy of Cowley's Works was in his library.

and Particularly to Sr Wm T. I never read his writings but I prefer
him to all others at present in England, Which I suppose is all but
a piece of selflove, and the likeness of humors makes one fond of
them as if they were ones own—I do not at all like your ordering
yr fortune, On my Conscience you'll be a beggar, and I was just
going to ask you the old musty question, what to you Propose &c?
I confess a persons happiness is a thing not to be slighted so much as
the world thinks, I mean with being too anxious for the future, but
I deny yours to be a present happiness, and I was going to call you
a poor ignorant contented Fellow for thinking [it is] but that if you
do, your very thoughts make it so, And I will not take the Pains to
lug you out only to give you demonstration that you are under
water, All that I can say is that I wish to God you were well provided for thô it were with a good living in the Church—This Virgil
sticks plaguily on my hands, I did about 200 lines and gave it to
my Lady G.^{1} for a Sample, and she and Sr W. T. like it as I would
have them, but He wont allow that I should leave out what I
mentiond to you. Which begins, In foribus lethum Androgeo &c^2
and so for about 10 lines, and about 3 lines in a place beyond it
Foliis tantum ne carmina manda &c,^{3} which perhaps I know the
meaning but 'tis confounded silly nonsense in English—prithee if
you can make better of either of them tell me, What I writt was not
worth transcribing to you, and besides I was dunnd for it,—I like
yr stile to the Girl, but you make no Conscience because 'tis to a
Woman, and therefore borrow from rich Mr Cowly, well 'tis
cleanlyly absurd, and if she has any sense yr entertainment is very
agreeable, but igad I can not write anything easy to be understood
thô it were but in praise of an old Shooo and sometime or other I
will send you something I writt to a young lady in Ireland which
I call the Ramble,^{4} and it will show what I say is true,

My Tutor promises me a Testimon: and I stay for him, but I

---

^{1} Lady (Martha) Giffard, Temple's sister, who lived with her brother and
his wife at Moor Park. The tragedy of her life was the death of her husband,
Sir Thomas Giffard, in 1662, within thirteen days of their marriage. In his poem
addressed to Temple on his illness Swift wrote of her:

Grief from Dorinda's face does ne'er depart
Further than its own palace in her heart.

There are frequent references to her in the *Journal to Stella*.
^{2} *Aen.* vi. 20.
^{3} *Aen.* vi. 74. Swift's attempted translation of Virgil has not survived.
^{4} This poem is not forthcoming.

have been often told that tho Midsummer was not the onely time yet it was the best time to commence, However, what makes me uneasy is for fear of coming off ill either in not getting that Testim.[1] or else ill performing acts, I have gott up my Lattin, pretty well, and am getting up my Greek, but to enter upon causes of Philosophy is what I protest I will rather dy in a ditch than go about. and so Adieu J. S.

Send me word how I shall direct hereafter.[2]

Address: To | Mr Swift at Sr John | Morgan's in Kinnersly, to | be left with John Griffith | in Wobbly | Hereford-shire

Orrery, Remarks

Swift to William Swift

Moore Park, Nov. 29, 1692

Sir,

My sister told me, you was pleased (when she was here)[3] to wonder, I did so seldom write to you. I [hope you have][4] been so kind, to impute it neither to ill mann[ers or want of] respect.[5] I

---

[1] For the *testimonium* from Trinity College see note, p. 12.

[2] Swift and his cousin must have met at Oxford soon after the writing of this letter, for Swift took his degree on 5 July and his cousin two days later.—Ball.

[3] Swift's sister was about eighteen months older than her brother. Her baptism is recorded in the register of St. Michan's Church, Dublin: 'Jane dau. to Jonathan Swift and Abigail his wife bapt. 1 May 1666.' The King's Inns, when Swift's father was the steward, stood near St. Michan's Church.

[4] The original letter from which Orrery made his transcript was mutilated. The words within square brackets are conjectural. Deane Swift, *Essay*, 1755, pp. 56–57 also printed this letter 'although very imperfect'.

[5] This letter is addressed to the fourth of Swift's paternal uncles. All his grandfather's sons except Thomas, who took holy orders, adopted a legal profession. Godwin and Dryden were students of Gray's Inn, and the former was called in 1660 to the English Bar, and, in 1663, to the Irish Bar. The other three were admitted solicitors in Ireland, William on 25 Nov. 1661. He was probably accompanied thither by Swift's father, who, although not admitted a solicitor until 26 Jan. 1665–6, is said to have been connected with the King's Inns from the time of the Restoration. William Swift, who acquired considerable property, seems to have devoted himself with great assiduity to his profession, and held at the time of his death the office of a filizer in the Court of Common Pleas. He was married four times, but only two children survived him, a son, possibly the 'Beau Swift' of the *Journal*, p. 117, and a daughter who married one of his brother Godwin's sons. William's will is dated 19 May 1703 and was proved 1 Mar. 1705–6.

always [have] thought that sufficient from one, who has always been but too troublesome to you: besides I knew your aversion to impertinences, and God Knows so very private a life as mine can furnish a letter with little else: for I often am two or three months without seeing any body besides the family; and now my sister is gone, I am likely to be more solitary than before. I am still to thank you for your care in my Testimonium,[1] and it was to very good purpose, for I never was more satisfied than in the behaviour of the University of Oxford to me.[2] I had all the civilities I could wish for, and so many [showed me] favours, that I am ashamed to have been more obliged in a few weeks to strangers, than ever I was in seven years to Dublin College. I am not to take orders till the King gives me a Prebendary: and Sir William Temple, tho' he promises me the certainty of it, yet is less forward than I could wish; because, I suppose he believes I shall leave him, and upon some accounts, he thinks me a little necessary to him [at present].[3] If I were . . . [affording you] entertainment, or doing you any satisfaction by my letters, I should be very glad to perform it that way, as I am bound to do it by all others. I am sorry my fortune should fling me so far from the best of my relations, but hope that I shall have the happiness to see you some time or other. Pray my humble service to my good aunt, and the rest of my relations, if you please.

[1] A reference to the alleged *testimonium* from the University of Dublin, which Orrery (*Remarks*, pp. 12–13) believed to have contained the words *speciali gratia*, which brought credit to Swift at Oxford, where it was taken to imply 'a degree conferred in reward of extraordinary diligence, or learning'. See, however, Barrett's *Essay*, p. 36, Forster, *Life*, pp. 28–29, 41–43.

[2] Swift had gone to Oxford in the preceding December, probably for the purpose of visiting his cousin, Thomas Swift, who had been with him at Kilkenny School, and at Trinity College, Dublin, and who was then studying at Balliol College, whence his father, Swift's uncle, the Rev. Thomas Swift, had graduated. It was probably then that Swift conceived the idea of taking his Master of Arts degree at Oxford. According to Delany (*Observations*, p. 48) he did so in order to show that he could succeed in a more difficult course, but no examination was then necessary for that degree. Swift's residence at Oxford, which has been sometimes magnified into months, can have been only very brief. On 14 June 1692 Swift, as a Bachelor of Arts of Dublin University, was incorporated a member of Oxford University from Hart Hall, which from its antiquity enjoyed a precedence in the right of inscribing strangers on its books (*Hertford College*, by S. C. Hamilton, p. 38). Three weeks later, on 5 July, he received his Master of Arts degree.—Ball.

[3] By this time Temple had become conscious of Swift's usefulness to him in the revision and further publication of his writings.

Swift to Thomas Swift

Dec^br 6th 1693—²

Y^r Letter speaks of so many Choices of Employment, that one would think you to[o] busy to be very unhappy tho the Pinch of a present uneasyness makes one a very ill Reasoner, and He that lyes ill on one side tho the Posture may help to his Health is very hardly dissuaded from turning on the other, This is enough to say on that score, in the Place this Letter finds you, For the rest, I think the advise of a Friend is very far from being disinterested, and to avoyd that was the very reason I forbore it. I cannot at this distance give a judgment near enough upon yr other hopes, but if they be not certain, I think there is no avoyding the Choice of what is; This I told you, or something like it before—I protest I cannot much Pity yr present Circumstances, which keep yr mind and yr body in Motion, and my self was never very miserable while my thoughts were in a Ferment for I imagine a dead Calm to be troublesomest part of our Voyage thro the World; If that Curacy were not disposed of which I once mentiond You, I think I should say it was; for it fits yr present Prospects almost as ill as it did your merit then—

Tho You are so crammd with business I must needs desire yr assistance in Paying 45 shill for Nan Swift & Matt Rooke³ and Me, for our Dictionary which is about this time to be delivered, or else my Bookseller (Simpson)⁴ may be careless in the choice of the Copyes in which there is difference enough—

I desire You would inform yr self what you mean by bidding me

¹ First printed by Ball, i. 367–8, among supplemental letters. The original passed from Mrs. More-Molyneux, Losely House, Surrey, to the Rothschild collection in 1937. An endorsement under the address reads 'D— Swift's Letter 1693 taken from Mrs Cathra[l]'s papers'. This letter was evidently written from Moor Park.

² As the address of this letter shows, Thomas Swift was then staying with his uncle, Charles Davenant, son of Sir William, the poet. Dr. Charles Davenant was a prolific writer of tracts on political economy. A letter from him addressed to Swift will be found under the date 3 Nov. 1713.

³ Nan (or Anne) Swift was a daughter of Swift's uncle Adam. She married a James Perry, of Perrymount, co. Down. In the *Journal*, p. 274, Swift mentions meeting in Pall Mall the 'little jackanapes . . . one Perry'. Matthew Rooke was apparently, from the post-script, a son of one of Swift's cousins (*Journal*, p. 582).

⁴ Ralph Simpson, bookseller in London, 1680–1704, Plomer, *Dictionary of Booksellers . . . 1668–1725*, p. 271. See also Dunton's *Life and Errors*, i. 224.

keep my Verses for Will Congreves next Play,[1] for I tell You they
were calculated for any of his, and if it were but acted when you
say, it is as early as ever I intended, since I onely design they should
be printed before it, So I desire you will send me word immediatly,
how it succeeded, whether well, ill or indifferently, because my
sending them to Mr Congreve depends upon knowing the Issue

They are almost 250 lines, not Pindarick—and if I could tell
what is become of Mr Thomas Swift whom I formerly knew I would
send them to Him for his Judgment, but for yr self, it is Ominous
and so I'll | Conclude | Yrs | J Swift

To Thwart business with Rhime, to spoyl its Witchcraft, and
My Ltr to Coz Rooke and Matt She must find money for those
Dictionarys but to show how rich I am I will send her my share my
self—

Address: For Mr Swift at | D^r D'avenant's | in Red-lyon Square | near Hol-
    born | London
Postmark: 7 DE

Deane Swift, Essay

Swift to Deane Swift

Leicester, June 3d, 1694.[2]
I received your kind Letter to day from your Sister, and am very
glad to find you will spare time from Business so far as to write a

[1] When six years old Swift was sent by his uncle, Godwin Swift, to Kilkenny
Grammar School. He was there joined by his cousin Thomas. In 1681, or 1682,
William Congreve, two years Swift's junior, was sent to the same school. There
is no evidence that they formed any acquaintance at this time. Later they were
together at Trinity College, Dublin, which Swift entered 24 Apr. 1682, and
Congreve 5 Apr. 1685. Swift is here referring to Congreve's second play, *The
Double-Dealer*, then appearing on the London stage. For Swift's verses *To Mr.
Congreve*, stated to have been 'Written November 1693', see *Poems*, pp. 43–50.
There is no record that Congreve ever received a copy of the poem.

[2] Deane Swift, *Essay*, 1755, p. 53, states in a footnote—'This letter is printed
exactly from an authentick copy taken from the original.'
Deane Swift was the father of Swift's biographer of the same name to whom
we owe the printing of this letter from a transcript. The elder Deane Swift was
a son of Swift's uncle Godwin, whose third wife was a daughter of Richard
Deane the regicide. His son Deane was her eldest child. Deane Swift was younger
than his cousin Jonathan. At the time this letter was written he could not have
been more than twenty. Before that time he had gone out to Portugal to join

long Letter to one you have none at all with but Friendship, which, as the World passes, is perhaps one of the idlest Things in it. 'Tis a pleasure to me to see You sally out of your Road, and take Notice of Curiosityes, of which I am very glad to have Part, and desire You to set by some idle minutes for a Commerce which shall ever be dear to Me, and from so good an Observer as you may easily be, cannot fail of being useful. I am sorry to see so much Superstition in a Country so given to Trade; I half used to think those two to be incompatible. Not that I utterly dislike your Processions for Rain or fair Weather, which, as trifling as they are, yet have good Effects to quiet common Heads, and infuse a gaping Devotion among the Rabble. But your burning the old Woman, unless she were a Duegna, I shall never be reconciled to; though it is easily observed that Nations which have most Gallantry to the Young, are ever the severest upon the Old. I have not Leisure to descant further upon your pleasing Letter, nor any thing to return You from so barren a Scene as this, which I shall leave in four Days towards my journey for Ireland.

I had designed a Letter to my Cosin Willoughby,[1] and the last Favour He has done me requires a great deal of Acknowledgment, but the Thoughts of my sending so many before, has made me believe it better to trust You with delivering my best thanks to Him, and that You will endeavour to persuade Him how extream sensible of his goodness and generosity I am. I wish and shall pray, He may

a stepbrother, a merchant in that country. About the year 1705 he returned from Portugal, and married a lady, like himself of Cromwellian descent. They settled in co. Meath within about six miles of Swift's living of Laracor. Deane Swift's will was dated 16 May 1713, and was proved on 17 May 1714. In his will he mentions his wife, his only child Deane, the future biographer of Jonathan, and his sister Hannah Maria, who lived with them, and is alluded to in this letter.

[1] Willoughby Swift was the stepbrother whom Deane Swift had joined in Portugal, and was at that time Godwin Swift's eldest surviving son by his first wife Elizabeth Wheeler. Deane Swift, the younger (*Essay*, p. 53) prints an interesting extract from a letter of the future Dean of St. Patrick's mother, dated 10 Aug. 1703, in which she writes: 'Pray be pleased to present my best service to my good nephew Swift [Willoughby] and tell him I always bear in my heart a grateful remembrance of all the kindness he was pleased to shew to my son.' Deane Swift adds the comment: 'A proof in my opinion that her son Jonathan was chiefly supported after the insanity of his uncle by this merchant at Lisbon.' Willoughby Swift's will was dated at Lisbon in Jan. 1709–10, with an added codicil executed shortly before his death in Mar. 1712–13. In the will he mentions his daughters, Honoria, wife of Ferdinand Swanton, and Hannah, wife of the Rev. Stafford Lightburne, who became Swift's curate.

be as happy as he deserves, and he cannot be more. My Mother desires her best Love to Him and to You, with both our Services to My Cosin his Wife.

I forgot to tell You I left Sir William Temple a month ago, just as I foretold it to You, and every thing happened thereupon exactly as I guest. He was extream angry I left Him, and yet would not oblige Himself any further than upon my good Behaviour, nor would promise any thing firmly to Me at all; so that every Body judged I did best to leave Him; I design to be ordained September next, and make what Endeavours I can for something in the Church. I wish it may ever lye in my Cosin's way or Yours to have Interest to bring me in Chaplain of the Factory.[1]

If any thing offers from Dublin that may serve either to satisfy or divert You, I will not fail of contributing, and giving You constant Intelligence from thence of whatever you shall desire.

I am your affectionate Cosin

and Servant

J. Swift.

Harvard

Swift to Sir William Temple

Dublin. Octbʳ 6ᵗʰ 1694

May it please Your Honor[2]

That I might not continue by any means the many Troubles I [have] given You; I have all this while avoyded one, which I fear proves necessary at last. I haven (*sic*) taken all due Methods to be ordayned, and one Time of Ordination is allready elapsed since my Arrivall, without effecting it: Two or three Bishops Acquaintance of our Family, have signified to me and them, that after so long a

---

[1] As a result of the treaties between England and Portugal during the reign of Charles II, a large body of English merchants and factors had settled in Lisbon, and, as appears from Swift's reference, a chaplain was attached, as in other cases of the kind, to the company.—Ball.

[2] This letter, as printed by editors before Ball, was taken from a transcript, not wholly accurate, made by the Rev. Robert Shipman, Fellow of All Souls and rector of Compton near Winchester. He was said to be a relation of the Temple family. The original was sold, 19 July 1867, at Sotheby's to Baker for £11. It thence passed into the possession of Frederick Locker-Lampson, and was printed by him in *Patchwork*, 1879, pp. 77–79. The original letter is now deposited in the Harvard University Library.

standing at the University, it is admired I have not entered upon
something or other (above half the Clergy in this Town being my
Juniors) and that it being so many Years since I left this Kingdom,
they could not admit me to the Ministry without some Certificate
of my Behavior where I lived: And my Lord ArchBishop of Dublin
was pleased to say a great deal of this Kind to Me Yesterday;
concluding against all I had to answer that He expected I should
have a Certificate from Your Honor of my Conduct in your Family.¹
The Sense I am in, how low I am fallen in Your Honor's Thoughts,
has denied Me Assurance enough to beg this Favor till I find it
impossible to avoyd:² and I intreat Your Honor to understand that
no Person is admitted to a Living here, without some Knowledge
of his Abilityes for it; which it being reckon'd impossible to judge
in those who are not ordained, the usuall Method is to admit them
first to some small Readers Place till by Preaching upon Occasions
they can value themselves for better Preferment: This (without
great Friends) is so generall, that if I were fourscore years old, I
must go the same Way, and should at that age be told, every one
must have a Beginning. I intreat that Your Honor will consider this,
and will please to send me some Certificate of my Behavior during
almost three Years in Your Family: Wheren I shall stand in need of
all Your Goodness to excuse my many Weaknesses and Follyes and
Oversights; much more, to say any Thing to my Advantage. The
Particulars expected of me, are what relate, to Morals and Learning,
and the Reasons of quitting your Honor's Family, that is, whether
the last was occasion'd by any ill Actions of mine. They are all
entirely left to Your Honor's Mercy, thô in the first, I think I cannot
reproach my self any further than for Infirmityes.

¹ Narcissus Marsh, born 1638, a studious scholar, became a Fellow of Exeter
College, Oxford. He was, by favour of the Duke of Ormonde, appointed Provost
of Trinity College, Dublin. He bestowed a gift of Oriental MSS. on the Bodleian;
and founded the library in Dublin which bears his name. In 1683 he was created
Bishop of Ferns and Leighlin. During the revolution he fled the country. On
the accession of William III he was presented to the Archbishopric of Cashel;
in 1694 he was translated to Dublin; and in 1703 to Armagh. See *D.N.B.*
Swift's 'Character' of Marsh (*Prose Works*, ed. Temple Scott, xi. 189) is evidence that he did not like him, possibly on two grounds—Marsh's insistence
upon a certificate from Temple and his disagreements with Archbishop King.
² This letter has been described as 'penitential', and by some it has been
assumed that Temple's treatment of Swift was stiff and unkindly. There is no
justification for this assumption. As time passed a sincere regard between the
two unfolded.

This is all I dare beg at present from Your Honor, under Circumstances of Life not worth your Regard: What is left me to wish (next to the Health and Felicity of Your Honor and Family) is that Heaven would one Day allow me the Opportunity to leave my Acknowledgments at Your feet, for so many Favors I have received, which whatever effect they have had upon my Fortune shall never fayl to have the greatest upon my Mind, in approving my self upon all Occasions | Your Honor's | most obedient and | most dutifull | Servant, | J. Swift.

I beg my most humble Duty and Service, be presented to my Ladyes, Your Honor's Lady and Sister.

The Ordination is appointed by the Arch-Bishop by the Beginning of November, so that if Your Honor will not grant this Favor immediatiy I fear it will come too late[1]

Address: For The Honorable Sr William | Temple, Bar^t; at His House at
    Moor-Park near Farnham | in Surrey | England | By way of London
Postmark: 12 OC

Forster copy[2]

Swift to Miss Jane Waring

29 April 1696.[3]

Madam,
    Impatience is the most inseparable quality of a lover, and indeed of every person who is in pursuit of a design whereon he conceives

---

[1] Nineteen days later, on 25 Oct. 1694, Swift was ordained deacon, and three months later, on 13 Jan. 1694-5, priest, by William Moreton, Bishop of Kildare. (See *Proc. of the Royal Irish Academy*, II. ii. 4.)—Ball.

[2] This letter was first printed in 1789 in George Monck Berkeley's *Literary Relics*, pp. 23-32. The original was then in the possession of Dr. Saunders of Dublin. In 1804, when the original was in the hands of Earl Macartney, Berkeley's text was collated with it by Edmund Malone. Now Forster Collection, 34. i. 2. So far as can be seen, despite Malone's claim to important corrections, Berkeley's transcript is not far astray. His corrections are, however, embodied. Inquiries have failed to discover the present whereabouts of the autograph letter. See further, Forster's *Life*, p. 78 n. Lyon, in his copy of Hawkesworth's *Life of Swift* (Forster Collection) states that three other letters, before the only other surviving letter, 4 May 1700, were addressed to Jane Waring at Belfast: 20 Dec. 1695 from Dublin; 29 June 1696 and 28 Aug. 1697, both from Moor Park. No trace of these letters remains.   *[For note 3 see opposite.*

his greatest happiness or misery to depend.[1] It is the same thing in war, in courts, and in common business. Every one who hunts after pleasure, or fame, or fortune, is still restless and uneasy till he has hunted down his game: and all this is not only very natural, but something reasonable too; for a violent desire is little better than a distemper, and therefore men are not to blame in looking after a cure. I find myself hugely infected with this malady, and am easily vain enough to believe it has some very good reasons to excuse it. For indeed, in my case, there are some circumstances which will admit pardon for more than ordinary disquiets. That dearest object upon which all my prospect of happiness entirely depends, is in perpetual danger to be removed for ever from my sight. Varina's[2] life is daily wasting, and though one just and honourable action would furnish health to her, and unspeakable happiness to us both, yet some power that repines at human felicity has that influence to

[1] In Swift's time there were two undergraduates of the name of Waring at Trinity College, Dublin, sons of William Waring of Waringstown, co. Down; William who matriculated 11 June 1681, and Richard who matriculated 9 Apr. 1684, but their relationship to Jane Waring, whom Swift addresses, was that of cousin. Deane Swift's statement (*Essay*, p. 31) that the lady 'who made some very considerable impressions upon the Doctor's heart in the days of his youth' was a sister of Westenra Waring, 'a gentleman of fortune in the neighbourhood of Belfast', is to be accepted, although he did not matriculate till 16 June 1692, more than three years after Swift had left (*Alum. Dub.*, pp. 859–60). They were children of the Rev. Roger Waring, Archdeacon of Dromore. His wife was a Westenra, Isabella, sister of Peter Westenra, who represented Athboy in William III's first Irish Parliament. Archdeacon Waring's will, proved by his widow, 23 July 1692, mentions Jane and Westenra as well as other children.

[2] A poetical transformation of the name Waring.

[3] This letter was dated either at Belfast or Carrickfergus. A fortnight after his admission to priest's orders, on 28 Jan. 1694–5, Swift had been appointed by the Irish Government, then vested in three Lords Justices, of whom Lord Capel, of Tewkesbury, was the chief, to the prebend of Kilroot, in the Cathedral of Connor. The corps of this prebend consisted of the vicarages of Kilroot and Templecorran, and the rectory of Ballynure, comprising an area of nearly sixteen hundred acres. The parish of Kilroot lies on the northern side of Belfast Lough, to the east of the parish of Carrickfergus. It has for its northern and eastern boundaries the parish of Templecorran; the parish of Ballynure, which lies to the north-west, is separated from it by the parish of Carrickfergus. The church of Kilroot was, in Swift's time, in ruins, but the churches of Templecorran and Ballynure were in use. ('Swift in Kilroot', *Ulster Biographical Sketches*, 2nd Series, by Classon Porter, p. 13.) See also Landa, *Swift and the Church of Ireland*, pp. 8–18.

hold her continually doating upon her cruelty, and me upon the
cause of it. This fully convinces me of what we are told, that the
miseries of man's life are all beaten out on his own anvil. Why was I
so foolish to put my hopes and fears into the power or management
of another? Liberty is doubtless the most valuable blessing of life;
yet we are fond to fling it away on those who have been these 5000
years using us ill. Philosophy advises to keep our desires and
prospects of happiness as much as we can in our own breasts, and
independent of anything without. He that sends them abroad is
likely to have as little quiet as a merchant whose stock depends upon
winds, and waves, and pirates, or upon the words and faith of
creditors, every whit as dangerous and inconstant as the other.

I am a villain if I have not been poring this half hour over the
paper merely for want of something to say to you:—or is it rather
that I have so much to say to you, that I know not where to begin,
though at last 'tis all very likely to be arrant repetition?

Two strangers, a poet and a beggar, went to cuffs yesterday in this
town, which minded me to curse heartily both employments. However, I am glad to see those two trades fall out, because I always
heard they had been constant cronies: but what was best of all, the
poet got the better, and kicked the gentleman beggar out of doors.
This was of great comfort to me, till I heard the victor himself was
a most abominable bad rhymer, and as mere a vagabond beggar as
the other, which is a very great offence to me, for starving is much
too honourable for a blockhead. I read some of his verses printed in
praise of my Lady Donegal,[1] by which he has plainly proved that
Fortune has injured him, and that he is dunce enough to be worth
five thousand pounds a-year. It is a pity he has not also the qualifications to recommend himself to your sex. I dare engage no ladies
would hold him long in suspense with their unkindness: one settlement of separate maintenance, well engrossed, would have more
charms than all the wit or passion of a thousand letters. And I'll
maintain it, any man had better have a poor angel to his rival than
the devil himself if he was rich.

[1] In the last twelve lines of *Apollo's Edict* (*Poems*, p. 269) Swift celebrates
Lady Donegal as 'The glory of the *Granard* Race'. She was Catherine, only
daughter of Arthur, first Earl of Granard. She married in 1685 Arthur Chichester,
third Earl of Donegal, who was killed near Barcelona, 1706, fighting under
the command of Peterborough. She died in 1743, and was buried at Carrickfergus (Lodge, *Peerage of Ireland*, i. 338–40).

You have now had time enough to consider my last letter, and to form your own resolutions upon it. I wait your answer with a world of impatience, and if you think fit I should attend you before my journey, I am ready to do it. My Lady Donegall tells me that 'tis feared my Lord Deputy will not live many days;[1] and if that be so, 'tis possible I may take shipping from hence;[2] otherwise I shall set out on Monday fortnight for Dublin,[3] and, after one visit of leave to his Excellency, hasten to England: and how far you will stretch the point of your unreasonable scruples to keep me here, will depend upon the strength of the love you pretend for me. In short, Madam, I am once more offered the advantage to have the same acquaintance with greatness that I formerly enjoyed, and with better prospect of interest. I here solemnly offer to forego it all for your sake. I desire nothing of your fortune; you shall live where and with whom you please till my affairs are settled to your desire: and in the mean time I will push my advancement with all the eagerness and courage imaginable, and do not doubt to succeed.

Study seven years for objections against all this, and by Heaven they will at last be no more than trifles and put-offs. 'Tis true you have known sickness longer than you have me, and therefore perhaps you are more loath to part with it as an older acquaintance: But listen to what I here solemnly protest, by all that can be witness to an oath, that if I leave this kingdom before you are mine, I will endure the utmost indignities of fortune rather than ever return again, though the king would send me back his deputy. And if it

---

[1] Henry Capel, second son of Lord Capel of Hadham, was created Lord Capel of Tewkesbury in 1692. In the following year he was named, with two others, one of the Lords Justices with whom was placed the government of Ireland. Finding favour in this position he was, in May 1695, installed Lord Deputy. His health had been failing for some time, and he died at Chapelizod, near Dublin, on 30 May 1696. In his fragment of autobiography (*Prose Works*, ed. Temple Scott, xi. 379) Swift says that he was recommended to Capel, whether by Temple or another is left uncertain, although we know that Capel was a near neighbour of his at Sheen.

[2] There was at that time a noble Jacobean mansion belonging to Lord Chichester in Belfast, and another, equally splendid, belonging to him in Carrickfergus. It is doubtful which Lady Donegal occupied at that moment. The mansion at Belfast was destroyed by fire in 1706, three of Lady Donegal's children perishing in the flames. *Ulster Journal of Archaeology*, i. ii. 1; vii. 1.

[3] Swift had visited Dublin at least once during his residence at Kilroot, as one of the missing letters addressed to Jane Waring was dated from there on 20 Dec. 1695. See above, p. 18, n. 2.

must be so, preserve yourself, in God's name, for the next lover who
has those qualities you love so much beyond any of mine, and who
will highly admire you for those advantages which shall never share
any esteem from me. Would to Heaven you were but a while sensible
of the thoughts into which my present distractions plunge me: they
hale me a thousand ways, and I not able to bear them. 'Tis so, by
Heaven: The love of Varina is of more tragical consequence than
her cruelty. Would to God you had treated and scorned me from
the beginning. It was your pity opened the first way to my misfortune; and now your love is finishing my ruin: and it is so then.
In one fortnight I must take eternal farewell of Varina; and (I
wonder) will she weep at parting a little to justify her poor pretences of some affection to me? and will my friends still continue
reproaching me for the want of gallantry, and neglecting a close
siege? How comes it that they all wish us married together, they
knowing my circumstances and yours extremely well, and I am sure
love you too much, if it be only for my sake, to wish you any thing
that might cross your interest or your happiness?

Surely, Varina, you have but a very mean opinion of the joys that
accompany a true, honourable, unlimited love; yet either nature and
our ancestors have hugely deceived us, or else all other sublunary
things are dross in comparison. Is it possible you cannot be yet
insensible to the prospect of a rapture and delight so innocent and
so exalted? Trust me, Varina, Heaven has given us nothing else
worth the loss of a thought. Ambition, high appearance, friends, and
fortune, are all tasteless and insipid when they come in competition;
yet millions of such glorious minutes are we perpetually losing, for
ever losing, irrecoverably losing, to gratify empty forms and wrong
notions, and affected coldnesses and peevish humour. These are the
unhappy incumbrances which we who are distinguished from the
vulgar do fondly create to torment ourselves. The only felicity
permitted to human life we clog with tedious circumstances and
barbarous formality. By Heaven, Varina, you are more experienced,
and have less virgin innocence than I. Would not your conduct
make one think you were hugely skilled in all the little politic
methods of intrigue? Love, with the gall of too much discretion, is a
thousand times worse than with none at all. 'Tis a peculiar part of
nature which art debauches, but cannot improve. We have all of us
the seeds of it implanted in ourselves, and they require no help
from courts or fortune to cultivate and improve them. To resist the

violence of our inclinations in the beginning, is a strain of self-denial that may have some pretences to set up for a virtue: but when they are grounded at first upon reason, when they have taken firm root and grown up to a height, 'tis folly—folly as well as injustice, to withstand their dictates; for this passion has a property peculiar to itself, to be most commendable in its extremes, and 'tis as possible to err in the excess of piety as of love.

These are the rules I have long followed with you, Varina, and had you pleased to imitate them, we should both have been infinitely happy. The little disguises, and affected contradictions of your sex, were all (to say the truth) infinitely beneath persons of your pride and mine; paltry maxims that they are, calculated for the rabble of humanity. Oh, Varina, how imagination leads me beyond myself and all my sorrows! 'Tis sunk, and a thousand graves lie open!—No, Madam, I will give you no more of my unhappy temper, though I derive it all from you.

Farewell, Madam, and may love make you a while forget your temper to do me justice. Only remember, that if you still refuse to be mine, you will quickly lose, for ever lose, him that is resolved to die as he has lived, All yours, Jon. Swift.

I have here sent you Mr. Fletcher's letter, wherein I hope I do not injure generosity or break trust, since the contents are purely my own concern. If you will pardon the ill hand and spelling, the reason and sense of it you will find very well and proper.

Deane Swift 1768[1]

Swift to ——

[1698]

I received your kind letter from *Robert* by word of mouth, and think it a vast condescension in you to think of us in all your great-

---

[1] This letter, first printed by Deane Swift in 1768, was dated 1696, and stated to have been addressed to Jane Swift, 'The Doctor's sister'. The letter was written from Moor Park, where Swift had returned soon after writing the preceding one. From internal evidence it was evidently written early in 1698, and addressed either to Stella or her mother. Temple with his sister, Lady Giffard, and their domestic following, were in London. Swift has received a kind letter delivered by 'Robert' by word of mouth. In reply he gives information about the state of affairs at Moor Park.

ness: now shall we hear nothing from you for five months but *We courtiers. Loory*[1] is well, and presents his humble duty to my Lady, and love to his fellow-servant: but he is the miserablest creature in the world; eternally in his melancholy note, whatever I can do; and if his finger does but ake, I am in such a fright you would wonder at it. I pray return my service to Mrs. *Kilby*,[2] in payment of her's by *Robert*.

Nothing grows better by your absence but my Lady's chamber-floor, and Tumble-down *Dick*. Here are three letters for you, and *Molly* will not send one of them; she says you ordered her to the contrary. Mr. *Mose*[3] and I desire you will remember our love to the king, and let us know how he looks.

Robert says the Czar[4] is there, and is fallen in love with you, and designs to carry you to *Muscovy*; pray provide yourself with muffs and sable tippets, *&c*.

Æolus has made a strange revolution in the rooks nests; but I say no more, for it is dangerous to meddle with things above us.

I desire your absence heartily; for now I live in great state, and the cook comes in to know what I please to have for dinner: I ask very gravely what is in the house, and accordingly give orders for a dish of pigeons, or, *&c*. You shall have no more ale here, unless you send us a letter. Here is a great bundle and a letter for you; both came together from *London*. We all keep home like so many cats.

[1] In the British Museum there is a unique privately-printed volume: *Poems by Sir W. T.* For further details of this volume see *The Early Essays and Romances of Sir William Temple Bt.*, ed. G. C. Moore Smith, 1930, pp. xxiii–xxvi. About half the poems in the book were printed in editions of Temple's works. Among poems not reprinted was one 'Upon My Lady Giffard's Loory', which appears in Professor Moore Smith's volume, pp. 183–5, together with explanatory notes, pp. 205–6. Temple's little book was probably printed some time after 1680. A loory, or lory, is a parrot-like bird of brilliant plumage.

[2] Probably a mistake for Filby. Anne Johnson, Stella's younger sister by over two years, married a man called Filby, described as a baker, who subsequently became a salt officer in the west of England. See *Journal to Stella*, pp. 39 n. and 576 n.

[3] Ralph Mose, Temple's steward, who afterwards married Stella's mother. They are both named for pecuniary legacies in Temple's will.

[4] On the invitation of William III, Peter the Great visited England during the early months of 1698. During this visit he occupied Evelyn's house at Deptford. The season is described as being exceptionally severe. He left England in April.

Forster No. 539[1]

Swift to the Rev. John Winder

More Park, Ap[r] 1st 1698

Since the Resignation of my Living and the noise it made amongst you, I have had, at least 3 or 4 very wise Letters unsubscribed, from the Lord knows who, declaring much sorrow for my quitting Kilroot, blaming my Prudence for doing it before I was possesst of something else, and censuring my Truth in relation to a certain Lady.[2] One or two of them talked of you as one who was less my Friend than you pretended, with more of the same sort, too tedious to trouble you or my self with. For what they say relating to my self, either as to my Prudence or Conscience, I can answer sufficiently for my own Satisfaction, or for that of any body else who is my Friend enough to desire it. But I have no way of convincing People in the Clouds; And for any thing of the Letters that relates to you, I need not answer the Objections because I do not believe them: For I was ever assured of your good Intentions, & justice & Friendship, and thô I might suspect them, Yet I do not find any Interest you can have either to wish or to use me ill.[3]

I am very glad you have finished the Affair and are settled in Possession: I think you may henceforth reckon your self easy, and have little [to] do besides serving God your Friends and your self, and unless desire of Place or Titles will interfere, I know nothing besides accidents can hinder you from being happy, to which if I have contributed either by chance or good will, I shall reckon it among the lucky adventures of my Life.[4]

---

[1] The original, once in the possession of Mr. John Young, of Vanbrugh Fields, Blackheath, is now in the Forster Collection, no. 539. There is a transcript of this letter in the National Library of Scotland, MS. 912, f. 222.

[2] Jane Waring.

[3] Swift had resigned Kilroot early in Jan. 1698. The Rev. John Winder, as Rector of Carmoney, had been his neighbour. He is said to have come to Ireland as a chaplain to William III, in whose army Winder's father, Colonel Cuthbert Winder, of Wingfield in Berkshire, was an officer. Winder succeeded Swift at Kilroot. See Cotton's *Fasti Eccl. Hib.* iii. 104, 266; v. 246; Landa, *Swift and the Church of Ireland*, pp. 13–14, 19, 24; and 'The Winders of Lorton', by F. A. Lorton, in the *Trans. of the Cumberland and Westmorland Antiq. and Archaeol. Society*, xiv. 199, 207; xv. 238.

[4] Evidently Swift had been instrumental in securing the prebend for his friend, who continued to hold Kilroot till 1717.

For what you say of my having no reason to repent any of my endeavours to serve you, I am and have always been of the same Opinion, and therein your self may bear me Witness, when you remember that my Promises and designs relating to your succeeding in the Prebend were not of a sudden, or by chance, but were the constant Tennor of what I said when we last parted, and of most of my Letters since. Neither did that enclosed Letter of the Bps hasten it at all, for S^r W[illiam] T[emple] desired to write for my further Licence, and I would not consent to it, besides I had severall Accounts from others that it was your Opinion I should not give it up so soon, and that what you supposed about a Visitation so soon was a mistake, & that you would write to me to the same Effect, which either never came to my hand, or else you justly omitted to do upon receipt of my Resolution and Resignation inclosed. This I thought fitt to say to set us both right and clear in each other's thoughts.

For my own Fortune, as late in my Life as it is, I must een lett it drive on its old Course. I think I told in my last that 10 days before my resignation, My Ld Sunderland fell and I with Him,[1] since that there have been other Courses, which if they succeed, I shall be proud to own the Methods, or if otherwise, very much ashamed.

I shall be loath any Affairs of mine should constrain you, Therefore I approve of your method in first adjusting my Accounts, wherein I neither suspect your Justice nor dislike your resolutions of exactness, for I am and ever was very much for that Custom of making Accounts the clearest especially with my nearest Friends. If my uncle Adam Swift should be down in the North[2] and would desire to state them with you, I entreat you would comply, and take the usuall Course in such Cases either for present or future Paymt,

[1] In his preface to the third part of Temple's *Memoirs* Swift stated that his patron continued until his death in 'intimate friendship' with the Earl of Sunderland. Although Courtenay, in his *Life of Temple*, ii. 248, casts doubt on this statement there was a relationship close enough to explain a passing acquaintance with Swift on the part of Sunderland.

[2] Adam Swift described himself in an unsigned will, proved on 27 May 1704, as of Greencastle in co. Down. As a practising solicitor he probably resided for the most part in Dublin, and it was there that he died of a seizure while writing his will. He was twice married. A son, called William, and two daughters survived him. The elder of these two daughters, Anne, married a James Perry, the 'little jackanapes' of the *Journal to Stella*, p. 274, who lived at Perrymount, co. Down. The younger daughter, Martha, became the Mrs. Whiteway who tended Swift in his latter years.

wherein I shall not be urgent, but desire you to chuse your own Time, and fix upon it, and I shall readily consent.

Mr Higgison[1] has writ to me about that Abatem^t and I wish you had easd me of that Concern, as you might have done from what I said. I thought the half was sufficient; I made no Promise of any at all. I would do nothing rigorous. I am not on the Spott to judge of Circumstances. I want money sufficiently; and have nothing to trust to but the little in your hands. I dealt easily with Him the Year before. The utmost I will say is this; I gave Him half a promise to endeavor He should be Farmer this Year, but that is now out of my Power; If you have disposed it to another, in consideration of that Disappointment let him take the whole Abatem^t in God's name, but if you have lett it to him this Year, e'en be kind to him your self if you please, for then he shall only be abated half; that's positive.

I never heard whether the Bp received my Lettr of Farewell; pray know, & present his Ldship with my humble Duty and Service.[2]

I assure you (for I am an understanding man in that Affair) that the Parish of Balinure upon a fair view, at eighteen pence per acre [of] Oats, amounts to better than 100^{11} a year, with Cows, Sheep, Cats and Dogs &c.[3]

I would have you send me a List of my Books, and desire you will not transmitt them to Dublin till you gett all together: I will not pardon you the loss of any; I told you the Method of collecting any that are not in your hands. Jack Tisdall[4] will do it. He has my Trunk & some Books and Papers which you are also to gett, pray use

---

[1] Not identified.

[2] Shortly after Swift's appointment to Kilroot Thomas Hacket, who had been promoted to the sees of Down and Connor, was deprived for gross neglect of duty. He was succeeded by Samuel Foley (see *D.N.B.*), a Fellow of Trinity College, Dublin, who died within nine months, 22 May 1695. His successor, Edward Walkington, also a Fellow of T.C.D., is the bishop to whom reference is here made. See also *Alum. Dub.*, pp. 295, 849.

[3] The corps of Swift's prebend was a union of three parishes, Kilroot, Templecorran, and Ballynure. Most, if not all, of his income was derived from tithes. Here Swift estimates the value of Ballynure alone as 'better than' £100 a year. If this estimate be accepted the total value must have been decidedly greater. See Landa, *Swift and the Church of Ireland*, p. 16, and notes.

[4] Ball suggests that he was probably a son of William Tisdall, Sheriff of Carrickfergus in 1690 and 1694, and a brother of Stella's lover, the Rev. William Tisdall.

Messengers & pay them at my Charge, and for Gd^s sake, see about paying Taylor of Loughbrickland[1] (I have been an hour thinking of the Town's name) for something about grazing a Horse and Farrier's bill it cannot be above 4 or 5 shill. and you may know by a Letter.

You will buy a wooden box for my Books, and gett the new ones put up in brown Paper, I told you enough of this in one of my last. Pray let me know if you want further Information, for I had rather you would take time than not finish as you and I shall like, thô it be but about a Trifle.

Pray give my service to your Wife and Family, I am,

Yours assuredly,

J. Swift.

Address: For R[ev. Mr. W]inder, Preb[endary of Kilroot], at Belf[ast in the county] of Ant[rim.][2]

Rothschild[3]

Swift to the Rev. John Winder

More Park. Jan^{ry} 13th 1698[9.]

I am not likely to be so pleasd with any thing again this good while, as I was with y^r Letter of Decb^r 20th, and it has begun to putt me into a good Opinion of my own Merits, or at least my Skill at Negotiation, to find I have so quickly restored a Correspondence that I feard was declining; As it requires more *charms and Address in Women* to revive one *fainting Flame* than to *kindle* a dozen *new ones.* But I assure You I was very far from imputing your silence to any bad Cause (having never entertained one single ill thought of You in my life) but to a custom which breaks off commerce between abundance of People after a long absence; At first one omitts writing for a little while, and then one stays a while longer to consider of Excuses and at last it grows desperate and one does not

---

[1] Loughbrickland is on the main road from Dublin to Belfast, in the county of Down, eight miles to the north of Newry. It was chosen by King William as the place of assembly for his army before the Battle of the Boyne.—Ball.

[2] Paper mutilated. The transcript in the National Library of Scotland adds: '[To be called] for'.

[3] The original of this letter, previously in the collection of Sir John Murray, passed into the library of Lord Rothschild in 1935. No. 2279.

write at all: At this rate I have served others and have been served my self. I wish I had a Lexicon by me to find whether Yr Greek word be spelt and accented right, and I am very sorry You have made an Acutum in ultima as if you laid the greatest Stress upon the worst part of the Word. However I protest against your meaning, or any Interpretation You shall ever make of that nature out of my Letters; If I thought You deserved any bitter Words, I should either deliver them plainly or hold my tongue altogether. For I esteem the Custom of conveying ones Resentments by hints or Innuendoes to be a Sign of Malice or Fear, or too little Sincerity; But I have told you *Coram* and *Absens*, that you are in your Nature more sensible, than you need be; And I find it is with Reputation as with all other Possessions, that those who have the greatest Portion are most covetous of it; and 'tis hard You can not be satisfied with the esteem of the best among y^r Neighbors, but lose y^r time in regarding what may be thought of You by one of my Privacy and Distance. I wish You could as easily make my Esteem and Friendship for You to be of any Value, as You may be sure to command them.

I should be sorry if you have been at an Inconvenience in hastening my Accounts, and I dare refer you to my Letters, that they will lay the Fault upon your self; For I think I desired more than once that You would not make more dispatch than stood with your ease because I was in no hast at all.

I desired of you 2 or 3 times that when you had sent me a Catalogue of those few Books You would not send them to Dublin till You had heard again from me; The reason was that I did believe there were one or 2 of them that might have been usefull to You, and one or 2 more that were not worth the Carriage; Of the latter sort were an old musty Horace, and Foley's Book;[1] of the former were Reynolds Works[2] with a Collection of Sermons in 4to. Stillingfleet's Grounds,[3] &c, and the Folio paper book; very good for

---

[1] It is uncertain which of the minor publications of Samuel Foley, Bishop of Down and Connor, Swift had in mind. The most probable is *Two Sermons*, printed for Moses Pitt in 1683. For a list of Foley's writings see Wing, ii. 61.

[2] Edward Reynolds (1599-1676), a moderate Anglican, who was prepared to accept the accommodation during the parliamentary period; but conformed at the restoration. A long list of sermons and short religious pieces stands to his credit in print. Two editions of his *Works* in folio appeared, 1658 and 1659. In 1661 he became Bishop of Norwich.

[3] Edward Stillingfleet (1635-99), whose output in controversial and religious

Sermons or a Receit book for yʳ Wife or to keep accounts for Mutton, Raisins &c. The Scepsis Scientifica[1] is not mine but old Mʳ Dobb's,[2] and I wish it were restored; He has Temple's Miscellanea[3] instead of it, which is a good book, worth your reading; If Scepsis Scientifica comes to me I'll burn it for a fustian piece of abominable curious Virtuoso Stuff. The books missing are few and inconsiderable, not worth troubling any body about. I hope this will come to yʳ hands before You have sent yʳ cargo; that you may keep those books I mention; and desire You will write my name and ex dono before them in large Letters.

I desire my humble service to Mrs Winder, and that You will lett her know that I shall pay a Visit at Carmony[4] some day or other How little soever any of You think of it. But I will as you desire excuse you the delivery of my Compliments to poor H. Clements[5] and hope You will have much better Fortune than poor Mʳ Davis,[6] who has left a Family that is like to find a cruell want of Him. Pray lett me hear Yᵘ grow very rich and begin to make Purchases. I never heard that H. Clements was dead. I was at his Mayorall feast;[7] has he been Mayor since? or did he dye then and every body forget to send me Word of it.

print was prodigious. His *Rational Account of the Grounds of the Protestant Religion* first appeared in 1665, and in a second edition 1681.

   [1] Joseph Glanvill (1636–80), whose *Scepsis Scientifica: Or, Confest Ignorance the Way to Science* (1665), directed towards the search for empirical grounds for our knowledge of the supernatural, would seem to Swift 'abominable, curious, Virtuoso Stuff'.

   [2] Richard Dobbs, High Sheriff of co. Antrim in 1664, lived in the principal house of Swift's parish of Kilroot. His eldest son, Arthur, became governor of North Carolina.

   [3] The first volume of Temple's *Miscellanea*, which appeared in 1680. *Miscellanea. The Second Part* came in 1690; and *Miscellanea. The Third Part*, edited by Swift, in 1701.

   [4] This allusion suggests that Winder, Swift's successor at Kilroot, preferred living at Carnmoney of which place he was rector. Tradition points to an oval cottage near the village of Kilroot as Swift's residence; but the evidence is not convincing. For a picture of the cottage see Ball, i. 176.

   [5] Henry Clements, who resided at Straid, near Carrickfergus, died 2 Nov. 1696, six months after Swift left Kilroot. He was Mayor and one of the representatives of Carrickfergus in parliament. See McSkimin, *History of Carrickfergus*, pp. 143, 328.

   [6] Probably John Davis, of Carrickfergus, whose will, dated 9 Apr 1693, and proved in 1694, shows that he left a wife and three daughters.—Ball.

   [7] According to McSkimin (op. cit., pp. 185, 375a) the installation of the Mayor

Those sermons You have thought fitt to transcribe will utterly disgrace You, unless you have so much credit that whatever comes from You will pass; They were what I was firmly resolved to burn and especially some of them the idlest trifling stuff that ever was writt, calculated for a Church without a company or a roof; like our [Chapel at][1] Oxford;[2] they will be a perfect lampoon upon me, [Whenever you][3] look on them & remember they are mine.

I remember those Letters to Elisa,[4] they were writt in my Youth. You might have held them up and no body of my friends would have opend them: Pray burn them. There were parcells of other Papers, that I would not have lost; and I hope you have packt them up so that they may come to me. Some of them were Abstracts and Collections from Reading.

You mention a dangerous Rival for an absent Lover. But I must take my Fortune: If the report proceeds pray inform me. And when You have leisure & humor, give me the Pleasure of a letter from You. And thô You are a Man full of Fastnings to the World, yet endeavor to continue a Friendship in Absence. For who knows but Fate may jumble us together again. And I believe had I been [assurd of your] Neighberhood, I should not have been so unsatisfied with the Region I was planted in. I am, and will be ever entirely yours &c | J. Swift

Pray lett me hear something of my debt being paid to Tailer the Inkeeper of —[5] I have forgot, the Town between Dromore and Newry:

Address: For the Reverend M^r | Windar, Preben d^{ry} of | Kilroot; to be left at Belfast in the County of Antrim | Ireland
Endorsement in a later hand: Dean Swift | to | The Revd John Winder | Jan: 13*th* 1698

of Carrickfergus was attended with much ceremony. The civic worthies and their friends were feasted by the Mayor, and the commonalty were entertained by the baiting of a bull in the market-place.—Ball.

[1] Paper mutilated.
[2] Winder is said to have been at Oxford with Swift. Hart Hall does not appear to have possessed a chapel till 1716.
[3] Paper mutilated.
[4] Possibly Betty Jones.
[5] Loughbrickland, see p. 28, n. 1.

Deane Swift, Essay 1755

Miss Jane Swift to Deane Swift

May 26, 1699[1]

My poor brother has lost his best friend Sir WILLIAM TEMPLE, who was so fond of him whilst he lived, that he made him give up his living in this country [*Ireland*] to stay with him at Moore-Park, and promised to get him one in *England*; but death came in between, and has left him unprovided both of friend and living.

Nichols 1779

Swift to Miss Jane Waring

Dublin, May 4, 1700.[2]

Madam, I am extremely concerned at the account you give of your health; for my uncle[3] told me he found you in appearance better than you had been in some years, and I was in hopes you had still continued so. God forbid I should ever be the occasion of creating

[1] This letter was addressed by Swift's sister to the cousin in Portugal, for whom see p. 14, n. 2. Jane was probably in Dublin when she wrote the letter. On 13 Dec. in that year a licence was issued for her marriage to Joseph Fenton, a currier in Dublin, a union to which Swift was opposed, possibly on social grounds; and almost certainly because he mistrusted the man's character. See *Journal to Stella*, pp. 101, 150, 368, and notes. For years, until Jane died, in the same lodging with Stella's mother, Mrs. Bridget Mose, in Farnham, Swift paid his sister an annuity (*Gentleman's Magazine*, xxiv. 491). The amount seems to have been £15. Lady Giffard also befriended her (*Journal*, pp. 150, 357, 366).

[2] Swift arrived in Dublin with Charles, second Earl of Berkeley, in the summer of 1699. Berkeley had been appointed a Lord Justice, and on the voyage Swift acted both as secretary and chaplain. According to his own statement it was intended that he should continue to hold both offices. After the arrival of the party in Dublin Swift was superseded as secretary by Arthur Bushe, who had not travelled over with Berkeley (B.M. Add. MS. 28,884, f. 167). It is doubtful if Berkeley can have intended his chaplain to retain his position as secretary, which would have been contrary to precedent. Swift had thus been in Ireland for the better part of a year before this letter was written; and it is evident that other letters had passed between him and Jane Waring.

[3] His uncle, Adam Swift (see p. 26, n. 2), was a friend of the Warings, and appears to have had property in the parish of Magheralin, adjoining that in which Waringstown is situated (see p. 19, n. 1).

more troubles to you, as you seem to intimate! The letter you desired me to answer I have frequently read, and thought I had replied to every part of it that required [it]; however, since you are
pleased to repeat those particulars wherein you desire satisfaction,
I shall endeavour to give it you as well as I am able. You would know
what gave my temper that sudden turn, as to alter the style of my
letters since I last came over. If there has been that alteration you
observe, I have told you the cause abundance of times. I had used a
thousand endeavours and arguments, to get you from the company
and place you are in; both on the account of your health and humour,
which I thought were like to suffer very much in such an air, and
before such examples. All I had in answer from you, was nothing but
a great deal of arguing, and sometimes in a style so very imperious
as I thought might have been spared, when I reflected how much
you had been in the wrong. The other thing you would know is,
whether this change of style be owing to the thoughts of a new
mistress. I declare, upon the word of a Christian and a gentleman,
it is not; neither had I ever thoughts of being married to any other
person but yourself. I had ever an opinion that you had a great
sweetness of nature and humour, and whatever appeared to the contrary, I looked upon it only as a thing put on as necessary before a
lover: but I have since observed in abundance of your letters such
marks of a severe indifference, that I began to think it was hardly
possible for one of my few good qualities to please you. I never knew
any so hard to be worked upon, even in matters where the interest
and concern are entirely your own; all which, I say, passed easily
while we were in the state of formalities and ceremony; but, since
that, there is no other way of accounting for this untractable behaviour in you, but by imputing it to a want of common esteem and
friendship for me.

When I desired an account of your fortune, I had no such design
as you pretend to imagine. I have told you many a time, that in
England it was in the power of any young fellow of common sense to
get a larger fortune than ever you pretended to. I asked, in order to
consider whether it were sufficient, with the help of my poor income,
to make one of your humour easy in a married state. I think it
comes to almost a hundred pounds a year;[1] and I think at the same

---

[1] Her father mentions in his will that she was entitled to charges on lands
producing £75 a year, as well as to household stuff and pictures, and bequeathed
her in addition £400.—Ball.

time that no young woman in the world of the same income would dwindle away her health and life in such a sink, and among such family conversation: neither have all your letters been once able to persuade that you have the least value for me, because you so little regarded what I so often said upon that matter. The dismal account you say I have given you of my livings I can assure you to be a true one;[1] and, since it is a dismal one even in your own opinion, you can best draw consequences from it. The place where Dr. *Bolton* lived is upon a living which he keeps with the deanery;[2] but the place of residence for that they have given me is within a mile of a town called *Trim*, twenty miles from hence; and there is no other way but to hire a house at *Trim*, or build one on the spot: the first is hardly to be done, and the other I am too poor to perform at present. For coming down to *Belfast*, it is what I cannot yet think of, my attendance is so close, and so much required of me; but our Government sits very loose, and I believe will change in a few months; whether *our part* will partake in the change, I know not, though I am very apt to believe it; and then I shall be at leisure for a short journey.[3] But I hope your other friends, more powerful than I, will

[1] Swift was appointed to Laracor on 16 Feb. 1699–1700. The union of Laracor consisted of the vicarages of Laracor and Rathbeggan and the rectory of Agher. The first two, adjoining each other, lie to the south-east of Trim. Agher was separated from the others by about eleven miles. The total area of the three was about 13,000 acres. The value of the three parishes, varying from year to year, amounted to about £230 annually, as may be deduced from Swift's own account books in the Forster collection. See Forster, *Life*, pp. 116–17; and Landa, *Swift and the Church of Ireland*, p. 36 and notes.

[2] The death of Coote Ormsby, Dean of Derry, early in Jan. 1700, left vacant a valuable ecclesiastical appointment. Dr. John Bolton, who had previously held the union of Laracor, also held the adjacent union of Ratoath. He was not anxious to accept the deanery of Derry, and was only prepared to do so when he received permission to retain Ratoath. Swift, in the last section of his fragment of autobiography, expresses the belief that the deanery ought to have come to him, and that Berkeley's 'secretary having received a bribe the deanery was disposed of to another'. There is no justification for this suspicion. In the correspondence which passed between William King, then Bishop of Derry, with the Lords Justices, Galway and Berkeley, and Narcissus Marsh, Archbishop of Dublin, there is no indication that Swift was ever considered. His name does not appear. The deanery was first offered to Bolton, who refused it; it was then offered to Dr. Synge of Cork, who also refused. Finally Bolton accepted the deanery if accompanied with the retention of Ratoath. This vexatious affair is fully discussed by Landa, pp. 27–34.

[3] The news of the proceedings in Parliament on the question of the resumption of the Irish land grants would then have reached Dublin. Swift's

before that time persuade you from the place where you are. I desire
my service to your mother, in return for her remembrance: but for
any other dealings that way, I entreat your pardon: and I think I
have more cause to resent your desires of me in that case, than you
have to be angry at my refusals. If you like such company and conduct, much good do you with them![1] My education has been otherwise. My uncle *Adam* asked me one day in private, as by direction,
what my designs were in relation to you, because it might be a
hindrance to you if I did not proceed. The answer I gave him
(which I suppose he has sent you) was to this effect: 'That I hoped
I was no hindrance to you; because the reason you urged against a
union with me was drawn from your indisposition, which still continued; that you also thought my fortune not sufficient, which is
neither at present in a condition to offer you: That if your health
and my fortune were as they ought, I would prefer you above all
your sex; but that, in the present condition of both, I thought it
was against your opinion, and would certainly make you unhappy:
That, had you any other offers which your friends or yourself
thought more to your advantage, I should think I were very unjust
to be an obstacle in your way.' Now for what concerns my fortune,
you have answered it. I desire, therefore, you will let me know if
your health be otherwise than it was when you told me the doctors
advised you against marriage, as what would certainly hazard your
life. Are they or you grown of another opinion in this particular?
Are you in a condition to manage domestic affairs, with an income
of less (perhaps) than three hundred pounds a year? Have you such
an inclination to my person and humour, as to comply with my
desires and way of living, and endeavour to make us both as happy
as you can? Will you be ready to engage in those methods I shall
direct for the improvement of your mind, so as to make us entertaining company for each other, without being miserable when we

anticipation proved true eight months after, when the Whig ascendancy gave way
to a Tory one.—Ball.

[1] Archdeacon Waring (see p. 19, n. 1) was the son of a Belfast merchant who had
been Sovereign of that town, and the Archdeacon's elder brother had followed
their father's steps (*Hist. of Belfast*, by George Benn, p. 249). Swift's remarks
originated, no doubt, in friendships, which led to a second marriage on the part
of the Archdeacon's widow. Whether there was cause for Swift's indignation it
is not possible to say, but the will of Mrs. Waring's second husband, Robert
Greene, of Belfast (dated 1 Oct. 1726 and proved 5 Apr. 1727), is evidence of
his having been a good husband and stepfather.—Ball.

are neither visiting nor visited? Can you bend your love and esteem and indifference to others the same way as I do mine? Shall I have so much power in your heart, or you so much government of your passions, as to grow in good humour upon my approach, though provoked by a ——? Have you so much good-nature as to endeavour by soft words to smooth any rugged humour occasioned by the cross accidents of life? Shall the place wherever your husband is thrown be more welcome than courts or cities without him? In short, these are some of the necessary methods to please men, who, like me, are deep-read in the world; and to a person thus made, I should be proud in giving all due returns towards making her happy. These are the questions I have always resolved to propose to her with whom I meant to pass my life; and whenever you can heartily answer them in the affirmative, I shall be blessed to have you in my arms, without regarding whether your person be beautiful, or your fortune large. Cleanliness in the first, and competency in the other, is all I look for. I desire, indeed, a plentiful revenue, but would rather it should be of my own; though I should bear from a wife to be reproached for the greatest.[1]

I have said all I can possibly say in answer to any part of your letter, and in telling you my clear opinion as to matters between us. I singled you out at first from the rest of women; and I expect not to be used like a common lover. When you think fit to send me an answer to this without ——, I shall then approve myself, by all means you shall command, Madam, | Your most faithful humble servant,

                                                    Jon. Swift.

Faulkner 1762

Swift to Bishop King

Dublin-Castle, July 16, 1700.

My Lord,[2]
   I was several Times to wait on your Lordship at your Lodgings; but you were either Abroad, or so engaged, that I could not be

---

[1] Varina died unmarried, from which, perhaps, evidential conclusions may be drawn. A grant of administration of her effects was issued to her stepfather, Robert Greene, on behalf of her mother and sister Fenekin, on 2 Nov. 1720.

[2] William King (1650–1729), of Scottish descent, was born in Ireland, whither

permitted the Honour to attend you. I have an humble Request to your Lordship, that you will please to excuse me if I cannot be at the triennial Visitation;[1] for my Lord and Lady[2] continually residing at the Lodge,[3] I am obliged to a constant Attendance there.

I am, with all Respect, | My Lord | Your Lordship's most obedient | And most humble Servant, |

Jon. Swift.

Deane Swift, Essay 1755

Mrs. Jonathan Swift to Deane Swift[4]

Aug. 10, 1703

Pray be pleased to present my best service to my good nephew Swift [Willoughby Swift] and tell him I always bear in my heart

his father had migrated. Despite his best endeavours he failed to obtain a fellowship at Trinity College, Dublin. After his ordination his abilities won him recognition. In 1689 he became Dean of St. Patrick's; and about the same time he embraced Whig opinions. When Swift's letter was addressed to King he was Bishop of Derry. Less than two years later he was translated to the Archbishopric of Dublin, in succession to Narcissus Marsh. For this, the first letter addressed by Swift to King, the beginning of a lengthy correspondence, we are dependent on Faulkner. Although King did not wholly favour the appointment of Swift to St. Patrick's, although for a number of years they were often at issue, each, recognizing the character of the other, exercised restraint. A period of better feeling set in when King supported Swift's agitation against Wood's coinage.

[1] It was the custom of the archbishops in the Church of Ireland to visit the dioceses of their suffragans once in every three years. On this occasion King was acting for Michael Boyle, Archbishop of Armagh, whose faculties were impaired by age. As the diocese of Meath lay within the province of Armagh it would have been Swift's duty to attend the visitation.

[2] Lord and Lady Berkeley.

[3] The Lodge was a Jacobean mansion in the village of Chapelizod. It had been built by Henry Power, first Viscount Valentia. After the Restoration it became the country house of the Viceroy. King William held his court there after the battle of the Boyne.

[4] This is a fragment of a letter addressed by Swift's mother to her nephew, De ne Swift in Portugal. Swift devotes a large part of his fragment of biography to his paternal ancestors. The account is not to be trusted. Only Section XIX is devoted to the lineage of his mother. Her parentage is in question. Swift tells us that his father married Abigail Erick of Leicestershire, 'descended from the most ancient family of the Ericks, who derive their lineage

a grateful remembrance of all the kindness he was pleased to shew to my son.

Hawkesworth 1766
Swift to the Rev. William Tisdall

London, December 16, 1703.[1]

I put great violence on myself in abstaining all this while from treating you with politics.[2] I wish you had been here for ten days, during the highest and warmest reign of party and faction that I ever knew or read of, upon the bill against Occasional Conformity, which, two days ago, was, upon the first reading, rejected by the Lords.[3] It was so universal, that I observed the dogs in the streets

from Erick the forester, a great commander, who raised an army to oppose the invasion of William the conqueror, by whom he was vanquished, but afterwards employed to command that prince's forces; and in his old age retired to his house in Leicestershire, where his family hath continued ever since'.

[1] Swift had been in Ireland from Oct. 1702 to Nov. 1703. He records in an account book (Forster Collection, no. 505) that he left Ireland on Thursday, 11 Nov. 1703, and landed in England on the following Sunday. According to Lyon (Forster, no. 579) he visited his mother at Leicester on his way to London. If so he could only have stayed a few days with her, for we know that he was in London before the great storm of 26 Nov. On this visit he remained in England till May 1704.

[2] William Tisdall (1669–1735) came of a family seated in co. Meath. He matriculated at Trinity College, Dublin, 16 Aug. 1688. The date given in the *D.N.B.* is incorrect. In 1696 he became a Fellow. He regarded himself as an outstanding controversialist, on a level with Swift himself, with whom a reasonable friendliness seems to have existed until he presented himself as a suitor for Stella's hand. This brought further intercourse to an abrupt end. Tisdall married a Miss Morgan, and became Vicar of Belfast and Rector of Drumcree. See, further, Deane Swift, *Essay*, 1755, pp. 87–99; Sheridan, *Life*, 1784, pp. 297–301; *Poems*, p. 1123.

[3] Upon the accession of Queen Anne a bill was introduced into the House of Commons designed to prevent the practice of 'occasional conformity', or acceptance of the Sacrament according to the rites of the Church of England in order merely to qualify for public office. The bill enacted that any person bearing office who resorted to a conventicle should forfeit £100, and £5 for every day that he should continue in office afterwards. The bill passed the Commons but met with strong opposition in the Lords. The upper house proposed amendments to which the lower house would not agree; and the bill was lost. Before the end of the year the bill was again brought forward. The bishops were divided, but the Lords again rejected the bill. Swift is here referring to the

much more contumelious and quarrelsome than usual; and the very
night before the bill went up, a committee of Whig and Tory cats,
had a very warm and loud debate upon the roof of our house. But
why should we wonder at that, when the very ladies are split
asunder into High Church and Low, and out of zeal for religion,
have hardly time to say their prayers? The masks will have a
crown more from any man of the other party, and count it a high
point of merit to a member, who will not vote on their side. For the
rest, the whole body of the clergy, with a great majority of the House
of Commons, were violent for this bill. As great a majority of the
Lords, amongst whom all the Bishops, but four,[1] were against it.
The Court and the rabble (as extremes often agree) were trimmers.
I would be glad to know men's thoughts of it in Ireland: for myself,
I am much at a loss, though I was mightily urged by some great
people to publish my opinion. I cannot but think (if men's highest
assurances are to be believed) that several, who were against this bill,
do love the Church, and do hate or despise Presbytery. I put it close
to my Lord Peterborough just as the bill was going up, who assured
me in the most solemn manner, that if he had the least suspicion the
rejecting this bill would hurt the Church, or do kindness to the
Dissenters, he would lose his right-hand rather than speak against it.
The like profession I had from the Bishop of Salisbury, my Lord
Somers, and some others; so that I know not what to think, and therefore shall think no more; and you will forgive my saying so much on
a matter, that all our heads have been so full of, to a degree, that
while it was on the anvil, nothing else was the subject of conversation.[2] I shall return in two months, in spite of my heart. I have here
the best friends in nature, only want that little circumstance of
favour and power; but nothing is so civil as a cast courtier. Pray let
the ladies know I had their letter, and will answer it soon; and that
I obeyed Mrs. Johnson's commands, and waited on her mother, and
other friend. You may add, if you please, that they advise her clearly
to be governed by her friends there about the renewing her lease,
and she may have her mortgage taken up here whenever she pleases,
second occasion upon which the bill was introduced. The return of a Whig
majority to the Commons in 1705 prevented its revival.

[1] Archbishop Sharp and five bishops were in favour of the bill.

[2] Swift's avowal of his authorship of his first political writing, *Contests and
Dissensions between the Nobles and the Commons in Athens and Rome*, 1701,
brought him the friendship of Somers, Peterborough, Bishop Burnet, and other
leaders of the Whig party.

for the payment of her fine; and that we have a project for putting out her money in a certain lady's hands for annuities, if the Parliament goes on with them, and she likes it.[1]

I will teach you a way to outwit Mrs. Johnson: it is a new-fashioned way of being witty, and they call it a *bite*.[2] You must ask a bantering question, or tell some damned lie in a serious manner, and then she will answer or speak as if you were in earnest: and then cry you, 'Madam, there's a *bite*.' I would not have you undervalue this, for it is the constant amusement in Court, and every where else among the great people; and I let you know it, in order to have it obtain among you, and teach a new refinement.

Nichols 1779

Swift to the Rev. William Tisdall

London, Feb. 3, 1703–4[3]

I am content you should judge the order of friendship you are in with me by my writing to you, and accordingly you will find yourself the first after the ladies;[4] for I never write to any other, either friend or relation, till long after. I cannot imagine what paragraph you mean in my former, that was calculated for Lord Primate; or how you could shew it him without being afraid he might expect to see the rest.[5] But I will take better methods another time, and you shall never, while you live, receive a syllable from me fit to be shewn a Lord Primate, unless it be yourself. *Montaigne* was angry to see his

[1] The lease referred to would almost certainly be that in connexion with property bequeathed to Stella by Sir William Temple, designated in his will as lands in Morristown, co. Wicklow. The certain lady alluded to was Lady Giffard.

[2] The equivalent phrase today would be 'a sell'. See *O.E.D.*

[3] A small portion of this letter was printed by Hawkesworth in 1766. See that part enclosed in half-brackets on p. 43. The complete letter was first printed by Nichols in his *Supplement*, 1779. Hawkesworth may have seen no more than the fragment of a draft.

[4] This reference to 'the ladies' suggests that Swift early adopted the guise, as in *The Journal to Stella*, of addressing his letters conjointly to Stella and Rebecca Dingley. From the first his account books enter the letters under the symbol MD.

[5] We may well understand Swift's resentment of Tisdall's indiscretion in showing the previous letter to a dignitary of the character of Narcissus Marsh.

Essays lie in the parlour-window, and therefore wrote a chapter that forced the ladies to keep it in their closets.¹ After some such manner I shall henceforth use you in my letters, by making them fit to be seen by none but yourself.

I am extremely concerned to find myself unable to persuade you into a true opinion of your own littleness, nor make you treat me with more distance and respect; and the rather, because I find all your little pretensions are owing to the credit you pretend with two ladies who came from *England*. I allow indeed the chamber in *William-Street*² to be *Little England* by their influence; as an ambassador's house, wherever it is, hath all the privileges of his master's dominions: and therefore, if you wrote the letter in their room or their company (for in this matter their *room* is as good as their company), I will indulge you a little. Then for the *Irish* legs you reproach me with, I defy you. I had one indeed when I left your island; but that which made it *Irish* is spent and evaporate, and I look upon myself now as upon a *new foot*. You seem to talk with great security of your establishment near the ladies; though perhaps, if you knew what they say of you in their letters to me, you would change your opinion both of them and yourself. A bite!—And now you talk of a bite, I am ashamed of the ladies' being caught by you, when I had betrayed you, and given them warning.—I had heard before of the choaking, but never of the jest in the church: you may find from thence that women's prayers are things perfectly by rote, as they put on one stocking after another, and no more.—But, if she be good at blunders, she is as ready at come-offs; and to pretend her senses were gone, was a very good argument she had them about her.—You seem to be mighty proud (as you have reason if it be

---

¹ The passage to which Swift alludes occurs in Montaigne's *Essais*, Livre III, chap. v, Sur des vers de Virgile: 'Je m'ennuye que mes Essais servent les dames de meuble commun suelement, et de meuble de sale: ce chapitre me fera du cabinet.' A copy of Montaigne in French appears in the list of Swift's books drawn in 1715, also in the Abbotsford list, and in the sale catalogue of 1745, no. 21. The entry 'Montaigne ses Essais' gives no date. Perhaps the title-leaf was missing. The absence of the statement of the number of volumes suggests that it was a single-volume edition. The first edition to contain the third book of the *Essays*, and the last published during the author's life, was that in quarto, 1588. See, further, *Dean Swift's Library*, 1932.

² William Street lies south of the Liffey, midway between Trinity College and St. Patrick's Cathedral. At the time of this letter the street was among fields; for, as it owes its name to the victory of the Boyne, it probably consisted of no more than a few houses.

true) of the part you have in the ladies' good graces, especially of her you call the *party*: I am very much concerned to know it; but, since it is an evil I cannot remedy, I will tell you a story. A cast mistress went to her rival, and expostulated with her for robbing her of her lover. After a long quarrel, finding no good to be done; 'Well,' says the abdicated lady, 'keep him, and stop him in your a—.' 'No,' says the other, 'that will not be altogether so convenient; however, to oblige you, I will do something that is very near it.'— *Dixi.*

I am mightily afraid the ladies are very idle, and do not mind their book. Pray put them upon reading; and be always teaching something to Mrs. *Johnson,* because she is good at comprehending, remembering, and retaining. I wonder she could be so wicked as to let the first word she could speak, after choaking, be a pun. I differ from you; and believe the pun was just coming up, but met with the crums, and so, struggling for the wall, could neither of them get by, and at last came both out together.

It is a pleasant thing to hear you talk of Mrs. *Dingley's*[1] blunders, when she has sent me a list with above a dozen of yours, that have kept me alive, and I hope will do so till I have them again from the fountain-head.—I desire Mrs. *Johnson* only to forbear punning after the *Finglas* rate when *Dilly* was at home.[2]

[1] The parentage of Rebecca Dingley was first unquestionably stated by Margaret Toynbee in an article contributed to *Notes and Queries*, cxcviii. 478–83 (Nov. 1953), on 'Sir John Dingley of Woolverton'. The marriage of one of Sir John's sons, Charles, to a first cousin is thus recorded in the registers of Kingston, Isle of Wight: 'Mr Charles Dingley of Shorwell, and Ms Elizabeth Hamond of S. Botolphes London were married October the 3: 1659.' She was the daughter of Colonel Thomas Hammond, one of the judges of Charles I, although he did not sign the death-warrant. Charles Dingley died 28 Sept. 1700, and was buried near his wife (who had predeceased him) in Winchester Cathedral. In his will the first legatee named is 'my Daughter Rebecca', who receives an annuity of £14. There can be no doubt but that this was the lifelong companion of Stella. Deane Swift, *Essay*, p. 86, informs us that she was older than Stella by fifteen years. This would place the date of her birth at about 1666. See, further, the article in *Notes and Queries* referred to above, which determines the facts of 'Rebecca Dingley's parentage, of her double relationship to the Hammonds and the Temples, and the origin of her Christian name'.

[2] The living of Finglas, about three miles to the north of Dublin, was held by the Rev. Dillon Ashe, who had been with Swift at Trinity College, Dublin. In 1704 he was promoted Archdeacon of Clogher; and in 1706 became Chancellor of Armagh (*Fasti Eccl. Hib.* iii. 40, 91, 95; iv. 92; Ball, *Hist. of County Dublin*, pt. vi, pp. 121–2). His elder brother, St. George Ashe, Bishop of Clogher,

I thank you for your bill, which was a cunning piece of civility to prevent me from wanting. However, I shall buy hats for you and *Tom Leigh*; for I have lately a bill of twenty pounds sent me for myself, and shall take up ten more here. I saw *Tom Leigh's* brother in the court of Requests, and, knowing him to be your friend, I talked with him; and we will take some occasion to drink your health together, and *Tom Leigh's*.[1] I will not buy you any pamphlets, unless you will be more particular in telling me their names or their natures, because they are usually the vilest things in nature. *Leslie* has written several of late, violent against Presbyterians and Low Churchmen.[2] If I had credit enough with you, you should never write but upon some worthy subject, and with long thought. But I look upon you as under a terrible mistake, if you imagine you cannot be enough distinguished without writing for the publick. Preach, preach, preach, preach, preach, preach; that is certainly your talent; and you will some years hence have time enough to be a writer. I tell you what I am content you should do: choose any subject you please, and write for your private diversion, or by way of trial; but be not hasty to write for the world. Besides, who that hath a spirit would write in such a scene as *Ireland*? You and I will talk an hour on these matters. [I have been so long and so frequently pursued with a little paltry ailment of a noise in my ears that I could never get humour and time to answer your letter.[3] Pox on the

---

had been Swift's college tutor, and is reputed to have married Swift and Stella in or about 1716. The eldest brother, Thomas Ashe, a man of property, resided from time to time at Ballygall in the parish of Finglas, and here Stella was entertained by him. Both Thomas and Dillon Ashe were inveterate punsters. The latter is frequently mentioned in the *Journal to Stella*.

[1] The two brothers Thomas and James Leigh are also frequently mentioned in the *Journal*. They also were punsters. James, who was on friendly terms with Stella, was an Irish landowner, seated at Walterstown, near Dundalk, but very much of an absentee with a liking for London life. The Rev. Thomas Leigh, whose formal ways annoyed Swift, held several preferments in the diocese of Armagh. See Leslie, *Armagh Clergy*, p. 309; *Fasti Eccl. Hib.* iii. 59, 298; *Poems*, pp. 217 n., 968 n.

[2] Charles Leslie, the famous non-juror and Jacobite, was a prolific writer of pamphlets. There was naturally little sympathy between him and Swift. In his *Examiner*, no. 15, Swift does, however, concede that Leslie's 'good Learning and Sense, discovered upon other Subjects, do indeed deserve Respect and Esteem'.

[3] The first sentence of the fragment of a letter printed by Hawkesworth in 1766—'I have been so long . . . letter'—does not appear in Nichols's text of 1779.

Dissenters and Independents! I would as soon trouble my head to write against a louse or a flea. I tell you what; I wrote against the bill that was against Occasional Conformity; but it came too late by a day, so I would not print it. But you may answer it if you please; for you know you and I are Whig and Tory. And, to cool your insolence a little, know that the Queen and Court, and House of Lords, and half the Commons almost, are Whigs; and the number daily increases.[1]

I desire my humble service to the Primate, whom I have not written to, having not had opportunity to perform that business he employed me in; but shall soon, now the days are longer. We are all here in great impatience at the King of *Spain's* delay, who yet continues in the *Isle of Wight*.[1]

My humble service to dean *Ryves*,[2] *Dilly*, *Jones*,[3] and other friends. And I assure you nobody can possibly be more, or I believe is half so entirely, yours, as

J. S.

Hawkesworth 1766
Swift to the Rev. William Tisdall

London, April 20, 1704.

Yesterday coming from the country I found your letter, which had been four or five days arrived, and by neglect was not forwarded as it ought. You have got three epithets for my former letter, which I believe are all unjust: you say it was unfriendly, unkind, and unaccountable. The two first, I suppose, may pass but for one; saving (as Capt. *Fluellin* says) the phrase is a little *variations*.[4]

[1] On his way from Holland to Lisbon the Archduke Charles, whose cause England was supporting, visited the country for a few days. On 5 Jan. 1704 he set sail for Portugal, but was driven back by tempestuous winds. He left finally on 12 Feb. and reached Lisbon on the 27th.
[2] Jerome Ryves, Dean of St. Patrick's since 1699. He died 1 Feb. 1704–5. *Fasti Eccl. Hib.* ii. 103.
[3] Ball is most probably justified in identifying Jones with the reciter of the Tripos printed in Barrett's *Essay*, p. 46. He had now become the Rev. John Jones, D.D., master of one of the principal schools in Dublin, which he carried on in a disused church called St. Michael le Pole. Jones was also Precentor of Kildare Cathedral. He died in 1715.
[4] *Henry V*, IV. vii. 16: 'Why, I pray you, is not pig great? The pig, or the

I shall therefore answer those two as I can; and for the last, I return it you again by these presents, assuring you, that there is more un-accountability in your letter's little finger, than in mine's whole body. And one strain I observe in it, which is frequent enough; you talk in a mystical sort of way, as if you would have me believe I had some great design, and that you had found it out: your phrases are, that my letter had the effect you judge I designed; that you are amazed to reflect on what you judge the cause of it: and wish it may be in your power to love and value me while you live, &c.,[1] In answer to all this, I might with good pretence enough talk starchtly, and affect ignorance of what you would be at; but my conjecture is, that you think I obstructed your insinuations, to please my own, and that my intentions were the same with yours. In answer to all which, I will upon my conscience and honour tell you the naked truth. First, I think I have said to you before, that if my fortunes and humour served me to think of that state, I should certainly, among all persons on earth, make your choice; because I never saw that person whose conversation I entirely valued but hers; this was the utmost I ever gave way to. And, secondly, I must assure you sin-cerely, that this regard of mine never once entered into my head to be an impediment to you; but I judged it would, perhaps, be a clog to your rising in the world; and I did not conceive you were then rich enough to make yourself and her happy and easy. But that objection is now quite removed by what you have at present; and by the assurances of *Eaton's* livings.[2] I told you indeed, that your authority was not sufficient to make overtures to the mother, with-out the daughter's giving me leave, under her own or her friend's hand; which, I think, was a right and a prudent step. However, I told the mother immediately, and spoke with all the advantages you deserve. But the objection of your fortune being removed, I declare I have no other; nor shall any consideration of my own misfortune

great, or the mighty, or the huge, or the magnanimous, are all one reckonings, save the phrase is a little variations.'
  [1] Since the preceding letter had reached Tisdall he had evidently acquainted Swift with his desire to marry Stella, and Swift had replied deprecating the suit on the ground of prudence.
  [2] This reference is to the Rev. Richard Eaton, who was beneficed in co. Donegal, and was rector of the parish in which the town of Dunfanaghy was situated, a living which, before the disestablishment of the Irish Church, was in the gift of Trinity College, Dublin. Administration of Eaton's goods was granted to his children on 9 Nov. 1705.—Ball.

of losing so good a friend and companion as her, prevail on me, against her interest and settlement in the world, since it is held so necessary and convenient a thing for ladies to marry; and that time takes off from the lustre of virgins in all other eyes but mine. I appeal to my letters to herself, whether I was your friend or no in the whole concern; though the part I designed to act in it was purely passive, which is the utmost I will ever do in things of this nature, to avoid all reproach of any ill consequence, that may ensue in the variety of worldly accidents. Nay, I went so far both to her mother, herself, and I think to you, as to think it could not be decently broken; since I supposed the town had got it in their tongues, and therefore I thought it could not miscarry without some disadvantage to the lady's credit. I have always described her to you in a manner different from those, who would be discouraging; and must add, that though it hath come in my way to converse with persons of the first rank, and of that sex, more than is usual to men of my level, and of our function; yet I have nowhere met with a humour, a wit, or conversation so agreeable, a better portion of good sense, or a truer judgment of men and things, I mean here in *England*; for as to the ladies of *Ireland*, I am a perfect stranger. As to her fortune, I think you know it already; and if you resume your designs, and would have farther intelligence, I shall send you a particular account.

I give you joy of your good fortunes, and envy very much your prudence and temper, and love of peace and settlement, the reverse of which has been the great uneasiness of my life, and is like to continue so. And what is the result? *En quis consevimus agros!*[1] I find nothing but the good words and wishes of a decayed ministry, whose lives and mine will probably wear out before they can serve either my little hopes, or their own ambition. Therefore I am resolved suddenly to retire, like a discontented courtier, and vent myself in study and speculation, till my own humour, or the scene here, shall change.[2]

[1] Virg. *Ecl.* i. 73.
[2] In allusion to Tisdall's desire to marry Stella, Dr. Johnson commented that Swift 'hindered a match sufficiently advantageous by accumulating unreasonable demands and prescribing conditions that could not be performed' (*Lives of the Poets*, ed. Birkbeck Hill, iii. 41). Johnson had borrowed his observation from Deane Swift, *Essay*, p. 89, where it is stated that Swift demanded of Tisdall that he 'should settle upon his wife an hundred pounds a year for pin-money', and that, when Tisdall agreed, he insisted further that 'he should live in Dublin, and keep a coach for his wife'. Tisdall 'had more honor than to promise what

Swift to Archbishop King

Trim, December 31, 1704.[2]

My Lord,

I did intend to have waited on your Grace before you went for *England*, but hearing your Voyage is fixed for the first Opportunity of the Wind, I could not forbear giving you a few Minutes Interruption, which I hope your Grace will believe to be without any other Design than that of serving you. I believe your Grace may have heard, that I was in *England* last Winter, when the Dean and Chapter of *Christ-Church* had, I think, with great Wisdom and Discretion, chosen a most malicious, ignorant, and headstrong Creature to represent them; wherein your Grace cannot justly tax their Prudence, since the Cause they are engaged in is not otherwise to be supported.[3] And, I do assure your Grace, (which perhaps others may have been cautious in telling you) that they have not been without Success. For not only the general Run in *Doctors'-Commons* was wholely on

he could not perform'. Sheridan, *Life*, 1784, p. 301, dismisses Deane Swift's story as a 'fabricated account' placing Swift in 'a mean selfish light'. The refusal, he avers, came from Stella herself.

 [1] This letter, for which we are dependent upon a printed text, first appeared in Faulkner, 1762, and in Bowyer of the same year. The text is here taken from Faulkner.

 [2] In the possession of Lord Rothschild is one of Swift's little account books covering 'Expences from Nov[br] 1st 1703 to Nov[br] 1st 1704'. In this book appears an entry, 'landed at Dublin. Thursday morn. Jun. 1. 1704. being my 16th Voyage.' Forster, *Life*, p. 131, says that it was Swift's tenth voyage between the two countries. This is a mistake for sixteenth, which Lyon mentions (Forster Collection, no. 579). Fourteen voyages can be identified. Case, *Modern Language Notes*, lx. 257–65, mistakenly supports Forster. See, however, Irvin Ehrenpreis, *M.L.N.* (Apr. 1950), lxv. 256–7, 'Swift's Voyages'.

 [3] Swift is here offering Archbishop King advice on a subject which was linked with recurring difficulties between the two in later years when he became Dean of St. Patrick's—the ecclesiastical standing of the Dean and Chapter of Christ Church Cathedral in relationship to Archbishop King. The originator of the present trouble seems to have been the Rev. John Clayton, a prebendary of Christ Church, who, after spending some part of his life in Virginia, had come to Ireland with Charles, second Duke of Bolton, on his appointment as a Lord Justice. Clayton's orthodoxy and rectitude of character were suspect by King as also his evil influence on the Bishop of Kildare and the Chapter of the Cathedral (King's Correspondence, 15 Aug. 1704). It is to Clayton that Swift refers when he writes of the representative of the Chapter.

their Side, which my Lord Bishop of *Cloyne*¹ observed as well as I; but that little Instrument of their's did use all his Power to misrepresent your Grace, and your Cause, both in Town and City, as far as his narrow Sphere could reach. And he spared not to say, that your Grace had personal Resentment against him; that you sought his Ruin, and threatened him with it.² And I remember at a great Man's Table, who hath as much influence in *England* as any Subject can well have, after Dinner came in a Master in Chancery, Whom I had before observed to be a principal Person in *Doctors-Commons*, when your Grace's Cause was there debating; and, upon Occasion of my being there, fell into Discourse of it, wherein he seemed wholly an Advocate for *Christ-Church*: for all his Arguments were only a Chain of Misinformations, which he had learned from the same Hand; insomuch as I was forced to give a Character of some Persons, which otherwise I should have spared, before I could set him right, as I also did in the Affair of the late Dean of *Derry*, which had been told with so many Falsehoods and Disadvantages to your Grace, as it is hard to imagine.³

I humbly presume to say thus much to your Grace, that, knowing the Prejudices that have been given, you may more easily remove them, which your Presence will infallibly do.

I would also beg of your Grace to use some of your Credit towards bringing to a good Issue the Promise the Queen made, at my Lord Bishop of *Cloyne's* Intercession, to remit the First Fruits

¹ Charles Crow, consecrated Bishop of Cloyne in 1702. He held the see till his death in 1726. There is some mention of him in the *Journal to Stella*. On 18 Feb. 1712 Swift writes of receiving a letter from Crow asking him 'to sollicit an Affair for him with Ld Treasr, . . . which I will do as soon as fly'.

² In a letter Archbishop King wrote: 'Mr. Clayton when in London last winter made it his business to go from coffee-house to coffee-house and make me and his cause the subject of his discourses there; he went to all persons of note to whom he could have access and made very free with my person and reputation.' From subsequent letters it appears that a libellous pamphlet was published by Clayton against King, in addition to one of which the Bishop of Kildare appears to have been the author, entitled: *An Account of the Innovations made by the Archbishop of Dublin both in respect of his entrance on the Archbishoprick and in regard of the Dean and Chapter of Christ Church.*—Ball.

³ The reference is to Dean Bolton's predecessor, Coote Ormsby, whose faculties deserted him with old age. He accused King of having on one occasion snatched the verge from its bearer and broken it 'with strange and passionate expressions' when the Dean and Chapter of Derry Cathedral went to conduct him to the vestry. King denied this ridiculous accusation.

and Tenths of the Clergy; unless I speak ignorantly, for Want of Information, and that it be a Thing already done. But what I would mind your Grace of is, that the Crown Rent should be added, which is a great Load upon many poor Livings, and would be a considerable Help to others. And, I am confident, with some Reason, that it would be easily granted; being, I hear, under a thousand Pounds a Year, and the Queen's Grant for *England* being so much more considerable than our's can be at best.[1] I am very certain, that, if the Bishop of *Cloyne* had continued to sollicit it in England, it would easily have passed; but his Lordship giving it up wholely to the Duke of *Ormond*, I believe it hath not been thought of so much as it ought.[2] I humbly beg your Grace's Pardon for the Haste and Hurry of this, occasioned by that of the Post, which is not very regular in this Country; and imploring your Blessing, and praying to God for your good Voyage, Success and Return, I humbly kiss your Grace's Hands, and remain | My Lord, | Your Grace's most obedient, | And most humble Servant,

J. Swift.

King's Letter-book
Trinity College, Dublin[3]

Archbishop King to Swift

London 30th Jan^ry 1704[5]

Rev^d S^r

I received the favour of yours of the 31st Decem^br last and am very much obliged to you for the concern you took in my affair of which I have had information from severall hands. I am satisfied that

---

[1] For Swift's success in obtaining the extension of Queen Anne's Bounty to Ireland see the *Journal to Stella*.

[2] James, second Duke of Ormonde, had been appointed Lord-Lieutenant in the previous year. His wealth, bearing, and expansive character had all the makings of popularity. Swift pays him high tribute in his *Enquiry into the Behaviour of the Queen's last Ministry* (*Prose Works*, ed. Davis, viii. 132–3); but both in home affairs and in the field Ormonde failed to distinguish himself.

[3] This letter is the first here printed from clerical copies made of letters written by Archbishop King to various correspondents. These are to be found in the library of Trinity College, Dublin. Many of the letters have suffered from damp, and possibly also from the nature of the ink used. Some, as for example the above letter, are in a good state.

great industry has been used to misrepresent me and my cause here, and that those imployed to do me ill offices have not bin altogether unsuccessfull. It was so in Dublin till my cause was heard, but I think I left every body possessed of another opinion,[1] and believe it will quickly be soe here. I reached London on the 13th instant and have in effect bin ever since confined by the Gout which has been a great hindrance to my affairs, but I hope it is near over.[2] Tis no small misfortune for us in Ireland to have our causes judged here by persons that neither understand or regard our affairs. For an instance of this, I do find that neither stationers' shops, publick or private Librarys can furnish so much as the Statutes or Canons of Ireland, tho' I have made a very diligent search for them, & I do now find that the reason my adversarys desire to be judged here, is in hopes their cause will never be understood, but that will not serve their turn. As to their prints they have a very different effect on all I have discoursed from what they designed. I shall be able to give a better account when my Commission is returned and opened; I am not very fond of saying any thing till I have full vouchers, and then their falshoods will turn to their shame.

As to the 20th parts and first fruits, I am not as yet to meddle in that affair. I suppose it must be done in parlement as it was in England. I doubt not but his Grace the Duke of Ormond thinks of it, and will make it his act as far as it can be, As to the Crown Rents they are a much greater burthen than the other, 20th parts and first fruits are not more than a 1000l per annum but the Crown Rents are of greater value. I have a book of them, and the matter being in my thoughts before I left Dublin, I ordered my servants to put up it and the book of first fruits to bring along with me, but my servants left the first behind them. I spoke to his Grace the Duke of Ormond about them and if what I said be seconded I hope we may see some effects of it, thô I am a little afraid to ask too much. Mr. Dean

[1] In his correspondence, writing on 19 Dec., King says there had been one hearing before the Duke of Ormonde, and three before the Lord Chancellor of Ireland about a petition lodged by Clayton, and that he had succeeded in disproving the statements made by his opponents.—Ball.

[2] As will be seen from subsequent letters King suffered from severe attacks of gout. When he became Chaplain to the Archbishop of Tuam, according to his own account, the sudden transition from the plain fare of Trinity College to 'the plentiful table and abundant wines' of the Archbishop's house brought on his lifelong complaint. To afford himself some ease it was his custom to visit Bath every three years.

Reader[1] designs soon to come over. I intend to write to him to bring my paper with him.

Tis not safe for me to be too busy, but you may assure your self and all your Brethren, that no endeavours that I judge usefull to them shall be wanting on my part. I recommend you to God's care & am &c.

W: Dublin.

Dr. Jonathan Swift

Church of Ireland Gazette[2]
Swift and Dean Reader to Archbishop King

March 22, 1704-5.

May it please y^r Grace,

y^r Chapter of St. Patrick's have given us instructions to present to you our new elected Dean in order to receive the usuall confirmation. For the particulars of the Election wee crave leave to referr you to the inclosed papers, being the Decretum Electionis. Wee doubt not but that y^r Grace will give all reasonable dispatch to this affaire, which seems to be very necessary in this juncture.

We are, may it please y^r Grace, y^r most obedient humble servants,

Enoch Reader.
Jonathan Swift.

My Lord,[3]

We and most of the Chapter are of opinion that if your Grace were here in Person, You would not by any means take the Subscription of the other Party, or at least not untill the Person we have

---

[1] The Rev. Enoch Reader, who was both Dean of Emly and Archdeacon of Dublin. *Fasti Eccl. Hib.* ii. 130; iii. 40, 173, 260.

[2] The draft was formerly in the possession of Dean (later Archbishop) Bernard. His transcript of the letter was first printed in the *Church of Ireland Gazette*, 11 Dec. 1908.

[3] The first letter is addressed to Archbishop King by Enoch Reader, Archdeacon of Dublin, and Jonathan Swift, then prebendary of Dunlavin in St. Patrick's Cathedral, on behalf of the Chapter. Dean Jerome Ryves had died on 1 Feb. 1704-5, and the Chapter, fearful lest their right of election should be set aside by the Crown, hastened to elect as successor their Chancellor, John Stearne (afterwards Bishop of Clogher). The election took place on 20 Mar. 1704-5. The purport of the letter is to request the Archbishop, who was then

elected were in full Possession, because there may be Arts used by lawyers to disturb possessions; of which we have not been without some Hints given us. We cannot explain our selves further at this Distance, and therefore we leave it to your Grace's great Prudence.

Endorsed by Swift: Letter to the ArBp about the Deanry of St. P. Mar. 22, 1704.

Rothschild[1]

Swift to John Temple

Dublin, June. 15. 1706.

S[r2]

I deferrd acknowledging the Favor of your Letter, till M[r] Ashenhurst and I had gott an Answer from the Colledge, we both were of Opinion to venture offering 20[ll] encrease of Rent for the Lease of Clounish,[3] w[ch] we might safely do, upon the Tenants themselves offering above 30[ll]. As to the Lease of Armagh, M[r] Ashenhurst could make no Offers, having received no Return, tho he says he has often writt for it. He tells me he has given you an Account of the Answer from the Colledge, and the Provost and Fellows gave it me separately before. neither did I expect any other. for You know there is Act obliding them not to sett under half Value wch thô it be not observed very exactly, yet where the difference

in London, to lose no time in confirming the election. It appears (Mason, *History of St. Patrick's*, p. 220) that the Government intended to nominate Dr. Edward Synge; but they refrained from pressing the matter. The second draft, in Swift's hand, shows how prominent a part Swift already took in the business affairs of the Chapter. The 'other Party' referred to was evidently Synge.

[1] The original of this letter was sold at Sotheby's, 19 July 1867, and bought by W. Mitchell for £8. 15s. 0d. It is now in Lord Rothschild's Library, no. 2280. There is a transcript in the Forster Collection (Box Case F. 44. E. 1); and Forster printed part of the letter, *Life*, pp. 181–3.

[2] John Temple, to whom this letter is addressed, was a nephew of Sir William. He married one of the daughters of Sir William's son who committed suicide, and succeeded his uncle at Moor Park. The leases were of lands belonging to Trinity College, Dublin, whose property was mainly leased to middlemen, and had been held by Sir William Temple, who bequeathed the lease of Armagh to his sister, Lady Giffard, and that of Clones to his nephew, John Temple.

[3] Clounish, i.e. Clones, which is pronounced as a dissyllable.

is very great, their Successors very certainly make the Lease voyd: However I am of opinion that they will not stand altogether to the Height of those Returns they have shewn us, provided we offer some considerable Advance of Rent. But this we can not possibly do of the reele Value of the Lands; which Mr Ashenhurst will endeavor to get by writing to the Receiver of the Lands at Clonish, and will desire him to do the same for those of Armagh, thô we doubt whether he be so well qualified for the latter; However it will do well to try; and You have time till next Michaelmas, after wch the Provost tells Mr Ashenhurst that they will expect an Encrease of the Fine; But if that Man cannot send Mr Ashenhurst such an Account as may be depended upon, I know not what you will do. You mistook my Advice when you supposed I meant a man should be sent down to take a Survey of the Lands, that would indeed be a matter of Expence (tho I think if you and all Gentlemen had such a Thing, you would find yr Accounts in it) What I designed was onely to get some body to go down there for ten days and pick out the Quantity and Quality of the Land in generall, and how it is sett in the Neighborhood, which would not be a Business of above 3 or 4 Pounds; and this is what Mr Reading and Mr Rotton thought absolutely necessary; and so you must do at last, unless we can gett such an Account as we desire, some other way.[1] Tis an Advantage to You, that Land in this Kingdom was never lower then now, I mean where it is far from Dublin; and therefore if you have a fair Return, you can not well be a loser whenever we have Peace; Nothing can be righter then yr Opinion not to sett yr Lands at a Rack-rent; they that live at yr distance from their Estates would be undone if they did it, especially in such an uncertain Country as this. Therefore I should advise you to sett it so easily to Y^r undertenants, when you renew, that they may be able to repay you in part of your Fine; and

[1] The persons referred to in connexion with the negotiations were either friends or men of business of the Temple family. Ralph Ashenhurst leaves in his will (dated 15 Apr. 1705, and proved on the 30th of that month) a remembrance to William Yarner, a kinsman of John Temple through his mother, and Daniel Reading, who represented Newcastle, a pocket borough in the county of Dublin, mentions in his will (dated 31 Jan. 1725-6, and proved 28 July following) the kindness shown to him 'when a fugitive in England at the time of the happy Revolution' by 'the then great Sir William Temple and his family'. John Rotton was a brother-in-law of Stearne the then lately elected Dean of St. Patrick's. His will is dated 12 Nov. 1709 and was proved 14 July 1713.— Ball.

then your Rent is Secure. If You have thoughts of selling it, Y^r best way will be to offer it among the Gentlemen of the Neighborhood, that will give you most: but I hope you will consider it a little longer: or else you may be in danger of selling you know not what; which will be as bad as buying so. I forgot to tell you, that no Accounts from y^r Tenants can be relyed on; If they payd you but a pepper corn a Year they would be readyer to ask Abatement than offer to advance; It is the universall Maxim throughout the Kingdom. I have known them fling up a Lease, and the next day give a Fine to have it again. It has not been known in the memory of Man that an Irish Tenant ever once spoke truth to his Landlord.[1]

Mr Elwood[2] one of the Fellows of the Colledge was recommended by Sr Wm Robinson[3] to y^r Brother[4] for a small Favor; it is, to promise him the grant of a certain Room in the Colledge wch is in Mr Temple's disposall; whenever it shall be vacant, or, whenever Mr Elwood can persuade the present owner to sell it him; It is a Thing of no value to Mr Temple, and he cannot dispose of it better then to one of the Fellows, and Mr Elwood is a very worthy Person, and when he comes to be Senior-Fellow it may lye in his Power to be serviceable to You; and he will take it for a great Obligation. Pray use your Power with y^r Brother to bring this to pass, and be so kind to present him my most humble Service.

I am extremely obliged by yr kind Invitation to More-Park, wch no time will make me forgot or love less.[5]

If I love Ireland better than I did, it is because we are nearer related, for I am deeply allyed to its Poverty. My little Revenue is sunk two Parts in three, and the third in Arrear. Therefore if I come to More-park it must be on foot; But then comes another difficulty; that I carry double the Flesh you saw about me at London; to

[1] In 1707 the authorities of Trinity College executed a lease of lands in co. Fermanagh in favour of John Temple. See, further, Ball, i. 56, n. 1.

[2] John Elwood became Vice-Provost and representative in the Irish Parliament of the University of Dublin. The question of his rooms in college arose once more when Swift wrote on the subject to Henry Temple, Viscount Palmerston, 15 Jan. 1725-6.

[3] William Robinson, attached to the army as Commissary-General, later became Receiver-General of Ireland. He was knighted by William III. At this time he was one of the representatives of the University in the Irish Parliament. He died in 1712.

[4] Henry Temple, later Viscount Palmerston.

[5] These words hardly bear out the suggestion of Macaulay that Swift was wholly unhappy during the period of his residence at Moor Park.

wch I have no manner of Title, having neither purchased it by Luxury nor good humor. I did not think Mr Percival[1] and I had agreed so well in our Opinion of Ireland; I believe it is the onely publick Opinion we agree in, else I should have had more of his company here, for I allways loved him very well, as a man of very good understanding and Humor. But Whig and Tory has spoild all that was tolerable here, by mixing with private Friendship and Conversation, and ruining both; tho it seems to me full as pertinent to Quarrell about Copernicus and Ptolemee, as about My Ld Treasurer,[2] and Ld Rochester, at least for any Private man, and especially in our remote Scene; I am sorry we begin to resemble England onely in its defects; about seven Years ago, Frogs were imported here, and thrive very well;[3] and 3 years after a certain great Man[4] brought over Whig and Tory which suit the soyl admirably.—But my Paper is at an End before I am aware. I desire my most humble Service to y^r Lady; and remain, S^r | Your most faithfull | humble Servt. | Jon: Swift

I was desired by a Person of Quality to gett him a few Cuttings of the Arboise and Burgundy Vines[5] mentioned by Sr W. T in his Essay on Gardening; because they ripen the easyest of any. Pray be so kind to order y^r Gardener to save some against the Season,

---

[1] John Percival of Knightsbrook in Swift's parish of Laracor. One of Swift's note-books records games of picquet with Percival as early as 1702. He was M.P. for the Borough of Granard and later for that of Trim. In 1716 he sold Swift twenty acres for the glebe of Laracor. He died in 1718.

[2] Earl of Godolphin, Lord High Treasurer, 1702–10.

[3] Frogs are, in fact, indigenous to Ireland. The legend of the introduction of frogs into Ireland varies in the assigned date. In this letter Swift places it about 1699. A letter addressed to *The Tatler*, no. 236, says that frog-spawn was brought over from Liverpool to Ireland 'about Two Years after the Battle of the Boyne' by an 'ingenious Physician'. Deane Swift, in a footnote to *Considerations about Maintaining the Poor*, says that a Dr. Gwythers introduced spawn into Ireland about 1720 (*Prose Works*, vii. 340).

[4] Presumably the reference is to Laurence Hyde, the Earl of Rochester, referred to above, who, unwillingly, came over to Ireland as Lord-Lieutenant in September 1700 and left in the following January.

[5] In Temple's essay *Of Gardening* he mentions four sorts of grape which he cultivated 'in our Climate', including 'the Arboyse from the Franche Comte' and 'The Burgundy, which . . . of all others is surest to ripen' in his country. His out-of-door culture of the vine seems to have met with a more than common success, although he avers that in his time these varieties were 'pretty common among some Gardeners in my Neighbourhood'. See *Works*, 1720, i. 184.

and I will direct they shall be sent to London, & from thence to Chester

Address: For John Temple Esqʳ; | at his House at Morepark | near Farnham in | Surrey | England
Postmark: 21 IV
Endorsed in a late hand: Dʳ Jon. Swift to J. Temple Esq. June 15. 1706.

Deane Swift, Essay 1755

The Rev. Thomas Swift to ——

Puttenham, Surry, February 5, 1706[-7].

[I should be glad to know] whether JONATHAN be married? or whether he has been able to resist the charms of both those gentle-women that marched quite from *Moore-Park* to *Dublin* (as they would have marched to the *north* or any where else) with full resolu-tion to engage him?[1]

The Library, Armagh[2]

Swift to Archbishop King

Leicester Decᵇʳ 6ᵗʰ 1707.

My Lord.

It was my misfortune that your Grace was abroad the night before I left Ireland where I attended at St Sepulchre's[3] to receive your last Commands and Instructions, therefore I am in the dark how

---

[1] Deane Swift in his *Essay*, p. 87, quoted this brief passage from a letter which he stated to be then lying before him. Thomas Swift had been Swift's school-fellow at Kilkenny and college companion at Trinity, Dublin (see p. 12, n. 2). He is also stated to have been Sir William Temple's chaplain. He witnessed Temple's will made shortly after the death of Lady Temple in the spring of 1696. He therefore appears to have been at Moor Park while Swift was at Kilroot. His residence with Temple was, however, probably of no long duration. His opportunities of forming a judgement upon the relationship of Swift, Stella, and Rebecca Dingley cannot be assigned much credit. Indeed, Deane Swift (*Essay*, the Appendix, p. 35) writes disparagingly of him: 'Unfortunately bred up like his father and grandfather, with an abhorrence and contempt for all *sectaries*; [he] continued *Rector* of *Putenham*, without any the least hope of rising in the church, for the space of threescore years, and died in the month of May 1752, in the eighty seventh year of his age.'
By 'the *north*' Thomas Swift refers to Swift's erstwhile living of Kilroot.

[For notes 2 and 3 see opposite

far My L^d L^t¹ is pleased to approve my having any share in solliciting that Business Your Grace spoke to me about. I confess I was
always of opinion that it required a sollicitor of my Level, after
Your Grace had done your part in it, and if my endeavors to do
service will be thought worth employing, I dare answer for every
thing but my own Ability; when your Grace thinks fitt to send me
the Papers I would humbly desire your opinion, whethr if occasion
should require, I may not with My L^d L^{t's} Approbation engage the
good offices of any great Person I may have credit with, and particularly my L^d S, and the E. of S.² because the former by his great
Influence, and the other by his employment and Alliance, may be

¹ Thomas Herbert (1656–1733), eighth Earl of Pembroke, had held many
high offices since the accession of William and Mary, including First Lord of
the Admiralty and Lord Privy Seal, and in 1707 he succeeded the Duke of
Ormonde as Viceroy of Ireland. Archbishop King held him in high esteem for
his learning and general knowledge; and Delany, *Observations*, 1754, pp. 211–
12, described him as 'the greatest benefactor to Ireland' the country had ever
seen, 'at least within the compass of this century'. Swift was on friendly terms
with the new Lord-Lieutenant who shared with him a fondness for punning.
He hoped to gain Pembroke's influence on behalf of the Irish clergy in favour
of a remission of the first fruits and twentieth parts; but he was eventually
disappointed.
² Lord Somers and the Earl of Sunderland. John, Lord Somers, born in
1651, the son of a country attorney, raised himself to high position by singular
ability. He became Lord Chancellor in 1697, and was raised to the peerage as
Baron Somers of Evesham. He was one of the four Whig lords impeached in
1701 for their share in the partition treaties. Swift's *Contests and Dissensions*,
1701, defended Somers under the name of Aristides. In later life Swift described
Somers as possessed of 'all excellent qualifications except virtue' (*Prose Works*,
ed. Temple Scott, x. 275). Charles Spencer, third Earl of Sunderland, son of
the Minister whom Swift had previously approached, hasty in temperament,
was a trial to the other Whig leaders. It was alleged that Somers was the only
man to whom he would listen. He had married, as his second wife, Lady
Anne Churchill, second daughter of Marlborough.

² In the Record Room of the Library of Armagh seven letters in Swift's
autograph addressed to Archbishop King and two addressed to Sheridan are
preserved. By permission of the Dean of Armagh copies of these letters were
made for me by the then librarian, Mr. K. M. Hamilton. Earlier copies were
used by Elrington Ball for his conventionalized text. There are also in the
Forster Collection copies made by Bishop Reeves.
³ St. Sepulchre's was the medieval palace of the Archbishops of Dublin,
and continued to be used by them until the close of the eighteenth century.
It adjoined the close of St. Patrick's Cathedral. King expended a large sum of
money on the fabric. King's Correspondence, 13 May 1708.

57

very instrumentall; I would not have mentioned this at such a distance if I had not forgott it when Your Grace discoursed this matter with me last.

I left my L^d L^t at Park-gate this day sennight, when he had just landed,[1] before the ship that carried his equipage, for which he was forced to stay, and it was said he could not think of beginning his journey till Wednesday the 3rd instant, he goes to Wilton,[2] and stays there a week, from thence to London where I design to attend him as soon as Sr Andrew Fountain[3] shall send me notice of his arrivall

I came round by Darby to this Toun (where I am now upon a short visit to my Mother) and I confess to Your Grace that after an absence of less than four years[4] all things appear new to me. The Buildings, the Improvement, the Dress and countenance of the People putt a new spirit into one et tacite circum praecordia ludit.[5] This long war has here occasioned no fall of lands, nor much Poverty among any sort of People, onely some complain of a little slowness in tenants to pay their rents, more than formerly. Here is a universall love of the present Government, and few animosityes except upon Elections of which I just arrive[d] to see one in the town upon a vacancy by the Death of a Knight of the Shire[6] They have been

[1] Parkgate, on the river Dee, was the port most used for passenger traffic to and from Dublin. Letters were sent by Holyhead over wild and rough country unsuitable for ordinary travellers. Lord Pembroke had sailed from Ireland on Friday, 28 Nov.

[2] Wilton House, Pembroke's residence in the country, where he gathered statuary and other objects of art with doubtful discrimination.

[3] Sir Andrew Fountaine, 1676–1753, descended from an old Norfolk family, knighted in 1699, formed at Narford a splendid collection of pictures, coins, and books. This naturally led to a friendship with Pembroke. At this time, also, Fountaine held an official position in the viceregal court at Dublin, and it was there, probably, that Swift made his acquaintance. For his collection of Swift autographs and other papers, now in the Pierpont Morgan Library, New York, see *Poems*, pp. xlix, 744, 1141–3.

[4] Swift's reckonings of time are frequently untrustworthy. These words may be taken to refer to England in general or be limited to Leicester, implying that although he visited England in 1705 he proceeded to London without visiting his mother. Evidence for an English visit in 1705 is lacking. From Oct. 1702 to Nov. 1703 Swift was in Ireland. From that date to May 1704 he was in England. From June 1704 to Nov. 1707 he was in Ireland.

[5] Persius, i. 117.

[6] On 4 Dec. 1707 George Ashby of Quenby was returned for Leicestershire in the room of John Verney deceased.

polling these three days, and the number of thousands pretty equall on both sides, the Partyes as usuall, High and Low, and there is not a Chambermaid Prentice or Schoolboy in the whole town, but what is warmly engaged on one side or tother.

I write this to amuse Your Grace, and relieve a dull letter of business. Others would make excuses for taking up so much of Your Grace's time to read the Impertinence but I shall offer none, I, who know that no man's time is worse taken up than Your Grace's; which I am sorry to say of so great a Person, and for whom upon all other accounts I have so high a veneration. The World may contradict me if they please; but when I see your Palace crowded all day to the very Gates with suitors, sollicitors, Petitioners, who come for Protection, Advice and Charity and when your time of sleep is misspent in perpetual Projects for the good of the Church and Kingdom how successful so ever they have been, I can not forbeur (*sic*) crying out with Horace, Perditur interea misero lux.[1] No doubt the Publick would give me little Thanks for telling your Grace of Yᵣ Fault, by which it receives so much Benefitt, But it need not fear, for I know you are incorrigeable and therefore I intend it purely as a Reproval, and your Grace has no remedy but to take it as it is meant. And so in perfect Pity to that very little remnant of Time which is left in your own disposall, I humbly kiss your Grace's Hands, and remain

My Lord | Your Grace's | most obedient | most humble and | most obliged servant | Jon: Swift.

I shall be at Sᵣ Andrew Fountain's house in Leicester Fields before your Grace's commands there directed will reach me.
Address: For His Grace, the Lord | Arch Bishop of Dublin. Ireland By way | of London.

King's Letter-book
Trinity College, Dublin

Archbishop King to Swift

Dublin Decemᵇʳ 16ᵗʰ 1707

Revd Sᵣ
I recd yours of the 6th inst from Leicester, I am heartily glad you got safe to land, for Saturday evening Sunday and Monday after
[1] Hor. *Sat.* ii. 6, 59.

you went proved here to be most violently stormy, threw down some houses strip'd many and did abundance of mischief. We were in pain for my Ld. Lt. and the other Gentlemen lest they shoud not have got to land before it happened.[1]

I told my Ld Lt that you would put his Excellency in mind of the business of the first fruits and 20th parts and he desired that it might be so.

The representation is not yet ready, and twil be hard to make it so as to answer our design and please everybody. there seems to me a strange spirit of jealousy to have possessed the Clergy, insomuch that they seem afraid to let any thing of their business be known, tho in order to assist them.[2] we know not (say they) what use will be made of it. But they do not consider that what they would conceal is known to all the world, and a great deal more believed concerning their affairs than is true, and that only a true representation of their state can remove the prejudices that are against them as for example a man that has 60 l. per annum is afraid to discover it, when at the same time the world believes he has an 100 l. and he suffers all the obloquy and envy that such an Income is apt to raise in those that grudge a maintenance to the Clergy. I have often compared such to a traveller that has a guinea in his pocket and dare not discover his Stock, lest he shou'd encourage robbers that in the meantime know he is on the road, and believe he has an 100 l. about him.

But there are some weaknesses ought to be concealed. I grant it, if they are secrets. But we ought to take care of the woodcock's folly that thinks none see him when he hides his head, one half of the pains wou'd mend those faults that some take to conceal them, in which after all they never succeed.

[1] As has been noted, on the authority of the *Dublin Gazette* (see p. 58, n. 1), Lord Pembroke sailed from Ireland on Friday, 28 Nov., and according to the same journal the storm did not occur until a week later: 'On Friday and Saturday last [5 and 6 Dec.] happened as terrible a storm of wind as has been known for some years past, which has blown down some Houses, several stacks of Chimnies, and done great damage throughout this City and Suburbs.' The wind came from WNW. and 'the Shoram Prize was overset in Clontarf Pool and several small boats were sunk.'—Ball.

[2] The purpose of the inquiry, as Archbishop King informed Pembroke in a letter of 21 Feb. 1707–8, was to provide a typical example of the state of the parishes in the diocese of Dublin, to be used in urging a measure of relief for the Irish clergy. At the same time King explained that conditions were worse elsewhere save in the six counties of the north where a more equitable tithing table had been established by James I in a settlement following Tyrone's rebellion.

But however I hope next week to send the representation, and I will direct it to you by which means you will have an opportunity to discourse my Ld about it, when you deliver it to him.

As to your other friends especially the two great Lds you mention, I think it of great moment, that they should be apprised of, and assured to the business, you need use no caution as to the Clergy here or to me, all the danger is of shocking my Ld. Lt. if he should take it ill, that we applyed to other interest it might be of ill consequence and therefore you must do this with due deference to him and such caution as prudence may direct, and in some cases there may be a supererogation in that, for I fancy this had bin done before had we not been unwilling to go otherwise than in the high road by the Government. If any thing be to be moved on my part I shall readily fall into it.

I am glad you find matters so pleasing to you in your Countrey; it is well that you can believe your eyes, for great pains I assure you are taken to give your Countrey affairs a grumbling aspect, I am glad to understand that they do not look so sour as represented.

I am too much tired now to answer the rallying part of your letter tho it please me the best of any part of it. I confess I deserve to be chid for my easiness in admitting suitors and am growing every day morose in that point but can't persuade people to believe me. However I can't allow that all my time is ill spent. I divide it into eating, sleeping, praying, studying business and trifling the two last are only liable to exception and yet both necessary, for I could not do the first without a little of the last I should be good for nothing without business, and unfit for it without relaxation *dulce est desipere in loco* pray do not grudge me the pleasure of serving my friends or refreshing my self or tell me which of these I shall abridge.

When the papers come to you you'l hear more in the mean time &c.

W. D.

Address: Dr Jonathan Swift at S^r andrew fountains in Leicester | fields

Swift to Archbishop King

My Lord.   London. Jan^{ry} 1. 170⅞

I had the Hon^r of Your Grace's Letter two Posts ago, and should not have given you the trouble of acknowledging it so soon, but that I was loth to leave yr Grace in an uncertainty, by one I writt lately to the Dean of St Patrick's[1] before yours came to Hand.

The storm Your Grace mentioned did not reach England and I remember about the same time four years ago I came just to have my share of a much greater in this town, when Ireland received no Damage.[2] I am glad Your Grace says nothing of any People killd or hurt.

I should be surprised at what your Grace tells me of the Clergy, if I were not sensible how extream difficult it is to deal with any Body of men, who seldom understand their true Interest or are able to distinguish their Enemyes from their Friends. Your Grace's Observation is so great a Truth that there is hardly a Clergyman in Ireland whose Revenue is not reckoned in the world at least double what he finds it, beside the Accidents to wch the Remaindr is subject.

For my own Part, I hope to live to see Your Grace very well used, that is in other words, I wish the Affair may succeed, and then you will be sure to be rewarded with a Good Conscience and Detraction; And then likewise those Woodcoks may have a better reason for hiding their Heads, they may hide them for shame.

I have heard it whispered by some who are fonder of politicall Refinements than I, that a new Difficulty may arise in this Matter, that it must perhaps be purchased by a Complyance with what was undertaken and endeavord in Ire^{ld} last Sessions, wch I confess I can

[1] Despite two major fluctuations a friendship between John Stearne and Swift was sustained throughout life. They became acquainted on Swift's appointment to Laracor, for then Stearne was Rector of the adjoining parish of Trim. Stearne, succeeding Jerome Ryves, preceded Swift as Dean of St. Patrick's. By Swift's instrumentality he was promoted Bishop of Dromore in 1713; and, succeeding St. George Ashe, he was translated to Clogher in 1717. A man of learning and piety, Stearne was also distinguished by his generous benefactions.

[2] The allusion is to the devastating tempest of 26 Nov. 1703, perhaps the most terrible on record in these islands. Defoe's *The Storm*, 1704, written in prison, is well known; and there is a vivid account of damage and loss of life suffered throughout the southern part of the country in Stanhope's *Hist. of the Reign of Queen Anne*, chap. iv.

not bring myself yet to believe nor do I care to think or reason upon it.[1]

When I have received the Representation, I shall as Your Grace directs, deliver it to My L^d L^t, and very heartily engage my Service in whatever I shall be thought fitt to be employed. And the cautions Your Grace is pleased to mention I shall observe with the utmost Exactness.

As to publick Affairs, all things are asleep during the Recess, and I am told, the two Houses seem resolved against busying themselves with Inquiry into past Miscarriages, concerning which the D. of M. made lately a speech with warmth unsuall to him, and with very great effect.[2] The Admiralty is certainly to continue in the same Hand, nor do I know of any change in the Prⁱ Council. The sea Commanders seem mightily pleased at a great Point gaind and speak hardly of the Merchants, who are yet louder against them, and those Gentlemen who go into the City return with melancholy Accounts from thence; I shall enter into the merits of either cause no further than by telling Y^r Grace a story which perhaps you may have already heard. After the Scots had sent their Colony to Darien, It was proposed here what methods should be taken to discourage that Project without coming to any open or avowed opposition. The Opinion of severall merchants was required to that Purpose, among the rest Haistwell advised to send over to them the Lds of the Admiralty, and if that would not ruin them, nothing could. Such a Liberty of Speech People are apt to take when they are angry.[3]

---

[1] While Lord Pembroke was in Ireland and the Irish Parliament sitting an attempt was made by the English Government to ascertain the opinion of members as to the repeal of the Test Act. The response was discouraging. The design is said to have been initiated by Lord Sunderland whose judgement of public feeling was untrustworthy.

[2] Parliament, meeting for the first time on 23 Oct. 1707 since the Act of Union with Scotland had come into force, was much occupied in discussing the conduct of the war and the provision of supplies. It was in the debate of 19 Dec., when Rochester proposed standing on the defensive in Flanders and transferring a strong force of men into Catalonia, and Nottingham expressed concurrence in these views, that Marlborough, deeply stirred, rose to explain the military dangers of 'such an undigested council'.

[3] The disastrous Darien scheme, projected by William Paterson, was sanctioned by the Scottish Parliament in 1695, and an expedition sailed in 1698. English commercial interests opposed the scheme. Edward Haistwell, a Quaker merchant, had extensive trade interests with the East Indies and China (B.M. Add. MS. 22852, f. 132).

I observe Your Grace's Artifice to bespeak my good Opinion by pretending to the merit of Trifling; But I who am a Strict Examiner, and a very good Judge, shall not be so ready to allow your Pretensions with out some better Title than I ever yet knew or heard you were able to sett up. And, if this Trifling you boast of were strictly enquired into it would amount to little more than talking with a Friend one hour in a week, or riding to Clontarf[1] in a fair Day: Would Socrates allow this, My Lord, Who at four score was caught whistling and dancing by himself, or Augustus who used to play at hucklebone with a parcel of Boys: Your Grace must give better Proof before I shall admit your plea.

It is reported about the Toun that a Clerk of Mr Secretary Harly's[2] is taken up on suspicion of corresponding with the French Court.

I beg Your Grace's Prayers, and am with all possible Respect | My Lord, | Your Grace's | most obedient and | most oblidged | humble Servt

Jon: Swift

Address: To His Grace, the Lord | Arch-Bishop of Dublin | at Dublin | Ireland

Rothschild[3]

Swift to Archdeacon Walls

London Jan^ry 22 170⅞

I have received y^r 3 Letters thô I have not had the manners to answer any of them sooner. By Manners we hear[4] mean Leisure but you Irish Folks must have Things explain'd to You; I thank you

---

[1] Clontarf, now a suburb, lies on the northern shore of the bay of Dublin. Its firm expanse of sand was then used by citizens of Dublin for equestrian exercise.

[2] William Gregg, a clerk in Harley's office, whose treasonable correspondence with the French Secretary of State was detected. See Swift's *Some Remarks upon a Pamphlet* (*Prose Works*, ed. Temple Scott, v. 30–53).

[3] This is the first of forty-six letters addressed by Swift to Thomas Walls, Archdeacon of Achonry, of which the originals survive. Previously in the possession of Sir John Murray they are now in Lord Rothschild's library. The letter is printed in part by Forster (*Life*, p. 197), in full by Stanley Lane-Poole (*Letters and Journals of Jonathan Swift*, p. 42).

[4] *Sic* 'hear'.

heartily for the Care and Kindness, and good Intentions of Y^r Intelligence, and I once had a Glimpse that Things would have gone otherwise, But now I must retire to my Moralls pretend[1] to be wholly without Ambition, and to resign with Patience.[2] You know by this time, who is the happy Man, a very worthy Person, and I doubt not but the whole Kingdom will be pleasd with the Choice: He will prove an Ornament to the Order, and a publick Blessing to the Church and Nation; And after this if you will not allow me to be a good Courtier, I will pretend to it no more; But let us talk no further on this Subject; I am stomach sick of it already; the rest when we meet ———[3]

I am glad the punning trade goes on: Sr Andr Fountain[4] has been at his Country house this Fortnight, and he has neither Influence nor Effluence from thence to London, else perhaps Things would not have gone as they did. Pray is yr Dorothy (as You call her) any Kin to Dr Thindoll, you know (h) is no Lett^r; She should have calld it Mrs Catherine Logg, not Katty Log; that leaves nothing to guess.[5] Tell her a Pun of mine, I saw a Fellow about a week ago hawking in the Court of Requests with a Parrot upon his Fist to

[1] The word 'and' before 'pretend' is scratched out.

[2] Swift is addressing himself to an Englishman, despite the reference to 'you Irish Folks'. Thomas Walls was entered at Trinity College, Dublin, in 1693, and there received his university education. On leaving he became master of a school attached to St. Patrick's Cathedral, which he held in conjunction with the Archdeaconry of Achonry. Later, resigning his schoolmastership, he became incumbent of Castleknock, near Dublin. For Swift's verses ridiculing the diminutive vestry of Castleknock see *Poems*, p. 125. There are frequent references to Walls in the *Journal to Stella*.

[3] The allusion is to the bishopric of Waterford to which Thomas Milles (1671–1740) had been appointed. Milles, Vice-Principal of St. Edmund Hall, 1695–1707, and Regius Professor of Greek, 1707, had come over to Ireland with Lord Pembroke. Swift had evidently entertained hopes of the bishopric himself. Sheridan (*Life*, p. 435) tells us that Swift conceived a 'particular dislike' of Milles and relates the story of a Latin jest upon him.

[4] Sir Andrew Fountaine (see p. 58, n. 3) shared with Swift and Lord Pembroke a delight in punning. Swift may have thought that if Fountaine had been at hand to influence Lord Pembroke the bishopric of Waterford might have come to him.

[5] The maiden name of Dorothy, Walls's wife, as this paragraph shows, was Newman. In writing to Swift, Walls had related a pun which he had made on the occasion of his being engaged on the cataloguing of Dean Stearne's books; and Swift retorts with several puns, including a play on the name of Matthew Tindal, the deistical writer, whose character and writings were about this time being attacked by him.

sell. Yesterday I mett him again, and said to him; How now Friend, I see that Parrot sticks upon the Hand still. When you had done with the Dean's Books I believe you were very glad of your *Liberty*, Your Catalogue puts me in mind of another Pun I made tothr day; a Gentleman was mightily afraid of a Cat: I told him it was a Sign he was Pus-ilanimous, and Lady Berkeley talking to her Cat, My Lord said she was very impertinent, but I defend[ed] her & said I thought her Ladyship spoke very much to the *poor-pus*[1] Do you call Dorothy's Puns a Spurious race quasi *Spew*rious because they turn yr Stomach? If you do not like them let the *Race* be to the Swift and I am content to father them all as you direct me. Tell her I thought she had been a New-man but I find she is the old Woman still. The Ladyes of St Mary's[2] are well, and talk of going to Ireld in Spring.[3] But Mrs Johnson cannot make a Pun if she might have the Weight of it in Gold. They desire me to give you their Service when I writt. As for Politicks, I know little worth writing: The Parlmt is this year prodigiously slow, and the Preperations for War, much slower, so that we expect but a moderate Campain, and People begin to be heartily weary of the War.[4] Pray give my humble Service to the Dean of St Patricks, I writt to him lately once or twice I hope he has received my Letters. I give no Service to Mrs Walls, because I write this to you both; Pray send me an Account of some smaller Vacancy than a Bishoprick in the Governmts Gift Y^r &c. | JS.

I do not remember that I desired Dr Smith[5] to take the Trouble he was pleasd to do, but I thank him for it, and wish you would desire him to speak to Dean Syng[6] as from himself, to enquire whether D^r

[1] The reference to Lady Berkeley is of interest. See 'A Ballad on the Game of Traffick' (*Poems*, p. 74) in which Swift depicts a family scene at Berkeley Castle. Lady Betty Berkeley, the daughter, added a stanza to the poem, describing how Swift used to 'deafen 'em with Puns and Rhime'.

[2] Stella and Rebecca Dingley are thus designated because they had changed their lodgings in Dublin from William Street (p. 41, n. 2) to Capel Street in the parish of St. Mary's.

[3] We have no certain evidence that Stella and Rebecca Dingley, after taking up their residence in Ireland, made more than one visit to England, and that in 1707–8. See *Journal to Stella*, pp. xviii, xxviii.

[4] A little earlier Swift had expressed the contrary opinion (see p. 58).

[5] William Smith, or Smyth, a Dublin physician, five times President of the College of Physicians. Mentioned in *Journal to Stella*.

[6] Samuel Synge, Dean of Kildare and Precentor of St. Patrick's Cathedral. For other members of a distinguished family see *D.N.B.*

Stearn designs really to give me the Parish that has the Church, for I believe I told you, that at parting he left me in doubt, by saying he would give me one of them; if he means that wch has the Church to build, I would not accept it, nor come for Ireld to be deceived, and let him desire Dean Syng (to whom I writt some time ago) to send me Word.[1]

Address: For the Reverend Mr Walls | at his House in Cavan | Street[2] | Dublin | Ireland
Postmark: 2? IA

Faulkner 1762

Swift to Archbishop King

London, *February* 5, 1707–8
My Lord,
I have been above a Month expecting the Representation your Grace was pleased to promise to send me, which makes me apprehend your Grace hath been hindered by what you complained of, the Clergy's Backwardness in a Point so very necessary to their Service;[3] And it is Time ill lost at this Juncture, while my Lord Lieutenant is here, and in great Credit at Court, and would perhaps be more than ordinarily ready to serve the Church in *Ireland*. If I have no Directions from your Grace by the End of this Month, I

[1] About sixteen months before that time the curacy of the parish of St. Nicholas Without, in Dublin, of which the Dean and Chapter of St. Patrick's were rectors, became vacant, and as the parishioners had greatly increased in number, the opportunity was taken to divide the parish, and to constitute the severed portion a separate parish under the name of St. Luke's. According to Swift, Stearne had given him reason to expect that he would benefit under the new arrangement. In a letter written to Stearne twenty-five years later, Swift alleged that Stearne had made him an absolute and frequent promise of the curacy of St. Nicholas Without; but from Swift's words here it would appear that Stearne was not explicit as to which parish he intended to give him. In the end neither one nor the other came to Swift, as Stearne found that there was not money enough available to carry through the scheme, and retained both parishes himself until he resigned the deanery, devoting the revenue to the erection of a church for St. Luke's parish. It is curious to note that Swift's friend, Delany (*Observations*, p. 27), was under the impression that Swift was actually given the curacy of St. Nicholas Without.—Ball.
[2] Otherwise Kevin Street, where Walls resided as master of the Cathedral School.—Ball.
[3] See p. 60.

shall think of my Return to *Ireland* against the 25th of *March*, to endeavour to be chosen to the Living of St. *Nicholas*, as I have been encouraged to hope;[1] but would readily return, at a Week's Warning, to sollicit that Affair with my Lord Lieutenant while he stays here, or in any other Manner your Grace will please to direct.

Your Grace knows long before this, that Dr. *Milles* is Bishop of *Waterford*. The Court and Archbishop of *Canterbury* were strongly engaged for another Person, not much suspected in *Ireland*, any more than the Choice already made was, I believe, either here or there.[2]

The two Houses are still busy in Lord *Peterborough*'s Affair, which seems to be little more than an Amusement, which it is conceived might at this Time be spared, considering how slow we are said to be in our Preparations; which, I believe, is the only Reason why it was talked the other Day about the Town, as if there would be soon a Treaty of Peace. There is a Report of my Lord *Galway*'s Death, but it is not credited. It is a perfect Jest to see my Lord *Peterborough*, reputed as great a Whig as any in *England*, abhorred by his own Party, and caressed by the Tories.[3]

The great Question, whether the Number of Men in *Spain* and *Portugal*, at the time of the battle of *Almanza*, was but 8,600, when there ought to have been 29,600, was carried on Tuesday in the Affirmative, against the Court, without a Division, which was occasioned by Sir *Thomas Hanmer*'s[4] Oratory. It seems to have been

[1] See p. 67.
[2] This, as Ball suggests, probably refers to Swift himself; and, as the Court and Archbishop Tenison supported him, he may not then have been suspected of being the author of *A Tale of a Tub*.
[3] On 19 Dec. 1707 the whole story of Peterborough's behaviour in Spain came up for discussion in the Lords. This developed into an extraordinary trial of strength between the political factions, the Tories supporting Peterborough, although he was a Whig, against a Whig government which denounced him. After an inquiry extending over several weeks the charges against him were dropped; but a vote of thanks for his services was declined. Swift greatly esteemed Peterborough—'I love the hang-dog dearly'; often mentions him in the *Journal to Stella*; and letters passed between them until within two or three years of Peterborough's death in 1735. For Swift's spirited lines addressed 'To the Earl of Peterborough' see *Poems*, p. 396.
[4] Sir Thomas Hanmer, 1677-1746, succeeded his father as fourth baronet in 1701. In 1714 he succeeded Bromley as Speaker of the House of Commons but the accession of George I soon terminated his occupancy of the chair. The question at this debate was 'where the rest [of the forces] were, and how the money was employed?' Harley and St. John spoke in favour of the Ministry.

no Party Question, there being many of both glad and sorry for it. The Court hath not been fortunate in their Questions this Session; and I hear some of both Parties expressing contrary Passions upon it. I tell your Grace bare Matters of Fact, being not inclined to make Reflections; and if I were, I could not tell what to make, so oddly People are subdivided, | I am, my Lord, | Your Grace's most obedient, | And most humble Servant, |

J. Swift.

Nichols 1801

Swift to Archbishop King

London, Feb. 12, 1707–8.

Having written what I had of business about three posts ago (whereof I wait an answer), perhaps it may be some amusement to you for a few minutes to hear some particulars about the turns we have had at Court. Yesterday the seals were taken from Mr. Harley, and Sir Thomas Mansell gave up his staff. They went to Kensington together for that purpose, and came back immediately, and went together into the House of Commons. Mr. St. John designs to lay down in a few days, as a friend of his told me, though he advised him to the contrary; and they talk that Mr. Brydges, and Mr. Coke the Vice-Chamberlain, with some others, will do the like.[1] Mr. Harley had been some time, with the greatest art imaginable, carrying on an intrigue to alter the Ministry, and began with no less an enterprise than that of removing the Lord Treasurer, and had nearly effected it, by the help of Mrs. Masham, one of the Queen's dressers, who was a great and growing favourite, of much industry and insinuation. It went so far, that the Queen told Mr. St. John a week ago, that she was resolved to part with Lord

[1] In Jan. 1708 Godolphin and Marlborough realized that the independent position in the Queen's favour which they had enjoyed during the crisis of the war had been replaced by her secret confidence in Harley. In the first week of February the Queen attempted to dismiss Godolphin. Marlborough addressed to her a vigorous remonstrance refusing under any conditions to serve with Harley. The moderate party among the Ministers refused to act without Marlborough. A Cabinet meeting on Sunday, 9 Feb., at which the Queen presided, brought matters to a head. Two days later Harley resigned. He was followed by St. John, Sir Thomas Mansell, Controller of the Household, and Sir Simon Harcourt. See Trevelyan, *England under Queen Anne*, ii. 326–9.

Treasurer; and sent him with a letter to the Duke of Marlborough, which she read to him, to that purpose; and she gave St. John leave to tell it about the town, which he did without any reserve; and Harley told a friend of mine a week ago, that he was never safer in favour or employment. On Sunday evening last, the Lord Treasurer and Duke of Marlborough went out of the Council; and Harley delivered a memorial to the Queen, relating to the Emperor and the war. Upon which the Duke of Somerset rose, and said, if her Majesty suffered that fellow (pointing to Harley), to treat affairs of the war without advice of the General, he could not serve her; and so left the Council. The Earl of Pembroke, though in milder words, spoke to the same purpose:[1] so did most of the Lords: and the next day the Queen was prevailed upon to turn him out, though the seals were not delivered till yesterday. It was likewise said, that Mrs. Masham is forbid the Court; but this I have no assurance of. Seven Lords of the Whig party are appointed to examine Gregg, who lies condemned in Newgate; and a certain Lord of the Council told me yesterday, that there are endeavours to bring in Harley as a party in that business, and to carry it as far as an impeachment.[2] All this business has been much fomented by a Lord whom Harley had been chiefly instrumental in impeaching some years ago. The Secretary always dreaded him, and made all imaginable advances to be reconciled, but could never prevail; which made him say yesterday to some who told it to me, that he had laid his neck under their feet, and they trod upon it. I am just going this morning to visit that Lord, who has a very free way of telling what he cares not who hears; and if I can learn any more particulars worth telling, you shall have them.[3] I never in my life saw or heard such divisions and complications of parties as there have been for some time: you sometimes see the extremes of Whig and Tory driving on the same thing. I have heard the chief Whigs blamed by their own party for want of moderation, and I know a Whig Lord in good employment who voted with the highest Tories against the Court, and the Ministry, with whom he is nearly allied. My Lord Peterborough's

---

[1] Lord Pembroke's firmness of utterance caused surprise, for, so far as Harley was concerned, he was judged to be complacent.

[2] See p. 64, n. 2.

[3] It has been suggested that the allusion is to Somers, but 'a very free way of telling' is inconsistent with the formality of his habitual manner. Ball suggests, with more probability, that it may have been Halifax.

affair is yet upon the anvil, and what they will beat it out to, no man can tell.[1] It is said that Harley had laid a scheme for an entire new Ministry, and the men are named to whom the several employments were to be given. And though his project has miscarried, it is reckoned the greatest piece of Court skill that has been acted these many years.

I have heard nothing since morning but that the Attorney either has laid down, or will do it in a few days.

King's Letter-book
Trinity College, Dublin

Archbishop King to Swift

Dublin Feb^ry 21st 1707[8]

Revd S^r

I have at last with great difficulty got the representation concerning the first fruits of Ireland and 20th parts signed by the archbps and Bȋps in town and send it by this post.[2] I intended to have sent it immediately to you, but found it may be very chargeable in the post Office, since I cou'd not get a private hand to send it by. and therefore I rather chose to send you the enclosed relating to a matter of near as great a value, and wch I hope may be so managed as to prove an Introduction to this of the 1st fruits and 20th parts.[3] I trust them both to your managem^t and am—&c.

Dr Swift   W:D:

King's Letter-book
Trinity College, Dublin

Archbishop King to Swift

Dublin Feb. 21st 1707[8]

Revd S^r

I am informed that Mr Burgh my Ld Bophins son is procuring an Act of Parlem^t that if it pass, will take away all those forfeited tiths

---

[1] See p. 68.   [2] See p. 67.
[3] The letter which follows.

that were given to the Church by former Acts of Parlem^t.[1] they
are in value at least 300^11 per annum, and are the chief fruit of
the Trustees Act that vested forfeited tiths in them for building
Churches. If you acquaint his Ex^cy the Ld L^t with this I am confident his Ex^cy will concern himself to prevent it. If any other means
be thought necessary, we shall on notice be ready to apply them. I
had writt to his Ex^cy on this subject, but having given him so great
trouble already ab^t the representation of the Archbps and Bĩps relating to their 1st fruits and 20th parts, I did not dare to multiply his
Ex^cys trouble at this time. I spake to him before he left Dublin to
permitt you to put him in mind on occasion of this affair. and his
Ex^cys goodness is so great that I persuade my self you may safely
venture to do it without offending. | I pray for etc
       Dr Swift   W:D:

King's Letter-book
Trinity College, Dublin

Archbishop King to Swift

                                          Dublin February 28th 1707[8].
Revd S^r
   I sent some posts ago the representation to My Ld Lt. and a
Pacquett to you[2] I am concerned they went so late, but when I
considered what the Ministry had on their hands, I am apt to think
that a pacqu^tt relating to Irish affairs will come time enuf for the
leisure of the Court.
   If the next pacquetts confirm the report of an Invasion[3] the

---

   [1] John Bourke, ninth Earl of Clanricarde, born 1642, was colonel of a regiment in the army of James II. He was created by that King, 2 Apr. 1689,
after his exclusion from the throne, Baron Bourke of Bophin, co. Galway. He
was taken prisoner at the battle of Aughrim, 12 July 1691, and attainted. In
1699 he conformed to the Established Church, and was in 1702 acquitted of all
treasons and attainders, and restored in blood and estate. He died 17 Oct. 1722,
aged eighty-two. G. E. C., *Complete Peerage*, iii. 234.
   [2] See previous letter.
   [3] On 17 Mar. o.s., 1708, an expedition of nearly thirty ships carrying the
Chevalier and 6,000 French infantry sailed from Dunkirk to effect a landing on
the Scottish coast. These preparations were well known to the English Government. The English admiral, Byng, came within sight of the French on the 24th,
and pursued them towards the north. In sad condition, sailing round Cape

Hurry in Ireland for aught I can see will be as great and universall as the fear of the Irish massacre was in England on the revolution, and some are so Imprudent as to parallell them, but the great cry is, that this was H[arle]y's plott, and if he had continued 3 days longer in his place, the French wou'd have landed at Greenwich. Others think it an amusement to divert the succours designed for Spain. That I find is the part of the war that most have at heart and there is really a dread on most lest it shou'd be lost. If it shou'd (which God forbid) whichever party shall have the misfortune to be reckoned the cause of it, will hardly be able to stand.

As to Dr. Milles' preferment you'l not expect from me any account how it [is] relished here. Some say if General Lanceston had been Primate it wou'd not have bin so, I did not ask what they meant.[1]

As to your own business I have discoursed the Dean about it and I doubt the thing can't possibly be done so soon as you expect.[2] we have not yet bin able to pay for the Act of Parlem^t much less purchase ground for a Church and least of all to lay a scheme for the building it. and some progress must be made in these before we can think of separating the parishes. but it will be time enough to concert these matters, when you come over. I can say no more but my— etc.

Dr Swift   W. D.

Wrath and Ireland, the abortive expedition made its way back to Dunkirk. See Trevelyan, *England under Queen Anne*, ii. 341–5. Evidently news of the preparations at Dunkirk had filtered through as far as Dublin by the end of February.

[1] For the appointment of Thomas Milles as Bishop of Waterford and Lismore see p. 65, n. 3. A man of learning and a generous benefactor of his diocese he was, nevertheless, unpopular in Ireland. He was suspected of Jacobite leanings; and was said to carry a crucifix on his breast. A visit he paid to the doctors of the Sorbonne was a move which laid his loyalty open to doubt. Lanceston is perhaps a slip for Lancaster, Vice-Chancellor of the University of Oxford; unless it has some hidden meaning in reference to John Lancaster, consecrated Bishop of Waterford one hundred years earlier. He was also suspected of unduly favouring Romanists. The *D.N.B.* article on Thomas Milles needs correction.

[2] See p. 67.

Joseph Addison to Swift

[29 February 1707–8]

Sir

Mr Frowde tells me, that you design me the Honour of a Visite to-morrow morning but my Lord Sunderland having directed me to wait on him at Nine a clock, I shall take it as a particular favour, if you will give me Your Company at the George in Pal-Mal about two in the After-noon when I may hope to enjoy your Conversation more at leisure, which I set a very great value upon. I am | Sir | Your most Obedient | Humble servant

J. Addison

Mr Steele & Frowde will Dine with us.[1]

Feb. 29. 1707/8.

King's Letter-book
Trinity College, Dublin

Archbishop King to Swift

Dublin. Ap[l]. 7th. 1708[2]

Rev[d] Sir

I have had yours of the 9th of March last some time by me but you'l excuse my not answering first post when you consider what we have bin doing since. All thoughts of fighting had bin laid aside in Ireland as much as if we would never be attacked, a militia was an abomination to many. what need for such when we have 12000 standing Troops on our Establishment and these punctually pd.

---

[1] Swift's acquaintance with Addison most probably began during the early part of that visit to England which lasted from Nov. 1707 to June 1709; and Sir Andrew Fountaine may have been instrumental in bringing them together (*Poems*, pp. 89–90). On the other hand, the mention of Philip Frowde, a pupil of Addison and author of *The Fall of Saguntum*, suggests that he was responsible for procuring the invitation. For Frowde see further, *Journal*, p. 81, n. 16. At this time Addison was an Under-Secretary of State for the Southern Department, for which Lord Sunderland was Secretary of State.

[2] This copy of King's letter in the library of Trinity College, Dublin (N. 3. 3), is preserved in good condition.

But soe it happens that we really have but 4400.[1] hardly a Gun mounted in the whole Kingdom, Forts generally slighted, no arms and little powder, And now on a sudden we must raise a Militia which after all has not proved impossible, for I doubt but in one month's time we shall have 40000 Listed, and these good hearty men, that generally understand Arms, if they had them.[2]

I am to inform you that great Art is used to advance the Dissenters Interest on this occasion, and the City of Dublin has bin surprised to put some thing that way in their address,[3] tho I do not know any Officer that has on accn[t] of the Test parted with his command & I do not believe that 3 will,[4] Tis hardly credible how working those people on all occasions are to promote their party. I do not think it proper to say any more on this subject, but twill phaps be of some use and satisfaction to observe the steps that are taken.

I know not what England might have done if this invasion made any progress but I am confident that the whole body of the pro-testants here would have bin firm to a man ag[t] it.

Pray do not forget to put my Ld Lieu[t] in mind of our first fruits and 20th parts. I had no answer from his Excy about it. If Mr. Burghs Bill goe on, let it be viewed by a Lawyer, but if my information be right the parlem[t] is already up & it can't proceed.

I am of your opinion that expectation of reversions is a cold Subsistance, I had many Arguments ag[t] the methods used in his case, but necessity has no Law, and till things be a little better I can

---

[1] Ball reads 'four thousand five hundred'.

[2] In connexion with the attempted invasion of Scotland (see p. 72, n. 3) a diver-sionary attack on Ireland evidently formed part of the original plan. Ball quotes from a letter of Archbishop King, 13 Mar., addressed to another correspondent, in which he says: 'People here are almost frightened out of their wits with the fear of an invasion.' He continues: 'The truth is we are in an ill condition, not above four thousand three hundred men in the army, many of those want arms . . . the militia absolutely neglected, no arms nor powder for them if raised . . . we reckon our security rather in the weakness of our enemy than in our own strength.'

[3] The address from the city of Dublin may be presumed to have been one congratulating the Queen on the failure of the French expedition against Scotland.

[4] King seems to have misconceived the situation. Froude, *The English in Ireland*, edition 1872, i. 326, after an examination of State Papers, formed the conclusion that the Test had a severe detrimental effect on recruitment. The Ulster militia, almost wholly Presbyterian, refused to enlist unless under officers of their own persuasion.

have no prospect of ordering it otherwise, I hope however that this may turn to your advantage, for to deal ingenuously with you I do conceive that you would have no prospect of temporall interest if you were to morrow put into one of those parishes.[1] And therefore that you lose no profit and secure your Ease whilst you are out of it. But this is soe far from being an argument ag^t you with others that on the contrary every good man will be uneasy till you be settled in that or a better. If a new Ld Lieu^t should be thought on with which we are threatned, pray be early to come in his family, for you see that is the only merit.[2] I heartily commend you to Gods favour & am etc

                                                                    W D

    Dr Swift

Hawkesworth 1766

Swift to Dean Stearne

                                                    London, April 15, 1708.

Sir,

I wonder whether, in the midst of your buildings,[3] you ever consider that I have broke my shins, and have been a week confined, this charming weather, to my chamber, and cannot go abroad to hear the nightingales, or pun with my lord *Pembroke*. *Pug*[4] is very well, and likes *London* wonderfully, but *Greenwich* better, where we could hardly keep him from hunting down the deer. I am told by some at Court, that the Bishop of *Kildare* is utterly bent upon a removal on this side, though it be to St. *Asaph*; and then the

---

[1] See p. 73.

[2] That is, Swift should busy himself to obtain the post of chaplain.

[3] The Deanery House, afterwards occupied by Swift, was built by Stearne. Since the Reformation, according to Archbishop King, no house had existed on the site. The sum expended by Stearne was said to be about £1,000. Unfortunately Swift's Deanery was almost entirely destroyed by fire in the latter part of the eighteenth century. The only portions remaining are the spacious basement rooms of stone, and a small part of the floor above. A few relics were rescued, the most important being the large portrait of Swift by Bindon, painted for the Chapter of St. Patrick's in 1739. See *Prose Works*, ed. Temple Scott, xii. 27. This portrait, framed in Irish oak, hangs in the Deanery.

[4] 'Pug' was probably the pet of Stella and Rebecca Dingley, who apparently had not yet left London.

question must be, whether Dr. *Pratt* will be Dean of *St. Patrick's*, minister of *St. Catherine's*, or Provost? For I tell you a secret, that the Queen is resolved the next promotion shall be to one of *Dublin* education: this she told the Lord Lieutenant.[1] Your new *Waterford* Bishop franks his letters, which no bishop does that writes to me; I suppose it is some peculiar privilege of that see.[2] The Dissenters have made very good use here of your frights in *Ireland* upon the intended invasion; and the Archbishop writes me word, that the address of *Dublin* city will be to the same purpose, which I think the clergy ought to have done their best to prevent, and I hope they did so. Here has the *Irish* Speaker been soliciting to get the *Test Clause* repealed by an Act here; for which I hope he will be impeached when your Parliament meets again, as well as for some other things I could mention.[3] I hope you will be of my opinion in what I have told the Archbishop about those addresses. And if his Grace and clergy of the province send an address, I desire I may present it, as one of the chapter, which is the regular way; but I beg you will endeavour among you, that the Church of *Ireland* gentlemen may

---

[1] The see of Kildare was then held by Welbore Ellis, an Oxford man, who was appointed to the bishopric in 1705, when over fifty years old. He regarded residence in Ireland as banishment, and made no secret of the fact. He was, however, unsuccessful in obtaining translation to England. In 1731 he became Bishop of Meath, died in less than three years, and was buried in Christ Church Cathedral, Dublin, where he is commemorated by a monument. He was not a man of remarkable parts. In the event of a vacancy occurring at Kildare Swift considered that those from whom a successor to Ellis was likely to be chosen were Dean Stearne, Dean Synge (see p. 66, n. 6), who held the incumbency of St. Catherine's in Dublin, and Dr. Peter Browne, since 1699 Provost of Trinity College. For the post vacated by any one of these who might be promoted Swift thought the obvious selection to be the Rev. Benjamin Pratt, who had entered Trinity College while Swift was an undergraduate there. When Browne was promoted to the see of Cork in 1710 Pratt succeeded him as Provost. A man of considerable fortune, he was something of a *bon vivant* and incurred criticism for spending too much of his time in London. See *Poems*, p. 289.

[2] See p. 65, n. 3.

[3] Alan Brodrick came of an able and wealthy family. He adopted the law as a profession, and in 1695, under William, he was appointed Solicitor-General for Ireland, an office in which he was continued under Queen Anne. He was at this time Speaker of the Irish House of Commons. In 1707 he was promoted Attorney-General. A man of advanced Whig views he was in favour of the repeal of the Test Act, and even crossed to England in an attempt to persuade the English Parliament, without success, to initiate a repeal there, a proceeding which led Swift, as will be seen in the following letter, to be at a loss to find terms 'bad enough' in which to denounce him.

send an address to set the Queen and Court right about the Test, which every one here is of opinion you should do; or else I have reason to fear it will be repealed here next session, which will be of terrible consequence, both as to the thing and the manner, by the Parliament here interfering in things purely of *Ireland*, that have no relation to any interest of theirs.

If you will not use me as your book-buyer, make use of Sir *Andrew Fountaine*, who sends you his humble service, and will carry over a cargo as big as you please toward the end of summer,[1] when he and I intend my Lord Lieutenant shall come into our company without fail, and in spite of *Irish* reports, that say we shall come no more.

I reckon by this time you have done with masons and carpenters, and are now beginning with upholsterers, with whom you may go on as slow and soberly as you please.

But pray keep the garden till I come. I am, Sir, |

Your most faithful humble servant,

Jon. Swift.

Direct the inclosed, and deliver it to the greatest person in your neighbourhood.[2]

The Library, Armagh

Swift to Archbishop King

London Apr. 15. 1708[3]

My Lord.

I had last Post the Hon[r] of Your Grace's of the 7th instant, and I must caution Your Grace once for all, that you must either resolve never to write to me, or be content that I answer immediately, tho I have nothing material to say, which I allow to be hard usage, and just the reverse of what all my other correspondents meet with.

[1] Stearne had collected a considerable library of printed books and manuscripts. The rarer books he gave to Archbishop Marsh's library; the manuscripts he bequeathed to Trinity College. Archbishop King made use of Sir Andrew Fountaine's knowledge in purchasing additions to the library.

[2] The letter which follows. In its concluding paragraph Swift explains his reason for not posting it direct.

[3] This letter, enclosed within the preceding one, shows no external address, nor even the beginning of one. It was closed with a small red seal.

But the Fault is in your Grace, who gives the Provocation, and whose Letters are full of everything that can inspire the meanest Pen with generous and Publick Thoughts.

Considering many reasons not proper to mention, I do not wonder at all, that Ireland was found in so ill a Posture of defense, But I hope all will be better upon My Ld Lt's return, which we certainly conclude will be towards the end of Summer, there being not the least talk of his removall. I was told in confidence three weeks ago by a Friend in Business, that the chief Whig Lords resolved to apply in a Body to the Queen, for my Ld Sommers to be made President; but tother day upon Tryall, the Ministry would not joyn, and the Qu. was resolute, and so it miscarried;[1]

We have been already surprised enough with two Addresses from the Dissenters of Ireld; but this from Dublin will, I fear be very pernicious;[2] and there is no other Remedy, but by another Address from the uncorrupted part of the City, which has been usuall in England from severall countyes, as in the case of the Tack;[3] and I should hope from a Person of Your Grace's vigilance, that Counter Addresses should be sent from the Clergy and Conforming Gentry of Ireland, to sett the Qu. right in this matter; I assure your Grace all Persons I converse with are entirely of this Opinion and I hope it will be done.

Some days ago, My Ld Sommers entered with me into discourse about the Test Clause, and desired my Opinion upon it, which I

[1] Lord Pembroke then held the office of President of the Council together with that of Lord Lieutenant of Ireland. After the Whigs had won the general election in May 1708, and before the meeting of Parliament later in that year, the victorious party pressed for further recognition in positions of office. Among demands put forward were the substitution of Lord Pembroke for the incompetent Prince Consort at the head of the Admiralty and the appointment of Lord Somers to the Presidency of the Council. The attack on her husband and the promotion of Somers were difficult for the Queen to countenance; for Prince George, quite unjustly, seems to have regarded Somers as the primary instigator of attacks on Admiralty measures. While the crisis was coming to a head the Prince died, 28 Oct. 1708, a fortnight before Parliament was due to assemble (Trevelyan, *England under Queen Anne*, iii. 388–91).

[2] See p. 77.

[3] The unsuccessful attempt which was made on its third introduction to attach the Bill against Occasional Conformity to a money bill in order to insure its acceptance by the Lords, excited even greater feeling in the country than has been described by Swift on the occasion of its second introduction. A division list showing how each member voted was published, which was very rarely done in that age.—Ball.

gave him truly, tho with all the Gentleness I could, Because as I am inclined and oblidged to value the Friendship he professes for me; so he is a Person whose Favor I would manage in this Affair of the First-fruits. I had consulted Mr Southwell[1] and some other Friends before; and they all agreed it necessary that I should have Access to Ld. Treasurer and sollicite the matter myself.[2] I told Ld Sommers the case, and that by Your Grace's Command and the desire of severall Bishops and some of the Principall Clergy, I undertook the matter; that the Qu. & Ld. Tr: had already fallen into it these 4 years; that it wanted nothing but sollicitation; that I knew His Ldship was a great Friend of Ld Sunderland,[3] with whom I had been long acquainted, but hearing he forbore common visits now he was in Business, I had not attended him. Then I desired his Ldship to tell Ld. Sunderland the whole matter and prevail that I might attend with him upon My Lord Tr. Yesterday My Ld. Sommers came to see me, and told me very kindly he had performed my commission, that Ld Sunderland was very glad we should renew our Acquaintance, and that he would whenever I pleased go along with me to Ld Tr. I should in a day or two have been able to give Yr Grace some further Account, if it were not for an accident in one of my Legs, wch has for some time confined me to my Chamber, and wch I am forced to manage for fear of ill consequences; I hope Yr Grace will approve what I have hitherto done. I told Ld. Sommers, the Nicety of Proceeding in a matter where the Ld. Lt was engaged, and design to tell it Ld Sund. & Ld Tr: and

---

[1] Edward Southwell was the eldest son of Sir Robert Southwell, to whom, when he was going as Secretary of State to Ireland in 1690, Temple recommended Swift. The son succeeded his father as Secretary for Ireland in 1702. The office did not entail residence in that country, and he spent most of his time in England, where he held the clerkship of the Privy Council; although later he was for many years M.P. for Kinsale, and through his wife, the only daughter of the Earl of Ardglass, he obtained a large property in co. Down. In writing to the Archbishop Swift was well aware that Southwell was a close friend and frequent correspondent of King.

[2] Over four months had passed (see Swift's letter to King, 6 Dec. 1707) since Swift had declared his intention of seeking the assistance of Lord Sunderland and Lord Somers in the affair of the First Fruits; but owing to intervening events time had slipped by ineffectually. He now realized the wisdom of going further and gaining an interview with Godolphin.

[3] Swift must have known Lord Sunderland since Moor Park days, for in *The Journal to Stella*, p. 476, he refers to a visit paid by him in company with Trimnel, who had been chaplain to the second Earl.

shall be sure to avoid any false step in that Point,[1] and Your Grace shall I hope soon know the Issue of this Negotiation, or whether there be any hope from it.

If it became me to give ill Names to all Things and Persons, I should be at a loss to find bad enough for Villany and Baseness of a certain Lawyr of Ireld, who is in a station the least of all other excusable for such Proceedings, and yet has been going about most industriously to all his Acquaintance in both Houses toward the end of the Session to shew the necessity of taking off the Test Clause in Ireld by an Act here, wherein you may be sure he had his Brother's Assistance.[2] If such a Project should be resumed next Session, and I in England; unless Yr Grace would send me your Absolute Commands to the contrary, wch I should be sorry to receive, I should hardly forbear publishing some Paper of opposition to it, or leaving one behind me, if there should be occasion.

I most humbly thank Your Grace for your favorable Thoughts in my own Particular, and I cannot but observe that you conclude them with a compliment in such a turn as betrays more skill in that part of eloquence than you will please to own, and such as we whose necessityes put us upon practising it all our lives, can never arrive to.

I send this Politick Letter inclosed, for fear some profound Person might know it by its weight, which will now be all imputed to the cover.

Sr A. Fountain presents his humble Duty to Yr Grace, and will gett you the Talmud if you please; he is gone this morning to Oxford for 3 or 4 days. Your Bill shall be made up when the Talmud is in it. I am with the greatest Respect My Lord

Your Grace's most obedient | and most oblidged humble Servt

J: Swift

I do suppose Your Grace intends to send an Address from the Clergy of Dublin, and of your Province, and I should be glad

---

[1] This passage is a reply to King's cautionary note in his letter of 16 Dec.

[2] As will be seen by reference to the previous letter the person here denoted is Speaker Brodrick. His brother Thomas was still more extreme in his views. It is to him Swift alludes as the man who 'had the Impudence, some Years ago, in Parliament Time, to shake my Lord Bishop of *Killaloo* by his Lawn Sleeve, and tell him in a threatening Manner, *That he hoped to live to see the Day, when there should not be one of his Order in the Kingdom.*' (*Letter concerning the Sacramental Test, Prose Works*, ed. Davis, ii. 117.)

to be the Deliverer of it, and I think the University should send
another, and Dr. Prat is here to deliver it, I am sure it would please
the Duke of Ormond.[1]

Hawkesworth 1766

Swift to Dean Stearne

[10] June 1708

Sir,

I writ to you some weeks ago,[2] and inclosed (as now) a letter to
your neighbour.[3] But I fear it was kidnapp'd by some privateer, or
else you were lazy or forgetful; or, which is full as good, perhaps, it
had no need of an answer; and I would not for a good deal, that the
former had miscarried, because the inclosed was wonderfully politic,
and would have been read to you, as this, I suppose, will, though it
be not half so profound. Now are you gone some summer ramble,
and will not receive this in a fortnight; nor send the inclosed in as
much more. I have often begged you would let me buy you one
fifty pounds worth of books; but now I have been here so long, I
believe you will have reason to apprehend I may sink the money.
Sir *A. Fountaine*[4] will never be satisfied till he gets into the little
room, with the three *Ashes*, the Bishop of *Killala*, and myself, to
be happy at the expence of your wine and conversation.[5] Here is a
sight of two girls joined together at the back, which, in the news-
monger's phrase, causes a great many speculations; and raises
ɐbundance of questions in divinity, law and physic.[6] The boys of our
town are mighty happy, for we are to have a beheading next week,

---

[1] The Duke of Ormonde was then Chancellor of Dublin University.
[2] 15 Apr.   [3] Archbishop King.
[4] See p. 65, n. 4.
[5] This sentence affords a pleasing testimony to the appreciation in which Swift
was held by friends of college days. St. George Ashe, Bishop of Clogher, had
been his tutor. Thomas Ashe, the Bishop's brother, and senior by one year, lived
on the family estate near Trim. As well as Dillon Ashe, Swift's contemporary,
he had been educated in Trinity College. William Lloyd, Bishop of Killala, who
matriculated before Swift was born, had been a Fellow. Stearne, who was attached
to the University by hereditary ties, eventually became its Vice-Chancellor.
[6] Ball quotes at some length an elaborate account from *Philosophical Transactions* of two sisters born at Szony in Hungary in 1702, joined together at the
small of the back. They were, in course of time, possessed of remarkable
accomplishments: they could read, write, sing, and speak several languages.

unless the Queen will interpose her mercy.¹ Here is a long lampoon publicly printed, abusing by name at length, all the young people of quality, that walk in the park.² These are effects of our liberty of the press.

I long to know what is become of your new house, whether there is yet a union between that and the little one, or whether the work stops for want of money; and you pretend it is only that the boards may have time to season.³ We are still in pain for Mr. *Dopping's* being in one of the pacqet-boats that were taken. He and many more have vowed never to return to *England* again; which, if they forget, they may properly be called vows written in water.⁴

Pray, Sir, let me hear from you some time this hot weather, for it will be very refreshing; and I am confined by business to this ugly town, which, at this season of the year, is almost insufferable. I am, |

Sir, your most faithful humble servant, |

J. S.

¹ Only eight days before James II was declared to have abdicated Edward Griffin, son and heir of Sir Edward Griffin, was created, 3 Dec. 1688, Baron Griffin of Braybrooke. He remained faithful to the Stuarts and followed the King overseas. On 13 or 14 Mar. 1707–8 he was taken prisoner off Leith when engaged upon an expedition to Scotland on the exiled King's behalf. He was tried and condemned to death 12 June 1708; but obtained from the Queen first a reprieve and then a remission of the death penalty. He died a prisoner in the Tower of London 10 Nov. 1710, aged about eighty. His son James seems never to have assumed the title. See G. E. C., *Complete Peerage*, vi. 202.

² According to John Nichols, *Swift's Works*, 1801, xi. 26, the reference is to a poem by William Oldisworth under the title of 'St. James's Park'. Oldisworth revived the Tory *Examiner* in Dec. 1711, and continued it until the death of the Queen. In recognition of his editorial labours he received twenty guineas from Lord Oxford in Mar. 1712. Commenting upon this recognition Swift (*Journal*, p. 637) wrote: 'He is an ingenious fellow, but the most confounded vain coxcomb in the world; so that I dare not let him see me, nor am acquainted with him.'

³ From this allusion it is evident that Stearne built the Deanery house in sections. The sum of £1,000 stated to be its cost by King can only have been a portion of the expenditure.

⁴ As appears from *The Journal to Stella*, in which he is several times mentioned, Samuel Dopping, if he ever made such a vow, failed to keep it. He was the eldest son of Anthony Dopping, Bishop of Meath (1681), and brother of Anthony Dopping, who became Bishop of Ossory (1740). Samuel, a man of independent means, and a strong Tory, sat in the Irish Parliament for Armagh in the reign of Queen Anne, and for Dublin University under George I. He died in 1720.

83

Swift to Archbishop King

London, June 10, 1708.

My Lord,

I sent your Grace a long Letter several Weeks ago, enclosed in one to the Dean.[1] I know not whether it came to your Hands, having not since been honoured with your Commands. I believe I told your Grace, that I was directly advised by my Lord *Sund—*, my Lord *Somers*, Mr. *Southwell*, and others, to apply to my Lord Treasurer, in Behalf of the Clergy of *Ireland*; and Lord Sunderland undertook to bring me to Lord Treasurer, which was put off for some Time on Account of the Invasion. For, it is the Method here of great Ministers, when any publick Matter is in Hand, to make it an Excuse for putting off all private Application. I deferred it some Time longer, because I had a Mind my Lord *Sunderland* should go along with me; but either the one or the other was always busy, or out of the Way; however, his Lordship had prepared Lord Treasurer, and engaged him (as he assured me) to think well of the Matter; and the other Day Lord Treasurer appointed me to attend him. He took me into a private Room, and I told him my Story, that I was commanded by your Grace, and desired by some other Bishops, to use what little credit I had, to sollicit (under the Direction of my Lord-Lieutenant) the remitting of the first Fruits, which from the favourable Representation of his Lordship to the Queen about four Years ago, the Clergy were encouraged to hope would be granted: That I had been told it might be of Use, if some Person could be admitted to his Presence, at his usual Times of being attended, in order to put him in Mind; for the rest, they relied entirely on his Excellency's good Office, and his Lordship's Dispositions to favour the Church. He said, in Answer, he was passive in this Business: That he supposed my Lord-Lieutenant would engage in it, to whom, if I pleased, he would repeat what I had said. I replied, I had the Honour of being well known to his Excellency, that I intended to ask his Leave to sollicit this Matter with his Lordship, but had not mentioned it yet, because I did not know whether I had Credit enough to gain that Access he was now pleased to honour me with: That upon his Lordship's Leave to attend him, signified to me by the Earl of *Sunderland*, I went to inform his Excellency, not doubting

[1] His letter of 15 Apr.

84

his Consent; but did not find him at Home, and therefore ventured to come; but, not knowing how his Excellency might understand it, I begged his Lordship to say nothing to my Lord-Lieutenant, until I had the Honour to wait on him again. This my Lord Treasurer agreed to, and entering on the Subject, told me, that since the Queen's Grant of the first Fruits here, he was confident, not one Clergyman in *England* was a Shilling the better. I told him, I thought it lay under some Incumbrances. He said, it was true; but besides that, it was wholly abused in the Distribution, that as to those in *Ireland*, they were an inconsiderable Thing, not above 1000 *l.* or 1200 *l.* a Year, which was almost nothing for the Queen to grant, upon two Conditions: First, That it should be well disposed of. And, secondly, That it should be well received with due Acknowledgments; in which Cases he would give his Consent, otherwise, to deal freely with me, he never would. I said, as to the first, that I was confident the Bishops would leave the Methods of disposing it entirely to her Majesty's Breast; as to the second, her Majesty, and his Lordship might count upon all the Acknowledgments that the most grateful and dutiful Subjects could pay to a Prince. That I had the Misfortune to be altogether unknown to his Lordship, else I should presume to ask him, whether he understood any particular Acknowledgments. He replied, by Acknowledgments, I do not mean any Thing under their Hands, but I will so far explain my self to tell you, I mean better Acknowledgments than those of the Clergy of *England*. I then begged his Lordship, to give me his Advice, what sort of Acknowledgments he thought fittest for the Clergy to make, which I was sure would be of mighty Weight with them. He answered, I can only say again, such Acknowledgments as they ought. We had some other Discourse of less Moment; and after Licence to attend him on Occasion, I took my leave.[1] I tell your Grace these Particulars in his very Words, as near as I can recollect, because I think them of Moment, and I believe your Grace may think them so too. I told [Mr.] Southwell all that had passed, and we agreed in our Comments, which I desired him now to inform you. He set out for *Ireland* this Morning.[2] I am resolved to see my Lord *Sund*[erland] in a Day or

---

[1] The nature of the acknowledgements expected Swift well understood to be the repeal of the Test. A visit to Lord Pembroke the same evening left him with the conviction that he was not being frankly used; and that he had better turn aside to study his own chances of ecclesiastical preferment.

[2] Southwell seldom visited Ireland. On this occasion he was engaged upon

two, and relate what my Lord Treasurer said (as he hath commanded me to do) and perhaps I may prevail on him to let me know his Lordship's Meaning, to which I am prepared to answer, as Mr. *Southwell* will let you know. At Evening, the same Day, I attended my Lord Lieutenant, and desired to know what Progress he had made; and at the same Time proposed that he would give me leave to attend Lord Treasurer only as a common Sollicitor, to refresh his Memory. I was very much surprised at his Answer, that the Matter was not before the Treasurer, but entirely with the Queen, and therefore it was needless; upon which I said nothing of having been there. He said, he had writ lately to your Grace an Account of what was done; that some Progress was made, that they put it off because it was a Time of War, but that he had some Hopes it would be done: but this is only such an Account as his Excellency thinks fit to give, although I sent it your Grace by his Orders. I hope that in his Letters he is fuller. My Lord Treasurer on the other Hand assured me, he had the Papers (which his Excellency denied) and talked of it as a Matter that had long lain before him, which several Persons in great Employments assure me is and must be true. Thus your Grace sees that I shall have nothing more to do in this Matter, further, than pursuing the cold Scent of asking his Excellency, once a Month, how it goeth on? Which, I think, I had as good forbear, since it will turn to little Account. All I can do is, to engage my Lord *Sunderland*'s interest with my Lord Treasurer, whenever it is brought before him; or to hint it to some other Persons of Power and Credit, and likewise to endeavour to take off that Scandal the Clergy of *Ireland* be under, of being the Reverse of what they really are, with Respect to the Revolution, Loyalty to the Queen, and Settlement of the Crown; which is here the Construction of the word Tory.

I design to tell my Lord Treasurer, that this being a Matter my Lord-Lieutenant hath undertaken, he doth not think proper I should trouble his Lordship; after which, recommending it to his Goodness, I shall forbear any further Mention. I am sensible how lame and tedious an Account this is, and humbly beg your Grace's Pardon: but I still insist, that if it had been sollicited four Years ago by no abler a Hand than my own, while the Duke of *Ormond* was in *Ireland*, it might have been done in a Month;[1] and I believe it may be so still, if his Excellency lays any Weight of his Credit upon it;

business connected with property which came to him through his wife. See p. 80, n. 1.   [1] See King to Swift, 30 Jan. 1704-5.

otherwise, God knows when. For myself, I have nothing more to do here but to attend my Lord-Lieutenant's Motions, of whose Return we are very uncertain, and to manage some personal Affairs of my own. I beg the Continuance of your Grace's Favour, and your Blessing, | And am with all Respect, |

Your Grace's most obedient &c.

King's Letter-book
Trinity College, Dublin

Archbishop King to Swift

Dublin June 12. 1708

Sir,

I cannot tell what you may think of my Long silence, nor can I well account for it, I am sure there is a reason for it, pray see if you can find it out, for my own part I profess I find my self in a wood, and do not know but in such a case it is best to stand still till the mist clear; by doing soe I shall at least avoyd the fatigue of wandring or falling into a pitt, we have been terrifyed with interception of Letters at the post office.[1] I am sure I can write nothing that I am solicitous to conceal and yet am desirous not to give so much interruption to any as the reading of a letter of no consequence in an ill hand may create: the good nature of mankind besides is such that they seldom search for nothing and therefore either find, or make something of, that nature in what they read.

I should not have ventured to have given you the trouble of this if I had not recd the honr of a Letter from his Excellency the Lord Lieut wherein he signifies that he has made some progress in the affair of the first fruits and 20th parts And that his Excy had good hopes of having it concluded in some time. This I intended immediately to have communicated to the Bps here, but such another accident in my foot as you mention to have happened to you in one of your Leggs has confin'd me to my chamber ever since I recd it.

[1] This is followed by many further complaints in this correspondence on the danger of the interception of letters passing through the post. Pope and Bolingbroke, to cite no others, frequently make the same complaint. Walpole had no scruple in opening the letters of a political rival. In 1723 he even came to an arrangement with the Postmaster-General in Brussels to send him copies of all the correspondence of Atterbury. Coxe's *Walpole*, ii. 284.

There is no manner of necessity that people in London should know that I have the Gout.[1]

As to the Test clause, if the repeated votes of parlement be not sufficient to show the sense of the people as to that point I can't tell how it shall be known, great industry has been used and great Art to drop some thing tending that way into 3 or 4 Addresses.[2] Those have been industriously printed and all others excluded. for my own part I can't have soe mean a soul as to stoop to such artifices. I have had the comfort to see many such defeated and their fine spun Webbs that had cost much time and pains, swept away at one brush, I hope the like success will follow the like endeavours. As to Addresses I have ever looked on them as an argument of the weakness of the Government, that the Addressers thought so & believed themselves suspected or feared. I hope this is not the case of her Majesty. I am of opinion that the great men you mention lay little weight on them, and make their computation not from such but from the reall affection and bent of the people, I believe that all schemes not built on these foundations will fall of themselves. I always except a standing Army, for that may support a Governm[t.] in Spite of the genius of the people so long as to change it and make them content with their slavery, but I cant suspect that any you have mentioned as friends can look that way, or can have any views but what are Founded on the naturall bent of the people's inclinations. Yet I can't but observe that there looks something like constraint in some people's managem[t.] of late and that if all were left to themselves they would not act altogether as they doe.

We know not what to think of his Ex[ys] long stay on that side of the water 'Tis true the Governm[t.] of Ireland is a very good sinecure, but we do not believe that it is his principle to make it soe.[3]

[1] As previously noted, this was an affliction from which King constantly suffered.
[2] See Swift to King, 15 Apr. 1708.
[3] In the reign of Queen Anne the Lord Lieutenants began to think that their residence in Ireland could be very well limited to the periods during which the Irish Parliament was in session, and established a precedent which was followed by almost all their successors until some time after George III ascended the throne. As the Irish Parliament usually met only every second year, and the session as a rule lasted under six months, the result was to permit the Viceroy to spend three-fourths of his time in England. The practice began with Queen Anne's uncle, Lord Rochester, who was Lord Lieutenant from 1701 to 1703, and whose residence in Ireland was under four months. His successor, James, second Duke of Ormonde, who was Lord Lieutenant from 1703 to 1707, owing

I must still entreat you to employ your care towards the pushing on our business. If you have success, it will reward your pains, & I will take care that the clergy shall not be ignorant to whom they are obliged.

I have always been of opinion that the Ministry have no mind that we should have any Militia in Ireland for the ardor of the people to raise it, is not encouraged as it would be if the Governm$^{t.}$ heartily designed it. And yet at this juncture it is of absolute necessity, since of the 5000 men that were left of the Army above a 1000 are to be transported. if the pretender had landed and our forces sent to Scotland as they must have been, we had been in an ill taking having nothing to trust to but a militia to be raised. I believe the providence of this disappointment is more than the generality are apprised of.

I take it for granted our parlement will hold one session more, for if that be not intended, it had been nonsense to continue it an hour. One thing there is remarkable that such as made the greatest noise to procure the papists to be confined on the invasion & quarrelled that they were not more severely used, at last became bail for the most obnoxious and dangerous amongst them.[1]

I find Sr Martin Marralls humour grows on me[2] & now my hand is in I know not when to cease. I judge others by my self, and being weary here I suppose you soe too before you come this farre and therefore I dismiss you with the prayers of Rev$^{d.}$ Sir Yrs &c

(Mr Swift)   W D

to his connexion with the country, managed to extend each of his two visits to about nine months. But Lord Pembroke had emulated Lord Rochester, and contrived to escape in exactly four months.—Ball.

[1] Ball extracts from papers (no longer extant) in the P.R.O. of Ireland details of an order of the Lords Justices and Privy Council, dated 5 Apr. 1708, directing that thirty-five gentlemen of 'the Popish Religion', who had been taken into custody under a previous order, when an invasion by the French was appre-hended, should be set at liberty on entering into recognizances of £2,000 each with sufficient security. Amongst those confined were two knights, ten colonels, three other officers, a barrister, and a doctor.

[2] The allusion is to the principal character in Dryden's comedy, *Sir Martin Mar-all, or the Feign'd Innocence*, 1668, which caused Pepys to laugh till his head ached. Macdonald, no. 71.

Forster No. 555

Swift to Ambrose Philips

London, July 10, 1708.[1]

I was very well pleased to hear you were so kind to remember me
in your letter to Mr. Addison, but infinitely better to have a line
from yourself.[2] your saying that you know nothing of your affairs
more than when you left us, puts me in mind of a passage in Don
Quixote where Sancho upon his master's first adventure, comes and
asks him for the Island he had promised, and which he must
certainly have won in that terrible combat: to which the Knight
replied in these memorable words:—Look ye, Sancho, all adventures
are not adventures of Islands, but many of them of dry blows, and
hunger, and hard lodging. However, take courage, for one day or
other, all of a sudden, before you know where you are, an Island will
fall into my hands as fit for you as a Ring for your finger.[3] In the
meantime the adventures of my Lord and you are likely to pass with
less danger and with less hunger, so that you need less patience to
stay till Midwife Time will please to deliver this Commission from
your *Womb of Fate.* I wish the victory[4] we have got, and the scenes
you pass through would put you into humour of writing a Pastoral
to celebrate the D. of Marlborough, who, I hope, will soon be your
General. My Lord and you may perhaps appear well enough to the
York ladies from the distance of a window, but you will both be
deceived if you venture any nearer. They will dislike his Lordship's
manner and conversation as too Southern by three degrees, and as
for your part, what notion have they of spleen or of sighing for an

[1] The original of this letter was sold at Sotheby's, 20 Apr. 1869, no. 949, to
Addington for £31. It has not been traced. The text has here been taken from
a copy in the Forster Collection, no. 555.
[2] This is the first of Swift's letters to Ambrose Philips, 1674–1749, whose
Pastorals opened the sixth volume of Tonson's *Miscellany*, 1709. His later
style, satirized by Henry Carey and others, earned for him the name of 'Namby
Pamby'. See *Poems*, p. 270 n. There is no record of service in the army by
Philips; but at this time, apparently, he was stationed at York, serving under
Lord Mark Kerr, wounded at Almanza, 25 Apr. 1707, who was the third son
of the fourth Earl and first Marquis of Lothian.
[3] A paraphrase, not the actual words.
[4] The battle of Oudenarde was fought 11 July, N.S. The difference between
the new style and the old style explains the transmission of the news to London
by the date at which Swift was writing.

absent mistress? I am not so good an astronomer to know whether Venus ever cuts the Arctic Circle, or comes within the Vortex of Ursa Major; nor can I conceive how Love can ripen where Gooseberries will not.

The Triumvirate of Mr. Addison, Steele, and me, come together as seldom as the Sun, Moon and Earth.[1] I often see each of them, and each of them me and each other; and when I am of the number Justice is done you as you would desire.

I hope you have no intentions of fixing for any time in the North. *Sed nec in Arctoo sedem tibi figeris orbe.*[2] But let my Ld. Mark though he is your North Star, guide you to the South. I have always had a natural antipathy to places that are famous for Ale. Wine is the liquor of the Gods and ale of the Goths. And thus I have luckily found out the reason of the Proverb—to have Guts in one's Brain, that is what a wise man eats and drinks rises upwards, and is the nourishment of his head where all is digested, and, consequently, a Fool's Brains are in his guts, where his Beef, and Thoughts, and Ale descend. Yes, your hours would pass more agreeably if you could forget every absent Friend and Mistress you have, because of that *impotens desiderium*, than which nothing is a more violent feeder of the Spleen, and there is nothing in life equal to recompense that.

Pray tell my Lord Mark Kerr I humbly acknowledge the honor of his remembrance, and am his most obedient servant, tell him I love him as *un homme de bien, honeste, dégagé, désinteressé, libéral, et qui se connoit bien en hommes.* As for you, I have nothing to wish mended but your fortune; and in the meantime, a little cheerfulness, added to your humor, because it is so necessary towards making your Court. I will say nothing to all your kind expressions, but that if I have deserved your friendship as much as I have endeavoured to cultivate it, ever since I knew you, I should have as fair pretensions as any man could offer. And if you are a person of so much wit and invention as to be able to find out any use for my service, it will encrease my good opinion both of you and my self.

St. James's Coffee house is grown a very dull place upon two accounts, first by the loss of you, and secondly, of every body else.[3]

[1] See Swift's letter to Addison, 29 Feb. 1707-8.
[2] Lucan, i. 53.
[3] An Irish visitor to London writes to a friend in Dublin on 8 Mar. in that year that 'St. James's Coffee-house is the rendezvous of our countrymen' (Departmental Correspondence in P.R.O. of Ireland).—Ball.

Mr. Addison's lameness goes off daily, and so does he, for I see him seldomer than formerly, and therefore cannot revenge myself of you by getting ground in your absence. Coll. Frowde[1] is just as he was, very friendly and *grand rêveur et distrait*. He has brought his Poems almost to perfection and I have great credit with him, because I can listen when he reads, which neither you nor the Addisons nor the Steeles ever can. I am interrupted by a foolish old woman; and besides here is enough. Mr. Addison has promised to send this, for I know not where to direct, nor have you instructed me. I am, | Ever your most faithful humble Servant, | J. Swift.

King's Letter-book
Trinity College, Dublin

Archbishop King to Swift

Dublin August 12th 1708

Revd S^r

Tis some time since I heard from you, which makes me a little uneasy. I have bin hindered from writing for near a month by the gout in my right hand which is a great mortification to me. I recd a letter from Mr. Dodington[2] in which he tells me that my Ld Lt has made some progress in the affair of our 20th parts and 1st fruits. I wish he may be able to put it in a good way, which I believe is all

---

[1] In the *Journal*, p. 81, 4 Nov. 1710, Swift mentions a 'colonel Proud'. There is every probability that what Swift wrote was 'Froud', that he was the same person as the 'colonel Freind' mentioned on 15 Sept. of the same year, and that, in both instances, the reference is to the Col. Frowde to whom we find Addison addressing a letter from Paris in Nov. 1699 (W. Graham, *Letters of Joseph Addison*, p. 9). On both occasions (when he met 'colonel Proud' and when he met 'colonel Freind') Swift was in Addison's company. William Frowde, son of Sir Philip Frowde, was appointed lieutenant-colonel in 1694 in Col. Thomas Farrington's Regiment of Foot. In 1702 he was appointed lieutenant-colonel in the First Foot Guards. Dalton's *English Army Lists*, ii. 28, 37; iii. 382; v. 42. There can be no doubt but that this is the Col. Frowde here mentioned.

[2] George Dodington, who came of an ancient Somersetshire family, was an uncle of the celebrated George Bubb Dodington, afterwards Lord Melcombe. He was serving as secretary to Lord Pembroke during his viceroyalty. Before coming to Ireland George Dodington was Treasurer to the Navy, and afterwards became a Lord Commissioner of the Admiralty.

will be done at present for my Ld did not encourage us to hope for it before a peace. I reckon if my Ld return to us again something will be done but if not, the Ministry will hardly be persuaded to gratify us in such a matter by a dying Ld. Lt.

I suppose you have an account of what past in the University about the vindication of K Wms memory. 'Tis really strange that any should be found so prodigiously ungratefull to him, at least in Ireland, where we owe all to him, but Mr. Forbes that used him so barbarously was from Scotland and had studyed in Aberdeen, and taken his degrees there.[1] I do own the Church of Scotland was hardly used in his time, but I reckon that his misfortune not fault, for had they espoused him as cordially as the other party, he wou'd never have altered any thing there more than in Ireland. But Government must be supported, and Tis a plain case if we will not do it those that will must be embraced and that was the case in Scotland. on serious reflection I am apt to think that there are hardly any men less politick for themselves than Clergymen and we perhaps least of any. I have revolved again and again the oraculous saying of the great man you mention in your last, and discoursed Mr. Southwell about it but cannot unriddle it.[2] I have thought of 2 or 3 meanings it may have, but they appear to me either so trifling or so wicked that I can't allow my self to think that I have hit right.

We have lately had 4 young men Candidates for Orders amongst the Dissenters here, that have deserted them, they seem sober and of good sense, but the difficulty is what to do with them we are overstocked already and we must either maintain them out of our own pockets or let them starve. I have engaged for one, My Ld Primate for another, and I hope some of our Brethren will come in for the other two. | I heartily recommend you etc

Dr Swift   W: D:

[1] In a letter to the Archbishop of Canterbury King says that at the Proctors' feast a young man Forbes, who was a candidate for an *ad eundem* M.A. degree, reflected 'most rudely and scandalously' on King William's memory. Unacquainted with the facts the heads of the College allowed Forbes to take his degree the next day. Afterwards, however, he was expelled the College; and subsequently at a meeting of the Senate, was deprived of his degree (King's Correspondence, 5 Aug. 1708).

[2] The reference is to the 'acknowledgments' stated by Godolphin to be a prior condition of a remission of the firstfruits to the clergy of Ireland. See Swift's letter to King of 10 June.

Swift to Archbishop King

Lond. Aug. 28. 1708[1]

I hope you will excuse my want of ceremony, occasioned by my desire to give a full Answer to yours of the 12th. What hindring my writing was the want of confidence to trouble you when I had nothing of Importance to say; but, if you give me Leave to do it at other times, I shall obey you with great satisfaction, and I am heartily sorry for the Occasion that hath prevented you, because it is a Loss to the Publick as well as to me. The Person who sent you the Letter about Progress made in that matter, is one who would not give threepence to save all the established Clergy in both Kingdoms from the Gallows.[2] And to talk of not encouraging you to hope for it before a Peace is literally *dare verba*, and nothing else. But in the small conversation I have had among Great men, there is one maxim I have found them constantly to observe, which is, that in any Business before them, if you enquire how it proceeds; they onely confide, what is proper to answer, without one single Thought whether it be agreeable to fact or no. For Instance, here is Ld. Tr. assures me, what you ask is a Trifle; that the Q. would easily consent to it, and he would do so too; then adds some generall conditions etc, as I told you before; then comes L. L[t]; assures me, that the other has nothing at all to do with it, that it is not to come before him, and that he has made some Progress in it,[3] and hints to you, it seems, that it will be hardly done before a Peace. The Progress he means, must be something entirely between the Q. and himself; for the 2 Chief Ministers assure me, they never heard of the Matter from him; and, in God's name, what sort of Progress can he mean.

In the mean time, I have not stirred a step further, being unwilling to ruin myself in any man's favor, when I can do the Publick no

---

[1] This letter to Archbishop King was probably, like that of 15 Apr., enclosed within a letter addressed to Dean Stearne. It begins without any formal 'My Lord', and ends without any courtesy conclusion. There is no external address, save the word 'For', which may have been a beginning. The letter was closed with a small red seal. The greater portion of the letter was printed by Forster, *Life*, p. 242.

[2] The Whig magnates regarded with strong disfavour the opposition of the Irish clergy to the repeal of the Test. Further, they suspected many of the Irish Protestants as imbued with Jacobite leanings.

[3] See p. 85.

Good. and therefore I had to much Art to desire LT. not to say anything to tother of what I had spoke, unless I could get Leave, wch was refused me; and therefore I omitted speaking again to L^d S—d;[1] which however I am resolved to do when he comes to Town, onely in order to explain something which I onely conjectured. Upon the whole I am of Opinion that the Progress yet made is just the same, with that of making me Generall of the Horse; and the D. of O. thinks so too,[2] and gave me some Reasons of his own. Therefore I think the Reason why this thing is not done, can be onely perfect neglect, or want of sufficient Inclination; or perhaps a Better Principle, I mean a dislike to the conditions, and unwillingness to own them—I think Mr S—[3] and I agreed in our Interpretation of that Oracular saying, which has perplexed you; and fixed it upon the Test, whether that be among the Trifles, or wicked meanings you thought of, I need not ask. Whatever method you would please to have me take in this, or any other matter for the service of the Publick or yourself, I shall readily obey. And if the matter does not stick at that mysticall point before mentioned, I am sure, with common Application, it might be done in a month.

I was told some time ago by a great Person, of that Business of Forbes, with much Aggravation, and abominable Additions, and having given him a true Account as I could, the next Time I saw him, he told me at dinner, among much company that he had further Intelligence, and made the matter still worse, and seemd inclined to think his Account was righter than mine. I had the same from severall others, and I have reason to know there are men in great Office on your side, who make it their Business, to do all the hurt they can, by misrepresenting the Clergy and University, of what I believe I have in former Letters given you Instances, that have been related to me by Persons I cannot mention at this distance.[4] I think a Particular Account of Forbe's matter ought to be transmitted, and published here. The Part which the A.Bp of Dublin had

---

[1] i.e. Sunderland.

[2] See p. 49, n. 2.

[3] i.e. Southwell. Archbishop King can hardly have been serious, in his letter of 12 Aug., in affecting to be puzzled by Godolphin's 'oraculous saying', which Swift divined at once to refer to the repeal of the Test.

[4] The English Government appears to have suspected an influential Jacobite faction in Trinity College at this time. It may have existed among younger men and some of the undergraduates; but the heads were without doubt loyal to the Hanover succession.

in prosecuting it, has been extremely well taken on this side, and I am glad of the City's gratitude to him.[1]

I congratulate with you for the converts you mention, and hope they are sincere, because they can propose little temporall Interest as you Circumstances are. However, I doubt whether on this side of the water, they would meet with so good Encouragment. We are now every day expecting news from abroad of the greatest Importance, nothing less than a Battle, a Siege raised, or Lille taken.[2] Wagers run 2 to one for the last In the last Gazette it was certainly affirmed that there would be a Battle, but the copy coming to the office to be corrected; I prevailed with them to lett me soften the Phrase a little, so as to leave some Room for Possibilityes, and I do not find the soldiers are so very positive. However it is a Period of the greatest expectation, I ever remember. and God in his Mercy send a good Issue. This is all I have to say at present, I will soon write again, if anything be worth sending, and it shall be in more form

King's Letter-book
Trinity College, Dublin

Archbishop King to Swift

Dublin, September 7. 1708

Rev[d] S[r]

I received yours of the 28th of August last, your letters are always very acceptable to me, and therefore you need [not] suspect that I will think them troublesome. The generality of the world writ in a mask and the want of a true knowledge of the humour of people on your side the water, cause many errors on this. One comes from England and tells with confidence that the Ministry and Court expect such a thing from us, that we shall be lost in their opinion if we do not comply, and vouch A and B etc. for what he says; none do inquire into the truth of what he affirms nor have the generality

[1] As Ball suggests, this sentence was probably framed to mislead the postal officials, in the event of their opening the letter, as to the person to whom it was written.

[2] For some weeks already Marlborough and Eugene had invested Lille, the strongest fortress in Europe and considered impregnable. Not till 22 Oct. did Boufflers, the French commander, surrender the city, and not till 9 Dec. the citadel, into which he had retired. Trevelyan, *England under Queen Anne*, ii. 368–73.

any way to do so, and therefore they run after him like a flock of
sheep, and very often into a pit. At first when this artifice was used,
I was surprised and thought I ventured much when [I] presumed to
oppose mischievous things, and when so recommended. But a little
experience taught me either that such allegations were absolutely
false, or if any truth in them they were procured by persuading
those great men, that either the humour of the people of Ireland
would be gratified by the recommendation, or that the necessity of
the affairs of Ireland in order to serve the Ministry required it. For
I found the good of Ireland has no weight at all. And it is a great
mistake in all the applications we make, to allege as we commonly
do that such a thing will help or mischief us, for perhaps those considerations will have a quite different effect from what we intend;
and therefore I have always advised those that have expressed their
fear of such a matter, and run into the detail of the inconveniences
that would follow it, to conceal their thoughts, and not discover that
it would have such consequences. Perhaps if those to whom they
make application to prevent them knew what would follow, it would
be an insuperable argument for their doing it. It moves one's spleen
to find a clergyman pressing the ruin of the Church if a certain
thing be done, when perhaps that is the reason that it is to be done.

As to the affair of our twentieth parts and first fruits, I partly
guess where it sticks. I have had another letter from Mr. Dodington
in very obliging terms;[1] but my Lord Lieutenant having hinted to
my Lord Primate and me, when we discoursed him about them, that
perhaps we were not to expect them till a peace, I have little hope of
them. I do not know but an immediate application of the Bishops
to L[ord] T[reasurer] might bring them. If there should happen
an interregnum of chief governors, I believe it would be a seasonable
opportunity to make such an application.

I sent a full account of Forbes's business to his Grace the Lord
Archbishop of Canterbury, who has acknowledged the receipt of it,
and adds that I have obliged him and many others that are hearty
friends to the Universities, against which he says this occasioned a
mighty cry.[2] We know there are not wanting good men, that make
it their business to lay hold on all such occasions and to aggravate
them; the design seems not against the Church, but against learning
in general, and all that is regular either in religion or polity. And
some amongst us are so wise as to think that the destroying of these

is a good argument against the design that infers it. But they do not consider that when Cromwell had destroyed the King and kingship, he did it with a design to get them for himself. I am, etc.,

W. D.

Query—Is there nothing of a comprehension designed on your side? May not the oracle hint something of that nature?

Dr Swift

Wellesley College Library[1]

Swift to Ambrose Philips

Lond. Sep^{br}. 14. 1708.

Nothing is a greater Argument that I look on my self as one whose Acquaintance is perfectly useless, than that I am not so constant or exact in writing to you, as I should otherwise be. and I am glad at heart to see Mr Addison who may live to be serviceable to you, so mindfull in your Absence. He has reproached me more than once for not frequently sending him a Lettr to conveigh to You. That Man has Worth enough to give Reputation to an Age, and all the Merit I can hope for with regard to you, will be my Advice to cultivate his Friendship to the utmost, and my Assistance to do you all the good Offices towards it in my Power.

I have not seen Ld Mark these 3 weeks nor have heard any thing of him but his Poetry, which a Lady shewed me some time ago, it was some Love verses, but I have forgot the Matter and the Subject, or rather the Object, tho I think they were to Mrs Hales.

I can fitt you with no Fable at present, unless it should be of the Man that rambled upon and down to look for Fortune, at length came home and saw her lying at a Man's feet who was fast asleep, and never stirrd a step, this I reflected on the other day when my Ld Treas^r gave a young Fellow a Friend of mine an Employmt sinecure of 400^{ll} a year added to one of 300^{ll} he had before; I hope thô you are not yet a Capt: L^d M[ark] has so much consideration to provide you with pay suitable to the Expence and Trouble you are at, or else you are the greatest Dupe, and he the greatest—on

---

[1] American Art Association sale, 20–21 Apr. 1921; now in the Wellesley College Library, Wellesley, Massachusetts. Ball took his text from the Aldine Edition of Swift's Poetical Works.

Earth; and I wish you would tell me plainly how that matter passes,
—You say nothing of the Fair one, I hope you are easyer on that
foot than when You left us, else I shall either wish her hangd or You
marryed, but whether to her or some Yorkshire Lady with ten
thousand Pounds, I am somewhat in doubt—There is some Comfort that you will learn your Trade of a Soldier, in this Expedition,
at least the most material part of it, long Marches, ill dyet, hard
lodging, and scurvey Company. . I wish you would bring us home
half a dozen Pastorals, thô they were all made up of Complaints of
y[r] Mistress and of Fortune. Lady Betty Germain[1] is upon all occasions stirring up L[d] Dorsett[2] to shew you some Marks of his Favor,
wch I hope may one day be of good Effect, or he is good for nothing
—L[d] Pembroke is going to be marryed to Lady Arundel[3]—We are
here crammd with hopes and Fears about the Siege of Lisle,[4] and the
Expectations of a Battle; but I believe you have little humor for
publick Reflections. For my Part I think your best Cause[5] is to try
whethr the Bp of Durham[6] will give you a Niece and a golden

[1] Lady Elizabeth Germain was the second daughter of Charles, second Earl
of Berkeley. When Lord Berkeley was going to Ireland as a Lord Justice in 1699
he took Swift with him as a chaplain. In that capacity Swift remained with him
for the best part of two years. Although he never held his patron in much
regard Swift formed a lifelong friendship with the Earl's daughter. Lady Elizabeth (1680–1769) married as his second wife, in 1706, Sir John Germain, a
soldier of fortune, reputed to be a son of William II, Prince of Orange. He died
in 1718, and she lived a widow for over fifty years. Germain inherited the
Drayton property in Northamptonshire from his first wife, Lady Mary Mor-
daunt, sister of Lord Peterborough. He left to Lady Betty the estate at Drayton
and the further large property he had inherited from his first wife. Lady Betty
spent her widowhood partly at Knole with her friends the Dorsets, partly at
Drayton, and partly in London. See *D.N.B.*; *Drayton House*, 1939, by N. V.
Stopford Sackville; *Poems*, pp. 62 n., 68, 74; *Journal to Stella, passim*.
[2] The only connexion between Germain and Lord Dorset is said to have
been the marriage of the latter to the daughter of his colleague in the Dutch
service, Field-Marshal Walter Philip Colyear, which took place four months
after the date of this letter. As he only then came of age Dorset's ability to
promote Philips's fortune cannot have been great.
[3] Lord Pembroke married 21 Sept. 1708, as his second wife, the widow of
John, second Baron Arundell of Trerice. She had been previously married.
[4] See p. 96, n. 2.
[5] Cause] Course *Ball*.
[6] Nathaniel Crew, third Baron Crew of Stene (1633–1721), who led a dis-
creditable career of sycophancy. The favourite Anglican ecclesiastic of the Duke
of York he was preferred to the see of Durham in 1674. When James II ascended
the throne he proved himself wholly subservient. After the flight of the King he

Prebend, unless you are so high a Whig, that yr Principles like yr Mistress are at Geneva.

I have nevr been a night from this Toun since you left, and could envy you if your mind were in a Condition to enjoy the Pleasures of the Country, But I hope you will begin to think of London, and not dream of wintring in the north, Scoticas pati pruinas—

Here[1] has been an Essay of Enthusiasm[2] lately publisht that has run mightily, and is very well writt, All my Friends will have me to be the Author, sed ego non credulus illis. By the free Whiggish thinking I should rather take it to be yours: But mine it is not; For thô I am every day writing my Speculations[3] in my Chamber, they are quite of anothr sort.—I expect to see you return very fatt with Yorkshire Ale, pray let us know when we are to expect you, and resolve this Winter to be a Man of Levees, and be a man of Hopes, and who knows what that may produce against Spring, I am sure no man wishes you better, or would do more in his Power to bring those Wishes to Effect, which thô they are Expressions usually offered most freely by those that can do least, I hope you will do me the Justice to believe them, and my self to be entirely | Yr most faithfull & | most humble Servt | J. Swift.

I saw Dr Englis to day who tells me Ld Mark has grace to consider you so far as not to travel at yr own charges.

Address: For Mr Philips
Endorsed: Jonathan Swift | 1708 | Resp. sept. 29.

was, however, pardoned, and remained in possession of the bishopric. See *D.N.B.*

   [1] Here] There *Ball.*
   [2] Anthony Ashley Cooper, Lord Shaftesbury's *Letter Concerning Enthusiasm*, published in this year.
   [3] The 'speculations' were probably the writings in which at this time Swift embodied his views on Religion and the Church. For a discussion of these tracts see *Prose Works*, ed. H. Davis, vol. ii. Here may be named those said to have been written in 1708 and 1709—*An Argument against abolishing Christianity, A Project for the Advancement of Religion, Remarks upon a Book, intitled 'The Rights of the Christian Church Asserted', A Letter Concerning the Sacramental Test, A Letter to a Member of Parliament. The Sentiments of a Church-of-England Man,* although attributed to 1708, was, in substance, probably written in 1704. See the essay by Irvin Ehrenpreis in *Review of English Studies*, N.S., July 1952, iii. 272-4.

Anthony Henley to Swift

Sept. 16th Grange[1]

Yesterday the weather Glass was att 28 inches, which is Lower than ever I saw it; The wind was att East, a very dull Quarter, the Garden so wett there was no Looking into it, And I my self, by consequence in the Spleen. Before night, the Glass rose, the wind changed, the garden dried, I recd your L^r, and was as well as ever I was in my life to my thinking, tho Perhaps you may think other wise. The reason why your L^r was so long a coming to my hands, was its being directed to mee near Winchester & Alresford is the Post town nearest to mee.[2] If the officers shoud come to you, D^r If you want a security, that your Children shant be troublesome to the Parish pray make use of mee. I will stand them all tho you were to have as many as the Holland Countesse.[3] We have had a tedious Expectation of the Success of the Siege of Lille; the Country people begin to think there is no such thing, and say the news Papers talk of it to make people bear paying Taxes a year Longer; I dont know how Steel will gett off of it, his veracity is att Stake in Hampshire; pray desire him to take the town thô hee shoud leave the Cittadel for a nest Egg.[4] I hant the Honour to know Coll: Hunter.[5] But I never saw him in so good Company as you have putt him, Ld Hall: Mr Add: Mr Cong: and the Gazettier: Since he is there lett him stay there.

[1] The ink of this letter is badly faded.

[2] Anthony Henley inherited considerable wealth which he improved by marriage with a well-endowed lady. This encouraged him to enter politics. He was Whig M.P. for Andover 1698–1700, and for Weymouth 1702–11; and he also enjoyed some reputation as a wit. As far as politics permitted Swift and Henley were on friendly terms for a few years. He is mentioned several times in the *Journal to Stella*.

[3] Margaret Countess of Henneberg, reputed to have given birth to 365 children at one lying-in.

[4] See p. 96, n. 2.

[5] Robert Hunter, who came of a Scottis family, fought at Blenheim, and afterwards was appointed lieutenant-colonel of a regiment of dragoons; and later, as Lieutenant-Governor of Virginia, he sailed for that province on 20 May 1707. On the voyage he was taken prisoner by a French privateer and carried to France. Two letters from Swift were addressed to him, 12 Jan. 1708–9, and 22 Mar. 1708–9. In the former Swift mistakenly attributed to him the authorship of Shaftesbury's *Letter Concerning Enthusiasm*. After his release Hunter was appointed Governor of New York; and in 1729 Governor of Jamaica.

Pray D^r lett mee know whether writing L^{rs} bee talking to ones self or talking to other folks. For I think the world has settled it, that talking to ones self wch offends nobody, is maddness and talking to other people wch generally is not Quite so harmless is Witt or good Breeding or Religion or I wont write a word more till you have satisfyd mee what I have been doing all this while Ime sure one need not have writt 2 pages to Introduce my assuring you that I am | Yr most Afft Humble Sert, |

A. Henley.

Address: For the Rev Dr Swifft att | St James's Coffee house | in Pall mall.
Frank: A Henley   *Postmark:* Illegible.
Endorsed by Swift: Mr Henly | Septr 16 1708, | I suppose

Nichols, Literary Illustrations[1]

Swift to Ambrose Philips

Havisham, Oct. 20, 1708

Sir,

I am glad at heart you are come to Town, where I shall be in a few days, having left it only as fastidious when I was weary of its emptyness and my own; but *quibus Hector ab oris?* You will be admirable company after your new refined travels. I hope you met subjects for new Pastorals, unless the new character as a soldier has swaggered those humble ideas, and that you consider the field no longer as a Shepherd, but a Hero.

I was ignorant of Lisle till your Letter came, and I hope you will so order it that we shall have no difficulty in the Citadel.[2] My Host Mr. Collier was your schoolfellow at Shrewsbury, and in that

---

[1] The original of this letter, and of Swift's letter to Philips of 30 Oct. 1709, were, when printed by Nichols, *Lit. Illustr.* iv. 730, in the possession of William Upcott (1779–1845), the antiquary. It appears from Swift's letter to King of 9 Nov. that he may, at this time, have been staying in Kent. No place of the name of Havisham can be traced in that county, nor anywhere in England. In Swift's day there was a manor-house in the Kent parish of Harrietsham. It is probable that 'Havisham' was a mistake on the part of the transcriber.
[2] The citadel of Lille did not capitulate till 9 Dec.

capacity presents you his service, and you will mine to Colonel Hunt[er], Mr. Addison, Mr. Steele, &c.

I am most sincerely yours,   J. S.

I must write your Christian name in the address, lest it should fall into the hands of the Irish poetical Captain.[1]

4804

Anthony Henley to Swift

Nov, 2ᵈ 1708

Dʳ Dʳ

Tho you wont send me yʳ Broomstick[2] I will send you as good a Reflection upon Death as even Adrians himselfe[3] Tho the Fellow was but an old Farmer of mine that made it. Hee had been ill a good while, and when his friends saw him going they all came croaking about him as usuall and one of 'em asking him how hee did, Hee replyd in great Pain If I coud but gett this same Breath out of my body, Ide take care by God How I lett it come in again.[4] This if it were put in fine Latine I fancy woud make as good a Sermo as any I have mett wth. I am Yr most Afft Humble Sert,

A. Henley.

Postmark: 3 N

---

[1] See Swift to Ambrose Philips 15 Mar. 1708–9.

[2] Swift's *Meditation upon a Broom-Stick*, probably written in 1702. Its first appearance in print was in 1710. *Prose Works*, ed. Davis, pp. xxxiii–xxxiv, 237–40, 302.

[3] The famous address to his soul, 'Animula, vagula, blandula', attributed to the dying Hadrian, of which innumerable translations in other tongues have appeared, including Prior's 'Poor little, pretty, flutt'ring Thing'. See *Translations, Literal and Free of the dying Hadrian's Address to his Soul*, by David Johnston.

[4] Swift relates this anecdote in 'Thoughts on Various Subjects', *Prose Works*, ed. Temple Scott, i. 278.

Swift to Archbishop King

London, Nov. 9, 1708

My Lord,

Your Grace's Letter of *September* 7, found me in *Kent*, where I took the Opportunity to retire during my Lord *Pembroke*'s Absence with his new Lady (who are both expected To-morrow,[1] I went afterwards to *Epsom*,[2] and returned but Yesterday: This was the Cause of my so long omitting to acknowledge your Letter. I am ready to agree with your Grace, that very wrong Representations are made of Things and Persons here, by People who reside on this Side but a short Time, converse at second or third Hand, and on their Return make a Vanity of knowing more than they do.[3] This I have observed myself in *Ireland*, even among People of some Rank and Quality; and I believe your Grace will proceed on much better Grounds, by trusting to your own Wisdom and Experience of Things, than such Intelligence.

I spoke formerly all I knew of the Twentieth Parts, and whatever Mr. *D*[odington] hath said in his Letters about staying until a Peace, I do assure your Grace, is nothing but Words. However, that Matter is now at an End. There is a new World here;[4] and yet I agree with you, that if there be an Interregnum, it will be the properest Time to address my Lord Treasurer; and I shall second it with all the Credit I have, and very openly; and I know not (if [no] difficulty lye in the way) but it may prove a lucky Juncture.

On my Return from *Kent* (the Night of the Prince's Death) I staid a few Days in Town before I went to *Epsom*: I then visited a certain great Man, and we entered very freely into Discourse upon the present Juncture.[5] He assured me, there was no doubt now of the Scheme holding about the Admiralty, the Government of *Ireland*, and presidency of the Council;[6] the Disposition whereof your Grace

[1] See p. 99, n. 3.
[2] Where it was then still 'pleasant to see' as in Pepys's day the visitors walking about 'without knowing almost what to do, but only in the morning to drink waters' (*Diary*, ed. Wheatley, iii. 224).—Ball.
[3] See King to Swift, 7 Sept. 1708.
[4] Owing to the death of Prince George on 28 Oct.
[5] Probably either Somers or Halifax.
[6] The office of Lord High Admiral, vacant through the death of the Prince,

knoweth as well as I; and although I care not to mingle publick Affairs with the Interest of so private a Person as myself: Yet upon such a Revolution, not knowing how far my Friends may endeavour to engage me in the Service of a new Government, I would beg your Grace to have favourable Thoughts to me on such an Occasion, and to assure you, that no Prospect of making my Fortune, shall ever prevail on me to go against what becometh a Man of Conscience and Truth, and an entire Friend to the established Church.[1] This I say, in Case such a Thing should happen; for my own Thoughts are turned another Way, if the Earl of *Berkeley*'s Journey to *Vienna* holds, and the Ministry will keep their Promise of making me the Queen's Secretary;[2] by which I shall be out of the Way of Parties, until it shall please God I have some Place to retire to, a little above Contempt: or, if all fail, until your Grace and the Dean of St. *Patrick*'s shall think fit to dispose of that poor Town-Living in my Favour.[3]

Upon this Event of the Prince's Death, the Contention designed with the Court about a Speaker is dropt, and all agree in Sir Richard Onslow, which is looked on as another Argument for the Scheme succeeding.[4] This I had from the same Hand.

As to a Comprehension which your Grace seems to doubt an Intention of, from what was told me, I can say nothing; doubtless, it must be intended to come to that at last, if not worse; but I believe at present, it was meant, that there should be a Consent to what was endeavoured at in your Parliament last Session.

went to Lord Pembroke, that of President of the Council to Somers, and that of Lord Lieutenant of Ireland to Lord Wharton.

[1] This may seem a needless affirmation on Swift's part, but his future was uncertain, and it was important to retain the favour of the Church dignitaries of Ireland.

[2] Lord Berkeley had been envoy to Madrid and also to the States of Holland before he went to Ireland as a Lord Justice in 1699. He returned to England in Apr. 1701 and took little further part in public life. It would appear, however, from Swift's statement, that Berkeley contemplated again diplomatic employment.

[3] The curacy of St. Nicholas Without, Dublin.

[4] Richard Onslow, 1654–1717, was the grandson of Sir Richard Onslow, the prominent parliamentarian and supporter of Cromwell. He had represented Surrey as a moderate Whig since 1689. Elected Speaker of the House of Commons on 16 Nov. 1708 he retained the office till 21 Sept. 1710. Under George I he became Chancellor of the Exchequer; and in 1716 was raised to the peerage. The Queen had, at this time, desired the appointment of William Bromley as Speaker, who was so elected in 1710, following the Tory victory.

I thought to have writ more largely to your Grace, Imagining I had much Matter in my Head; but it fails, or is not convenient at present. If the Scheme holds, I shall make bold to tell your Grace my Thoughts as formerly, under cover, because I believe there will be a great Deal to be thought of and done. A little Time may produce a great Deal. Things are now in great Suspense both at Home and Abroad. The Parliament, we think, will have no Prorogation. There is no Talk of the Duke of Marlborough's Return yet. Speculative People talk of a Peace this Winter, of which I can form no Prospect, according to our Demands. | I am, my Lord, Your Grace's | Most Obedient, Humble Servant,

J. S.

Your Grace will please to direct your Commands to me at St. *James*'s Coffee-house, in St. *James's-street*.

Rothschild[1]

Swift to Archdeacon Walls

Lond. Nov^br. 9. 1708

Why: I was told five months ago that you had about six or seven and twenty Pounds of mine from Parvisol,[2] and has the Puppy never encreast it since? and have I lived here like a poor Rogue in hopes of a Sum to putt out to Interest? and is it all come to this? You Irish Folks ly under an ill name for Honesty; not that I suspect you, but, perhaps you are upon a Purchase, and make use of some of my money; You can do no less than pay me Interest.

S^r, if Mr King dyes, I have desired people to tell the A. Bp that I will have the Living; for I like it and he told me I should, have the first good one that fell, & you know, great mens Promises never fail.[3] Ay, ay; look among my Books for Livy; and if it be there, let

[1] Previously in the possession of Sir John Murray. Since 1935 in Lord Rothschild's Library.

[2] Isaiah Parvisol, Swift's steward and tithe-collector, is frequently mentioned in the letters from 1708 onwards and in the *Journal to Stella*. The references nearly always display dissatisfaction or contempt; and for a time he seems to have been dismissed. He died in Swift's service, 1718.

[3] The living was that of Swords, which formed the corps of a prebend, known in ancient times as the golden one, in the Cathedral of St. Patrick. The village of Swords, which is situated seven miles to the north of Dublin on the main road to Belfast, occupies the site of a medieval town, the property of the

the Provost have it.¹ Mʳ Wally² was an idle man if he represented any Answer of mine wrong; all that I could say was that I thought I had sent it, but would give order it should be lookt for among my Books, and so I did, in one of my Lettrs³ to Mrs Dingley or Mrs Johnson. We have dropt writing because he has now no Occasion for me, as he thought he had &c—I need not tell you more; but I can have him when I will, and if that be the least bitt of Service to you, most⁴ infallibly I will resume it, and with-out the least surmise of yr having any Share.⁵

I am heartily glad of Raymds good Fortune;⁶ and I write this Post to congratulate him upon it; I hope you will advise him to be a good manager, without wᶜʰ the greatest Fortune must run out.

see of Dublin, and is well known as containing one of those possessions typical of Ireland, a round tower, as well as remains of a residence of the early Arch-bishops of Dublin. A year after his translation to Dublin Archbishop King had conferred this living on one of his kinsmen, the Rev. Thomas King (see *Journal of the Royal Society of Antiquaries of Ireland*, xxxiii. 258, 439). It is evident that the death of the latter was expected at the time this letter was written, and it occurred before 8 Feb. in the following year, when his successor was appointed. The successor, as Swift seems to have suspected would be the case, was another relation of the Archbishop.—Ball.

¹ The Provost of Trinity College at this time was Dr. Peter Browne. In 1710 he was appointed Bishop of Cork and Ross. His *Letter in Answer* (1697) to Toland's *Christianity not Mysterious* won him high esteem. He was more generally known as strongly opposed to the practice of drinking to the immortal memory of William III, which he regarded as a superstitious rite. See *D.N.B.*; *Fasti Eccl. Hib.* i. 231.

² The Rev. Randolph Walley, elected a Fellow of Trinity College, Dublin, in 1703, died in 1709. He was chaplain to Lord Cutts, the subject of Swift's 'Description of a Salamander' (*Poems*, p. 82).

³ A constant correspondence had been maintained between Swift and 'the Ladies' since he came to England in the preceding year. This appears by a list of letters written and received, entered in one of his little account-books, 1 Nov. 1708 to 1 Nov. 1709 (Forster, no. 506). See Appendix I.

⁴ Ball omits the word 'most' which is in the original.

⁵ As this letter, and remarks in the *Journal to Stella*, p. 596, indicate Swift regarded Dr. Browne doubtfully, although he mentioned him particularly as a friend of Stella (*Prose Works*, xi. 134).

⁶ The Rev. Anthony Raymond succeeded John Stearne as Rector of Trim, on the promotion of the latter to the Deanery of St. Patrick's. Three miles to the south of Trim lay Swift's living of Laracor. Raymond held the living of Trim till his death in 1726. Shortly before his death he issued the prospectus of a 'History of Ireland', but the work was never published. Deane Swift (*Essay*, 1755, p. 90) says that Raymond enjoyed 'the advantage of a tall handsome and graceful person'.

When you see Parvisol be so kind to wonder why he pays in no more money to you. I have sent the Ladyes I think one Bill on him for some of their money I received here; but I have had onely twenty Pounds of him since I came over, even including this I had from You.

My Journy to Germany depends on Accidents as well as upon the Favor of the Court; if they will make me Queens Secretry when I am there, as they promise, I will go;[1] unless this new change we expect on the Prince's Death should alter my Measures for it is thought that most of those I have Credit with will come into Play; but yet if they carry things too far I shall go to Vienna, or even to Laracor, rather than fall in with them.

My most humble Service to yr punning Spouse; The Dean of St P— repeats strange ones after her & the other Ladyes, they wash their hands of it, but how clean I cannot tell. Lett them look to that.

I fancy the Ladyes are come to Toun, pray let them continue to be part of yr Club; and remember my Saturday dinner against I return; it was a cunning Choice that of Saturday; for Mrs Walls remembred that 2 Satyrdays in four I was at Laracor.[2] Yrs—&c

Address: For the Reverend, Mr | Archdeacon Walls at his House | in Cavan Street | Dublin | Ireland
Postmark: 9 NO
Later Endorsement: Novr 9th: 1708 | Dr Swift

Rothschild
Swift to Charles Ford

London. Novbr 12. 1708.

[3] One Reason why I can not believe a word of what you say about your self, is because you write to me; for if you were not very ill

[1] See p. 105, n. 2.
[2] The kindly care and attention shown by Dean Stearne and Archdeacon and Mrs. Walls while he was absent in England was deeply appreciated by Swift.
[3] This is the first of the letters in the correspondence between Swift and Charles Ford, printed for the first time as a whole in 1935 by Professor David Nichol Smith, extending to sixty-nine letters. Of these, forty-three original letters by Swift are now in Lord Rothschild's Library, no. 2282. They were for some time in the hands of Sir John Hyde Cotton (d. 1752), Ford's executor. Charles Ford, son of Edward Ford, or Forth, and grandson of Sir Robert Forth, was born in Dublin on 31 Jan. 1681–2. He was left with a moderate fortune

entertaind, and much in the Spleen, you would neglect me as you did here, except¹ when you were in those Circumstances, which was just all the time that you were neither eating, drinking, sleeping, nor seeing the Opera, and if I had a mind to be rigorous I would substract a good deal even from each of those. When you talk morally about Mʳˢ Tofts,² Lᵈʸ Mounthermer,³ and the rest, I think upon what Sᵗ Evremont says of Devotes, that when they call their Sins to mind in order for Repentance, the truth of the Matter is, they take a delight in remembring them.⁴ I laugh at what You say of the glorious Life you led here, when I remember how often You told me it was a Life You wisht to Your Enemyes. But I have observed from my self and others (and I think it the wisest Observation I ever made in my Life) that Men are never more mistaken, than when they reflect upon passt things, and from what they retain in their Memory, compare them with the Present. Because, when we reflect on what is past, our Memoryes lead us onely to the pleasant side, but in present things our Minds are chiefly taken up with reflecting on what we dislike in our Condition. So I formerly used to envy my own Happiness when I was a Schoolboy, the delicious Holidays, the Saterday afternoon, and the charming Custards in a blind Alley; I never considered the Confinement ten hours a day, to nouns and Verbs, the Terror of the Rod, the bloddy Noses, and broken Shins. —This is exactly your Case, as I find by your Recollections, and in short I never knew a more imperfect Repentance, or more agreable to what I expected from You. Thus much for You, Now for Publick Affairs. On the Prince's death, the Ministry resolved to bring Lᵈ Sommers to the Head of the Council, and make Lᵈ Wharton | Lieuᵗ of Ireland, therefore Lᵈ Pemb— must be made Admirall. The Thing we all reckon is determind; But Lᵈ Pemb— is unwilling, and would

and the small estate of Woodpark, co. Meath. He became one of Swift's most trusted friends. In 1712 Swift procured for him the office of Gazetteer. He was an absentee landlord who spent most of his time in London, where he died in 1741. For the best account of Ford see *Letters of Swift to Ford*, ed. D. Nichol Smith. See also *Poems*, pp. 309–10, 720.

¹ MS. 'expect'.

² Katherine Tofts, of Drury Lane Theatre.

³ The youngest daughter of Marlborough, Lady Mary Churchill, married 2 Mar. 1705 to Lord Monthermer, who succeeded his father as second Duke of Montagu 9 Mar. 1709.

⁴ 'Une Dévotion nouvelle plaît en tout, jusqu'à parler des vieux Pechés dont on se repent.' Saint-Evremond, *Œuvres Meslées*, 1709, iii. 56, 'Que la Dévotion est le dernier de nos Amours'.

stave it if he could. If this Scheam holds, either my Journey to Vienna[1] will vanish, or at least be upon such a Foot as I would have it, unless my old Friends turn Courti[e]rs every way, which I shall not wonder at, tho I do not suspect. If they do, I will return to Laracor, and in my way talk moralls, and rail at Courts, at Wood-Park,[2] till You are weary.

To my great Surprise I had tother day a Letter from M[r] Domvil,[3] thô he faithfully promised to write to me. It was dated from Geneva.

Here was some time ago publisht an Essay upon Enthusiasm,[4] which all my Friends would persuade me to have been the Author of; sed ego non credulus illis;[5] For upon my word I was not. Some other Things people have been fathering on me with as little Truth, for I have publisht nothing since I saw you.

Pray give your self the Trouble of presenting my most humble Service to your Mother and Sister.

If you had told me you began to take a Relish in planting and improving the Scene,[6] I should begin to have favorable Thoughts of your Conversion.

Address: For M[r] Ford, at M[r] Westgarth's | House on Ormond Key | in | Dublin | Ireland
Added by another hand: at m[r] tody in sheep streete.
Postmark: 13 NO

[1] See Swift's letter to Archbishop King, 9 Nov. 1708.

[2] Ford's residence, eleven miles from Dublin on the road to Trim, two miles north of Dunboyne. For a description and illustration see Sir Frederick Falkiner's essay on 'The Portraits of Swift', *Prose Works*, ed. Temple Scott, xii. 68–70.

[3] William Domville, grandson of the distinguished Sir William Domville, Attorney-General for Ireland (d. 1689), inherited a large estate in co. Dublin; but he spent most of his time in England or abroad (Ball, *County Dublin*, pt. i, pp. 90–92). He is frequently mentioned in the *Journal*. Swift heard from him on 10 Nov. and replied on 2 Dec.

[4] See p. 100, n. 2.

[5] Virgil, *Eclog*. ix. 34.

[6] At Woodpark. Swift had been 'planting and improving the scene at Laracor'.

Archbishop King to Swift

Dublin, Nov. 20, 1708.

Revd S[1]

I have yours of the 9th instant, and if the scheme of alteration holds, as represented, I despair of our twentieth parts in the present method; yet I can't think it proper to move in any new course till the declaration of what is intended be more authentic. I have no good ground for my doubt; and yet, in my own mind, I make some question, whether all things will be just as surmised. If I find this to be so in earnest, I will then endeavour to obtain an address to my Lord Treasurer, which, I suppose, has been hitherto wanting: but, if the matter stick on any considerations not agreeable, there is an end of it. To deal freely, I have very little hope of succeeding any way; but it will not make things worse to try the experiment.

I understand some Dissenters from hence will apply to the Parliament of *England* this session, to obtain a repeal of the Test, and for a toleration on a larger foot than in *England*; and that a fund is raised, and agents appointed to solicit their affairs, by the presbyters of the North. I have had some intimation, that all Dissenters are not of a mind in this point; the other sects, if I am rightly informed, being as much afraid of them as of us; and that they would rather be as they are, than run the hazard of coming under the *jus divinum* of Presbytery. Something pleasant enough is said to have happened on this occasion: a certain person endeavoured to comfort them, and remove their jealousy; by telling them they needed not to fear; for that the greatest friends to Dissenters, and who would be most zealous for toleration, never designed to establish any church, but only to destroy that, which had the protection of the laws. Whether this will give them satisfaction I can't tell; but am certain, that if any have so wicked a design, they will fail in it.

I am often alarmed with the fears of some good men, who would persuade me, that religion is in danger of being rooted out of the hearts of men; and they wondered to see me so sanguine in the cause. But I tell them, that I believe it is with religion, as with paternal affection; some profligate wretches may forget it, and some may dose

[1] The copy of this letter in the manuscript room of Trinity College, Dublin, is badly injured by damp, and only partly legible. The text, in the main, here follows that printed by Hawkesworth in 1766.

themselves so long with perverse thinking, as not to see any reason for it: but in spite of all the ill-natured and false philosophy of these two sorts of people, the bulk of mankind will love their children. And so it is, and will be with the fear of God and religion: whatever is general hath a powerful cause, though every one cannot find it out.

But I have forgot my Dissenters: the reason of their applying in *Great Britain* is, because they see little reason to hope for success here; and if I can judge of the sense of gentlemen that compose the Parliament, they never seemed to be farther from the humour of gratifying them.

As to your own concern, you see hardly anything valuable is obtained any otherwise than by the government; and therefore, if you can attend the next Lord Lieutenant, you, in my opinion, ought not to decline.[1] I assure myself that you are too honest to come on ill terms; nor do I believe any will explicitly be proposed. I could give several reasons why you should embrace this, though I have no exception against your secretaryship;[2] except that you may lose too much time in it, which, considering all things, you cannot so well spare at this time of the day.

As to my own part, I thank God, I was never much frightened by any alterations: neither King *James* nor the Earl of *Tyrconnel*, shocked me.[3] I always comforted myself with the 112th psalm, 7th verse.[4] I never was a favourite of any Government, nor have I a prospect of being so, though I believe I have seen forty changes; nor would I advise any friend to sell himself to any, so as to be their slave. I could write some other things, that you would desire to know; but pen and ink are dangerous tools in some men's hands, and I love to leave a friend with an appetite. I am, &c.

W. D.

[1] King's suggestion is that Swift should seek the appointment of chaplain to Lord Pembroke's successor as Lord Lieutenant. He and King would have in mind the preferment of Pembroke's chaplain, Thomas Milles, to the see of Waterford.

[2] To accompany Lord Berkeley to Vienna in the event of his Lordship receiving the appointment.

[3] Archbishop King, who was then Dean of St. Patrick's Cathedral, unlike most of his brethren, remained in Ireland while King James was in that country. He was twice imprisoned in Dublin Castle by that monarch, and during his first incarceration kept a diary which has been carefully edited with illuminating notes by Professor Lawlor for the *Journal of the Royal Society of Antiquaries of Ireland* (vol. xxxiii, *passim*).—Ball.

[4] 'He shall not be afraid of evil tidings: his heart is fixed, trusting in the Lord.'

Swift to Dean Stearne

Nov. 30, 1708.

Sir,

I received a letter from you the Lord knows when, for it has no date; but I conceive it to have been a month ago, for I met it when I came from *Kent*, where, and at *Epsom*, I passed about six weeks,[1] to divert myself the fag end of the summer, which proved to be the best weather we had. I am glad you made so good a progress in your building; but you had the emblem of industry in your mind, for the bees begin at the top and work downwards, and at last work themselves out of house and home, as many of you builders do.[2]

You know before this the great revolution we have had at court; and that Dr. *Lambert* is chaplain to the Lord Lieutenant: the Archbishop of *Canterbury*, several other Bishops, and my Lord Treasurer himself would needs have it so. I made no manner of application for that post, upon certain reasons, that I shall let you know, if ever I have the happiness to see you again.[3]

My Lord *Sunderland* rallied me on that occasion, and was very well pleased with my answer, that I observed one thing in all new *ministries*: for the first week or two they are in a hurry, or not to be seen; and when you come afterwards, they are engaged. What I have to say of the public, *&c.* will be inclosed, which, I suppose, will be shewn you, and you will please to deliver as formerly.[4] Lord *Pembroke* takes all things mighty well, and we pun together as usual; and he either makes the best use, or the best appearance with his philosophy of any man I ever knew; for it is not believed he is pleased at heart upon many accounts.

Sir *Andrew Fountaine* is well, and has either writ to you last post, or designs it soon.

[1] See Swift to King, 9 Nov.　　　　　[2] See p. 83, n. 3.
[3] Thomas Wharton, 1648–1715, the son of a puritanical father, became a notorious profligate. He was, however, a man of ability and strong character; and, in the Whig interest, an efficient political organizer. On his appointment, 16 Nov. 1708, as Lord Lieutenant it was generally understood that his chief aim would be the removal of the test in Ireland. He chose as his chaplain the Rev. Ralph Lambert as a hopeful coadjutor, for on 23 Oct. 1708 he preached a sermon urging closer unity with the Nonconformists. Later Swift delivered uncompromising attacks on Wharton's character as 'Verres' in the *Examiner*, no. 17, and, about the same time in *A Short Character of His Excellency Thomas Earl of Wharton*.　　　[4] That is to say a letter for Archbishop King.

Dr. *Pratt* is buying good pennyworths of books for the college, and has made some purchases that would set you a longing. You have heard our mighty news is extreamly dwindled in our last pacquets. However we expect a very happy end of the campaign, which this sudden thaw, and foul weather, begun here yesterday, will soon bring to an issue.[1] I am *&c.*

Faulkner 1762

Swift to Archbishop King

London. Nov. 30, 1708.

My Lord,

I Writ to you about a Fortnight ago, after my Return from the Country, and gave you some Account of an intended Change at Court, which is now finished. Care was taken to put Lord *Pembroke* in Mind of the First Fruits before he went out of his Office; but, it was needless, for his Excellency had it at Heart, and the Thing is done, of which, I suppose, you have an Account.[2] You know who goes over Chaplain; the Archbishop of *Canterbury*, and several other Bishops, and the Lord Treasurer himself, sollicited that Matter in a Body: It was thought absolutely necessary, considering the dismal Notion they have here of so many High Church Archbishops among you; and your Friend made no Application, for Reasons left you to guess.[3] I cannot yet learn whether you are to have a new Parliament; but I am apt to think you will, and that it must be thought necessary.[4] The affair of *Drogheda* hath made a Noise here, and like every Thing else on your Side, is used as a Handle: I have had it rung in my Ears from certain Persons.[5] I hope you are prepared to take off the

[1] On 23 Nov. it was reported in London that Marlborough and his ally, Prince Eugene, had beaten the forces of the Elector of Bavaria, who was then besieging Brussels, out of their lines with a loss of seventeen battalions taken prisoner; but on 27 Nov. it was found that although the siege had been raised the loss to the Elector was only 200 men killed and 800 taken prisoners.—Ball.

[2] In this assumption Swift was mistaken.

[3] Lambert's conciliatory attitude towards the Dissenters.

[4] The Irish Parliament then in being had been returned on the accession of Queen Anne. Wharton retained this Parliament believing it to be amenable to persuasion in favour of the repeal of the Test. A dissolution was not proclaimed till five years later, and then by the Tories.

[5] Two Presbyterian ministers had been prosecuted for preaching in Drogheda. According to J. S. Reid (*Hist. of the Presbyterian Church in Ireland*, iii. 3–6)

Sacramental Test, because that will be a Means to have it taken off here among us; and that the Clergy will be for it, in Consideration of the Queen's Bounty; and that Men in Employment will be so wise as to please the Court, and secure themselves: But, to think there is any Design of bringing the *Scotch* into Offices, is a mere Scandal.

Lord *Pembroke* is to have the Admiralty only a few Months, then to have a Pension of 4000 *l.* a Year, and to retire; and, it is thought Lord Orford will succeed him, and then it is hoped, there will be an entire Change in the Admiralty; that Sir *John Leake* will be turned out, and the *Whigs* so well confirmed, that it will not be in the Power of the Court, upon a Peace, to bring the Ballance on the other Side.[1]

One Mr. *Shute* is named for Secretary to Lord *Wharton*: He is a young Man, but reckoned the shrewdest Head in *England*; and the Person in whom the *Presbyterians* chiefly confide: and, if Money be necessary towards that good Work in *Ireland*, it is reckoned he can command as far as 100,000 *l.* from the Body of *Dissenters* here. As to his Principles, he is truly a moderate Man, frequenting the Church and the Meeting indifferently, *&c.*[2]

The Clergy are here in an Uproar upon their being prorogued: The Archbishop of Canterbury taketh pains to have it believed it was a Thing done without his Knowledge. A Divine of Note (but of the wrong Side) was with me the other Day, and said, he had it from a good Hand, that the Reason of this Proceeding was an Intention

a non-conforming congregation had been established in Drogheda since the time of Cromwell. On the contrary William Tisdall, *Conduct of the Dissenters of Ireland with Respect to the Church and State,* 1712, asserts that there had been no conventicle in Drogheda for some years before the accession of King William. Wharton, aided by Dodington, exercised his influence in favour of the two ministers. One was released after six weeks' confinement, and the prosecution of the other was dropped.

[1] Towards the end of 1709 Pembroke resigned the office of Lord High Admiral, and was succeeded by Lord Orford. Sir John Leake, instead of being turned out, was, in Nov. 1709, advanced from his patent rank of Rear Admiral of Great Britain to be a Lord of the Admiralty.

[2] John Shute, 1678–1734, Christian apologist and polemical writer, was sent to the University of Utrecht; and on his return to England was called to the bar. He had the good fortune to gain the friendship of Locke. At the instance of Lord Somers he was sent to Scotland to win Presbyterian support for the Union. For his political services he was, in 1720, created Baron Barrington of Newcastle in the county of Meath, and Viscount Barrington of Ardglass in the county of Down, in the peerage of Ireland.

of putting the Parliament on examining and correcting Courts Ecclesiastick, &c.

The Archbishop of *Dublin* is represented here as one that will very much oppose our Designs; and, although I will not say that the Observator[1] is paid for writing as he doth; yet I can positively affirm to you, that whatever he says of that Archbishop, or of the Affairs of *Ireland*, or those here, is exactly agreeable to our Thoughts and Intentions.

This is all I can recollect, fit to inform you at present.—If you please I shall from Time to Time send you any Thing that cometh to my Knowledge, that may be worth your notice. I am, &c.

Faulkner 1762

Swift to Archbishop King

London, Jan. 6, 1708–9

My Lord,

Before I received the Honour of your Grace's of *Nov.* 20, I had sent one enclosed, &c. with what Account I could of Affairs. Since that Time, the Measures are altered of dissolving your Parliament, which doubtless, is their wisest Course, for certain obvious Reasons, that your Grace will easily apprehend and I suppose you have now received Directions about proroguing it, for I saw the Order some Days ago.[2] I should have acknowledged your Grace's Letter, if I had not been ever since persecuted with a cruel Distemper, a Giddiness in my Head, that would not suffer me to write or think of any Thing; and of which I am now slowly recovering.[3] I sent you Word of the Affair of the first Fruits being performed, which my Lord *Pembroke* had the Goodness to send me immediate Notice of. I seldom see his Lordship now, but when he pleaseth to command me, for he sees No-body in Public, and is very full of Business. I

[1] The first number of the *Observator*, a Whig paper, was issued by John Tutchin on 1 Apr. 1702. It started as a weekly, but from 23 May it appeared twice weekly. After Tutchin's death, 23 Sept. 1707, it was continued for the benefit of his widow, and lingered on till it succumbed to the stamp tax. 'The Observator is fallen', wrote Swift, 7 Aug. 1712 (*Journal*, p. 554).

[2] A dissolution of the Irish House of Commons would probably have resulted in a decrease in the number of members favouring a repeal of the Test.

[3] This is the first mention of the disease from which Swift was to suffer at frequent intervals throughout life. See, further, Appendix.

fancy your Grace will think it necessary that in due Time his Lordship should receive some Kind of Thanks in Form: I have a fair
Pretence to merit in this Matter, although, in my own Conscience,
I think I have very little (except my good Wishes, and frequent
reminding my Lord *Pembroke*). But, two great Men in Office,
giving me Joy of it, very frankly told me, that if I had not smoothed
the Way, by giving them and the rest of the Ministry a good Opinion
of the Justice of the Thing; it would have met with Opposition:
upon which I only remarked what I have always observed in Courts,
that when a Favour is done, there is no Want of Persons to challenge
Obligations. Mean Time I am in a Pretty Condition, who have
Bills of Merit given me, that I must thankfully acknowledge, and
yet cannot honestly offer them in payment. I suppose the Clergy
will in due Time send the Queen an Address of Thanks for her
Favour.

I very much applaud your Grace's sanguine Temper, as you call
it, and your Comparison of Religion to paternal Affection; but the
World is divided into two Sects, those that hope the best, and those
that fear the worst; your Grace is of the former, which is the wiser,
the nobler, and most pious Principle; and although I endeavour to
avoid being of the other, yet upon this Article I have sometimes
strange Weaknesses. I compare true Religion to Learning and
Civility which have ever been in the World, but very often shifted
their Scenes; sometimes entirely leaving whole Countries where
they have long flourished, and removing to others that were before
barbarous; which hath been the Case of Christianity itself, particularly in many parts of *Africa*, and how far the wickedness of a
Nation may provoke God Almighty to inflict so great a Judgement,
is terrible to think. But as great Princes, when they have subdued all
about them, presently have universal Monarchy in their Thoughts;
so your Grace, having conquered all the Corruptions in a Diocese,
and then pursued your Victories over a Province, would fain go
farther, and save a whole Kingdom, and would never be quiet, if
you could have your Will, until you had converted the World.

And this reminds me of a Pamphlet lately come out, pretended to
be a Letter hither from *Ireland*, against repealing the Test; wherein
your Grace's Character is justly set forth: For the rest, some Parts
are very well, and others puerile, and some Facts, as I am informed,
wrong represented. The Author hath gone out of his Way to reflect
on me as a Person likely to write for repealing the Test, which I am

sure is very unfair Treatment. This is all I am likely to get by the
Company I keep. I am used like a sober Man with a Drunken Face,
have the Scandal of the Vice without the Satisfaction. I have told the
Ministry with great Frankness, my Opinion, that they would never
be able to repeal it, unless such Changes should happen as I could
not foresee; and they all believe I differ from them in that Point.[1]

Mr. *Addison*, who goes over first Secretary, is a most excellent
Person; and being my most intimate Friend, I shall use all my
Credit to set him right in his Notions of Persons and Things.[2] I
spoke to him with great Plainness upon the Subject of the Test;
and he says, he is confident my Lord *Wharton* will not attempt it,
if he finds the Bent of the Nation against it. I will say nothing
further of his Character to your Grace at present, because he hath
half persuaded me to have some Thoughts of returning to *Ireland*,
and then it will be Time enough: But if that happens otherwise, I
presume to recommend him to your Grace as a Person you will
think worth your Acquaintance.

My Lord *Berkeley* begins to drop his Thoughts of going to
Vienna; and indeed I freely gave my Opinion against such a
Journey for one of his Age and Infirmities.[3] And, I shall hardly
think of going Secretary without him, although the Emperor's
Ministers here think I will, and have writ to *Vienna*. I agree with
your Grace, that such a design was a little too late at my Years;[4]

[1] In December Swift had written and published his *Letter from a Member
of the House of Commons in Ireland to a Member of the House of Commons in
England, Concerning the Sacramental Test* as a challenge to the 'low party' and
the attitude adopted by Lambert, chaplain to Wharton. If not exactly a Tory
pamphlet it came near it. Swift pointed out that political alignments were
differently drawn in Ireland to those in England, that in Ireland the real danger
was from the Presbyterians rather than from the Papists. Readers of the pamphlet
in London were deceived into believing it to be a genuine letter written by some
one in Dublin. King was not deceived. Twenty-five years later the tract was
included in Swift's collected *Works* with a note indicating that it still expressed
his views. See *Prose Works*, ed. Davis, ii, pp. xxi–xxiv, 109.

[2] Biographers have found difficulty in explaining the association of the
reserved and eminently respectable Addison with the profligate Wharton. The
only observable link between them was Whig political principle. See, further,
the *Life of Addison*, 1954, by Peter Smithers, in which the character of Wharton
is drawn in kindlier outline.

[3] Lord Berkeley, at this time sixty years of age, was in failing health. In the
Journal to Stella, 19 Sept. 1710, Swift mentions having received a letter from
Lady Berkeley 'begging me for charity to come to Berkeley-castle, for company
to my lord'. Five days later his lordship died.   [4] See p. 112.

but considering myself wholly useless in *Ireland*, and in a Parish with an Audience of half a Score, and it being thought necessary that the Queen should have a Secretary at that Court, my friends telling me it would not be difficult to compass it, I was a little tempted to pass some time abroad, until my Friends would make me a little easier in my Fortunes at Home. Beside, I had hopes of being sent in Time to some other Court, and in the mean while the Pay would be forty shillings a Day, and the Advantage of Living, if I pleased, in Lord *Berkeley's* Family. But, I believe, this is now all at an End. | I am, my Lord, | With the greatest Respect. |

Your Grace's most obedient, and | most humble Servant,

J. Swift.

My Lord *Wharton* says, he intends for *Ireland* the Beginning of *March*.

Haverford College Library

Swift to Robert Hunter

London. Jan^r 12. 170⅞

I know no People so ill used by your Men of Business as their intimate Friends. About a fortnight after Mr Addison had received the Letter you were pleased to send me, he first told me of it with an Air of Recollection, and after ten days further, of Grace, thought fitt to give it me, so you know where to fix the whole Blame that it was no sooner Acknoledged.[1] Tis a delicate Expedient you Prisoners have of Diverting your selves in an Enemyes Country, for which other men would be hangd. I am considering whether there be no way of disturbing your quiet by writing some dark Matter that may give the French Court a Jealosy of you, I suppose, Mon^s Chamillard[2] or some of his Commrs must have this Letter interpreted to them before it comes to your Hands; and therefore I here think good to warn them that if they exchange you under six of their Lieutenant Generals, they will be Losers by the Bargain. but that

[1] According to Swift's account-book (Forster 506) the letter from Hunter was received on 7 Jan. For Hunter see p. 101, n. 5.

[2] Michel de Chamillard (1651–1721), in 1699 named by Louis XIV Controller General of Finance. Incompetent and opinionated he died with the reputation of a man honourable in private life and a bad Minister.

they may not mistake me, I do not mean as Vice-roy de Virginia, mais comme le Colonel Hunter. I would advise you to be very tender of Your Honor, and not fall in Love because I have a Scruple whether you can keep your Parole if you become a Prisoner to the Ladyes. At least it will be a scandal for a free Briton to drag two Chains at once. I presume you have the Liberty of Paris and fifty miles round, and have a very light pair of Fetters, contrived to ride or dance in, and see Versailles, and every Place else except St Germains[1]—I hear the Ladyes call you already Notre prisonnier Hunter, le plus honnête garzon du monde.—Will you[r] French yet own us Brittons to be a brave People? will they allow the D. of Marlborough to be a great Generall? or are they all as partiall as their Gazetters? Have you yett met any French Collonell, whom you remember to have formerly knockt from his Horse, or shivered at least a Lance against his Breastplate? Do you know the Wounds you have given when you see the Scars! Do you salute your old enemyes with, Stetimus terra aspera contra, contulimus manus[2] vous savez Monsr d'Addison notre bon ami est fait Secretaire d'etat d'yrlande,[3] and unless you make hast over, and get me my Virginian Bishoprick,[4] he will persuade me to go with him; for th[e] Vienna Project is off, which is a great disappointment to the design I had of displaying my Politicks at the Emperor's Court.[5]—I do not like the Subjects[6] you have assigned me to entertain you with. Crowder[7] is sick to the comfort of all quiet People, and Frowd[8] is Reveur á peindre. Addison and I often drink your Health, and this day I did it with Will Pate, a certain Adorer of yours, who is both a bel esprit, and a wollen Draper.[9] The Whigs carry all before them, and how far they will pursue their Victoryes, we moderate Whigs can hardly tell. I have not yet observed the Toryes Noses, Their number is not to be learned by telling of Noses, for every Tory has

---

[1] Where the Pretender resided.
[2] Virg. *Aen.* XI. 282–3; 'terra' should be 'tela'.
[3] Addison's office was that of Secretary to the Lord Lieutenant, Wharton.
[4] Sheridan, *Life*, p. 57, followed by Scott, *Memoirs*, p. 98, interpret this as a serious proposal; but, as the tone of the allusion indicates, Swift was jesting. There is no evidence that Swift was ever considered for a colonial bishopric.
[5] See p. 108.
[6] Ball mistakenly reads 'subject'.
[7] Thomas Crowther, who commanded a regiment of horse at the battle of Blenheim, and became a major-general.   [8] See p. 92, n. 1.
[9] This is the first mention of William Pate by Swift. He is also referred to

not a Nose.—Tis a Loss you are not here to partake of three weeks
Frost, and eat Gingerbread in a Booth by a Fire upon the Thames.
Mʳˢ Floyd lookt out with both her Eyes and we had one Days
Thaw, but she drew in her Head, and it now freezes as hard as ever.¹
As for the Convocation, the Queen thought fitt to prorogue it,
thô at the Expence of Dʳ Atterbury's Displeasure, who was designed
their Prolocutor, and is now raging² at his disappointment.—I
amuse my self sometimes with writing Verses to Mʳˢ Finch,³ and
sometimes with Projects for uniting of Partyes, which I perfect
over night, and burn in the morning; Sometimes Mʳ Addison and I
steal to a pint of bad wine, and wish for no third Person but you,
who if you were with us, would never be satisfied without three
more;—You know, I believe, that poor Dʳ Gregory is dead, and
Keil sollicites to be his Successor. But Party reaches even to Lines
and Circles, and he will hardly carry it being reputed a Tory, wᶜʰ
yet he wholly denyes.⁴—We are here nine times madder after
Opera's than ever, and have gott a new castrato from Italy calld
Nicolini who exceeds Valentini I know not how many Bars length.⁵
Lᵈ Sommers and Hallifax are as well as busy Statesmen can be in
Parlmᵗ time. Lord Dorset is nobody's Favorite but yours and Mʳ
Prior's, who has lately dedicated his Book of Poems to him, which

three times in the *Journal to Stella*, 17, 24 Sept., 6 Oct. 1710. Known as 'the
learned tradesman', he was on friendly terms with men of letters, including
Swift, Arbuthnot, and Steele. He was probably the original of the woollen-
draper described in the *Guardian*, no. 141, 22 Aug. 1713. He died in 1746. See,
further, *D.N.B.*, Nichols, *Lit. Anec.* i. 98 n., and *Journal to Stella*, p. 20, n. 37.

¹ A severe frost, which began on 26 Dec., continued, with intermissions,
until March. Mrs. Biddy Floyd was Lady Betty Germain's friend and companion. She was a noted beauty (*Journal to Stella*, 12 Oct. 1711). See *Poems*, pp.
117–18, for Swift's verses addressed to her.

² Ball mistakenly reads 'raving'.

³ Anne Finch, later Countess of Winchilsea. See 'Apollo Outwitted', *Poems*,
p. 119.

⁴ David Gregory, b. 1661, was chosen Savilian Professor of Astronomy in
1691. He died 10 Oct. 1708. John Keill, a pupil of Gregory, though not an
immediate successor, became Savilian Professor in 1712, a delay which may be
attributed to 'Party'.

⁵ Operas on the Italian model were first introduced into England in 1705.
They were first sung in English by English performers, later by Italian *castrati*
who were answered in English by subordinate characters; but after a short
time the operas became wholly Italian (Lecky, *England in the Eighteenth Century*,
i. 532). Nicolini was one of the most famous of the Italian opera singers. See
Poems, ii. 598 n.

is all the Press has furnisht us of any value since You went.[1] Mʳ Bringle,[2] a Gentleman of Scotland succeeds Mʳ Addison in the Secretary's Office. And Mʳ Shute,[3] a notable young Presbyterian Gentleman under thirty years old, is made a Commissioner of the Customs. This is all I can think of, either publick or private, worth telling you, perhaps you have heard part or all of both from other Hands, but you must be content: Pray let us know what hopes we have of seeing you, and how soon, and be so kind or just to believe me always | Your most faithfull | humble Servᵗ.|

                                                              Jon: Swift.

Mʳ Steel presents his most humble Service to you. And I can not forbear telling you of yʳ Mechancete to impute the Lettr of Enthusiasm to me; when I have some good Reasons to think the Author is now at Paris

Address: A Monsieur | Monsieur Hunter | á Paris[4]

Hawkesworth 1766
Archbishop King to Swift

                                                  Dublin, Feb. 10, 1708–9.
Rev. Sir,[5]

I received yours of last *January* the 6th, and you will find but a sorry correspondent of me. I have been confined near two months this winter, and forbid pen and ink by my physician; though, I thank God, I was more frightened, as it happened, than hurt. I had

---

[1] Priors' *Poems on Several Occasions*, 1709, opens with a lengthy dedication 'To the Right Honourable Lionel, Earl of Dorset and Middlesex', who was created Duke of Dorset on 17 June 1720. The dedication is overloaded with compliments to the father, Charles Sackville, sixth Earl of Dorset (d. 1706), who had been an early patron of Prior.

[2] Robert Pringle, third son of Sir Robert Pringle, first baronet of Stitchel, studied at Leyden, and afterwards took service under William, Prince of Orange. He was appointed Under-Secretary of State for Scotland; and in 1718 Secretary at War. He died at Rotterdam in 1736.

[3] See p. 115, n. 2.

[4] After 'Monsieur Hunter' Sheridan, Nichols, and Ball introduce 'Gentilhomme Anglois', or 'Anglais', which is not in the manuscript.

[5] The copy of this letter in the manuscript room of Trinity College, Dublin, is legible only in part. The text is here printed from Hawkesworth, 1766.

a colic about the year 96, that brought me to extremity, and all despaired of my life, and the news-letters reported me dead. It began at the same time of the year, and the same way it did then, and the winters were much alike; and I verily believe had I not had the assistance of my old physician Sir *Patrick Dun*, I should have run the same course, which I could not have supported. But with a little physic, and the Spaw and Bath waters, I escaped without other hardships than keeping at home; and so much for private affairs.[1]

As to the public, I had a letter from my Lord *Pembroke*, wherein he told me the first fruits and twentieth parts were granted, and that my Lord Lieutenant will bring over the Queen's letter for them. I returned him my thanks, and as soon as the order comes, he will have a public acknowledgment.[2]

I have seen a letter, that passes as from a Member of the House, *&c*. I think your judgement concerning it is very just. But pray by what artifice did you contrive to pass for a Whig? As I am an honest man, I courted the greatest Whigs I knew, and could not gain the reputation of being counted one.

But you need not be concerned; I will engage you will lose nothing by that paper. I wish some facts had been well considered before vouched: if any one matter in it prove false, what do you think will come of the paper? In short, it will not be in the power of man to hinder it from a warm entertainment.[3]

As to the Test, I believe that matter is over for this season. I was much for dissolving this present Parliament, and calling a new one this spring.[4] I had a pretty good account of the future elections, which, as far as my acquaintance reached, were settled; and I was sure, that without great force and artifice, the new members would never have repealed the Test; but I did not know what the influence of a Lord Lieutenant (when well acquainted in the kingdom, and who knew how to take his measures justly) might have effected, and we know very well what force, management and timing matters have; and there is hardly anything but powerful persuasions, terror,

---

[1] It appears from King's correspondence, when he was Bishop of Derry, that he was taken seriously ill in Oct. 1696. In the following March he came to stay in the village of Rathfarnham, under the Dublin mountains, to find repose. Ball presumes that he may there have been tended by Sir Patrick Dunn, the eminent Dublin physician, who had rendered notable services to William III's army during the Irish campaign.

[2] See p. 114.   [3] See p. 118.   [4] See p. 115.

and ostentation of interest may effect, especially in popular elections. And to confess the truth to you, I am not altogether easy in that matter yet, especially if things take any new turn in *England*. It is whispered, but I know not by what authority, that the Queen herself was at the bottom of what passed in the House of Commons with you, and that the Ministry screened her in that affair, for reasons that may be guessed at.

I am wonderfully pleased at the good character you give Mr. *Addison*. If he be the man that you represent him to be (and I have confidence in your judgment), he will be able to serve his Lord effectually, and procure himself love and respect here. I cannot say it will be in my power to do him any service: but my good wishes and endeavours shall not be wanting.

Mr. *Stoughton* preached *a sermon* here, on the 30th of *January*, King *Charles's* Martyrdom, that gives great offence: the Government heard it, but I was ill at home, which Dean *Stearne* will needs have a providence. If the representation I have of it be true, I am sure I should have suspended him, if it had cost me both my reputation and interest. I have represented what I have heard of it, and have discoursed my Lord Chancellor about it, and told him of what consequence I think it to be, both to him and us, and that it should not pass without censure. I have not as yet seen my Lord Primate. Wise men are going all they can to extinguish faction; and fools and elves are throwing firebrands. Assure yourself this had an ill effect on the minds of most here; for, though they espouse the Revolution, they heartily abhor forty-one. And nothing can create the Ministry more enemies, and be a greater handle for calumny, than to represent them, and those that espoused them, to be such as murdered King *Charles I* and such are all, that approve or excuse it.[1]

As to your own affairs, I wish you could have come over chaplain as I proposed; but since a more powerful interest interposed, I believe you had best use your endeavours there; but if nothing happens before my Lord Lieutenant comes over, you had best make

[1] In his sermon, which was printed, William Stoughton, Prebendary of St. Patrick's, told his hearers that respect for the Queen impelled him, in speaking of Charles I, 'to pass his faults and errors over with gentle touch and light reflection'. The 'ill effect' of these words will be understood. The Primate, Narcissus Marsh, at that time one of the Lords Justices, could hardly ignore them.

us a visit. Had you been here, I believe something might have been done for you before this. The deanery of *Down* is fallen, and application has been made for it to my Lord Lieutenant, but it yet hangs, and I know not what will become of it;[1] but if you could either get into it, or get a good man with a comfortable benefice removed to it, it might make present provision for you. I have many things more to say; but they are so much of a piece with these I have writ already, that you may guess at them all by this sample. God be with you: Amen.

William Dublin.

Rothschild

Swift to Charles Ford

London. Mar. 8. 170$\frac{8}{9}$

I am of late grown into debt with severall Correspondents, and You among the rest,[2] which I can impute to nothing but my having so little to do which has taken up all my Time, nothing being so great an Engrosser of it as Idleness. I shall be very far from endeavoring to persuade you that you are not happy; onely I cannot apprehend the Reason of your dating your Happiness from February last year: that being not the Period distinguisht either by your coming to or leaving London. I believe by this Time you are satisfyed that I am not grown great, nor like to do so very soon: for I am thought to want the Art of being thourow paced in my Party, as all discreet Persons ought to be, and some time this Summer you may not improbably see me alighting at your House in my way to Residence;[3] and you will find, when I promised to take you into my Family, it was with a politick Design to strengthen my Title of being taken into Yours. Whether I am agreeably entertained here or no, I would not tell you for the World, unless I were assured I should never be blesst again with a Return to Ireland. I must learn to make my Court to that Country and People better than I have done, thô to lett you into one Secret, (and it is a great one) I doubt at my return I shall pass my Time somewhat different from what I formerly did, wherein I will explain my self no further

[1] In May the Deanery of Down went to Ralph Lambert, Lord Wharton's chaplain.   [2] Swift had heard from Ford on 19 Jan.
[3] At Laracor, about two miles south of Trim.

than by telling you of the humor of a Gentleman I knew, who having eat Grapes in France, never lookt up towards a Vine after he came back for England. And if you find I pass for a morose Man, find some Excuse or other to vindicate me. But the fault will not be Ireland's, at least I will persuade my self so; For I am grown so hard to please, that I am offended with every unexpected Face I meet where I visit, and the least Tediousness or Impertinence gives me a Shortness of Breath, and a Pain in my Stomack. Among all the Diversions you mention among you, I desire to know whether a Man may be allowed to sitt alone among his Books, as long as he pleases. You destroy my Opinion of your Content, by the abundance of your Moral Reflections, which you may find have given me the Spleen, and which I observe men seldom trouble themselves about when they are as they would be.

The Account you give me of Peoples Inclinations with relation to the Test, agrees with what I have from all the best Hands. I believe little can be attempted that way among you this Session. I know not what may be done in the next Parliament, of which I suppose you will endeavor to be a Member.[1]

My Journy to Vienna is dropt as you are pleased to wish. We all advised My Ld Berkeley against it, tho in my own particular, I should not have disliked it. I thought I could be more usefull abroad, than I believe I shall ever be at home; and I was not unwilling to be at as great a Distance as I could from the Factions of the Age. My onely dreed was the Ill Payment from the Court, which might have utterly ruined me. No, the Report of my Answering Tindall's Book[2] is a Mistake; I had some thoughts that way, but they are long layd aside.

I have had a second Letter from Mr. Domvile,[3] who is still at

---

[1] In his *Letter Concerning the Sacramental Test* Swift had said that the party in favour of the repeal of the Test 'will hardly, I am confident, amount to above Fifty Men in Parliament, which can hardly be worked up into a Majority of Three Hundred'. He expected that Wharton would dissolve the Irish Parliament at once, but it was not dissolved till May 1713; and at that time Ford was Gazetteer in London.

[2] *The Rights of the Christian Church asserted against the Romish and all other Priests*, 1706, followed by a *Defence*, 1707, and a *Second Defence*, 1708. Swift had begun an answer after Easter 1707, and before the publication of the first *Defence*, but he soon abandoned it. The fragment he had written was published by Faulkner in 1758 as *Remarks upon a Book intituled The Rights*, &c.

[3] Received 12 Feb.; Swift replied 31 Mar.

Geneva, and tells me, he is grown a Whig in Point of Government, by observing the Plenty, Spirit, and Trade, and Improvement wherever Liberty prevails. I approve of his Conversion; and would have him stick there, without proceeding further. How liberall you are in your Pity, to bestow it from Dublin upon him in Geneva, which I am told is the pleasantest Place almost in Europe to pass away the Time.

Pray present my most humble Service to Mrs Ford,[1] and your Sister, and to Mr Elwood,[2] if he comes in your way; that is a Man I have an esteem for, and in my London Phrase, will suffer his Acquaintance.

Address: For Charles Ford, Esqr, at | Lucas's Coffee-House | in | Dublin
         Ireland
Postmark: 8 MR

Rothschild[3]

Swift to Ambrose Philips

London. Mar. 8th 170⅞. O.S.

I give you Joy of all the difficultyes in your Journey, since they ended in a safe Arrivall; and I pity you the less, since Mr Molsworth[4] told me of the present he made you of a warm Fur cap for Y^r Composition, You know Horaces Rule, dissolve frigus ligna

---

[1] Ford's mother.

[2] John Elwood, sometime Vice-Provost of Trinity College, Dublin, and University member in the Parliament of 1713–14. *Alum. Dub.*, p. 264.

[3] This letter was sold in Puttick's auction rooms in the summer of 1857. It next appeared in the Clumber Library sale at Sotheby's, 16 Feb. 1938, whence it passed into the Rothschild Library. Ball, i. 141–2, took his text from a transcript in the Forster Collection, evidently taken from the letter while in Puttick's rooms. The transcript, not wholly accurate, represents only about one-quarter of the original, divided into two portions: (1) 'Your versifying in a sledge . . . Northern Sea', (2) 'The Town is run mad . . . always going to'. Furthermore, Ball dates this letter 15 Mar., presuming it to be of that date and written in reply to a letter received from Philips 22 Feb. 1709 (Swift's Account Book, Forster Collection, no. 506).

[4] It is doubtful whether the reference here is to Robert Molesworth, later (1719) Viscount Molesworth of Swords, to whom Swift addressed the fifth Drapier's Letter (*Drapier's Letters*, ed. H. Davis, pp. 287–9), or to his son John, whom Swift met occasionally in 1710 (*Journal*, p. 26, n. 1). In 1692 the father was envoy extraordinary to Denmark. The son was envoy to the Grand Duke of Tuscany in 1710.

super foco large reponens, and merum diota,[1] which last, is a Receit
I suppose Denmark may teach you. At worst, a good reception and
friendly Treatment, will remove the Clymate ten degrees southward.
Your Dane of a refined Tast is somewhat Extraordinary, unless it be
a Tast of Second Hand, but I desire, whoever admires or blames the
Book, you will not think me to have any concern in the Matter, tho
since People will in spight of my disarming suspect me for an
Author, I cannot but be better pleased with those who think me so
to my Advantage—Your versifying in a Sledge seems somewhat
parallell to singing a Psalm upon a Ladder, and when you tell me it
was upon the Sea, I suppose it might be a Pastorall, and that you had
got a Calenture,[2] which makes men think they behold green Feelds,
and Groves on the Ocean. I suppose the Subject was Love, and then
came in naturally your burning in so much cold, and that the Ice
was hott Iron in comparison of her disdain. Then there are frozen
Hearts, and melting Sighs, or Kisses, I forget which, But I believe
your Poeticall Faith could never arrive at allowing that Venus was
born on the Belts[3] or any Part of the Northern Sea.—Treve des
bagatelles. This same Mistress of y^{rs} is a very usefull Amusement
takes all your Passions by turns and putts them into Motion, which
may not be amiss in a cold Clymate; therefore I hope she will step
once more to France and ply you with a Rival or two while Winter
lasts.

As to what you enquire about me, I can only tell you that L^d
Berkeley has at last refused going to Vienna,[4] wherein all his Friends
think him in the Right, and my self among the rest; so that the
Peace with the Hungarian Rebels is like to be made without me;
let the Emperor look to it.[5] I shall return to Ireland in Summer and
have desired Mr Steel to take care of any Letters you will please to
send me: therefore pray direct to him, who shall know my Address.
This is onely meant as long as you shall think fitt to keep up the
Humor of remembering absent Friends especially of so short a

[1] Hor. *Odes* I. ix. 5, 6 and 8.
[2] Swift alludes again to this form of tropical fever and its effect on seamen
in *The Bubble*. See *Poems*, p. 251 and note.
[3] The name given to two straits, the Great and the Little Belt, which, with
the Sound, connect the Cattegat with the Baltic.
[4] For Lord Berkeley's contemplated mission to Vienna see Swift to King,
9 Nov. 1708.
[5] Joseph I, a more liberal Emperor than his predecessors, granted privileges
to the Protestants of Hungary.

standing, and so little Use as I. Mr Addison will go for Ireland in a Month. Colonell Froud[1] has received y^r Lett^r, and his Lady commanded me this day to give you her Service and began Y^r Health to me. Mr Addison and I drink it often; He loves you very well, and you can hardly have a better Possession, upon every Account imaginable. You do not expect I shall send you News or Politicks, and if you did, you would be deceived; and therefore a Lett^r from Irel^d will be full as valuable as from hence. All your Friends here are well, and howvr transitory the rest of the World may be, St James Coffee house still continues as you left it. Dr King has reprinted all his Works together and the Volume begins with his Answer to Mr Molesworth's Book   of Denmark.[2] Your Pastorals will appear at the head of the new Miscellany in a month.[3] Nic Row is with great difficulty coming in to be Secretary to the Duke of Queensbury, much against his Grace's Inclination.[4] The Town is run mad after a new Opera. Poetry and good Sense are dwindling like Echo into Repetition and Voice. Critick Dennis vows to G— these Opera's will be ruin of the Nation and brings Examples from Antiquity to prove it.[5] A good old Lady five miles out Town, askt me tother day, what these *Uproars* were that her Daughter was always going to. I wish I had the Hon^r to be known to the Envoy, that I might end my Letter with desiring You to present my most humble Service to Him; It is so necessary a Part in the conclusion

[1] William Frowde, in 1694 lieutenant-colonel in Col. Thomas Farrington's Regiment of Foot. In 1704 he was appointed lieutenant-colonel in the First Foot Guards (Dalton's *English Army Lists*, ii. 28, 37; iii. 382; v. 42). Cf. *Journal*, p. 81 n.

[2] Robert Molesworth, when envoy to Denmark in 1692, gave serious offence to the court of Copenhagen. He withdrew from the country and expressed his indignation in writing *An Account of Denmark as it was in the Year 1692* (1694). The statements expressed incensed not only the Danish authorities but also the Tories of England. The Danish envoy supplied William King with material for his anonymous rejoinder *Animadversions on a Pretended Account of Denmark* (1694). This, occupying over 200 pages, was reprinted at the beginning of King's *Miscellanies in Prose and Verse*, which had, as Swift implies, just appeared. For the date of publication see Colin J. Horne in *The Library*, Fourth Series, xxv. 37-45. A word has here been obliterated by Swift.

[3] Tonson's *Poetical Miscellanies. The Sixth Part.* 1709.

[4] On 5 Feb. 1708-9 Rowe became under-secretary to James Douglas, second Duke of Queensberry, who held office as Secretary of State for Scotland.

[5] In his *Essay on the Operas after the Italian Manner*, 1706, John Dennis attacked operas for encouraging a tendency to effeminacy. Later he returned to the attack, stigmatizing them as a corrupting influence.

of an Epistle that I do not know how to supply it. His Brother that dyed last Year was my particular Friend. His Father is also my Acquaintance, so that I seem to have some sort of Title—I am a scurvy Writer, and as I remember you are not very expert at reading an ill Hand; which if I had thought on sooner I would have made mine a little worse, for now you are growing to be a Minister you must learn to decypher.

Let me know if there are any Country houses of Men of Quality in Denmark; because I have a Notion that in all arbitrary[1] Governments they are very scarce.

I forgot you are a Man of Business, but you may read this Letter at three or four reprises you will break no Connection—I am | Your most faithfull | humble Servant | J: Swift.

Address: For Mr Philips, at Copenhagen
Endorsed by Philips: Jonathan Swift—1709—Resp. May. 21.[2]

Hawkesworth 1766[3]
Archbishop King to Swift

Dublin, March 12, 1708[9]

Rev. Sir,

The business of the twentieth parts and first-fruits is still on the anvil. We are given to understand that her Majesty designs, out of her royal bounty, to make a grant of them for charitable uses, and that it is designed this grant should come over with his Excellency the Lord Lieutenant. The Bishops in this town at present thought it reasonable to apprise his Excellency of the affair, and to address him for his favour in it, which accordingly is done by this post. We have sent with this address the representation made at first to her Majesty about it; the reference to the Commissioners of the Revenue here, and their report, together with the memorial to the Lord *Pembroke.* In that there is mention of the state of the diocese of *Dublin,* as a specimen of the condition of the clergy of *Ireland,* by

[1] In his account of Denmark Molesworth represented the Government as arbitrary.
[2] In his account-book, Forster, no. 506, Swift enters after the date 28 May 1709, 'a little before Mr. Philips (From Copenhagen)'.
[3] The text is taken from Hawkesworth 1766. The copy in the manuscript room of Trinity College, Dublin, is not decipherable.

which it will appear how much we stand in need of such a gift. This we could not well send to his Excellency, because it is very long, and we apprehend, that it might be improper to give him so much trouble at first, before he was any way apprised of the matter; but if you think that his Excellency may judge it agreeable that it should be laid before him, I entreat the favour of you to apply to my Lord *Pembroke*'s Secretary, with whom it is, for the original, or a copy of it, and present it to my Lord Lieutenant, or leave it with his Secretary. I have engaged for you to my brethren, that you will be at this trouble; and there is a memorial to this purpose, at the foot of the copy of the representation made to the Earl of *Pembroke*, transmitted with the other papers. What charges you are at upon this account, will be answered by me.

The good impression you have given me of Mr. *Addison*, my Lord Lieutenant's Secretary, has encouraged me to venture a letter to him on this subject, which I have inclosed, and make you the full and sole judge whether it ought to be delivered. I can't be competently informed by any here, whether it may be pertinent or no; but I may and do depend on your prudence in the case, who, I believe, will neither omit what may be useful, nor suffer me to do an officious or improper thing. I mix no other matter with this, besides what agrees with all occasions, the tender of the hearty prayers and wishes for you of, Sir, your, &c.

Will. Dublin.

The reversal of my Lord *Slane*'s outlawry makes a mighty noise through this kingdom: for aught I can remember, the destroying of our wollen manufactory did not cause so universal a consternation.[1]

Address: Care of Sir Andrew Fountaine, Leicester Fields

---

[1] Christopher Fleming, seventeenth Baron of Slane, in Ireland, took up arms for King James. He was attainted, his estate and peerage forfeited. About the time of this letter the English Parliament reversed the attainder. Those who had purchased his property from the Trustees of Forfeited Estates were alarmed. A notice was therefore issued that Protestant purchasers under the authority of an Act of Parliament need fear no invasion of their property rights. Lord Slane was, in Nov. 1713, created Viscount Longford.

Faulkner 1762
Swift to Robert Hunter

London, March 22, 1708–9.

Sir,

I am very much obliged to you for the Favour of a kind Reproach you sent me, in a Letter to Mr. *Addison*, which he never told me of till this Day, and that accidentally; but I am glad at the same Time, that I did not deserve it, having sent you a long Letter, in Return to that you was pleased to honour me with; and, it is a Pity it should be lost; for as I remember, it was full of the *Diei fabulas*, and such Particularities as do not usually find Place in News Papers. Mr. *Addison* hath been so taken up for some Months, in the amphibious Circumstances of premier *C——* to my Lord *Sunderland*, and Secretary of State for *Ireland*, that he is the worst Man I know, either to convey an idle Letter, or deliver what he receiveth; so that I design, when I trust him with this, to give him a Memorial along with it; for if my former hath miscarried, I am half persuaded to give him the Blame. I find you a little lament your Bondage; and indeed in your Case it requires a good Share of Philosophy: But, if you will not be angry, I believe I may have been the Cause you are still a Prisoner, for I imagine my former Letter was intercepted by the French Court, when the most Christian King reading one passage in it, (and duly considering the Weight of the Person who wrote it), where I said, if the *French* King understood your value as well as we do, he would not exchange you for Count *Tallard*, and all the *débris* of *Blenheim* together; for I must confess, I did not rally when I said so.[1]

I hear your good Sister, the Queen of *Pomunki*, waiteth with Impatience until you are restored to your Dominions: and that your Rogue of a Viceroy returneth Money fast for *England*, against the Time he must retire from his Government. Mean Time *Philips* writeth verses in a Sledge, upon the frozen Sea, and transmits them hither, to thrive in our warmer Clime, under the Shelter of my Lord *D***t*.[2] I could send you a great deal of news from the

---

[1] It had been reported in the previous August that Hunter was to be exchanged for the Bishop of Quebec (Luttrell, *Brief Relation*, vi. 336). Marshal Tallard, who had been taken prisoner at Blenheim, remained a prisoner in this country till 1712.

[2] The poem is introduced into the *Tatler*, no. 12, as coming from Copenhagen,

Republica Grubstreetaria, which was never in greater Altitude. though I have been of late but a small Contributor. A Cargo of Splinters from the *Arabian* Rocks have been lately shipwrecked in the *Thames*, to the irreparable Damage of the Vertuosi. Mrs. *Long* and I are fallen out. I shall not trouble you with the Cause, but do not you think her altogether in the Wrong?[1] But Mrs. *Barton*[2] is still in my good Graces; I design to make her tell me when you are to be redeemed, and will send you Word. There it is now, you think I am in Jest; but I assure you the best Intelligence I get of publick Affairs is from Ladies, for the Ministers never tell me any Thing; and Mr. Addison is nine Times more secret to me than any Body else, because I have the Happiness to be thought his Friend. The Company at St. *James*'s Coffee-house is as bad as ever, but it is not quite so good. The Beauties you left are all gone off this Frost, and we have got a new Set for Spring, of which Mrs. *Chetwynd*[3] and Mrs. *Worsley*[4] are the principal. The Vogue of Operas holdeth up wonderfully, altho' we have had them a Year; but I design to set up a Party among the Wits to run them down by next Winter, if true *English* Caprice doth not interpose to save us the Labour. Mademoiselle *Spanheim* is going to marry my Lord *Fitzhardinge*, at least I have heard so;[5] and if you find it otherwise at your Return, the

and 'as fine a Winter-piece, as we have ever had from any of the Schools of the most learned Painters'.

[1] Miss Anne Long was a sister of Sir James Long, Bt., of Draycott, Wiltshire. She was a celebrated beauty and a toast of the Kit-Cat Club. Swift seems to have made her acquaintance through the Vanhomrighs to whom she was related. Owing to financial difficulties she retired to King's Lynn, where she died (*Journal*, 25 Dec. 1711). In Dec. 1707 or Jan. 1708 Swift drew up 'A Decree for concluding the Treaty between Dr. Swift and Mrs. Long', which was printed by Curll in a miscellany collection entitled *Letters, Poems, and Tales: Amorous, Satyrical, and Gallant*, 1718. See *Prose Works*, ed. Temple Scott, xi. 383-6; *Portland MSS.* vii. 284; *Poems*, p. 913 n.

[2] Catherine Barton, niece of Sir Isaac Newton, was a companion of Anne Long. She was a beautiful woman and her relations with Lord Halifax aroused comment. See *Notes and Queries*, 1 S. viii. 258, 429, 543, 590; and *Westminster Abbey Registers* (*Publications of the Harleian Society*), p. 354.

[3] She was the wife of Walter Chetwynd of Ingestre in Staffordshire, afterwards created a Viscount in the Irish peerage, and was daughter of John, fourth Viscount Fitzhardinge. She was appointed a maid of honour to Queen Anne. See *The Chetwynds of Ingestre*, by H. E. Chetwynd-Stapylton.

[4] Frances, only daughter of Sir Robert Worsley, Bt., of Appuldercombe, Isle of Wight, who was married to Lord Carteret on 17 Oct. 1710.

[5] Viscount Fitzhardinge, the father of Mrs. Chetwynd above mentioned,

consequences may possibly be survived; however, you may tell it the *Paris* Gazetteer, and let me have the Pleasure to read a Lye of my own sending. I suppose you have heard, that the Town hath lost an old Duke, and recovered a mad Duchess.—The Duke of *Marlborough* hath at Length found an Enemy that dareth face him, and which he will certainly fly before with the first Opportunity, and we are all of Opinion it will be his wisest Course to do so. Now the Way to be prodigiously witty, would be by keeping you in Suspense, and not letting you know that this Enemy is nothing but this North-east Wind, which stoppeth his Voyage to *Holland*. This Letter going in Mr. *Addison*'s Pacquet will, I hope, have better Luck than the former. I shall go for *Ireland* some Time in Summer, being not able to make my Friends in the Ministry consider my Merits, or their Promises, enough to keep me here; so that all my Hopes now terminate in my Bishoprick of *Virginia*; in the mean Time I hold fast my Claim to your Promise of corresponding with me, and that you will hence-forward address your Letter for me at Mr. *Steele*'s Office at the Cockpit, who hath promised his care in conveying them. Mr. *Domvile*[1] is now at *Geneva*, and sendeth me Word he is become a Convert to the Whigs, by observing the good and ill Effects of Freedom and Slavery Abroad.

I am now with Mr. *Addison*, with whom I have fifty Times drunk your Health since you left us. He is hurrying away for *Ireland*, and I can at present lengthen my Letter no farther; and I am not certain whether you will hear from him or no, until he gets thither. How-ever, he commandeth me to assure you of his humble Service; and, I pray God, too much Business may not spoil *Le plus honnête Homme du Monde*; for it is certain, which of a Man's good Talents he em-ployeth on Business, must be detracted from his Conversation. I cannot write longer in so good Company, and therefore conclude Your most faithful, and most humble Servant,

                                                    J. Swift.

Address: A Monsieur Monsieur Hunter, Gentilhomme Anglois a Paris.

lost his wife six months before this letter was written. Mademoiselle Spanheim, daughter of the Prussian ambassador, did not marry him.
    [1] William Domville. (See note Swift to Ford, 12 Nov. 1708.)

Swift to Primate Marsh

London March. 24. 170⅞

My Lord.[1]

I am commanded by His Excellency the Lord Lieutenant to send the enclosed to Your Grace, in answer to a Letter His Excellency lately received from your Grace, and severall Bishops, relating to the First-fruits of Ireland.[2] This will spare Your Grace and their Lordships the Trouble of any farther Account from me. I shall therefore onely add, that His Excellency commanded me to assure Your Grace of his hearty Inclination in favor of the Church of Ireland. | I am with great Respect | My Lord | Your Grace's | most dutifull and | most obedient Servant, |

J. Swift.

Endorsed by Swift: Copy of a Lett^r to the | Ld Primate of Ired | by Ld Whartons Order | Mar. 24. 170⅞

Faulkner 1762

Swift to Archbishop King

March 26, 1709.

My Lord,

I should have acknowledged your's of *Feb.* 10. long ago, if I had not stayed to see what became of the First Fruits. I have likewise your's of the 12th Instant. I will now tell you the Proceeding in this unhappy Affair. Some Time after the Prince's Death, Lord *Pembroke* sent me Word by Sir *Andrew Fountaine*, that the Queen had granted the Thing, and afterwards took the Compliment I made him upon it. He likewise (I suppose) writ to the same Purpose himself to the

---

[1] Several deletions appear, and alterations of wording, in this draft, before Swift was satisfied with its final form. The draft is written on a sheet folded to form two quarto leaves. The letter appears on the first page; pages 2 and 3 are blank; the endorsement is written on the fourth page.

[2] The letter received by Wharton was the address referred to in Archbishop King's letter to Swift of 12 Mar. On receipt of the Archbishop's letter Swift waited on Wharton, and was, apparently, commissioned by him to forward his reply to the Primate.

Archbishop of *Dublin*.[1] I was then for a long Time pursued by a cruel Illness, that seized me at Fits, and hindered me in meddling in any Business;[2] neither, indeed, could I at all suspect there was any Need to stir any more in this, until, often asking Mr. *Addison* whether he had any Orders about it? I was a little in Pain, and desired Mr. *Addison* to enquire at the Treasury, whether such a Grant had then passed? And, finding an unwillingness, I enquired myself; where Mr. Taylour[3] assured me there was never any Orders for such a Grant. This was a Month ago, and then I began to despair of the whole Thing. Lord *Pembroke* was hard to be seen; neither did I think it worth talking the Matter with him. What perplexed me most was, why he should tell me, and write to *Ireland*, that the Business was done (For if the account he sent to *Ireland* were not as positive as what he gave me, I ought to be told so from thence.) I had no Opportunity of clearing this Matter until the Day I received your last Letter; when his Explanation was, that he had been promised he should carry over the Grant when he returned to *Ireland*, and that his Memorial was now in the Treasury. Yet, when I had formerly begged Leave to follow this Matter with Lord Treasurer only, in the Form of common solliciting, he was uneasy, and told me Lord Treasurer had nothing at all to do with it; but that it was a matter purely between the Queen and himself, (as I have told you in former Letters) which however I knew then to be otherwise, from Lord Treasurer himself. So that all I had left me to do was only the cold Amusement of now and then refreshing Lord *Pembroke*'s Memory, or giving the Ministry, as I could find Opportunity, good Dispositions toward the Thing. Upon this Notice from Lord *Pembroke*, I immediately went to Lord *Wharton* (which was the first attendance I ever paid him.)[4] He was then in a great Crowd; I told him my Business; he said, he could not then discourse of it

---

[1] As on previous occasions when writing to Archbishop King, Swift enclosed this letter in one to Dean Stearne. See Appendix I.

[2] See p. 116, n. 3.

[3] In a letter dated from Treasury Chambers, Whitehall, on 1 Mar. 1704-5, John Taylor writes to Edward Southwell in a jocular strain thanking him for his annual remembrance of him, and reminding him of an account of fees for which he would have seized Southwell's secretary if the secretary had not got away by stealth (B.M. Add. MSS. 21474, f. 88).—Ball.

[4] In his *Memoirs relating to that Change which happened in the Queen's Ministry in the Year 1710* (*Prose Works*, ed Davis, viii. 121) Swift is even more emphatic: 'It was the first time I was ever in company with the Earl of Wharton.'

with me, but would the next Day. I guessed the Meaning of that, and saw the very Person[1] I expected, just come from him. Then I gave him an Account of my Errand. I think it not convenient to repeat here the Particulars of his Answer; but the formal part was this: That he was not yet properly Lord Lieutenant until he was sworn; That he expected the same Application should be made to him, as had been done to other Lord Lieutenants; That he was very well disposed, &c. I took the Boldness to begin answering those Objections, and designed to offer some Reasons; but he rose suddenly, turned off the Discourse, and seemed in Haste; so I was forced to take my Leave.[2] I had an Intention to offer my Reasons in a Memorial; but was advised, by very good Hands, to let it alone, as infallibly to no Purpose. And, in short, I observe such a Reluctance in some Friends whose Credit I would employ, that I begin to think no further of it.

I had writ thus far without receiving[3] a former Letter from the Archbishop of *Dublin*, wherein he tells me positively that Lord *Pembroke* had sent him Word the first Fruits were granted, and that Lord *Wharton* would carry over the Queen's Letter, &c. I appeal to you, What any Man could think after this? Neither, indeed, had I the least Suspicion, until Mr. *Addison* told me he knew nothing of it: And that I had the same Account from the Treasury. It is wonderful a great Minister should make no Difference between a Grant and the Promise of a Grant; and it is as strange that all I could say would not prevail on him to give me Leave to sollicit the finishing of it at the Treasury, which could not have taken the least Grain of Merit from him. Had I the least suspected it had been only a Promise, I would have applied to Lord *Wharton* above two Months ago; and so I believe would the Archbishop of *Dublin* from *Ireland*; which might have prevented, at least, the present Excuse, of not having had the same Application; although others might, I suppose, have been found.

I sent last Post by the Lord Lieutenant's Commands an inclosed

[1] Ball suggests that this person may have been Thomas Brodrick, who had a residence near London, and afterwards became a member of the English House of Commons.

[2] The *Memoirs relating to that Change*, above mentioned, may be further read for an account of Wharton's reception of Swift at their first and subsequent meetings.

[3] The reference is to Archbishop King's letter of 10 Feb., which reached Swift on the 19th.

Letter, from his Excellency to the Lord Primate. In Answer to a Passage in your former Letter; Mr. *Stoughton* is recommended for a Chaplain to the Lord Lieutenant.[1] His Sermon is much recommended by several here. He is a prudent Person, and knows how to time Things. Others of somewhat better Figure are as wise as he. A bold Opinion is a short easy way to Merit, and very necessary for those who have no other.

I am extremely afflicted with a Cold, and Cough attending it, which must excuse any Thing ill-expressed in this Letter.[2] Neither is it a Subject in the present Circumstances very pleasant to dwell upon. I am, &c.

4804

Joseph Addison to Swift

[22 April 1709]

Dear Sir

I am in a very great Hurry of Business but can not forbear thanking you for your Letter at Chester wch was the only good[3] Entertain^mt I met with in that place. I hope to see you very suddenly and will wait on our Friend the Bp of Clogher as soon as I can possibly.[4] I have had just time to tell him en passant that you were well. I long to see you and am

Dear Sir |
Yo^r most Faithfull and most obed^t Servt |
J. Addison

We arrived yesterday
at Dublin[5]
Apr. 22. 1709.

Endorsed: Mr Addison
Apr. 22^d 1709

[1] Honorary chaplain. See p. 124, n. 1.
[2] In his account book, Forster, no. 506, Swift records under March 'headache frequent; towards the end cough a week but ends in a cold', and under April, 'begins with cough, turned to cold, well by the 6th'.
[3] The word 'good' struck through.
[4] Swift's list of letters for this period (Forster, no. 506) shows that when Addison was leaving London Swift handed him a letter for Bishop Ashe dated 9 Apr. The letter received at Chester by Addison was dated the 15th.
[5] Wharton was sworn into office on that day.

The Earl of Berkeley to Swift

Cranford[1] Friday night [22 April 1709][2]

I hope you continue in the mind of coming hither tomorrow: for, upon my sincerity, which is more than most people's, I shall be heartily glad to see you as much as possible before you go for Ireland. Whether you are or are not for Cranford, I earnestly intreat you, if you have not done it already, that you would not fail of having your bookseller enabling the Archbishop of York to give a book[3] to the Queen; for, with Mr. Nelson, I am entirely of opinion, that Her Majestys reading of the book of the Project for the increase of Morality and Piety, may be of very great use to that end. I am, | Entirely yours, | B.

Address: For Dr. Swift at his lodgings in the Haymarket, London
Endorsed by Swift: Old Earl of Berkeley about 1706 or 1707.

Pierpont Morgan Library[4]

Swift to the Earl of Pembroke

Leicester.[5] June. 13. 1709

My Lord.

I am informed, Your Lordship has been pleased to railly upon my Misfortunes, because I have gott an Ailment incommodious for

---

[1] Cranford, the seat of Lord Berkeley, which Swift visited on several occasions, was situated near Hounslow. Nothing remains of the house Swift knew.

[2] The endorsement of this letter, a later guess on Swift's part, has misled editors prior to Ball. There can be no doubt that the letter was written about the above date, which fell on a Friday. Further, in Swift's list of letters (Forster no. 506) he records the receipt of a Letter from Berkeley on 23 Apr. and a reply written on the same day.

[3] The allusion is to Swift's *Project for the Advancement of Religion and the Reformation of Manners*, which was published about the beginning of April. Steele accorded it a complimentary paragraph in the *Tatler*, no. 5, 20 Apr. Swift attributed to the influence of John Sharp, Archbishop of York, the Queen's refusal of any English preferment for him. Robert Nelson was the author of the popular *Companion for the Festivals and Fasts of the Church of England*, 1704. Cf. Nelson's letter to Swift 22 Feb. 1710-11. Nelson had married a sister of Berkeley.

[For notes 4, 5 see overleaf

Riding: But had Your Excellency been Lieutenant of Ireland, if Pelion had been *Piled* upon Ossa, I would have been there before now: But the Truth is, I was ready to fling my Cross or *Pile* (which last is the old Name for a Ship)[1] whether I should go or no; especially at this Juncture, when the Case is what Lucan expresses in the War between Cesar and Pompey; Et *Pila* minantia *Pilis.*

I sent S[r] Andrew Fountain a very learned Description of an old Roman Floor, (I hope he has communicated to D[r] Sloan and D[r] Woodward) which is to be sold a Pennyworth. There are onely two Objections against buying it; First, that it can not be taken up without breaking, and secondly, that it will be too heavy for Carriage.[2] He has fallen out with me, because I can not prevail with a Fellow here to part with three Saxon Coins,[3] which the Owner values as I did My Alexander Seal, and with equall Judgment. There were some Fellows here last Year, that could make Medals faster than

[1] Ball suggests that Swift may have had some mistaken idea as to the origin of the word pilot.

[2] Nichols, *Hist. Leic.* i. 11, 12, mentions Roman pavements found in Leicester in the eighteenth century. See further, for more exact details, *Victoria County History, Leicestershire*, i. 188–97. Sir Hans Sloane was at this time Secretary of the Royal Society, and John Woodward, 1665–1728, was a member of the Council. In the following year, however, he insulted Sloane at a Council meeting and was thereupon expelled.

[3] There was a mint at Leicester in Saxon times, and many coins of the period have been found there (Nichols, *Hist. of Leicestershire*, i. 1. xli). Swift appears to have spent his time at Leicester with the vendors of curios and books. He records while there the purchase of the works of Plato and Xiphilinus for £1.10s., and of five books which he does not describe for £1. 1s. 6d.—Ball.

---

[4] Ball took his text from a copy made by Forster from the original, sold by Sotheby's, 15 Dec. 1906, with other papers and letters from the family collection of Sir Andrew Fountaine at Narford in Norfolk. These manuscripts are now in the Pierpont Morgan Library, New York.

[5] In his account-book, Forster, no. 506, Swift records that he left London on Thursday, 5 May, and reached his mother's house in Leicester on the following Saturday, that is travelling just over thirty miles a day. His route lay through St. Albans, Dunstable, Newport Pagnell, Northampton, and Market Harborough. On the succeeding Friday he started on a five days' visit to Throckmorton in Worcestershire, where he stayed apparently with a relation of Archdeacon Walls (see p. 64, n. 3) whose family belonged to that county. During the last week of May he was the guest of Sir George Beaumont at Stoughton Grange, near Leicester. In the *Journal*, 13 Apr. 1711, Swift recounts calling him out from a dinner of the October Club.

the Padua Brothers,[1] onely they dealt altogether in modern ones; and equally struck them upon the high Road; I desire to know whether they were not properly Pad-way Brothers.

I beg Your Excellency[2] will send me a Commission to be Cap^{tn} of a Man of War of fifty Guns for a Fortnight, till I gett to Ireland. But I can do without it. For if the Coasting Privateers dare ac*coast* me I will so rattle out Your Excellency's Name, that it shall fright them as much as ever Your Ancestor's[3] did at Boulogne. I allways thought Ships had Rats enough of their own without being troubled with Py-R*a*ts. Hence comes the old Proverb; Poison for Rats, and Powder for Py-rats. There is another Proverb in Your Lordship's own Calling, which I suppose You know the Originall of. Ships when they are in Dock are quiet, but at Sea they sting all they come near. Hence came the saying, In Dock, out Nettle.

I shall be at the Sea Side in two days, and shall wish heartily for some of Your Excellency's Snuff against the Bilch Water. In the mean time I humbly beg Your Excellency will order Your Fleets to beat the French this Summer, that we may have a Peace about Michaelmas, and see Your Lordship again in Ireland by Spring: For which a Million of People in that Kingdom would rejoyce as much as my self; and Mr Ash[4] assures me, that whenever Your Excellency comes over, the whole Island will be so enflamed with Joy and Bonfires, that it will all turn to Ashes to receive You.

I am with the greatest Respect | My Lord | Your Excellency's | most obedient, | most oblidged and | most humble Servant

J: Swift

Addressed: For the Right Honorable the | Earl of Pembroke, Lord High | Admirall, &c, at His House in | St James's Square | London
Postmarks: IV 15 LEICESTER
Endorsed by Sir Andrew Fountaine: My L^d with his service to you thanks you not only for your Memoirs but for your punnaide which he is glad you take it being the best cure for your ailment his L^d has left it to me to give you a further dose

---

[1] Juan Cavino of Padua, d. 1570, joined with Alexandre Bassiano to engrave numerous imitations of Greek and Roman coins and medallions.
[2] The title, familiar during Pembroke's viceroyalty, was now inappropriate to Pembroke's office of Lord High Admiral.
[3] Swift is probably referring to the first Earl of the Herbert line of the second creation, a favourite of Henry VIII and an executor of his will. He died in 1570.
[4] The reference will be to the Rev. Dillon Ashe, or his brother Thomas Ashe, who, like Pembroke, found amusement in punning.

B.M. Add. MS. 7121, f. 71¹

Swift to Lord Halifax

Leicester, Jun. 13th, 1709

My Lord.²

Before I leave this Place (where ill Health has detained me longer than I intended), I thought it my Duty to return Your Lordship my Acknowledgments for all Your Favors to me while I was in Town; and at the same time, to beg some share in Your Lordship's Memory, and the Continuance of Your Protection. You were pleased to promise me Your good Offices upon Occasion; which I humbly challenge in two Particulars, One is, that you will sometimes putt, My Lord President³ in mind of me; the other is, that Your Lordship will duly once every Year wish me removed to England. In the meantime, I must take leave to reproach Your Lordship for a most inhuman piece of Cruelty; for I can call Your extreme good Usage of me no better, since it has taught me to hate the Place where I am banished, and raised my Thoughts to an Imagination, that I might live to be some way usefull or entertaining, if I were permitted to live in Town, or, (which is the highest punishment on Papists) any where within ten miles round it. You remember very well, My Lord, how another Person of Quality in Horace's time, used to serve a sort of Fellows who had disoblidged him; how he sent them fine Cloaths, and money, which raised their Thoughts and their Hopes, till those were worn out and spent; and then they were ten times more miserable than before. Hac ego si compellar imagine, cuncta resigno. I could cite severall other Passages from the same Author, to my Purpose; and whatever is applyed to Mecenas I will not

---

¹ The original of this letter is in the British Museum, Add. MS. 7121, f. 71. It has attracted several editors. It was printed in the *New Monthly Magazine*, 1842, lxiv. 3; by Peter Cunningham (who gave the date as 13 Jan.) in his edition of Johnson's *Lives of the English Poets*, iii. 201; and in Ellis's *Original Letters of Eminent Literary Men*, Camden Society, p. 338.

² Charles Montagu entered Parliament in 1689. He displayed a genius for finance; and held several important offices under William III. In 1700 he was created Baron Halifax of Halifax. Swift won his friendship with *Contests and Dissensions* (1701), in which Halifax appears as Pericles and Alcibiades. No real cordiality appears in the friendship, for Swift's two letters to Halifax, this and that of 13 Nov. 1709, are forced in tone. During Queen Anne's reign Halifax remained out of office.

³ Lord Somers.

thank Your Lordship for accepting; because it is what you have
been condemned to these twenty Years by every one of Us qui se
mêlent d'avoir de l'esprit. I have been studying how to be revenged
of Your Lordship, and have found out the way. They have in
Ireland the same idea with Us, of Your Lordship's Generosity,
Magnificence, Witt, Judgment, and Knowledge in the Enjoyment
of Life.[1] But I shall quickly undeceive them, by letting them plainly
know, that you have neither Interest nor fortune which You can call
your own; both having been long made over to the Corporation of
deserving Men in Want, who have appointed You their Advocate
and Steward, which the World is pleased to call Patron and Protector. I shall inform them, that my self and about a dozen others
kept the best Table in England, to which because we admitted Your
Lordship in common with us, made You our Manager, and sometimes allowed you to bring a Friend, therefore ignorant People
would needs take you to be the Owner. And lastly, that you are the
most injudicious Person alive, because, thô you had fifty times more
Witt than all of Us together, you never discover the least Value for
it, but are perpetually countenancing and encouraging that of others.
I could add a great deal more, but shall reserve the rest of my
Threatenings till further Provocation. In the mean time I demand
of Your Lordship the Justice of believing me to be with the greatest
respect | My Lord, |

Your Lordship's | most obedient and | most oblidged humble
Servant |

Jon: Swift.

Pray, My Lord, desire Dr South to dy about the Fall of the
Leaf,[2] for he has a Prebend of Westminster which will make me
your neighbor, and a Sinecure in the Country, both in the Queen's
Gift; which my Friends have often told me would fitt me extreamly.
And forgive me one Word, which I know not what extorts from me;

---

[1] Halifax was a munificent patron of learning. Macky in his *Characters of
the Court of Queen Anne* said of him: 'He is a great encourager of learning and
learned men.' On this Swift wrote a note: 'His encouragements were onely
good words and dinners. I never heard him say one good thing or seem to
taste what was said by another.' *Prose Works*, ed. Temple Scott, x. 275.

[2] The death of the well-known controversialist and preacher, Dr. Robert
South, who was born in 1634, had been rumoured (Luttrell, *Brief Relation*,
vi. 417). He survived till 1716. He was installed Prebendary of Westminster in
1663. The 'Sinecure in the Country' was the rectory of Islip, Oxfordshire.

that if my Ld President would in such a Juncture think me worth
laying any Weight of his Credit [on], you cannot but think me persuaded that it would be a very easy matter to Compass: and I have
some sort of Pretence, since the late King promised me a Prebend
of Westminster, when I petitioned him in Pursuance of a Recommendation I had from Sr William Temple.

Address: For the Right Honorable | the Lord Hallifax at his House | in the New
    Palace Yard in | Westminster | London.
Endorsed: 13 June 1709 from Dr Swift

4804

Joseph Addison to Swift

Dublin Castle June 25, 1709
Dear Sir
    I am heartily glad to hear that you are so near us.¹ If you will
deliver the Enclosed to the Cap^n of the Wolf I dare say he will
accomodate you with all in his power. If he has left Chester I have
sent you a Bill according to the Bp. of Clogher's desire, of whom
I have a thousand good things to say. I do not ask your excuse about
the Yacht because I don't want it as you shall hear at Dublin. If
I did I should think my self Inexcusable.² I long to talk over all affairs
with you and am Ever |

Dear Sir |
Yo^rs most Entirely |
J. Addison
The Yacht will come over wth the Acts of Parl^t, and a Convoy³

¹ Swift's account-book (Forster, no. 506) records that he left Leicester on
Tuesday, 14 June. He travelled that day as far as Stone, stopping for dinner at
Burton on the Hill. The next day, stopping at Nantwich for dinner, he reached
Chester. He remained at Chester twelve days, possibly on account of contrary
winds. On the 27th his boxes were carried to Parkgate; and he embarked on the
29th at Dawpool on the river Dee.
² After arriving at Chester Swift had written to Addison, and to Ashe,
Bishop of Clogher. In his letter to the former he had evidently asked for a
passage in the Government yacht. The yacht was not then available, and Addison
offered him a passage in the *Wolf*, a sloop-of-war guarding the channel. Addison's
letter did not reach Chester until Swift had left, and was sent back after him to
Ireland.
³ Quoting from P.R.O. papers of Ireland, not now extant, Ball notes that—
The officials in London were then 'under great impatience' for bills coming

about a week hence, wch opportunity you may lay hold of if you do
not like the Wolfe. I will give orders accordingly.

Endorsed by Swift: Mr Addison
                           Jun. 25 1709

4804

Joseph Addison to Swift

                              [Dublin Castle, Monday, July 4, 1709][1]
Dear Sir
    I think it is very hard I shoud be in the same Kingdome with
Dr Swift and not have the Happinesse of his Company once in three
days. The Bp of Clogher[2] intends to call on you this morning as will
your Humble Servt in my return from Chappel lizzard[3] whither I
am just now going
                                             Y^r H. Servt
                                                 J. Addison
9. a clock
Munday morning
Endorsed by Swift: Mr Addison | About 1709

over from the Irish Parliament for the approval of the Privy Council in England,
and as no doubt there was equal impatience in Dublin for their return the yacht
had to wait at Parkgate until the messenger came back with them. The necessity
of a convoy was great at that time; shortly before one of the packet-boats had
been captured by a French privateer, and a fleet of ships carrying wool from
Ireland to Bristol, although under the convoy of two men-of-war, had been
attacked by 'seven privateers of the enemy' which were only beaten off with
difficulty.
    [1] The ship in which Swift crossed reached Dublin Bay on Thursday evening,
30 June. The next morning he landed at Ringsend at the mouth of the Liffey,
and 'went straight to Laracor without seeing anybody'. On the following
Monday he returned to Dublin. This letter may have been written on that day,
or a little later.
    [2] Bishop Ashe appears to have seen much of Addison while he was in Ireland.
    [3] Chapelizod on the south side of Phoenix Park, where stood a mansion
used by the Viceroys as a country house (see p. 37, n. 3).

Anthony Henley to Swift

Εὐδαιμονεῖν καὶ Εὐπραττεῖν

[July 1709.][1]

Rev^d S^r.

It is reported of the Famous Regiomontanus, that he framed an Eagle so artfully of a certain wood, that upon the Approach of the Emperor Maximilian to the Opulent City of Neuremberg, it took wing, and flew out of the Gates to meet him: And (as my author has it) appear'd as tho alive. Give me leave to Attribute this excellent invention to the vehement desire he had to Entertain his Master, with something Extraordinary: And to say with the Poet, Amor Addidit Alas. I am trying a like Experiment, whither I cannot make this Composition of Old Raggs, Galls & Vitriol fly to Dublin: And if (as the moving Lion which was compos'd by an Italian Chymist and open'd his breast, and showed the Imperial Arms Painted in its heart) this could disclose it self and discover to you the high Esteem and Affection I have for you, I should attain my End, and not only Sacrifice an Hecatomb, but cry out, with Extatic Archimedes, εὕρηκα.

I should not have presumed to Imagin, that you'd Deign to cast an Eye on any thing proceeding from so mean an hand as mine, Had I not been Incouraged by that Character of candor & Sweetness of temper for which you are so Justly Celebrated and esteem'd by all good men as the Deliciae Humani generis; And I make no Question but like your Predecessor[2] You Reckon Every Day as Lost in which You have not an Opportunity of doing some Act of Beneficence. I was moreover Embolden'd by the Adage which does not stick to Affirm that one of the most despicable of Animals may look upon the Greatest of Queens: As it has been prov'd to a Demonstration by A late most Judicious Author whom (as I take it, you have vouch-

---

[1] Only three letters from Henley to Swift have survived—this and the two earlier letters, 16 Sept. 1708 and 2 Nov. 1708. In Swift's list of letters, 1 Nov. 1708 to 1 Nov. 1709 (Forster, no. 506), the only letter from Henley recorded is under 10 Nov. 1708. Hawkesworth, Sheridan, and Nichols place the above letter under Nov. 1708. The reference to Dublin, however, rules this out, for Swift was not in Dublin during the whole of that year. Scott marks the letter as 'About 1709 or 1710'. The reference to the *Tatler*, which began with the number of 12 Apr. 1709, and the contents of the letter as a whole leave no doubt but that it was written during the summer of 1709.

[2] The words 'an Emperor again' have been struck out.

safd to Immortalize by Your Learned Lucubrations;[1] And as Proverbs are the Wisdom of A Nation, soe I take the Naturalizing such a Quantity of very Expressive ones as we did by the Act of Union, to be one of the Considerablest Advantages wee shall reap from it: And I doe not Question but the Nation will be the Wiser for the future.

But I have digress'd too far and therefore resume my thread. I know my own unworthyness to deserve Your Favour but lett this attempt pass on any Account for some merit. In magnis voluisse sat est.[2] And thô all cannot be sprightly like F—d wise like T—rs Agreeable like B—th Polite like P—r—de, or to summ up all tho there be but one Phœnix and One Lepidissimus Homuncio T—p—m[3] Yet since a Cup of Cold water was not an Unacceptable Present to a Thirsty Emperor, I may flatter my self, that this tender of my Services (how mean soe ever) may not be contemn'd and thô I fall from my great attempt, spero trovar pieta non che Perdono, As that mellifluous Ornament of Italy, Franciscus Petrarcha sweetly has it. Mr Crowther[4] I have often heard affirm, and the fine thinkers of all Ages have constantly held, that much good may be attain by Reading of History, And Dr Sloane is of Opinion, that modern Travels are very behovefull towards forming the mind and Inlarging the thoughts of the Curious part of Mankind.[5]

Give me leave to speak a little from both these Topicks. In the Roman Triumphs which were doubtless the most August Spectacles that were ever Seen it was the Constant custom, that the Publick Executioner should be behind the Conqueror to remind him (says my author) from time to time, that these Honors were Transitory, and could not secure him from the severity of the Laws.[6] Coll:

---

[1] For discussions of Swift's contributions to the *Tatler* see *Prose Works*, ed. Temple Scott, ix. 3; ed. Davis, ii. Introd.

[2] In magnis et voluisse sat est—Propertius ii. 10, 6.

[3] Identifications can be no more than empty surmise. Ball offers improbable guesses.

[4] See p. 120, n. 7.

[5] In 1707 Sir Hans Sloane published the first volume of his famous work, *A Voyage to the Islands of Madera, Barbadoes, Nieves, St. Christopher's, and Jamaica*, dedicated to Queen Anne. The second volume did not appear till 1725.

[6] In Isodorus the part taken in the triumphs by a public slave is said to have been performed by the executioner: 'Quod vero a carnifice contingebantur, id erat judicio, ut ad tantum fastigium evicti mediocritatis humanae commonerentur.'

Morrison of the Guards[1] [He lives next door to Tart-Hall] His
Father was in Virginia and being like to be starv'd, the company had
recourse to a Learned Master of Arts, his name was Venter; He
advis'd them to Eat one another Pour passer le Tems, and to begin
with A fatt Cook-maid. She had Certainly gone to Pott had not a
Shipp arriv'd Just in the nick with a Quantity of Pork, which
Apeasd theyr Hunger, & sav'd the Wenches Bacon.

To apply these; Did you never? [when rioting in the Costly
Daintys of my Lord High Admiral's[2] table, when the Polutasted
wine excited Jovial thoughts & banish'd Serious reflexions] did you
never forget your frail mortal Condition? or when att another tyme,
you have wipd the point of a knife, or perhaps with a little spoon
taken some Attic salt out of Mrs F—s[3] Cadenat; and as the Poet
sings, qui sedens adversus identidem—spectat et audit?[4] Did you
not think your self Par Deo? Pray God you did not; pray God you
did not think your self Superare Divos. Confess the truth, D[r], you
did; Confess it and repent of it, if it be not too late; But, alas I
fear it is.

And now methinks I look down into that Bog all Flaming with
Bonny-clabber & Usquebaugh, & hear you gnashing your teeth
& crying: oh! what would I give now for a glass of that small Beer
which I usd to say was sowre! or a pinch of that Snuff which I
us'd to say was the Cursedst stuff in the world? and Borrow as much
as would Lye on a shilling the minute after; Oh what would I give to
have had a Monitor in those moments to have put me in mind of the
Sword hanging by a twine-thread over my head, and to have cry'd
in a voice as loud as S-th-lls. Memento Doctor, quia Hibernus es
et in Hiberniam reverteris. Every man in the midst of his Pleasures
shoud Remember the Roman Executioner: And I have been assurd
that had it not been for the unfortunate Loss of his R.H. the Prince,
S[r] Charles Duncomb would have reviv'd that usefull Ceremony
which might be very properly introduc'd in the L[d] Mayor's Caval-
cade.[5]

[1] Henry Morryson, captain in the Coldstream Guards. Later he commanded
the 8th Foot, and died in 1720.
[2] Lord Pembroke.
[3] See p. 121, n. 1.
[4] Qui sedens adversus identidem te spactat et audit—Catullus 51, 3–9.
[5] Sir Charles Duncombe, the banker, knighted in 1699, elected Lord Mayor
of London in 1708, died the richest commoner in England (Hearne's *Collections*,
iii. 146). On account of Prince George's death the usual procession was laid

I woud not be mistaken either in what has gone before, or in that which is to follow, as if I took you to be a Belly God, an Apicius, or him that wish'd his neck as long as a Cranes, that he might have the greater pleasure in swallowing; Noe Dear Dʳ far be it from me to think you Epicuri de grege Porcum. I know indeed, you are Helluo, but 'tis Librorum, as the learned Dr. *Accepted Frewen*, sometime A Bp of York was, and *Ingenii*, as the Queint Dr. Offspring Blackall now Bp of Exeter, is.¹ Therefore lett us returne to the Use which may be made of modern Travels, and apply Mr. Morrisons to your Condition.

You are now Cast on an Inhospitable Island, noe Mathematical figures on the Sand, noe Vestigia hominum to be seen, perhaps at this very time reduc'd to one single Barrel of Damag'd Biscuit, and short allowance even of salt-water.² What's to be done? Another in your condition woud look about, perhaps he might find some Potatoes, or gett an old piece of Iron and make a Harpoon and if he found Higgon³ sleeping near the Shoar, strike him and eat him. The Western Islanders of Scotland say tis good meat, and his train oyl, Bottled till it mantles, is a delicious beverage if the Inhabitants of Lapland are to be credited.

But this I know is too gross A Pabulum for one who (as the Camelion lives on air) has allways hitherto livd on Wit; and whose friends God be thanked designe he should continue to doe soe, and on nothing else; Therefore Ide advise you to fall upon Old Joan, Eat Doe I live to bid thee! Eat Addison and when you have eat every body else Eat my Lᵈ Lieutenant [he something lean God help the while]⁴ and thô twill for ought I know, be Treason, there will be noe body left to hang you unless you should think fitt to doe your self that favour; which if you shoud, pray dont write me word

---

aside, and the Mayor, accompanied by some of the alderman, went without ostentation to Westminster Hall to take the oaths. Henley, as a Whig, enjoyed the thrust at a Tory Mayor.

¹ These prelates seem to have been selected by Henley merely from the singularity of their Christian names.

² Forster, *Life*, p. 264 n., observes: 'Though six or seven years were to pass before De Foe's immortal masterpiece was written, there are whimsical foreshadowings of *Crusoe* in Henley's quaint letter.'

³ Henley appears to be referring to the Rev. Francis Higgins, 1669–1728, a violent High Churchman, who was prosecuted for seditious preaching in London in 1707. See *Journal to Stella*, p. 408 and note.

⁴ Lord Wharton.

of it, because I should be very sorry to hear of any Ill that shoud happen to You, as being with a profound Veneration, one of the Greatest of Your Admirers,

> T.B. or any other two
> L^rs you like better.

Pray Direct your answer to me, att the Serjeants head in Cornwall or att Mr Sentiments a Potty Carrier in Common Garden in the Phhs.

4804

Lord Halifax to Swift

6 Octb^r 1709

S^r

Our friend Mr Addison telling Me that He was to write to You to night,[1] I would not let His Packet go away with out telling you how much I am concerned to find them returned without you. I am ashamed for my selfe and my Friends to see you left in a Place, so incapable of tasting you, and to see so much Merit, and so great Qualitys unrewarded by those who are sensible of them. Mr Addison and I are enter'd into a New Confederacy, never to give over the pursuit, nor to cease reminding those, who can serve you, till your worth is placed in that light where it ought to shine. Dr South holds out still, but He can not be immortal,[2] the situation of his prebendary would make me doubly concern'd in serving you, and upon all occasions, that shall offer I will be your constant solicitor, your sincere Admirer, and your unalterable Friend. I am |

Your most humble and | Obedient serv^t |

Halifax.

Endorsed by Swift on page 3: I kept this lett^r as a true | Original of Courtiers & | Court promises.
Endorsed by Swift on page 4: Ld Hallifax | Octr. 6. 1709

[1] Addison had reached England on 19 Sept. (*Philological Quarterly*, Apr. 1937). We find him writing a letter from Chester to Joshua Dawson on the 21st (*Letters of Addison*, ed. Graham, p. 185). In his notebook, Forster, no. 506, Swift recorded the receipt of this letter from Halifax on 23 Oct.

[2] This was a reply to the postscript of Swift's letter to Halifax, written from Leicester, 13 June 1709.

Richard Steele to Swift

Ld Sunderland's Office, Oct^{br} 8th 1709

Dear S^r

Mr. Secretary Addison went this morning out of town, and left behind Him an agreeable command for Me, vizt: to forward the Enclos'd, which Ld Hallifax sent Him for You.[1] I assure You no man could say more in praise of another than He did in Y^r behalfe at that noble Lord's Table on Wednesday last: I doubt not but you will find by the enclos'd the effect it had upon Him: No opportunity is omitted among Powerfull Men to upbraid 'em for your stay in Ireland. The Company that day at Dinner Were Ld Edward Russel Ld Essex, Mr. Maynwaring[2] Mr. Addison, and my self. I have heard such things said of that same Bishop of Clogher,[3] with you, that I have often said that He must be enter'd ad Eundem in our House of Lords. Mr. Philips din'd with me yesterday. He is still a Shepheard,[4] and walks very lonely through this unthinking Crowd in London. I wonder you do not Write sometimes to Me.[5] The Town is in great Expectation from Bickerstaffe.[6] What passed at the

---

[1] The preceding letter from Lord Halifax.

[2] Lord Edward Russell, better known as Lord Orford, and in Nov. 1709 Lord High Admiral. Lord Essex, Algernon Capel, second Earl of Essex. Arthur Mainwaring, or Maynwaring, born in 1668, came of a good and at one time moneyed family. His early sympathies were Jacobite. Later he transferred his pen to the Whig service. Godolphin rewarded him with the auditorship of the imprests in 1705, carrying an income of £8,000. Steele dedicated to him the first volume of the *Tatler*.   [3] St. George Ashe.

[4] The allusion is to Ambrose Philips's *Pastorals*. The first four were first published in Jan. 1708 in Fenton's *Oxford and Cambridge Miscellany Poems*, and later reprinted with two more in Tonson's *Poetical Miscellanies*, vi. 1709.

[5] The table of letters entered by Swift as sent and received during 1708 and 1709 may be accepted as careful and fairly full. While in Leicester in 1709 Swift had sent three letters to Steele on 11 and 26 May and 13 June, and had received one from him on 14 June. Thereafter not till October does Steele's name appear again. On the 23rd of that month Swift noted that he received this letter and dispatched a reply on the 30th.

[6] The paucity of the correspondence between Swift and Steele at this time suggests that the extent of Swift's contribution to the *Tatler* is less than has often been supposed. A full discussion of the question in a footnote would occupy pages. See *Prose Works*, ed. Temple Scott, ix. 1–66; ed. Herbert Davis, ii, pp. xxvi–xxxii, 235–47; Rae Blanchard, *Correspondence of Richard Steele*, p. 34 n.; and Ball, *Corresp.* of Swift, i. 167 n.

Election for His first Table¹ being to be publish'd this day sen'night:
I have not seen Ben Tooke² a Great while but long to Usher you
and Yours into the World not that there can be any thing added by
me to Yʳ Fame, but to walk bareheaded before you.

I am, | Sʳ,
Yʳ Most Obedient & | Most Humble Servant |
Richᵈ Steele

Roger Barrett

Swift to Ambrose Philips

Octᵇ 30ᵗʰ 1709

Sʳ3

I was surprised to find in a Letter from Mʳ Steel, that you are
now in London,⁴ and am at a Loss whether publick or private
Business hath brought you over. Your comeing over has spoilt a
Letter I had half writt to send you to Copenhagen. It was not
Lazyness, Spleen or Neglect that made me omitt acknoledging two
of yours so long;⁵ but downright Sickness, which after a years
pursuing, now I hope begins to leave me, when I am, in the Country,

---

¹ A reference to the *Tatler*, no. 81, which has been attributed to Swift, as
also other papers of the series, numbers 67, 68, and 74. He may have supplied
the hint but it is more likely that Steele and Addison wrote these papers.

² Swift's bookseller to whom he had sold the copyright of the third part of
Temple's *Memoirs*. There was evidently at this time some thought of an introduction by Steele to a collection of Swift's miscellaneous writings; but by the
middle of the following year this proposal had ceased to commend itself to
Swift. On 29 June 1710 he wrote to Tooke: 'I would not have you think of Steele
for a publisher . . . I will, one of these days, send you some hints . . . and you
may get some friend to dress them up.' The volume was finally published by
John Morphew, on 27 Feb. 1711, as *Miscellanies in Prose and Verse*.

³ This letter was first printed by Nichols, *Lit. Illustr.* iv. 730–1. The original,
as was also Swift's letter to Philips of 20 Oct. 1708, was then in the possession
of William Upcott, antiquary and collector, for whom see *D.N.B.* This later
letter is now in the collection of Mr. Roger Barrett, of Kenilworth, Illinois, to
whom acknowledgement is due for permission to print from it.

⁴ In the previous letter Steele mentions that Philips dined with him in London.

⁵ From Swift's list of letters, Forster no. 506, it appears that he had received
letters from Philips 22 Feb. 1709 (Copenhagen), again from Copenhagen,
towards the end of May, on 16 Aug., and a letter on 30 Oct., which arrived
while Swift was writing this letter to Philips.

cultivating half an Acre of Irish bog.[1] The Tasts you sent me of Northern Eloquence are very extraordinary; They seem to have heard there is such a Thing in the World as Witt and Sublime; and not knowing better they supply the want of both with sounding words; That which vexes me is the Difficulty in construing their Latin, and keeping my Breath so long between a Relative and antecedent, or a Noun and a Verb . . . I could match you with Irish Poetry, and printed Latin Poetry too, but Mr Addison shewd it me, and can give you the best Account of it.

You are a better Bickerstaff than I; for you foretold all the Circumstances how I should receive your last Pacquet with the honorary Memoriall of Monsieur I don't know who. My Ld Wharton gave me the Letter. I went aside and opened it, and people throngd about me to ask what it was; and I shewd it His Excellency.

My Heart is absolutely broke with the Misfortunes of K. of Sweden nothing pleased me more in the Thoughts of going abroad than some hopes I had of being sent to that Court. And now to see that poltroon Augustus putting out his Manifestoes and pretending again to Poland after the tame Submissions he made![2] It puts me in mind of the sick Lyon in the Fable, among all the Insults offered him nothing vexed him so much as the Spurns of an Ass. I hope you are laying in new Stocks to revive your Poeticall Reputation. But I am wholly in the dark about you, whether you have left the North, or are onely sent back on an Ambessy from the Envoy. You have the best friend in the World, Mr Addison, who is never at ease while any man of worth is not so; and Mr Steel is alter ab illo. What says Ld Dorset. You had not me for a Councellr when you chose him for a Patron. Is Coll Hunter gone to his Governmt;[3] he is mechant homme, and he never writt to me since he came from France, and I came to Ireld. Your Coll Wayly[4] and I

---

[1] In his account-book, Forster no. 506, Swift notes that during August he suffered from giddiness. This, however, did not prevent him from spending more time away than in residence at Laracor.

[2] The allusion is to the defeat of Charles XII of Sweden at Pultawa by Peter the Great on 8 July 1709; the flight of Charles across the Turkish frontier; and the revocation of the Treaty of Altranstadt by Augustus II of Poland.

[3] Hunter, who had been appointed Governor of New York whither he sailed early in 1710.

[4] The reference is probably to Bernard Whaley. According to Dalton (*English Army Lists*, v. 182) his regiment was stationed in Ireland for some years before 1707, when it embarked for the West Indies. It may not have sailed until a

are mighty good Acquaintance, he loves and esteems you much, and I am sorry that Expedition did not hold. When you write any more Poetry do me honor, mention me in it: tis the common Request of Tully and Pliny to the great Authors of their Age; and I will contrive it so, that Pr.[1] Posterity shall know I was favored by the Men of Witt in my Time. Pray send me word how your Affairs are, that I may order my manner of writing to you accordingly, and remember me sometimes in your walks up the Park, and wish for me amongst you. I reckon no man is throughly miserable unless he be condemnd to live in Ireland; and yet I have not the Spleen; for I was not born to it. And let me know whether the North has coold your Geneva flames, but you have one Comfort that the Loss of the Ladyes Fortunes will encrease her Love, and assure you her Person, and you may now be out of Pain of y^r Rival Monsr le Baron.

Pray write to me, and remember me, and drink my health sometimes with our Friends, and believe me ever your most Faithfull & | most humble Ser^vt | J: Swift

Address: To Mr Philips
Endorsed (by Ambrose Philips?) Dr Swift | 1709 | Resp. March 8. 1710[2]

Alfred Morrison Catalogue
Swift to Lady Giffard

Nov^br 10th 1709
Madam.[3]

I had some time ago the Honor of a Letter from Your Ladyship, which I could not acknowledge so soon as I intended, because I was in the Country (as I still am) and had onely heard of an Advertise-

later date; or Whaley was left behind for special duty. He did not become lieutenant-colonel of his regiment until 1712, but may previously have been given brevet rank.—Ball.   [1] i.e. Prince.

[2] There is no trace of any reply to Swift by Philips in Mar. 1710. The above letter is the last forthcoming of any addressed to Swift.

[3] The original of the facsimile in the Morrison *Catalogue of Autograph Letters and Historical Documents*, vi. 218, has not been traced. This letter, with the omission of the two opening sentences, was printed by Courtenay in his *Life of Temple*, ii. 243. The letter of 10 Nov. 1709 is the only one passing between Swift and Lady Giffard which has come down to us. In his letter list (Forster, no. 506) he records the receipt of a letter from Lady Giffard on 6 Aug. 1709. To this he replied on 17 Aug. Her next letter he received on 6 Oct., and to

ment you were pleased to putt out against me, and in order to ruin my Reputation. In a short time after, severall of my Friends in London sent me that Advertisement, but, their Pacquets[1] coming to the Secretaryes Office[1] here, they were not conveyd to me till very lately. The Writer of the Postman, pleads for his Excuse that the Advertisement was taken in and printed without his Knowledge, and that he refused to repeat it, tho urged by that same Mr Wilcocks from My Lord Berkeleys[2] in Dover street, in Your Ladyship's name. He thought it too unChristian a Thing for him to defend. But all that shall not provoke me to do a disrespectfull Action to Y^r Ladyship, or any of Sr Wm Temple's Family; and therefore I have directed an Answer wholly consistent with Religion and good Manners.

I wonder why your Ladyship will please to see a Contradiction where I hope there is none. By particular Commands, one thing is understood, and by generall ones another. And I might insist upon it, that I had particular Commands for every Thing I did, though more particular for some than for others. Your Ladyship says, if ever they were designed to be printed, it must have been from the Originall. Nothing of his ever printed in my Time was from the Originall; the first Memoirs was from my Copy; so were the Second Miscellanea: so was the Introduction to the English History: so was every Volume of Letters,[3] They were all copied from the Originals by Sr Wm Temples direction, and corrected all along by his Orders; and it was the same with these last Memoirs: So that whatever be

this he is now replying, writing from Laracor. He had also received a copy of the *Postman* in which Lady Giffard had published an advertisement accusing him of having printed the third part of Temple's *Memoirs* from an unfaithful copy. The publication of this volume of the *Memoirs* was advertised in the *Daily Courant*, 30 June 1709, and frequently thereafter. The whole story is not before us. In his will Temple left no directions as to the disposal of his writings; and the autographs remained with his representatives. It may be, however, that Lady Giffard's objection to the publication was the disparagement of Arthur Capel, first Earl of Essex, whose widow was one of Lady Giffard's close friends.

[1] The packets were probably sent by Addison with his official letters to Dublin Castle to save postage. Under date of 30 Oct. Swift notes the receipt of letters from Addison, Philips, and Fountaine. Morrison read the words 'Secretary's Office' as 'Surcharge Office'.

[2] The reference is not to Swift's patron, the Earl of Berkeley, but to William, fourth Baron Berkeley of Stratton, who had married a niece of Lady Giffard, a daughter of her brother Sir John Temple.

[3] The three works first mentioned were published in Temple's lifetime; the *Letters* in 1699, 1700, and 1701.

printed since I had the Honor to know him, was an unfaithfull Copy if it must be tryed by the Originall. Madam; I pretend not to have had the least Share in Sr Wm Temples Confidence above his Relations, or his commonest Friends; (I have but too good Reason to think otherwise). But this was a thing in my way; and it was no more than to prefer the Advice of a lawyer or even of a Tradesman before that of his Friends, in Things that related to their Callings. Nobody else had conversed so much with his Manuscripts as I, and since I was not wholly illiterate, I cannot imagine whom else he could leave the Care of his Writings to.

I do not expect Your Ladyship or Family will ask my Leave for what you are to say; but all People should ask leave of Reason and Religion rather than of Resentment. And will your Ladyship think indeed that is agreeable to either to reflect in print upon the Veracity of an innocent Man. Is it agreeable to Prudence or at least to Caution, to do that which might break all Measures with any Man who is capable of retaliating. Your Nephews[1] say the printed Copy differs from the Originall in fourty Places, as to words, and manner of Expression; I believe it may in a hundred;[2] It is the same or more in all he ever printed in my memory; And that passage about my Ld Sunderland was left out by his Consent; thô to say the Truth at my Intreaty; and I would fain have prevailed to have left out another.[3] Your Ladyship is misinformed by those who told you I ever left any Papers in Booksellers Hands or any others, which I protest I never did a Minute, nor ever shall; I had too much warning by the Papers left with Sr Ro^bt Southwell, which fell into Booksellers Hands.[4] I might add a great deal more to what I have s^d; and I

---

[1] The reference is to Henry and John Temple, sons of Sir William's younger brother Sir John Temple.

[2] The original is in the British Museum (Add. MS. 9804). The variants between the original and the printed text are trifling, and not above twenty in number. The insinuation that Swift garbled the text will not bear examination.

[3] The words relating to Lord Sunderland which were omitted described him as 'breaking all measures' with Temple when both were members of the revived Privy Council, 1679. Swift himself, it should be noted, was anxious to gain the patronage of Charles Spencer, third Earl of Sunderland, and would naturally avoid any disparaging allusion to his father. In his own preface to the *Memoirs* he refers to Temple's readiness to 'commend the Abilities and Virtue' of deserving statesmen 'particularly of the late Earl of Sunderland'. This commendation does not appear in the *Memoirs*.

[4] Presumably the allusion is to the second part of Temple's *Memoirs*. See Courtenay's *Life of Temple*, ii. 152–3.

cannot accuse my self of one single Action of Disrespect to Y^r Lady-ship or family; Those Memoirs were printed by a correct Copy exactly after the same manner as the Authors other works were: He told me a dozen times, upon asking him, that it was his intention they should be printed after his Death, but never fixed any thing about the Time. The Corrections were all his own, ordering me to correct in my Copy as I rec^d it, as he allways did. Knowing y^r Lady-ship's Opinion was against their publishing, I did it without y^r Knowledge, on purpose to leave you wholly without Blame; and I humbly conceive it would have been enough to have S^d so in the Advertisement, without adding the Words (unfaithfull Copy) to wch I should have been content to Submitt. I am with great Respect Madam

    Your Ladyships | most obedient | humble Servant |

                                   J. Swift.

I forgot to answer one thing y^r Ladyship says; You wonder why I should complain of y^r refusing me those Papers when I was pos-sessed of correct Copyes: It was because I could not possibly be secure while there were any Copyes out of my Possession, and those sometimes as your Ladyship owned to me, lent abroad; and besides I knew that they justly belonged to me, and it was the Fear of that uncorrect Originall getting abroad, made me publish mine; which I might still have deferred, had the other been in my Power, and had I been sure no straggling Copy were in the hands of any body else.

Address: For my Lady Giffard at her | House in Dover Street | London.
Endorsed: Dr Jon. Swift to | Lady Giffard. | Nov: 10. 1709.

B.M. Add. MS. 7121, f. 71¹

Swift to Lord Halifax

                                 Dublin Nov^{br} 13. 1709.²
My Lord

I cannot but pity Your Lordships misfortune in being a great Man, by which Disadvantage You are never qualifyed to receive

¹ The original of this letter is in the B.M. Add. MS. 7121, f. 71. There is also a transcript in the Forster Collection, no. 555. As in the previous letter of Swift to Halifax, 13 June 1709, this letter was first printed in the *New Monthly Magazine* for 1842 (vol. lxiv); thereafter in Peter Cunningham's edition of

[For note 2 see overleaf.

such Letters as You write; but instead of them onely tedious Expressions of Respect and Gratitude; wherein you are generally deceived too: For I believe it is with Gratitude as with Love, the more a Man has of it at heart, he is but the worse at expressing it. Such Reflections as these were occasioned by the Honor of Your Lordship's Letter;[1] and what is yet worse, I am afraid I have discovered through all Your Lordship's Civilityes, that I have some Share in your Favor; and God knows what Deductions a Man may draw from thence, tho he had no Vanity to assist him: I ever thought it a mighty Oversight in Courts to let the honête homme, the homme d'esprit, and the homme de bien gain ground among them, because those Qualityes will be sure to predominate over Business and Greatness, as they now do with Your Lordship, who against all Forms is pleased to remember a useless Man at so great a Distance, where it would be pardonable for his idlest Friends, and of his own Level to forget Him. I Joyn with your Lordship in one Compliment, because it is grounded on so true a Knoledge of the Tast of this country, where I can assure you, and I call Mr Addison for my Witness, I pass as undistinguished, in every Point that is Merit with Your Lordship, as any Man in it. But then I do them impartiall Justice; for except the Bishop of Clogher, and perhaps one or two more, my Opinion is extremely uniform of the whole Kingdom.[2] However, I retire into my self with great Satisfaction, and remembering I have had the Honor to converse with Your Lordship, I say as Horace did when he meant Your Predecessor; Cum magnis vixisse invita fatebitur usque invidia.[3] Yet for all this, if I had a mind to be malicious, I could make a Vanity at your Lordships Ex-

[1] 6 Oct. 1709.
[2] Bishop Ashe was a man of more than average attainments. Educated at Trinity College, Dublin, he became a Fellow in 1679, and Provost in 1692, at the age of about thirty-five. He was a Fellow of the Royal Society, interested both in science and mathematics. In 1695 he was appointed Bishop of Cloyne; translated to Clogher in 1697; and to Derry in 1716–17, not long before his death.
[3] Hor. *Sat.* II. i. 76.

Johnson's *Lives of the English Poets*, vol. iii; and in Ellis's *Letters of Eminent Literary Men*, Camden Society.
[2] Swift's account-book shows that at this time, until 18 Nov., he was at Laracor. Ball suggests that as 13 Nov. in 1709 was a Sunday Swift may have gone up to Dublin to preach as a prebendary of St. Patrick's; or he may have thought Dublin a more imposing address than Laracor when writing to Halifax.

pence, by letting People here know that I have some Share in Your Esteem. For I must inform You to Your great Mortification; that Your Lordship is universally admired by this tastless People. But not to humble You too much, I find it is for no other Reason, than that for which Women are so fond of those they call the Witts, meerly for their Reputation. They have heard wonderful Things of Your Lordship, and they presently imagine You to possess those Qualityes they most esteem in themselves, as the Asses did when they discoursed about Socrates. For if Your Lordship were here in disguise, perhaps it would be just as if you sent your Pictures and Statues to a Country Fair; where One would offer half a crown for a Piece of Titian to stick on a Sign-post, Another a shilling for a Grecian Statue to fright away the Crows. Which Thought I have a Mind to make into a Fable and putt it on Mr Addison for an old one, in revenge for his putting that of Socrates and the Asses upon me, because it scaped his Reading.

Can your Lordship pardon so tedious a Letter in Parliament time. Put it under Your Couch, I advise you My Lord, as I remember you use to do the dull Poems and Pamphlets that come out, till the End of the Sessions: Otherwise I shall be tempted to laugh with Pride when I consider my own Power. How I was able at this distance to putt a Stop to the whole Course of Publick Business. How I deferred some new Scheam for supplying the war in all these Exigencyes without burthening the Subject; how I suspended some Law wherein the Welfare of ten Millions was concerned; and how I withheld the Peace of Europe for four minutes together.

Yet all these are Trifles in comparison of having such a Sollicitor as Your Lordship of which I will make this use, that if you think this gentle Winter will not carry off Dr South,[1] or that his Reversion is not to be compassed Your Lordship would please to use your Credit, that as My Lord Somers thought of me last year for the Bishoprick of Waterford, so my Lord President may now think on me, for that of Cork,[2] if the Incumbent dyes of the Spotted Fever he is now under; and then I shall be sure of the Honor to pass some Winters at your Lordship's Levee; though not with equall Satisfaction as in the former Case. | I am, with the greatest Respect | my

---

[1] Dr. South, see p. 143, n. 2.
[2] Dive Downes, then Bishop of Cork and Ross. Born in England, he was educated at Trinity College, Dublin, of which he was elected a Fellow in 1675. He died on the very day on which Swift was writing this letter.

Swift to Lord Halifax   *13 November 1709*

Lord | Your Lordships | most obedient | most oblidged and | most
humble Servt

                                                              J. Swift.

Endorsed: 13 Novemb^r 1709 | From Dr Swift.

Nichols 1801

Swift to the Earl of Pembroke

                                                    [December 1709.]¹

My Lord,

It is now a good while since I resolved to take some occasions
of congratulating with your Lordship, and condoling with the
publick upon your Lordship's leaving the Admiralty;² and I thought
I could never choose a better time, than when I am in the country
with my Lord Bishop of Clogher, and his brother the Doctor;³ for
we pretend to a *triumvirate* of as humble servants and true admirers
of your Lordship, as any you have in both islands. You may call
them a *triumvirate*; for, if you please to *try-um*, they will *vie* with
the best, and are of the first *rate*, though they are not *men-of-war*,
but men of the Church. To say the truth, it was a pity your Lordship should be confined to the *Fleet*, when you are not in debt.
Though your Lordship is *cast away*, you are not *sunk*; nor ever will
be, since nothing is out of your Lordship's *depth*. Dr. Ashe says, it
is but justice that your Lordship, who is a man of *letters*, should be
placed upon the *post-office*; and my Lord Bishop adds, that he hopes
to see your Lordship tossed from that *post* to be a *pillar* of state

¹ As has been mentioned Swift set out on 18 Nov. from Laracor to pay
a visit to Bishop Ashe at his episcopal residence which was situated at
Clogher in the county of Tyrone. He arrived there four days later, and remained
the Bishop's guest until 19 Dec., when he returned to Laracor. It is evident
from the contents that this letter was written by Swift while on this visit. In
connexion with his journey to Clogher it is curious to note that the portion of
the journey from Virginia to Cavan, a distance of some fifteen miles, was performed on a Sunday. At both of those places Swift stayed at an inn.—Ball.
² On Lord Pembroke's retirement from that office. Lord Orford succeeded
him as Lord High Admiral on 8 Nov.
³ Allusion has been made to the fondness for puns and plays upon words of
Lord Pembroke and Dillon Ashe the Bishop's brother.

160

again; which he desired I would put in by way of *postscript*. I am, my Lord, &c.

4804

Joseph Addison to Swift

No 5 St Jame's Place. Apr. 11th 1710

Sir

I have run so much in debt with you that I don't know how to excuse my self and therefore shall throw my self wholly upon your good nature and promise if you will pardon what is passed to be more punctual with you for the future. I hope to have the Happinesse of waiting on you very suddenly at Dublin, and do not at all regrette the leaving of England whilst I am going to a place where I shall have the satisfaction and Honour of Dr. Swift's conversation. I shall not trouble you with any occurrences here because I hope to have the pleasure of talking over all affaires with you very suddenly. We hope to be at Holy-Head by the 30th Instant.[1] Lady Wharton stays in England. I suppose you know that I have obeyed yours and the Bishop of Clogher's commands in relation to Mr Smith,[2] for I desired Mr Dawson[3] to acquaint you with it. I must beg my most Humble Duty to the Bishop of Clogher. I heartily long to eat a dish of Bacon and Beans in the best company in the world. Mr Steel and I often drink your Health. I am forced to give my self Airs of a punctual Correspond^{ce} with you in discourse with your friends at St James's Coffee-house[4] who are always asking me Questions about you when they have a mind to pay their Court to me, if I may use so magnificent a Phrase. Pray Dear Doctour continue your

---

[1] Addison arrived in Dublin for the second time with Lord Wharton on 7 May.

[2] The reference may be, but doubtfully, to William Smith, or Smyth, a Dublin physician, who received his doctorate at Trinity College in 1692. He was five times President of the College of Physicians. He died in 1732. He is mentioned twice in the *Journal to Stella* on 17 June 1712.

[3] Joshua Dawson, Under-Secretary at Dublin Castle. There are many references to him in Swift's letters, for it was one of his privileges to issue, on payment of a fee, licences for absence from Ireland. A street in Dublin is named after him. After the accession of George I he was displaced from office.

[4] St. James's Coffee-house stood at the lower end of St. James's Street. It was a resort of Whigs and a favourite meeting-place of Irish visitors to London. See *Memorials of St. James's Street*, E. Beresford Chancellor, pp. 170-5.

friendship towards one who Loves and esteems You, if possible, as much as you deserve. |

I am ever Dear Sir |
Yo^{rs} Entirely |
J. Addison

Endorsed by Swift: Mr Addison |
Apr. 11th, 1710

4804

Swift to Dean Stearne

Laracor, Apr 17 1710[1]

S^r

You have putt me under a necessity of writing you a very scurvy Lettr, and in a very scurvy manner. It is the wont of Horses, and not of Inclination, that hinders me from attending you at the Chapter; but I would do it on foot to see you Visit in your own Right. But if I must be visited by Proxy, by Proxy I will appear.[2] The Ladyes of St Mary's deliver'd me your Commands, but Mrs Johnson had dropd half of them by the shaking of her Horse. However I have made a shift by the Assistance of two Civilians, and a Book of Presedents to send you the Jargon annexed, with a Blank for the name and Title of any Prebendary who will have the Charity to answer for me; Those two words, *gravi incommodo*, are to be translated, the want of a Horse.[3] In a few days I expect to hear the two Ladyes lamenting the Flesh-pots of Cavan Street.[4] I advise them since they have given up their Title and Lodgings of St Mary's, to buy each of them a palfrey, and take a Squire and seek Adventures. I am here quarrelling with the frosty weather, for spoiling my poor half dozen of Blossoms. Spes anni collapsa ruit, whether those words be mine or Virgils, I cannot determine. Pray

---

[1] During the first three months of this year Swift divided his time between Trim, Laracor, and Dublin. On 8 Apr. he came to Laracor and there remained till June, as his account-book (Forster, no. 507) informs us. The 'Ladyes of St. Mary's', Stella and Rebecca, joined him on the day before this letter was written, possibly occupying a cottage to which Stella's name was later attached.

[2] Swift was seeking a proxy for his appearance as Prebendary of Dunlavin at Archbishop King's visitation.

[3] Swift records, however, Nov. 1709, before his visit to Clogher, the purchase of a horse for £6. 5s.

[4] The Deanery of St. Patrick's is situated in Cavan, otherwise Kevin Street.

S^r favor me so far as to present my Duty to my Lord Bishop of Cork,¹ and I wish he knew how concerned I was not to find him at home when I went to wait on him before I left the Town. I am this minute very busy, being to preach to day before an Audience of at least 15 People, most of them Gentle, and all Simple.

I can send you no News; only the Employment of my Parishioners may for memory-sake be reduced under these Heads, Mr Percivall is ditching,² Mrs Percivall in her Kitchin, Mr Wesly switching,³ Mrs Wesley stiching, Sr Arthur Langford,⁴ riching, which is a new word for heaping up Riches; I know no other Rhime but Bitching, and that I hope we are all past. Well Sir, long may you live the Hospital Owner of good Bits good Books and good Buildings. The Bp of Clogher would envy me for those three B's. I am Y^r most obedient humble Servt

J. Swift.

Addressed: To the Reverend Dr John Stearne | Dean of St Patrick's, at his House | in Cavan-Street | Dublin.
Postmark: 17 AP

Faulkner 1762

Joseph Addison to Swift

Dublin, June 3, 1710.⁵

Dear Sir,

I am just now come from *Finglas*, where I have been drinking your Health and talking of you with one who loves and admires you

---

¹ Dr. Peter Browne, Provost of Trinity College since 1699, was consecrated Bishop of Cork and Ross on 8 Apr. 1710. He was held in high esteem for his learning and piety. Although named as one of Stella's friends (*Prose Works*, ed. Temple Scott, xi. 134), Swift seems to have regarded him doubtfully (*Journal*, p. 596).
² John Percival of Knightsbrook in Swift's parish. In 1716 he sold twenty acres for the glebe of Laracor.
³ Dangan, the paternal home of the Duke of Wellington, was at this time the residence of Garrett Wesley, M.P. successively for Trim and the county of Meath in the Irish Parliament.
⁴ Sir Arthur Langford, who inherited a baronetcy from his father, belonged to an English family which had migrated to Antrim. He resided at Summerhill in the parish of Laracor. As will be seen later he distressed Swift by the establishment of a Presbyterian chapel at Summerhill.
⁵ Addison, as stated before, had arrived in Dublin on 7 May.

better than any Man in the World, except your humble Servant.[1]
We both agree in a Request, that you will set out for *Dublin* as soon
as possible.[2] To tell you truly, I find the Place disagreeable, and
cannot imagine, why it should appear so now, more than it did last
Year.[3] You know, I look upon every Thing that is like a Compliment
as a Breach of Friendship; and therefore, shall only tell you, that I
long to see you, without assuring you, that I love your Company
and value your Conversation more than any Man's, or that I am,
with the most inviolable Sincerity and Esteem, | Dear Sir, | Your
most faithful, | Most humble, and | Most Obedient Servant, |

J. Addison.

4804

Sir Andrew Fountaine to Swift

June 27. 1710

I neither can nor will have patience any longer, and Swift you are
a confounded son of a —. May your halfe acre turn to a Bog, and
may your Willows perish; May the worms eat your Plato,[4] and may
Parvisoll break your snuff-box. What! because there is never a Bp
with halfe the Wit of St George Ash, nor ever a Secretary of State
with a quarter of Addisons good sense, therefore you cant write to
those that love you as well as any Clogher or Addison of 'em all.[5]

---

[1] Dillon Ashe, who seems to have been a good and constant resident at his
rectory. At this time Thomas Ashe, his brother, lived at a place called Ballygall
in the parish of Finglas. Stella had stayed for the last week in the previous
January at Ballygall.

[2] On 10 May, 'between seven and eight in the evening', Swift received at
Laracor the news of the death of his mother (*Prose Works*, ed. Temple Scott, xi.
387). As Ball suggests, this may have induced him to linger longer at Laracor
than he had originally intended.

[3] Finglas appears to have been the favourite haunt of Swift and Addison in
the previous year (Forster Collection, no. 506). Although tradition connects
Addison's residence in Ireland with the suburb of Glasnevin through which
the road to Finglas passes, his normal residence was in official apartments in
Dublin castle, and any significant association with Finglas is questionable.

[4] Two folio editions of Plato appear in the sale catalogue of Swift's books—
no. 78, *Platonis Opera Grae-Lat. cum notis Jo: Serrani, in 3 vol. Curâ Hen.
Steph. 1578*, and no. 588, *Platonis Opera omnia Latinè, studio Mons. Ficini Basil.
1546*. The former of these two was a highly esteemed edition.

[5] After he had left London Swift and Fountaine corresponded with fair

You have lost your reputation here, and that of your Bastard the Tattler is going too; and there is no way left to recover either but your writing. Well! tis no matter; Ile een leave London; Kingsmill is dead, and you dont write to me; Adieu.

Address: To the Revd Dr. Swift at Mr Currys | over agst the Ram in Capell-Street | Dublin | Ireland.[1]
Endorsed by Swift: S[r] And Fountaine

Deane Swift 1765

Swift to Benjamin Tooke

Dublin, June 29, 1710.

Sir,

I was in the country when I received your letter with the Apology inclosed in it; and I had neither health nor humour to finish that business. But the blame rests with you, that if you thought it time, you did not print it when you had it.[2] I have just now your last, with the complete Key.[3] I believe it is so perfect a Grub-street-piece, it will be forgotten in a week. But it is strange that there can be no satisfaction against a Bookseller for publishing names in so bold a manner. I wish some lawyer could advise you how I might have satisfaction: For, at this rate, there is no book, however so vile, which may not be fastened on me. I cannot but think that little

regularity in May, June, July 1709. One letter was dispatched to Fountaine in August and one in October. Between Nov. 1709 and Nov. 1710 Swift ceased to keep a full list of letters, and we have no means of knowing how many, if any, passed between them.

[1] Capel Street was named after Arthur Capel, Earl of Essex, Lord Lieutenant 1672-7. Here Swift was near the lodgings of Stella and Rebecca Dingley.

[2] The fifth edition of *A Tale of a Tub* did not appear till late in the year 1710. The 'Apology' prefixed to it was a thought which occurred to Swift as early as Oct. or Nov. 1708. From Leicester, in 1709, Swift had written several letters to Tooke, and it is probable that a copy of the 'Apology' was enclosed in one of these and was now returned by Tooke. Swift's letter to Tooke and Tooke's reply leave no doubt as to the authorship of the 'Apology'. Consult, further, *A Tale of a Tub*, ed. Guthkelch and Nichol Smith, pp. xix-xxi and *Prose Works*, ed. Davis, vol. i, Introduction.

[3] Curll's *Complete Key to the Tale of a Tub*, advertised as published 20 June 1710, attributed the composition of *A Tale* to Thomas Swift and Jonathan conjointly, the more important part to the former. This worthless story has long been disproved. See Guthkelch and Nichol Smith, op. cit., pp. xiv-xvi. In the same work *A Complete Key* is reprinted in full, pp. 325-42.

Parson-cousin of mine is at the bottom of this; for, having lent him a copy of some part of, &c. and he shewing it, after I was gone for Ireland, and the thing abroad, he affected to talk suspiciously, as if he had some share in it. If he should happen to be in town, and you light on him, I think you ought to tell him gravely, that, if he be the author, he should set his name to the &c. and rally him a little upon it: And tell him, if he can explain some things, you will, if he pleases, set his name to the next edition. I should be glad to see how far the foolish impudence of a dunce could go. Well; I will send you the thing, now I am in town, as soon as possible. But, I dare say, you have neither printed the rest, nor finished the cuts,[1] only are glad to lay the fault on me. I shall, at the end, take a little contemptible notice of the thing you sent me; and I dare say it will do you more good than hurt.[2] If you are in such haste, how came you to forget the Miscellanies? I would not have you think of Steele for a publisher: he is too busy.[3] I will, one of these days, send you some hints, which I would have in a preface, and you may get some friend to dress them up. I have thoughts of some other work one of these years; and I hope to see you ere it be long; since it is like to be a new world, and since I have the merit of suffering by not complying with the old. Yours, &c.

Deane Swift 1765

Benjamin Tooke to Swift

London, July 10, 1710.

Sir,

Inclosed I have sent the Key, and think it would be much more proper to add the notes at the bottom of the respective pages they refer to, than printing them at the end by themselves.[4] As to the

[1] For a note on the 'cuts' see the following letter.
[2] See Swift's 'Postscript' to the 'Apology' prefixed to the fifth edition of *A Tale*.   [3] See Steele to Swift, 8 Oct. 1709.
[4] A passage lower down in this letter shows that Tooke was of opinion that the Key should be distributed in the form of footnotes. This plan was adopted. The unsigned notes represent Swift's commentary on his own work. These same notes, along with the 'Apology', were also printed together as a pamphlet, issued in the following year, which could be bound up with earlier editions of *A Tale*. The notes signed 'W. Wotton' were a humorous and ironical revenge on *A Tale's* chief critic. See Guthkelch and Nichol Smith, op. cit., pp. xx–xxxiii.

Cuts, Sir Andrew Fountaine has had them from the time they were designed, with an intent of altering them. But he is now gone into Norfolk,[1] and will not return till Michaelmas; so that, I think, they must be laid aside: For, unless they are very well done, it is better they were quite let alone. As to the Apology, I was not so careless but that I took a copy of it before I sent it to you, so that I could have printed it easily, but that you sent me word not to go on till you had altered something in it. As to that Cousin of yours which you speak of, I neither know him nor ever heard of him till the Key mentioned him. It was very indifferent to me which I proceeded on first, the Tale or the Miscellanies: But, when you went away, you told me there were three or four things should be sent over out of Ireland, which you had not here;[2] which, I think, is a very reasonable excuse for myself in all these affairs. What I beg of you at present is, that you would return the Apology and this Key, with directions as to the placing it: Although I am entirely of opinion to put it at the bottom of each page; yet shall submit. If this be not done soon, I cannot promise but some rascal or other will do it for us both; since you see the liberty that is already taken. I think too much time has already been lost in the Miscellanies; therefore hasten that: And whichever is in the most forwardness, I would begin on first. All here depend on an entire alteration. I am, &c.

4804

Joseph Addison to Swift

Dublin Castle July. 23. 1710.

Dear Sir.

About two days ago I received the Enclosed that is sealed up and yesterday that of my friend Steele, which requiring a speady Answer I have sent you Expresse. In the mean time I have let him know that you are out of Town and that he may expect your Answer by the

---

[1] On the subject of the original designs for the illustration of *A Tale* and the subsequent engravings see Guthkelch and Nichol Smith, op. cit., pp. xxiii–xxvi.

[2] Subjects for a miscellany volume had been dotted down by Swift on the back of a letter now lost addressed to him at Lord Pembroke's in Leicester Fields, Oct. 1708. A copy of the list is inserted between pp. 36 and 37 of Lyon's copy of Hawkesworth's *Life of Swift* in the Forster Collection, South Kensington. See Guthkelch and Nichol Smith, op. cit., p. xviii; Forster, *Life*, pp. 257–8.

next post. I fancy he had my L Halifax's Authority for writing. I hope this will bring you to town:[1] for your Amusement by the way I have sent you some of this days news. to wch I must adde that Drs Bysse and Robinson are likely to be the B^{ps} of Bristoll and St Davids,[2] that our Politic^{ns} are startled at the Breaking off the Negociations and fall of stocks insomuch that it is thought they will not venture at dissolving the Parlam^t in such a Crisis. I am Ever Dear Sir

Yours Entirely
J. Addison

Mr Steele desires me to seale yours before I deliver it but this you will excuse in one who wishes you as well as He or any Body can do.

Endorsed: Mr Addison
July 23. 1710.

Rothschild

Swift to Joseph Addison

Dublin. August 22. 1710[3]

I lookt long enough at the Wind to sett you safe on tother side and then I . . . own Conduct, very unwillingly, for fear you . . . up to a Post horse, and hazard your Limbs to be made a Member. I believe you had the displeasure of much ill news almost as soon as you landed. Even the moderate Toryes here are in pain at these Revolutions, being what will certainly affect the D. of Marlborough,

[1] In his account-book (Forster, no. 507) Swift notes that from the 17th to the 22nd of the month he was at Laracor. He was probably in Dublin again when he visited Finglas on the 25th.

[2] These two bishoprics had been vacant for several months. Philip Bisse, a Fellow of New College, Oxford, was consecrated Bishop of St. David's in Nov. 1710. He was translated to Hereford in Feb. 1712–13. Dr. John Robinson was for years an accredited representative of this country in Sweden. After his return to England in 1709 he was granted the Deanery of Windsor; and on 19 Nov. 1710 he was consecrated Bishop of Bristol. Swift, looking for preferment himself, would be interested in such items of news.

[3] First printed by Scott, 1814, xix. 345–7; thence Ball, i. 187–90; Graham, *Letters of Addison*, pp. 464–5. The original was sold among Tickell Papers, 16 July 1928. Now Lord Rothschild's library, no. 2284. The earlier part of this letter has been badly effaced, and the paper has also been torn. These injuries are indicated in the text.

and consequently the Success of the War. My L^d L^t askt me yesterday whether I intended for England; I said, I had no Busyness there
now, since I suppose in a little Time I should not have one Friend
left that had any Credit and his Excellency was of my Opinion.[1]
I never once begun Your [Task] since you [left this] being perpetually prevented by all the Company [I kept and especially] Capt
Prat,[2] to whom I am almost a Domestick upon Your Account. I am
convinced that whatever Governm^t come over you will find all
marks of Kindness from any Parl^mt here, with respect to Your
Emplym^t,[3] the Toryes contending with the Whigs, which should
speak best of You. Mr Prat says he has received such marks of your
Sincerity and Friendship, as he never can forget. And in that, if you
will come over[4] when you are at Leisure, we will raise an Army, and
make you King of Ireland. Can you think so meanly of a Kingdom
as not to be pleased that every Creature in it who hath one Grain of
Worth has a veneration for you. I know there is nothing in this to
make you add any value to your self, but it ought to put you upon
valuing them, and to convince you that they are not an undistin-
guishing People. On Thursday the Bp of Clogher the two Prats and
I are to be as happy as Ireland will now give us Leave; We are to
dine with Mr Paget,[5] at the Castle, and drink your Health. The Bp
shewd me the 1st Volume of the small Edition of the Tatler,[6]

[1] When Swift was writing these words it is difficult to believe he can have
entertained for Wharton the savage distaste which developed into his *Short
Character* of the Lord Lieutenant (*Prose Works*, Davis, iii. 175), which he dated
30 Aug. 1710; but it is to be remembered that this letter, addressed to Addison,
demanded caution.

[2] Captain John Pratt was Deputy Vice-Treasurer of Ireland and Constable
of Dublin Castle, a position he owed to the influence of the Duke of Ormonde.
For a number of years Swift was on friendly terms with him and trusted him
with money affairs. Unfortunately in 1725 Pratt was adjudged guilty of defalca-
tions in the public accounts and committed to prison. Ball was of opinion that
Swift owed the facts used by him in his *Short Character of Wharton* to John
Pratt and Sir Richard Levinge, Attorney-General in Ireland, 1711–14.

[3] The employment to which reference is made was that of 'Keeper of her
Majesty's Records' in Ireland, a sinecure with a nominal salary of ten pounds,
which was, however, raised to £400. These records were in bad condition and
poorly housed. Addison proposed that they should be examined and catalogued;
but to the day of his death nothing seems to have been done. See Smithers's
Life of Addison, pp. 164–7.

[4] After the word 'over' Scott and Ball introduce 'again', which is not in the
original.   [5] Gentleman Usher of the Black Rod.

[6] The first two volumes of the collected *Tatler* in duodecimo format were

where there is a very handsom Compliment to me; but I can never pardon the printing the News of every Tatler, I think he might as well have printed the Advertism^ts; I know it was a Booksellers piece of Craft to encrease the Bulk and Price of what he was sure would sell but I utterly disapprove it. I beg you would freely tell me whether it will be of any Account for me to come [to] England. I would not trouble you for Advice if I knew where else to ask it. We expect every day to hear of My L^dTreasurer^s Removal;[1] if he were to continue I might perhaps hope for some of his good Offices. You ordered me to give you a Memoriall of what I had in my Thoughts. There were two Things D^r So—th's Prebend and Sinecure;[2] or the Place of Historiographer. But if Things go on in the Train they are now; I shall onely beg you when there is an Account to be depended on for a new Governmt here, that you will give me early Notice, and then I will make what Applications I can so as to get favor enough[3] to procure so[me] Addition to my Fortunes. And with saying this I take Leave of troubling you with my self.

I do not desire to hear from [you till you are out of the hurry at] Malmesbury;[4] I long till you have [some good Account of] your Indian Affairs,[5] so as to make Publick Business depend upon You, and not you upon that. I read your Charact^r in Mrs Manly's noble Memoirs of Europe.[6] It seems to me as if she had about two thousand Epithets, and fine words putt[7] up in a bag, and that she puled

published on 10 July. In the dedication to Arthur Maynwaring by Steele tribute was paid to 'a Gentleman' who had made the name of Bickerstaff 'famous through all parts of *Europe*'.
  [1] Godolphin was dismissed from office on 8 Aug. Contrary winds probably accounted for delay in the receipt of the news in Ireland.
  [2] See p. 143, n. 2.
  [3] Scott and Ball omit the words 'and then I will make . . . favor enough'.
  [4] Addison represented Cavan in the Irish Parliament in addition to his seat in the English Parliament, in which he represented successively the boroughs of Lostwithiel and Malmesbury. A general election in England appeared to be imminent. This accounted for Addison's hurried departure.
  [5] In July 1710 news reached England that Gulston Addison, a prosperous India merchant, had died, and that 'his fortune, which is very considerable, devolves upon his brother, Joseph Addison Esq.' See Smithers's *Life of Addison*, pp. 181-2 *et passim*.
  [6] Swift has been credited with the writing of the *Tatler*, no. 63, which contains an attack on Mrs. Manley. See *Prose Works*, ed. Temple Scott, ix. 15-17. The attribution should not be accepted. Steele also denied authorship of the paper. Further to Swift's part in the *Tatler* see *Prose Works*, Davis, vol. ii.
  [7] For 'putt' Scott and Ball read 'packed'.

them out by handfull, and strewed them on her Paper, where about
once in five hundred times they happen to be right.

My L^d L^t we reckon will leave us in a fortnight. I led him by a
Question to tell me, he did not expect to continue in the Governmt,
nor would when all his Friends are out. Pray take some Occasion to
let my [L^d] Hallifax know the [sense]^1 I have of the Favor he in-
tended me.^{2} | I am with great Respect | S^r | Your most obedient
and | most oblidged | humble Servt | J: Swift

4804

Primate Marsh and Others to the Bishops of Ossory and Killaloe

[Dublin, 31 August 1710]

Our very good Lords^3

Whereas severall Applications have been made to her Majestie
about the first Fruits and Twentieth parts payable to her Majestie
by the Clergy of this Kingdome, beseeching her Majestie that she
wou'd be gratiously pleased to Extend her bounty to the Clergy here
in such manner as the Convocation have humbly laid before her
Majestie, or as her Majestie shall in her Goodnes and Wisdome think
fitt, and the Said Applications lye still before her Majestie and We
do hope from her Royal Bounty a favourable answer.

We do therefore Entreat your Lordships to take on you the
Solicitation of that affair, and to use such proper Methods, and
Applications, as you in your prudence shall Judge most like to be
effectual. We have likewise desired the Bearer Doctor Swift to
Concern himself with you being persuaded of his Diligence and good
affection, And We desire that if your Lordships occasions require
your leaving London before you have brought the business to effect,
that you wou'd leave with him the papers relateing to it, with your
Directions for his Management in it if you think it advisable so to do^4

---

¹ Paper torn.
² The cold nature of the acknowledgement is apparent.
³ The commission is in the hand of a scribe, four quarto pages, the commission on the first page, the second and third pages blank, Swift's endorsement
on the fourth page.
⁴ On 8 Aug. Godolphin received a letter from the Queen desiring him to
break his staff. The receipt of this news in Dublin accelerated Wharton's

We are your Lordships most | humble Servants and Brethren

	Narcissus Armath
Dublin August the ⎱	Will. Dubliniensis
Thirty first 1710— ⎰	W. Cassel
To the Right Revd fathers in God	W. Meath
John Lord Bishop of Ossory and Thomas	W. Kildare
Lord Bishop of Killalo²	Wm. Killala¹

Endorsed by Swift: Commission from | the Bps of Ireld to me | about the first Fuits | Aug. 31st. 1710

Faulkner 1762

Swift to Archbishop King

London, Sept. 9, 1710

My Lord

I arrived here on Thursday last, and enquireing for the two Bishops, I found my Lord of *Ossory*, was gone some Time ago, and the Bishop of *Killaloe*³ I could not hear of till next Day, when I found he was set out early in the Morning for *Ireland*; so that the Letter to their Lordships is so far to no Purpose. I cannot yet learn whether they left any Papers behind them; neither shall I much enquire; and to say the Truth, I was less sollicitous to ask after the Bishop of *Killaloe*, when I heard the other was gone. They tell me,

departure for London to look after his own interests. On the 28th the Irish Parliament was prorogued. The Archbishops of Armagh, Dublin, and Cashel, and three bishops were alone available to attend the adjournment of Convocation on the 31st. They decided to continue with the new Ministry their plea for the remission of the First Fruits in favour of the Irish clergy. On this mission two bishops were already in London. It was resolved to strengthen their efforts by an enabling commission handed to Swift. The commission was drafted and signed only just in time to enable him to catch the Lord Lieutenant's yacht before its hurried sailing.

¹ The three archbishops were Narcissus Marsh of Armagh, William King of Dublin, and William Palliser of Cashel; the three bishops were William Moreton of Meath, Swift's diocesan, Welbore Ellis of Kildare, and William Lloyd of Killala.

² Swift reached London on Thursday, 7 Sept., missing the Bishops of Ossory and Killaloe, John Hartstonge and Thomas Lindsay, who were returning to Ireland. This, it may be surmised, caused him no regrets.

³ Here and below Faulkner misprints the name as 'Killala'.

all Affairs in the Treasury are governed by Mr. *Harley*,¹ and that he is the Person usually applied to; only of late, my Lord *Poulett*, upon what People have talked to him that Way, hath exerted himself a little, and endeavours to be as significant as he can.² I have Opportunities enough of getting some Interest with his Lordship, who hath formerly done me good offices, although I have no personal Acquaintance with him. After which I will apply to Mr. *Harley*, who formerly made some Advances towards me, and unless he be altered, will, I believe, think himself in the Right to use me well: But, I am inclined to suspend any particular Sollicitations until I hear from your Grace, and am informed what Progress the two Bishops have made; and, until I receive their Papers, with what other Directions your Grace will desire to send me.

Upon my Arrival hither, I found myself equally caressed by both Parties, by one as a Sort of bough for drowning men³ to lay hold of; and by the other as one discontented, with the late Men in Power, for not being thorough in their Designs, and therefore ready to approve present Things. I was to visit my Lord *Godolphin*, who gave me a Reception very unexpected, and altogether different from what I ever received from any great Man in my Life; altogether short, dry, and morose, not worth repeating to your Grace, until I have the Honour to see you. I complained of it to some of his Friends, as having, as I thought, for some reasons, deserved much the contrary from his Lordship: They said, to excuse him, that he was over-run with Spleen and Peevishness upon the present Posture of Affairs, and used No-body better.⁴ It may be new to your Grace to

---

¹ Harley had been appointed Chancellor of the Exchequer.

² John, fourth Baron and first Earl Poulett (1663–1743), was inactive and possessed of mediocre abilities. From 8 Aug. 1710 to 30 May 1711 he was nominally first Lord of the Treasury. Macky described him as 'one of the hopefullest gentlemen in England; is very learned, virtuous, and a man of honour'; upon which Swift comments 'this Caracter is fair enough'. Anthony Henley and Lord Poulett were married to sisters, daughters of Peregrine Bertie, and it was this relationship which contributed to Swift's 'interest' with Lord Poulett.

³ Instead of 'Bough for drowning men' Faulkner misread the words, 'Purge for drawing men'.

⁴ It is possible, though doubtful, that Godolphin, who favoured the Occasional Conformity Bill, knew that Swift was the author of *A Letter . . . Concerning the Sacramental Test*, 1709. If so, it is not surprising that his manner was forbidding. Writing to Stella (*Journal*, 9 Sept. 1710) Swift further mentions his cold reception, and adds, 'I am almost vowing revenge'. The revenge took the form of his lampoon, *Sid Hamet* (*Poems*, pp. 131–5).

tell you some Circumstances of his Removal. A Letter was sent him by the Groom of the Queen's Stables, to desire he would break his Staff, which would be the easiest Way, both to her Majesty and him. Mr. *Smith*, Chancellor of the Exchequer,¹ happening to come in a little after, my Lord broke his Staff, and flung the Pieces in the Chimney, desiring Mr. *Smith* to be Witnes s that he had obeyed the Queen's Commands, and sent him to the Queen with a Letter, and a Message, which Mr. *Smith* delivered, and at the same Time surrendered up his own Office. The Parliament is certainly to be dissolved, although the Day is yet uncertain. The Remainder of *Whigs* in Employment are resolved not to resign; and a certain Lord told me, he had been the Giver of that Advice, and did in my Presence prevail on an Acquaintance of mine in a great Post to promise the same Thing; only Mr. *Boyle*, they say, is resolved to give up.² Every Body counts infallibly upon a general Removal. The Duke of *Queensberry*, it is said, will be Steward;³ my Lord *Cholmondeley* is gone over to the new Interest, with great Indignation of his Friends.⁴ It is affirmed by the *Tories*, that the great Motive of these Changes was the absolute Necessity of a Peace, which they thought the *Whigs* were for perpetually delaying. Elections are now managing with greater Violence and Expence, and more Competitors than ever was known; yet the Town is much fuller of People, than usually at this Time of the Year, waiting until they see some Issue of the Matter. The Duke of *Ormond* is much talked of for *Ireland*, and I imagine he believeth something of it himself.⁵ Mr. *Harley* is looked upon as first Minister, and not my Lord *Shrewsbury*,⁶ and

¹ John Smith, 1655–1723, sat as Member of Parliament for several constituencies from 1678 till the year of his death. A strong Whig and friend of Godolphin, he was Chancellor of the Exchequer, 1708–10.

² Henry Boyle, youngest son of Lord Clifford of Lanesborough, was persuaded to remain in office. He had been Principal Secretary of State for the Northern Department since 1708. On the accession of George I he was created Baron Carleton. Against Macky's characterization of Boyle Swift wrote, 'Had some very Scurvy Qualities, particularly avarice'.

³ James Douglas, second Duke of Queensberry, Secretary for Scotland in Harley's administration. He died 6 July 1711.

⁴ Hugh Cholmondeley, *c.* 1662–1725, was created Baron Cholmondeley in the peerage of England in 1689. He was Treasurer of the Household, 1708–13, and again, 1714–15. 'Good for nothing as far as I ever knew' was Swift's opinion of him (*Prose Works*, ed. Temple Scott, x. 280).

⁵ See p. 49, n. 2.

⁶ When in Apr. 1710 the Queen dismissed the Marquis of Kent and appointed

his Grace helps on the Opinion, whether out of Policy or Truth; upon all Occasions professing to stay until he speaks with Mr. *Harley*. The Queen continues at *Kensington* indisposed with the Gout, of which she hath frequent Returns.

I deferred writing to your Grace as late as I could this Post, until I might have something to entertain you: But there is such an universal Uncertainty among those who pretend to know most, that little can be depended on. However, it may be some Amusement to tell you the Sentiments of People here, and, as bad as they are, I am sure they are the best that are stirring; for it is thought there are not three People in *England* entirely in the Secret, nor is it sure, whether even those three are agreed in what they intend to do. I am with great Respect, | my Lord, | Your Grace's | Most Obedient, and | Most Humble Servant, |

J. Swift.

I have not Time to read this and correct the literal Mistakes. I was to wait on the Duke of *Ormond*, and to set him right in the Story of the College, about the Statue, *&c.*[1]

Hawkesworth 1766
Archbishop King to Swift

Dublin, Sept. 16, 1710.
Reverend Sir,

I received yours by the last pacqets, of *September* the 9th; and because you have missed the two Bishops, I send you, with this, the papers relating to the first fruits, and twentieth parts. I send them in two bundles, being too big for one letter. The Bishops, so far as I

the Duke of Shrewsbury Lord Chamberlain, the event marked the first step in her move to replace the Whig government. Although Swift regarded Shrewsbury as 'timorous' he acted firmly on Queen Anne's death and assured the Hanoverian succession.

[1] This reference is to an outrage committed in the previous June on the statue of William III in Dublin by three college students, who removed the truncheon from the King's hand and plastered his face with mud. Owing to the strong feeling at the time, 'that barbarous fact' was viewed as a very serious offence, and as confirmation of the report that Trinity College was a hotbed of Jacobitism (see p. 95, n. 4). As Chancellor Ormonde was interested.—Ball.

can learn from the Bishop of *Ossory*, have not made any step since I left *London*. I will endeavour to get you a letter from the Bishops to solicit that affair. In the mean time, open the letter to the two Bishops, and make use of it as occasion shall serve. The scheme I had laid for them is crossed by my Lord Treasurer's being out; though, perhaps, that would not have done; but her Majesty's promise I depended on, and I had engaged the Archbishop of *York*[1] in it. When he comes to *London*, I will give you a letter to him. I can likewise find means, I believe, to possess my Lord *Shrewsbury* and Mr. *Harley*, with the reasonableness of the affair. I am not courtier enough to know the properness of the thing; but I had once an imagination to attempt her Majesty herself by a letter, modestly putting her in mind of the matter; and no time so proper, as when there is no Lord Lieutenant of *Ireland*, which perhaps may be soon; but this needs advice.

There are great men here as much out of humour, as you describe your great *visitee* to have been; nor does the good news from *Spain*[2] clear them. I believe, however, they are glad at it, though another would have served their occasions as well.

I do not apprehend any other secret in all this affair, but to get Whigs out of all places of profit and trust, and to get others in them. As for peace, it must be on no other terms than the preliminaries; and you will find a Tory Parliament will give money as freely, and be as eager to prosecute the war, as the Whigs were, or they are not the wise men I take them to be. If they do so, and take care to have the money well disposed of when given, they will break the King of *France's* heart, and the Whigs together, and please the nation. There's an ugly accident, that happens here in relation to our twentieth parts and first-fruits: at *Midsummer*, 1709, there was ready money in the Treasury, and good solvent debts to the Queen to the value of 70000 *l*. Now I am told, by the last week's abstract, there is only 223 *l*. in the Treasury, and the army unpaid, at least uncleared for a year; and all others, except pensioners, in the same condition. Now the great motive to prevail with her Majesty to give the clergy the bounty petitioned for, was the clearness of the revenue here; but

[1] John Sharp, to whose opposition Swift attributed later the refusal of the Queen to give him preferment in England. See *Poems*, p. 193.
[2] The outstanding victory of Saragossa, 20 Aug. 1710, in which the allied forces under the leadership of Stanhope and Starhemberg routed the Spanish army.

if that be anticipated, perhaps it may make an objection. I will add no more, but my prayers for you. I am, &c.

Will. Dublin.

Hawkesworth 1766

Swift to Dean Stearne

London, Sept. 26, 1710

Sir,

One would think this an admirable place from whence to fill a letter; yet when I come to examine particulars, I find they either consist of news, which you hear as soon by the public papers, or of persons and things, to which you are a stranger, and are the wiser and happier for being so. Here have been great men every day resigning their places; a resignation as sincere, as that of a usurer on his death-bed. Here are some, that fear being whipt, because they have broken their rod; and some that may be called to an account, because they could not cast one up. There are now not much above a dozen great employments to be disposed of, which, according to our computation, may be done in as many days. *Patrick*[1] assures me his acquaintance are all very well satisfied with these changes, which I take for no ill symptom, and it is certain the Queen has never appeared so easy or so chearful. I found my Lord *Godolphin* the worst dissembler of any of them that I have talked to; and no wonder, since his loss and danger are greater, beside the addition of age and complexion.[2] My Lord Lieutenant is gone to the country, to bustle about elections.[3] He is not yet removed; because they say it will be requisite to supersede him by a successor, which the Queen has not fixed on; nor is it agreed whether the Duke of

---

[1] Swift's Irish servant, against whom we meet with many complaints in the *Journal to Stella* for drunkenness and irregular habits. He had redeeming features, however, for he came to Swift a second time on 9 Feb. 1709-10, as Swift noted in his 'Account of Expences From Novbr. 1. 1709 to Novbr. 1. 1710' (Forster 507). He left Swift finally in Apr. 1712 (*Journal*, p. 529).

[2] Godolphin was just over sixty-five. He died 15 Sept. 1712.

[3] Wharton was a first-rate electioneering agent. In this crisis he busied himself immediately in trying to stem the tide which was running against the Whigs. On 11 Sept. Swift writes to Stella, 'Lord Wharton expects every day to be out: he is working like a horse for elections'.

Shrewsbury or *Ormond* stand fairest.¹ I speak only for this morning, because reports usually change every twenty-four hours. Mean time the pamphlets and half sheets grow so upon our hands, it will very well employ a man every day from morning till night to read them; and so out of perfect despair I never read any at all. The Whigs, like an army beat three quarters out of the field, begin to skirmish but faintly; and deserters daily come over. We are amazed to find our mistakes, and how it was possible to see so much merit where there was none, and to overlook it where there was so much. When a great Minister has lost his place, immediately virtue, honour, and wit, fly over to his successor, with the other ensigns of his office. Since I left off writing, I received a letter from my Lord Archbishop of *Dublin*,² or rather two letters upon these memorials. I think immediately to begin my soliciting; though they are not very perfect, for I would be glad to know, whether my Lord Archbishop would have the same method taken here, that has been done in *England*, to settle it by Parliament; but, however, that will be time enough thought of this good while.

I must here tell you, that the Dean of *St. Patrick's* lives better than any man of quality I know; yet this day I dined with the Comptroller, who tells me, he drinks the Queen's wine to-day.³ I saw Collector Stearne,⁴ who desired me to present his service to you, and to tell you he would be glad to hear from you, but not about business; by which, I told him, I guessed he was putting you off about something you desired.

I would much rather be now in *Ireland* drinking your good wine, and looking over, while you lost a crown at penny ombre. I am weary of the caresses of great men out of place. The Comptroller expects every day the Queen's commands to break his staff. He is the last great household officer they intend to turn out. My Lord

¹ On 19 Oct. the Duke of Ormonde was, for the second time, appointed Lord Lieutenant of Ireland in place of Lord Wharton.
² See the previous letter.
³ Sir John Holland, grandson and heir of Sir John Holland, the first baronet of Quidenham, Norfolk, whom he succeeded in 1701. He retained his place as Comptroller of the Household till 1711, when he was succeeded by Sir Thomas Mansell. Sir John Holland was regarded by Swift with sincere respect, despite his Whiggism.
⁴ Enoch Stearne, a cousin of the Dean of St. Patrick's, was collector of Wicklow and Clerk of the Irish House of Lords. He appears to have taken to loose courses. See *Journal*, pp. 385, 420.

Lieutenant is yet in, beause they cannot agree about his successor. I am | your most obedient humble servant,

J. Swift.

4804 and Portland Manuscript

Swift's Memorials to Robert Harley concerning the First-Fruits

From the draft in the British Museum[1]

In Ireland hardly one Parish in ten hath any Glebe, and the rest very small, and scattered, except a very few, & then have seldom any Houses.

There are in Proportion more Impropriations in Ireland than in England, which added to the Poverty of the Country make the Livings of very small and uncertain Value, so that five or six are often joyned to make a Revenue of 50 ll per a $\overline{ann}$. but these have seldom above one Church in repair, the rest being destroyed by frequent Wars &c.

The Clergy for want of Glebes are forced in their own or neighboring Parish to take farms to live on Rack Rents.

The Queen having some years since remitted the First Fruits to the Clergy of England, the Bishop of Cloyn being then in London did petition Her Majesty for the same Favor in behalf of the Clergy of Ireland and received a Gracious Answer, But this Affair, for want of solliciting, was not brought to an Issue during the Governmts of the Duke of Ormond and Earl of Pembroke.

Upon the Earl of Wharton's succeeding, Dr Swift (who had sollicited this matter in the preceding Governmt) desired by the Bishops of Ireland to apply to His Excy., who thought fit to receive the Motion as wholly new, and what he could not consider till he

---

[1] A draft of the memorial which Harley put into his pocket on 7 Oct. is in the British Museum (Add. MS. 4804, ff. 36, 37). In 1766 it was printed from this draft in Hawkesworth's edition of the *Letters*. On 16 Oct. Swift left with Harley another and more careful copy, now among the Portland papers. This copy bears Harley's endorsement of receipt on that day. The British Museum draft is written in a small hand on the first two pages of a sheet folded to four pages, small quarto. The Portland copy is written on four quarto pages with two lines on the third page. On the fourth page are endorsements by Swift and Harley. Both versions of the memorial are here printed.

were fixt in the Governmt. and till the same Application were made to Him as had been to his Predecessors. Accordingly an Address was delivered to his Ldship with a Petition to the Queen and a Memoriall annexed, from both Houses of Convocation; But a dispute happening in the Lower House, wherein his Chaplain concerned and which was represented by the sd Chaplain as an affront designed to His Excy; who was pleased to understand and report it to Court, the Convocation was suddenly prorogued, and all further thoughts about the First fruits, lett fall as desperate.

The Subject of the Petition was to desire that the 20th Parts might be remitted to the Clergy, and the First fruits made a Fund for purchasing Glebes and Impropriations, and rebuilding of Churches.

The twentyth Parts, are twelve pence in the Pound paid annually out of all Eccliasticall Benificy, as they were valued at the Reformation. they amount to about 500 ll p ann. but of little or no value to the Queen, after the Officers and other Charges are paid, tho of much trouble and Vexation to the Clergy.

The first Fruits paid by Incumbents upon their Promotion amount to about 450 p añ so that Her Majesty in remitting about 1000 ll p añ to the Clergy will really lose not above 500 ll.

Upon Aug. 31. 1710. The two Houses of Convocation being met to be further prorogued; the Arch-Bishops and Bishops conceiving there was now a favorable Juncture to resume their Applications, did in their private Capacityes sign a Power to the sd Dr Swift to sollicite the Remitting the First Fruits and Twentyth Parts.

But there is a greater Burthen than this and almost intollerable upon severall of the Clergy in Ireland, the easing of which, the Clergy only lookt on as a Thing to be wisht, without making it part of their Petn.

The Queen is Impropriator of severall Parishes, and the Incumbent pays her half-yearly a rent generally to the third Part of the reall Value of the Living, and sometimes half; some of their Parishes by the encrease of Graziers are seised on by the Crown, and cannot pay the required Rent. The Value of all their Impropriations are about two Thousand Pounds p añ to Her Majesty.

If the Queen would graciously please to bestow likewise these Impropriations to the Church; part to be remitted to the Incumbent, where the Rent is large, & the Living small; and the rest to be layd out in buying Glebes and Impropriations, & building of Churches It would be a most pious and seasonable Bounty

The Utmost value of the 20th Parts, First Fruits and Crown rents, is 3000 ll per anñ. of which about 500 ll per anñ is sunk among Officers; so that her Majesty by this great Benefaction would lose but 2500 ll per anñ.

Endorsed by Swift: Copy of Memorial to Mr Harley—about 1st Fruits

From the Portland Manuscript

There are in Proportion more Impropriations in Ireland than in England, which added to the Poverty of the Country, makes the Livings of very small and uncertain Value, so that five or six united do often hardly amount to 50 ll p anñ; but these have seldom above one Church in repair, the rest being destroyed by the Wars. &c.

Hardly one Parish in ten hath any Glebe, and the rest, very small ones, and scattered, except very few; and even these have seldom any Houses; For want of which, the Clergy are forced to take Farms at Rack-rents in their own or some neighboring Parish.

The Queen having some years since remitted the First-fruits to the Clergy of England, the Bishop of Cloyn being some time after in London, petitioned her Majesty to grant the same Favor for Ireland, and received a gracious Answer; But this Affair for want of solliciting, was not brought to an Issue during the Government of the Duke of Ormond or Earl of Pembroke.

Upon the Earl of Wharton being nominated Lord Lieutenant, Dr Swift (having sollicited the Matter in the preceding Government) was desired by the Bishops of Ireland to apply to his Excellency; who thought fit to receive the Motion as wholly new, and what He could not consider (as He said) till he were fixed in the Governmt, and till the same Application were made to Him, as had been to His Predecessors. Accordingly, soon after His Arrival in Ireland, an Address was delivered to His Lordship, from both Houses of Convocation, with a Memoriall, and Petition to the Queen annexed to it. But a dispute happening in the lower House, wherein His Chaplain was concerned, and which was represented by the sd Chaplain as an Affront designed to His Excellency; He was pleased to understand and report it so to the Court: Upon which the Convocation was suddenly prorogued, and all further Thoughts about First-fruits, let fall as desperate.

The Subject of the sd Petition was to desire, that the Twentyth Parts might be remitted to the Clergy, and the First-fruits made a Fund for purchasing Glebes and Impropriations, and building Churches.

The Twentyth Parts, are twelvepence in the Pound yearly out of all Eclesiasticall Benefices, as they were valued at the Reformation; they amount to about 500 ll p ann̄, but of little or no value to the Queen, after the Officers and other Charges are payd; though of much Trouble and Vexation to the Clergy.

The First-fruits payd, by Incumbents upon their Promotion amount to about 450 ll p ann̄; so that Her Majesty in remitting near 1000 ll p ann̄ to the Clergy, will really lose onely 500 ll p ann̄.

But there is a greater Burthen than this, and almost intolerable upon severall of the Clergy in Ireland; the easing of which, the Convocations for some Reasons, of weight at that Time, did not make a Part of their Petition.

In certain Dioceses the Queen is Impropriator of many Parishes, and the Incumbent pays Her Majesty a yearly Rent, generally to the third Part of the reall Value of the Living; and often, a full half. Nay, some of these Parishes are sunk so low by the Increase of Graziers, that they are seised on by the Crown, which out of the whole Profits cannot make the reserved Rent. The Value of all these Impropriations is about 2000 ll p ann̄ to Her Majesty.

If the Queen would graciously please to bestow likewise these Impropriations to the Church; part to be remitted to the Incumbent, where the Rent is large and the Living small, and the rest to be layd out in purchasing Glebes, &c; it would be a most pious and seasonable Bounty.

The utmost Value of the Twentyth Parts, First-fruits and Impropriations together, is 3000 ll p ann̄; of which above 500 ll is sunk by Salaryes, and other Charges of collecting; so that Her Majesty by this great Benefaction to the Church would lose but 2000 ll p ann̄.

Upon August 3d, 1710, the two Houses of Convocation being met onely to be further prorogued, the Arch-Bishops and Bishops conceiving there was now a favorable Juncture to resume their Applications, did in their private Capacities sign a Power to the sd Dr Swift, to sollicite the remitting the First-fruits and Twentyth Parts.

Endorsed by Swift: Dr Swift's Memoriall about the First-fruits of Ireland.
Octbr. 7. 1710
Endorsed by Harley: ℞ octo: 16: 1710

Swift to Archbishop King

London. Oct^br 10. 1710.

My Lord.[1]

I had the Honor of Your Grace's Letter of Septr 16. but I was in no pain to Acknowledge it, nor shall be at any other Time, till I have something that I think worth troubling you; because I am very sensible how much an insignificant Letter is worse than none at all. I had likewise the Memoriall etc in another Pacquet; and I beg Your Grace to inclose whatever Pacquets you send me (I mean of bulk) under a Paper directed to Mr Steel at his Office in the Cock-pit, and not for me at Mr Steel's. I should have been glad the Bishops had been here, though I take Bishops to be the worst Sollicitors in the world, except in their own Concerns; They cannot give themselves the little Trouble of Attendance that other men are content to swallow; else I am sure their two Lordships might have succeeded easier than men of my level can reasonably hope to do.

As soon as I received the Pacquets, I went to wait upon Mr Harley, I had prepared him before by another Hand where he was very intimate, and got my self represented (which I might justly do) as one extreamly ill used by the last Ministry, after some obligations, because I refused to go certain Lengths they would have had me.[2]

---

[1] This letter presents textual variants, illustrating Swift's desire to acquaint the Archbishop of Harley's reception of him and recount the trend of political affairs with accuracy and restraint. A draft of the first portion of the letter, in Swift's hand, is in the British Museum (Add. MS. 4804, f. 38). The original letter, as sent, extending to greater length, is in the Library, Armagh. Faulkner, 1746, viii. 356–9, printed the letter from the draft. In 1762 he printed the letter from the Armagh text. Bowyer, and others of the trade, printed in 1760 from the draft. In 1762 they followed the Armagh original. Hawkesworth in 1766 printed from the draft. The letter is here printed from the Armagh autograph.

[2] It was owing to King's influence with his fellow prelates that on 31 Aug. Swift received his commission to plead with the new government the cause of the Irish clergy. Within forty days, thirty-one of reaching London, he had carried his mission so far that he had presented the earlier of his two memorials to Harley. This was on Saturday, 7 Oct. Harley put the memorial in his pocket to show the Queen. On Tuesday, 10 Oct. (*Journal*, 10 Oct.) he dined with Harley, who informed him that the memorial had been shown to the Queen, a statement repeated on Sunday, the 15th, in the form that the memorial had been left with the Queen. On Monday, the 16th, he left the revised copy at Harley's door. This was the copy marked by Harley himself as received that day. It may

This happened to be in some sort Mr. H's own case. He had heard very often of me, and received me with the greatest Marks of Kindness and Esteem, as I was whispered that he would, and the more, upon the ill usage I had met with. I sate with him two hours among Company, and two Hours we were alone; where I gave him a History of the whole Business, and the steps that had been made in it, which he heard as I could wish, and promised with great readyness his best credit to effect it. I mentioned the Difficultyes we had met with from Lds Lts and their Secretaryes, who would not suffer others to sollicite and neglected it themselves. He fell in with me entirely, and said, neither they nor Himself should have the merit of it, but the Queen, to whom he would shew my Memorial with the first opportunity, in order if possible to have it done in this Interregnum. I said, it was a great encouragement to the Bps that He was in the Treasury, whom they knew to have been the chief Adviser of the Queen to grant the same favor in England. That the Hon^r and merit of this, would certainly be his next to the Queen but that it was nothing to him, who had done so much greater Things, and that for my Part, I thought he was oblieged to the Clergy, for giving him an Occasion of gratifying the Pleasure he took in doing Good to the Church. He received my Compliment ex-treamly well, and renewed His Promises with great kindness. I for-got to tell Your Grace that when I sd I was impowered etc, He desired to see my Powers and then I heartily wish they had been a little ampler: and I have since wondred what Scruple a number of Bishops could have of empowring a Clergyman to do the Church and them a service, without any Prospect or Imagination of Interest for himself, further than about ten shillings a-year.—Mr. H[arley] has invited me to dine with him to-day; but I shall not putt him upon this discourse so soon. If he begins it himself I will add at bottom, whatever there is of moment. He sayd, Mr. Sectry St. John desires to be acquainted with me, and that he will bring us together, which may be further help; though I told him I had no Thoughts of applying to any but himself; wherein he differed from me, desiring I would speak to others, if it were but for Form and seemed to mean

further here be mentioned that Swift's approach to Harley had been arranged by Erasmus Lewis—

a Cunning Shaver,
And very much in Harley's Favour
(*Poems*, p. 171).

as if he would avoid the envy of doing things alone. But an old Courtier (an intimate Friend of mine) with whom I consulted, advised me still to let him know, I relyed wholly upon his good Inclinations, and Credit with the Queen. I find I am forced to say all this very confusedly, just as it lyes in my memory; but perhaps it may give Your Grace a truer notion of what passed than if I had writt in more order. Besides I am forced to omitt the greatest Part of what I said, being not proper for a Letter at such a Distance; For I told very freely the late causes which had stoppt this matter, and removed many odious Misrepresentations etc.

I Beg, whatever Letters are sent to Bishops or others here in this matter by Your Grace or the Primate, may be inclosed to me, that I may stifle or deliver them as the course of the Affair shall require. As for a Letter from Your Grace to the Queen, you say it needs Advice; and I am sure it is not from me, who shall not presume to offer, but perhaps from what I have writt you may form some Judgment or other.

As for publick Affairs, I confess I began this Letter on a half-sheet merely to limit my self on a subject with which I did not know whether Your Grace would be entertained. I am not yet convinced that any Access to men in Power gives a man more Truth or Light than the Politicks of a Coffee House, I have known some great Ministers who would seem to discover the very inside of their Hearts, when I was sure they did not value whether I had proclaimed all they had said, at Charing cross. But I never yet knew one great Minister who made any scruple to mould the Alphabet into whatever words he pleased; or be more difficult about any Facts, than his Porter is about that of his Lord's being at home. So that whoever has so little to do as to desire some Knowledge in Secrets of State, must compare what he hears from severall great men, or from one great man at severall Times, which is equally different. People were surprised when the Court stopt its hand as to farther removalls; the Controller, a Lord of the Admiralty, and some others told me they expected every day to be dismisst, but they were all deceived, and the higher Toryes are very angry: But some time ago at Hampton Court, I pickt out the Reason from a dozen Persons; and told Sr J.[ohn] Holland, I would lay a wager he would not lose his staff so soon as he imagined. The new Ministry are afraid of too great a Majority of their own side in the H. of C. and therefore stopt short in their changes; yet some Refiners think they have gone too far already; for of 30 new members in the present Elections, about 25 are Toryes. The D. of O. seems still to stand the fairest for Ireld; tho I hear some faint hopes they will not nominate very soon.— The Ruin of the late Party was owing to a great number, and complication of causes, which I have had from Persons able enough to inform me, and that is all we can mean by A good Hand, for the veracity is not to be relyed on. The Dutchess of M's Removall has been 7 years working, that of the Tr. above three, and he was to have been dismisst before Ld. Sund—. Beside the many Personall causes, that of breaking measures settled for a Peace four years ago, had a great weight, when the French had complyed with all Terms etc. In short, they apprehended the old Party to be entirely against a Peace for some Time till they were rivetted too fast to be broke, as they otherwise expected if the War should conclude too soon. I cannot tell (for it just comes into my head) whether some unanimous Addresses, from those who love the Church in Ireland, or from Dublin, or your Grace and the Clergy might not be seasonable; or whether my Ld. Wharton's being not yet superseded may yet hinder it.

I forgot to tell your Grace, that the memoriall I gave Mr H— was drawn up by my self, and was an Abstract of what I had said to Him, it was as short as I could make it, that which you sent being too long, and of another Nature.

I dined to-day with Mr H— but I must humbly beg Your Grace's Pardon if I say no more at present, for Reasons I may shortly let you know. In the mean time I desire Your Grace to believe me with the greatest Respect, | My Lord | Your Grace's most dutifull | and most humble Servt |

J: Swift

Address: To His Grace the Lord | Archbishop of Dublin at | Dublin | Ireland

Faulkner 1746

Archbishop King to Swift

Dublin, Oct. 24, 1710

Reverend Sir,[1]

I thank you for yours of the 10th Instant, and send you inclosed a farther Power[2] by my Lord Primate and me. My Lord is not able to

[1] The copy in King's Correspondence, T.C.D., is injured by damp, and only partly decipherable. The text is printed from Faulkner.

[2] The 'farther Power' from the Primate and Archbishop King, bearing the

come to Town, which obliged me to wait on him at *Johnston*,[1] and hindered the joining of two or three Bishops in it who are yet in Town: But I suppose our signing is sufficient. I went in the Morning to wait on his Grace, and intended when he had signed it, to have applied to other Bishops; but he was abroad taking the Air, and I could not get it till it was late, and thought it better to sign and send it, as it is, than wait for another Post. You may expect by the next a Letter to his Grace of *Canterbury*, and another to the Archbishop of *York*.[2] I apprized them both of the Business. The latter, if I remember right, spoke to her Majesty about it; I am not sure that her Majesty remembers what I said on the Subject; but am sure she was pleased to seem satisfied with it, and to scruple only the Time, I suppose, not thinking it fit to confer the Favour she designed the Clergy of *Ireland* by the Hands it must then have passed through, but said, that in the Interval of a Change, or Absence of a Chief Governor, it should be done. I hope, now is the proper Time, and that her Majesty will rather follow the Dictates of her own bountiful Inclinations, than the Intrigues of cunning covetous Counsellors.

I thought to have troubled you with a great many Things, but such a Crowd of Visitors have broken in upon me before I could lock my Gates, that I am forced to break off abruptly, recommending you to GOD's Care. | *I am, &c.* |

William Dublin.

4804

Primate Marsh and Archbishop King to Swift

[Dublin, 24 October 1710]

We directed a Letter to the Bishops of Ossory and Killaloe last August, desiring and empowering Them to Solicite the Affair of our

same date as this letter, is printed below. In the previous letter Swift refers to Harley as having expressed a wish that his powers 'had been a little ampler'. On this point Harley was probably indifferent; and King did not realize that the success of the mission was more dependent on Harley's desire to secure Swift's services than any proof that he enjoyed the support of Irish prelates.

[1] Archbishop Marsh had no residence in his cathedral city of Armagh. Johnstown, where he was then residing, was in Dillon Ashe's parish of Finglas.

[2] Archbishop Tenison and Archbishop Sharp.

First Fruits and Twentyeth Parts, with Her Majesty, which has
depended so long, notwithstanding Her Majesty's Good Inclinations
& several Promises of the Chief Governours how to lay our Addresses
before Her Majesty in the best Manner; We were then apprehensive
that These Bishops might return from England before the Busyness
could be effected, and therefore We desired Them to concern You
in it: having so good Assurance of your Ability, prudence and fitness
to prosecute such a Matter; We find the Bishops returned before you
came to London, for which We are very much concerned, and
judging this the most proper Time to prosecute it with Success, We
intreat you now to take the full Management of it into your Hands,
and do commit the care of Solliciting It to your Dilegence and
Prudence; desiring You to let us know from Time to Time, what
Progress is made in it; and if any Thing further be necessary on our
Part, On your Intimation We shall be ready to do what shall be
judged reasonable, This with our Prayers for You and the Good
Success of your Endeavours is all from | Sr. Your affectionate,
Humble | Servants and Brothers |

Dublin. October[1]   Narcissus Armath
ye 24th: 1710.   Will. Dublin

Address: To | The Revd Dr. Jonathan Swift | these
Endorsed by Swift: Power from the Ld | Primate and Ar Bp Dublin | Octbr.
          24th. 1710. | First fruits
and again: Primate & AB, Dublin

Hawkesworth 1766
Archbishop King to Swift

Dublin, Nov. 2, 1710
Reverend Sir,[2]
   The declaration of his Grace the Duke of *Ormond* to be our Lord
Lieutenant has stopped the further letters of recommendation[3]
designed to be sent to you, because the Bishops were unwilling to
solicit the affair of the first-fruits and twentieth parts by any other

---

[1] This document is in a clerical hand, written upon a sheet folded to make
four quarto pages.
[2] There is a copy in King's Correspondence, T.C.D., but it is only partly
decipherable.
[3] To the Archbishops of Canterbury and York.

hand.[1] I gave them some account how far you had been concerned in it; and they ordered a letter to Mr. *Southwell*,[2] to give him an account, that the papers were in your hands, and to desire you to wait on him with them, and take your own measures in soliciting the affair. I am not to conceal from you, that some expressed a little jealousy that you would not be acceptable to the present courtiers, intimating that you were under the reputation of being a favourite of the late party in power. You may remember I asked you the question before you were engaged in this affair, knowing of what moment it was; and by the coldness I found in some, I soon perceived what was at the bottom. I am of opinion, that this conjuncture in circumstance will oblige you to exert yourself with more vigour; and if it should succeed, you have gained your point; whereas, if you should fail, it would cause no reflections, that having been the fate of so many before you.[3]

I can be very little useful to you at this distance; but if you foresee any thing, wherein I may be serviceable to the business or yourself, you may command, sir, Yours, &c.

Will. Dublin.

Faulkner 1762

Swift to Archbishop King

London, Nov. 4, 1710.

My Lord,

I am most unhappily engaged this Night, where I cannot write to your Grace so long a Letter as I intended:[4] But, I will make it up in a Post or two. I have only now to tell you, that Mr. *Harley* hath given me Leave to acquaint my Lord Primate and your Grace, that the

---

[1] That is, any other hand than that of Ormonde.

[2] Edward Southwell, who was acting under Ormonde as Chief Secretary for Ireland.

[3] On 21 Oct. Harley informed Swift that 'the queen has now granted the First-Fruits and Twentieth Parts'. Writing to Stella, Swift added 'but he will not yet give me leave to write to the archbishops, because the queen designs to signify it to the bishops in Ireland in form'. On 3 Nov. he received permission from Harley to write to the Primate and Archbishop King (*Journal*, pp. 66, 80). King's letter of 2 Nov. did not reach Swift till 23 Nov. (*Journal*, p. 102), and naturally roused him to indignation, for he saw himself being deprived of credit for the success of his mission.

[4] Swift was dining at Kensington with Addison and Steele (*Journal*, p. 81).

Queen hath granted the first Fruits and twentieth Parts to the Clergy of *Ireland*. It was done above a Fortnight ago, but I was then obliged to keep it a Secret, as I hinted to your Grace in my last Letter.[1] He hath now given me Leave to let your Grace and my Lord Primate know it, only desires you will say nothing of it until a Letter cometh to you from my Lord *Dartmouth*, Secretary of State.[2] All I know yet is, that the Bishops are to be made a Corporation for the disposal of the first Fruits, and that the twentieth Parts are to be remitted. I will write to your Grace the Particulars of my Negotiation, and some other Amusements very soon. I humbly beg your Grace to acquaint my Lord Primate with this. I had your Grace's Letter last Post, and you will now see, that your Letters to the Archbishops here are unnecessary. I was a little in Pain about the Duke of *Ormond*, who, I feared might interpose in this Matter, and be angry it was done without him: But, Mr. *Harley* has very kindly taken this Matter upon himself. It was Yesterday I dined with him, and he told me all this; and To-morrow I dine with him again, where I may hear more. I shall obey your Grace's Directions whether my Stay here be further necessary, after you have had the Letter from the Secretary's Office. I know not what it will be; but if any Forms remain to finish, I shall be ready to assist in it as I have hitherto done. I have all the Reason in the World to be satisfied with Mr. *Harley*'s Conduct in this whole Affair. In three Days he spoke of it to the Queen, and gave her my Memorial, and so continued until he got her Grant. I am now in much Company, and steal this Time to write to your Grace. The Queen was resolved to have the whole Merit of this Affair to herself. Mr. *Harley* advised her to it, and next to her Majesty he is the only Person to be thanked. I suppose it will not be many Days before you have the Letter from my Lord *Dartmouth*,[2] and your Grace will afterward signify your commands, if you have any, for me. I shall go to the Office and see that a Dispatch be made as soon as possible. I am with the greatest Respect, | my Lord, | Your Grace's most dutiful, and | Most obedient humble Servant, |

Jon. Swift.

[1] Cf. 10 Oct. 1710.

[2] On 14 June 1710 William Legge, who had succeeded his father in the barony of Dartmouth in 1691, was appointed Secretary of State for the Southern Department in place of Lord Sunderland. In the *Examiner*, no. 27 (26), Swift characterized him as 'a man of letters, good nature and honour, of strict virtue and regularity in life'. He was Lord Keeper of the Privy Seal, 1713–14.

King's Letter-book and Hawkesworth 1766
Archbishop King to Swift

Dublin, Nov. 16, 1710.

Reverend Sir,[1]

I have before me yours of the 4th instant, which I received two posts ago. It was very grateful to me, and I hope it will have a good effect as to the Church in general, and be of use to you in particular, which I heartily wish. My Lord Primate is out of town, and I have not seen him since I received your's, nor do I see any haste to communicate it to him; but in due time there will be no need to make a secret of it. I durst not have said any thing of it, if you had not given me the caution, lest any accident should intervene, to which all matters of this nature are liable. It puts a man out of countenance to raise expectations, if he should not be able to satisfy them. I understand that her Majesty designed this should be her own act; but the good instruments, that have been subservient, ought not to be forgot; and, with God's help, I will do my endeavour that they shall not. I shall be impatient to see the accomplishment of this charitable work.

We are here in as great a ferment about choosing Parliament men, on a supposition that this Parliament will be dissolved as soon as yours in *England*.[2] And it is remarkable, that such as design to betray their country, are more diligent to make votes, than those that have some faint intentions to serve it. It would prevent a great deal of needless charges and heats, if we certainly knew whether we should have a new Parliament or no.

All business in Chancery, and in truth all public business, is at a stand, by the indisposition of my Lord Chancellor.[3] I would tell you, that I am engaged most unhappily this night, to excuse this short letter; but the plain truth, I think, will do as well; which is, that I have no more to say but my prayers for you, &c.

Will. Dublin.

---

[1] The copy in King's Correspondence, T.C.D., is only partly decipherable.

[2] The Irish Parliament was not dissolved for three years.

[3] Richard Freeman, a Whig, who owed his advancement to Somers, had been sent over from England in 1706 to fill the position of Chief Baron of the Exchequer in Ireland. In the following year he was appointed Lord Chancellor. His abilities seem to have been moderate. See Ball, *Judges in Ireland*, ii. 30–31, 67–68.

Swift to Archbishop King

London, Nov. 23, 1710.

My Lord,

I had your Grace's Letter not until this Day: Whether it lay in the Secretary's Office, or was kept by the Wind I cannot tell; but I would have exposed it immediately whenever it had come.[1] Mr. Southwell told me two Days ago of the Letter your Grace mentions,[2] which surprised me a good deal, when I remembered I had writ to your Grace three Weeks ago, that the Queen had absolutely granted the First Fruits and Twentieths, and that Mr. *Harley* had permitted me to signify the same to the Primate and your Grace. Perhaps that Letter might not have reached your Grace before that Resolution of sending to the Duke of *Ormond*;[3] but however, I gave you such an Account of my Reception from Mr. *Harley*, and his Readiness to undertake this Affair, and what Steps he had already made in it, as I thought would have given you some Sight in what Way the Business was; but, Mr. *Harley* charged me to tell no Body alive, what the Queen had resolved on, till he gave me Leave; and, by the Conclusion of a former Letter, your Grace might see you were to expect some farther Intelligence very soon.[4] Your Grace may remember, that upon your telling me how backward the Bishops were in giving me a Power, I was very unwilling to go at all, and sent the Dean of *St. Patrick's* to tell you so; but, you thought I could not

[1] Swift was naturally enraged when he received King's graceless letter of 2 Nov., exhibiting, as it did, a meek surrender to the jealous interference of the bishops, and even suggesting that Swift would do well to exert himself with more vigour. This was hard to bear in face of his surprisingly quick success with the Ministry. He penned this angry reply at once; and, when he had given himself time to re-read the Archbishop's letter, a more considered, if equally indignant, answer, 28 Nov.

[2] In the *Journal*, 24 Nov., Swift refers to this letter, reported to him 't'other day' by Southwell, 'with an address to the duke of Ormond, to intercede with the queen, to take off the First-Fruits'. On the 24th Swift dined with Southwell and saw 'another letter to him from the bishop of Kildare, to call upon me for the papers, &c.' On seeing this letter Swift was further enraged.

[3] Swift should have remembered that King's letter, just received by him, was written two days before his own of 4 Nov.

[4] Swift in his letter to King, 10 Oct., hinted that he had something to say which he could not declare at the moment 'for Reasons I may shortly let you know'.

192

handsomely put it off, when Things were gone so far. Your Objection then about the Disadvantage I lay under in Point of Party, I knew well enough how to answer, otherwise nothing should have prevailed on me to come hither; and, if my Lords the Bishops doubt whether I have any Credit with the present Ministry, I will, if they please, undo this Matter in as little Time, as I have done it. I did reckon your Grace understood and believed me in what I said; and I reckon so still, but I will not be at the Pains of undeceiving so many. I never proposed to myself either Credit or Profit by my Labour, but the Satisfaction of doing Good, without valuing whether I had the Merit of it or no: But the Method now taken was the likeliest Way to set all Things backward if it were not past danger.

It shall be my Business (until my Lords the Bishops forbid me to engage farther) to prevent any Misunderstanding with Mr. *Harley* by this sudden Step. The Thing was all done before the Duke of *Ormond* was named for Lord Lieutenant, so there was no Affront at all to him; and Mr. *Harley* told me more than once, that such an Interest was the properest, because he thought the Queen herself should have the Doing it: But, I said a great Deal of this in former Letters. If your Grace hath any Commands for me of your own, I shall obey them with all Chearfulness, being, with great Respect, | My Lord, | Your Grace's most obedient, and | Most humble Servant, |

Jon. Swift.

Faulkner 1762

Swift to Archbishop King

London, November 28, 1710

My Lord,

A Day or two after I received your Grace's Letter, of the 2nd Instant, I dined with Mr. *Southwell*,[1] who shewed me the Letter of the Bishop's, to the Duke of *Ormond*, and another Letter from the Bishop of *Kildare* to Mr. *Southwell* to desire him to get the Papers from me, which I shall send him as soon as I have looked them out. Mr. *Southwell* said, that a Month or two hence, when the Duke began to think of his Journey, it would be Time enough to sollicit this Affair. Upon this I told him frankly, that the Queen had

---

[1] It was on the day after the preceding letter had been dispatched that Swift dined with Southwell (*Journal*, p. 102).

already granted the first Fruits, and that I had writ to your Grace by
Mr. *Harley*'s Directions, but that my Letter did not reach you until
your's was sent to the Duke and him; and, that therefore I thought
it would be a very odd Step to begin again. He said, he was glad it
was done, and that he did not design to take any of the Credit from
me, *&c.* I told him sincerely, it was what I did not regard at all, and
provided the Church had the Benefit, it was indifferent to me how it
came about, and so we parted.[1] I had told the Duke of *Ormond* at
first, that I would apply myself to *Mr. Harley* if his Grace advised
it, which he did; and I afterward told Mr. *Southwell*, that Mr.
Harley had been very kind in promising his good Offices: Further
I durst not speak, being under an Engagement of Secrecy to Mr.
Harley; and the whole Thing was done before the Duke was declared Lord Lieutenant. If your Grace considers the Time you sent
me the Paper, you will judge what Dispatch was made; in two
Days after, I delivered a Memorial, I drew up, to Mr. *Harley*, and in
less than a Fortnight he had treated the Matter four Times with the
Queen, and then told me she had granted it absolutely as my
Memorial desired, but charged me to tell no Man alive; and your
Grace may remember, that one of my Letters ended with something
as if I were limited, and would say more in a short Time. In about
a Week after I had leave to inform the Primate and your Grace, as I
did in my Letter of the 4th instant. It is to be considered, that the
Queen was all this while at *Hampton-Court* or *Windsor*, so that I
think the Dispatch was very great. But, indeed, I expected a Letter
would have been sent from the Secretary's Office, to signify this
Matter in due Form, and so it will; but Mr. *Harley* had a Mind first to
bring me to the Queen, for that and some other Matters; and, she
came to Town not a Week ago, and was out of Order one Day when
it was designed I should attend her, and, since the Parliament's
Beginning hath taken her up; but in a few days, Mr. *Harley* tells
me, he will introduce me.[2] This I tell your Grace, in Confidence
only to satisfy you in particular, why the Queen hath not yet sent a
Letter in Form. Upon that Dispatch to Mr. *Southwell*, I was

[1] On 24 Nov. Swift wrote to Stella: 'As I hope to live, I despise the credit
of it, out of an excess of pride, and desire you will not give me the least merit
when you talk of it; but I would vex the bishops, and have it spread that Mr.
Harley had done it: pray do so.'
[2] So far as is known Swift was never presented to Queen Anne. Although
there can be no doubt that he would have valued an introduction to the royal
presence he is content to make little of it. On 29 Dec. 1710 he tells Stella that

perplexed to the last Degree. I did not value the slighting Manner of
the Bishop of *Kildare*'s Letter, barely desiring Mr. *Southwell* to call
on me for the Papers, without any Thing further, as if I had been
wholly insignificant; but I was at a Loss how to behave myself
with the Duke and Mr. *Harley*. I met the latter Yesterday in the
Court of Requests, and he whispered me to dine with him. At
dinner I told him of the Dispatch to Mr. *Southwell*, and raillied him
for putting me under Difficulties with his Secrets, that I was running my Head against a Wall; that he reckoned he had done the
Church and me a Favour; that I should disoblige the Duke of
Ormond, and that the Bishops in *Ireland* thought I had done
nothing, and had therefore taken away my Commission. He told me
your Lordship had taken it away in good Time, for the Thing was
done, and that as for the Duke of *Ormond*, I need not be uneasy, for
he would let his Grace know it as soon as he saw him, which would
be in a Day or two at the Treasury, and then promised again to
carry me to the Queen, with the first opportunity.[1] Your Grace now
sees how the Affair stands, and whether I deserve such Treatment
from the Bishops, from every Part whereof I wholly exclude your
Grace, and could only wish my first Letter, about the Progress I had
made, had found so much Credit with you, as to have delayed that
Dispatch until you heard once more from me. I had at least so much
Discretion, not to pretend I had done more than I really did, but
rather less; And if I had consulted my own Interest, I should have
employed my Credit with the present Ministry another Way. The
Bishops are mistaken in me; it is well known here, that I could have
made my Markets with the last Ministry if I had pleased; and the
present Men in Power are very well apprised of it, as your Grace
may, if I live to see you again; which I certainly never would in
Ireland, if I did not flatter myself that I am upon a better Foot with
your Grace, than with some other of their Lordships. Your Grace is

he took St. John aside and complained to him that Harley, after promising to
bring him to the Queen, 'had not done it in six weeks, and I was in danger to
lose reputation' (*Journal*, p. 143). Nothing came of this. It may be surmised
that the Queen was unwilling to see him, or, at the least, indifferent. Before
this, on 14 Dec., he says that Harley and St. John were 'resolved' that he should
'preach before the Queen', but he hoped that they would forget it. Nothing
more is heard of this (*Journal*, p. 126).

[1] The purpose of this paragraph is, of course, to impress upon King his
standing with the Ministry, and his indifference to the opinion of the Irish
bishops.

pleased to command me to continue my Sollicitations, but as now
there will be no Need of them, so I think my Commission is at an
End, ever since I had Notice of that Dispatch to Mr. *Southwell.*
However, in Obedience to your Grace, if there be any Thing to be
done about expediting the Forms, wherein my Service can be of
Use, I will readily perform as far as I am able: But I must tell your
Grace what gives me the greatest Displeasure, that I had Hopes to
prevail that the Queen should in some Months be brought to remit
the Crown-rents, which I named in my Memorial, but in an Article
by itself, and which Mr. *Harley* had given me some Hopes of, and
I have some private Reasons to think, might have been brought
about.[1] I mentioned it in the Memorial, only as from myself; and
therefore, if I have an Opportunity, I shall venture to mention it to
the Queen, or at least repeat it to Mr. *Harley.* This I do as a private
Man, whom the Bishops no longer own. It is certainly right to pay
all Civilities, and make Applications to a Lord Lieutenant; but,
without some other Means, a Business may hang long enough, as
this of the first Fruits did for four Years under the Duke of *Ormond*'s last Government, altho' no Man loves the Church of *Ireland*
better than his Grace; but such Things are forgot and neglected
between the Governor and his Secretaries, unless sollicited by
Some Body who has the Business at Heart. But I have done, and
shall trouble your Grace no farther upon this Affair; and on other
Occasions, while I am here, will endeavour to entertain you with
what is like to pass in this busy Scene, where all Things are taking
a New, and, I think, a good Turn; and where, if you please, I will
write to you, with that Freedom I formerly did; and I beg your
Grace to employ me in any Commands you may have here, which I
shall be prouder to obey, than to have ever so much Merit with some
others; being with perfect Respect, my Lord, | Your Grace's | Most
dutiful and | Most obedient Humble Servant,

Jon. Swift.

Your Grace will please to direct for me, St. *James*'s Coffee-house
in St. *James*'s-*Street.*

Two hundred Members supped last Night at the Fountain Tavern,
where they went to determine about a Chairman for Elections.
Medlicott and Manly were the two Candidates;[2] but the Company

[1] The crown rents are named in both memorials. See pp. 181, 182, and
Journal, pp. 677–80.
[2] Thomas Medlycott was M.P. for Westminster, and John Manley for Bossiney.

could not agree, and parted in an ill Humour. It is a Matter of some Moment, and I hope it will be amicably made up; but the great Rock we are afraid of, is a Dissention among the Majority, because the weakest Part, when they grow discontented know where to retire, and be received.

King's Letter-book and Hawkesworth 1766

Archbishop King to Swift

Dublin, Nov. 30, 1710.

Reverend Sir,

I received yours of the 23^d, by last packet. I was aware of what you observed, when the letter to his Grace[1] was signed; but it was before I received yours of the 4th instant, wherein you tell me, that the business was in effect done; nor could I have any certain prospect that it would be done from any intimation that I had before from you. You must know that this was not the only thing displeased me in the letter; it was drawn and signed by some before I saw it. I looked on it as a snare laid in my way; nor must you wonder that some are better at making their court, than serving the Church; and can flatter much better, than vote on the right side. Those, that had rendered themselves justly obnoxious by deserting his Grace's friends and interest in notorious instances, think they have salved all by this early application, and perhaps it may prove so.[2]

But if the matter be done, assure yourself it will be known by whom, and what means it was effected.

In the mean time, God forbid you should think of slacking your endeavours to bring it to perfection. I am yet under an obligation not to say any thing of the matter from your letter; and whilst so, it would be hard to me to refuse to sign such a letter as that you mention, or find a pretence for so doing: but when the business is done, the means and methods will likewise be known, and everybody have their due that contributed to it.

I shall reckon nothing done till the Queen's letter come here. You may remember how we were borne in hand in my Lord

---

[1] The letter from the bishops to the Duke of Ormonde, see p. 192, n. 2.

[2] The desire on the part of certain bishops to propitiate the Duke of Ormonde arose no doubt from votes given by them in the House of Lords during the two previous viceroyalties.—Ball.

Pembroke's time, that the Queen had passed the grant, which, after a whole year's expectation and solicitation, proved only a mouthful of moonshine.[1] But, if it succeeds better now, we must owe it, next to the Queen's goodness and bounty, to the great care of the great man to whom you have applied, and to your management. It is seven or eight years since we first attempted this affair,[2] and it passed through several hands; yet no progress was made in it, which was certainly due to the ill methods taken to put it forward; which, in truth, instead of promoting, obstructed it. At the very first motion, it was promised, and in a fair way; but the Bishops here, out of their abundant deference to the Government, made the same wrong step they would have done now; and we could never make the least progress since, till now, and I pray God we have not put it back again.

You must not imagine, that it is out of any disaffection to you, or any distrust of your ability or diligence, that the Bishops here were so cold in their employing you; but they reckon on party; and though several knew what you were, yet they imagined, and some vouched, that you were looked on at Court as engaged on the other side; and you cannot do yourself a greater service than to bring this to a good issue, to their shame and conviction. I heartily recommend you and your business to God's care. I am, *&c.*

Will Dublin

Faulkner 1746

Archbishop King to Swift

Dublin, Dec. 16, 1710

Sir,[3]

This is to acknowledge the receipt of yours of the 28th[4] past, which came not to my hands till *Thursday* last,[5] by Reason of Winds that kept the Pacquets on the other Side.[6]

---

[1] See Swift to King, 26 Mar. 1709.

[2] Swift, writing to King, 31 Dec. 1704, expresses a hope that a remission of the First Fruits to the Irish clergy might 'be easily granted'.

[3] There is an illegible copy of this letter in the manuscript room of Trinity College, Dublin. The text is here printed from Faulkner, 1746.

[4] Faulkner and Hawkesworth misprint '20th'.

[5] 14 Dec.

[6] Communication with Ireland was irregular at this time, On 6 Dec. Swift

I find the Matter of our First Fruits, &c. is talked of now.¹ I reckon on nothing certain till her Majesty's Letter Comes in Form: and Quære, Why should not you come and bring it with you? It would make you a very welcome Clergyman to *Ireland*, and be the best Means to satisfy Mankind how it was obtained, although I think it will be out of Dispute. I am very well apprized of the Dispatch you gave this Affair, and well pleased, that I judged better of the person fit to be employed, than some of my Brethren. But now it is done, as I hope it is effectually, they will assume as much as their Neighbours; which I shall never contradict.

Things are taking a new Turn here as well as with you; and I am of Opinion, by the Time you come here, few will profess themselves *Whiggs*. The greatest Danger I apprehend, and which terrifies me more than perhaps you will be able to imagine, is the Fury and Indiscretion of some of our own People; who never had any Merit but by *imbroiling* things; they did, and I am afraid will yet do Mischief. You will soon hear of a great conspiracy discovered in the county of Westmeath. I was used to so many discoveries of plots in the latter end of King Charles's time, and the beginning of King James's, that I am not surprised at this discovery. I must not say any thing of it, till all the witnesses be examined: so many as have deposed are not decisive. The design of it is to show all the gentlemen of Ireland to be a pack of desperate Whigs, ready to rise up in arms against her Majesty, for the old Ministry, associating to that purpose. Whether it be for the interest of Ireland to have this believed you may judge; and sure there must be good evidence to make any reasonable man believe it. Mr. Higgins has drawn up the narrative, and sent it to England, and will pawn all he is worth to make it good.² I heartily recommend you to God's favour; and am, &c.

                                             Will Dublin.

had not received the Archbishop's letter of 16 Nov., and the letter of 28 Nov. did not come to hand till 14 Dec.

¹ On 24 Nov. Swift had written to Stella: 'I give you free leave to say, on occasion, that it is done, and that Mr. Harley prevailed on the queen to do it, &c. as you please.'

² Hawkesworth quotes from a letter of Archbishop King, which, being illegible, is otherwise lost. 'That four or five gentlemen of small fortunes are said to have signed an association to fight up to the knees in blood against the new ministry. The discoverer was one Langton, who swore to it: he was a converted priest.' The direct informer is stated to have been a servant of one of the gentlemen, who denied, however, that he had seen a signed compact. 'Some seditious words spoken by some of those gentlemen at dinner in their

Swift to Archbishop King

London, Dec. 30, 1710.
My Lord,

I have just received your Grace's Letter of the 16th, and I was going however to write again to your Grace, not upon Business, but to amuse you with something from hence, which no Man wants more than your Grace, considering the Variety of other People's Affairs you have always on your Hands, as well as the Church's and your own, which are the same Thing. The Duke of *Ormond* told me the other Day, that the Primate declined very fast, and was hardly able to sign a Paper. I said, I wondered they would put him in the Government, when every one knew he was a dying Man this Twelvemonth past.[1] I hope, for the Church's Good, that your Grace's Friends will do their Duty in representing you, as the Person the Kingdom wisheth to succeed him. I know not how your Dispositions stand that Way. I know my Lord President hath great Credit at present, and I have understood him to be a Friend to your Grace.[2] I can only say, I have no Regard to your Interest in this, but that of the Church; and therefore should be very glad to drop in a Word where it lieth in my Way, if I thought it would not be disagreeable to you. I dread their sending a Person from hence, which I shall venture to prevent with all the little Credit I have, and should be glad to see a Primate of our own Kingdom and University; and that is all I shall venture to say on this Subject.

Marshal *Staremberg* hath certainly got to *Saragossa* with 7000 Men, and the Duke of *Vendome* hath sent him his Equipage. Mr. *Stanhope* was positive to part Forces with *Staremberg*, which occasioned this Loss; and when the Battle was, they were several

cups, or conversation, so far as I can remember, is the sum of the evidence for the plot.' The grand jury declined to find true bills upon the evidence. Langton was a creature of Francis Higgins, the violent High Church clergyman.

[1] On the appointment of Ormonde as Lord Lieutenant Marsh had again been named a Lord Justice. He was seventy-two years of age. He died 2 Nov. 1713.

[2] Lord Rochester had succeeded Somers, 21 Sept. 1710, as Lord President of the Council. Ball conjectures that Rochester may have been instrumental in King's translation from Derry to Dublin, as he resigned the office of Lord Lieutenant only a few weeks before the letters patent, 11 Mar. 1702–3, were issued to King.

Miles asunder.[1] The Duke of *Marlborough* was Yesterday an Hour with the Queen; it was set him at twelve at Noon, when it was likely his Visit should be shortest.[2] Mr. *St. John* was with her just before, and Mr. *Harley* just after. The Duke's Behaviour was with the most abject Submission; that he was the meanest of her Majesty's Instruments; her humble Creature, a poor Worm, &c. This I had from a Lord to whom the Queen told it: For the Ministers never tell any Thing; and, it is only by picking out and comparing, that one can ever be the Wiser for them. I took Leave Yesterday of Lord *Peterborow*, who is going in a Day or two to *Vienna*: I said I wished he were going to *Spain*; he told me, he hoped his present Journey would be to more Purpose; and, by what I can gather, they will use all Means to make as speedy a Peace as possible, with Safety and Honour.[3] Lord *Rivers* tells me he will not set out for *Hanover* this Month: I asked him about his late Reception there, because the Town was full of Stories about it: He assured me he could not desire a better; and, if it were otherwise, I believe he would be hardly pitched upon to be sent again.[4] The young People in Parliament are very eager to have some Enquiries made into past Managements, and are a little angry with the Slackness of the Ministry upon that Article; they say, they have told those who sent them, that the Queen's calling a new Parliament was to correct and look into former Abuses; and, if something of the latter be not done, they know not how to answer it. I am not altogether satisfied how the Ministry

---

[1] Four thousand British troops, under Stanhope, trapped within the walls of Brihuega, surrendered to Vendome, Starhemberg, moving too slowly to the relief, had then no alternative but to resume his retreat to Barcelona. See Trevelyan, *England under Queen Anne*, iii. 85–87.

[2] Marlborough reached London on 28 Dec., and was received by the populace with acclamation. In the evening he waited on the Queen, who gave him a cold reception. The next day at noon he was again received, and informed by the Queen that he was not to expect a vote of thanks to be moved in Parliament.

[3] Peterborough was appointed Ambassador Extraordinary to Vienna on a mission designed to promote a better understanding between the Emperor and the Duke of Savoy; but his departure was delayed till 13 Jan. on a representation from the House of Lords, who wished to stage an investigation into miscarriages in Spain. The result was a vote of censure on Lord Galway and a vote of thanks to Peterborough for his 'great and eminent services'.

[4] Richard Savage, fourth Earl Rivers (whom Richard Savage, the poet, claimed as father), though a Whig, anticipated the fall of that party and ingratiated himself with Harley. He was sent to Hanover in August to allay the Elector's apprehensions caused by the Tory reaction.

is disposed in this Point. Your Grace hath heard there was much Talk lately of Sir *Richard Levinge*'s design to impeach Lord *Wharton*; and several Persons of great Consideration in the House, assured me they would give him all Encouragement; and, I have Reason to know, it would be acceptable to the Court: But Sir *Richard* is the most timorous Man alive, and they all begin to look upon him in that Character, and to hope nothing from him.[1] However, they talk of some other Enquiries when the Parliament meets after this Recess; and it is often in people's Mouths that *February* will be a warm Month; but this I can affirm nothing of, and I hope, your Grace will distinguish between what I affirm, and what I report: As to the First, you may securely count upon it; the other you will please to take as it is sent.

Since the letter from the Bishops to the Duke of *Ormond*, I have been a much cooler Sollicitor; for I look upon myself no longer a deputed Person. Your Grace may be fully satisfied that the Thing is granted, because I had Orders to report it to you from the Prime Minister; the rest is Form, and may be done at any Time: As for bringing the Letter over myself, I must again profess to your Grace, that I do not regard the Reputation of it at all;[2] perhaps I might if I were in *Ireland*; but, when I am on this side, a certain Pride seizeth me, from very different Usage I meet with, which maketh me look on Things in another Light. But besides I beg to tell your Grace in Confidence, that the Ministry have desired me to continue here some Time longer, for certain Reasons, that I may some Time have the Honour to tell you.[3] As for every Body's knowing what is done in the First Fruits, it was I that told it; for, after I saw the Bishops' Letter, I let every one know it in perfect Spight,[4] and told Mr. *Harley* and Mr. Secretary *St. John* so. However, in humble

---

[1] Sir Richard Levinge, called to the English Bar and M.P. for Chester, went to Ireland, where he enjoyed a distinguished career. He was Solicitor-General of Ireland 1690–5 and 1704–9; Speaker of the Irish House of Commons 1692–5. Levinge had returned to the English Parliament at the recent general election as member for Derby, and wisely realized the wisdom of caution. He was rewarded by promotion to the office of Attorney-General for Ireland, 1711. See *Historical Notices of the Levinge Family*, 1853, by Sir Richard Levinge, pp. 5–6; Ball, *Judges in Ireland*, ii. 195–6; *D.N.B.*; and *Poems*, p. 67, n.

[2] See p. 194, n. 1.

[3] The reason was his instalment as editor of the *Examiner*, which he had taken up before the negotiations about the First Fruits had been concluded.

[4] See p. 199, n. 1.

Deference to your Grace's Opinion, and not to appear sullen, I did Yesterday complain to Mr. Secretary *St. John*, that Mr. *Harley* had not yet got the Letter from the Queen to confirm the Grant of the First Fruits; that I had lost Reputation by it; and that I took it very ill of them both; and that their excuses of Parliament Business, and Grief for the Loss in *Spain*, were, what I would bear no longer. He took all I said very well, and desired I would call on him To-morrow Morning, and he would engage, if Mr. *Harley* had not done it, he himself would in a Day or two.[1] As soon as there is any Issue of this I shall inform your Grace; and I have Reason to think it is a Trifle they will not refuse me.

I have had from other hands some Accounts of that ridiculous Plot your Grace mentions, but it is not yet talked of here, neither have any of the Ministry mentioned a Word of it to me, altho' they are well apprized of some Affairs in *Ireland*; for I had two Papers given me by a great Man, one about the Sentence of the Defacers of the Statue,[2] and the other about a Trial before the Lord Chief Justice Broderick, for some Words in the North, spoke by a Clergyman against the Queen. I suppose your Grace reckons upon a new Parliament in *Ireland*, and some Alterations in the Council, the Law, and the Revenue. Your Grace is the most exact Correspondent I ever had, and the Dean of *St. Patrick*'s directly contrary, which I hope you will remember to say to him upon the Occasion. | I am, with the greatest Respect, | my Lord, your Grace's most dutiful, | and most humble Servant,

J. Swift

I have read over this Letter, and find several Things relating to Affairs here, that are said in perfect Confidence to your Grace: If they are told again, I only desire it may not be known from what Hand they came.

[1] Swift was not introduced to St. John till 11 Nov. 1710; but on the day before this letter was written he had dined with him for the fifth time. As early as 7 Oct. Harley told Swift that he must bring him acquainted with St. John, but in the end he owed his introduction to Erasmus Lewis.

[2] The college students who had injured King William's statue in Dublin (p. 175, n. 1) had been sentenced to stand before it in penitential guise, to pay a fine of £100 each, and to be imprisoned for six months.—Ball.

Swift to Archbishop King

London, January, 4, 1710–11.

My Lord,

Having writ to your Grace so lately, I only now make bold to let you know, that on *Tuesday* I was to wait on Mr. Secretary *St. John*, who told me from Mr. *Harley*, that I need not be in Pain about the First-Fruits, for the Warrant was drawn in Order towards a Patent; but, must pass several Forms, and take up some Time, for the Queen designeth to make a Grant by her Letters Patent.[1] I shall take all due Methods to hasten it as far as I am able, but in these Cases they are generally pretty tedious. Mr. *Harley* likewise sent me the same Day by another Person, the same Message. I dined with him about four Days ago, but there being much Company, and he going away in haste pretty soon after Dinner, he had not Time to tell me so himself.[2] Indeed he hath been so ready to do every Thing in this Matter as I would have him, that he never needed pressing, which considering both the Weight and Difficulty of Affairs, at present on his Shoulders, is very extraordinary, and what I never met from so great a Minister before. I had thought, and so Mr. Harley told me, that the Queen would have sent a Letter to the Bishops; but, this is a shorter Way, and I hope your Grace will like it. I am, | with the greatest Respect, | My Lord, | Your Grace's most Dutiful, | and most humble Servant, |

Jon. Swift.

I am told from a good Hand, that in a short Time, the House of Commons will fall upon some Enquiries into the late Management.

[1] On the previous Sunday, 31 Dec., Swift waited on St. John, 'and gave him a memorial to get the queen's letter for the First-Fruits', who then promised to obtain it 'in a very few days'. On Tuesday, 2 Jan., he waited again on St. John, who assured him 'that the warrant was now drawn, in order for a patent for the First-Fruits', and that ''tis granted and done past all dispute'. See *Journal*, pp. 145, 150.

[2] It was on Sunday, 31 Dec., that Swift had dined with Harley. There was 'much company' and Swift confessed himself to Stella 'not merry at all'. Ball conjectures that Swift's ambiguous statement, 'about four Days ago', and his uneasiness at the dinner, betray, perhaps, 'a consciousness that he would have been better elsewhere'. There seems to be no reason for this suggestion. The date was correctly stated; and Swift was not always pleased with the company in which he found himself.

I took leave Yesterday of Lord *Peterborow*, who, I suppose is this Day set out on his Journey to *Vienna*;[1] he is a little discouraged, and told me, he did not hope for any great Success in what he went upon. He is one of those Many who are mightily bent upon having some such Enquiries made, as I have mentioned.

4804

Henry St. John to Swift

Sunday past twelve. Jany $17\frac{11}{10}$[2]

there are few things I would be more industrious to bring about than opportunitys of seeing you. since you was here in the morning,[3] I have found means of putting off the engagement I was under for tomorrow, so that I expect you to dine with me att three a clock

I send you this early notice to prevent you from any other appointment. I am ever Reverend S^r | Y^r obedient humble | Servant
H. St. John.

Address: To the Reverend | Dr Swift

Swift to Henry St. John

[7 January, 1710–11.]

S^r . . .[4]

Tho I should not value such usage from a Secretary of State and a great Minister, yet when I consider the person it comes from I can endure it no longer; I would have you know S^r. that if the Queen gave you a Dukedom and the Gart^r to morrow with the Treasury just at the end of them . . . I would regard you no more than if you were not worth a groat. I could almost resolve, in spight, not to find fault with my Vittals or be quarrelsome to morrow at y^r

[1] As already mentioned (p. 201, n. 3) Peterborough's departure was delayed by the inquiry of the House of Lords into the Spanish campaign.
[2] The date, written very small, is in Swift's hand. Sunday fell on 7 Jan.
[3] On the previous Friday Swift was sent for so early by St. John that he 'was forced to go without shaving'. St. John had little of importance to say, and on this Sunday morning Swift shaved first 'for fear of missing church'. Later he received the above note inviting him to dine on the following day.
[4] This draft of a reply was written by Swift on the back of the preceding letter.

Table: but if I do not take the first Opportunity to lett all the world know some Qualityes in y that you take most Care to hide may my right Hand forgett its Cunning. After which threatening believe me if you please, to be with the greatest Respect | S^r yr most obedient & | most humble serv^t

J: Swift

Endorsed by Swift: Ld Bolingbroke | Jan^ry 1710–11— | with an Answer

Hawkesworth 1766 and Copy
Archbishop King to Swift

Dublin, Jan. 9, 1710 [–11.]

Reverend Sir,[1]

I received yours of *December* the 30th by the last pacquets: it found me in the extremety of the gout, which is the more cruel, because I have not had a fit of it for two years and a half. I strain myself to give you an answer to-night, apprehending that as both my feet and knees are already affected, my hands may perhaps be so by the next post; and then, perhaps, I may[2] not be able to answer you in a month, which might lose me some part of the praise you give me as a good correspondent.

As to my Lord Primate, he is much better since he was put into the government; and I reckon his life may be longer than mine; but, with God's help, hereafter I will say more on this subject.

As to what is reported of Mr. *Stanhope*'s obstinacy, I demur, till satisfied how far the kindness to him, as a manager, influences the report.[3]

We have received an answer from his Grace the Duke of *Ormond* to our letter.[3] It is in a very authentic and solemn form, *that his Grace will take a proper time to lay our request before her Majesty, and know her pleasure on it.* By which I conclude two things: first, that his Grace is not informed of any grant her Majesty has made; for if he had, he would have applied immediately and sent it; and then it would have passed for his, and he would have had the merit of it. Secondly, that his Grace is in no haste about it. And therefore let me

---

[1] The clerical copy of this letter in King's correspondence is severely injured by damp, and, save for the part which can be deciphered, we are dependent on Hawkesworth.

[2] Hawkesworth reads 'might'.   [3] See p. 201.

beseech you to solicit and press it, and get the letter dated, as when first it was promised; but I confess I have still some scruple in my mind about it.

I acknowledge you have not been treated with due regard in *Ireland*, for which there is a plain reason, *praegravat artes infra se positas*, &c. I am glad you meet with more due returns where you are; and as this is the time to make some use of your interest for yourself, do not forget it.

We have published here a Character of the Earl of *Wharton*, late Lord Lieutenant of *Ireland*.[1] I have so much christianity[2] and justice as to condemn all such proceedings. If a governor behave himself ill, let him be complained of and punished; but to wound any man thus in the dark, to appeal to the mob, that can neither inquire nor judge, is a proceeding that I think the common sense of mankind should condemn. Perhaps he may deserve this usage, but a good man may fall under the same.

We expect a new Parliament and many changes, but I believe some we hear of will not be. Your observation of the two sentences is just.[3] You will pardon this gouty disjointed letter, and believe my respects are better than the expressions here. I am, *&c*.

W. D[ublin].

Hawkesworth 1766 and Copy

Archbishop King to Swift

Jan. 13, 1710 [–11.][4]

My gout gives me leave yet to answer yours of the 4th instant, which was very acceptable to me; because I find by it some farther

[1] Swift's attack on Wharton in his *A Short Character of His Ex. T.E. of W.* was first printed (without imprint) in Dec. 1710. No copy of this private issue has survived. The first edition with an imprint was that of 'William Coryton', dated '1711'. This attack was written about the same time as Swift's *Examiner* of 30 Nov. 1710, in which he imitated Cicero's speech against Verres. 'The character', says Swift, 'is here reckoned admirable, but most of the facts are trifles' (*Journal*, 1 Jan. 1711). In other words, he acknowledged the characterization as his own writing; the continuation, confirmatory facts from Ireland, was not his compilation. See *Prose Works*, ed. Davis, iii, pp. xix–xxi, 175–84, 229–40.
[2] Ball misread the word as 'charity'.
[3] The sentence on the two undergraduates who had defaced the statue of King William. See p. 203.   [*For note 4 see overleaf.*]

steps are made in our business. I believe it will take up some time and thoughts to frame a warrant, and much more a patent for such an affair. Except your lawyers there be of another humour than ours here, they will not write a line without their fees; and therefore I should think it necessary some fund should be thought of to fee them. If you think this motion pertinent, I can think of no other way at present to answer it, than, if you think it necessary, to allow you to draw upon me, and any bill to this purpose, less than an 100 *l.* shall be punctually answered. I write thus, because I have no notion how such a thing should pass the offices without some money; and I have an entire confidence in you, that you will lay out no more than what is necessary.

I think your Ministers perfectly right to avoid all enquiry, and every thing that would embroil ⌐them before the funds are found and agreed on. When this is over they may do what they please; and sure it will please them to see the crow stripped of her rapareed feathers. We begin to be in pain for the Duke of *Marlborough.*

I hear an answer is printing to the Earl of *Wharton*'s Character. Pray was there ever such licentiousness of the press as at this time? Will the Parliament not think of curbing it?⌐1 I heartily recommend you, *&c.*

W. D[ublin]

Your friends have their hands full; pray God direct and support them.

---

¹ These words make it unlikely that King suspected Swift's authorship of the *Character.*

---

⁴ When this and the preceding letter from King were printed by Hawkesworth the copies in the Archbishop's letter-book seem already to have suffered injury, and he confused the concluding portions. The sentences included above in half brackets were printed as part of the letter of 9 Jan. When Ball was engaged on his edition of the *Correspondence* the manuscripts were still sufficiently legible to enable him to detect the confusion. Nothing now remains.

Swift to Thomas Staunton

London. Feby. 10. 17$\frac{11}{10}$

S^r.[1]

I wish you and all men of Business would observe one Rule of sending People word of where to direct to you; For I do not think that when any body has been 5 Months in London, they remember where any body lodges in Dublin. I had y^r Letter yesterday; and you are to know that I am fallen out with the whole Temple Family, on account of something I publisht Last Year of Sr Wm Temples without their Consent: However I went this morning to see Henry Temple, and it is the first time I have done so since I came to Engld, as indeed the first Visit I ever made him in my Life, thô we were very well acquainted before he was marryd. I began with asking him how Mr Mall[2] did, he sd, very well, and no appearance of his dying: Then I told him y^r Story, s^d you were a Person I had long known, and for whom severall People of Consideration would be bound—and I gave the Character I am sure you deserve. I told him that all I said was more for his Service than Yours: That whenever he got that Office, if he thought of any Removals, he would find it his Interest to make use of You. He s^d, he had been already applyed to by many People; but he would make no promise to any body; He agreed with me that if any Removals were made, You would be the Person fittest to be put in, and he very readily writt your Name and your Pretensions in a large Paper-book that was in his Scrutore. I desired him, when ever He had that Office, to enquire y^r Character; and if it did not answer, I would ask nothing in y^r Behalf. I read that part of y^r Letter to him which I thought proper; and by what he s^d to me I am almost confident you may reckon upon some Benefit by it. However; I will try one Trick more; I will find out who has Power with him, and see whether by the promise of one of your two

---

[1] This letter, not in Ball, was first printed by A. Martin Freeman in *Vanessa and her Correspondence with Swift*, pp. 193–5. It was addressed to Thomas Staunton, who for many years carried out legal business for Swift. The dispatch of this letter of 10 Feb. 1710–11 is mentioned to Stella, *Journal*, p. 188. Henry Temple had evidently taken Staunton into his service, for on 15 Jan. 1725–6 we find him, then Viscount Palmerston, stating that Staunton had been dismissed for demanding an increase of salary which he was not prepared to grant.

[2] Presumably Mall transacted business for Temple.

Friends, (I mean 100¹¹ Guinees) we may not engage him. but that must be as time and Opportunity offers: And if you have any other Proposals or Scheam, I desire you will let me know, for I will be sure either to serve You, or tell you frankly that I can not . . But what you desire in Your Letter was exactly in my way, being in my Opinion as much for his Advantage as Yours. And I will make it my business to watch Mr Malls health, if he be in Town. The Expression I always used was that in case there should be any removals, You might have the Benefit of it. And this is all the Account I can give You.

Mrs Percivall¹ has desired me these 2 Years to buy her a Watch and Chain & [h]ook² they will come to about 38¹¹. He has sent me a Bill for 23¹¹ and I am to receive 10¹¹ more from a Legacy, which may not be paid these 20 Years and the other 5¹¹ I know nothing of. He may be sure I cannot advance a farthing for him. I am not so rich here; and therefore [un]less³ he sends me a Bill for 15¹¹ I will let Mr Tompion sell the Watch, and I shall be shamed into the bargain. A P— of his little stingy Temper. I will send it by the D. of Ormond if I get the money: Pray let him know all this ——

I desire my humble Service to yr Lady, and that you will get me a Pint of Wine and a Chicken against I come for Ireld, which I suppose will be in Summer. | I am Yr | most faithfull | humble Sert | J. Swift

4804

Robert Nelson to Swift

[14 February 1710–11.]⁴

Reverend Sr

I beg leave to put you in mind of the Inscription which you are to prepare for the Earl of Berkeley's Monument;⁵ my Lady Dowager

---

¹ The wife of John Percival of Knightsbrook. See p. 55, n. 1.
² Hole in the paper.   ³ Hole in the paper.
⁴ Previous editors have dated this letter 22 Feb., the date of Ash Wednesday in 1710. In 1711 Ash Wednesday fell on 14 Feb. In the *Journal* on 15 Feb. Swift mentions that he is writing an inscription for Berkeley's tomb.
⁵ The Earl of Berkeley had died on 24 Sept. 1710 at Berkeley Castle in Gloucestershire. Robert Nelson, author of the *Companion for the Festivals and Fasts of the Church of England*, had married a sister of the Earl, and he therefore writes to remind Swift of the inscription he had promised to compose. On the verso of Nelson's letter Swift has written a draft of the inscription. See Appendix.

has determined to have it in Latin so that I hope you want no Farther directions towards the finishing of it. The workman calls upon me for me;¹ which is the reason of this trouble given you by | Reverand Sʳ | your most Humble | Servant | Rob: Nelson Ash-wenesday

1710

Address: To the Reverend | Dʳ Swift at his | Lodgings in | Sᵗ Albans street²
Endorsed by Swift: Mʳ Nelson | Ashwednesday 1710

Deane Swift 1765
Swift to the Earl of Peterborough

[19] February 1710–11.

My Lord,

I envy none of the Queen's subjects as those who are abroad; and I desire to know, whether, as great a soul as your Lordship has, you did not observe your mind to open and enlarge, after you were some leagues at sea, and had left off breathing party-air. I am apt to think this schism in politics has cloven our understandings, and left us but just half the good sense that blazed in our actions: And we see the effect it has had upon out wit and learning, which are crumbled into pamphlets and penny-papers. The October-club, which was in its rudiments when your Lordship left us, is now growing up to be a party by itself,⁴ and begins to rail at the Ministry as much as the Whigs do, but from topics directly contrary. I am sometimes talked into frights, and told that all is ruined; but am immediately

---

¹ Thus written for 'it'.

² This was Swift's second change of residence since he came to London. St. Albans Street was demolished in 1815, and is now covered by parts of Waterloo Place and Lower Regent Street (Wheatley and Cunningham, *London Past and Present*, i. 11).

³ On 3 Jan. 1710–11 Peterborough and Swift had agreed to be 'mighty constant correspondents'. On 13 Jan. Peterborough left for Vienna. On 18 Feb. Swift writes: 'Lord Peterborow is now got to Vienna, and I must write to him tomorrow.' This gives us the date of the letter. See *Journal*, pp. 152, 194.

⁴ A gathering of about 100 country squires took its name from the custom of drinking October beer. They met at the Bell Tavern in King Street, Westminster. The Club attracted influential members, and its extremist character, including a call for harsher measures with Whig leaders, made it a cause of anxiety to the Ministry. For Swift's letter of *Advice* to the Club see *Prose Works*, ed. Davis, vi. 67-80.

cured when I see any of the Ministry: Not from the satisfaction
they give me in any one point, but because I see them so perfectly
easy, and I believe they could not be so if they had any fear at heart.
My comfort is, they are persons of great abilities, and they are
engaged in a good cause. And what is one very good circumstance,
as I told three of them the other day, they seem heartily to love one
another, in spite of the scandal of inconstancy which Court-friendships lie under.¹ And I can affirm to your Lordship, they heartily
love you too; which I take to be a great deal more than when they
assure you so themselves. For even statesmen will sometimes discover their passions, especially their good ones.

Here is a pamphlet come out, called, a *Letter to Jacob Banks*,
shewing that the liberty of Sweden was destroyed by the principle
of passive obedience.² I know not whether his quotation be fair, but
the piece is shrewdly written: and in my opinion, not to be answered,
otherwise than by disclaiming that sort of passive obedience which
the Tories are charged with. This dispute would soon be ended, if
the dunces who write on each side, would plainly tell us what the
object of this passive obedience is in our country. For, I dare swear,
nine in ten of the Whigs will allow it to be the legislature, and as
many of the Tories deny it to the Prince alone: And I hardly ever saw
a Whig and a Tory together, whom I could not immediately reconcile on that article, when I made them explain themselves.

My Lord, the Queen knew what she did, when she sent your
Lordship to spur up a dull northern court: Yet, I confess I had
rather have seen that activity of mind and body employed in con-
quering another kingdom, or the same over again. | I am, | My
Lord, | &c.

¹ Two days before this Swift had been admitted for the first time to what may
be described as Harley's inner cabinet meetings. In his *Memoirs relating to that
Change in the Queen's Ministry* (*Prose Works*, ed. Davis, viii. 105) Swift gives
some further account of these Saturday dinners.

² This pamphlet, which was noticed in the *Examiner*, no. 31, was entitled
The History or Present State of Sweden in a Letter to Sir J[aco]b B[ank]s, 1711,
in which William Benson, the author, contested that kings were only account-
able to God, and that subjects should obey them whatever happened. He was
at one time surveyor-general of works, but was suspended upon false advice
tendered about the state of the House of Lords. He figures in *The Dunciad*.
See that work, ed. Sutherland, pp. 188, 336, 352.

Swift to Archbishop King

My Lord,   *London, March* 8, 1710–11

I write to your Grace under the greatest Disturbance of Mind for the Publick and Myself. A Gentleman came in where I dined this Afternoon, and told us Mr. *Harley* was stabbed, and some confused Particulars.[1] I immediately ran to Secretary *St. John's* hard by, but no body was at home; I met Mrs. *St. John* in her Chair, who could not satisfy me, but was in Pain about the Secretary, who as she heard, had killed the Murderer. I went straight to Mr. *Harley's* where Abundance of People were to enquire. I got young Mr. *Harley* to me; he said his Father was asleep, and they hoped in no Danger, and then told me the Fact, as I shall relate it to your Grace. This Day the Marquis *De Guiscard* was taken up for High-Treason, by a Warrant of Mr. *St. John*, and examined before a Committee of Council in Mr. *St. John's* Office, where were present, the Dukes of *Ormond, Buckingham, Shrewsbury*, Earl *Poulett*, Mr. *Harley*, Mr. *St. John*, and others. During examination, Mr. *Harley* observed *Guiscard*, who stood behind him, but on one Side, swearing and looking disrespectfully. He told him he ought to behave himself better, while he was examined for such a Crime, Guiscard immediately drew a Penknife out of his Pocket, which he had picked out of some of the Offices, and reaching round, stabbed him just under the Breast, a little to the Right side; but, it pleased God, that the Point stopped at one of the Ribs, and broke short half an Inch.[2]

[1] On this fateful day Swift was dining with the eldest daughter of Lord Pembroke, Lady Catherine, who had married Sir Nicholas Morice of Werrington, Devon, when 'young Arundell came in with the story' (*Journal*, pp. 210–12). The bearer of the news may have been Henry Arundell, son of Henry Arundell, who succeeded his father as fifth Baron Arundell of Wardour.

[2] Antoine de Guiscard, born in 1658, came of a good French family. In 1703 licentious misconduct compelled him to leave France. After various adventures he took refuge in England. He won the ear of Godolphin, Marlborough, and other influential persons, was placed in command of a regiment of refugees, and granted a pension. Harley reduced his pension, and Guiscard entered into treasonable correspondence with France. His letters were intercepted, and he was brought up for examination. He succeeded in stabbing Harley with a penknife which he had secreted. In the uproar which followed Harley showed great composure. See further accounts of the incident by Swift in the *Examiner*, no. 33, and in *Memoirs Relating to that Change*. See also Boyer, *Political State*, i. 275–314; Burnet, *Own Time*, vi. 37–40; *Wentworth Papers*, pp. 185–7.

Immediately Mr. *St. John* rose, drew his Sword, and ran it into *Guiscard*'s Breast. Five or six more of the Council drew and stabbed *Guiscard* in several Places: But, the Earl *Poulett* called out, for God's Sake, to spare *Guiscard*'s Life, that he might be made an Example; and Mr. *St. John*'s Sword was taken from him, and broke; and the Footmen without ran in, and bound *Guiscard*, who begged he might be killed immediately; and, they say, called out three or four Times, 'my Lord *Ormond*, my Lord *Ormond*.' They say *Guiscard* resisted them a while, until the Footmen came in. Immediately *Buissière* the Surgeon[1] was sent for, who dressed Mr. *Harley*: and he was sent home. The Wound bled fresh, and they do not apprehend him in Danger: He said, when he came home, he thought himself in none; and when I was there he was asleep, and they did not find him at all feverish. He hath been ill this Week, and told me last *Saturday*, he found himself much out of Order, and hath been Abroad but twice since; so that the only Danger is, lest his being out of Order should, with the Wound, put him in a Fever; and I shall be in mighty Pain 'till Tomorrow Morning. I went back to poor Mrs. *St. John*, who told me, her Husband was with my Lord Keeper,[2] at Mr. Attorney's,[3] and she said something to me very remarkable: That going To-day to pay her Duty to the Queen, when all the Men and Ladies were dressed to make their appearance, this being the Day of the Queen's Accession, the Lady of the Bed-chamber in waiting told her the Queen had not been at Church, and saw no Company; yet, when she inquired her Health, they said she was very well, only had a little Cold. We conceive, the Queen's Reason for not going out, might be something about this seizing of *Guiscard* for High Treason, and that perhaps there was some Plot, or something extraordinary. Your Grace must have heard of this *Guiscard*: He fled from *France* for Villanies there, and was thought on to Head an Invasion of that Kingdom, but was not liked. I know him well, and think him a Fellow of little Consequence, although of some Cunning, and much Villainy. We passed by one

---

[1] Paul Buissière, a French refugee, who gained reputation in London; but Radcliffe, who was called in later, insisted upon consulting with Green, his own surgeon (*Journal*, pp. 225, 239).

[2] On the advent of the Tories to power Harcourt was first restored to place as Attorney-General, but on 9 Oct. 1710, before the meeting of Parliament, he was named Lord Keeper and sworn of the Privy Council. Swift calls him 'trimming Harcourt' (*Poems*, p. 190).

[3] Sir Edward Northey succeeded Harcourt as Attorney-General.

another this Day in the Mall, at two o'Clock, an Hour before he was
taken up, and I wondered he did not speak to me.

I write all this to your Grace, because I believe you would desire
to know a true Account of so important an Accident; and besides,
I know you will have a Thousand false ones, and I believe every
material Circumstance here is true; having it from young Mr. *Harley.*
I met Sir *Thomas Mansell,*[1] (it was then after Six this Evening) and
he and Mr. *Prior*[2] told me, they had just seen *Guiscard* carried by
in a Chair, with a strong Guard, to *Newgate,* or the *Press-Yard.*[3]
Time perhaps, will shew who was at the Bottom of all this; but
Nothing could happen so unluckily to *England,* at this Juncture, as
Mr. *Harley's* Death, when he has all the Schemes for the greatest
Part of the Supplies in his Head, and the Parliament cannot stir a
Step without him. Neither can I altogether forget myself, who, in
him, should lose a Person I have more Obligations to, than any other
in this Kingdom; who hath always treated me with the Tenderness
of a Parent, and never refused me any Favour I asked for a Friend;
therefore I hope your Grace will excuse the Disorder of this Letter. I
was intending this Night to write one of another Sort.

I must needs say, one great Reason for writing these Particulars
to your Grace, was, that you might be able to give a true Account
of the Fact, which will be some Sort of Service to Mr. *Harley.* I am,
with the greatest Respect, | my Lord, |
Your Grace's most dutiful, | and most humble Servant,

                                                            Jon. Swift.

I have read over what I writ, and find it confused and incorrect,
which your Grace must impute to the violent Pain of Mind I am in,
greater than ever I felt in my Life.—It must have been the utmost
Height of desperate Guilt which could have spirited that Wretch
to such an Action; I have not heard whether his Wounds are dangerous; but I pray God he may recover to receive his Reward, and
that we may learn the Bottom of his Villany. It is not above ten

---

[1] Comptroller of the Household to Queen Anne. Though Swift was ready to
walk with Mansell in the park and accepted his dinners, he thought his intellec-
tual gifts moderate and his dinners wretched.
[2] Since their first meeting at Harley's table, 15 Oct. 1710, the friendship
between Swift and Prior had quickly gained ground. The stabbing of Harley
was followed by an outpouring of verses in his honour, among them a poem by
Prior. See *Journal*, p. 228 and note.
[3] The Press Yard lay between the Old Bailey Sessions House and Newgate.

Days ago, that I was interceding with the Secretary, in his Behalf, because I heard he was just starving; but, the Secretary assured me he had 400 *l.* a Year Pension.[1]

Hawkesworth and Copy
Archbishop King to Swift

Dublin, March 17, 1710–11.
Rev. Sir,[2]
I return you my thanks for yours of the 8th instant. I do not wonder that you were in some confusion when you writ it; for I assure you I read it with great horror, which such a fact is apt to create in every body, that is not hardened in wickedness. I received several other letters with narratives of the same, and seen some, that came to other hands; but none so particular, or that could be so well depended upon. I observe, that, among them all, there is no account of the matters laid to *Guiscard*'s charge, of his design, or how he came to be discovered. I suppose those are yet secrets, as it is fit they should be. I do remember something of this *Guiscard*, and that he was to head an invasion; and that he published a very foolish narrative;[3] but neither remember exactly the time, or under what Ministry it was, or who were his patrons. It seems convenient, that these should be known; because it is reported, that Mr. H[arley] and Mr. St. J[ohn] were those who chiefly countenanced him, and he their peculiar favourite. One would think this should convince the world, that Mr. H[arley] is not in the *French* interest, but it has not yet had that effect withal: nay some whisper the case of *Faenius Rufus*, and *Scaevinus* in the 15th book of *Tacitus*,[4] *quem eundem conscium et inquisitorem non tolerabant*. Mr. St. J[ohn] is condemned for wounding *Guiscard*: and had he killed him, there would not have

---

[1] It was, however, irregularly paid.

[2] The copy in King's letter book was partly decipherable by Ball, and details noted by him are incorporated in the text of this letter, though of no peculiar significance.

[3] *Mémoires du marquis de Guiscard, dans lequels est contenu le récit des entreprises qu'il a faites dans le royaume et hors du royaume pour le recouvrement de sa patrie*, Delft, 1705. It is remarkable that King had seen this rare duodecimo book.

[4] *Annals*, xv. c. 66.

wanted some to suggest, that it was done on purpose, lest he should tell tales.

We had a strange piece of news by last pacqet, that the address to her Majesty met with but a cold reception from one party in the House of Commons; and that all the Lords, spiritual and temporal, of that party, went out when it passed in the Lords' House. But I make it a rule, never to believe party news, except I have it immediately from a sure hand.

I was in hopes to have heard something of our first-fruits and twentieth parts; but I doubt that matter sleeps, and that it will be hard to awaken it.

You will expect no news from home. We eat and drink as we used to do. The parties are tolerably silent, but those for the late Ministry seem to be united, keep much together, and are so wise as not to make much noise; nor have I heard anything of their sentiments of late, only what has happened on this accident. I heartily recommend you to God's care. I am, *&c.*

W. D[ublin]

4804

The Earl of Peterborough to Swift

Vienna, April 18 [O.S. 7], 1711.[1]

S^r

I have often with pleasure reflected upon the glorious possibilitys of the English Constitution, but I must apply to politicks a french Expression appropriated by them to Beauty, there is a (*je ne scay quoy*) among us, which makes us troublesome with our Learning, dissagreeable with our Witt, poor with our wealth, & insignificant with our power.[2]

---

[1] This is a reply to Swift's letter of 19 Feb. It reached Swift on 20 Apr., O.S (*Journal*, pp. 246–7).

[2] The nominal purpose of Peterborough's mission, as already mentioned, was to bring about more cordial relations between the Emperor Joseph I and the Duke of Savoy; the primary object of the Ministry was to get him out of the country. Without properly completing his task in Vienna Peterborough dashed off to Turin. While he was there the Emperor died, 6 Apr. 1711, N.S. This explains why there is no mention of the event in his letter, written though it was one day later. On 17 Apr., O.S., an express reporting the Emperor's death reached London. This was a blow to the Whig programme of 'No peace without

I could never despise any body for what they have not, and am only provoked, when they make not the right use of what they have, this is the greatest mortification to know the advantages we have by art & nature, & see them dissappointed by self conceit and faction, what patience could bear the dissappointment of a good scheme by the October Clubb?

I have with great uneasinesse received imperfect accounts of a disagrement among ourselves, the party we have to struggle with has strength enough to require our united endeavours, We should not attack their firm body like Hussars, let the Victory be secure before we quarrel for the Spoils, let it be considered whether their yoock were easy, or their burthen Light, what! must there ever be in St Stephen's chapel, a majority either of knaves or fools.

But seriously I have long aprehended the effects of that universall corruption, which has been improved with so much care, and has so fitted us for the Tyranny design'd, that we are grown I fear insensible of Slavery, & almost unworthy of liberty.

The gentlemen who give you no other satisfaction in politicks than the appearances of ease and mirth, I wish I could partake with them in their good humour, but Tokay itself has no effect upon me while I see affairs so unsettled, Faction so strong & credit so weak, and all services abroad under the truest difficulties by past miscarriages, and present want of money, but we are told here, that in the midst of victory, orders are given to sound a parley I will not say a retreat, give me leave to tell the churchman, that there is not in . . . . [1]

I have rid the Resty Horse you say they gave me, in plowed Lands till I have made him tame, I wish they manage the Dull jades as well att home, and gett them forward either with whipp or spur, I depend much upon the three you mention, if they remember me with kindnesse, I am theirs by Two the strongest ties, I love them, & hate their Ennemies.

Yet you seem to wish me other work, it is Time the Statesmen employ me in my own Trade, not theirs If they have nothing else for mee to subdue, let me command against that rank Whiggish puppet show, Those Junto pigmies if not destroyed will grow up to Giants, Tell St. John, he must find me work in the old world or the new.

Spain'; for the heir of Joseph I was his brother, already acknowledged by the allies as Charles III of Spain. Few could be found to urge that England should go on fighting to add Spain and half America to the vast possessions Charles would inherit.   [1] Some words are here obliterated.

I find Mr Harley forgetts to make mention of the most important part of my Letter to him, which was to let him know that I expected immediately for one Dr Swift, a Lean Bishoprick, or a fat Deanery, if you happen to meet that gentleman att dinner tell him that he has a Friend out of the way of doing him good, but that he would if he could, whose name is

Peterborow

Vienna the 18th 1711. April.

Address: For the Reverend Dr Swift Bishop of or Dean of &c
Frank: Ld Peterborow
Endorsed by Swift: Earl of Peterborow | Vienna. 1711. | Apr. 18th

Faulkner 1762
Swift to Archbishop King

London, April 10, 1711.

My Lord,
    I had lately the Honour of a Letter from your Grace,[1] and waited to acknowledge it until something material should happen, that might recompence the Trouble. My Occasion of writing to you at present is purely personal to your Grace. A Report was beginning to run here, by some Letters from *Ireland*, that your Grace had applyed the Passage you mention of *Rufus*, in a Speech you made to your Clergy, which I ventured to contradict, as an Impossibility, and inconsistent with your general Opinion, and what was in your Letter. Mr. *Southwell*[2] and Mr. *Dopping* were of the same Mind, and the former says, he hath writ to your Grace about it. I should have thought no more of the Matter, but let it spend like an idle Story below Notice; only dining last *Sunday* with one of the principal Secretaries of State, he gave me a Letter to read, which he had just received from the Printer of the News-Paper called the Post-Boy, in which was a Transcript of a Letter from *Dublin*, and the Secretary being mentioned in that Transcript, the Man would not publish it without his Advice. It contained an Account how the News of Mr. *Harley*'s being stabbed had been received by the Whigs in *Dublin*; of which he produced some Instances. Then he mentions the Passage out of *Tacitus*, and concludes thus: *The First that mentioned it, was the Archbishop of Dublin, who took Notice of it first at a Meeting*

---

[1] King's letter of 17 Mar.   [2] See p. 189, n. 2

of his Clergy; and, afterwards in the Hearing of several Persons, was reprimanded for it in a civil, though sharp Manner, by one of the chief Ministers there, well known for his steady Loyalty to Her Majesty, and his zealous Service to the Church of England, under her late perilous Tryal. I immediately told the Secretary, that I knew this must be false and misrepresented, and that he must give me Leave to scratch out that Passage, which I accordingly did; and for fear of any Mistake, I made him give me afterwards, the whole Letter, that I might have it in my Power. The next Day, I sent for the Printer, and told him what I had done, and upon further Thoughts, I stifled the whole Letter, and the Secretary approved of it.[1] I likewise told the Printer, that when he had any Thing relating to *Ireland*, I had the Secretary's Order (which was true) to send it me, that he might not do Injury to Men's Reputations, by what was represented to him from ignorant or malicious Hands in that Kingdom. The Letter was to have been printed this Day in the Post-Boy with that Conclusion reflecting on your Grace, which is happily prevented; for, although your Character and Station, place you above the Malice of little People, yet your Friends would be extremely concerned to see your Name made so bold with in a common News-Paper.

I humbly hope your Grace will not disapprove of what I have done; at least I have gratified my own Inclination, in the Desire of serving you, and besides, had the opportunity of giving Mr. Secretary some Part of your Character.

I dare lay a Wager, that all this happened by the gross Understandings of some People, who misunderstood and misapplied something very innocent that came from your Grace. I must be so bold to say, that People in that Kingdom do very ill understand Raillery. I can railly much safer here with a great Minister of State

---

[1] Under 8 Apr. (*Journal*, p. 237) Swift tells Stella: 'I dined to-day with Mr. secretary St. John; he gave me a letter to read, which was from the publisher of the newspaper called the *Post-boy*; in it there was a long copy of a letter from Dublin, giving an account of what the Whigs said upon Mr. Harley's being stabbed, . . . and at the end there was half a dozen lines, telling the story of the archbishop of Dublin, and abusing him horribly.' This refers to King's remarks in his letter of 17 Mar. to Swift, and his allusion to Tacitus. The Archbishop's meaning in that letter was that some insinuated that Harley denounced Guiscard to conceal his own intrigues with France. A report got about that King had cited the passage in public. In this letter Swift explains the trouble he has been at to prevent the story being published. The *Post-Boy* was at this time the leading Tory newspaper, conducted by Abel Roper.

or a Dutchess, than I durst do there with an Attorney or his Wife.: And, I can venture to railly with your Grace, although I could not do it with many of your Clergy. I myself have been a Witness, when Want of Common Sense hath made People offended with your Grace, where they ought to have been the most pleased. I say Things every Day at the best Tables, which I should be turned out of Company for, if I were in *Ireland*.

Here is one Mr. *Richardson*, a Clergyman, who is solliciting an Affair that I find your Grace approveth, and therefore I do him all the service I can in it.[1]

We are now full of the Business of the *Irish* Yarn and I attend among the rest, to engage the Members I am acquainted with in our Interest. To-morrow we expect it will come on.[2]

I will shortly write to your Grace, some Account how publick Affairs stand: We hope Mr. *Harley* will be Abroad in a week. We have news from *Brussels* that the Dauphin is dead of an apoplexy.[3]

I am, with the greatest Respect, | My Lord, |

Your Grace's most dutiful, | And most humble Servant,

Jon. Swift.

I wish your Grace would inclose your commands to me, directed to *Erasmus Lewis*, Esq.[4] at my Lord *Dartmouth*'s Office at *Whitehall*; for I have left off going to Coffee-Houses.

---

[1] The Rev. John Richardson, 1664–1747, distinguished himself by his constant endeavours to convert the native Irish by means of Irish-speaking clergy and the distribution of Bibles and Prayer Books printed in the Irish language. His proposals met with opposition in the Upper House of Convocation lest they should injure the English interest in Ireland; and his claims to preferment were neglected (*D.N.B.*; *Fasti Eccl. Hib.* iv. 204).

[2] A bill for imposing a duty on Irish yarn was at this time before the English House of Commons. Irishmen in London, including Swift, spent much time in lobbying. See *Journal*, pp. 235, 237, 239, 241, 245.

[3] The Dauphin, then fifty years of age, died of the smallpox.

[4] Erasmus Lewis was Under-Secretary of State to Lord Dartmouth.

Swift to the Duke of Argyle

London, *April* 16, 1711

My Lord,[1]

This comes to interrupt your Grace a few minutes in the con-
quest of a kingdom, and to let the Duke of Anjou keep the crown
so much longer on his head. I owe you this piece of malice, because
you have ruined the reputation of my pride, being the first great
man for whose acquaintance I made any great advances; and you
have need to be what you are, and what you will be, to make me
easy after such a condescension. Remember, my Lord, I have pointed
you out these six years to make a hero. Take some care of your life,
and a great deal of your health; and if Spain be to be conquered,—
si Pergama dextra defendi possint[2]—you are the man. The greatest
of the Scipios began his glories at your age, in that country. But I
am afraid the Spaniards, when your Grace has conquered them, will
remember the climate you came from, and call you Goth.

I am glad to find the Ministry here upon all occasions talking with
so much justice and friendship of your Grace; and, as much as one
can promise from the dispositions of a Court, I have reason to
believe your Grace's expectations will be answered from hence as
fully as possible. The talk is hot among us of some sudden changes
and promotions, and I am inclined to believe something of it. We
expect Mr. Harley will be Treasurer, and, by that and other steps,
the Ministry more fixed than it seems at present. Mr. Harley now
sees some of his friends, begins to talk of business, and will take the
air in a day or two. Mr. St. John has been out of order with gravel,
and we have forbid him burgundy and champagne wines, which he
very unwillingly complies with. The Queen is well enough to go

---

[1] John Campbell, 1680–1743, second Duke of Argyle, whose acquaintance
Swift may have made on his previous visit to London. He had served with valour
and distinction under Marlborough. On 20 Dec. 1710 he was installed a Knight
of the Garter. On 11 Jan. 1711 he was appointed ambassador extraordinary to
Spain and commander of the English forces in that country. During the period
of the *Journal* Swift was on friendly terms with Argyle; but the Duke was
irreconcilably incensed by *The Publick Spirit of the Whigs* (*Prose Works*, ed.
Davis, viii, pp. xvii–xx, 27–68). In a note on Macky's *Characters* Swift stigmatized Argyle as an 'Ambitious, covetous, cunning Scot', who was without
principle.
[2] Si Pergama dextra Defendi possent—Virg. *Aen.* ii. 291–2.

abroad every day. The October Club grumbles still, and wants a thorough change. New toasts arise daily, and I am afraid, if your Grace be two years conquering Spain, you will meet, at your return, with a set entirely new.

I send this by Mr. Harris, your Grace's chaplain, and I desire he may be your historian.[1] I have known him these three years. He has a great deal of merit, and I envy his being so near your Grace, who will be sure to distinguish it. You will find him full of good manners, and good sense, and possessed with the highest veneration for your Grace's person and virtues. I am, with the greatest respect, my Lord, |

Your Grace's most obedient, and most humble servant, |

Jon. Swift.

Hawkesworth 1766

Archbishop King to Swift

Dublin, April 19, 1711.

Rev. Sir,

I had the favour of yours of the 10th instant, by which I understand how much I am obliged to you for the justice you did me as to the report you let me know was about to be printed in the Post-boy relating to Mr. *Harley*.

I think there is no man in this kingdom, on which such a report could be fixed with less colour of truth, having been noted for the particular regard I have always had for him. I have suffered in some cases too, for my zeal to defend him in the worst of times; for I confess I never could, with patience, bear the treatment he met with in *Gregg*'s affair. The truth is, when I received the news of this last barbarous attempt made on him, I with indignation insulted some with whom I used to dispute about the former case, and asked them, whether they would now suspect that he was in the conspiracy to stab himself? The turn they gave it was what I wrote to you, that they imagined he might be in it notwithstanding that; and that his discovering *Guiscard*, and pressing so hard on the examination, was the thing that provoked the man to such a degree of rage, as

[1] Probably Samuel Harris, who would at this time be about twenty-eight years of age. In 1724 he became first regius professor of modern history at Cambridge.

appeared in that villanous act. And they instanced the story of *Piso* in *Tacitus*, and the passage of *Rufus*.¹ I know very well that they did not believe themselves, and among other things I applied that passage of *Hudibras*, he that beats out his brains, *&c*.² I believe I have told this passage to several as an example, to shew into what absurdities the power of prejudice, malice, and faction will lead some men, I hope with good effect; and added, as several gentlemen that heard me can witness, that it was a strange thing, that Mr. *Harley* should discover *Gregg*, and have him hanged, and yet be suspected to be partaker of his crime; but altogether unaccountable, that in a cause, wherein his life was so barbarously struck at it was a thousand to one if he escaped, he should still be under the suspicion of being a party with his murderer; so that I could never imagine, that any one should report, that I spoke my own sense in a matter wherein I expressed so great an abhorrence, both of the fact, and the vile comment made upon it.

As to any speech at the meeting of the clergy, or any reprimand given me by any person on this account, it is all, assure yourself, pure invention.

I am sensible of the favour you did me, in preventing the publishing of such a false report, and am most thankful to Mr. Secretary *St. John* for stopping it. I have not the honour to be known to him, otherwise I would give him the trouble of a particular acknowledgment. As to Mr. *Harley*, I have had the happiness to have some knowledge of him, and received some obligations from him, particularly on the account of my Act of Parliament, that I obtained for the restitution of *Seatown* to the see of *Dublin*.³ I always had a great honour for him, and expected great good from his known abilities, and zeal for the common interest; and, as I believe he was the

¹ Taciti Annalium, lib. ii et xv.
²   For he that hangs, or beats out's brains,
                     The devil's in him if he feigns.

                                             Hudibras, Part II. i. 498.
³ These lands which are situated near Swords had been granted by the Crown after the Restoration in augmentation of the see of Dublin. From neglect and legal difficulties, the occupants of the see never obtained any benefit from them, and finally, in 1703, they were sold by the Trustees of Forfeited Estates. Archbishop King became the purchaser for £3,105, and with characteristic generosity took steps immediately to obtain an Act of the English Parliament to secure them for all time to his successors (15th Report of the Commissioners of the Public Records of Ireland, p. 359).—Ball.

principal instrument of settling things on the present foot; so I believe every one, that wishes well to these kingdoms, is satisfied, that there is not any man, whose death would be a greater loss to the public than his. The management of this Parliament has, if not reconciled his worst enemies to him, at least silenced them; and it is generally believed that his misfortune has much retarded public affairs.

I partly can guess who writ the letter you mention: it must be one of two or three, whose business it is to invent a lye, and throw dirt, ever since I was obliged by my duty to call them to account for their negligence and ill practices: they have published and dispersed several libellous prints against me, in one of which I marked forty-three downright falsehoods in matters of fact. In another, it is true, there was only one such; the whole and every part of it, from beginning to end, being pure invention and false-hood. But, to my comfort, they are despised by all good men; and I like myself nothing less for being the object of their hate. You will excuse this long letter, and I hope I may, by next, apprise you with something of consequence. In the meantime, I heartily recommend you, *&c.*

William Dublin.

I held my visitation on the 9th instant, where you were excused,[1] as absent on the public business of the Church.

Deane Swift 1765
Swift to the Earl of Peterborough

May 4, 1711.

My Lord,

I have had the honour of your Lordship's letter;[2] and by the first lines of it have made a discovery that your Lordship is come into the world about eighteen hundred years too late, and was born about half a dozen degrees too far to the north, to employ that public virtue I always heard you did possess: which is now wholly useless, and which those very few that have it are forced to lay aside, when they would have business succeed.

Is it not some comfort, my Lord, that you meet with the same

---

[1] As a prebendary of St. Patrick's.

[2] Peterborough's letter from Vienna, 18 Apr., N.S.

degeneracy of manners, and the same neglect of the public, among the honest Germans, though in the philosopher's phrase, differently modified, and I hope, at least, we have one advantage, to be more polite in our corruptions than they.

Our divisions run farther than perhaps your Lordship's intelligence hath yet informed you of, that is [to] a triumvirate of our friends whom I have mentioned to you: I have told them more than once, upon occasion, that all my hopes of their success depended on their union, that I saw they loved one another, and hoped they would continue it, to remove that scandal of inconstancy ascribed to Court-friendships. I am not now so secure.[1] I care not to say more on such a subject, and even this *entre nous*. My credit is not of a size to do any service on such an occasion: But, as little as it is, I am so ill a politician, that I will venture the loss of it to prevent this mischief; the consequence of which I am as good a judge of as any Minister of State, and perhaps a better, because I am not one.

When you writ your letter, you had not heard of Guiscard's attempt on Mr. Harley: Supposing you know all the circumstances, I shall not descant upon it. We believe Mr. Harley will soon be Treasurer, and be of the House of Peers;[2] and then we imagine the Court will begin to deal out employments, for which every October-member is a candidate; and consequently nine in ten must be disappointed: The effect of which we may find in the next session. Mr. Harley was yesterday to open to the House the ways he has thought of, to raise funds for securing the unprovided debts of the nation, and we are all impatient to know what his proposals are.[3]

---

[1] Swift had begun to realize that the Ministry was no longer a united body. Writing to Stella on 27 Apr. he confesses himself 'heartily sorry to find my friend the secretary stand a little ticklish with the rest of the ministry'. St. John suspected the wisdom of Harley's trimming policy. While Harley lay ill he spoke with an indiscreet heat in the House in defence of his friend James Brydges, Paymaster-General of the forces abroad, to clear him of a charge of peculation. This speech appeared to lean in favour of the Whigs. See Cobbett, *Parliamentary History*, vi. 1016–19; Leadam, *Political History of England*, ix. 180.

[2] These rumours were getting abroad. See *Wentworth Papers*, p. 191. On 10 Apr. Swift wrote to Stella cautiously: 'They talk of great promotions to be made; that Mr. Harley is to be lord treasurer, and Lord Poulet master of the horse, &c.'

[3] The war had raised the country's annual expenditure to thirteen millions. By the winter of 1709–10 the Government was heavily in debt. On 2 May 1711 Harley introduced his financial scheme for meeting the crisis. It consisted of

As to the imperfect account you say you have received of disagreement among ourselves, your Lordship knows that the names of Whig and Tory have quite altered their meanings. All who were for turning out the late Ministry, we now generally call Tories; and in that sense, I think it plain that there are among the Tories three different interests. One of those, I mean the Ministry, who agree with your Lordship and me, in a steady management for pursuing the true interests of the nation; another is, that of warmer heads, as the October-Club and their adherents without doors; and a third is, I fear, of those who, as your Lordship expresses it, would sound a parley, and who would make fair weather in case of a change, and some of these last are not inconsiderable.

Nothing can be more obliging than your Lordship's remembering to mention me in your letters to Mr. Harley and Mr. St. John, when you are in the midst of such great affairs. I doubt I shall want such an advocate as your Lordship: for, I believe, every man who has modesty or merit, is but an ill one for himself. I desire but the smallest of those titles you give me on the outside of your letter.[1] My ambition is to live in England, and with a competency to support me with honour. The Ministry know by this time whether I am worth keeping; and it is easier to provide for ten men in the Church, than one in a civil employment.

But I renounce England and deaneries, without a promise from your Lordship, under your own hand and seal, that I shall have the liberty to attend you whenever I please. I foresee we shall have a peace next year, by the same sagacity that I have often foreseen when I was young, I must leave the town in a week, because my money is gone, and I can borrow no more. Peace will bring your Lordship home; and we must have you to adorn your country, when you shall be no longer wanted to defend it, I am, | My Lord, &c.

funding the national debt, allowing the proprietors a yearly interest of 6 per cent., and incorporating them to carry on the trade in the South Seas under the name of the South Sea Company. For the state of the national finances at the end of the Session, June 1711, see Trevelyan, *England under Queen Anne*, iii. 324–5.

[1] See the form of address on Peterborough's letter to Swift, 18 Apr., N.S.

Swift to Archbishop King

Chelsea,[1] *May* 10, 1711.

My Lord,

I have had your Grace's Letter, of *April* 19, some Time by me, but deferred my Answer until I could give some Account of what Use I had made of it. I went immediately to Mr. Secretary *St. John*, and read most of it to him; he was extremely satisfied, and very glad that scandalous Account designed to be printed in the Post-Boy, was suppressed. Mr. *Harley* was not then quite well enough; so I ventured (and hope your Grace will not disapprove it) to show your Letter to a Gentleman who hath a great Respect for your Grace, and who told me several others of *Ireland* were possessed of that Report. I trusted the Letter with him, and gave him Leave to read it to them, which he told me he did, and that they were all entirely convinced: And, indeed, as far as I can find, the Report is quite blown over, and has left no Impression. While your Grace's Letter was out of my Hands; dining with Mr. *Harley*, he said to me, almost as soon as he saw me; *How came the Archbishop of Dublin and I to fall out?* I told him, I knew what he meant; but your Grace was altogether misrepresented; and it must come from some infamous Rascals, of which there never wants a Set in that Kingdom, who make it their Business to send wrong Characters here, &c. He answered, that he believed, and knew it was as I said. I added, that I had the Honour to be long known to your Grace, and that you were the last Man in the Kingdom upon whom such a Report could be fixed with any Probability; and that, since he was pleased to mention this Matter first, he must give me Leave, the next Time I saw him, to read a Letter I had from your Grace, in Answer to one of mine, wherein I had told you of such a Report; he said, there was no need, for he firmly believed me. I answered smiling, that should not do, for I would never suffer a Person for whom I had so great an Esteem, to lye under the least Suspicion of any Thing wrong.[2]

[1] On 26 Apr. 1711 Swift left St. Albans Street and moved to the riverside village of Chelsea, whence he could enjoy the pleasure of country walks to and from town. He remained at Chelsea till 5 July when he moved to Suffolk Street to be near the Vanhomrighs.

[2] Despite what Swift here says he suspected that the Archbishop was 'a little guilty'; and nearly a year later he accepted Lord Anglesey's statement that King *had* compared Harley with Piso (*Journal*, pp. 253, 488).

Last *Saturday*, after Dinner, I was again to wait on him. On that Day of the Week, my Lord Keeper, my Lord *Rivers*, and Mr. Secretary *St. John*, always used to dine with him before this Accident; and sometimes they used to let me be of the Company.¹ This was the first *Saturday* they had met since his Recovery; and I was in such Joy to see the old Club met again, that it affects me still, as your Grace sees by my Impertinence in mixing it with an Account that only relates to yourself. I read those Parts of your Letter to him, which I thought proper, and both he and the Company did very frankly acquit your Grace, and Mr. *Harley* in particular spoke a good deal of his Respect and Esteem for you; and then he repeated, that it was no new thing to receive Lies from *Ireland*; which I doubt is so true, that no Man of Distinction in that Kingdom is safe; and I wish it were possible to take some Course to prevent the Evil.

As for Libels upon your Grace, bating my Concern for the Souls of the Writers, I should give you Joy of them. You would less deserve your Station, if Knaves and Fools did not hate you; and while these Sects continue, may your Grace and all good Men be the Object of their Aversion.

My Lord Keeper, Mr. *Harley*, and one or two more, are immediately to be made Peers: The Town hath been expecting it for some Time, altho' the Court make it yet a Secret; but I can assure your Grace of the Truth, for the Preambles to their Patents are now drawing, and I saw a very handsome one for Mr. *Harley*.² You will please not to mention this Particular, although it will be soon publick, but it is yet kept mighty private. Mr. *Harley* is to be Lord Treasurer. Perhaps before the Post leaves this Town, all this will be openly told, and then I may be laughed at for being so mysterious; but so capricious are great Men in their Secrets. The first authentick Assurances I had of these Promotions was last *Sunday*, though the Expectation hath been strong for above a Month. We suppose likewise that many Changes will be made in the Employments as soon

¹ Swift can only have been present at the 'cabinet' dinners three times before Guiscard's attack on Harley.

² *The Reasons Which induc'd Her Majesty to Create the Right Honourable Robert Harley, Esq; A Peer of Great-Britain. London. Printed for J. Morphew . . . 1711.* This quarto pamphlet has a Latin preamble, followed by an English translation; or, in another edition, with the Latin and English facing each other. The Latin was probably composed by Robert Freind, headmaster of Westminster school. The English translation has been attributed to Swift. Harley met with censure on account of its pompous style and the fact that it was published.

as the Session endeth, which will be, I believe, in less than a Fortnight.

Poor Sir *Cholmondeley Deering* of *Kent*, was Yesterday in a Duel shot through the Body, by one Mr. *Thornhill*, in *Tothill-fields*, and died in some Hours.[1] I never mention any Thing of the First Fruits either to Mr. *Harley* or the Duke of *Ormond*. If it be done before his Grace goes over, it is well, and there's an End: If not, I shall have the best Opportunity of doing it in his Absence; if I should speak of it now, perhaps it would be so contrived as to hinder me from solliciting it afterwards; but as soon as the Duke is gone. I shall learn at the Treasury what he hath done in it.

I am with the greatest Respect, my Lord, | Your Grace's most dutiful, and | obliged humble Servant, | Jon. Swift.

I have been at this Town this Fortnight for my Health, and to be under a Necessity of walking to and from *London* every Day. But your Grace will please still to Direct your Letter under Cover to Mr. *Lewis*.

Deane Swift 1765

Swift to Henry St. John

Chelsea, May 11, 1711

Sir,

Being convinced by certain ominous prognostics, that my life is too short to permit me the honour of ever dining another Saturday with Sir Simon Harcourt, Knight, or Robert Harley, Esq; I beg I may take the last farewell of those two gentlemen to-morrow.[2] I made this request on Saturday last, unfortunately after you were

---

[1] Sir Cholmeley Dering, fourth Baronet of Surrenden Dering, Kent, and Richard Thornhill came to blows on 27 Apr., and Thornhill had some teeth knocked out. Thornhill refused an apology and sent Dering a challenge. They fought with pistols at sword's length, and Dering fell mortally wounded. Thornhill was found guilty of manslaughter. Shortly after he was assassinated. See *Journal*, pp. 264, 337; Hist. MSS. Com., 15th Report, iv. 686; Ashton's *Social Life in the Reign of Queen Anne*, ii. 192–4. Tothill Fields was a favourite duelling spot in Westminster.

[2] The following day was Saturday. It was not, however, until the 24th of that month that the patent creating Harley a peer, as Earl of Oxford, was passed.

gone; and they, like great statesmen, pretended they could do nothing in it without your consent; particularly my Lord-Keeper, as a lawyer, raised innumerable difficulties, although I submitted to allow you an hour's whispering before dinner, and an hour after. My Lord Rivers would not offer one word in my behalf, pretending he himself was but a tolerated person.[1] The Keeper alleged, you could do nothing but when all three were capitularly met, as if you could never open but like a parish-chest, with the three keys together. It grieves me to see the present Ministry thus confederated to pull down my great spirit. Pray, Sir, find an expedient. Finding expedients is the business of Secretaries of State. I will yield to any reasonable conditions not below my dignity. I will not find fault with the victuals; I will restore the water-glass that I stole, and solicit for my Lord-Keeper's salary. And, Sir, to show you I am not a person to be safely injured, if you dare refuse me justice in this point, I will appear before you in a pudding-sleeve gown, I will disparage your snuff, write a lampoon upon Nably Car,[2] dine with you upon a foreign post-day; nay, I will read verses in your presence, until you snatch them out of my hands.[3] Therefore pray, Sir, take pity upon me and yourself; and believe me to be, with great respect, | Sir, | Your most obedient, and | most humble servant.

Hawkesworth 1766

Archbishop King to Swift

Dublin, May 15, 1711.

Rev. Sir,[4]

I had the favour of yours of the 10th Instant, by the last pacquets, and cannot return you sufficient acknowledgment for your kind and

[1] On the first occasion, 17 Feb. 1710–11, upon which Swift attended a 'cabinet' dinner 'Lord Rivers was got there' before him and was chid by Swift 'for presuming to come on a day when only lord keeper and the secretary and I were to be there' (*Journal*, p. 193).

[2] Possibly Billy Carr, who was appointed a Groom of the Bedchamber to George I (*Wentworth Papers*, p. 419).—Ball.

[3] The allusion is presumably to the occasion, 31 Dec. 1710, when Prior took exception to Swift's reading of some of his verses, and Swift admitted, whether in jest or not, that he 'was famous for reading verses the worst in the world' (*Journal*, p. 145).

[4] The clerical copy of this letter in King's correspondence in the manuscript

prudent management of that affair so much to my advantage. I confess that I did not much fear that such a vile report would do me any great injury with Mr. *Harley*; for I was persuaded he is too wise to believe such an incredible story. But the publishing it to the world might have influenced some to my disadvantage; and no man can be well pleased to be the subject of a libel, though it often happens to be the fate of honest men.

I doubt not but you will hear of an unlucky contest in the city of *Dublin* about their mayor. You may remember (I think whilst you were here, that is, in 1709) alderman *Constantine*, by a cabal, for so I must call it, lost his election; and a junior alderman, one *Forrest*, was elected mayor for the ensuing year. *Constantine* petitioned the Council-Board not to approve the election; for you must know, by the new rules, settled in pursuance of an Act of Parliament, for the better regulation of Corporations, their chief officers must be approved of by the Governor and Council after they are elected, before they can enter into any of their respective offices; and if not approved of in ten days, the Corporation that chose them must go to a new election. Now, Alderman *Constantine*, upon the Corporation's return of *Forrest*, complained of it as wrong, and desired to be heard by counsel; but my Lord *Wharton*, then Lord Lieutenant, would not admit it. This passed on to the year 1710, and then the present mayor was chosen, alderman *Eccles*, another junior alderman; and this year one alderman *Barlow*, a tailor, another junior. *Constantine*, finding the government altered, supposed he should have more favour, and petitions again of the wrong done him. The city replied, and we had two long hearings. The matter depended on an old bye-law, made about the 12th of Queen *Elizabeth*; by which the aldermen, according to their ancientry, are required to keep their mayoralty, notwithstanding any licences or orders to the contrary. Several dispensations and instances of contrary practices were produced; but with a salvo, that the law of succession should stand good; and some aldermen, as appeared, had been disfranchised for not submitting to it, and holding their mayoralty. On the contrary, it was urged, that this rule was made in a time when the mayoralty was looked upon as a great burthen, and the senior aldermen got licences from serving it, and by faction and interest got it put on the junior and poorer, and most of the aldermen were then papists, and

room of Trinity College, Dublin, is scarcely decipherable. The text follows Hawkesworth, 1766.

being obliged, on accepting the office, to take the oath of supremacy, and come to church, they declined it; but the case was now altered, and most were ambitious of it, and a rule or bye-law, that imposed it as a duty and burthen, must be understood to oblige them to take it, but could not oblige the electors to put it on them; that it was often dispensed with, and, as alledged, altogether abrogated by the new rules, that took the election out of the city, where the charter places it, and gave it to the aldermen only; [and] that since those rules, which were made in 1672, the elections have been in another manner, and in about 36 mayors, eight or nine were junior aldermen. On the whole, the matter seemed to me to hang on a most slender point; and being Archbishop of *Dublin*, I thought I was obliged to be for the city; but the majority was for the bye-law, and disapproved alderman *Barlow*, who was returned for mayor. I did foresee that this would beget ill blood, and did not think it for my Lord Duke of *Ormond*'s interest to clash with the city; and I went to several of his Grace's friends, whom I much trust, before the debate in Council, and desired them to consider the matter; and laid the inconveniency I apprehended before them, and desired them to take notice, that I had warned them; but they told me, that they did not foresee any hurt it would be to his Grace. And I pray God it may not; though I am afraid it may give him some trouble.

The citizens have taken it heinously; and, as I hear, met to-day, and in common council repealed the bye-law, and have chosen alderman *Barlow* again. I think them wrong in both, and [it is] a declaration of enmity against the Council and Government, which feud is easier begun than laid. It is certain the Council must disapprove their choice, it being against the new rules, as well as good manners: and what other steps will be made to correct them, I cannot say; whereas if they had appointed a committee to view and report what old obsolete bye-laws were become inconvenient, and repealed this among the rest, it would not have given offence; and if they had chosen another instead of *Barlow*, I believe he would have been approved, and there had been an end of the contest.

You must know this is made a party affair, as *Constantine* sets up for a High-Churchman, which I never heard he did before: but this is an inconveniency in parties, that whoever has a private quarrel, and finds himself too weak, he immediately becomes a zealous partisan, and makes his private a public quarrel.

Perhaps it may not be ungrateful, nor perhaps altogether useless to you, to know the truth of this matter; for I imagine it will be talked of.[1]

I believe the generality of the citizens and gentlemen of *Ireland* are looked on as friends to the Whiggish interest. But it is only so far as to keep out the Pretender, whom they mortally fear with good reason; and so many villanous papers have been spread here, and so much pains taken to persuade them that the Tories design to bring him in, that it is no wonder they are afraid of them; but, God be thanked, this Ministry and Parliament has pretty well allayed that fear, by their steady and prudent management. And if his Grace the Duke of *Ormond* prosecutes the same measures [as] the Ministry doth in Britain (as I believe he will) I persuade myself, that the generality here will be as zealous for this as any Ministry we ever had.

The death of the Earl of *Rochester* is a great blow to all good men, and even his enemies cannot but do justice to his character.[2] What influence it will have on public affairs, God only knows. I pray let me have your thoughts on it, for I have some fears, that I do not find affect other people; I was of opinion, that he contributed much to keep things steady; and I wish his friends may not want his influence. I conclude with my prayers for you, |

Will. Dublin.

[1] The civic dispute, to which King devotes the larger part of his letter, developed into a political war between Whigs and Tories. The mayoral battle is now a laughable comedy; but it has left behind a mass of correspondence and pamphlet literature. Ball draws attention to the complete absence of any sense of humour on either side: 'We find the Recorder gravely urging that the unpopularity of Constantine's wife with her own sex, for whom the Recorder professes the deepest respect, was a sufficient reason for the rejection of her husband'. For a comment by Swift on this civic quarrel see *Journal*, p. 113.

[2] On 21 Sept. 1710 Rochester succeeded Somers as Lord President of the Council. He died 2 May 1711, and was succeeded by his son, styled Lord Hyde, born in 1672. On Lord Rochester's death Buckingham was appointed Lord President of the Council.

The Earl of Peterborough to Swift

Hanover, 21 June [O.S. 10] 1711.

Sʳ

You were returning me to Ages past for some expressions in my letter. I find matter in yours[1] to send you as far back as the Golden Age. How came you to frame a System (in the Times we Live in) to govern the world by Love.

I was much more surprised att such a Notion in your first, than to find your opinion alter'd in your last letter, my hopes were founded more reasonably upon the contrary principle, I wish we could keep our selves steady by any, but I confess it was the hatred & contempt so justly conceived against our late Governors, that gave me some little Expectations we might unite att least in order to prevent a Relapse.

The consequences of places not given were apparent, the whole party were then dissatisfyed, and when given, those are only pleased who have them. This is what the honest management of past Administrations has brought us to, but I should not yett despair if your Loving principle could but have it's force among three or Fower of your acquaintances, never persons had more reason to agree, nor was it ever in the power of a few men to bring greater Events to bear, or prevent greater inconveniences, for such are Inevitable without the Nicest Management, & I believe no person was ever better prepared to make this out than my self.

I wish before I left England that I had mett with either in your letters, or discourse, any thing like what you hint in your last, I should have found great Ease & you some satisfaction, for had you passed these six months with mee abroad, I could have made you sensible that it were Easy to have brought the character & influence of an English peer equall to that of a Senator in Old Rome, methinks I could have brought itt to that pass, to have seen a Levee of Suppliant Kings & Princes, expecting their destinies from us & submitting to our decrees, but if we come in politicks to your necessity of Leaving the Town for want of money to Live in itt, Lord, how the case will alter.

You Threaten mee with law & tell me I might be compelld to make my words good, remember your own insinuations what if I

[1] Of 4 May.

should leave England in a week's Time & summon you in quality of chapplen & secretary, to be a witnesse to Transactions perhaps of the greatest importance, so great that I should think you might deserve the Bishoprick of Winchester at your return, let me know in a letter directed to Parsonsgreen the moment you receive this, whether you are ready & willing, but you must learn to Live a month now and then, without Sleep,[1] as to all other things, we should meet with no Mortifications abroad, if we could Scape them from home.

But, without raillery if Ever I can propose to my self to be of any great use I foresee this will be the case, this is so much my opinion, that I conclude, if it falls out otherwise, I shall never concern my self in any public business in England, That I shall either leave itt for a better Climate, or Marry in a Rage, and become the hero of the October Clubb Yours |

Peterborow.

Hannover June the 21th 1711

Address: For Dr Swift
Endorsed by Swift: Ld Peterborow | Earl of Peterborow | Hannover June · 21 · 1711

Faulkner 1762

Swift to Archbishop King

London,[2] *July* 12, 1711.

My Lord,

I now conceive your Grace begins to be a busy Person in Council, and Parliament, and Convocation;[3] and perhaps may be content to

---

[1] On 24 June 1711 Swift in the *Journal*, p. 297, records the receipt of this letter 'four days ago'. He continues: 'The Earl of Peterborow is returned from Vienna without one servant: he left them scattered in several towns of Germany.' When asked, in this letter to send an answer to Peterborough's country house at Parson's Green Swift wondered what was meant till he heard that already he had arrived. Two stanzas in Swift's verses to Peterborough (*Poems*, pp. 396–8) may be a recollection of this return to England.

> Mordanto gallops on alone,
> The Roads are with his Foll'wers strown,
> This breaks a Girth, and that a Bone.
>
> .   .   .   .
>
> So wonderful his Expedition,
> When you have not the least Suspicion,
> He's with you like an Apparition.

[2] Swift, as noted before, left Chelsea on 5 July for lodgings in Suffolk Street.
[3] The Irish Parliament had been summoned for 9 July, but was not formally

be diverted now and then by an idle Letter from hence. We have an empty Town, the Queen being settled at *Windsor*, and the Ministers often there. We are so weary with expecting farther Removals, that we begin to drop the Discourse: Neither am I sure, whether those in Power may not differ a little in Opinion as to the Matter. However, it seemth generally agreed, that there will be many Changes before next Session, and that it is necessary there should be so.[1] My Lord *Peterborow* hath been some Time returned, and I have had a good Deal of Talk with him; or rather, he hath talked a good Deal to me. He is mightily discontented with what I writ to him, and which he findeth to be true, that there seemeth a general Disposition among us towards a Peace. He thinketh his successful Negotiations with the Emperor and the Duke of *Savoy* have put us in a better Condition than ever to continue the War, and will engage to convince me, that *Spain* is yet to be had, if we take proper Measures.[2] Your Grace knoweth he is a Person of great Talents, but dashed with something restless and capricious in his Nature. He told me he came over without being recalled, and without one Servant, having scattered them in several Parts of *Germany*. I doubt he will not have Credit enough with the Ministry to make them follow his Plans; and he is such a Sort of Person as may give good Advice, which wise Men may reasonably refuse to follow.

It seemeth to me that the Ministry Lie under a grievous Dilemma, from the Difficulty of continuing the War, and the Danger of an ill Peace; which I doubt, whether all their Credit with the Queen and

---

opened by Ormonde till the 12th. Bad weather delayed the sailing from Parkgate of the official yacht and the escorting man-of-war.

[1] That section of the Tory party represented by the October Club was pressing for 'a thorow Change of Employments', meaning the dismissal of every minister and government official suspected of moderate views. Though Harley himself lay under this suspicion Swift, writing at a later date, attributes the difficult situation to the Queen, who, he says, 'entertained the Notion of forming a modest and comprehensive Scheam', that she became slow and suspicious, 'difficult to be *advised*', and that Harley took 'the Burthen of Reproach upon himself' rather than permit the Queen to bear it. (*An Enquiry into the Behaviour of the Queen's Last Ministry*, *Prose Works*, ed. Davis, viii. 143–4.)

[2] As has been noted before the death of the Emperor Joseph I and the succession of Charles placed the Whig programme of 'No peace without Spain', outside the policy of all but a few. It may be, however, that Peterborough foresaw the renunciation of Spain by Charles, and was nursing his scheme for placing the Duke of Savoy on the Spanish throne.

Country would support them under: But, my Lord Treasurer is a Stranger to Fear, and has all that Courage which Innocence and good Sense can give a Man, and the most Free from avarice of any one living; both which are absolutely necessary for his Station in this Juncture. He was saying a Thing to me some Days ago, which I believe is the great Maxim he proceedeth by; That Wisdom in publick Affairs, was not what is commonly believed, the forming of Schemes with remote Views; but the making Use of such Incidents as happen. It was thought my Lord *Marr* would have succeeded as Secretary upon the Duke of *Queensberry's* Death; but the Court seemeth now disposed to have no third Secretary, which was a useless Charge.[1] The Queen has been extremely ill, so as for four and twenty Hours People were in great Pain; but she hath been since much better, and voided Abundance of Gravel, &c.[2] Our Expedition under Mr. *Hill* is said to be towards the South-Seas, but nothing is known: I told a great Man, who is deepest in the Project of it, that I had no good Opinion of these Expeditions, which hitherto never succeeded with us. He said, he would venture ten to one upon the Success of it, provided no ill Accident happened by Storms; and that it was concerted with three or four great Princes Abroad.[3]

As to the First Fruits, I must inform your Grace, that the whole Affair lyeth exactly as it did for some Months past. The Duke and his People never thought, or at least never meddled in it, until some Days before they went, and then they were told it was already done; and, my Lord Treasurer directed, that it should be an instruction

[1] James Douglas, second Duke of Queensberry, was appointed a third Secretary of State in Feb. 1709. He died six days before Swift wrote this letter. Lord Mar was not, however, appointed a Secretary of State till 13 Sept. 1713.
[2] Queen Anne had not been in health, suffering in the earlier part of the year from gout complicated by attacks of ague. On 10 July Swift expressed fears that all the Queen's physicians would 'kill her among them'. On the 14th bank stock was falling, but soon began to rise again. On the 17th Swift could report that the Queen 'is very well now, and all the story of her illness, except the first day or two, was a lie' (*Journal*, pp. 311, 313, 315-16).
[3] While Harley was lying ill from the effects of his wound St. John took the opportunity of forwarding a scheme which he thought would redound to his credit—the capture of Quebec. Under the command of Mrs. Masham's brother, General 'Jack' Hill, 5,000 men were convoyed in transports by a squadron of ships commanded by Sir Hovenden Walker; and about the middle of August they entered the mouth of the St. Lawrence. A storm cast eight transports on the rocks with the loss of about 900 men; and the expedition returned home a complete failure (Trevelyan, *England under Queen Anne*, iii. 118-

to the Lord-Lieutenant to mention in his Speech to Parliament, that the Queen had done it, &c. But they took no Sort of Care to finish the Matter, and carry the Instrument over with them, which they might have done, had they began timely, and applied themselves; and as the Bishops superseded me, I did not presume to meddle further in it: But, I think this may be a Lesson, that in all such Cases as these, it is necessary to have some good Sollicitor, and not leave Things wholly to great Men: Nay, so little did the Duke engage in this Matter, that my Lord Treasurer told me Yesterday (although that is a Secret) that the very Draught they had made upon my Application was some Way or other mislaid between the Queen and himself, and could not be found; but, however, that another should soon be drawn: And, his Lordship commanded me to inform your Grace, and my Lords the Bishops, that with the first Convenience the Instrument should be prepared and sent over, which your Grace will please to let them know. I was of Opinion with my Lord Treasurer, that it should be done by a Deed from the Queen, without an Act of Parliament, and that the Bishops should be made a Corporation, for the Management of it. Your Grace sees I write with much Freedom, because I am sure, I can do it safely.

I have been engaging my Lord Treasurer and the other great Men in a Project of my own, which they tell me they will embrace, especially his Lordship. He is to erect some kind of Society or Academy under the Patronage of the Ministers, and Protection of the Queen, for correcting, enlarging, polishing, and fixing our Language. The Methods must be left to the Society; only I am writing a Letter to my Lord Treasurer, by Way of Proposals, and some general Hints, which I design to publish, and he expecteth from me.[1] All this may come to nothing, although, I find, the ingenious and learned Men of all my Acquaintance fall readily in with it; and, so I hope, will your Grace if the Design can be well executed. I would desire at Leisure some of your Grace's Thoughts on this Matter.

I hope, your Grace will take Advantage of the Times, and see,

[1] This pamphlet occupied Swift's thoughts for some time (*Journal*, pp. 295–6, 493), and finally appeared as *A Proposal for Correcting Improving and Ascertaining the English Tongue; In a Letter to the Most Honourable Robert Earl of Oxford and Mortimer, . . . London: Printed for Benj. Tooke, at the Middle-Temple-Gate, Fleetstreet,* 1712. It is dated 'Feb. 22. 1711, 12.'; and was published on 17 May 1712 (the *Post Boy*, 15–17 May; the *London Gazette*, 17 May).

whether your violent House of Commons will fall in with some
good Law for the Benefit of the Church, as their much betters have
done it here:[1] And, I think the Convocation could not be better
employed, than in considering what good Law is wanting for the
Church, and endeavour to have it passed, rather than in brangling
upon Trifles. The Church hath so few happy Occasions, that we
ought to let none of them slip. I take up too much of your Grace's
Time, and therefore begging your Prayers and Blessing, I remain
with the greatest Respect, | Your Grace's | Most dutiful, humble
Servant,

J. Swift.

Hawkesworth 1766

Archbishop King to Swift

Dublin, July 25, 1711.

Rev. Sir
    You must not wonder that I have been so ill a correspondent of
late, being, as I find, in debt to you for yours of *June* the 8th[2] and
July the 12th. This did not proceed from any negligence, but from
the circumstances of things here, that were such, that I could not
return you any satisfactory answer.
    We have now got over the preliminaries of our Parliaments and
convocation; that is to say, our addresses, *&c.*, and as to the Parliament, so far as appears to me, there will be an entire compliance
with her Majesty's occasions, and my Lord Duke of *Ormond's*
desire; and that funds will be given for two years from *Christmas*
next; by which we shall have the following summer free from
parliamentary attendance, which proves a great obstruction both to
Church and country business. As to the Convocation, we have no

---

    [1] During the previous session the English Parliament had voted funds for
the building of fifty churches to meet the increasing needs of the population of
London. Swift had contributed an impulse to the scheme in his *Project for the
Advancement of Religion and Reformation of Manners* published in Apr. 1709.
The bill received the royal assent 12 June 1711. See *Prose Works*, ed. Temple
Scott, iii. 21-47.
    [2] This letter is not forthcoming. It was written at the time Swift's last
Examiner appeared (*Journal*, p. 291 and note). He was on the point of going
out of town to stay with Lord Shelburne, and he remained out of London for
about twelve days.

licence as yet to act. I have heard some whispers, as if a letter of licence had come over, and was sent back again to be mended, especially as to direction about a President. I may inform you, that the matter is in her Majesty's choice: we have on record four licences; the first directed to the Archbishop of *Dublin* in 1614; the other three, that are in 1634, 1662, 1665, directed to the then Lords Primates. I have not at present the exact dates; but I have seen the writs, and find the Convocation sat in these years.

His Grace the Duke of *Ormond*, in his speech to the Parliament (which I doubt not but you have seen), mentioned the remittal of the twentieth parts, and the grant of the first-fruits, for buying impropriations; but did not assume to himself any merit in the procuring of them;[1] nor, that I can find by any intimation, so much as insinuated that the grant was on his motion; notwithstanding, both in the House of Lords and Convocation, some laboured to ascribe the whole to his Grace; and had it not been for the account I had from you, his Grace must, next to her Majesty, have had the entire thanks. You'll observe, from the Lords' address and Convocation, that his Grace is brought in for a share in both.[2] But if the case should be otherwise, yet his Grace is no way to be blamed. The current runs that way; and perhaps neither you nor I have bettered our interest here at present, by endeavouring to stop it.

The conclusion was, that all the Archbishops and Bishops agreed to return thanks to my Lord Treasurer of *Great Britain*, by a letter, which all in town have signed, being convinced, that, next to her Majesty's native bounty, and zeal for the Church, this favour is due to his Lordship's mediation.

But they have employed no agent to solicit the passing the act through the offices, believing his Lordship will take care of that of his own mere motion, as he did of the grant. This is meant as an instance of their great confidence in his Lordship's concern for them, which makes it needless that any should intermeddle in what he has undertaken.

If his Lordship thinks fit to return any answer to the Bishops, I

[1] The actual words used by Ormonde in his address to Parliament did not claim any special merit to himself.

[2] The Lords voted two addresses to the Queen, and an address to the Duke of Ormonde. In the addresses to the Queen there is no allusion to Ormonde's help in gaining remission of the First Fruits. In the address to Ormonde his 'particular care and mediation' in the matter is definitely acknowledged. King was one of those responsible for drafting the addresses.

wish he would take some occasion to mention you in it; for that would justify you, and convince the Bishops, some of whom, perhaps, suspect the truth of what you said of the first-fruits and twentieth parts being granted before his Grace the Duke of *Ormond* was declared Lord Lieutenant of *Ireland*.[1]

I can't at present write of several matters, that perhaps I may have opportunity to communicate to you. I have sent with this the Lords' and the Convocation's address to my Lord Duke.

If it may be proper, I would have my most humble respects to be laid before my Lord Treasurer. You may be sure I am his most humble servant, and shall never forget the advantages he has been the author of to the Church and State; and yet I believe, if it please God to prolong his life, greater things may be expected from him; my prayers shall not be wanting.

As for yourself, I will say more some other time: and for the present shall only assure you, that I am, sir, your affectionate humble servant, and brother, |

Will. Dublin.

Hawkesworth 1766

Archbishop King to Swift

Lissenhall,[2] July 28, 1711.

Since my Lord Duke of *Ormond*'s arrival, I have been so continually hurried with company, that I retired here for two or three days. The preliminaries of our Parliament are now over; that is to say, addresses, &c., and I find the usual funds will be granted, I think unanimously for two years from *Christmas* next, which is all the Duke of *Ormond* desires. I do not see much more will be done. You will observe several reflections are in the addresses on the late management here, in which the Earl of *Anglesey* and I differed.[3]

[1] The Archbishop's letter did not reach Swift's hands till 14 Aug. In reference to it he remarked sardonically, writing to Stella, that the Duke 'had less share in it than MD' (*Journal*, p. 333).

[2] Lissen Hall, in the parish of Swords, about seven miles from Dublin, was at this time the residence of Robert King, a member of the Irish Parliament and brother of Thomas King, rector of Swords, who were related to the Archbishop.

[3] The Lords moved addresses to the Queen expressing satisfaction upon the change of government and reflecting unfavourably on Wharton. The words to

If we could impeach, as you can in *Great Britain*, and bring the malefactors to account, I should be for it with all my endeavour; but to show our ill-will when we can do no more, seems to be no good policy in a dependent people, and that can have no other effect, than to provoke revenge without the prospect of redress; of which we have two fatal instances. I reckon, that every chief governor who is sent here comes with a design to serve first those who sent him; and that our good only must be so far considered, as it is subservient to the main design. The only difference between governors, as to us, is to have a good-natured man, that has some interest in our prosperity, and will not oppress us unnecessarily; and such is his Grace. But I doubt, whether even that will not be an objection against him on your side of the water: for I have found, that those governors, that gained most on the liberties of the kingdom, are reckoned the best; and therefore it concerns us to be on our guard against all governors, and to provoke as little as we can. For he, that cannot revenge himself, acts the wise part, when he dissembles, and passes over injuries.

In my opinion, the best that has happened to us, is, that the Parliament grants the funds for two years; for by these means we shall have one summer to ourselves to do our Church and country business. I have not been able to visit my diocese *ecclesiatim*, as I used to do, the last three years, for want of such a recess. I hope the Parliament of *Great Britain* will not resume the yarn bill whilst they continue the same.[1] The Lords have not sat above four or five days, and are adjourned till *Monday* next;[2] so we have no heads of bills brought into our House as yet: but if any be relating to the Church, I will do my endeavour to give you satisfaction.

Our letter[3] is come over for the remittal of the twentieth parts, and granting the first-fruits for buying impropriations, and purchasing glebes, which will be a great ease to the clergy, and a benefit to the Church. We want glebes more than the impropriations; and I

which King objected were contained in the unfortunate phrasing of an acknowledgement to the announcement of a grant towards the building of a library for Trinity College. In opposition to the terms, however, the Archbishop had only two supporters.

[1] See p. 221, n. 2.
[2] The Lords, who had met eight times, had adjourned on Tuesday the 24th to Monday the 30th.—Ball.
[3] It was dated 17 Feb., about seven weeks after St. John had assured Swift that the warrant was drawn.

am for buying them first, where wanting; for without them, residence is impossible: and besides, I look upon it as a security to tithes, that the laity have a share in them; and therefore I am not for purchasing them, but where they are absolutely necessary.

We shall, I believe, have some considerations of methods to convert the natives; but I do not find, that it is desired by all, that they should be converted. There is a party amongst us, that have little sense of religion, and heartily hate the Church: these would have the natives made Protestants; but such as themselves are deadly afraid they should come into the Church, because, say they, this would strengthen the Church too much. Others would have them come in, but can't approve of the methods proposed, which are to preach to them in their own language, and have the service in *Irish*, as our own canons require. So that between them, I am afraid that little will be done.[1] I am, sir, yours, &c.

Faulkner 1762

Swift to Archbishop King

London, August 15, 1711.

My Lord,

I have been at *Windsor* for a Fortnight, from whence I returned two Days ago,[2] and met a Letter at my Lodging, from your Grace, dated *July* 25. I was told it was sent to Mr. Manly's House, (your Postmaster's son)[3] and by him to me; so that I suppose your Grace

[1] Reference has already been made (p. 221) to the devoted endeavours of the Rev. John Richardson for the conversion of the native Irish by the publication of books printed in Irish and the ordination of an Irish-speaking clergy. He often himself preached in Irish. In 1712 he published in London *A Short History of the Efforts for the Conversion of the Popish Natives of Ireland*. A committee was appointed by the Irish House of Commons to further his plans; but, to their shame, the Upper House of Convocation opposed his efforts as likely to injure the English interest.

[2] Swift was taken to Windsor for the first time by Harley on Saturday, 21 July, and returned to London the next day. On the following Saturday he went down with St. John and remained at Windsor till Tuesday 14 Aug. (*Journal*, pp. 318, 321, 332). It is probable that during this stay he wrote the whole or part of *Some Remarks upon a Pamphlet, Entitl'd, A Letter to the Seven Lords* (*Prose Works*, ed. Davis, iii, pp. xxix–xxxi, 158–205), which appeared on 18 Aug. See, further, *Journal*, p. 340.

[3] Possibly the handsome young Manley with an 'indifferent' wife mentioned in the *Journal*, 12 July 1711.

did not direct to Mr. *Lewis* as formerly,[1] otherwise I should have had it at *Windsor*. The Ministers go usually down to *Windsor* on *Saturday*, and return on *Monday* or *Tuesday* following. I had little Opportunity of talking with my Lord Treasurer, seeing him only at Court, or at Suppers at third Places, or, in much Company at his own Lodgings. Yesterday I went to visit him after Dinner, but did not stay above an Hour, because Business called him out. I read to him that Part of your Grace's Letter which expresseth your Grace's Respects to him, and he received them perfectly well. He told me, he had lately received a Letter from the Bishops of *Ireland*, subscribed (as I remember) by Seventeen, acknowledging his Favour about the First-Fruits. I told his Lordship, that some People in *Ireland* doubted, whether the Queen had granted them before the Duke of *Ormond* was declared Lieutenant; yes, he said, sure I remembered it was immediately upon my Application. I said, I heard the Duke himself took no Merit on that Account. He answered, no, he was sure he did not, he was the honestest Gentleman alive: But, said he, it is the Queen that did it, and she alone shall have the Merit; and, I must be so free as to tell your Grace, that the grudging, ungrateful Manner of some People, which upon several Occasions, I could not but give him Hints of for my Justification, hath not been prudent. I am sure it hath hindered me from any Thoughts of pursuing another Affair of yet greater Consequence, which I had good Hopes of compassing.[2] What can be the Matter with those People? Do I ask either Money or Thanks of them? Have I done any Hurt to the Business? My Lord Treasurer told me, he had sent the Letter over about the First Fruits. I never enquired into the Particulars: He says, he will very soon answer the Bishops' Letter to himself, and will shew me both Letter and Answer; but I shall not put him in Mind, unless he remembers it of his own Accord. Nor, with great submission to your Grace, can I prevail on my own Pride to desire he would make any Mention of me in his Answer. Your Grace is convinced, that unless I write a heap of lies, the Queen had granted that Affair before my Lord Duke was named. I desire to convince no Body else, and since the thing is done, it is not of any Consequence who were instrumental in it. I could not forbear Yesterday reminding my Lord Treasurer of what I said to Mr.

---

[1] Erasmus Lewis.

[2] The remission of the crown rents, which, on his own initiative, Swift included in his memorial submitted to Harley.

Southwell[1] before his Lordship, when he came to take his Leave before he went to *Ireland*; which was, that I hoped Mr. *Southwell* would let the Bishops and clergy of *Ireland* know, that my Lord Treasurer had long since (before the Duke was governor) prevailed on the Queen to remit the First Fruits, *&c.* and that it was his Lordship's Work, as the Grant of the same Favour in *England* had formerly been. My Lord Treasurer did then acknowledge it before Mr. *Southwell*, and I think Mr. *Southwell* should have acted accordingly; but there is a great deal of Ignorance, as well as ill Will, in all this Matter. The Duke of *Ormond* himself, had he engaged in it, could only act as a sollicitor. Every body knows that the Lord Treasurer in such Cases, must be applied to, (and only He) by the greatest Persons. I should think the people of *Ireland* might rather be pleased to see one of their own Country able to find some Credit at Court, and in a Capacity to serve them, especially, one who doeth it without any other Prospect than that of serving them. I know not any of the Bishops from whom I can expect any Favour, and there are not many upon whom a Man of any Figure could have such Designs; but, I will be revenged; for, whenever it lieth in my Power, I will serve the Church and Kingdom, although they should use me much worse. I shall dine To-morrow with Lord Treasurer, and perhaps I may then see the Answer he is to write. I thought to have sent this Letter away to Night; but, I have been interrupted by Business. I go to *Windsor* again on *Saturday* for a Day or two, but I will leave this behind to be sent to the Post

Aug. 21. I had wrote thus far, and was forced to leave off, being hurried away to *Windsor*, by my Lord Treasurer,[2] from whence I returned but last Night. His Lordship gave me a Paper, which he said, he had promised me; I put it in my Pocket, thinking it was about something else we had been talking over; and, I never looked into it until just now, when I find it to be my Lord Primate's Letter to his Lordship, with an enclosed one from the Bishops. With Submission, I take it to be dry enough, although I shall not tell his Lordship so. They say *they are informed his Lordship had a great*

---

[1] See King's letter to Swift of 2 Nov. 1710.

[2] The earlier part of this letter was written by Swift on Wednesday, 15 Aug., the day after his return from Windsor. He went to Windsor again on Saturday the 18th. His departure for Windsor can therefore hardly have been the cause of his failing to complete the letter on the 15th. He was back in London on Monday, 20th, and the next day wrote to King, 'and inclosed a long politick paper by itself' (*Journal*, p. 336).

part in, &c. I think they should either have told who it was informed them so, since it was a Person commissioned by themselves; or, at least, have said they were *assured*. And, as for those Words, *a great part*, I know no Body else had any, except the Queen herself. I cannot tell whether my Lord hath writ an Answer, having said nothing to him of it, since he gave me the letters, nor shall I desire to see it.

As to the Convocation, I remember both my Lord Treasurer, and Mr. *St. John*, spoke to me about the Matter, and were of the same Opinion with your Grace, that it was wholly in the Queen's Choice; I excused giving my opinion, being wholly uninformed; and, I have heard nothing of it since.

My Lord Keeper gave me Yesterday, a Bundle of *Irish* Votes at *Windsor*, and we talked a good deal about the Quarrel between the Lords and Commons:[1] I said, the Fault lay in not dissolving the Parliament; which I had mentioned to the Duke of *Ormond*, and often to some of those who were thought to have most Credit with him. But, they seemed to believe, as I did, that any *Irish* Parliament would yield to any Thing that any chief Governor pleased; and so it would be a needless Trouble.

We reckon for certain, that Mr. *Hill* with his Fleet is gone to *Quebec*.

Mrs. *Masham* is every Minute expecting to Lye in. Pray God preserve her Life, which is of great Importance. I am with the greatest Respect, | My Lord, | Your Grace's most dutiful | and most humble Servant,

The Queen hath got a light fit of the Gout. The Privy Seal is not yet disposed of.

---

[1] The Irish Upper House adopted in their addresses to the Queen an extreme Tory attitude. The Commons, alarmed by what they regarded as unfavourable reflections on 'sound Revolution principles', declared in their address that these words could bear no other construction than their strict relationship to 'the late happy Revolution'.

Swift to Archbishop King

[26 August 1711][1]

My Lord,

Perhaps you will be content to know some Circumstances of Affairs here. The Duke of *Somerset* usually leaves *Windsor* on *Saturday*, when the Ministers go down thither, and returns not until they are gone. On *Sunday* 7-Night, contrary to Custom, he was at *Windsor*, and a Cabinet Council was to be held at Night; but, after waiting a long Time, Word was brought out, that there would be no Cabinet. Next Day it was held, and then the Duke went to a Horse-Race about three Miles off. This began to be whispered; and at my return to Town they had got it in the City; but, not the Reason; which was, that Mr. Secretary *St. John* refused to sit if the Duke was there.[2] Last *Sunday* the Duke was there again, but did not offer to come to the Cabinet, which was held without him. I hear the Duke was advised by his Friends of the other Party to take this Step. The Secretary said to some of his Acquaintance, that he would not sit with a Man who had so often betrayed them, *&c.* You know the Dutchess of *Somerset* is a great Favourite, and has got the Dutchess of *Marlborough*'s Key. She is insinuating, and a Woman of Intrigue; and will, I believe, do what ill Offices she can, to the Secretary. They would have hindered her coming in; but, the Queen said, if it were so, that she could not have what Servants she liked, she did not find how her Condition was mended. I take the Safety of the present Ministry to consist in the Agreement of three great Men, Lord Keeper, Lord Treasurer, and Mr. Secretary, and so I have often told them together, between Jest and Earnest, and two of them separately with more Seriousness. And, I think, they intirely love one another; their Differences are not of Weight to break their

[1] This letter, printed by Faulkner in 1762, carried a conjectural date '—, 1712', which cannot be correct. Nichols, 1801, has '26 August 1711', which is confirmed by the subject-matter of the letter.

[2] Swift, writing to Stella, 13 Aug., tells her that St. John refused to sit with Somerset at a cabinet meeting. Charles Seymour, sixth Duke of Somerset, although a Whig, began in May 1710 to intrigue with Harley against Godolphin and Marlborough (Portland MSS. iv). St. John always suspected Somerset's good faith. His Duchess was the Queen's confidante (*Poems*, pp. 145-8). For Swift's estimate of the Duke at large see *Four Last Years of the Queen* (*Prose Works*, ed. Davis, vii. 13-15).

Union. They vary a little about their Notions of a certain General. I will not say more at this Distance. I do not see well how they can be without the Secretary, who hath very great Abilities, both for the Cabinet and Parliament.¹ The Tories in the City are a little discontented, that no further Changes are made in Employments, of which I cannot learn the Secret, although I have heard several, and from such who might tell the true one if they would: One is, that Lord Treasurer professeth he is at a Loss to find Persons qualified for several Places: Another, (which is less believed) that the Queen interposeth: A third, that it is a trimming Disposition.² I am apt, to think, that he finds the Call for Employments greater than he can answer, if there were five Times as many to dispose of; and I know particularly, that he dislikes very much the Notion of People, that every One is to be turned out. The Treasurer is much the greatest Minister I ever knew: Regular in Life, with a true Sense of Religion, an excellent Scholar, and a good Divine, of a very mild and affable Disposition, intrepid in his Notions, and indefatigable in Business, an utter Despiser of Money for himself, yet frugal, (perhaps to an Extremity) for the Publick. In private Company, he is wholely disengaged, and very facetious, like one who has no Business at all. He never wants a Reserve upon any Emergency, which would appear desperate to others; and maketh little Use of those thousand Projectors and Schematists, who are daily plying him with their Visions, but to be thoroughly convinced, by the Comparison, that his own Notions are the best. I am, my Lord, | with the greatest Respect, | your Grace's | most obedient, &c.

Hawkesworth 1766
Archbishop King to Swift

Swords, Sept. 1, 1711.

Rev. Sir,

I have before me yours of the 15th and 21st, for which I return you my hearty thanks. I perceive you have the votes of our Commons

¹ This suggests that for the time being Swift was more in the confidence of St. John than he had previously been. His lengthy visit to Windsor seems to have been at St. John's suggestion. The reference to 'a certain General' may mean that St. John, working for a peace, had hinted the obstacle presented by Marlborough.   ² See p. 237, n. 1.

here, and I suppose the address of the Lords, that gave occasion to them. I must let you know, that I was very positive against the clause that provoked them, and kept the House in debate about it at least an hour, and spoke so often, that I was ashamed of myself; yet there were but three negatives to it.[1] I used several arguments against the Lords concurring with their committee, and foretold all that has happened upon it; upon which I was much out of favour with the House for some time; and industry has been used, as I was informed, to persuade my Lord Duke, that what I did was in opposition to his interest; but when I had the opportunity to discourse his Grace last, he was of another opinion. And, in truth, my regard to his Grace's interest was the principal reason of opposing a clause, that I foresaw might embarrass his business here.

There happened another affair relating to one *Langton*, of whom I formerly gave you some account.[2] The Commons found him on the establishment for a small pension; and having an ill notion of him and his informations, they took this occasion to examine his merits. In order to which, they sent up a message to the Lords, to desire leave of Judge *Coote*,[3] who had taken his examinations, and those of his witnesses, to come down, and inform the committee: and this seemed the more necessary, because the examinations taken by the Council were burned:[4] but the Lords refused to let the Judge go down, as desired, and passed a vote to take the examination of the matter into their hands. This, I foresaw, might prove another bone of contention, and did oppose it, but with the same success as the former. *Langton* pleaded privilege, as chaplain to the Bishop of *Ossory*,[5] and refused to appear before the Commons: on which they passed the angry resolves you will find in their votes. The examination of this matter has employed much of the Lords' time to very

[1] See p. 242, n. 3.
[2] See King to Swift, 16 Dec. 1710, and note.
[3] The Hon. Thomas Coote, third son of Lord Coote of Coloony, Recorder of Dublin, 1690, and M.P. for that city in 1692. The soundness of his politics was suspect, and, on an occasion, he sought to justify himself with Swift (*Journal*, 28 Dec. 1711). He had been appointed a Justice of the King's Bench in 1693, but was superseded after the accession of George I. Ball, *Judges in Ireland*, ii. 60–62; Lodge's *Peerage of Ireland*, iii. 215; Dunton, *Life and Errors*, 1818, p. 521.
[4] In the previous April public papers and records had been destroyed by a fire.
[5] John Hartstonge, frequently mentioned in the *Journal to Stella*.

little purpose. My opposing this was made an objection against me by some, that wish now my advice had been taken.

The business of the city of *Dublin*, of which I gave you an account formerly,[1] embroils us very much. We have at the council rejected four mayors and eight sheriffs, all regularly elected by the city, some of them the best citizens in the town, and much in the interest of the Government. We begin to be sick of it, and I am afraid, that it may beget ill blood, and come into Parliament here. We have rejected the elected magistrates in four other corporations, which adds to the noise. I own there were good reasons for rejecting some of them; but I cannot say the same for *Dublin*. I wish this may not prove uneasy to us.

There was a motion made at the session for the county of *Dublin* at *Kilmainham*, for an address of thanks to her Majesty for sending his Grace the Duke of *Ormond* to be our chief governor. Nine of the justices, that is, all that were then present, agreed to it, and an address was ordered to be drawn, which was brought next morning into court, and then there were above a score, that seemed to have come on purpose, and promised that it should be rejected by a majority; for this reason only, that it would entail a necessity on them to address in favour of every new Lord Lieutenant, or disoblige him. For which reason it was rejected also in my Lord *Wharton*'s time. This no ways concerns his Grace himself; but in my opinion, ought to lessen the esteem of some persons' management, that attempt things, which would be better let alone, where they cannot be carried without opposition.

The House of Commons seem to have received ill impressions of some. They reckon my Lord Duke's advisers, as if they were secretly his enemies, and designed to betray him. They generally seemed persuaded, that his Grace is a sincere honest man, and most in the interest of the kingdom of any chief governor they can ever expect; and that, therefore they ought to support him to the utmost of their power, and declare, that the quarrels his enemies raise, shall not hinder them from doing whatever he shall reasonably desire from them, or her Majesty's service require; and as an instance of their sincerity in this, they have granted funds for two years from *Christmas* last; whereas at first they intended only two years from the 24th of *June* last.

I have been preaching a doctrine that seems strange to some: 'tis,

[1] In his letter of 15 May.

that her Majesty, and the Ministry, will be inclined to employ such as may be a help and support to their interest, and not a clog. I mean, that these subalterns should, by their prudence and dexterity, be able to remove any misunderstandings, that may be between the Government and the people, and help to beget in them a good notion of the Ministry; and by all means, avoid such things as may embarrass or beget jealousies; so that the burthen or odium may not fall on the Ministry, where any harsh things happen to be done: that it seems to me to be the duty of those in posts, to avoid unnecessary disputes, and not to expect that the Ministry will interpose to extricate them, when they, without necessity, have involved themselves. But some are of a different opinion, and seem to think, that they have no more to do when they meet with difficulties, perhaps of their own creating, than to call in the Ministry, and desire them to decide the matter by power: a method that I do not approve, nor has it succeeded well with former governors here: witness Lord *Sydney*, and Lord *Wharton* in the case of the Convocation.[1]

There really needs but one thing to quiet the people of *Ireland*, and it is to convince them, that there is no eye to the Pretender. Great industry has been, and still is, used to bugbear them with that fear. I believe it is over with you; but it will require time and prudent methods to quiet the people here, that have been possessed for twenty-two years with a continual apprehension, that he is at the door, and that a certain kind of people designed to bring him in. The circumstances of this kingdom, from what they saw and felt under King *James*, make the dread of him much greater than it can be with you.

As to our Convocation, a letter came from her Majesty to give us licence to act; but it no ways pleased some people, and so it was sent back to be modelled to their mind, but returned again without alteration. It came not to us till the day the Parliament adjourned. I was at that time obliged to attend the Council, there being a hearing of the Quakers against a Bill for Recovering Tithes. In my absence they adjourned till the meeting of the Parliament, without so much as voting thanks, or appointing a committee. The things that displeased some in the licence were, first, that my Lord Primate was not the

---

[1] In 1692 Viscount Sydney, afterwards Earl of Romney (*Poems*, pp. 64–65), caused the utmost indignation by quelling a noisy session of the Irish Parliament by the simple process of dissolution. Similarly Wharton prorogued Convocation, when the conduct of his chaplain, Lambert, was under debate.

sole president, so as to appoint whom he pleased to act in his absence; the second was, the consideration of proper methods to convert the natives, against which some have set themselves with all their might;[1] the third is, what concerns pluralities, and residence, which some have not patience to hear of. The Lower House seem to have the matter more at heart; for they have appointed committees during the recess, and are doing something.

I can't but admire, that you should be at a loss to find what is the matter with those, that would neither allow you, nor any one else, to get any thing for the service of the Church, or the public. It is, with submission, the silliest query I ever found made by Dr. *Swift*. You know there are some, that would assume to themselves to be the only churchmen and managers, and can't endure that any thing should be done but by themselves, and in their own way; and had rather that all good things proposed should miscarry, than be thought to come from other hands than their own, whose business is to lessen every body else, and obstruct whatever is attempted, tho' of the greatest advantage to Church and State, if it be not from their own party. And yet, so far as I have hitherto observed, I do not remember an instance of their proposing, much less prosecuting with success, anything for the public good. They seem to have a much better hand at obstructing others, and embarrassing affairs, than at proposing or prosecuting any good design.

These seem as uneasy that more alterations are not made here, as those you mention are with you.[2] The reason is very plain, they would fain get into employments, which can't be without removes; but I have often observed, that none are more eager for posts, than such as are least fit for them. I do not see how a new Parliament would much mend things here; for there is little choice of men: perhaps it might be for the worse, *rebus sic stantibus*; though I always thought the honest part is, to allow the people to speak their sense on the change of affairs by new representatives. I do not find that those that have embarrassed the present, designed a new one; but they thought the Commons so passive, that they might carry what they pleased, whatever their design might be. If they prosecute the present measures, I believe they will make new ones necessary, when there shall be occasion to have a new session.

I pray most heartily for her Majesty, and her Ministers; and am inclined to believe, that it is one of the most difficult parts of their

---

[1] See p. 221.   [2] you] them *Hawkesworth*.

present circumstances, to find proper instruments to execute their good intentions, notwithstanding the great crowds that offer themselves; particularly, my Lord Treasurer's welfare is at heart with all good men: I am sure, with none more than, Reverend Sir, &c.

                                                            Will. Dublin.

Hawkesworth 1766

Archbishop King to Swift

                                            Swords, Sept. 1, 1711.
Rev. Sir,
    I got a little retirement here, and made use of it, to write you by the present pacquet. I promised to say something as to your own affairs; and the first thing is, not to neglect yourself on this occasion, but to make use of the favour and interest you have at present to procure you some preferment that may be called a settlement. Years come on, and after a certain age, if a man be not in a station that may be a step to a better, he seldom goes higher. It is with men as with beauties, if they pass the flower, they grow stale, and lie for ever neglected. I know you are not ambitious; but it is prudence, not ambition, to get into a station, that may make a man easy, and prevent contempt when he grows in years. You certainly may now have an opportunity to provide for yourself, and I entreat you not to neglect it.[1]
    The second thing that I would desire you to consider, is, that God has given you parts and learning, and a happy turn of mind; and that you are answerable for those talents to God: and therefore I advise you, and believe it to be your duty, to set yourself to some serious and useful subject in your profession, and to manage it so, that it may be of use to the world. I am persuaded, that if you will apply yourself this way, you are well able to do it; and that your knowledge of the world, and reading, will enable you to furnish such a piece, with such uncommon remarks, as will render it both profitable and agreeable, above most things that pass the press. Say not,

---

[1] Writing to Stella (*Journal*, 12 Sept. 1711) Swift summarizes King's letter scornfully, as he had done previously in his letter to Ford, *post* 8 Sept. The ineptness of the letter is a curious illustration of King's misunderstanding of Swift's true character. Swift's answer, written from Windsor, 1 Oct., is a model of dignified restraint.

that most subjects in divinity are exhausted; for, if you look into Dr. *Wilkins*'s Heads of Matters, which you will find in his Gift of Preaching,[1] you will be surprized to find so many necessary and useful heads, that no authors have meddled with. There are some common themes, that have employed multitudes of authors; but the most curious and difficult are in a manner untouched, and a good genius will not fail to produce something new and surprizing on the most trite, much more on those that others have avoided, merely because they were above their parts.

Assure yourself, that your interest, as well as duty, requires this from you; and you will find, that it will answer some objections against you, if you thus shew the world that you have patience and comprehension of thought, to go through with such a subject of weight and learning.

You'll pardon me this freedom, which I assure you proceeds from a sincere kindness, and true value that I have for you. I will add no more, but my hearty prayers for you. I am, Dr. *Swift*, yours, |

Will. Dublin.

Nichols 1801

Swift to Dean Atterbury

Sept. 1, 1711.

Sir,

I congratulate with the College, the University, and the kingdom, and condole with myself, upon your new dignity.[2] The virtue I would affect, by putting my own interests out of the case, has failed me in this juncture. I only consider that I shall want your conversation, your friendship, your protection, and your good offices, when

---

[1] *Ecclesiastes; or, a Discourse concerning the Gift of Preaching as it falls under the Rules of Art*, by John Wilkins (1614–72), Bishop of Chester, first published in 1646. It ran into a seventh edition before the end of the century, and into an eighth, 'much enlarged', in 1704.

[2] Francis Atterbury had been Dean of Carlisle since 1704. The Deanery of Christ Church became vacant by the death on 14 Dec. 1710 of Henry Aldrich. After a long delay Atterbury was appointed to fill the vacancy, and installed 27 Sept. 1711. It is probable that Swift made his acquaintance late in 1710 or early in 1711. In the *Journal*, p. 156, he speaks of visiting him on the morning of 6 Jan. 1710–11. When Swift went to lodge in Chelsea he found himself 'just over against Atterbury's house'. Here they spent many hours together and formed a close friendship.

I can least spare them. I would have come among the crowd of those who make you compliments on this occasion, if I could have brought a cheerful countenance with me. I am full of envy. It is too much, in so bad an age, for a person so inclined, and so able to do good, to have so great a scene of showing his inclination and abilities.

If great Ministers take up this exploded custom of rewarding merit, I must retire to Ireland, and wait for better times. The College and you ought to pray for another change at Court, otherwise I can easily foretell that their joy and your quiet will be short. Let me advise you to place your books in moveable cases: lay in no great stock of wine, nor make any great alterations in your lodgings at Christ Church, unless you are sure they are such as your successor will approve and pay for. I am afraid the poor College little thinks of this, *qui nunc te fruitur credulus aureâ.*

I am going to Windsor with Mr. Secretary; and hope to wait on you either at Bridewell[1] or Chelsea. I am, with great respect and esteem, Sir, Your most obedient and most obliged humble servant,

J. Swift.

Rothschild

Swift to Charles Ford

London. Sep[tr]. 8. 1711[2]

I have two Letters[3] of yours to acknolidge, one of a very old date, and when I was going to write, your second stopt me, because you gave me a Commission in it about your Lotteryes. Ben Took[4] has been out of Town these three weeks, and at last I had no Patience, but was resolved to write to You, and let you know I will obey your Commands when he comes home. The last Lottery you know has been all drawn already; and I am apt to guess that this Curiosity of

[1] For many years Atterbury officiated as chaplain to the prison known as the Bridewell. In the *Tatler*, no. 66, a generous tribute is paid to him as a preacher to a difficult congregation.
[2] Swift's list of letters shows that he had heard from Ford on 24 Apr. 1709 and replied on 28 Apr. Both letters are lost.
[3] These two letters also are lost. Ford left London for Ireland at the end of June: see *Journal*, 24 June 1711.
[4] Swift had recently, July 1711, got Tooke appointed printer of the *Gazette*.

desiring the Lists[1] is not yours, but a near Relation's of the other Sex; For I cannot imagine what use they will be to You. You know L[d] Abercorn's Second Son[2] has got a Prize of 4000[11] besides two small ones.—Now to your former Letter, where you say the Publick requires my Leisure. The Publick is a very civil Person, and I am it's humble Servant, but I shall be glad to shake hands with it as soon as I can. Tis probable I may sett out for Ireland about the same Time You begin your Journey here. I tell the great Men so, but they will not believe me. You are in the right as to my Indifference about Irish Affairs, which is not occasioned by my Absence, but contempt of them; and when I return my Indifference will be full as much. I had as live be a Beau in Dublin as a Politician,[3] nay, I had as lieve be an Author there; and if ever I have any thoughts of making a Figure in that Kingdom, it shall be at Laracor. I will talk Politicks to the Farmers, and publish my Works at Trim.—Thanks of the Convocation to me![4] Why, the whole Sett of Bishops except four or five are angry with me, because the D. of O's merit is lessened. However they had the Grace to write L[d] Tr a Letter of thanks signed by 17 Bishops: but I was not mentioned. My L[d] Tr lent it me.—I will not say any thing to You in defence of the A.Bp Dubl— but I must believe they were all mistaken, for Raillery is very little understood in Ireland. You know, you and I do not always agree in eodem tertio. One thing is that I never expect Sincerity from any man; and am no more angry at the Breach of it, than at the colour of his Hair. That same A.Bp told me in severall Letters that he would shortly mention something about my self, which would be to my Advantage; I have heard from others that he resolved to provide for me before any man. Two days ago he performs his Promise, which consists of two Parts, first to advise me to get some Preferment now I have so many Friends. Secondly, because I have Parts and Learning, and a happy Pen, he thinks it my Duty to engage in some usefull Subject of Divinity untouched by others, which he doubts not, I should manage with great Success &c. He was afraid, I expected something from him: He had got some other

---

[1] The amounts of the prizes and the numbers of the successful tickets in the 'Two Million Lottery', drawn at Guildhall from 1 to 15 Aug. 1711, are given in the *Evening Post*, 4 to 16 Aug. See also the *Gazette*, 16–18 Aug.

[2] The Hon. John Hamilton (1694–1714), second surviving son. Educated at Trinity College, Dublin. Collins, *Peerage of England*, 1812, ii. 530.

[3] Cf. *Twelfth Night*, III. ii. 34—one of Swift's few allusions to Shakespeare.

[4] For his part in procuring the remission of the First Fruits.

View: and so takes care to undeceive me.[1] Now do You imagine I take this ill, or think the worse of him for it? or would avoid his Company if I liked it, for such Trifles as this. Perhaps indeed I may answer so as to let him see I very well understand him, and so we shall go on as before.

I have been at Windsor these six Sundays past, except one; and I stayd there once a fortnight together. I go this afternoon[2] again, with Ld Treas^r, and I believe shall continue there a Week; For our Society[3] meets this day Sennight at Mr Secr^ty's Lodgings there. Was that Society begun before you left us? I think it was, and so will say nothing of it.—You hear I suppose, that Prior has been in France; tis certainly true; and I believe you may reckon that we shall soon have a Peace.[4] How do the Whigs in Ireland relish a Bishop's being Ld Privy Seal?[5] They rejoice at it here, as a Thing that will one day ly against the present Ministry. We are weary of expecting Removals in the Excise, Customs, &c. yet they say something must be done before the Sessions. I was last night at the Christning of Mr Mashams young Son,[6] Ld Treas^r and Ld Rivers stood God-fathers, and Mrs Hill Godmother, the Dean of Rochester[7] did the Office, there was no other Company but Ld Duplin[8] and Ld Harley.[9]

  [1] Cf. King's letter of 1 Sept.
  [2] Saturday; he returned to London with Oxford on Monday, but went back to Windsor the following Saturday with St. John.
  [3] St. John, writing to the Earl of Orrery, 12 June 1711, speaks of 'a club which I am forming' to be composed of members who have 'wit and learning' or 'power and influence', and of others 'who from accidental reasons may properly be taken in' (*Letters*, 1798, i. 150, 171). There are many references to this club in the *Journal*. It became better known as 'The Society'. For its membership see *Journal*, p. 505, n.
  [4] Prior was in Paris negotiating peace, 12-24 July. See Portland MSS. v. 34-42.
  [5] John Robinson, 1650-1723, a Fellow of Oriel College, was, about 1680, appointed chaplain to the English embassy in Sweden, and there remained for over twenty-five years. He became Bishop of Bristol in 1710, and in 1711 Lord Privy Seal; and he was thus the last English ecclesiastic to hold diplomatic and political office. Later he went to Utrecht as first English plenipotentiary at the peace conference. [6] See *Journal*, 7 Sept. 1711.
  [7] Samuel Pratt (1659-1723), Dean of Rochester since 1706.
  [8] George Henry Hay, Viscount Dupplin (1689-1758), the Lord Treasurer's son-in-law. He had married Abigail, Oxford's younger daughter, in 1709. He was one of the twelve peers created at the close of 1711; and succeeded his father as eighth Earl of Kinnoul in 1719.
  [9] Edward Harley, the Lord Treasurer's son.

It was at Kensington. What abundance of Lords have dyed since You left us. Ld Jersey[1] would have had the Privy seal if he had lived a few hours longer, the M—rs were a month bringing the Qu— to consent. She is a little stubborn now and then, or they would have us think so, thô I believe the former. She is now in a Fit of the Gout. I find no body expects she can live long; and that is one great Reason why they would hasten a Peace.

I have not time at present to write you more Politicks nor have you been long enough absent to want much Information. Tis thought by State Astronomers that we shall have a scribbling Winter; but perhaps I shall then be far enough off. Pray let me know how I am to direct to You; I send this inclosed to M^r· Deering,[2] of whom I am a very humble Servant. M^r· Philips[3] goes constantly to L^d T^r's Levee; and I believe will get something: I took Occasion to mention him as favorably as I could. I can give You no account of the *Spectator*; for I never go to a Coffeehouse, and seldom see them any where else. M^r· Lewis[4] is your humble Servant, and talks often of you with great kindness. I am at least twice oftner with the M—rs than when you was here, yet you see nothing comes of it, nor I believe will; but every body else pretends to believe otherwise: And this is all I shall say of my self. Adieu.

Address: To Charles Ford Esqr.

Faulkner 1762

Swift to Archbishop King

Windsor-Castle, October 1, 1711.

My Lord,

I had the Honour of a long Letter from your Grace, just a month ago,[5] which I forbore acknowledging sooner, because I have been ever since perpetually tossed between this and *London*,[6] and

---

[1] Edward Villiers, born in 1656, first Earl of Jersey. In 1704 he was dismissed from the office of Lord Chamberlain. He died 26 Aug. 1711. See *Journal to Stella* of that date.

[2] Charles Deering, or Dering, M.P. for Carlingford and Auditor of the Exchequer in Ireland.   [3] Ambrose Philips.

[4] Erasmus Lewis.   [5] King's letter of 1 Sept.

[6] Swift spent every Sunday in the September of that year in Windsor, and also stayed there for the weeks beginning on the third and fifth Sundays.

partly because there had nothing happened that might make a Letter worthy the Perusal. It is the Opinion of some great Persons here, that the Words which the House of Commons took amiss in your Address, might very well bear an Application that concerned only my Lord *Wharton*.[1] I find they are against my Opinion that a new Parliament should have been called; but, all agree, it must now be dissolved: But, in short, we are so extremely busy here, that nothing of *Ireland* is talked on above a Day or two; that of the City Election I have oftenest heard of; and the Proceeding of your Court in it, it is thought, might have been wiser. I find your Grace seemeth to be of my Opinion, and so I told my Lord Treasurer. I think your *Kilmainham* Project of an Address was a very foolish one, and that for the Reason of those who were against it. I hope, *Ireland* will soon be equally convinced with us here, that, if the Pretender be in any Body's Thoughts, it is of those they least dream, and who now are in no Condition of doing Mischief to any but themselves. As for your Convocation, I believe every Thing there will terminate in good wishes. You can do nothing now, and will not meet again these two Years, and then, I suppose, only to give Money and away. There should, methinks, in the Interval, be some Proposals considered and agreed upon by the Bishops and principal Men of the Clergy, to have all ready against the next Meeting; and, even that I despair of, for a Thousand Reasons too tedious to mention.

My admiring at the odd Proceedings of those among the Bishops and Clergy who are angry with me for getting their First-Fruits, was but a Form of Speech. I cannot sincerely wonder at any Proceedings in Numbers of Men, and especially (I must venture to say so) in *Ireland*. Mean Time, it is a good Jest to hear my Lord Treasurer saying often, before a deal of Company, that it was I that got the Clergy of *Ireland* their First-Fruits; and, generally, with this Addition, that it was before the Duke of *Ormond* was declared Lord Lieutenant. His Lordship hath long designed an Answer to the Letter he received from the Bishops; he hath told me ten Times, he would do it To-morrow. He goeth to *London* this Day, but I continue here for a Week. I shall refresh his Memory, and engage my Lord *Harley* his Son to do so too.

I suppose your Grace cannot but hear in general, of some Steps that are making toward a Peace. There came out some Time ago an Account of Mr. *Prior*'s Journey to *France*, pretended to be a Transla-

[1] See p. 242, n. 2.

tion, and is a pure Invention from the Beginning to the End.[1] I will let your Grace into the Secret of it. The Clamours of a Party against any Peace without *Spain*, and railing at the Ministry, as if they designed to ruin us, occasioned that Production, out of Indignity and Contempt, by way of furnishing Fools with something to talk of; and it has had a very great Effect. Mean time your Grace may count that a Peace is going forward very fast.—Mr. *Prior* was actually in *France*; and there are now two Ministers from that Court in *London*, which you may be pretty sure of, if you believe what I tell you, that I supped with them myself in the House where I am now writing, *Saturday* last:[2] Neither do I find it to be a very great Secret; for, there were two Gentlemen more with us beside the Inviter. However, I desire your Grace to say nothing of it, because it may look like Lightness in me to tell it: Mr. *Prior* was with us too, but what their Names are I cannot tell; for, I believe, those they passed by when I was there are not their real ones. All Matters are agreed between *France* and us, and very much to the Advantage and Honour of *England*; but, I believe no farther Steps will be taken without giving Notice to the Allies. I do not tell your Grace one Syllable, as coming from any great Minister; and therefore I do not betray them. But, there are other Ways of picking out Things in a Court: However, I must desire you will not discover any of these little Particulars, nor cite me upon any Account at all; for, great Men may think I tell Things from them, although I have them from other Hands; in which last Case only, I venture to repeat them to one I can confide in, and one at so great a Distance as your Grace.

    I humbly thank your Grace for the good Opinion you are pleased

---

[1] It is doubtful how far Swift was in the confidence of Oxford and St. John as regards the negotiations for peace proceeding at this time. At a later stage he was certainly not cognizant to the full of St. John's moves. Prior, an experienced diplomat, was sent over in July 1711 to negotiate with Torcy. He maintained an unyielding attitude, had a private interview with Louis XIV, and thereafter returned (Trevelyan, *England under Queen Anne*, iii. 183), accompanied by Gaultier and Mesnager. A custom-house official, suspecting them for spies, took them in charge. The affair got abroad, and Swift came to the rescue with a fictitious narrative of the event, *A New Journey to Paris*, which appeared on 11 Sept. (*Prose Works*, ed. Davis, iii, pp. xxx–xxxi, 207–18); *Journal*, pp. 349, 351, 357, 366).

[2] Throughout Aug. and Sept. negotiations for a peace continued, now in London. The English demands were extensive. On the whole the English Ministers succeeded in making a good bargain. 'Preliminary Articles' were signed on Thursday, 27 Sept., o.s. See, further, *Trevelyan*, op. cit. iii. 184–7.

to have of me; and for your Advice which seemeth to be wholely grounded on it. As to the First, which relateth to my Fortune, I shall never be able to make myself believed how indifferent I am about it. I sometimes have the Pleasure of making that of others; and, I fear it is too great a Pleasure to be a Virtue, at least in me. Perhaps, in *Ireland*, I may not be able to prevent Contempt any other Way than by making my Fortune; but, then it is my Comfort, that Contempt in *Ireland* will be no Sort of Mortification to me. When I was last in *Ireland*, I was above half the Time retired to one scurvy Acre of Ground, and I always left it with Regret. I am as well received and known at Court, as perhaps any man ever was of my Level; I have formerly been the like. I left it then, and will perhaps leave it now (when they please to let me) without any Concern, but what a few Months will remove. It is my Maxim to leave great Ministers to do as they please; and, if I cannot distinguish myself enough by being useful in such a Way, as becometh a Man of Conscience and Honour, I can do no more; for, I never will solicit for myself, although I often do for others.

The other Part of your Grace's Advice, to be some Way useful to the Church and the Publick, by any Talent you are pleased to think I possess, is the only Thing for which I should desire some Settlement that would make me full Master of my Time. I have often thought of some Subjects, wherein I believe I might succeed: But, my Lord, to ask a Man floating at Sea, what he designed to do when he gets ashore, is too hasty a Question: Let him get there first, and rest, and dry himself, and then look about him. I have been pretty well known to several great Men in my Life; and, it was their Duty, if they thought I might have been of Use, to put me into a Capacity for it; but, I never yet knew one great Man in my Life, who was not every Day swayed by other Motives in distributing his Favours, whatever Resolutions he had pretended to make to the contrary.[1] I was saying a Thing the other Day to my Lord Keeper, which he approved of, and which I believe may be the Reason of this: It was, that Persons of transcendent Merit forced their Way in Spight of all Obstacles; but those whose merit was of a second, third, or fourth Rate, were seldom able to do any Thing; because the Knaves and Dunces of the World, had all the Impudence, Assiduity, Flattery, and servile Compliance divided among them,

---

[1] The restraint and dignity of Swift's reply to King's blundering advice in his letter of 1 Sept. deserve note.

which kept them perpetually in the Way, and engaged every Body to be their Sollicitors. I was asking a great Minister, a Month ago, how he could possibly happen to pick out a certain Person to employ in a Commission of discovering Abuses, who was the most notorious for the constant Practice of the greatest Abuses in that very Kind, and was very well known not to be at all reformed? He said, he knew all this; but, what would I have him to do? I answered, send any one of your Footmen, and command him to chuse out the first likely genteel Fellow he sees in the streets; for such a one might possibly be honest, but he was sure the other was not, and yet they have employed him.

I promise your Grace that this shall be the last Sally I shall ever make to a court, and that I will return as soon as I can have Leave. I have no great Pleasure in my present Manner of Living, often involved in Things that perplex me very much, and which try my Patience to the utmost; teized every Day by Sollicitors, who have so little Sense as to think I have either Credit or Inclination to be theirs, although they see I am able to get nothing for myself. But, I find I am grown very tedious, and therefore conclude, with the greatest Respect, |My Lord, your Grace's | Most dutiful, and most humble Servant.

Hawkesworth 1766

Archbishop King to Swift

Dublin, Oct. 27, 1711.[1] [or 29 Oct.]

Rev. Sir,

I have before me yours of the 1st instant, but have been so employed with attending Parliament, Convocation and Privy Council, that I could neither compose my thoughts to write, nor find time. Besides, our business is all in a hurry; and I may say in fine, that things admit of no perfect account. On *Wednesday* the Corn Bill, which the Commons seemed to value most, was thrown out;[2] because it reserved a power to the Lord Lieutenant and Council

---

[1] Hawkesworth dates this letter 'Oct. 27'. This must be a misdating or a misreading of the original; or perhaps the letter was not completed on 27 Oct.; for King refers to a motion debated in the House on 29 Oct.

[2] On Wednesday the 25th 'An Act for the Encouragement of Tillage' was rejected by the Commons.—Ball.

here, to prohibit or permit the transportation of grain at any time. There was a design to fall on the Privy-Council upon this occasion; but gentlemen would not come into it; which shewed they had some wit in their anger. And I am still of opinion, that, with tolerable good management, this would have been as quiet a session as has been in *Ireland*; but the *Dublin* business, the address of the Lords, *Langton*'s affair,[1] and now *Higgins*'s, have exasperated the Commons to such a height, that will, as you observe, make this Parliament to be impracticable any longer. It is true, the Lords' address might have been interpreted to aim at Lord *Wharton*, and was partly so intended; but it was ill expressed to bear that sense; and besides, what did it signify for us to shew our resentment, when it could only provoke a great man to revenge, and could not reach him?

As to the first-fruits and twentieth parts, no body here dare say, that any body, beside the Duke of *Ormond*, procured them, but his Grace himself; who, for aught I can learn, never assumed, either publicly or privately, any such merit to himself: and yet I confess it is not amiss that it should be thought he did those things. For he could not think of governing the kingdom, if it be not believed, that he has great interest at Court; and if that did not appear by some favours of moment obtained for the kingdom, none would suppose it. He is truly a modest, generous, and honest[2] man; and assure yourself, that whatever disturbance he has met with, proceeds from his sticking too close to his friends. It is a pity such a fault should hurt a man. I send you enclosed the papers that relate to Mr. *Higgins*.[3] Lord *Santry*[4] was heard against him, before the Lord Lieutenant and Council, October 27: he was allowed only to prove the articles

[1] See p. 199, n. 2.

[2] King's characterization of Ormonde as 'modest, generous, and honest' is just. He was not, however, a man of remarkable gifts.

[3] In this letter and that following King refers to papers which he was forwarding relating to the affair of Higgins. The Rev. Francis Higgins, a turbulent High Churchman, was prosecuted for seditious preaching in London in 1707. In 1709 he was superseded as a J.P. for the County of Dublin for offending Lord Sunderland, then Secretary of State. Again he made himself notorious by supporting Dominick Langton, a converted friar, who brought charges against Whig gentlemen of Westmeath. At a sessions at Kilmainham, 5 Oct. 1711, a grand jury presented Higgins as 'a common disturber of her Majesty's peace'. See *Political State of Great Britain*, ii. 346–66; *A Full and Impartial Account of the Tryal of the Reverend Francis Higgins*, 1712; *Poems*, pp. 1090 ff.

[4] Henry, 1680–1735, third Lord Santry, an ardent Whig, was one of Higgins's foremost prosecutors.

in his petition, that are marked with P, and he seemed to prove them pretty fully; but Mr. *Higgins* not having yet made his defence, I can give no judgment. By the testimony of the Lower House of Convocation in his favour, you will see how heartily they espouse him.[1] And surely both pains and art have been used to screen him: with what effect you shall hear when the matter is concluded. I wish every good man may meet with as good and as fast friends as he hath done. I send you likewise the votes, that kept the Commons in debate, from eleven in the morning till seven at night. The question was carried in the negative, by two accidents: the going out of one member, by chance, to speak to somebody at the putting the question; and the coming in of another, in his boots, at the very minute. If either had not happened, it had gone the other way.[2] The personal affection to the Duke of *Ormond* divided the House. If they could have separated him from some others, the majority had been great. You may easily from this see, what way the bent of the kingdom goes; and that garbling corporations no way pleases them.

We have several printed accounts of preliminaries of the peace; but I believe them all amusements; for, I imagine, none of the common scribblers know any thing of them at all. I pray God they may be such as may secure us from a new war; though, I believe, the death of the Emperor makes a lasting peace much more difficult than before. That depends on a balance, and to that three things seem so necessary, that any two may stop the third; but now all is reduced to two. I reckon, as soon as the peace is settled, the Dauphin will be taken out of the way, and then *France* and *Spain* will fall into one hand: a surmise I have had in mind ever since *Philip* got *Spain*; and I was of opinion, that if we could have been secured against this accident, there had been no need of a war at all.

As to the Convocation, I told you formerly how we lost all the time of the recess,[3] by a precipitate adjournment made by five Bishops, when the Archbishop of *Tuam*, and as many of us as were

---

[1] That House passed a resolution in which they declared that Higgins had always 'behaved himself agreeably to the character of the sacred function of a clergyman'.—Ball.

[2] On 29 Oct., on a motion being made for returns relating to the disputed elections of mayors and sheriffs, the previous question was moved, and on a division the yeas numbered 108, and the noes 109. To enter the House in outdoor dress and vote was considered a transgression of order.

[3] In order to permit transmission of bills for approval of the English Privy Council adjournments were usual.

of the Privy-Council, were absent, attending at the board, upon a hearing of the Quakers against the Bill for Recovery of Tithes. Since the meeting of the Parliament, after the recess, we have attended pretty closely, have drawn up and agreed to six or seven canons,[1] and have drawn up a representation of the state of religion as to infidelity, heresy, impiety, and Popery. We have gone through likewise, and agreed to, a part of this; but I doubt we shall not be able to finish it. We have also before us the consideration of residence, and the means of converting Papists. This last sent up from the Lower House. But I reckon it not possible to finish these things this session.[2] I need not tell you, that my Lord Primate's indisposition is a great clog to dispatch; but he is resolved none else shall have the chair. So we dispense with many things, that otherwise I believe we should not. We had only two Church-bills at this time: one for unions, which was thrown out in our House; and another for recovery of tithes, which I understand will be thrown out by the Commons. Our session draws near an end, and every body is tired of it.

Will. Dublin.

Hawkesworth 1766

Archbishop King to Swift

Oct. 31, 1711.

To-day we had another hearing at Council, concerning Mr. *Higgins's* business. Some of his witnesses were examined. So far as we have yet heard, it doth not appear to me, that they have cleared him of tampering with witnesses, shifting recognizances, or compounding felonies; but, it is said, these things are common in the country; and, perhaps, that will save him. And I know not how far his other witnesses, that are yet to be examined, may clear him. The

---

[1] The canons related to proceedings of the Ecclesiastical Courts.

[2] As appears from an interesting letter from Richardson to the Secretary of the Society for Promoting Christian Knowledge (B.M., Sloane 4276, f. 100) time was found in the Upper House of Convocation to consider resolutions about converting the Irish sent up by the Lower House, but 'they were rejected', says Richardson, 'by the influence of a prelate whom I need not mention'. An effort, during the same session, to introduce a bill to the same purpose into the House of Commons came to nothing through an early adjournment.—Ball.

hearing lasted above three hours.[1] I was unwilling to make this pacquet too large, so I have inclosed the other prints in another. I want some affidavits of gentlemen, in which they depose Mr. *Higgins*'s case to contain many falshoods. I am, *&c.* |

Will. Dublin.

Hawkesworth 1766
Archbishop King to Swift

Dublin, Nov. 1, 1711.

Rev. Sir,

    I have considered that part of your letter that relates to your own concerns.[2] I find you, in earnest, very indifferent as to making your fortune; but you ought not to be so, for a weighty reason you insinuate yourself, that you cannot, without a settlement, be master of your time in such a manner, as to apply yourself to do something that may be useful to the Church. I know it is not in your power to do it when you please; but yet something may be done towards it. Get but a letter to the Government,[3] from my Lord Treasurer, for the first good preferment; and you will, at the same time, fill it with a good man, and perhaps prevent a bad one from getting into it. Sure there is no immodesty in getting such a recommendation. Consider that years grow upon you; and, after fifty, both body and mind decay. I have several things on the anvil, and near finished, that perhaps might be useful, if published; but the continual avocation by business, the impositions on me by impertinent visits, and the uneasiness of writing, which grows more intolerable to me every day, I doubt, will prevent my going any farther. Therefore lose no time: *Qui non est hodie, cras minus aptus erit.*[4] I am sure, you are able to do good service; and give me leave to be importunate with you to go about it. *Caesar* wrote his Commentaries under the hurry and fatigues of a general; and perhaps a man's spirit is never more awakened, nor his thoughts better, than in the intervals of a hurry

---

    [1] On the two following days there were further hearings. The subject at issue was whether Higgins should be continued in the commission of the peace. A majority voted in the affirmative. King voted in the minority on the ground that the clergy should not be employed in civil offices.

    [2] See Swift to King, 1 Oct. 1710.   [3] That of Ireland.

    [4] Ovid, *Rem. Am.* 94.

of business. Read *Erasmus*'s life, and you will find it was almost a continual journey. You see how malicious some are towards you, in printing a parcel of trifles, falsely, as your works.¹ This makes it necessary that you should shame those varlets, by something that may enlighten the world, which I am sure your genius will reach, if you set yourself to it. If I had the honour to have any correspondence with my Lord Treasurer, I would certainly complain of you to him, and get his Lordship to join in this request, which, I persuade myself, he would readily do, if put in mind. I do not in the least fear that you will be angry with me for this, since you cannot suspect my sincerity and kindness in it: and though I shall be angry with you, if you neglect yourself and interest, yet it shall go no farther, than to be a trouble to myself, but no abatement of the real friendship of yours, &c.

Will. Dublin.

B.M. Add. MS. 39839

Swift to Sir Andrew Fountaine

[7 November 1711.]²

All that may be; but I stayd yesterday at home for you till two, and if ever I trust to yʳ Appointments again, may I stay till two and twenty. What made yr Hangdog tell mine, that he had orders to send Doctr I know not who after you to Ld Pembroke, and that from thence you were to come and call upon me. . For, not trusting

---

¹ On 14 May 1711 Swift complained to Stella (*Journal*, p. 269) that 'Curl has scraped up some trash and calls it Dr. Swift's miscellanies, with the name at large: and I can get no satisfaction of him'. Morphew's edition of Swift's *Miscellanies* appeared at the end of February. Curll's *Miscellanies by Dr. Jonathan Swift*, a made-up volume consisting of the previously published *Meditation upon a Broom-Stick*, 1710, with a 'Complete Key to the Tale of a Tub', and other matter prefixed, was probably brought out in April. It is a rare publication. There is a copy in the British Museum, 12350.b.16.

² This letter was first printed by Freeman in *Vanessa and her Correspondence with Jonathan Swift*, p. 196. Presumably it found its way into that correspondence (B.M. Add. MS. 39839) directly from Sir Andrew Fountaine's hands, who was one of the Vanhomrigh circle. The date may be deduced from Swift's reference to the incident in the *Journal to Stella*, 6 Nov. 1711: 'Here was I staying in my room till two this afternoon for that puppy Sir Andrew Fountain, who was to go with me into the city, and never came.'

to you, I sent my man, & he brought me this Answer. Why; Ld Dartmouth and Mr St John are neither of them yet come to Town; and I shall not go fetch them. As to breakfasting; I will infallibly breakfast with you this morning, and come exactly at ten. To morrow we will tantavy[1] as you say; And I will wait for you infallibly till you come. We will drink our Punch on Friday exactly at four a Clock without fail.

P.S. Pray get all things ready for Breakfast. have the Coffee Tee and Chocolate cut and dry in so many Pots, for I will most infallibly come this morning, and very early.—The Scoundrel you sent is gone to Bloomsbury, so that I fear I shall be with you before my Letter; If I do, pray let me know it by a Line. And be so kind to burn this before you read it; I am in such hast I have not time to correct the Style, or adjust the Periods; And I blush to expose my self before so great a Critick. You know I write without the assistance of Books, and my man can witness that I began and finisht this in three quarters of an hour.—Knowing that your man will infallibly come back for this Letter; I have sent it by Patrick, who is not yet returned; pray dispatch him as soon as you can, that when y^r Man comes back Patrick may know of him whether he will call or no.

Address: To Sr Andrew Fountain

Hawkesworth 1766

Archbishop King to Swift

Dublin, Nov. 10, 1711.

Rev. Sir,

Perhaps it will not be ungrateful to you, to know our session of Parliament ended on *Friday* last.[2] We threw out, in the House of Lords, two bills: that against fines in the city of *Dublin*, and about quit-rents; and voted an address, in opposition to the Commons address about Revolution principles.[3] We likewise burned Mr. *Stoughton*'s sermon, preached at *Christ-church* on the 30th of *January*, some

---

[1] Freeman reads the word as 'tantony' and strangely conjectures its meaning as 'to eat pork'. Swift wrote 'tantavy', usually spelled 'tantivy', with the meaning 'to ride at full gallop'. See *O.E.D.*

[2] The previous day.

[3] In this address the Lords asserted that the words used by the Commons, 'the encouragement of sound Revolution Principles' could not 'in good sense or good grammar be referred to the late Revolution'.—Ball.

years ago.[1] The House were pleased to vote me thanks for prosecuting him, which, you may remember, I did in a difficult time, notwithstanding the opposition I had from the Government, and his protection by Lord *Ikerrin*,[2] which he pleaded in court: and yet I followed him so close, that I forced him out of his living. After this, we burned Mr. *Boyse*'s book of A Scriptural Bishop;[3] and some Observators. Our address was brought in yesterday; in which sure we are even with the Commons. I forgot to tell you, we agreed to another address against Dissenting ministers, and their twelve hundred pounds *per annum*.[4] The Commons made an address to my Lord Lieutenant, in which they bring him in for Revolution principles.[5] The memorial of the Church of *England*[6] was reprinted here and dedicated to my Lord Lieutenant. This was brought into the House of Commons; and, I doubt, would not have escaped, if the Usher of the Black Rod had not called them up to the prorogation. *Langton*'s business came likewise into the House of Lords, and when the House was full of ladies, an offer was made to receive the report of the committee, which contained many sheets of paper.[7]

[1] For Stoughton's sermon, which had been preached 31 Jan. 1708–9, see p. 124. By order of the House of Lords it was condemned to be burned before the door of the House and of the Tholsel as a seditious libel reflecting on the honour of 'the Royal Martyr King Charles I'.

[2] If this was Pierce, fourth Viscount Ikerrin, and no other identification seems possible, his protection of Stoughton is difficult to explain, as he had been outlawed himself for his adherence to James II.

[3] Joseph Boyse, 1660–1728, Presbyterian minister and controversialist, settled in Dublin, published in 1708 a volume of fifteen sermons, of which the last was a discourse on 'The Office of a Scriptural Bishop', with a polemical appendix. A reprint of this sermon was ordered by the House of Lords to be burned before the Thosel by the common hangman. The copies of the Whig *Observator* ordered to be burned were those of 18–22 and 22–25 Aug. See *D.N.B.*

[4] The grant, known as the Regium Donum, was first made by William III. It remained unpaid for the rest of Queen Anne's reign.

[5] The address of the Commons thanked Ormonde for his 'great and early share' in the 'late happy Revolution'.

[6] *The Memorial of the Church of England humbly offered to the Consideration of all True Lovers of our Church and Constitution*, which was first published in London in 1705, was presented soon after its appearance by the Grand Jury of London and Middlesex, and burned by the hangman.—Ball.

[7] *The Whole Report of the Right Honourable Committee of the House of Lords in Ireland appointed by their Lordships to take into Consideration the Examination of Dominick Langton, Clerk, against Lewis Meares, and other Gentlemen of the County of Westmeath, and the Proceedings thereupon*, was published in London

A great debate happened upon it: but at last it was waived, and ordered to be laid before the Lord Lieutenant.

In short, we parted in very ill humour: and I apprehend that the minds of the generality are not easy. My Lord Duke of *Ormond*, so far as I could take it, made a very modest and healing speech; and his grace seemed in it to be altogether disinterested in parties.[1] All these you have in public; and if you think it worth while, I will take care to send them as they are printed.

As to our Convocation, those who had loitered and done nothing before last week, pressed on the representation of the state of religion, as to infidelity, heresy, impiety, and popery: it will, in some time, be printed. I had many reasons, but insisted only on two; first, its imputing all vices to us, as if we were the worst of people in the world; not allowing any good amongst us. Secondly not assigning it a cause of the natives continuing Papists, that no care was ever taken to preach to them in their own language, or translating the service into *Irish*. You will find the matter in *Heylyn's Reformation*, 2d *Eliz.* 1560, p. 128.[2] I was forced to use art to procure this protest to be admitted, without which they would not have allowed me to offer reasons, as I had cause to believe.

Both the Parliament and Convocation have been so ordered, as to make us appear the worst people in the world, disloyal to her Majesty, and enemies to the Church; and I suspect, with a design to make us appear unworthy to have any countenance or preferment in our native country. When the representation is printed, I will, if you think it worth your while, send you my protest. We agreed likewise in some canons of no great moment,[3] and some forms of prayer,[4] and forms of receiving Papists and sectaries; which, I think, are too

by John Morphew in 1713. In their findings the committee . . . gave Langton a high character as a faithful minister . . . and suggested that her Majesty should be asked to restore Langton's pension of which the Commons had deprived him.—Ball.

[1] The Duke urged compromise, impartiality, and good feeling.

[2] Dr. Peter Heylyn, 1600–62, sub-dean of Westminster, published in 1661 *Ecclesia Restaurata, Or the History of the Reformation*. A second edition appeared in 1670, a third in 1674. Heylyn reflects unfavourably upon the omission to provide the Irish with translations of the Bible and the Book of Common Prayer into the native language.   [3] See p. 269, n. 1.

[4] Three new forms of prayer were added by Convocation to the Irish Book of Common Prayer; (1) for the visitation of prisoners; (2) for prisoners under sentence of death; (3) for imprisoned debtors. See Mant, *History of the Church of Ireland*, ii. 233.

271

strait. I brought in a paper about residence; but here was no time to consider it, nor that which related to the means of converting Papists. I did not perceive any zeal that way. A great part of our representation relates to sectaries; and many things, in the whole, seem to me not defensible. I told you before, how we lost six weeks, during the adjournment of the Parliament;[1] and since it sat, we could only meet in the afternoon, and I was frequently in Council; so that I was neither present when it was brought into the House, when it passed for the most part, or was sent down in parcels, in foul rased papers, that I could not well read, if I had an opportunity; and never heard it read through before it past.

I believe most are agreed, that if my advice had been taken, this would have been the peaceablest session ever was in *Ireland*; whereas it has been one of the most boisterous. I believe it was his Grace the Duke of *Ormond*'s interest to have it quiet; but then the managers, conduct has shewed themselves to be necessary.[2] I have wearied myself with this scroll, and perhaps you will be so likewise. I am, *&c.*

W. Dublin.

B.M. Add. MS. 4804, ff. 50–51 and f. 52

Henry St. John to Swift

Hampton Court Nov: 16 1711

I return you the sheet which is I think very correct.[3]

Sunday morning I hope to see you. I am sincerely your hearty friend | and obed^t Servent | H. S^t J.

I have a vile story to tell you of the moral Philosopher Steele.

Endorsed by Swift: Ld Bolingbroke | Nov. 16th 1711.

---

[1] See p. 265.

[2] The system of managing the Irish Parliament through 'undertakers', which became so marked a feature in the Irish government fifty years later, had apparently already begun.—Ball.

[3] St. John was evidently referring to a proof of *The Conduct of the Allies*, published on 27 Nov., one of the most effective of political pamphlets. It discredited the war, and hastened a decline in Marlborough's popularity. Four more editions appeared before the end of 1711, dated that year, and a sixth edition in Jan. 1712. There were also Dublin and Edinburgh editions. See *Journal*, 27 Nov. 1711.

Henry St. John to Swift

[17 November 1711]

Dear S^r

I ask pardon for my mistake, & I send you the right paper.
I am in sickness & in health ever y^r faithfull friend and obedient
servt | H St John

Address: To | the reverend | Dr Swift
    Mr Secty St John
Endorsed by Swift: Ld Bolingbroke | 1712[1]

Deane Swift 1768

Miss Anne Long to Swift

Nov. 18, 1711.

If you will again allow me the pleasure of hearing from you, without murmuring, I will let you enjoy that of laughing at me for any
foolish word I misapply; for I know you are too reasonable to
expect me to be nicely right in the matter; but then when you take a
fancy to be angry, pray let me know it quietly, that I may clear my
meanings, which are always far from offending my friends, however
unhappy I may be in my expressions. Could I expect you to remember any part of my letters so long ago, I would ask you, that you
should know where to find me when you had a mind to it; but I
suppose you were in a romantick strain, and designed to have surprised me talking to myself in a wood, or by the sea.[2] Forgive the
dulness of my apprehension, and if telling you that I am at *Linn* will
not do, I will print it, however inconvenient it may yet be to me; for
I am not the better for the old lady's death, but am put in hopes of

[1] Undated by St. John. Probably written on the same or the next day. Swift's
endorsement, mistaken in date was written after St. John's advancement to the
peerage.

[2] Reference has already been made (p. 133, n. 1) to Anne Long and *The Decree
for a Treaty*. She was a sister of Sir James Long, Bt., of Draycott, Wiltshire
(*Complete Baronetage*, iii. 259). Swift became acquainted with her through the
Vanhomrighs to whom she seems to have been distantly related. She was a
celebrated beauty and a toast of the Kit-Cat Club. Owing to financial difficulties
she had retired to King's Lynn, where she died on 22 Dec., shortly after writing
this letter. The old lady upon whose death Miss Long was entitled to £2,000
was Dorothy, daughter of Sir Edward Leach, one of the Masters in Chancery.

being easy at *Christmas*; however, I shall still continue to be Mrs. *Smyth*, near *St. Nicholas*'s Church in the town aforesaid; so much for my affairs.—Now as to my health, that was much out of order last *Summer*; my distemper was a dropsy or asthma (you know what I mean, but I cannot spell it right) or both, lazy distempers, which I was too lazy to molest while they would let me sit in quiet; but when they grew so unreasonable as not to let me do that, I applied myself to Dr. *Inglis*,[1] by whose advice I am now well enough. To give you the best account I can of this place, the ladies will make any returns, if one may believe what they say of one another; the men I know little of, for I am here, what you have often upbraided me with, a Prude in everything but censuring my neighbours; a couple of divines, two aldermen, and a custom-house officer, are all my men acquaintance; the gay part of the town I know nothing of, and although for the honour of the place I will suppose there are good poets, yet that I never inquired after. I have a shelf pretty well filled at home, but want a *Miscellany* Mr. *Steele* put out last year; Miss *Hessy* promised it me, but has forgot it: I fancy you have interest enough with him to get it for me.[2] I wish too at your leisure you would make a pedigree for me; the people here want sadly to know what I am; I pretend to no more than being of *George Smyth*'s family of *Nitly*, but do not talk much of it, for fear of betraying myself; so they fancy some mystery to be in the matter, and would give their rivals place to be satisfied. At first they thought I came hither to make my fortune, by catching up some of their young fellows; but having avoided that sort of company, I am still a riddle they know not what to make of. Many of them seem to love me well enough; for I hear all they say of one another without making mischief among them, and give them tea and coffee when I have it, which are the greatest charms I can boast of: the fine lady I have left to *Moll* (who I suppose was at the *Bath*)[3] or any other that will take it up; for I am grown a good house-wife; I can pot and pickle, sir, and handle a needle very prettily; see Miss *Hessy*'s scarf, I think that is improving mightily. If Miss *Hessy* keeps company with the eldest

[1] John Inglis, Physician in Ordinary to Queen Anne.

[2] The reference is to Swift's *Miscellanies in Prose and Verse*, published by Morphew towards the end of Feb. 1711. There was an original intention that it should be prefaced with an introduction by Steele (see p. 166, n. 3).

[3] Moll was Vanessa's younger sister. She was baptized in St. Andrew's Church, Dublin, on 7 Sept. 1694. She seems always to have been delicate, and may have been at Bath for her health.

Hatton,[1] and is still a politician, she is not the girl I took her for; but to me she seems melancholy. Sure Mr. *St. John* is not so altered but he will make returns; but how can I pretend to judge of any thing, when my poor cousin is taken for an hermaphrodite; a thing I as little suspected her for as railing at any body; I know so little cause for it, that I must be silent. I hear but little of what is done in the world, but should be glad the Ministry did themselves the justice to distinguish men of merit: may I wish you joy of any preferment? I shall do it heartily: but if you have got nothing, I am busy to as much purpose as you, although my employments are next to picking straws. Oh, but you are acquainted with my Lord *Fitzhardinge*,[2] for which I rejoice with you, and am your most obedient servant,

Anne Long.

Endorsed by Swift: Poor Mrs. Long's last letter, written five weeks before she died.

B.M. Add. MS. 39839

Swift to Esther Vanhomrigh

[18 December 1711.][3]

[4]I have writ three or four lyes in as many Lines; pray seal up the Letter to M^rs L[ong] and let nobody read it but your self. I suppose

---

[1] Unidentified.   [2] See p. 133, n. 5.

[3] Ball prints this letter from Scott, xix. 396, and assigns it to 'November 7, 1711' in the belief that it was intended to cover a letter of that date which appears in the list of letters (Forster no. 508), but is not now forthcoming. The letter it was intended to cover was more probably that of 18 Dec. to Miss Long, which follows. This appears in the list under 19 Dec.

[4] Bartholomew Vanhomrigh, of Dutch extraction, established himself in Dublin, and in 1686 married Hester Stone, daughter of a commissioner of the Irish revenue. During the Revolution he became Commissary·General to the forces. After the campaign he resumed his position in Dublin, and in 1697 he was nominated Lord Mayor. When he died, 29 Dec. 1703, he left his widow, two daughters, Esther and Mary, and two sons, Bartholomew and Ginkell, in comfortable circumstances. In the hope of social advancement Mrs. Vanhomrigh moved to London towards the end of 1707. Swift may have met Mrs. Vanhomrigh in Ireland. He was certainly an early London acquaintance. In 'The Decree for Concluding the Treaty between Dr. Swift and Mrs. Long', contained in Curll's *Letters, Poems, and Tales: Amorous, Satyrical, and Gallant*, 1718, there is a double mention of Mrs. Vanhomrigh 'and her fair Daughter Hessy'. In the 'Decree' Swift is described as 'of Leicester-fields'. Swift was

this Pacquet will lye two hours till you awake. and pray let the outside starched Letter to you be seen, after you have seald that to
M^rs L[ong] see what Art people must use, thô they mean ever so
well. Now are You and Puppy lying at your ease, without dreaming
any thing of all this, Adieu till we meet over a Pott of Coffee, or an
Orange and Sugar in the Sluttery, which I have so often found to
be the most agreeable Chamber in the World

Address: To little Misessy.

B.M. Add. MS. 39839

Swift to Miss Anne Long

London. Decbr. 18th 1711[1]

Madam.

There is nothing I take kinder than Reproaches of Unkindness
from those I value, and yet there is nothing I would willingly less
deserve .. I do not remember you ever misapplyed a word at all,
much less out of Ignorance, which is not one of your Faults. I was
sensible I began to grow a dull Correspondent, as all busy People
are; I passed a scurvy Summer between Court and Country, and
Sickness, and never found my self in a humor to say any thing that
you would take the Pains to read—I remember you promised to let
me know where you are, but you never actually did so till your last
which I am now answering.[2] All your Letters are in my Cabinet (I
mean a Box but the word is not so genteel) and I remember them
better than you, neither is there any need for your printing the

staying with Sir Andrew Fountaine at his residence in Leicester Fields between
the middle of Dec. 1707 and the first week of Jan. 1708, when Sir Andrew
left for the country. If therefore Swift was not already acquainted with the
Vanhomrighs he must have been introduced to them almost as soon as they
moved to London. When he left London in May 1709 they were already on
corresponding terms as his list of letters shows, Forster no. 506. It is clear that
from the first Esther was the chief attraction. She was born towards the end
of 1687 or beginning of 1688, and would at the time of this letter be in her
twenty-fourth year. Swift mistakenly supposed her to be about three years
younger (*Journal*, 14 Aug. 1711).

[1] This letter, first printed by Freeman, pp. 65–69, is in Swift's list of letters
assigned to 19 Dec.   [2] Her letter of 18 Nov.

Places name where you are, your Pen makes a much more[1] lasting Impression, though you lean softer on it than any one I know. And after all I take it to be a Gasconnade; for I dare be hanged if ever there was a Printer at Lynn; I fear, not so much as a Printer of Calicoes. What can old Ladyes be good for, if[2] we are neither the better for their Lifes, nor their Deaths? You are put in hopes of being easy at Christmas. I shall be heartily glad to see it. But see how perverse you are, for that is just the time that I am in fear of being miserable. Your Brethren the Whigs are endeavouring to make another Change at Court, and we who stand for the present Ministry are under all imaginable Apprehensions. In a very short time, the matter will be decided, either to the Ruin of all my Friends at Court, or to that of their Adversaryes. But I shall not enlarge upon Politicks, nor would have s^d so much if my own Interests were not so deeply involved in the good or ill Event. Your Illness is the Effect of too little Exercise. I fence against the same Distemper you complain of, by perpetually walking when the Weathr will permit me. You must not eat Supper, nor drink at all at night; nor swill small beer. Pray be my Patient, for Health is worth preserving, tho Life is not.[3] —I approve of your Male Acquaintance, onely you want the Dancing master. I suppose the Custom-house Officer is a[4] genteeler name for the Excise-man. Censure is the growth of all little Towns: and I dare say the Ladyes may be virtuous enough, if you have no other Cavaliers besides Aldermen and Divines. There was a Miscellany put out last Summer, but not by Mr Steel, nor do I know by whom. They have raked up all they could gather of mine, without my Knowledge,[5] and Mishessy has cheated you in not sending you one of them, which I gott on purpose and delivered to her with my own

---

[1] The word 'more' is written above the line.

[2] A word erased after 'if'.

[3] In his account-book for 1711–12 (Forster, 508), on a page otherwise blank, Swift made the following entry:

'Decbr. 22. 1711

'On Saterday. at 4 in the morn. dyed Mrs. Ann at Lynn in Norfolk, where she had retired about 2 years before, and lived under the Name of Smyth. the News of it came to Town on Monday night following, wch was Xmas Eve and I heard it on Xmas day at Noon, wch was Tuesday. She was the most beautifull Person of the Age, she lived in, of great Honr and Virtue, infinite Sweetness and Generosity of Temper, and true good Sense.   J. Swift.'

[4] 'the' scored out, and 'a' written above the line.

[5] See p 268, n. 1.

Hand. But that Fault shall soon be mended. You could not pitch upon a fitter man than me to make your Pedigree, who have so often been your Herald. and it is fit, somebody should take it out of your Hands, for you have chosen most horribly for your self; but upon second thoughts it was the wisest Course for one who would be sure to be concealed, as the safest Disguise for a Prince is the Habit of a Beggar.—I am thinking of you, if you and I were together at Lynn, how little the Brutes would suspect what a Figure we have both made in the grand monde in severall ways. But what should I do to change my Talents like you, and fit them to the Country? I can neither pot nor pickle: but I can write Receits, and Papers to stick upon Bottles. Mishessy is but like her Neighbors, she is a Politician because everybody else is so, and a Tory out of Principle, without hopes of an Employment. Mistress Hatton[1] visits them, but is not her Companion. She Poor girl between sickness, domestick Affairs, and State Speculations has lost a good deal of her Mirth: but I think there is not a better Girl Upon Earth. I have a mighty Friendship for her: she had good Principles, and I have corrected all her Faults; but I cannot persuade her to read, tho she has an Understanding, Memory and Tast, that would bear great Improvement: but she is incorrigibly idle and Lazy: thinks the world made for nothing but perpetual Pleasure; and the Deity she most adores is Morpheur. Her greatest Favourites at present are Ldy Ashburnham,[2] her Dog, and my self. She makes me of so little Consequence that it almost distracts me. She will bid her Sister go down stairs, before my face, for she has some private Business with the Doctor. In short there would never be an end of telling you the Hardships she puts on me; onely because I have lived a dozen or fifteen years too much. I thank you for your Concern about my Fortune; the Ministry never had it yet in their Power; neither do I rely on their Promises if they had. I hope Misessy sends you all the little Town News. But pray do not go away with it that I am acquainted with Ld Fitzharding.[3] Tho he be your Admirer, I cannot be his, nor was ever in the same Room with him in my Life—I have sd enough for a man in an ill humor,

[1] This is a reply to the words in Miss Long's letter to Swift of 18 Nov. 1711: 'If Miss Hessy keeps company with the eldest Hatton . . . she is not the girl I took her for.' This has been interpreted to mean that an unidentified Hatton was Vanessa's suitor. It now transpires that she was a woman.

[2] Daughter of the second Duke of Ormonde.

[3] See p. 133, n. 5.

and I know you will be glad to be relieved. I am with great Respect and Truth, Madam |

> Your most obedient and most humble Servt |
>
> J. S.

Address: To Mrs Long.

Nichols 1801[1]

Swift to the Rev. Thomas Pyle

London, Dec. 26, 1711.

Sir,[2]

That you may not be surprised with a letter utterly unknown to you, I will tell you the occasion of it. The lady who lived near two years in your neighbourhood, and whom you was so kind to visit under the name of Mrs. Smyth, was Mrs. Ann Long, sister to Sir James Long, and niece of Col. Strangwayes:[3] she was of as good a private family as most in England, and had every valuable quality of body and mind that could make a lady loved and esteemed. Accordingly she was always valued here above most of her sex, and by most distinguished persons. But, by the unkindness of her friends and the generosity of her own nature, and depending upon the death of a very old grandmother, which did not happen till it was too late, contracted some debts that made her uneasy here, and in order to clear them was content to retire unknown to your town, where I fear her death has been hastened by melancholy, and perhaps the want of such assistance as she might have found here. I thought fit to signify this to you, partly to let you know how valuable a person you have lost, but chiefly to desire that you will please to bury her in some part of your church near a wall where a plain marble stone may be

---

[1] This letter, first printed by Nichols, 1801, xix. 17, has also been printed in *Notes and Queries*, II. ii. 182.

[2] The Rev. Thomas Pyle, 1674–1756, a Whig, and a Low Church divine, who scarcely disguised his Unitarian leanings, held a living at King's Lynn for the greater part of his life. He gained a reputation as a preacher and controversialist, but failed to receive preferment. Nichols, *Lit. Anec.* ix. 433–44, has a long account of him. See also *D.N.B.*

[3] Miss Long's brother, Sir James Long, of Draycott, Wiltshire, had succeeded to the baronetcy in 1697. Their father's first wife was a daughter of Col. Strangways, a well-known royalist. Swift probably refers to him, mistaking the relationship.

fixed, as a poor monument for one who deserved so well, and which, if God sends me life, I hope one day to place there, if no other of her friends will think fit to do it. I had the honour of an intimate acquaintance with her, and was never so sensibly touched with any one's death as with hers. Neither did I ever know a person of either sex with more virtues, or fewer infirmities; the only one she had, which was the neglect of her own affairs, arising wholly from the goodness of her temper. I write not this to you at all as a secret, but am content your town should know what an excellent person they have had among them. If you visited her any short time before her death, or knew any particulars about it, or of the state of her mind, or the nature of her disease, I beg you will be so obliging to inform me; for the letter we have seen from her poor maid is so imperfect by her grief for the death of so good a lady, that it only tells the time of her death; and your letter may, if you please, be directed to Dr. Swift, and put under a cover, which cover may be directed to Erasmus Lewis,[1] esq. at the earl of Dartmouth's Office, at Whitehall. I hope you will forgive this trouble for the occasion of it, and give some allowances to so great a loss, not only to me, but to all who have any regard for every perfection that human nature can possess; and if any way I can serve or oblige you, I shall be glad of an opportunity of obeying your commands. I am, &c.

J. Swift.

Address: To the Rev. Mr. Pyle, Minister of Lynn, Norfolk.

Hawkesworth 1766

Swift to Dean Stearne

London, Dec. 29, 1711

Sir,

The reason I have not troubled you this long time with my letters, was, because I would not disturb the quiet you live in, and which the greatest and wisest men here would envy, if they knew; and which it is one part of your happiness that they do not.[2] I have

---

[1] Erasmus Lewis, a friend of the Vanhomrighs, was remembered by Vanessa in her will.

[2] On 6 Nov. (*Journal*, p. 405) Swift wrote: 'I design to write to your dean one of these days, but I can never find time, nor what to say.' This is the first letter since that time which Swift addressed to him. The last surviving letter before this one was written on 26 Sept. 1710.

often sent the Archbishop political letters, of which I suppose you
have had part. I have some weeks ago received a letter from his
Grace, which I design to acknowledge in a short time (as I desire
you will please to tell him) when things here come to some issue; and
so we expect they will do in a little time. You know what an unexpected thing fell out the first day of this session in the House of
Lords, by the caprice, discontent, or some worse motive of the Earl
of *Nottingham*.¹

In above twenty years, that I have known something of Courts, I
never observed so many odd, dark, unaccountable circumstances in
any public affair. A majority against the Court, carried by five or
six depending Lords, who owed the best part of their bread to
pensions from the Court, and who were told by the public enemy,
that what they did would be pleasing to the Queen, though it was
openly levelled against the first Minister's head; again, those, whose
purse-strings and heart-strings were the same, all on a sudden
scattering their money to bribe votes:² a Lord, who had been so far
always a Tory, as often to be thought in the Pretender's interest,
giving his vote for the ruin of all his old friends, caressed by those
Whigs, who hated and abhorred him:³ the Whigs all chiming in with
a Bill against Occasional Conformity; and the very Dissenting
ministers agreeing to it, for reasons that nobody alive can tell;⁴
a resolution of breaking the treaty of peace, without any possible
scheme for continuing the war; and all this owing to a doubtfulness,
or inconstancy in one certain quarter, which, at this distance, I dare
not describe;⁵ neither do I find any one person, though deepest in
affairs, who can tell what steps to take. On *January* the second, the
House of Lords is to meet, and it is expected, they will go on in their
votes and addresses against a peace.

On the other side, we are endeavouring to get a majority, and
have called up two Earls' sons to the House of Peers;⁶ and I thought

¹ Although the Earl of Nottingham was a staunch Tory it was known, before
Parliament reassembled, that he had agreed with the Whigs to support their
opposition to peace if they would assist him in passing his Occasional Conformity Bill. See also *Poems*, pp. 141–5; and *Journal*, p. 432, n. 16.
² The allusion is to bribery attributed to the Duke and Duchess of Marlborough.   ³ Nottingham.
⁴ For an exception see Appendix V for a letter addressed to Oxford by the
Rev. John Shower, and a reply which has been attributed to Swift.
⁵ The allusion is to the Duchess of Somerset's influence with the Queen.
⁶ James Compton, 1678–1754, eldest son of the fourth Earl of Northampton,

six more would have been called, and perhaps they may before *Wednesday*. We expect the Duke of *Somerset* and Lord *Cholmondeley* will lose their places; but it is not yet done, and we wish for one more change at Court, which you must guess.[1] To know upon what small circumstances, and by what degrees, this change has been brought about, would require a great deal more than I can or dare write.

There is not one which I did not give warning of, to those chiefly concerned, many months ago; and so did some others, for they were visible enough. This must infallibly end either in an entire change of measures and ministry, or in a firm establishment of our side. Delay, and tenderness to an inveterate party, have been very instrumental to this ill state of affairs. They tell me you in *Ireland* are furious against a peace; and it is a great jest to see people in *Ireland* furious for or against anything.

I hope to see you in spring, when travelling weather comes on. But I have a mind to see the issue of this session. I reckon your hands are now out of mortar, and that your garden is finished:[2] and I suppose you have now one or two fifty pounds ready for books, which I will lay out for you, if you will give me directions.

I have increased my own little library very considerably; I mean, as far as one fifty pounds, which is very considerable for me. I have just had a letter from the *St. Mary* ladies, &c. I thought they were both dead; but I find they sometimes drink your claret still, and win your money. I am,

Sir, your most obedient humble servant,

You know *who*.

P.S. I had sealed my letter, but have broke it open, to tell you, and all that love the Church and Crown, that all things are now well. The Queen has turned out the Duke of *Somerset*, and has created twelve new Lords, of which three are Peers' eldest sons, the rest new created; so that a majority is past dispute.[3] We are all in the greatest joy imaginable to find her Majesty declare herself so seasonably.

was summoned to the House of Lords as Baron Compton, 28 Dec.; and Charles Bruce, 1682–1747, eldest surviving son of the second Earl of Ailesbury, was, 29 Dec., summoned in his father's barony of Bruce of Whorlton.

[1] The removal of the Duchess of Somerset. See *Poems*, pp. 145–8, for Swift's lampoon upon her, 'The Windsor Prophecy'.   [2] See p. 83.

[3] To form a group of twelve new peers necessary to ensure a majority in the Upper House the Queen, advised by her Ministers, took the following steps.

Swift to Archbishop King

London, Jan. 8, 1711–12.[1]

My Lord,

I cannot in Conscience take up your Grace's Time with an empty Letter; and it is not every Day one can furnish what will be worth your Reading. I had all your Grace's Packets,[2] and I humbly thank your Grace for your good Instructions to me, which I shall observe as soon as ever it shall please God to put me into a Way of Life where I can have Leisure for such Speculations.

In above twenty Years that I have known something of Courts and Ministers, I never saw so strange and odd a complicated Disposition of Affairs, as what we have had for six Weeks past. The Facts, your Grace may have met with in every common News-Paper; but the Springs of them are hardly discoverable even by those who had most Opportunity of observing. Neither do I find those who should know best, agree upon the Matter. There is a perpetual Tryal of Skill between those who are out and those who are in; and the former are generally more Industrious at watching Opportunities. Last *September*, at *Windsor*, the Duke of *Somerset*, who had not been at Cabinet-Council for many Months, was advised by his Friends of the late Ministry to appear there, but the rest refused to sit with him; and the Council was put off until next Day, when the Duke went to a Horse

---

The eldest sons of two Earls, Northampton and Ailesbury, were called up by writ. A barony was conferred on Henry Paget, eldest son of Lord Paget, and another barony on Viscount Dupplin, Lord Oxford's son-in-law. Viscount Windsor, an Irish peer, was created Baron Mountjoy in the English peerage. Two baronets, Sir Thomas Mansell and Sir Thomas Willoughby, became respectively Baron Mansell and Baron Middleton. Sir Thomas Trevor, Chief Justice of the Common Pleas, became Baron Trevor. George Granville was created Baron Lansdown, Thomas Foley, Baron Foley, Allen Bathurst, Baron Bathurst, and Samuel Masham, husband of the Queen's favourite, Baron Masham. Masham came in as an afterthought, for the Queen did not approve of making his wife, who was a 'useful servant', into a 'great lady'. At last, however, she consented.

[1] Faulkner dated this letter '*Nov.* 8, 1711'; but Lord Ranelagh's death did not occur till 5 Jan. 1712.

[2] The reference is to three letters from King in close sequence, 27 and 31 Oct. and 1 Nov. Swift was nettled because the Archbishop's secretary forgot to enclose the printed matter about Higgins under cover to Erasmus Lewis, which cost him four shillings (*Journal*, 9. Nov.).

Race.[1] This was declaring open War, and ever since both he and his Dutchess (who is in great Favour) have been using all Sorts of Means to break the present Ministry. Mrs. *Masham* was absent two Months from *Windsor*, with Lying-in at *Kensington*, and my Lord Treasurer six Weeks by Indisposition. Some Time before the Session, the Duke above-mentioned, went to all those Lords, who, by the Narrowness of their Fortunes, have depended on the Court, and engaged them to vote against the Ministry, by assuring them it was the Queen's Pleasure. He is said to have added other powerful Motives. *Bothmar*'s Memorial was published just at that Juncture,[2] as *Hoffman* the Emperor's Resident had some Time before printed the *French* King's Propositions.[3] It is confidently affirmed, by those, who should know, that Money was plentifully scattered. By these and some other Accidents, the Vote was carryed against the Ministry; and every Body of either Party, understood the Thing as intended directly against my Lord Treasurer's Head. The House of Lords made a very short Adjournment, and were preparing some Resolutions and Addresses of the most dangerous Importance. We had a very melancholy *Christmas*, and the most fearless Persons were shaken: For, our great Danger lay where I cannot tell your Grace at this Distance. The Thing wished for was, the Removal of the *Somerset* Family; but that could not be done, nor yet is.[4] After some Time the Queen declared herself as you have heard, and twelve new Lords were created. My Lord *Nottingham*'s Game in this Affair hath been most talked off, and several hard Things said of him, are affirmed to be true. The Dissenting Ministers in this Town, were consulted about the occasional Bill, and agreed to it, for what Reasons I

[1] Swift had forgotten that he had given an account of the affair to King in his letter of 26 Aug.; and he here makes a mistake as to the month.

[2] Johann Caspar von Bothmar, the Elector of Hanover's envoy to the Court of St. James, presented an outspoken memorial against the preliminary articles of peace.

[3] Swift appears to have confused Johann Philipp von Hoffman with his predecessor Count de Gallas, the previous Imperial Minister in London, who had openly associated himself with the Whigs in opposition to the peace. He was thereupon forbidden the Court in Her Majesty's name; and a message was directed to the Emperor requesting the appointment of another Austrian Minister (*Journal*, 29 Oct. 1711; *Wentworth Papers*, pp. 205, 207; Bolingbroke's *Letters*, i. 253, 278, 293, 295).

[4] Within a few days the Duke of Somerset was dismissed from his position of Master of the Horse. 'The Duke of Somerset is out' wrote Swift on 19 Jan. (*Journal*, p. 467). The Duchess retained her office as Mistress of the Robes.

cannot learn; that which is offered not satisfying me, that they were afraid of worse.[1] I believe they expected an entire Change of Ministry and Measures, and a new Parliament, by which it might be repealed, and have instead some Law to their Advantage. The Duke of *Marlborough*'s Removal hath passed very silently; the particular Reasons for it I must tell your Grace some other Time:[2] But, how it will pass Abroad I cannot answer. People on both Sides conclude from it, that the Peace is certain; but the Conclusion is ill drawn: The Thing would have been done, although we had been sure of continuing the War. We are terribly afraid of Prince *Eugene*'s coming, and therefore it was put off until the Resolutions were taken. Before he came out of his Yacht, he asked how many Lords were made. He was a Quarter of an Hour with the Queen, on *Sunday* about seven at Night.[3] The great Men resolve to entertain him in their Turns; and we suppose it will all end in a journey of Pleasure. We are so confidently told of the Duke of *Somerset*'s being out, that I writ so to the Dean of *St. Patrick*'s. A Man of Quality told me he had it from my Lord Keeper, whom I asked next Day, and found it a Mistake; but it is impossible to fence against all Lies: However, it is still expected that the Duke will be out, and that many other Removes will be made. Lord *Ranelagh* died on Sunday Morning: He was very poor and needy, and could hardly support himself for want of a Pension, which used to be paid him, and which his Friends solicited as a Thing of perfect Charity. He *dyed hard*, as the Term of Art is here, to express the woeful State of Men who discover no Religion at their Death.[4]

The Town-Talk is that the Duke of *Ormond* will go no more to *Ireland*, but be succeeded by the Duke of *Shrewsbury*, who is a very

---

[1] See p. 284.

[2] The *London Gazette* of 31 Dec. 1711 announced the dismissal of Marlborough from all his employments. The letter he received from the Queen was so offensively worded that he flung it into the fire (*H.M.C.*, R. 8, *Marlborough Papers*, p. 16).

[3] Charles VI, the new Emperor of Austria, in the hope of preventing a peace without Spain, sent Prince Eugene to England. He was received with acclamation; but he did not reach London till 6 Jan., 'too late to do the Whigs any good' as Swift observed (*Journal*, p. 456).

[4] Richard Jones, 1641?–1712, third Viscount Ranelagh, created an Earl in 1674, came of a family long connected with Ireland. In 1668–74 he was Chancellor of the Irish Exchequer. As Paymaster-General, 1689–1702, he was convicted of defalcation, but escaped prosecution. The famous Ranelagh Gardens were formed out of his estate at Chelsea.

great and excellent Person; and, I will hold a Wager, that your Grace will be an Admirer of his Dutchess: If they go, I will certainly order her to make all Advances to you; but, this is only a general Report, of which they know nothing at Court, although I think it not altogether improbable.[1]

We have yet heard nothing of my Lord Privy Seal.[2] *Buys*[3] the Dutch Envoy went to *Holland*, I think, at the same Time. *Buys* is a great Pretender to Politicks, and always leaves the Company, with great Expressions of Satisfaction that he hath convinced them all: He took much Pains to persuade me out of some Opinions; and, although all he said did but fix me the deeper, he told the Ministry how successful he had been. I have got poor Dr. *King*[4] who was some time in *Ireland*, to be Gazetteer, which will be worth 250 *l.* per Annum to him, if he be diligent and sober, for which I am engaged. I mention this, because I think he was under your Grace's Protection when he was in *Ireland*.

By what I gather from Mr. *Southwell*, I believe your Grace stands very well with the Duke of *Ormond*; and it is one great Addition to my Esteem for Mr. *Southwell*, that he is entirely your Grace's Friend and humble Servant, delighting to do you Justice upon all Occasions.[5] | I am, with the greatest Respect, | Your Grace's most dutiful | and most humble Servant.

[1] Ormonde replaced Marlborough as Commander-in-Chief and was allowed to hold the position in conjunction with that of Lord Lieutenant until the following year as meanwhile the Irish Parliament was not sitting. Swift had made the acquaintance of the Duke and Duchess of Shrewsbury at Windsor, where the Duke, as Lord Chamberlain, was in attendance on the Queen.

[2] John Robinson, Bishop of Bristol and Lord Privy Seal, was appointed plenipotentiary for the peace conference at Utrecht; and Lord Strafford accepted the post of second plenipotentiary. The Bishop was the first to arrive at Utrecht, 15 June 1712.

[3] Monsieur de Buys came to England as Dutch Envoy in consequence of the terms for peace with France negotiated by Prior. He was the principal representative of Holland at Utrecht. Swift thought little of his abilities.

[4] William King, wit and author, was Judge of the Admiralty Court in Ireland, 1701–7.

[5] Despite these fair words Swift knew that Archbishop King was not regarded with favour at this time by friends of the Government, nor was he by Swift himself. On 29 Dec. he told Stella that people coming from Ireland complained of King 'and scold me for protecting him'; and on the following 7 Jan. that he was going 'to write a long letter' to the Archbishop 'but not so politickly as formerly: I won't trust him'. This letter of 8 Jan., it will be noted, reveals nothing that King might not have learned elsewhere.

4804

The Rev. Henry Sacheverell to Swift

[Southwark, 31 January 1711–12]

Reverend Sir,[1]

Since You have been pleas'd to undertake the Generous Office of Soliciting My Good Lord Treasurer's Favour in my behalf, I should be very ungratefull if I did not Return You my most hearty Thanks for it, & my humblest Acknowledgments to his Lordship for the Success it has mett with.

I receiv'd last Monday a Message by my Pupil, M^r· Lloyd (Representative of Shropshire)[2] from M^r· Harley, by his Lp's order, to enquire w^t my Brother was Qualified for. I told him, having Fail'd in his Trade, He had been out of business for some Years, during wch time I had entirely Maintain'd Him & his Family. That his Education had not Qualified him for any considerable or nice Post, but that if His Lordship thought him an Object of his Favour, I entirely submitted him to his Disposal, & should be very Thankfull to his Goodness to Ease Me of Part of that Heavy Burthen of my Family, that requir'd more than my Poor Circumstances could allow of.

I am inform'd also that I am very much Indebted to my Great Country-Man, M^r. Secretary St. Johns, for his generous Recommendation of this Matter to his Lp. I should be proud of an Opportunity of expressing my Gratitude to That Eminent Patriot for whom no one that wishes the Welfare or Honour of his Church or Country can have too Great a Veneration.

But for Your Self (Good D^r) who was the First Spring to move it, I can never sufficiently acknowledge the Obligation. I should be Glad, if you will Command Me in any Time or Place to do it, w^ch

---

[1] Swift and Sacheverell met for the first time on 22 Jan. 1711–12. On 31 Jan. Swift alludes to the receipt of this letter. Sacheverell had expected preferment from the new Ministry; but as Swift was fain to acknowledge: 'He hates the new ministry mortally, and they hate him, and pretend to despise him too.' See *Journal*, pp. 342, 469, 477. Swift was accustomed to attribute the downfall of the Whigs to the result of the Sacheverell trial. Cf. *Memoirs Relating to that Change in the Queen's Ministry, Prose Works*, ed. Davis, viii.

[2] During the progress of the trial Robert Lloyd of Aston in Shropshire presented Sacheverell to the rectory of Selattyn in that county.

will be a Farther Favour conferr'd on Rev^d S^r | Your most faithfull
Servt,

H. Sacheverell

Southwark }
Jan: 31. 17$\frac{11}{12}$}

I am told there's a Place in the Custom-house void call'd the
Searchr's, wch if proper to Ask I would presume, but rather leave
it to his Lp's Disposal.[1]

Endorsed by Swift: D Sacheverell | Jan. 31st 1712–13

Longleat xiii

Swift to the Earl of Oxford

[5 February 1711–12]

My Lord,
   I most humbly take leave to inform your Lordship, that the Dean
of Wells dyed this morning at one oClock;[2] I entirely submit my
good Fortune to your Lordship, and remain with greatest Respect
My Lord | Your Lordship's | most obedient and | most obliged
humble Servt |

J: Swift.

Jan^ry. 5th

---

[1] The application was successful, and on 17 Mar. Sacheverell called to thank
Swift, who found him 'not very deep' (*Journal*, p. 516).

[2] Three English deaneries fell vacant during the earlier half of 1712—Wells,
Ely, and Lichfield. Immediately upon the vacancy at Wells through the death
at his lodgings in Hampton Court of William Graham, the holder, on Monday,
4 Feb. 1711–12, Swift applied to Oxford for the deanery. This letter comes from
the Harley manuscripts at Longleat, xiii, f. 44. In the *Bath MSS*. i. 228, it is
misdated '1712–13, January 5'. Writing in haste Swift put 'Jan^ry. 5th', and the
editor presumed the year to be '1712–13'. Without question, however, Graham
died in Feb. 1711–12. See Sir Charles Firth's paper, 'Dean Swift and Ecclesiastical Preferment', in the *Review of English Studies*, 1926, ii. 6–10. Ball, following
the erroneous dating of the *H.M.C.* report, places the letter at *Corresp*. ii. 4,
a year out of place. To Swift's annoyance persistent rumours ran that he was
to be Dean of Wells. See *Journal*, pp. 518, 552, 630, 660 and n., 664.

Archbishop King to Swift

Dublin Feb: 16. 1711[12]

Rev[d] S[r]

Yours of the 8th of January has lain by me some time for want of something to answer, not that our Country is altogether barren of news, but the accidents here are of so little consequence to you there, that it can hardly be pertinent to write them; what [is] of moment is in the public newspapers.

I doubt not, but you hear of vile practice of houghing and destroying cattle, that is spread in Sev[ll] Countys sev[ll] thousand Sheep and Bullocks have been thus destroyed. It began in Connaught, and has spread into Clare, Fermanagh and sev[ll] other Countys. The pretence is this, Lands of late have been raised mightily in their rates, and the poor people not being able to pay when demanded are turn'd out of their farms, and one man stocks as many as ten, twenty, or perhaps an 100 inhabited, these poor people are turned to stock-slaying or starve, for the Land will yield a great deal more when there is found only a shepherd or cowherd to pay out of it than it can yield when some inhabitants are first to be fed out of it, this turning the poor people to grazing has made them desperate, and they every where endeavour to destroy whole stocks of Cattle, that they may get Land to plow at the former rate. That is the pretence, and [to] show that this is no quarrel between Protestants and Papists, they destroy the Papists flocks and herds generally first, but it is much suspected that there is a deeper design hid under this [practice] and both Whigs and Papists seem to suggest that the Pretender is at the bottom. We have published several proclamations to discover and seize houghers but wholly up to [now] without success.[2]

---

[1] The secretarial manuscript in Trinity College, Dublin, severely injured by damp, is now only partly legible.

[2] The practice of houghing or slaughtering cattle broke out in the early part of 1711 in co. Galway and spread rapidly through the counties of Mayo and Clare and parts of Roscommon and Sligo. The reason of this agrarian outbreak was the increase of pasture in place of tillage, bearing hardly upon the subsistence of the people. Disciplined bands of houghers roamed the country and the magistrates were quite unable to control the situation. The movement seems to have had no religious or political significance. In 1713 the houghing suddenly ceased. See Lecky, *History of England*, 1879, ii. 351-6.

We wait impatiently for some acc^t from Utrecht, if my Lord Treasurer carry his point, he has surely done the greatest thing that ever statesman did in England for he has against [him] all the Allies, the moneyed men in England, the army and the fleet, and the majority of the old Lds; and everybody saw the pinch he was at when the new Lds were made, his choice must be approved by every body the Estates and familys well deserving honour; I hope he will never again be under the like necessity.

No body seems to say anything against her Majesty laying aside the Duke of M[arlborough], that being her prerogative, but if an Impeachment had followed I know not how it would have been, I believe it is wisdom to stop where things are as to him—*Magni nomen abrumpat.*

None here must talk of any change of our chief Governor: if that should happen at any time, none would [be more] grateful to the Kingdom than the person you name, I in particular have a great Veneration for him; and as to his lady, tho you know I have but an awkward way of address to ladies, yet assure your self I will if her Grace come here endeavour by all possible services to merit her esteem, my notion of her Grace is, that she is well able to distinguish between sincere respect and flattery, I can promise the first, though a stranger to the latter. But pray take you a care not to promise too much, for that will be a disadvantage as happens wherever expectation is raised, and for fear I should forfeit your recognisance as I am afraid poor Dr. King will.[1]

The Pretender runs in the heads of most of the people of Ireland; the Papists seem to have great hopes and the Protestants generally great fears, and it is the business of some to persuade all that [he] is at the door, and perhaps the perseverance of these men's suggestions, is the cause of these expectations and fears that serves them to good purposes, but when the falseness of their surmises once appears all Ireland will be unanimous for the new Ministry, for they are well convinced that the other had ill designs.

I had the good fortune to suppress a great many in their clamours for a war, by telling them that if it were known in England that Ireland were for the war, they would certainly exact from them a

---

[1] In Dec. 1711 William King was appointed to succeed Steele as gazetteer. For an amusing account of the occasion see King's *Works*, 1776, vol. i, pp. xxiii–xxiv. King, neither diligent nor sober, finding the post uncongenial, soon relinquished it.

tax towards it, and defied them to even [say] if this were not justice
and how they could either refuse or make a proportionable contribution; and that if they would avoid this they must hold their [peace]
which I think they chose to do; I recommend [you etc.]

Dr. Swift.   W. D.

Address: Under cover to Erasmus Lewis, Esq., at Lord Dartmouth's.

King's Letter-book and Ball[1]
Archbishop King to Swift

Revd Sr   Killbrew[2] March 27. 1712

I give you the trouble of this on account of our Government,
which I understand from all hands is to be changed. I am sorry to
find that it is the general opinion that no kindness is intended in the
change to his Grace the Duke of Ormond,[3] I suspected it would be
so when the struggles happened here in the Parliament and was so
open as to intimate my fears to his Grace himself, with the methods
I thought proper to prevent them, but other Counsels prevailed,
perhaps more to his Grace's advantage, but I am sure they would
not be given with more sincere affection and zeal for his Grace's
service. I heartily pray for his success in the great post in which he
is placed.

My Ld Duke of Shrewsbury will come here with great advantage,
the generality being possessed with a great opinion of his probity
and capacity, and besides they have reckoned his Grace to be a
friend to this countrey, for my own part I do not see how it can be in
the power of any Chief Governour to do us any great good, but any
one may do us a great deal of mischief, and if [we] have such a one
as will have so much affection for those he Governs that he will do
us no more hurt than he must, that he will not out of malice or

[1] The manuscript is severely injured by damp.
[2] At Kilbrew in county Meath, about eighteen miles from Dublin, Lieut.-
Gen. Richard Gorges had his seat. For Swift's *Elegy* on him and his wife,
'Countess Doll of Meath', see *Poems*, pp. 429-31.
[3] Ormonde's appointment as Captain-General of the Forces in Flanders
revived the rumour that he was to be superseded as Viceroy in Ireland. It was
generally expected that the Duke of Shrewsbury would take his place. At this
time he declined the offer (*Bath MSS.* i. 218). He was, however, induced to
accept it in Sept. 1713.

ignorance wilfully injure us, we ought and must be thankfull to God
for him.

I suppose in his Grace's time there may [be] occasion for a new
Parliament, for I believe he will hardly take up with the present
after such declared feuds between the two houses, not but I believe he
might with prudent management have influence enuff to oblige them
to do all the Service his Grace might have occasion for, but because
I do not think it worth the pains that must be taken in it; and as it
would not be pleasing to the Kingdom, so it would not be so serviceable to his Grace, for their acquiescence in his Grace's designs would
be looked on as a great merit and if not answered by some definite
return on his Grace's part it would disgust agst [him] many, whereas
the calling of a new Parliament will be reckoned as a favour from his
Grace and oblige the new Members to make suitable returns to their
creator. I do not see anything that anyways embarrass[es] his
Grace's government, except it be the jurisdiction of the House of
Lords. I understand that a cause judged by them last sessions is
carried before the Lords in Great Britain, this may breed disgusts,
and therefore I think it were advisable that his Grace should be
apprised of it.[1] If it may be prevented it will turn much to the ease of
his Grace's government, and entirely gain him the House of Lords
here and [he may] announce himself welcome with all.

I was in hopes to have [wished] you joy of a good preferment in
England and heartily wish it, and pray be not wanting to yourself at
[making] every venture, perhaps you may not in time have one so
serviceable. I recommend you, &c.   W. D.

Dr. Swift.

Faulkner 1762

Swift to Archbishop King

London, March 29, 1712.

My Lord,
    I cannot ask Pardon for not sooner acknowledging your Grace's
Letter,[2] because that would look as if I thought mine were of Con-

---

[1] This question was the one which gave rise seven years later to the well-
known constitutional conflict between the two Parliaments, and led to an
enactment of the English Parliament denying all power of appellate jurisdiction
to the Irish House of Lords.—Ball.   [2] That of 16 Feb.

sequence. Either I grew weary of Politicks, or am out of the Way of
them, or, there is less stirring than usual;¹ and, indeed, we are all
in Suspence at present; but, I am told that in ten or twelve Days
Time, we shall know what the Issue will be at *Utrecht*. I can only
tell your Grace, that there are some unlucky Circumstances not
proper to be trusted to a Letter, which have hitherto retarded this
great Work.² *Mihi ludibria rerum mortalium cunctis in negotiis
obversantur.*³ Mean Time we are with great Difficulty raising Funds
upon which to borrow five Millions. One of those Funds is a Tax
upon Paper, and I think, 30 per Cent. upon imported Books, and of
such a Nature as I could not Yesterday forbear saying to my Lord
Treasurer and the Chancellor of the Exchequer, that instead of
preventing small Papers and Libels, it will leave nothing else for the
Press.⁴ I have not talked to the Duke of *Argyle* upon the Affairs of
Spain, since his return; but, am told, he affirms it impossible for us
to carry on the War there by our former Methods. The Duke of
Ormond is expected to go in two or three Days for *Flanders*.⁵ And
what I writ to your Grace some Months ago of the Duke of *Shrewsbury* succeeding to govern *Ireland*, will, I suppose, be soon declared. I was the other Day to see the Dutchess, and reported your
Grace's Compliments, which she took very well; and, I told her, I
was resolved your Grace and she should be very good Acquaintance.
I believe the Spirit of your *Houghers* has got into our *Mohocks*, who
are still very troublesome, and every Night cut some body or other
over the Face; and commit a hundred insolent Barbarities.⁶

¹ Since his last letter to the Archbishop, 8 Jan. 1711–12, Swift had published
the cleverly written *Some Advice to the October Club* and *Some Remarks on the
Barrier Treaty*, published 21 Feb., and helped Hanmer to draw up the 'Representation of the State of the Nation', which was presented to the Queen on
4 Mar., and which he included later in the *Four Last Years of the Queen*.
² Swift alludes to the endeavours of the Dutch to interpose obstructions to
any 'reasonable Temper upon the Barrier-Treaty, or to offer a Plan in concert
with the Queen, for a General Peace' (*Four Last Years, Prose Works*, ed. Davis,
vii. 121).
³ Tacitus, *Ann.* iii. 18.
⁴ An Act was passed 10 June 1712, to come into force 1 Aug., whereby all
newspapers on a half-sheet or less were to be taxed a halfpenny, if on a whole
sheet, and not more, one penny. The intention of the Act was the suppression
of libels.
⁵ As Commander in Chief of the Forces.
⁶ Swift's belief that the Mohocks were incited by the Whigs need not be
accepted. That they were dangerous cannot be questioned. On 17 Mar. 1711-12

There was never the least Design of any Impeachment against the Duke of *Marlborough*; and it was his own great Weakness, or the Folly of his Friends, that the Thing went so far as it did.[1]

I know not whether it is, that People have talked themselves hoarse, but for some Weeks past we have heard less of the Pretender than formerly. I suppose it is, like a Fashion, got into *Ireland*, when it is out here: But, in my Conscience, I do not think any one Person in the Court or Ministry here, designs any more to bring in the Pretender, than the great Turk. I hope, Mr. *Harley*, who is now on his Journey to *Hanover*, will give that Court a truer Opinion of Persons and Things than they have hitherto conceived.[2] And, if your Grace knew the Instrument, through which these false opinions have been infused, you would allow it another Instance of the *Ludibrium rerum mortalium*. And, your Grace cannot but agree, that it is something singular for the Prince in Possession to make perpetual Advances, and the presumptive Heir standing off, and suspicious.

I know not whether your Grace hath considered the Position that my Lord Treasurer is visibly in. The late Ministry, and their Adherents, confess themselves fully resolved to have his Head, whenever it is in their Power, and were prepared upon the Beginning of the Sessions, when the Vote was carried against any Peace without *Spain*, to move that he should be sent to the Tower: At the same Time his Friends, and the Tories in general, are discontented at his Slowness in the changing of Commissions and Employments, to which the Weakness of the Court Interest in the House of Lords is wholly imputed: Neither do I find, that those in the greatest Stations, or most in the Confidence of my Lord Trea-

a proclamation of £100 reward for the discovery of any offenders appeared. See the *Spectator*, nos. 324, 332, 347; Gay's play, *The Mohocks*; *Trivia*, iii. 321–34.

[1] The Commissioners of Public Accounts reported, 21 Dec. 1711, to the House of Commons that between 1702 and 1711 Marlborough had received over £63,000 from Sir Solomon Medina, bread contractor for the allied armies, and his predecessor (*Journals of the House of Commons*, xvii. 15–18). The Duke, admitting the fact, declared that he had followed precedent, and that the money had been devoted to the public service. Swift states that it was designed to censure him as gently as possible 'provided his friends will not make head to defend him' (*Journal*, 23 Jan. 1711–12).

[2] Thomas Harley, a cousin of Lord Oxford, was sent to Hanover as an emissary of the Queen; and, further, he carried fresh instructions to the plenipotentiaries at Utrecht.

surer, are able to account for this Proceeding, or seem satisfied with it. I have endeavoured to solve this Difficulty another Way; and, I fancy, I am in the right, from Words I have heard let fall: But, whatever be the Cause, the Consequences may be dangerous.

The Queen is in very good Health, but doth not use as much Exercise as she ought. Pray God preserve her many Years!

A Projector hath lately applied to me to recommend him to the Ministry, about an Invention for finding out the Longitude. He hath given in a Petition to the Queen by Mr. Sec. *St. John.* I understand nothing of the Mathematicks, but I am told it is a Thing as improbable as the Philosopher's Stone, or perpetual Motion.[1]

I lately writ a Letter of about thirty Pages to Lord Treasurer, by way of Proposal for an Academy, to correct, enlarge, and ascertain the *English* Language.[2] And, he and I have named above twenty Persons of both Parties to be Members. I will shortly print the Letter, and I hope something will come of it. Your Grace sees I am a Projector too. I am, | with great Respect, | my Lord, | Your Grace's most dutiful, and most humble Servant, |

J. Swift.

Faulkner 1762

Swift to Archbishop King

London, May 20, 1712.

My Lord,

When I had the Honour of your Grace's Letter of *March* 27, I was lying ill of a cruel Disorder, which still pursueth me, altho' not with so much Violence;[3] and I hope your Grace will pardon me, if you find my Letter to be that of one who writeth in Pain. You see, my Lord, how Things are altered. The talk of a new Governor for *Ireland* is dropped. The Secret is, that the Duke of *Ormond* had a

---

[1] The allusion may be to William Whiston, who, on 30 Oct. 1710, was deprived of the Lucasian professorship at Cambridge for heterodox views.

[2] Swift's Proposal for *Correcting, Improving and Ascertaining the English Tongue* occupied his thoughts for some time. It is dated 'Feb. 22. 1711, 12.', and was published on 17 May 1712.

[3] From the end of March till the middle of September Swift has many references in the *Journal* to the severe attack of shingles from which he was suffering.

Promise of a Pension in Case he lost his Government; but my Lord
Treasurer is so excessively thrifty, that, to save Charges, he lets the
Duke keep it; and besides, there are some other Circumstances, not
proper for a Letter, which have great Weight in this Matter. I count
upon it, that whatever Governor goeth over under this Ministry, a
new Parliament will be called. Yet, I was told that the Duke of
Shrewsbury was pitched on, as a Sort of Medium between, &c.[1] He
is a Person of admirable Qualities: and if he were somewhat more
active, and less timorous in Business, no Man would be thought
comparable to him.

The Moderate of the other Party seem now content to have a
Peace, and all our Talk and Expectation are full of it: But I protest
to your Grace I know not what to write upon this Subject, neither
could I tell what to say if I had the Honour to be with you. Upon
Lord *Strafford*'s coming over the Stocks are fallen, although I
expected, and I thought with Reason, that they would rise.[2] There
is a Trade between some here and some in *Holland*, of Secrets and
Lies, and there are some among us whose Posts let them into an
imperfect Knowledge of Things, which they cannot conceal. This
Mixture maketh up the Town Talk, governs the Price of Stocks, and
hath often a great deal of Truth in it: Besides, publick Affairs have
often so many sudden Turns and Incidents, that even those behind
the Curtain can hardly pronounce for a Week. I am sensible that
I have often deceived your Grace with my wise *Innuendoes*. Yet,
I verily think that my Intelligence was very right at the Moment I
sent it. If I had writ to your Grace six Days ago, I would have
ventured to have given you Hopes that a Peace would soon appear,
and upon Conditions wholly surprizing and unexpected. I say this
to you wholly in Confidence, and I know nothing yet to change my
Opinion, except the desponding Talk of the Town, for I see nothing
yet in the Contrivances of the Ministers. It seems generally agreed
that the present Dauphin[3] cannot live, and upon that depend many
Measures to be taken. This Afternoon the Bill for appointing Commissioners to enquire into the Grants &c. was thrown out of the
House of Lords, the Voices being equal, which is a great Dis-

[1] Swift means that Shrewsbury was regarded as a moderate in politics.
[2] Lord Cowper, replying to an attack on Marlborough by Lord Strafford,
when he was temporarily in England, accused him of being unacquainted with
the language and constitution of his native country.
[3] The future Louis XV.

appointment to the Court, and Matter of Triumph to the other Party.[1] But it may possibly be of the worst Consequence to the Grants next Session, when it is probable the Ministry will be better settled, and able to procure a Majority. I am, with great Respect, | My Lord, Your Grace's | Most dutiful, and | Most humble Servant, |

J. Swift.

King's Letter-book

Archbishop King to Swift

Castleslaugh,[2] May 29. 1712

Revd Sr

I recd yours of the 20th inst since I left Dublin on my triennial visitation.[3] I made it more early by two months than it used to occur. I had, God be thanked, a very good state of health all last winter and spring, and having mist any fit of the gout at the usual time, apprehended it might seize me in July as sometimes it doth in that month wherein I used to visit, and therefore I was resolved to prevent it if possible, lest it should prevent me. I likewise have visited parochially such churches in my own Diocese as lay near my road and confi[rmed in many] of them. I go on from hence to Kilkenny and visit there to June, God willing, and shall return through the County of Wicklow, which is in my own diocese of Dublin. I find both Churches and Congregations much [mended] since my last visitation which is a very great comfort to me. . . . Things seem very quiet here and all persons desirous of [peace which] surely will be a common good, tho [my] opinion has always been that Ireland will lose by it, in which I now find that I am not singular.

I always imagined the terms of peace to be a matter of great difficulty, tho all partys shou'd heartily desire and endeavour it, and

---

[1] The inquiry under this bill was limited to grants of land, often extravagant, made by William III; and it was therefore in the main directed at Whig recipients.

[2] The transcript of this letter in the manuscript room of Trinity College, Dublin, is badly injured; but the place of writing is clearly legible, 'Castleslaugh', for which Ball prints 'Carlow'.

[3] It was customary at this time for Archbishops to visit their suffragans trienially.

if it were left to our own choice to settle the terms, it would require, as seems to me, a consummate wisdom to find out what would be expedient. It seems to me that by the rott in the Bourbon family,[1] the case is much altered since the negotiations were set on foot, and that the conditions of peace must be much another thing than they ought to have been then, and I should not wonder if so extraordinary a change should puzzle the wisest Ministry; but I am much surprised to hear that Philip should stick at renouncing his pretensions to France, that not suiting with the methods formerly used by that family. The only thing that can stick with him seems to me the fear [that] his brother Berry[2] should keep him to his word and take the advantage of his renunciation to step into the throne of France and exclude him; but he may set his heart at rest as to that, the French are so intent on their interest and glory, that if only one life stood between the union of the two crowns, they would soon find means to remove it out of the way. It is a maxim in France that the Hereditary right is indefeasible, and who ever endeavoured to put it by would be looked on as a usurper and by other maxims might be removed any way, especially when his removal would be so fair a step to the universall monarchy.

As to the conditions of peace I never heard of any yet, that had any, [so] to look, testimony of their being genuine, and perhaps no negotiations were ever managed with so much secrecy as this, which has made [people] not well affected say that this peace is like that of God and passes all understanding.

As to the government of Ireld, considering all things it had surely been in effect to destroy the Duke of Ormond to remove him, and some did not fail to suggest that he was only made Captain-General to get him out of Court on that consideration. I think it was not amiss to continue both as they were till other circumstances offer. I laid a wager last November that the peace would not be proclaimed before August; [it] was only a treat, and I am afraid I shall win it.

As to your Bill of Inquiries about Grants, I wonder how it

---

[1] In 1711 the Dauphin, then fifty years of age, had died of smallpox. In Feb. 1712 that Dauphin's eldest son and successor, the Duke of Burgundy, died also; and on 8 Mar. 1712, *his* eldest son, the Duke of Brittany, died, leaving Louis, a sickly infant, as heir to the throne of France. The next heir after him was Philip V, King of Spain. A situation threatening the peace of Europe thus arose. The infant, however, scarcely expected to live, became Louis XV, and did not die till 1774. See Trevelyan, *England under Queen Anne*, iii. 213-15.

[2] Charles, Duc de Berry, third grandson of Louis XIV, died in 1714.

passed so far considering that the legislators were generally the men that were to suffer by it, and besides Courtiers expect the like hereafter, and to resume the past is to cramp the hands of the Crown for the future, and make the gifts less valuable and the donors more cautious, and therefore the bringing the matter so near to bear satisfies me that those are mistaken in their count that reckon my Lord Treasurer to stand much alone—that he neither has nor desires assistance, which I assure you is the great foundation of some men's expectations that he cannot stand long; and I hope this will somewhat mortify them and stop their cant of woe to him that is alone.

I heard you were ill, and am heartily concerned for it, I can only give you the assistance of my prayers, which I assure you I do with constancy. I have several other matters to write about relating to your project of an academy for Language and other affairs, but I have not time having only stole this moment to signify to you that I am &c. |

W. D.

Dʳ Swift

Faulkner 1762

Swift to Archbishop King

Kensington, [26 June 1712]¹

My Lord,

I have two or three Times begun Letters to your Grace, and have torn what I writ, hoping I might send you something decisive about the Peace. But all still continues to lie very loose, and I continue to be very desponding, altho' the People in Affairs laugh at me for it. I have one plain Maxim in dealing with those, who have more Cunning, and less Honesty than myself, which is, what we call keeping the Staff in my own Hand, and contriving that they shall trust me rather than I them. A Man may reason until he is weary upon this Proceeding of the *Dutch*. The Soldiers tell me that the Duke of *Ormond* could not possibly take Possession of *Dunkirk*, since the foreign Troops have refused to march, and that the States

---

¹ Faulkner and editors previous to Ball date this letter 30 Sept. The contents of the letter are clearly incompatible with so late a date; and King's letter of 29 July fixes its true date with certainty.

will not suffer us to go through their Towns. But, I had a Whisper from one who should know best, that *Dunkirk* might now have been ours if right Methods had been taken. And, another great Man said to a Friend of mine, about a Fortnight ago, that the least wrong Step on that Side the Water might have very ill Consequences at this Juncture.[1] Mean Time, the discontented Party seems full of Hopes, and many of the Court Side beside myself, desponding enough. The Necessity of laying the Proposals before the Parliament drew us into all this; for, now we are in a Manner pinned down, and cannot go back an Inch with any good Grace: So that if the *French* play us foul, I dread the Effects, which are too visible to doubt. And, on the other Side, if the Peace goeth smoothly on, I cannot but think that some severe Enquiries will be made; and, I believe, upon very manifest Grounds. If there be any Secret in this Matter of *Dunkirk*, it must be in very few Hands; and those who most converse with Men at the Helm, are, I am confident, very much in the Dark. Some People go so far as to think that the *Dutch* will hinder even the English Forces under the Duke of *Ormond* from going by the *French* Country to *Dunkirk*: But I cannot be of that Opinion. We suppose a few Days will decide this Matter; and I believe your Grace will agree, that there was never a more nice Conjuncture of Affairs; however, the Court appears to be very resolute: Several Changes have been made, and more are daily expected. The *Dutch* are grown so unpopular, that, I believe, the Queen might have Addresses to stand by her against them with Lives and Fortunes.

I had your Grace's letter of *May* 29, written in the Time of your Visiting; from which, I hope, you are returned with Health and Satisfaction.

The Difficulties in the Peace, by the Accidents in the *Bourbon* Family, are, as your Grace observeth, very great, and what indeed our Ministers chiefly apprehended. But we think *Philip*'s renouncing to be an effectual Expedient; not out of any Regard he would have for it, but because it will be the Interest of every Prince of the Blood in *France* to keep him out, and because the *Spaniards* will never assist him to unite the two Kingdoms.

---

[1] For Swift's account of the negotiations leading to the occupation of Dunkirk on 8 July (o.s.) by a small force of troops from England under General Jack Hill see *Four Last Years of the Queen*, *passim*. Swift was not acquainted, however, with the perfidy of Bolingbroke and his secret communications with Torcy (Trevelyan, *England under Queen Anne*, iii. 217, 218, 221–2).

I am in Hopes yet that your Grace may pay your Treat, for it is yet four Weeks to [August[1]]: at least I believe we shall be happy, or ruined, before that Time.

It is certain that there is something in what People say; but the Court is so luckily constituted at present, that every Man thinks the chief Trust cannot be any where else so well placed, neither do I know above one Man that would take it, and it is a great deal too soon for him to have such Thoughts.[2]

I humbly thank your Grace for your Concern about my Health: I have still the Remainder of some Pains, which hath partly occasioned my removing hither about three Weeks ago; I was recommended to Country Air, and chose this, because I could pass my Time more agreeably near my Friends at Court. We think the Queen will go to *Windsor* in three Weeks; and, I believe I shall be there most of the Time I stay in *England*, which I intend, until towards the End of Summer.

My Lord Treasurer hath often promised he will advance my Design of an Academy; so have my Lord Keeper,[3] and all the Ministers; but they are now too busy to think of any Thing beside what they have upon the Anvil. My Lord Treasurer and I have already pitched upon twenty Members of both Parties; but perhaps it may all come to nothing.

If Things continue as they are another Session, perhaps your Grace may see the Bill of Resuming the Grants[4] carried on with a great deal more Rigour than it lately was. It was only desired that the Grantees should pay six Years Purchase, and settle the Remainder on them by Act of Parliament, and those Grants are now worse than other Lands by more Years Purchase than six; so that in Effect they would have lost nothing. | I am, with great Respect, | Your Grace's most dutiful, and | Most humble Servant.

J. Swift.

----

[1] Faulkner here substituted '*Nov.*'; for we can hardly suppose it to have been a slip on the part of Swift. In his letter of 29 May King wrote: 'I laid a wager last November that the peace would not be proclaimed before August.'

[2] Swift is alluding to Bolingbroke.

[3] Harcourt.

[4] See p. 297.

King's Letter-book[1]
Archbishop King to Swift

Dublin July 23. 1712

Revd. S[r]

The bearer Mr. Foley is a very hopefull young man and being well related to persons in power at Court it is in hopes of advancing of himself by their interest [that he goes to London].[2] I know no fault he has except his youth, which will mend every day, he was under my guardianship till he came to age, and since he has found his interest to consult me in the management of himself. I had a prospect of preferring him, but it failed me and that has put him on going to London to try another way. He will need advice and direction and some body to have an eye over him. I have ventured to recommend him to you, as to one, that knows perfectly well how to counsel him, and that has goodness to assist a young man in so critical a time. He may give you a tolerable account of matters here, and perhaps the better because 'tis to be presumed that he has not yet the art of dissembling his thoughts.

I came from my Visitation a month ago, but immediately after got the gout in my right hand, which has been very inconvenient to me, particularly in disabling me from writing, which I do with great pain and uneasiness or you had heard sooner from Revd S[r] yours &c. |

D[r] Swift   W. D.

King's Letter-book[3]
Archbishop King to Swift

Dublin 29th July 1712

Rev[d] Sir

I rec[d] yours of 26th June soon after my return from my Triennial; and you had rec[d] an answer to it with my acknowledgments long

---

[1] The transcript in King's correspondence is badly injured.

[2] The son of Samuel Foley, who was Bishop of Down and Connor when Swift was instituted to Kilroot. Foley died within a few months of his installation, and King, who was one of the executors of his will, made every effort to assist his friend's family. The Bishop was a cousin to the father of Harley's first wife, Elizabeth Foley, who died in 1691. She was the mother of the second Earl of Oxford.

[3] The copy of this letter in King's correspondence is badly injured.

agoe, but on my coming home I was seized with the gout in my right hand in soe severe a manner, that I with difficulty yet hold my pen. I did not think fit to use another hand in my letters to you, for as I communicate what you write to no mortal, so I did not care to make any privy to my answers tho they contain no secrets.

I never was in any fear but the French would give us up Dunkirk, and I laughed at those that pretended to believe the contrary, but perhaps you will not like my reason, which to deal ingenuously with you was this, that I reckoned the securing Spain to the House of Bourbon was of such moment that the King of France had been inexcusable if he had stuck at ten Dunkirks to obtain it, not to say anything of the prospect of uniting the two crowns if the Dauphin die, whom I have already condemned. If things be once prepared for it, I cannot believe that you imagine that the two obstacles you mention can hinder it. Pray how is it the interest of the Princes of the blood to keep out Philip? Sure if they and every man in France have not lost their senses, they must see that it is every individual's interest to make him their King, rather than the Duke of Berry, who can give them nothing but what they have, when the other will put the riches of the world in their hands, and can and will make them governors in all lands. Would it not be a pretty advantage for France and Frenchmen to be masters of all the gold and silver of the world, and for a poor Prince of the blood to be vice-regent of Mexico? Assure yourself they will break through every obstacle which may be cross to such a prospect. As to the Spaniards not assisting him, even that may be accomplished as well as Portocarero[1] will, but it is no matter whether they assist or no. I am sure they are not able to hinder it, and if the present King of France survive the peace but three years, he will be able to mould matters so that one may reckon on the thing as certain, if God do not in his providence prevent it, who often defeats the best laid schemes.

I am sure I would write this to none but your self, and pray let it be only to your self. I believe my wager is now secure,[2] for which I am heartily sorry. I durst venture on the same terms that we shall have no universal peace in Europe till this time next year, nor do I see any prospect of it so near, except some extraordinary unforeseen event procures it. And now Britain has made peace for it self me

[1] The Cardinal Archbishop of Toledo, who induced Charles II of Spain to designate King Philip as his successor.
[2] See p. 301.

thinks it is not much our interest there should be one abroad, let the confederates and France fight it out two or three years, in the meantime we shall gather strength and increase in men and money, both which we want at present, and then may be very good mediators, or force either party to a peace, which we cannot safely do at present. I admire what prospects they have that are so zealous to have a peace immediately. I have asked this Question of several and they referred me to some reviews, but I could find no sense either in those or from the Zealots, nor can I see how the continuance of the war by the parties abroad can hurt the Ministry.

I have under consideration the matter of an academy. I believe the close of a war is the more proper time to begin it, but I wish some other name were given it, for I find the generality so prejudiced against all French precedents that as parties are more formed I apprehend the name will be of great disadvantage. You will expect little assistance from Ireland in such a work; the best English writ or spoke here [is] patavineral,[1] and though we should in some things be in the right yet a provincial courtier would cram down always *mou't* instead of *might* as I observed when last in London.

I hope I may wish you joy of preferment [which] I hear her Majesty has bestowed on you,[2] but I reckon nothing sure till I understand your pattent be past, none will congratulate you more heartily than your | Humble serv^t

W. D.

Dr Jon: Swift.

B.M. Add. MS. 39839

Swift to Miss Esther Vanhomrigh

[1 August 1712][3]

Mishessy is not to believe a Word Mr Lewis says in his Letter, I would have writt to you sooner, if I had not been busy, and idle, and

---

[1] Characteristic of Patavium, now Padova. Hence provincial in style. See *O.E.D.*

[2] The deanery of Wells had been vacant since the preceding February. In Ireland, no less than in England, Swift's appointment to Wells was regarded as certain. The Lords Justices of Ireland went so far as to nominate a successor to Laracor.

[3] Scott left this letter undated. Ball gives *July* 31, 1712, but this would be a

out of humor, and did not know how to send to You without the
Help of Mr Lewis my mortal Enemy.[1] I am so weary of this Place,
that I am resolved to leave it in two days, and not return in 3 weeks.
I will come as early on Monday as I can find Opportunity; and will
take a little Grubstreet Lodging;[2] pretty near where I did before;
and dine with you thrice a week; and will tell You a thousand
Secrets provided You will have no Quarrells to me | adieu

Friday at Mr Lewis's office
Don't remember me to Moll; but
humble service to y^r Mother.

Address: To Misheskinage
Endorsed: 1st

Deane Swift 1765

Swift to John Hill

Windsor-Castle, August 12, 1712.[3]

Sir,[4]

With great difficulty I recovered your present of the finest box in
France out of the hands of Mrs. Hill:[5] She allowed her own to be

Thursday, and Swift names the day of the week as Friday. The true date must
have been 1 Aug. 1712.

[1] Swift's account-book (Forster 508) has this note: 'Jul 19. went to Windsr.'
If the date be correct (*Journal*, p. 550) perhaps Lord Oxford took him down after
dinner. But there may be a mistake; for the Queen did not move to Windsor
till 22 July (*Wentworth Papers*, p. 292). Thereafter, in any event, Erasmus
Lewis would be at Windsor in attendance on his chief, Lord Dartmouth.

[2] Writing to Stella on 7 Aug. Swift says: 'I left Windsor on Monday last.'
This would be 4 Aug. He adds: 'I am now in a hedge Lodging' (*Journal*, pp.
552, 553). At this time he was occupied with the composition of the *Four Last
Years of the Queen*. Further, and in connexion with his history, he wished to
see St. John, Viscount Bolingbroke as he had now become, who was entering
upon his negotiations with France. On the day after this letter was written he
set out on his journey to Paris.

[3] Swift had returned to Windsor from London two days before.

[4] After the failure of the Quebec expedition Swift had done all he could to
reinstate Jack Hill in public estimation—'we lay it all to a storm, &c.' At the
same time he was ready to admit: 'I doubt Mr. Hill and his admiral made
wrong steps' (*Journal*, p. 378).

[5] Lady Masham's sister Alice, who was then a woman of the Bedchamber
to Queen Anne.

the prettiest, but then mine was the handsomest; and in short, she would part with neither. I pleaded my brotherhood, and got my Lord and Lady Masham to intercede:[1] And, at last, she threw it me with a heavy sigh: But now it is in my possession, I wish you had sent a paper of directions how I shall keep it. You that sit at your ease, and have nothing to do but keep Dunkirk, never consider the difficulties you have brought upon me: Twenty ladies have threatened to seize or surprise my box;[2] and what are twenty thousand French or Dutch in comparison of those: Mrs. Hill says, it was a very idle thing in you to send such a present to a man who can neither punish nor reward you, since Grub-street is no more: For the Parliament has killed all the Muses of Grub-street, who yet, in their last moments, cried out nothing but Dunkirk.[3] My Lord Treasurer, who is the most malicious person in the world, says you ordered a goose to be drawn at the bottom of my box, as a reflection upon the clergy; and that I ought to resent it: But I am not angry at all, and his Lordship observes by halves: For the goose is there drawn pecking at a snail, just as I do at him, to make him mend his pace in relation to the public, although it be hitherto in vain. And besides, Dr. Arbuthnot,[4] who is a scholar, says, you meant it as a compliment

---

[1] Swift had early formed a friendship with Lord and Lady Masham, and this friendship was lasting. As late as 1733 we find them inviting him to stay with them.

[2] General Hill's present is mentioned in the *Journal*, 18 Sept. 1712. Deane Swift (*Essay*, 1755, pp. 163–4) also refers to the goose and snail device on the bottom of the box, and tells us that 'a prospect of the rialto of *Venice*', with many figures in carnival dress, was painted on the inside of the lid. Two snuff-boxes are mentioned in Swift's will, neither, apparently, this gift from Hill.

[3] In the *Journal*, 7 Aug. 1712, Swift says of Grub-street: 'I playd it pretty close the last Fortnight, and publisht at least 7 penny Papers of my own.' By 'the last Fortnight' Swift means, presumably, the last two weeks before 1 Aug., when the paper tax came into force. On 17 July (*Journal*, p. 548) Swift names (1) *Toland's Invitation to Dismal*; (2) *A Hue and Cry after Dismal*; (3) 'A Ballad on Dunkirk', by which he means *Peace and Dunkirk*; and 'An Argument that Dunkirk is not in our Hands'. No copy of this last has been discovered. On 19 July 'anothr Grub' is named—*A Letter from the Pretender to a Whig-Lord*, which was a broadside, dated *July 8. 1712*. This leaves two more of the '7 penny Papers' to be found. *A Letter of Thanks . . . To the Lord Bp of S. Asaph*, has been conjectured to be one of these; but this cannot have been printed later than 5 July, and probably came out a few days before that date. See *Journal*, pp. 548, 553, and notes; also John C. Stephens in *Notes and Queries*, vol. 197, pp. 139–40.

[4] This is the first reference to Arbuthnot in this correspondence. A reference

for us both: That I am the goose who saved the Capitol by my cackling; and that his Lordship is represented by the snail, because he preserves his country by delays. But my Lord Masham is not to be endured: He observed, that, in the picture of the inside, which represents a great company dancing, there stands a fool with a cap and bells; and he would needs understand that figure as applied to me. And the worst of it was, that I happened, last night, to be at my Lady Duchess of Shrewsbury's ball;[1] where, looking a little singular among so many fine ladies and gentlemen, his Lordship came and whispered me to look at my box; which I resented so highly, that I went away in a rage without staying for supper. However, considering of it better, after a night's sleep, I find all this is nothing but envy, and a design to make a quarrel between you and me: But it shall not do so; for I hope your intentions were good, however malice may misrepresent them. And though I am used ill by all your family, who win my money and laugh at me; yet, to vex them more, I will forgive them for your sake; and as soon as I can break loose, will come to Dunkirk for a fortnight, to get a little ease from my many persecutions, by the Harleys, the Mashams, and the Hills: Only I intend to change my habit, for fear Colonel Killigrew should mistake me for a chimney-sweeper.[2] In the mean-time, I wish you all success in your government, loyal French subjects, virtuous ladies, little champaign, and much health: And am, with the truest respect and esteem, | Sir, | Your most obedient | Humble servant, and brother.

to him in the *Journal*, 19 Mar. 1710–11, shows that they must then have been acquainted for some time. In a letter written to Arbuthnot in 1734 Swift speaks of 'above five-and-twenty years' acquaintance' with him, which would carry the date back to 1709. A doubtful anecdote recorded by Scott (*Works*, 1814, i. 83 n.) suggests that they met as early as 1702; but this is most unlikely. John Arbuthnot, 1667–1735, took his medical degree at St. Andrews. In 1709 he was appointed Physician in Ordinary to the Queen.

[1] The names of some of those present at this ball will be found in the *Wentworth Papers*, p. 296.

[2] The reference is almost certainly to Henry Killigrew, a lieutenant-colonel of the dragoons, who has a part to play in Swift's broadside *A Hue and Cry after Dismal*.

B.M. Add. MS. 39839

Swift to Miss Esther Vanhomrigh

Windsor-Castle. Aug. 15. 1712

I thought to have written to little Misessy by the Colonell,[1] but at last I did not approve of him for a Messenger. Mʳ Ford[2] began your Health last night under the name of the Jilt, for which I desire You to reproach him. I do neither study nor exercise so much here as I did in Town. The Colonell will intercept all the News I have to tell you, of my fine Snuff box, and my being at a Ball, and losing my Money at Ombre with the Duke and Dutchess of Shrewsbury.[3] I cannot imagine how you pass your time in our Absence, unless by lying a Bed till twelve, and then having Your Followers about You till Dinner. We have Dispatches to day from Lord Bolingbroke,[4] all is admirably well, and a Cessation of Arms will be declared with France in London on Tuesday next. I dined with the Duke of Shrewsbury to day, and sate an Hour by Mʳˢ Warburton[5] teaching her when she playd wrong at Ombre, and I cannot see her Defects. Either my Eyes fail me, or they are partiall. But Mʳˢ Touchet[6] is an ugly awkward Slutt. What do you do all the Afternoon? How came you to make it a Secret to me, that you all design to come for 3 or 4 days. five Pounds will maintain you and pay for your Coach backwards and forwards. I suppose the Captain will go down with you now, for want of better Company. I will steal to Town one of these Days and catch You napping. I desire you and Moll will walk as often as You can in the Park, and do not sitt moping at home, You that can neither work nor read nor play, nor care for company. I long to drink a dish of Coffee in the Sluttery,

---

[1] It is to Bartholomew that Swift refers in this letter under the titles of Colonel and Captain. So far as is known he was never in the army. He was for a time at Christ Church, Oxford. He seems to have accompanied Swift to Windsor and stayed with him for a few days.

[2] On 1 July 1712 Swift told Stella that, 'I have made Ford Gazetter, and got 200¹¹ a year settled on the Employmt'.

[3] See the previous letter.

[4] See p. 305, n. 2.

[5] A maid of honour to the Queen. Apparently there was a design to marry her 'to one of a great estate and a great Whig' (*Wentworth Papers*, p. 244).

[6] Miss Touchet appears to have been a member of the Duchess of Shrewsbury's household. She may have been a daughter of Mervyn Touchet, fourth Earl of Castlehaven.

and hear you dun me for Secrets, and—drink your Coffee—Why don't you drink your Coffee. My humble Service to your Mother, and Moll, and the Collonel | adieu

Address: To Mrs Esther Van-Homrigh Junior | att her Lodgings over against | Park-Place in St James's Street | London.
Endorsed: 2nd
Postmark: Windsor, AU

B.M. Add. MS. 39839

Miss Esther Vanhomrigh to Swift

London, Sept. ye 1st: 1712[1]

Had I a Correspondant in China I might have had an answer by this time[2] I never could think till now that London was so far off in your thoughts and that 20 miles were by your computation equall to some thousands—I thought it a piece of Charity to undeceive you in this point and so lett you know if you'l give your self the trouble to write I may probably receive you[r] letter in a day. t'was that made me venture to take pen in hand the 3^d time sure you'l nott let it be to no purpose, you must needs be extreamly happy where you are to forgett your absent friends and I believe you have formed a new system and think there is no more of this world passing your sensible Horizon. if this be your notion I must excuse you if not you can plead no other excuse, and if it be so I must reckon my self of another world butt I shall have much a do to be persuaded till you send me some convincing arguments of it, dont dally in a thing of this consequence but demonstrate that tis possible to keep up a correspondance between Friends thô in different worlds and assure one another as I do you that I am, | Your most obed^t and most humble Servant | E VanHomrigh[3]

Endorsed: 1st

[1] Vanessa's letters to Swift, as preserved to us, were 'foul copies', with frequent scorings and deletions. Punctuation is little in evidence. It has been supplied with reserve, and only where necessary to clarify her meaning.
[2] On the evidence of the preceding letter and the two which follow it can be concluded that the suggestion of a visit to Windsor by the Vanhomrighs was an invention on Swift's part. Vanessa, doubtless, caught at it. Swift, realizing the dangerous inconvenience for himself, refrained from a reply.
[3] This appears to be the only autograph signature of Vanessa now remaining, except that in her will. In the Swift-Vanessa correspondence the name is written

B.M. Add. MS. 39839

Miss Esther Vanhomrigh to Swift

London, Sept: ye 2ᵈ 1712

Mʳ Lewis tells me you have made a solemn resolution to leave Windsor the moment we come there. tis a noble Res: pray keep it, now that I may be now ways accessory to your breaking it I design to send Mʳ Lewis word to a minnute when we shall leave London that he may tell you. and might I advise you it shoud be to sett out from Windsor just at the same ti[me]¹ that we leave London and if there be a by way you had better take it for I very much apprehend that seeing us will make you break through all, at least I am sure it woud make you heartily repent and I woud not for the world could I avoid it give you any uneasiness upon this score because I must infallibly upon an other. for when Mʳ Lewis told me what you had don (which I must needs say was not in so soft a manner as he ought both out of friendship to you and compassion to me) I immediately swore that to be revenged of you I woud stay at Windsor as long as Mʳˢ H—l² did and if that was not long enough to tease you I woud follow her to Hampton Court and then I shoud see which would give you most vexation seeing me but some times or not seeing her at all, besides Mʳ Lewis has promised me to intercept all your letters to her and hers to you. at least he says I shall read them en passant and for sealing them again let him look to that. I think your ruin is ample contrived for which dont blame me but your self for twas your rashness prompted to this malice which I shoud never else have thought of

Endorsed: 2ᵈ

in a dozen different ways. The practice of writing it as one word developed early. Orrery (*Remarks*, 1752, p. 105) tells us that the name was pronounced 'Vannummery'.

¹ Paper injured.
² This would be Alice Hill, younger sister of Abigail Hill. As a woman of the royal Bedchamber she would be in attendance at Windsor. Previous printed versions have 'Mrs. H—e'.

B.M. Add. MS. 39839

Swift to Miss Esther Vanhomrigh

Windsor Castle. Sep^tr 3. 1712

I send this Haunch of Venison to Your Mother, and to you, and this letter, to You, not your Mother; I had your last, and your Bill, and know your Reasons—. I have ordered Barber to send you the Overplus sealed up.[1] I am full of Business and ill Humor.[2] Some End or other shall be soon put to both . . . I thought You would have been here yesterday. Is your Journy hither quite off. I hope Moll is recovered of her Illness and then You may come. Have you scaped your share in this new Feaver:[3] I have hitherto; thô of late I am not very well in my Head. You railly very well;[4] Mr Lewis allows you to do so. I read your Letter to him. I have not time to answer you. The Coach and Venison being just ready to go. Pray eat half an Ounce at least of this Venison. and present my humble Service to your Mother, Moll, and the Colonell. I had his Letter, and will talk to him about it when he comes . . . This Letter I doubt will smell of Venison, I wish the Hang-dog Coachman may not spoil the Haunch in the Carriage | Je suis à vous &c

Address: To Mrs Esther Van-homrigh the | younger, at her Lodgings over
     against | Park-place in St James's Street
          Carriage paid   London
Endorsed: 3rd

---

[1] Had Vanessa enclosed a money bill in one of her letters? John Barber, Swift's lifelong friend, was often used by him in various transactions. Barber, frequently mentioned in the *Journal*, became Printer to the City of London in 1710 (Nichols, *Lit. Anec.* iii. 571 n.). He was elected a city alderman in 1722; and Lord Mayor of London in 1732-3. See Plomer's *Dictionary of Booksellers and Printers, 1668-1725.*

[2] Swift was occupied with the composition of the *Four Last Years of the Queen*; and the vacant deaneries, for one of which he hoped, weighed on his mind.

[3] On 7 Aug. 1712 Swift informed Stella: 'We have a Feaver both here and at Windsor, which hardly any body misses, but it lasts not above 3 or 4 days, and kills nobody. The Qu— had 40 Servants down of it at once' (*Journal*, p. 553).

[4] Cf.   She railly'd well, he always knew,
          Her Manner now was something new.
                    Cadenus and Vanessa, ll. 660-1.

The Countess of Orkney and Miss Ramsay
to Swift

Cleefden¹ monday [15 September, 1712]
I have had great satisfaction in the favour of yʳ letter, tho' dis-
apointed, since not occasion'd by yʳself,² when one is too quick, mis-
judgeing commonly follows, att first I fear'd Mʳ Collier³ was taken
with a fit of an appoplexey, the next line I read, I wished he had one
if I did not apprehend by yʳ knowing me but a little that I might grow
troublesome, where I distinguished, you should not want any con-
veniency to bring you hither to Mʳˢ Ramsay⁴ & I, who are both,
without compliment truely mortified, intending ever to be sir, yʳ
sincere | humble servants | E: Orkney | Eliz: Ramsay we designe to
be att windsor
a wenesday, where I hope
you will meet⁵ me in the
drawing room to tell me when
you can dine with us

Endorsed by Swift: Lady Orkeney | 1712—I suppose *and* Countess Orkny

¹ Cliefden, or Cliveden, near Taplow. The original house was built by George
Villiers, Duke of Buckingham. See Lipscomb's *Buckingham*, iii. 296–7.
² Writing on 18 Sept. Swift tells Stella: 'Lady Orkney the late King's Mistress,
who lives at a fine place 5 miles from here called Cliffden, and I are grown
mighty Acquaintance' (*Journal*, p. 557). Elizabeth Villiers, 1657?–1733,
daughter of Sir Edward Villiers, Knight Marischal of England, accompanied
Princess Mary to Holland, and became mistress of the Prince of Orange. As
William III he granted her a large estate in Ireland; but cast her off in 1694.
In the following year she married Lord George Hamilton, who in 1696 was
created Earl of Orkney in the peerage of Scotland. For a character of Lady
Orkney from Swift's hand see *Bath MSS*. i. 226.
³ Presumably the Collier mentioned as his host by Swift when writing to
Ambrose Philips, 20 Oct. 1708.
⁴ On 30 Dec. 1712 Swift refers to 'one Mrs. Ramsay . . . an old lady of about
55 that we are all very fond of' (*Journal*, p. 590). From Sir Thomas Hanmer's
Correspondence, 1838, she appears also, at one time, to have lived with his wife,
the Duchess of Grafton.
⁵ Ball adds 'with' after 'meet'. The word is not in the original.

The Countess of Orkney to Swift

monday morning [22 September, 1712]

I am sure you are very ill-natier'd, (I would not a bein so cross to you), to have known Mr Lewes and me so long, and not a made us acquaited[1] sooner, when you know too, that I have bein in search of a reasonable conversation[2] I have no way to excuses you, but doubting his to be so agreeable, att a secound meeting, which I desire you will make when tis most convenient to both, itt is not from custome I say, I am extremly sir | your humble | servant | E: Orkney

when you read this
I fancy you will think
what dos she writ
to me, I hate a letter
as much as my lord
Treasurer dos, a petition

Endorsed by Swift: Countess of Orkeney | 1712 (I believe)

B.M. Add. MS. 39839

Swift to Miss Esther Vanhomrigh

[28 September 1712][3]

I did not forget the Coffee; for I thought you should not be robbed of it. John does not go to Oxford, so I send back the Book as you desire. I would not see you for a thousand Pounds if I could; but I am now in my Night gown writing a dozen Letters, and packing up Papers.—Why then you should not have come;[4] and I knew

[1] *Sic.*
[2] Lady Orkney had doubtless come to Windsor as she intended, and been introduced to Erasmus Lewis by Swift.
[3] In a note on this letter (i. 344) Ball, dating it 8 Sept., which was not a Sunday, but a Monday, concludes that Vanessa had come to Windsor, and that Swift, to escape the acquaintances by whom he was surrounded, had consented to go with her to Oxford. But, as Freeman (*Correspondence of Swift and Vanessa*, p. 77) observes, the more natural interpretation of the letter is that he is sending a book to London by her messenger which he would have sent to Oxford if John had been going there.
[4] To Windsor.

that as well as you. My Service to Molkin. I doubt you do wrong to go to Oxford, but now that is past, since you cannot be in London to night, and if I do not inquire for Acquaintance but let somebody in the Inn go about with you among the Colledges, perhaps you will not be known, adieu

Sunday nine.	John presents his
yr fellow has been	humble Service to you both
long coming.	

Address: To Missessy
Endorsed: 7th[1]

Faulkner 1762

Swift to Archbishop King

London, October 21, 1712

My Lord,

Since I had the Honour of your Grace's Letter of *July* 29, which found me at *Windsor*, I have been extremely out of Order with a Giddiness in my Head, which pursued me until very lately, that by an uneasy Course of Physic, I hope, I have in some Sort overcome it.[2]

We are now in very near Expectation of a Peace; and your Grace, I hope, will believe it as good a one as the Circumstances of Things would allow. I confess I agree with your Grace, that the great Difficulty was about the Danger of *France* and *Spain* being united under one King. To my Knowledge all possible Means have been taken to secure that Matter; and yet, after all, the weakest Side will be there. Renunciations by *France* havel very justly, so little Credit, that I do not wonder so little Weight is aid on them. But, *Spain*, we are sure, will, for their own Sakes, enter into all Securities to prevent that Union; and all the Allies must be Guarantees. If you still object, that some Danger still remains, what is to be done? Your Grace is altogether misinformed, if you think that this is at all the

---

[1] The endorsement shows that three of Swift's letters are missing between this and the letter of 3 Sept. Probably some letters from Vanessa had also intervened, to one of which this is an answer.

[2] Swift, writing to Stella 9 Oct. 1712, tells her that he left Windsor 'these ten days, and am deep in Pills with Assa Fetida, and a Steel bitter drink'. He was suffering again from one of his recurrent fits of dizziness.

Difficulty, which so long made the *Dutch* untractable. It was nothing less: Neither have they once mentioned during all the negociations at *Utrecht*, one Syllable of getting *Spain* out of the *Bourbon* Family, or into that of *Austria*, as the chief Men have assured me not three Days ago. *Buys* offered last Winter, to ease us immediately of the Trouble we were in by Lord *Nottingham*'s Vote, if we would consent to let them share with us in the Advantages we had stipulated with *France*, which Advantages however, did by no Means clash with *Holland*, and were only conditional if Peace should ensue. But, my Lord, we know further, that the *Dutch* made Offers to treat with *France*, before we received any from thence; and were refused, upon the ill Usage they gave Mr. *Torcy* at the *Hague*, and the *Abbé de Polignac* afterward at *Gertruydenberg*:[1] and, we know that *Torcy* would have been forced to apply to them again, if, after several Refusals, we had not hearkened to their Overtures. What I tell your Grace is infallibly true; and Care shall be taken very soon to satisfy the World in this, and many other Particulars at large, which ought to be known. For, the Kingdom is very much in the Dark, after all the Pains hitherto taken to inform it.[2] Your Grace's Conjectures are very right, that a General Peace would not be for our Interest, if we had made ours with *France*. And, I remember a certain great Man used to say two Months ago, *Fight on, fight on, my merry Men all.* I believe likewise that such a Peace would have happened, if the *Dutch* had not lately been more compliant; upon which our Ministers told those of *France*, that since the States were disposed to submit to the Queen, her Majesty must enter into their Interests: And I believe they have as good Conditions as we ever intended they should. *Tournay*, I hope, will be yielded to them: And *Lille* we never designed they should have. The Emperor will be used as he deserves; and having paid nothing for the War, shall get nothing by the Peace. We are most concerned (next to our regard to *Holland*) for *Savoy*, and *France* for *Bavaria*. I believe we shall make them both Kings, by the help of *Sardinia* and *Sicily*. But I know not how Plans may alter every Day. The Queen's whole Design, as your

---

[1] The Marquis de Torcy and Cardinal de Polignac represented France at the Utrecht Congress which dragged on during the autumn of 1712 and spring of 1713. The Treaty was finally signed 31 Mar., O.S., and 11 Apr., N.S. See Trevelyan, *England under Queen Anne*, iii. 219–26.

[2] These subjects are discussed at length by Swift in the *Four Last Years of the Queen*.

Grace conjectureth, is to act the Part of a Mediator, and our Advantages, too many to insert here, must be owned very great.

As for an Academy to correct and settle our Language; Lord Treasurer talketh of it often very warmly; but, I doubt, is yet too busy until the Peace be over. He goes down to *Windsor* on *Friday*, to be chosen of the Garter, with five more Lords.

I know nothing of Promises of any Thing intended for myself; but, I thank God, I am not very warm in my Expectations, and know Courts too well to be surprised at Disappointments; which, however, I should have no great Reason to Fear, if I gave my Thoughts any Trouble that Way, which, without Affectation, I do not; although I cannot expect to be believed when I say so.   I am, &c.

4804

The Duchess of Ormonde to Swift

3 Nov. [1712][1]

D[r]

I hope yr servant has told you I sent to beg the favour of you to come hither to night, but since you cou'd not conveniently, I hope you won't deny me the satisfaction of seeing you, to morrow morning My Ld joyns with me in that request & will see no company, but you, I hope you'l come before ten aclock, because he is to go at that hour to Windsor I beg yr pardon for sending so early, as I have ordered 'em to carry this, but the fear of yr being gon abroad if they went latter, occasioned that trouble given you by S[r] | Yr most sincere & | most faithfull humble | Servant | M Ormonde

Nov: the 3[d]
    11 a clock at night

Endorsed by Swift: Dutchess Orm | Nov[r] 3[d] 1713

[1] There can be little doubt but that the year date affixed to this letter was a slip of the pen. As Ball has pointed out, vi. 233, a passage in the *Journal*, 30 Oct. 1712, makes it probable that it was written on the return of the Duke of Ormonde from his command in Flanders, which took place on 3 Nov. Four days earlier, 30 Oct., Swift wrote: 'The Duchess of Ormond found me out to-day, and made me dine with her. . . . The Duke of Ormond will not be over these three or four days. I design to make him join with me in settling all right among our people. I have ordered the duchess to let me have an hour with the duke at his first coming, to give him a true state of persons and things.'

Archbishop King to Swift

Dublin Novem^{br} 4. 1712

Revd S^r

I have read yours of Octo^{br} 21 6 or 7 times and confess that nothing has happened to me this many years, that gave me so great mortification. I am unwilling, nay I cannot for my life bring myself to think that our affairs are in so ill a posture as you represent them.

I do not wonder that the French were more willing to treat with England than Holland, for it has been observed that Holland has commonly made their party good with them in treatys, whereas England is famous for being bubbled in all transactions with them from the time of Pharamond to the treaty of Ryswick inclusive. I hope this will be an instance to the contrary.

I think the views of the Confederates and France as to a peace are very different. The confederates desire a peace that they may disband their armys and save the charges of their pay, but France desires it in order to recruit theirs by those soldiers of fortune that the confederates disband, and if care be not taken they will effectually so do. It is plain to any that will consider the state of Europe for the last age, that the great Source of all the wars and miseries that have effected it have had their rise from the great standing army kept by France; and whilst he has in pay about 400000 men, no leagues, no promises, no oaths can bind him, nor Frontiers, Garrisons or Guarantees secure his neighbours from him; for before they can raise or discipline their armies he has done his work and some of the confederates against him will always be bought off by some particular advantages granted to them to sell all the rest, and let him keep what he has got, and perhaps restore what by any has been got from him. And therefore if no care be taken in the treaty to confine him to certain Conditions, to a certain number of ships and troops, it seems that all treaties, articles, leagues and conditions of peace entered in by him are mere delusions designed by him to put those with whom he treats off their guard, and then to surprise them, which has actually been the case in all the peaces this French King ever entered into: and rest satisfied that it will of this, if not under these obligations.

I am told there is a book writ by your friend Sir William Temple called Memoirs that talks at this rate, and gives an account of the peace of Nimeguen, which they say was treated the same way, and the barrier articles and every thing was in it as in this, and the men that managed it were of the same principles; though I am not fond of reading politic books, I have a great mind to buy this, if you assure me that it is worth my while.

I was yesterday on horseback to take the air: the horse fell and has much bruised my foot. I am sorry to hear of your indisposition. I wish you were settled and a little more your own man. Pray lay aside your modesty and push it. I do not encourage ambition, but think it very lawful for a man to endeavour by lawfull means to settle himself in a station wherein he may be easy to himself, and useful to the public; pray make hay whilst the sun shines—*post est occasio salva*—and be sure you do not call these quotations pedantry for they are grave wise sentences and nobody can say the thing better.

You may pass over the other parts of this letter as you please, but pray read the last twice. I heartily recommend yrs &c.

W. D.

Dr Swift

Deane Swift 1765

Swift to Miss Alice Hill

[November,] 1712[1]

Madam,

I was commanded some days ago to do what I had long a mind to, but avoided because I would not offend your prudence, or strain your eyes.[2] But my Lord Masham assures me there is no danger of either; and that you have courage enough to read a letter, though it comes from a man, provided it be one of no consequence, which his Lordship would insinuate to be my case; but I hope you will not affront me so highly as to understand it so. There is not a grain of news in this town, or five miles about it, worth sending you; and what we receive from Windsor is full as insignificant, except the accounts of the Queen's health, and your housekeeping. We are

---

[1] The references in this letter (which has by editors prior to Ball been dated May or July 1712) to the band-box plot and to Lady Masham show that it must have been written early in November.

[2] The Court had not yet left Windsor, and Miss Alice Hill was carrying out her own duties and three of her sister, Lady Masham, who at the time was unable to be in attendance.

assured that you keep a constant table, and that your guests leave
you with full stomachs and full pockets: That Dr. Arbuthnot sometimes leaves his beloved green cloth, to come and receive your
chidings, and pick up your money. We intend shortly to represent
your case to my Lord Treasurer, as what deserves commiseration;
but we hope the matter is already settled between his Lordship and
you, and that you are instructed to be thus magnificent, in order to
carry on the cause. We reckon his Lordship's life is now secure, since
a combination of band-boxes and ink-horns, the engines of late
times, were employed in vain to destroy him.¹ He will do me the
justice to tell you, that I never fail of toasting you under the name
of the Governess of Dunkirk, and that you have the honour to be
very particularly in my good graces. My Lady Masham still continues in a doubtful state of neither up nor down; and one of her
servants told mine, that they did not expect she would cry out this
fortnight.² I saw yesterday our brother Hill,³ who promises to be
more thrifty of his health, and seems to have a pretty good stock of it.
I hope you receive no visits from the head-ache and the spleen:
And one who knows your constitution very well, advises you, by all
means, against sitting in the dusk at your window, or on the ground,
leaning on your hand, or at see-saw in your chair. I am, | Madam,
&c.

4804
The Countess of Orkney to Swift

London November ye 21 1712

this key will open treasures, but vain in me to know them, yʳ
convenience is my satisfaction, if I can or may read what will be in
this table,⁴ itt ought & shall be my happyness, you must discerne

¹ For Swift's account of this affair see the *Journal*, 15 Nov. 1712. The story
of the band-box plot was related at length in the Tory *Post Boy*, 11–13 Nov.
On 4 Nov. Oxford received a box containing two pistols, with 'artificial barrels',
of 'two large ink-horns charged with powder and ball'. Swift, however, succeeded in opening the box without mishap. The Whig *Flying-Post* ridiculed
the whole affair. See also Boyer's *Political State of Great Britain*, iv. 370–4.
² Lady Masham was expecting to lie in.
³ Hill was Governor of Dunkirk, but preferred to discharge his duties at a
distance.
⁴ On 30 Oct. 1712 Swift wrote to Stella: 'Lady Orkney is making me a

this comes from the most intrested joyner that ever made a thing of this natuer peruse narrowly, and what faults you find, they shall be mended in every particular, to the utmost capacity of, Sir yr obliged | humble servant,

E: Orkney.

Endorsed by Swift: Countess of Orkney's Letter | and | Nov^{br} 21. 1712
  Sent with a Present | of a Writing Table, |
  Seal, Paper, Wax &c

Deane Swift 1765

Swift to the Countess of Orkney

November 21, 1712.

Madam,

When, upon parting with your Ladyship, you were pleased to tell me I should find your present at home, natural justice prompted me to resolve, that the first use I made of it should be in paying acknowledgments to my benefactor. But, when I opened the writing-table, which I must now call mine, I found you had neither sent pens, ink, nor paper, sufficient for such an undertaking. But I ought to tell your Ladyship in order, that I first got there a much more valuable thing: And I cannot do greater honour to my scrutoire, than to assure your Ladyship that your letter is the first thing I have put in it, and shall be the last I will ever take out. I must tell your Ladyship, that I am this moment under a very great concern. I was fully convinced that I should write with a new spirit, by the influence of the materials you sent me; but it is quite otherwise: I have not a grain of invention, whether out of the confusion which attends us when we strive too much to acquit ourselves, or whether your pens and ink are sullen, and think themselves disgraced, since they have changed their owner. I heartily thank your Ladyship, for making me a present that looks like a sort of establishment. I plainly see, by the contrivance, that if you were first Minister, it would have been a cathedral. As it is, you have more contributed towards fixing me, than all the Ministry together; for it is difficult to travel with this equipage, and it will be impossible to travel or live without it. You have an undoubted title to whatever papers this table shall ever

writing table of her own contrivance, and a bed night-gown. She is perfectly kind, like a mother.'

contain, (except your letter) and I desire you will please to have another key made for it; that when the Court shall think fit to give me a room worth putting it into, your Ladyship may come and search it whenever you please.

I beg your Ladyship to join in laughing with me, at my unreasonable vanity, when I wished that the motto written about the wax was a description of yourself. But, if I am disappointed in that, your Ladyship will be so in all the rest; even this ink will never be able to convey your Ladyship's note as it ought. The paper will contain no wonders, but when it mentions you; neither is the seal any otherwise an emblem of my life, than by the deep impression your Ladyship has made, which nothing but my death can wear out. By the inscription about the pens, I fear there is some mistake; and that your Ladyship did not design them for me. However, I will keep them until you can find the person you intended should have them, and who will be able to dispose of them according to your predictions. I cannot find that the workman you employed and directed, has made the least mistake: But there are four implements wanting. The first two I shall not name, because an odd superstition forbids us to accept them from our friends;[1] the third is a spunge, which the people long have given so ill a reputation to, that I vow it shall be no gift of your Ladyship: The last is a flat ivory instrument, used in folding up letters, which I insist you must provide.

See, Madam, the first fruits this unlucky present of yours has produced. It is but giving a fiddle to a scraper, or a pestle and mortar to an apothecary, or a Tory pamphlet to Mrs. Ramsay.[2] Nothing is so great a discouragement to generous persons as the fear of being worried by acknowledgments. Besides, your Ladyship is an unsufferable kind of giver, making every present fifty times the value, by the circumstances and manner. And I know people in the world, who would not oblige me so much, at the cost of 1000 *l.* as you have done at that of 20 *l.* which, I must needs tell you, is an unconscionable way of dealing, and whereof, I believe nobody alive is so guilty as yourself. In short, you deceive my eyes, and corrupt my judgment; nor am I sure of anything, but that of being, *&c.*

[1] A knife and scissors.
[2] See p. 312, n. 4.

4804

The Countess of Orkney to Swift

No. 22. 1712[1]

You are extremly obliging to writ how well you take my whim, in telling my true thoughts of your mind, for I was ashamed when I reflected & hoped I should see you soon after expresing the value I have of you in an uncommon way,[2] but this I writ with assurance that I am very sincerely S[r] yr obliged humble servant,

E. Orkney.

Address: For Dr. Swift.
Endorsed by Swift: Countess of Orkney | Nov[br] 22[d] 1712

H.M.C. Report 11

Swift to the Earl of Dartmouth

Saturday noon [13 December 1712]

My Lord,[3]

I am writing almost in the dark in my Lady Duchess of Hamilton's bedchamber.[4] Her Grace is on one side, and My Lady Oglethorpe on the other.[5] The latter commands me to write to your Lordship, and to entreat that you would hasten her daughter's pass, the maid being to go away at two o'clock to-day, and her daughter to-morrow with the Duchess of Shrewsbury.[6] Therefore I desire to use my

---

[1] The date is in Swift's hand. Ball gives the date as 'Saturday, *November* 23'.
[2] On Feb. 8 [?9] 1712-13 Swift wrote to tell Stella: 'Ldy Orkney has given me her Picture a very fine Originall of Sr Godfrey Knellers it is now a mending. He has favored her squint admirably, & you know I love a Cast in the Eye.'
[3] See p. 190, n. 2.
[4] Writing to Stella on the same day, Swift says: 'I must see my Brother Ormd at 11, & then the Duchess of Hamilton, with whom I doubt I am in disgrace, not having seen her these ten days.' After the death of her husband Swift was a constant visitor in his efforts to console her.
[5] Lady Oglethorpe is mentioned several times in the *Journal*. She was a daughter of Richard Wall of Rogane, Tipperary. She married Brig.-Gen. Sir Theophilus Oglethorpe, bore him seven children, and died in 1732. One of her children was James Edward Oglethorpe, the colonist of Georgia, and friend of Dr. Johnson.
[6] Writing to Stella during the morning of 13 Dec. 1712 Swift says, 'D Shrewsbury goes in a day or 2 for France, perhaps to day.' This fixes the date of the letter.

little credit with your Lordship to do what my Lady Oglethorpe
desires, that the pass may be signed as soon as possible, by which I
find she means by two o'clock to-day. I am with the greatest respect,
&c. | J. Swift.

4804

William Harrison to Swift

Utrecht ye 16ᵗʰ Decʳ 1712

Your thanks of the 25th. of Novᵇʳ., Sir,[1] come before their time,
the condition of the obligation being, that you should receive 12
shirts, which number shall be completed by the first proper occasion.
Your Kind letter however is extremely seasonable, and (next to a
Note from the Treasury) has proved the most vivifying cordial in
the world; if you please to send me now & then as much of the same
as will lye upon the top of your pen, I shall be content to take sheets
for shirts to the end of the chapter.

Since you are so good as to enter into my affairs, I shall trouble
you with a detail of them, as well as of my Conduct since I left
England, which, in my opinion, you have a right to inspect, &
approve or condemn as you think fit. During my State of Probation
with the Earl of Str— it was my endeavour to recommend myself to
his Exʸ. rather by fidelity, silence, & an entire submission, than by
an affectation to shine in his service, & whatever difficulties, whatever
discouragements fell in my way, I think it appears that they were
surmounted in the end; & my advancement followed upon it,
sooner than I expected, another would say, much sooner than I deserved, which I should easily agree to, were it not, that I flatter my
self there is some merit in the behaviour I kept when the hopes and

[1] William Harrison, educated at Winchester and New College, Oxford,
became a fellow of his college in 1706. His talents were not remarkable, but he
won the regard of Addison, Swift, and of other men of letters. St. John, through
the influence of Swift, gave him, in May 1711, the appointment of secretary to
Lord Raby, Ambassador Extraordinary to The Hague (Bolingbroke, *Letters*,
1798, i. 77, 90, 94, 95). He returned to England with the Barrier Treaty in
Jan. 1713, and died on the following 14 Feb. 'No loss', wrote Swift to Stella
on the same day, 'ever grieved me so much.'

temptation of being preferd glitterd in my eyes. All the world knows upon what foot Mr. Watkins thought himself with my Lord Strafford,[1] & though all the world does not know what Ime going to tell you, yet Mr. Watkins does on one hand, & my Lord Strafford on the other, that all the credit I had with either, was heartily & without reserve, employ'd to make matters easy, & to cultivate in my humble station, that good understanding, which our Court desired should be between them. I had my reasons for this; & such perhaps as flowed from an inclination to promote my own interest. I knew as well as any man living almost, how much Mr. Watkins was valued by my Ld Bolingbroke & others; I foresaw the danger of standing in Competition with him, if that case should happen; &, to tell you the truth, I did not think my self ripe in regard of interest at home, or of any service I could pretend to have done abroad, to succeed Mr. Watkins in so good an Employment. Above all, I protest to you Sir, that if I know my own heart, I am capable of suffering the utmost extremities rather than violate the infinite duty & Gratitude I owe My Lord B— by doing an ill office to a Person honoured with such particular marks of his Lordship's esteem. I might add to this that I really lovd M^r· Watkins, & I beg you, Sir, to urge him to the proof, whether my whole behaviour was not such as might justifye the warmest professions I can make of that kind. After all this how comes it that he, either in raillery or good earnest, accuses me of having any resentment against him? By word of mouth when he left us, by letters so long as he allowd me to correspond with him, and by all the people that ever went from Utrecht to Flanders, have I importund him for the continuance of his friendship, perhaps, even in his absence (if he pleases to reflect) given him a very essential proof of mine. If any body has thought it worth their while to sow division between us, I wish he thought it worth his to let me into the secret; & nothing, he may be sure, shall be wanting on my side to defeat a stratagem, which, for aught I know, may end in the starving of his

[1] Lady Strafford, writing from London to her husband, shortly before Harrison's death, refers to the young man as 'your favourite' (*Wentworth Papers*, p. 319), whereas 'Mr. Watkins' was not altogether in his good books (op. cit., p. 187). He was, however, a person of ability. Educated at Christ Church, Oxford, he proceeded to his B.A. degree in 1688 and his M.A. degree in 1691. He was secretary to the Duke of Ormonde, and in Jan. 1712 he was appointed secretary to the English representatives at the Utrecht Conference. He died in Mar. 1727, aged sixty-one. See further Aitken's note, *Life and Works of Arbuthnot*, p. 96.

humble servant. Which leads me naturally to the 2ᵈ thing proposd
to be spoken to in my text, namely, my circumstances; for between
you & me, Sir, I apprehend that the Treasury will issue out no
money on my account, till they know what is due on that of Mʳ·
Watkins; & if he has any pretensions I have none that I know of but
what are as precarious to me, as a stiver I gave away but now to a
beggar, was to him. Is it possible that Mʳ W. can demand the pay
of a commission which is, by the Queen her self, actually superseded,
during his absence from his Post? or is it not as plainly said in mine
that I am Her Majesty's Secretary during such his absence, as in his
that he was so, whilst he resided here? If I must be crushed, Sir, for
god's sake let some reason be alledged for it; or else an ingenuous
confession made, that, stat pro ratione voluntas. If you can fix
Mʳ· W. to any final determination on this subject, you will do me a
singular service, & I shall take my measures accordingly. Though I
know yʳ· power I cannot help distrusting it on this occasion. Before
I conclude, give me leave to put you in mind of beating my thanks
into my Lord Bolingbrokes ears, for his late generosity, to the end
that his Ldship may be wearied out of the evil habit he has got, of
heaping more obligations & goodness on those he is pleasd to favour,
than their shoulders are able to bear. For my own part, I have so
often thankd his Ldship, that I have now no more ways left to turn
my thoughts; & beg if you have any right good compliments, neat
& fine by you, that you will advance the necessary, and place them,
with the other helps you have given me, to my account; which I
question not but I shall be able to acknowledge at one and the same
time, ad Græcas Calendas.

In the mean time, I shall do my best to give you just such hints as
you desire, by the next post; though I cant but think there are some
letters in the office, which would serve your turn a good deal better
than anything I can tell you about the people at the Hague. Yr access
there abundantly prevents my attempting to write you any news
from hence; & I assure you, Sir, you can write me none from
England (however uneasy my circumstances are) which will be so
agreeable to me as that of yr long expected advancement. It grieves
me to the soul that a Person, who has been so instrumental to the
raising of me from obscurity & distress, should not be yet set above
the power of fortune & the malice of those enemies your real merit
has created. I beg, Dear Sir, the continuance of yr kind care &
inspection over me, & that you would in all respects, command,

reprove, or instruct me, as a father, for I protest to you, Sir, I do, & ever shall, honour & regard you with the affection of a Son.[1]

Endorsed by Swift: Th. Harrison Esqr | Sec^rty of the Ambassy. | since dead —the same year | Utrecht Decr 16. 1712

Deane Swift 1765

Swift to the Duchess of Ormonde

December 20, 1712.

Madam,

Any other person, of less refinement and prudence than myself, would be at a loss how to thank your Grace, upon the surprise of coming home last night, and finding two pictures where only one was demanded.[2] But I understood your Grace's malice, and do here affirm you to be the greatest prude upon earth. You will not so much as let your picture be alone in a room with a man, no not with a clergyman, and a clergyman of five-and-forty, and therefore resolved my Lord Duke should accompany it, and keep me in awe, that I might not presume to look too often upon it. For my own part, I begin already to repent that I ever begged your Grace's picture; and could almost find in my heart to send it you back: For, although it be the most beautiful sight I ever beheld, except the original, yet the veneration and respect it fills me with, will always make me think I am in your Grace's presence; will hinder me from saying and writing twenty idle things that used to divert me; will set me labouring upon majestic, sublime ideas, at which I have no manner of talent; and will make those who come to visit me, think I am grown, on the sudden, wonderful stately and reserved. But, in life we must take the evil with the good; and it is one comfort, that I know how to be revenged. For the sight of your Grace's resemblance will perpetually remind me of paying my duty to your person;

---

[1] Swift's list of letters for 1712 (Forster 508) shows that on a number of occasions in that year Swift wrote to Harrison while he was abroad.

[2] On the previous evening Swift wrote to Stella: 'the Dutchess of Ormd promised me her Picture, & coming home to night I found hers & the Dukes both in my Chamber, was not that a pretty civil surprise; yess & they are in fine gilded Frames too. I am writing a Letter to thank her, which I will send to morrow morning.'

which will give your Grace the torment, and me the felicity, of a more frequent attendance.

But, after all, to deal plainly with your Grace, your picture (and I must say the same of my Lord Duke's) will be of very little use, further than to let others see the honour you are pleased to do me. For all the accomplishments of your mind and person are so deeply printed in the heart, and represent you so lively to my imagination, that I should take it for a high affront, if you believed it in the power of colours to refresh my memory: Almost as high a one, as if your Grace should deny me the justice of being, with the most profound respect and gratitude, | Madam, | Your Grace's, *&c.*

Faulkner 1762
Swift to Archbishop King

London, Jan. 3, 1713.[1]

My Lord,

Since I had the Honour of your Grace's Letter,[2] we have had a dead Time of News and Politics, and I make a Conscience of writing to you without something that will recompence the Trouble of Reading. I cannot but grant that your Grace, who are at a Distance, and argues from your own Wisdom and general Observations and Reading, is likely to be more impartial than I, who, in spight of my Resolutions and Opinion to the Contrary, am forced to converse only with one Side of the World, which fasteneth Prejudice to me, notwithstanding all I can do to avoid them. Your Grace hath certainly hit upon the weak Side of our Peace, but I do not find you have prescribed any Remedies. For, that of limiting *France* to a certain Number of Ships and Troops was, I doubt, not to be compassed. While that mighty Kingdom remaineth under one Monarch, it will be always in some Degree formidable to its Neighbours. But we flatter ourselves it is likely to be less so than ever, by the Concurrence of many Circumstances too long to trouble you with. But, my Lord,

[1] Faulkner, printing this letter in 1762 dates it 'Jan. 3'. King's letter of 22 Jan. in reply refers to it as 'yours of the 8th inst.' Although the copy of the letter in King's correspondence is in part severely damaged the early portion is perfectly legible, and reads '8th'. The true date therefore remains in doubt; but the alternatives are not significant.

[2] King's letter of 4 Nov. 1712.

what is to be done? I will go so far with your Grace as to tell you, that some of our Friends are of Opinion with the other Party, that if this last Campaign had gone on with the Conjunction of the *British* Troops, *France* might have been in Danger of being driven to great Extremes. Yet, I confess to you, at the same Time, that if I had been first Minister, I should have advised the Queen to pursue her Measures towards a Peace.

Some Accidents and Occasions have put it in my Way to know every step of this Treaty better, I think, than any Man in *England*.[1] And I do assert to your Grace that if *France* had been closely pushed this Campaign, they would, upon our Refusal, have made Offers to *Holland*, which the Republic would certainly have accepted; and in that Case the Interest of *England* would have been wholely laid aside, as we saw it three Years ago at the *Hague* and *Gertruydenberg*. The Marshal *D'Uxilles*, and *Mesnager*, two of the *French* Plenipotentiaries, were wholely inclined to have begun by the *Dutch*; but the third, *Abbé de Polignac*, who hath most Credit with Monsieur *Torcy*, was for Beginning by *England*.

There was a great Faction in *France* by this Proceeding: and it was a meer personal Resentment, in the *French* King and Monsieur *Torcy*, against the States, which hindered them from sending the first Overture there. And, I believe your Grace will be convinced, by considering that the Demands of *Holland* might be much more easily satisfied than those of *Britain*. The States were very indifferent about the Article of *Spain* being in the *Bourbon* Family, as Monsieur *Buys*[2] publicly owned when he was here, and among others to myself. They valued not the Demolition of *Dunkirk*, the Frontier of *Portugal*, nor the Security of *Savoy*. They abhorred the Thoughts of our having *Gibraltar* and *Minorca*, nor cared what became of our Dominions in *North-America*. All they had at Heart was the Sovereignty of *Flanders*, under the Name of Barrier, and to stipulate what they could for the Emperor, to make him easy under their Encroachments. I can further assure your Grace, before any Proposals were sent here from *France*, and ever since, until within these

---

[1] The arguments advanced by Swift in this letter were borrowed from the material he was gathering for the compilation of his *History of the Four Last Years of the Queen*. The allusions to the work in the *Journal to Stella*, his relationship with the English ministers, and papers now available in the Public Record Office, which were used by Swift, testify to the truth of his claim to have used original documents. See *Prose Works*, ed. Davis, vii, Appendix C.

[2] See what Swift has to say about Buys in his letter to King of 8 Jan. 1711/12.

few Months, the *Dutch* have been endeavouring constantly by private
Intrigues with the Court, to undermine us, and put themselves at the
Head of a Treaty of Peace, which is a Truth which perhaps the
World may soon be informed in, with several others that are little
known. Besides, my Lord, I doubt, whether you have sufficiently
reflected on the Condition of this Kingdom, and the Possibility of
pursuing the War at that ruinous Rate. This Argument is not the
weaker for being often urged. Besides, *France* is likely to have a long
Minority; or, if not, perhaps to be engaged in a civil War. And I do
not find that in publick Affairs, human Wisdom is able to make
Provisions for Futurity, which are not liable to a Thousand Accidents. We have done all we can; and, for the rest, curent posteri.

Sir *William Temple*'s Memoirs,[1] which you mentioned, is his first
Part, and was published twenty Years ago; it is chiefly the Treaty
of *Nimeguen*, and was so well known, that I could hardly think your
Grace hath not seen it.

I am in some Doubt whether a Fall from a Horse be suitable to
the Dignity of an Archbishop. It is one of the chief Advantages in
a great Station that one is exempt from common Accidents of that
Kind. The late King indeed got a Fall; but, his Majesty was a Fox-
hunter. I question whether you can plead any Precedent to excuse
you; and therefore, I hope, you will commit no more such Errors:
And, in the mean Time, I heartily congratulate with your Grace that
I can rally you upon this Accident.

I am in some Fear that our Peace will hardly be concluded in
several Weeks, by Reason of a certain Incident[2] that could not be
foreseen; neither can I tell whether the Parliament will sit before the
Conclusion of the Peace, because, some Persons differ in their Politicks about the Matter. If others were no wiser than I, your Session
should not be deffered upon that Account. | I am, with the greatest
Respect, | Your Grace's | Most dutiful, | And humble Servant. | ——

[1] The volume of Temple's *Memoirs* referred to was published in 1692.
[2] The incident appears to have been the quarrel between the French plenipotentiary Mesnager and the Dutch plenipotentiary Rechteren. See *Prose
Works*, ed. Davis, vii. 154, 158, 159.

Swift to the Duke of Argyle

January 20, 1712-13.

My Lord,

I would myself have delivered the answer I sent yesterday to your Grace at court, by Dr. Arbuthnot, if I had not thought the right of complaining to be on my side: For, I think it was my due, that you should have immediately told me whatever you had heard amiss of my conduct to your Grace. When I had the honour to be first known to those in the ministry, I made it an express condition, that whoever did me ill offices, they should inform me of what was said, and hear my vindication; that I might not be mortified with countenances estranged of the sudden, and be at a loss for the cause.[1] And, I think, there is no person alive, whose favour or protection I would purchase at that expence. I could not speak to the disadvantage of your Grace without being ungrateful, (which is an ill word) since you were pleased, voluntarily, to make so many professions of favour to me for some years past; and your being a Duke and a General, would have swayed me not at all in my respect for your person, if I had not thought you to abound in qualities, which I wish were easier to be found in those of your rank. I have indeed sometimes heard what your Grace was told I reported; but as I am a stranger to coffee-houses, so it is a great deal below me to spread coffee-house reports. This accusation is a little the harder upon me, because I have always appeared fond of your Grace's character; and have, with great industry, related several of your generous actions, on purpose to remove the imputation of the only real fault (for I say nothing of common frailties) which I ever heard laid to your charge. I confess, I have often thought that Homer's description of Achilles bore some resemblance to your Grace, but I do not remember that ever I said so. At the same time, I think few men were ever born with nobler

---

[1] After an occasion when St. John appeared to be 'out of temper' with him Swift warned him 'never to appear cold' but to let him know it in 'plain words' (*Journal*, 3 Mar. 1711). The reason for this remonstrance addressed to Argyle seems to have been based on similar grounds, springing from the Duke's imperious nature. In a note on Macky's *Characters* Swift stigmatized him as an 'Ambitious, covetous, cunning Scot'; and elsewhere he speaks of his 'unquiet and ambitious spirit' (*Prose Works*, ed. Davis, viii. 115). The final break with Argyle followed the publication of *The Publick Spirit of the Whigs*.

qualities to fill and adorn every office of a subject, a friend and a protector, &c.

King's Letter-book

Archbishop King to Swift

Dublin January 22th 1712[1]

Revd S^r

I recd yours of the 8th[2] inst by last pacquets. I may tell you that I never could prevail with my self to confine my self to the conversation of any one party of men of any one sort, but have acquaintance of all, Papists, Protestants, Dissentors, Whiggs, Torys, Tradesmen, Gentlemen, even loose and wicked men as well as religious and devout provided that I am satisfied that their business is not to betray and do me mischief, and even then [I] have not always declined them, and I think my present station, not only Justifys me in this but obliges me to it, for the whole need not a Physician so much as the sick, and I thank God I have this comfort from it, and that many have been benefited by it and I never knew one was the worse. I know this is a great objection against me by some, but I am resolved never to remove it, I have been acquainted with a man many years and never can tax him with an ill Office, but [if] he differs from me in some opinions must I turn his Enemy on that account? This is to leave him in his errors, if they chance to be errors. No, surely to continue my friendship is in my Judgement the way to gain on him, and if not to reclaim him, yet to make him easy and moderate in his conversation, which is a great step gained, if a sett of men fall under the displeasure of the Government shall I immediately look on them as abandoned wretches, and avoid their conversation as infected? when then I must have no friends at all, for the Government changes perhaps in 3 or 4 Years and then those that I broke with are favourites, and men of the former sort brow-beaten. If a man therefore will follow this method he must have no friends at all in 10 or 12 years, these are measures I never followed, nor ever will with God's help. I will choose conversation for myself, and no man shall ever have it in his power to choose for me. If a man find it his interest

---

[1] The copy of this letter in King's correspondence is badly damaged. Ball's text is followed with such revision as is possible.

[2] For a note on this date see Swift's letter to King, 3, or 8, Jan. 1712/13.

to avoid me, I am not concerned, and that will allow him to come again. I receive him as if no such thing had happened, provided he has not bin guilty of treachery; [there]fore I dispense with a man to pursue an interest which I cannot serve as [well as the] person he applies to, so he only do[es] good to himself without doing mischief to others. I know all must not follow my rules, but I reckon it an unhappiness when they cannot, and perhaps that is your case.

As to the affair you write of in yours I conceive there are two ways of showing things, that is to say, they have a fair and plausible side generally and another that is not so popular, now in my opinion the great[est] care ought to be taken especially in publick businesses to put them in the most advantageous light and show that face of them that is most defensible. If a man have a good design to carry on, which must be secret in concealing it, he must advance by fair and specious colours that may both satisfy the world and if possible the true and real purposes. But I have no rule for those that design ill, but to lay aside their evil intention. Now I have observed of the French that they have the advantage of all Europe in this particular, for be their designs good or bad, they never want colours & Glosses to set them off, and thô they satisfy no body, yet they silence them and I find it true, what has often been said, one plausible reason is harder to be answered than ten reall ones. I would wish a little more dexterity this way in some of my friends than they have in my [opinion] shown hitherto, and that they would not show the ugly shocking face of things, and make the honourable and fair altogether a secret. Perhaps if it were proper I would give you a great many instances of this sort, that in my view of things might and ought to have been avoided. I and the world at a distance and in reality see only the outside of affairs, and when that is not lovely we are apt to conclude as the Poet doth in a contrary case *si quae latent pejore putant.* You say that I have *hit upon* one. I can by no means allow you that word, it looks as if there were something of chance in it, assure yourself that I believe there is hardly a man between Cape Clear and Rushpoint in the north, Papists or Protestants, but he has hit on this very thing: the former repeat it with triumph, and the latter with dread and amazement, they reckon their all depends on this point and the fear they are in distracts them in some degree, if there were not something of this nature they would never be guilty of such mad practices as I believe you have account of from hence.[1]

[1] Since the parliamentary session of 1711 political feeling in Ireland had con-

As to the minority of a King of France, I am mistaken if ever you see it, or if it happen, that it will be of long continuance. As to security of one Prince from encroachments of another, I know only two ways to obtain it effectually. One is to disenable him from hurting his neighbours, another to make it his interest not to do it, I wish somebody would as earnestly show the world that Europe on the peace will have either of those securities, it would be of great Service.

I remember formerly it has been a maxim to make peace with sword-hand, which the French King has always pursued with the exactest care and carried his point in every treaty by it. I find several here join with your friends in their opinion that if the French had been pushed last campaign, and we had redoubled our attempts against him, it would have got a better and [general] peace for all the confederates than we are like to have, and the nearer to [Paris] the Confederate armys had got, still the better. as to what you say of the Dutch tricking us, they say 'tis to be considered whether the Dutch or French are most in interest engaged to preserve the balance of power in Europe, and which have broken their faith and treatys oftenest and in prudence trusted them, but they pretend there neither was nor would be any danger, for it would have been in our power to turn short on them when we pleased, and if they began to falter. If the French had been soundly beaten, we might at any time [have] turned to them and they would have embraced us on any terms whatsoever, nor say they doth it appear that the demands of Holland were so easily satisfyed, witness the treaty at the Hague and Gertruydenberg. They pretend from this that England was never asked till Holland twice refused.

These are the pretences I have met with, and perceive that amongst people that see only the outside of things they carry some show, especially since even the best affected seem to be in the dark and can say nothing to them. There were two Gentlemen with me not long ago and they fell into a dispute (the occasion I need not tell you) whether it was easier to send a fleet and army from the Downs to Calais on the French Coast or to the Mediterranean. He that main-

tinued to run high. 'The rage and folly' of the Whigs, according to Secretary Southwell, knew no bounds (Departmental Correspondence in P.R.O. of Ireland). Their chief offence was that on the anniversary of King William's birthday in the previous year, when according to custom *Tamerlane* was acted in the Dublin theatre, they had insisted on the recitation of the prologue written by Garth, which the Lords Justices had prohibited as offensive to England's new allies.—Ball.

tained the latter to be more difficult called for a map, and began to
show the way they must sail, and the winds that are necessary, the
other cut him short, and told him none but a Whigg would maintain
such a Paradox, which struck him silent, but whether it satisfied him
I did not ask.

I have two notions (when or how I come by them or whether I was
born with them I cannot tell) but they are these that to prefer the
public to private interest is virtue and what a man loses that way will
be made good to him by the author of goodness, the other is, that to
prefer the future good of my self and posterity to the present is
wisdom, perhaps I had this from my own practice and other children's with their butter cakes. I remember we would thrust off the
butter from one part of the cake and eat it without any, that we might
have the more on the last, and that it might be the more pleasing and
relishing. how this will agree with your *curent posteri* I cannot say,
but I think all wise States have had the greatest regard to posterity,
and though they would not prevent all mischiefs, yet they never left
gaps open to chance which was visible and which with any care
would probably be stopped. A good gamester leaves as little to
chance as he can. In short I never saw any great thing done without
a certain scheme and plan of the whole business adjusted before
hand. What is done in such a way is regular and steady, and rewards
at last generally. Such as trust to time, place and occasions often
want necessaries. I am, etc.

[Dr. Swift.]   [W.D.]

4804

Robert Hunter to Swift

[1 Nov. 1712. Received 1 March 1712-13.]

I think I am indebted to you for two letters and should have continued so, had it not been for the apprehension of your putting a
wrong construction upon my neglect, My Friends being few in
Number, I would not willingly, or by my own fault lose those I have.
The true cause is this, My Unhappy Circumstances have so soured
me that whatever I write must be vinegar and gall to a Man of Your

Mirth,[1] For the better understanding of which be pleased to read them in the words of one of my most renowned predecessors. *Cuando pensé venir á este gobierno á comer caliente y á beber frio, y á recrear el cuerpo entre sábanas de holanda sobre colchones de pluma, he venido á hacer penitencia como si fuera ermitanno, y como no la hago de mi voluntad, pienso que al cabo al cabo me ha de llevar el diablo.*[2] This worthy was Indeed but a type of me, of which I could fully convince you by an exact paralell between our administrations and Circumstances, which I shall reserve to another opportunity.

The truth of the matter is this I am used like a dog after having done all that is in the power of Man to deserve a better treatment, so that I am now quite jaded. Male vehi malo alio gubernante, quam tam ingratis rectoribus bene gubernare.

The approaching peace will give leisure to the Ministry to think of proper remedys for the distracted state of all the Provinces but of this more particularly, the Importance of it by its situation being greater, and the danger by their conduct more Imminent than that of the rest I have done my duty in representing their proceedings and warning them of the consequences and there I leave it. *Neque tam me εὐελπιστία consolatur ut antea quam ἀδιαφορία. qua nulla in re tam utor quam in hac civili et publica.*

I have purchased a seat for a Bishop and by orders from the Society have given direction to prepare it for his reception. You once upon a day gave me hopes of seeing you there,[3] It would be to me no small reliefe to have so good a friend to complain to, what it would be to you to hear me when you could not help me I know not. *Cætera desunt*—for the post cannot stay. Adieu. I am, | Very sincerely | Yours,

Ro: Hunter

In another hand: N York Nov^br | 1^st(?) 1712
Endorsed by Swift: Governr of New York | New York Mar. 1st 1712

---

[1] Robert Hunter, for whom see p. 101, n. 5, sailed for New York as Governor early in 1710. Under great difficulties and against much opposition he distinguished himself as a singularly able and discerning colonial governor. He returned home in 1719.

[2] This passage occurs in Sancho Panza's letter from his island to Don Quixote.

[3] These words have been interpreted as implying that Swift at one time entertained the idea of a colonial bishopric. There is no ground for this suggestion.

Pierpont Morgan Library

Swift to Sir Andrew Fountaine

Good Sr Andrew.[2]

Friday morning[1]
the 6th of
March. Anno Domini 17$\frac{12}{13}$

I received your kind and friendly Letter last night,[3] indeed I think I may truly say I received it this morning, for it was past twelve a clock, for the Belman had gone about, for I had been abroad a playing at Cards with some good friends that you know and love,[4] now as to what you say of hoping I will excuse your Boldness and the Trouble, I do not take it in good part that you should please to think that I think, that any thing that you think to commend me in is any Bouldnesse or Trouble. I hope I am better bred than so, and that I know how to behave my self to my Betters as well as another. Now as to what you say that you desire my good Company (as you are pleased to call it so, much above my deserts) (unless you will accept the will (as we say) for the Deed) at Madam Vanhumree's at the Hour of three to morrow (for so it was when you wrote it, although it be now to day.) I stand very much bounden to Madam's good will and frendly Invitation (if so be she desired you to tell me (as I suppose she did) to come) But so it is, that I did in some sort make a kind of a Promise to eat a bit of Bief with a friend of mine in York-building, but if my said friend will by any means have me excused; I will accept Madam Vanhumrees invitation with many thanks. But now as to what you say that I am to decide whether Madam Hessy or you be most sillyest. I am sure it is but a Jest for Madam Hessy is a very ripe witted young Gentlewoman: and Sr Andrew as for you all the world knows that you are a Bookish Gentleman and admired far and near for your Forwardlyness in deep learn-

---

[1] The letter was first dated by Swift 'Thursday' and '26th'. Struck out and corrected.

[2] Ball printed this letter from a copy made by Forster from the original at Narford. The original has since passed into the possession of the Pierpont Morgan Library, New York. It is here used for the text.

[3] Swift probably made the acquaintance of Sir Andrew Fountaine in Dublin in 1707. Their friendship was renewed in London. Fountaine was frequently a visitor at Mrs. Vanhomrigh's house (*Journal, passim*).

[4] The day before Swift had visited Lord Pembroke 'to see some curious Books' (*Journal*, p. 633).

ing. But now if you mean that you will both strive to counterfit your selves silly, may hap to pass away the time and make your Friends merry, if I am to decide, why then I am a Judge, I must be sillyer than you both and so good Sʳ Andrew you call me Fool by Craft. Now as to what you say in your Postscript, I cannot answer all your fine Compliments, but I wish you as well as those who can, and would go as far by night or by day to serve my honored Friend Sʳ Andrew, as any he that wears a head, for I will not be behind hand with the best in well doing or in well wishing, when it lyes in my power, I desire you will present my Service to the good Gentlewoman and her two daughters, and the same to your self, who am | Good Sʳ Andrew | yours to command in all | faithfull Service | Jonathan Swift.

Good Sʳ Andrew when I say you call me Fool by craft I pray you take it not amiss as though I should take it unkindly that you should take me for a fool, for fool enough I am God he knows, but I know you do but jest, and pray pardon me that I indite no better, and I pray pardon these many Blots and this sad Scrawl.

Address: For his honored frend Sʳ Andr-|-ew fountaine Knight at his Dwe-|lling house in Sᵗ James his Place-|e, near Sᵗ James his Street, on the r-|-ight hand at the upper end of all bef-|-ore you turn to the right hand up again |
     These Present- in London

Faulkner 1762

Swift to Archbishop King

London, March 28, 1713

My Lord,

Although your humour of delaying, which is a good Deal in Fashion, might serve me for Authority and Example in not sooner acknowledging your Grace's Letter,[1] I shall not make that Use of it, but naturally tell you, that the publick Delay hath been the Cause of mine. We have lived almost these two Months past, by the Week, expecting that Parliament would meet, and the Queen tell them that

---

[1] King's letter of 22 Jan. 1712/13.

the Peace was signed. But unforeseen Difficulties have arisen, partly by some Mistakes in our Plenipotentiaries, as well as of those of *France*, too long to trouble your Grace with, since we now reckon all will be at an End;[1] and the Queen hath sent new Powers to *Utrecht*, which her Ministers there must obey, I think, or be left without Excuse. The Peace will be signed with *France*, *Holland*, the Emperor, *Savoy*, *Portugal*, and *England*; but *Spain* has yet no Minister at *Utrecht*, the *Dutch* making Difficulties about the Duke *d'Ossuna*'s Passports, but the Marquis de *Monteleon* will soon begin his Journey, at least he tells me so.[2] However, it is of no great Moment whether *Spain* cometh in now, or a Month hence, and the Parliament will be satisfied with the rest. People here have grumbled at those Prorogations until they are weary,[3] but they are not very convenient, considering how many Funds are out, and how late it is in the Year. They think of taking off two Shillings in the Pound from that Land Tax,[4] which I always argued earnestly against: But the Court has a Mind to humour the Country Gentlemen, and the Thing is popular enough; but then we must borrow upon new Funds, which it will be of the last Difficulty to invent, or to raise. The other Party are employed in spreading a Report most industriously, that the Lord Treasurer intends, after the Peace, to declare for the Whigs. They have spread it in *Scotland*, to prepare people for the next Election; and Mr. *Annesley*[5] told me the other Day at my Lord Steward's,[6] that he had heard I writ the same to my Friends in *Ireland*; which, as it is wholly without Ground, so the Fact is what I never had the least Belief of, although his Lordship is somewhat of your Grace's Mind, in not refusing to converse with his greatest Enemies; and

---

[1] The English plenipotentiaries delayed the signing of the treaty. They were anxious to include smaller princes, for example the Duke of Savoy, whose pretensions were far from moderate.

[2] Monteleon had arrived in England during 1712 as ambassador of Philip V of Spain. He was expected to act as Spanish plenipotentiary at Utrecht (*Journal*, p. 640). His place was, however, taken by Ossuna.

[3] Parliament had been eleven times prorogued.

[4] During the war the rate rose to four shillings, which produced a revenue of about two millions.

[5] Francis Annesley, 1663/1750, was a grandson of the first Viscount Valentia of that family. He was a member of the English Parliament and a prominent member of the October Club. In the reign of William III he sat in the Irish Parliament. He and Archbishop King were close friends. In the *Journal*, 22 Mar. 1712/13, Swift had already told this same story on Annesley's authority.

[6] Earl Poulett.

therefore he is censured, as you say you are, upon the same Account.[1] And, to those who charge him with it (as some are free enough to do it) he only says, his Friends ought to trust him; and, I have some Reason to believe, that after a Peace, the direct contrary will appear. For my own Part, I entirely agree with your Grace, that a free Man ought not to confine his Converse to any one Party; neither would I do so, if I were free; but, I am not, and perhaps much less is a great Minister in such a Juncture as this. Among many Qualities I have observed in the Treasurer, there is one which is something singular, that he will be under an Imputation, how wrong soever, without the Pains of clearing himself to his nearest Friends, which is owing to great Integrity, great Courage, or great Contempt of Censure. I know he hath abundance of the two last, and I believe he has the first.

Your Grace's Observations on the *French* Dexterity in Negotiation, as well as their ill Faith, are certainly right; but let both be as great as possible, we must treat with them one Time or other; and if Ministers will not be upon their Guard against such notorious Managers, they are altogether inexcusable. But I do assure your Grace, that as it has fallen in my Way to know more of the steps of this whole Treaty, than perhaps any one Man besides, I cannot see that any Thing in the Power of human Prudence, under many difficult Conjunctures, hath been omitted. We have been forced to conceal the best Side, which I agree has been unfortunate and unpopular; but you will please to consider that this Way of every Subject interposing their Sentiments upon the Management of foreign Negotiations, is a very new Thing among us; and the Suffering it hath been thought, in the Opinion of wise Men, too great a Strain upon the Prerogative; especially giving a Detail of Particulars, which, in the Variety of Events, cannot be ascertained during the Course of a Treaty.—I could easily answer the Objection of your Grace's Friends in relation to the *Dutch*, and why they made those Difficulties at the *Hague* and *Gertruydenberg*. And when the whole Story of these two last intriguing Years comes to be published, the World will have other Notions of our Proceedings. This perhaps will not be long untold, and might already have been, if other People had been no wiser than I.[2] After all, my Lord, I grant that from a distant

---

[1] In the *Journal*, 21 Mar., Swift states categorically that Oxford had been 'at a meeting at Ld Hallifax's House with 4 principall Whigs'.

[2] Swift had been making slow progress with the *Four Last Years of the Queen*. Oxford and Bolingbroke displayed little enthusiasm. In Feb. 1712/13 he had

View of Things, abundance of Objections may be raised against many Parts of our Conduct. But, the Difficulties which gave room to these Objections are not seen, and perhaps some of them will never appear; neither may it be convenient they should. If, in the End, it appears that we have made a good Bargain for you, we hope you will take it without entering too nicely into the Circumstances. I will not undertake to defend our Proceedings against any Man who will not allow this Postulatum, that it was impossible to carry on the War any longer; which, whoever denies, either hath not examined the State of the Nation with respect to its Debts, or denies it from the Spirit of Party. When a Friend of mine objected this to Lord *Nottingham*, he freely confessed it was a Thing he had never considered. But, however, he would be against any Peace without *Spain*; and why? Because he was not Privy Seal. But then, why does he Vote with the Whigs in every Thing else, although Peace hath no concern? because he was not Privy Seal. I hope, my Lord, we shall in Time unriddle you many a dark Problem, and let you see that Faction, Rage, Rebellion, Revenge, and Ambition, were deeply rooted in the Hearts of those who have been the great Obstructors of the Queen's Measures, and of the Kingdom's Happiness; and, if I am not mistaken, such a Scene may open, as will leave the present Age, and Posterity little Room to doubt who were the real Friends and real Enemies of their Country. At the same Time, I know nothing is so rash as predicting upon the Events of publick Councils, and I see many Accidents very possible to happen which may soon defeat all my wise Conjectures. | I am, | my Lord, | Your Grace's | Most dutiful, and | Most obedient humble Servant,

4804

Matthew Prior to Swift

Paris the 8 Ap. 1713 [O.S. 28 March.]

Pray take this word writ after our Pacquets closed and the Messenger staying for it, as an equivalent for yours dispatched at Midnight

placed part of the manuscript in Sir Thomas Hanmer's hands, where it remained for three months. The procrastination of Swift's friends delayed the completion of the *History* beyond the political occasion for which it was written—the justification of the Queen and her Ministry in their negotiations for peace.

& when the Writer was half a sleep[1] hang Me if I know how to go on, thô I am in a Country where Every body does not only write letters, but prints them: Our great affair goes on very successfully. We transmit the Spanish treaty concluded at Madrid for your approbation in End:[2] and transmission to Utrecht: after wch: I think Pax sit will become authentic Latin; after wch, I suppose our Society[3] will flourish, and I shall have nothing to do but to partake of that Universal Protection wch it will receive: in the mean time, pray give my great respects to our Brethren, and tell them that while in hopes of being favoured they are spending their own money, I am advancing my own Interests in the French Language and forgetting my own Mother Tongue, but We have done with other matters. I want mightily to hear from Ld Treas.ʳ, tell Him so; I owe brother Arburthnot[4] a Letter, excuse my not writing to him, till I know what to say: I cant find Van Humrigh[5] since he brought Me your Letter; I have a rarity of a book to send you by the first fair Occasion; I make but little of the English wit, the Guardian,[6] but possibly I do not yet enter into his design: let Ld Bolingbroke know I love him mightily, and pray do you as much for Dick Shelton.[7] Adieu, my good friend, I am, very truly | Your obedient and faithful Servt |

M. Prior

Address: To Dr Jonathan | Swift.
Endorsed by Swift: Mʳ Prior

[1] In Aug. 1712 Prior went to Paris with Bolingbroke in connexion with the suspension of hostilities while the Treaty of Utrecht was under negotiation. He remained in Paris after Bolingbroke's return to England; and later was invested with plenipotentiary powers.   [2] i.e. England.

[3] The inception of 'The Society', whose members addressed each other as 'Brother', appears to have owed itself to Bolingbroke (*Letters*, 1798, i. 150, 171). Later Swift played a large part in the proceedings; and there are many references to it in the *Journal*. Prior was an original member, as was Arbuthnot who is mentioned in this letter. Beginning with twelve the Society finally mustered twenty-two members. See *Journal*, p. 505, n. 43. From the end of 1712 meetings became less frequent and its fortunes declined.

[4] Swift was frequently in Arbuthnot's company.

[5] Bartholomew Vanhomrigh was then in Paris, where he took to extravagant courses. See Prior to Swift, 16 Aug. 1713, N.S.

[6] On 1 Apr. 1713 Swift informed Stella: 'Steel has begun a new daily Paper calld the Guardian, they say good for nothing.' The *Guardian* ran to 175 numbers, 12 Mar. to 1 Oct. 1713. Steele wrote 82 numbers.

[7] Prior's friend, who appears in the opening lines of *Alma*:
> Matthew and Richard, when or where
> From story is not mighty clear.

341

The Earl Poulett to Swift[1]

Sunday afternoon [29 March 1713].

I was called away presently after chappel upon some business which hinder'd my going upstairs at St James's & occasions Dr Swift the trouble of this to make my excuse for not returning the paper which I here send you, & tho' its not in my power to serve you in any proportion to my unfeigned respects for you, yet I would not be wanting of my part in any opportunity where I can to expres my self | S^r | y^r most faithfull | humble servant |

Poulett

Endorsed by Swift: Ld Steward— | 1713

King's Letter-book

Archbishop King to Swift

Dublin Apr. 14. 1713

S^r

I return you my hearty thanks for yours of the 28: of March last— it was a little shocking to find her Majestys Plenipotentiaries made any demurr of signing the peace but I find all that is over. I have not heard from any hand one word of the articles but assure your self if there be sufficient security agst the Pretender the people of Irld will receive it gratefully and not trouble their minds about any thing else, but the fear of him put them almost out of their witts and hurrys them into many inconveniencys.

I can't imagine what grounds any would have to say that you had wrote into Ireld that my Ld T—r after the peace intended to declare for the Whiggs. I am sure you never hinted any such thing to me, but the contrary, but if you had, it would have remained with me, for you may rest satisfied, that for above this twelve months, no one ever saw any letter you wrote to me nor did I so much as hint that I had any correspondence with you, partly for fear of importunity and partly of pumping, nay there want not such as would make

[1] Swift's application to Earl Poulett was probably in connexion with an unsuccessful effort which he made at that time to obtain a dispensation for a Fellow of Trinity College, Dublin, from the obligation to take Holy orders. The Fellow was one of the Grattans, who became Swift's great friends. This appears to have been his first acquaintance with the family.—Ball.

no scruple to quote me that were thought to have a good correspondent for a piece of news of their own inventing, of which I have
instances. I cannot conceive what great occasion there will be for
money considering we have had little campaigning these last two
years.

The Ministers as you observe had need to look sharp, considering
with whom they have to deal, for if you look back on all the treaties
that have been between England and France for the last four hundred years, you will not find one in which they have not notoriously
overreached us; and this is I reckon the great ground of the jealousies
of the people which is increased by the secrecy with which it is
transacted. And if you reflect on the management of former Ministries, particularly of those of the four last reigns, you will be of
opinion that these kingdoms have no great reason to be over confident
of their Ministers, or trust much to them.

I find that few here grant your postulatum, they say that the confederates were content to carry on the war, if Brittain would have for
the future contributed but 4000000. yearly towards it, which they
say we might have done for 20. years, without running one shilling
in debt. This is a matter of which I am no Judge and therefore can
say nothing to it.

I have nothing to add but my hearty prayers, that this may prove
a firm and lasting peace that may answer the Expectations of good
people and be for the honour of those that have negotiated it.

I have been extremely ill all this winter and intend God willing
[for] the Bath after my visitation is over. I hope to be there the latter
end of this month, or the beginning of the next. I am unwilling to
go to London because there are already too many of the Bishops and
other clergy of Ireld there. I have a cause in the House of Lords
between Christ Church and me.[1] Judgement has been given for me
in the Common Pleas and Queen's Bench here and Queen's Bench
in Engld unanimously by all the Judges in every Court, but it is
now removed by them into the Lords' House in Great Brittain; pray
speak to such Lords as you are acquainted with to be there at the
hearing.

Dr. Swift

[1] Almost as soon as King became Archbishop of Dublin, 1703, he was
involved in litigation with the Dean and Chapter of Christ Church about his
right of visitation. The case was transferred to England, and finally in 1724, on
appeal to the English House of Lords, decided in his favour.

Dean Atterbury to Swift

Chelsea Tuesd. morn. [21 April 1713]

Mr Dean,

Give me leave to tell you, that there is no man in England more pleasd with your being preferred than I am.[1] I would have told you so myself at Your Lodgings, but that my waiting[2] confines me. I had heard a flying report of it before, but my L Bolingbroke yesterday confirmd the Welcome Newes to me. I could not excuse my self without saying thus much; & I have not time to say more, but that I am Your most aff^ce & faithful Servt

Fr. Atterbury

Address: To | the Reverend Dr Swift
Endorsed by Swift: Bp Rochester | Apr. 21st 1713; *and also under the address—*
D. Attrby. Apr. 21. 1713. | about 11 in morning.

Faulkner 1762

Swift to Archbishop King

London, April 30, 1713.

My Lord,

I had the Honour of your Grace's Letter of the 14th, which at present I cannot answer particularly: I send this to welcome your Grace to the *Bath*, where we conclude you are now arrived, and, I hope, the Design of your Journey is more for Prevention than Cure. I suppose your Grace hath heard that the Queen hath made Dr. *Stearne* Bishop of *Dromore*, and that I am to succeed him in his Deanery. Dr. *Parnell*, who is now in Town, writ last Post to your Grace, to desire the Favour of you that he may have my small Prebend:[3] He thinketh it will be some Advantage to come into the Chapter, where it may possibly be in my Power to serve him in a Way agreeable to him, although in no Degree equal to his Merits;

---

[1] On this same day Swift wrote to Stella: 'D. Ormd has told the Qu— he is satisfied that Stearn should be Bp, & she consents I shall be Dean, and I suppose the Warrants will be drawn in a day or two.'

[2] As the Queen's chaplain.

[3] Parnell's letter to King asking for the prebend of Dunlavin is in the library of Trinity College, Dublin (MS. No. 1122).

by which he hath distinguished himself so much, that he is in great Esteem with the Ministry, and others of the most valuable Persons in this Town.¹ He hath been many Years under your Grace's Direction, and hath a very good Title to your Favour; so that I believe it will be unnecessary to add how much I should be obliged to your Grace's Compliance in this Matter:² And I flatter myself that his being agreeable to me, will be no Disadvantage to him in your Grace's Opinion. | I am, with the greatest Respect, | My Lord, | Your Grace's most dutiful, and | Most humble Servant, |

Jon. Swift.

Forster No. 555³
Swift to the Rev. William Diaper

London Apr. 30. 1713

S⁴

I am ashamed to tell you how ill a Philosopher I am, that a very ill situation of my own affairs for three weeks past, made me, utterly incapable of answering your obliging letter, or thanking you for your most agreeable copy of verses,⁵ the Prints will tell you that I am

¹ Thomas Parnell, the poet, and Archdeacon of Clogher, married in 1706 Anne, daughter of Thomas Minchin of Tipperary. He was subject to fits of depression, and his wife's death in Aug. 1711 seems to have led to a craving for relief in drink. His charm of character won him a large circle of friends. Swift, to forward his interests, introduced him to Oxford and Bolingbroke. See Johnson's *Lives of the Poets*, ed. Birkbeck Hill, ii. 49 ff.

² King who had been a guardian of Thomas Parnell and his brother, John Parnell, an Irish judge, would naturally be predisposed in Parnell's favour.

³ The original of this letter was sold at Sotheby's, 10 June 1869. The text is taken from a copy in the Forster Collection, No. 555 (48.E.26).

⁴ William Diaper, the son of Joseph Diaper of Bridgwater, was sent to Balliol College, Oxford, in 1699. He took orders in 1715, became curate of Brent, Somerset, and died in 1717. See *The Complete Works of William Diaper*, ed. Dorothy Broughton, 1952.

⁵ *Nereides: Or, Sea-Eclogues*, 1712, described by Swift (*Journal*, p. 512) as 'Poems of Mermen'. These were reprinted in Nichols's *Select Collection*, v. 209–55. Towards the end of 1712 Diaper published, under the date 1713, *The Dryades: Or, The Nymph's Prophecy*; and in 1714 he addressed to Swift an imitation of 'Horace, Book I. Ep. xvii', published as a quarto pamphlet, and reprinted in Nichols's *Supplement to Swift's Works*, 1779. Swift engaged 'The Society' to befriend Diaper financially (*Journal*, pp. 512, 513, 519).

condemned to live again in Ireland, and all that the Court and Ministry did for me, was to let me chuse my station in the country where I am banished. I could not forbear shewing both Your letter & verses to our great men, as well as to the men of wit of my acquaintance: and they were highly approved by all. I am altogether a stranger to your friend Oppian, and am a little angry when those who have a genius lay it out in translations.[1] I question whether res angusta domi be not one of your motives. Perhaps you want such a bridle as a translation, for your genius is too fruitful as appears by the frequency of your similes, and this employment may teach you to write like a Mortal man, as Shakespeare expresseth it.[2]

I have been minding my Ld Bolingbroke, Mr. Harcourt and Sir Wm Windham to solicit my Lord Chancellor[3] to give you a living, as a business which belongs to our Society, who assume the title of Rewarding of merit. They are all very well disposed, and, I shall not fail to negotiate while I stay in England, which will not be above six weeks but I hope to return in October, and if I am not then provided for, I will move Heaven and Earth that something may be done for you. Our Society hath not met of late, else I would have moved to have two of us sent in form to request a living for you from my Ld Chancellor, and if you have any way to employ my Service, I desire you will let me have it, and believe me to be | Very sincerely | S^r | Y^r Most | faithful humble Ser^t | J: Swift

Address: To the Reverend Mr William Diaper | at Dean near | Basingstoke | Hampshire

Rothschild

Provost Pratt and Swift to Edward Southwell

[5 May 1713.][4]

The Rectory of Moimed within two Miles of Trim in the County of Meath, value about 40^11 per Annum in the Gift of Lady

[1] At the time of his death Diaper left behind him in manuscript a translation of three books of Oppian's *Halieutica*, which were printed by subscription in 1722. The remainder of the work was completed by John Jones, also of Balliol College.

[2] 'How many years a mortal man may live' (*3 Hen. VI*. ii. 5).

[3] Harcourt had been recently advanced to the position of Lord Chancellor.

[4] In the last letter of the *Journal to Stella*, 6 June 1713, Swift writes from Chester: 'I spoke again to D. Ormd about Moimed for Raymd and hope he may

Roscommon,[1] but now on Dr Stearn's Promotion, in the Gift of the Governmt. It hath usually been given to the Minister of Trim, and is no Sinecure, but the Bishop will oblige whoever has it to keep a Curate. It is onely convenient for the Minister of Trim, being hardly worth while for any Body else to pass patent for it. Therefore his Grace is desired to bestow it to Dr Raymond Minister of Trim, ⌜if none of His Grace's Chaplains⌝ unless any Body whom His Grace hath a mind to oblige, think it worth their Acceptance.

The Cure of Trim is very great, and Profits small.[2]

Endorsed by Swift: Memoriall about | Dr Raymond. | May. 5. 1713 | Dr Prat & · Dr Swift

Deane Swift 1765

Swift to Joseph Addison

May 13, 1713

Sir,

I was told yesterday, by several persons, that Mr. Steele had reflected upon me in his Guardian,[3] which I could hardly believe, until, sending for the paper of the day, I found he had, in several parts of it, insinuated with the utmost malice, that I was author of the Examiner; and abused me in the grossest manner he could possibly invent, and set his name to what he had written.[4] Now, Sir,

yet have it. for I laid it strongly to the Duke, & gave him the Bp of Meath's Memoriall.' The draft memorial in Swift's handwriting, now in Lord Rothschild's library, No. 2262, would presumably be intended for submission by Dr. Benjamin Pratt, Provost of Trinity College, Dublin, and by Swift to Edward Southwell, Ormonde's Chief Secretary in Ireland. Words in half-brackets are scrawled over.

[1] Lady Roscommon, widow of the well-known fourth Earl of Roscommon (*D.N.B.*), was his second wife, whom he had married in 1674. He died in London in Jan. 1684–5. She afterwards married Thomas Carter of Robertstown, co. Meath. The gift of Moymet may have come to her through her second husband.

[2] It is to be noted that Stearne, on his promotion from Trim to the deanery of St. Patrick's, retained the emoluments of Moymet. The application on behalf of Raymond was successful. See Swift to Joshua Dawson, 29 June 1713.

[3] See p. 341, n. 6.

[4] The chief ground of the quarrel, now of some standing, between Steele and Swift, is to be found in the latter's reiterated attacks on Marlborough in the *Examiner* and elsewhere. Steele held Marlborough in the highest regard and veneration. The *Guardian*, No. 53 (12 May), contained a letter signed by Steele

if I am not author of the Examiner, how will Mr. Steele be able to defend himself from the imputation of the highest degree of baseness, ingratitude, and injustice? Is he so ignorant of my temper, and of my style? Has he never heard that the author of the Examiner (to whom I am altogether a stranger) did a month or two ago vindicate me from having any concern in it? Should not Mr. Steele have first expostulated with me, as a friend? Have I deserved this usage from Mr. Steele, who knows very well that my Lord Treasurer has kept him in his employment upon my intreaty and intercession?[1] My Lord Chancellor and Lord Bolingbroke will be witnesses, how I was reproached by my Lord Treasurer, upon the ill returns Mr. Steele made to his Lordship's indulgence, &c.

Journal to Stella

Appointment of Isaiah Parvisol

London May. 16. 1713

I do hereby appoint Mr Isaiah Parvisol my Proctor to sett and let the Tyths of the Deanry of St Patricks to witness whereof I have hereunto sett my Hand and Seal the day and Year above written

Jonat: Swift.

These are the last words of Letter LXIV of the *Journal to Stella*. A facsimile appears in Wilson's *Swiftiana*, vol. i.

---

unmistakably directed at Swift, although he had long ceased to have any connexion with the *Examiner*. The first *Examiner* written by him was No. 14, for 2 Nov. 1710, and thereafter he wrote the successive numbers to No, 45, 7 June 1711, then severing his editorial connexion with it, although he wrote the first part of No. 46. Mrs. Manley took over the editorship, but for a few numbers only, ending with No. 52. William Oldisworth revived the *Examiner* on 6 Dec. 1711.

[1] Swift made this assertion on several occasions. Here he is presumably referring to specific words in the *Guardian*, No. 53. Steele wrote: 'I apprehend by reading the *Examiner* over a second Time, that he insinuates, by the words close to the Royal Stamp, he would have the Man turned out of his office.' See further *Correspondence of Richard Steele*, ed. Rae Blanchard, pp. 70–72.

Archbishop King to Swift

Chester May 16: 1713.[1]

Revd S^r

This is to welcome you to my neighbourhood at St. Sepulchers. I have a very great loss in the removal of the Bi͠p of Dromore who was not only a neighbour but a bosom friend. I understand that was not much his advantage[2] but I am sure it was to mine and the Churchs. I hope that will not discourage you from reckoning your self amongst my friends, which I earnestly desire; I had wrote sooner to you but expected every day a wind to bring me here, it continued cross for many days, and gave me opportunity to consecrate your Predecessor before I came away.[3] I go directly from hence to the Bath, my health requiring it, where I shall be glad to hear from you. I know not whether I shall be obliged to go to London before I return. I will not if I can avoid it, for considering the great number of Irish Bishops and clergy that are there, I am ashamed to add to the number. I should be very much pleased to have an hour or two of your conversation before I returned or you went to Ireland, but am afraid I can hardly expect it, though perhaps it might be of use to us both.

I have a cause before the Lords in the Parliament to be heard this session. It is between Christ Church and me. I think I gave you an account of it before, you may do me good service in it if you would speak to Mr. Annesley who manages for me and knows when it comes on, and get some number of the states of the case when printed and distribute them to your friends, with a request to be present at the hearing. I would reckon [it] a great obligation. I have

---

[1] Writing to Southwell Archbishop King informed him that he had only reached Chester the previous day having been prevented from crossing from Dublin by three weeks of continuous easterly wind.

[2] There was difficulty in gaining Ormonde's consent to the promotion of Dean Stearne to the bishopric of Dromore on personal grounds, and because, so he asserted, Stearne was influenced by Archbishop King. He only consented in order to create a vacancy at St. Patrick's to which Swift could be presented (*Journal*, 19–21 Apr. 1713).

[3] King lost no time in consecrating his friend. Stearne's patent is dated 1 May, and his consecration took place in St. Patrick's Cathedral on 10 May. As a suffragan of the Armagh province Stearne ought to have been consecrated by Primate Marsh, but owing to the Primate's infirmities the duty fell to King.

had the unanimous judgement of all the judges in the Common Pleas and Queen's Bench in Ireland, and likewise of the Queen's Bench in England, for me; what weight those will have with the Lords I cannot tell, but the cause seems so plain to all that heard it argued that they say there is no colour against me.

Your Predecessor in St. Patrick's did a great deal to his church and house but there is still work for you, he designed a spire for the steeple, which kind of ornament is much wanting in Dublin, he has left your Œconomy clear and 200ll in bank for this purpose. The Steeple is 120 feet high, 21 feet in the clear wide where the spire is to stand. the design was to build it of brick, 120 feet high, the scaffolding we reckoned to be the principall cost, which yet is pretty cheap in Dublin, the brick and Lime are good and cheap. But we have no workman that understands any thing of the matter. I believe you may be acquainted with several that are conversant with such kind of work, and if you would discourse some of them, and push on the work as soon as settled, it might be of use to you, and give the people there an advantageous notion of you, *dimidium facti, qui bene capit habet*.[1]

I add no more, but my hearty prayers for you, and that you may enjoy with comfort and reputation the provision her Majesty has made for you,[2] which shall be the study and endeavour of etc. |

Dᵣ Swift   W:D:

[1] The imposing tower which stands at the north-west corner of St. Patrick's Cathedral was built in the fourteenth century. Fortunately the spire which was ultimately built, some years after Swift's death, was constructed of stone. Horace, *Ep*. I. ii. 40: 'dimidium facti, qui coepit, habet'.

[2] In actual fact King was not wholly pleased by Swift's appointment as Dean, although he preferred that appointment to a bishopric on the ground that as a dean he could do less mischief than as a bishop. See Landa, *Swift and the Church of Ireland*, pp. xiv, xv. Swift himself regarded the preferment as exile. His nearer friends would have been happier had he remained in England. And Robert Molesworth, writing to his wife, 28 Apr. 1713, commented: 'They have made Swift Dean of St. Patrick's. This vexes the godly party beyond expression' (*H.M.C.*, *Report on Various Collections*, viii. 262).

Richard Steele to Swift

May 19. 1713.

Sir,

Mr. Addison shewed me your letter, wherein you mention me.[1] They laugh at you, if they make you believe your interposition has kept me thus long in office. If you have spoken in my behalf at any time, I am glad I have always treated you with respect; though I believe you an accomplice of the Examiner's.[2] In the letter you are angry at, you see I have no reason for being so merciful to him, but out of regard to the imputation you lie under. You do not in direct terms say you are not concerned with him; but make it an argument of your innocence that the Examiner has declared you have nothing to do with him. I believe I could prevail upon the Guardian to say there was a mistake in putting my name in his paper: But the English would laugh at us, should we argue in so Irish a manner. I am heartily glad of your being made Dean of St. Patrick's. I am, | Sir, | Your most obedient | Humble servant, | Richard Steele.

4804

Sir Thomas Hanmer to Swift

Tuesday [19 May 1713.]

Sr3

I keep only the last book which I shall have gone through before night.[4] The rest I send you with the very few observations I made upon them which yet were as many as I cou'd see any occasion for

---

[1] Addison, characteristically, handed on the letter to Steele, declining to involve himself in the dispute.

[2] It is, perhaps, not easy to believe that Swift was never in touch with Oldisworth's *Examiner*. On 15 Jan. 1712-13 he told Stella: 'I gave the Examiner a hint about this Prorogation, & to praise the Qu— for her tenderness to the Dutch in giving them still more time to submitt. It fitted the Occasions at present.' On 31 Jan. he said: 'I was in the City with my Printer to alter an Examiner about my Friend Lewis's Story, which will be told with Remarks.' On these two occasions, at least, and within a few months of his difference with Steele, he supplied the *Examiner* with hints. See further *Correspondence of Richard Steele*, ed. Rae Blanchard, p. 73.

[For notes 3, 4 see overleaf.

351

thoe I doe assure you I read with the same strictness & ill-nature as in the former part. I am | Y^r most humble servant, |

Tho: Hanmer

Address: To | Dr Swift.
Endorsed by Swift: Sr T. Hanmer
Sr T. Hanmere | about May. 1713

Deane Swift 1765

Swift to Lord Harcourt

[23] May, 1713.

My Lord,[1]

I wonder your Lordship would presume to go out of town, and leave me in fear that I should not see you before I go to Ireland, which will be in a week. It is a strange thing, you should prefer your own health, and ease, and convenience, before my satisfaction. I want your Lordship for my solicitor: I want your letter to your younger brother of Ireland, to put him under my government.[2] I want an opportunity of giving your Lordship my humblest thanks, for a hundred favours you have done me: I wanted the sight of your

---

[1] Swift's mind was grievously disturbed by the increasing bitterness of the relations between Oxford and Bolingbroke. He hoped that Harcourt's judicial temper might allay these disputes.

Come trimming Harcourt; bring your Mace;
And squeeze it in, or quit your Place.

Poems, 'The Faggot', pp. 188–91.

[2] 'Dr. Swift is not only all our favourite, but our governor' said Harcourt on 7 Oct. 1711 (*Journal*, p. 379). Was Swift recalling these words when soliciting an introduction to the Lord Chancellor of Ireland, Sir Constantine Phipps, who had been Harcourt's junior when defending Sacheverell?

[3] Sir Thomas Hanmer, M.P. for Suffolk from 1708 to 1727, although a Tory adopted an independent attitude, refused office under Oxford, and in 1713–14 played an important part as leader of the 'Hanoverian Tories'. In 1714 he succeeded Bromley as Speaker of the House of Commons; but the accession of George I soon terminated his occupancy of the chair. In Feb. 1711/12 Swift assisted Hanmer in drawing up a 'Representation' to the Queen on the subject of the war (*Journal*, p. 493; *Journals of the House of Commons*, xvii. 119–23).

[4] In Feb. 1712/13 (*Journal*, p. 629) Swift had placed in Hanmer's hands, for his opinion, the earlier part of the *History of the Four Last Years of the Queen.* Hanmer now refers to the last book. Swift was in haste to finish the work before his departure for Ireland.

352

Lordship this day in York-buildings.[1] Pray, my Lord, come to town before I leave it, and supply all my wants. My Lord-Treasurer uses me barbarously; appoints to carry me to Kensington, and makes me walk four miles at midnight. He laughs when I mention a thousand pound, which he gives me; though a thousand pound is a very serious thing, *&c.*[2]

Faulkner 1762

Swift to Archbishop King

London, May 23, 1713.

My Lord,

I had the Honour of a Letter from your Grace, the 18th Instant, from *Chester*. I was confidently told about three Weeks ago, that your Grace was expected every Day at the Bath; and you will find a Letter there as old as that, with a Requisition in Favour of Dr. *Parnell*, who, by his own Merit, is in the Esteem of the Chief Ministers here. I am very sensible, that the Loss your Grace hath suffered in the Removal of Dr. *Stearne*, will never be made up by me, upon a great many Accounts; however, I shall not yield to him in Respect and Veneration for your Grace's Character and Person; and, I return you my most grateful Acknowledgments for the Offer you make me of your Favour and Protection. I think to set out for *Ireland* on *Monday* Seven-night, to be there before the Term endeth; for so they advise me, because the long Vacation follows, in which I cannot take the Oaths, unless at a Quarter Sessions, and I had better have two Chances than one. This will hinder me from paying my Respects to your Grace at the *Bath*; and indeed my own Health would be better, I believe, if I could pass a few Weeks there: But my Remedy shall be Riding, and a Sea Voyage. I have been enquiring, and am told your Grace's Cause will hardly come on this Session; but indeed I have been so much out of Order for these ten Days past, that I have been able to do nothing.

---

[1] Oxford's Cabinet dinners were given at York Buildings.

[2] Swift expected that on assuming his new dignity he would be expected to pay £600 to £800 on account of the house built by Stearne, £150 in respect of First Fruits, and £50 for his patent, making £1,000 in all. He hoped that a grant of the total sum might be made to him. See *Journal*, pp. 664, 669.

As to the Spire[1] to be erected on *St. Patrick's* Steeple, I am apt to think it will cost more than is imagined; and, I am confident that no Bricks made in that Part of *Ireland*, will bear being exposed so much to the Air: However, I shall enquire among some Architects here.

I hope your Grace will find a Return of your Health in the Place where you are. I humbly beg your Blessing; and remain, with great Respect, | my Lord, |

Your Grace's | most dutiful, | and most humble Servant, |

Jon. Swift.

Deane Swift 1765

Swift to Richard Steele

[23 May 1713.][2]

Sir,

* * * * *[3] I may probably know better, when they are disposed * * * * * The case was thus: I did with the utmost application, and desiring to lay all my credit upon it, desire Mr. Harley (as he was then called) to shew you mercy. He said he would, and wholly upon my account: That he would appoint you a day to see him: That he would not expect you should quit any friend or principle. Some days after, he told me, he had appointed you a day, and you had not kept it; upon which he reproached me, as engaging for more than I could answer; and advised me to more caution another time.[4] I told him,

---

[1] Faulkner has a footnote in which he states that when the spire was finally built it was in the form of an 'Octagon many Feet high, built of white hard Mountain Stone, with a gilt Ball at the Top of it, which may be seen at the Distance of many Miles'.

[2] The date may be accepted, for on this day Steele published another *Guardian* paper (No. 63) under his own name, in which he commented on the *Examiner* of 22 May. See Blanchard, *Correspondence of Richard Steele*, p. 75.

[3] It has unluckily happened that two or three lines have been torn by accident from the beginning of this letter; and, by the same accident, two or three lines are missing towards the latter part, which were written on the back part of the paper which was torn off.—Deane Swift.

[4] Steele had communicated with Oxford directly. In Steele's letter of resignation (B.M., Lansdowne MSS. 1236, f. 263; Blanchard, op. cit., p. 79) there is reference to a visit: 'When I had the honour of a short conversation with you, you were pleased not only to signifie to me that I should remain in this Office, but to add that if I would name to you one of more value. . . you would favour me in it.'

and desired my Lord Chancellor and Lord Bolingbroke to be witnesses, that I would never speak for or against you as long as I lived;
only I would, and,[1] that it was still my opinion, you should have
mercy till you gave further provocations. This is the history of what
you think fit to call, in the spirit of insulting, 'their laughing at me':
And you may do it securely; for, by the most inhuman dealings, you
have wholly put it out of my power, as a Christian, to do you the
least ill office. Next I desire to know, whether the greatest services
ever done by one man to another, may not have the same turn as
properly applied to them? And, once more, suppose they did laugh
at me, I ask whether my inclinations to serve you merit to be rewarded by the vilest treatment, whether they succeeded or no? If
your interpretation were true, I was laughed at only for your sake;
which, I think, is going pretty far to serve a friend. As to the letter
I complain of, I appeal to your most partial friends, whether you
ought not either to have asked, or written to me, or desired to have
been informed by a third hand, whether I were any way concerned
in writing the Examiner? And, if I had shuffled, or answered in-
directly, or affirmed it, or said I would not give you satisfaction; you
might then have wreaked your revenge with some colour of justice.
I have several times assured Mr. Addison, and fifty others, that I had
not the least hand in writing any of those Papers; and that I had
never exchanged one syllable with the supposed author in my life,
that I can remember, nor ever seen him above twice, and that in
mixt company, in a place where he came to pay his attendance. One
thing more I must observe to you, that, a year or two ago, when some
printers used to bring me their papers in manuscript, I absolutely
forbid them to give any hints against Mr. Addison and you, and
some others; and have frequently struck out reflexions upon you in
particular, and should (I believe) have done it still, if I had not
wholly left off troubling myself about those kind of things.

I protest I never saw anything more liable to exception, than every
part is of the letter you were pleased to write me. You plead, that I do
not, in mine to Mr. Addison, in direct terms, say I am not concerned
in the Examiner: And is that an excuse for the most savage injuries
in the world a week before? How far you can prevail with the
Guardian I shall not trouble myself to inquire; and am more concerned how you will clear your own honour and conscience, than
my reputation. I shall hardly lose one friend by what you[2] * * * * *

[1] and] add *Ball.*   [2] Here the manuscript is torn.—Deane Swift.

I know not any * * * * * laugh at me for any * * * * * absurdity of yours. There are solecisms in morals as well as in languages; and to which of the virtues you will reconcile your conduct to me, is past my imagination. Be pleased to put these questions to yourself. If Dr. Swift be entirely innocent of what I accuse him, how shall I be able to make him satisfaction? And how do I know but he may be entirely innocent? If he was laughed at only because he solicited for me, is that a sufficient reason for me to say the vilest things of him in print under my hand, without any provocation? And, how do I know but he may be in the right, when he says I was kept in my employment at his interposition? If he never once reflected on me the least in any paper, and hath hindered many others from doing it; how can I justify myself, for endeavouring in mine to ruin his credit as a Christian and a clergyman? I am, Sir, | Your most obedient humble servant,

J.S.

King's Letter-book

Archbishop King to Swift

Bath May 25. 1713.

Revd Sʳ¹

I gave you the trouble of a Letter from Chester² and proposed beginning my journey to this place the Monday after, but it pleased God to afflict me with a relapse into the gout which being both in my knee and foot hindered me venturing on it, however I ventured to set out on Wednesday and got here on Saturday³ thro most insufferable ways, my gout still continues but I thank God, it is more easy. I met here yours of Apl the 30th in favour of Dr. Parnell, there is no person I would more willingly oblige and am very glad to find it would be grateful to you, but I promised that prebend long ago to Mr. Espin that has the Cure and is very ill provided of a maintenance, and before I left Ireld gave order for his titles as soon as it should be vacant.⁴ I have laid a scheme for the supplying the Cures

¹ Part of this letter is now quite illegible.
² That of 16 May.
³ Archbishop King was writing on Monday.
⁴ Joseph Espin, educated at Trinity College, Dublin, and a man of scholarly attainments, remained a prebendary of St. Patrick's until his death. *Alum. Dub.*, p. 266.

of the diocese, the best that the present circumstances will afford and of which I shall be glad to have your opinion and approbation in due time.

I reckon the first care of a Bishop ought to be the provision for the cures of his diocese, and the next a proper encouragement for some clergyman of a superior form, that may be able to subsist not only in parochial offices, but also in managing the more general and political part of his pastoral charge. I find myself by the improportionable scantiness of the provision for Church ministers, both as to the number and duty required of them, unable in any measure to accomplish either of these, but I must do the best I can, and I think it necessary in many places to grant the prebends that are in my gift to those that serve the Cures, by which means I obtain both their attendance at the Cathedral in their turns, and likewise encourage better men to undertake the Cures, whereas when they are given to persons that have no other obligation to keep them in the Diocese, I intirely lose their service in both places. By this means you may have a chapter of ten or twelve members at any time in a day's warning, and there are generally six or seven resident in the City whose advice and assistance is of great moment both to the Dean and me in the affairs of the Church, and I hope you will find it so.

I find Dr. Parnell can't be very useful where he is, tho I gave him effectuall help to obtain what he has,[1] and perhaps it may be in my way (as I have it in my thought) to give him a removall where he may be more easy to himself and serviceable to the publick. But this must be a work of time. I add no more but my hearty prayers for &c.

                                                            W.D.

Since the writing of this I received yours of the 23rd instant. I have nothing to add but my prayers for your good journey into Ireland, as I take it if you be not installed before the next term, you must stay till Quarter Sessions or next term to take the oaths as the law requires. I should be sorry my cause were delayed till next session, which must be another year. Our Irish brick will do very well for the steeple, and five or six thousand will finish it.

Dr. Swift.

[1] See p. 345.

Richard Steele to Swift

Bloomsbury, May 26, 1713.

Sir,

I have received yours,[1] and find it impossible for a man to judge in his own case. For an allusion to you, as one under the imputation of helping the Examiner, and owning I was restrained out of respect to you, you tell Addison under your hand, you think me the vilest of mankind, and bid him tell me so. I am obliged to you for any kind things said in my behalf to the Treasurer; and assure you, when you were in Ireland, you were the constant subject of my talk to men in power at that time. As to the vilest of mankind, it would be a glorious world if I were. For I would not conceal my thoughts in favour of an injured man,[2] though all the powers on earth gainsaid it, to be made the first man in the nation. This position, I know, will ever obstruct my way in the world; and I have conquered my desires accordingly. I have resolved to content myself with what I can get by my own industry, and the improvement of a small estate, without being anxious whether I am ever in a Court again or not. I do assure you, I do not speak this calmly, after the ill usage in your letter to Addison, out of terror of your wit or my Lord Treasurer's power, but pure kindness to the agreeable qualities I once so passionately delighted in, in you. You know, I know no body but one that talked after you, could tell Addison had bridled me in point of party.[3] This was ill hinted, both with relation to him, and, | Sir, |

Your most obedient | humble servant, |

Richard Steele.

I know no party; but the truth of the question is what I will support as well as I can, when any man I honour is attacked.[4]

---

[1] That of 23 May.

[2] Marlborough.

[3] Miss Rae Blanchard (op. cit., p. 76, n.) suggests that this may be a reference to the *Examiner*, 1 May 1713, a paper on the recent performance of Addison's *Cato*. In that paper it was stated that Steele had organized a party of Whigs to clap at his signals, and that Addison tried by a judicious hint to save him from 'exposing himself to the Service of Faction'. This suggestion, Steele may have thought, was communicated to the *Examiner* by Swift.

[4] The postscript announces that Steele will on no occasion endure attacks upon Marlborough.

Swift to Richard Steele

May 27, 1713.

Sir,

The reason I give you the trouble of this reply to your letter, is because I am going in a very few days to Ireland; and, although I intend to return towards winter, yet it may happen, from the common accidents of life, that I may never see you again.

In your yesterday's letter, you are pleased to take the complaining side, and think it hard I should write to Mr. Addison as I did, only for an allusion. This allusion was only calling a clergyman of some little distinction an infidel. A clergyman who was your friend, who always loved you, who had endeavoured at least to serve you; and who, whenever he did write any thing, made it sacred to himself never to fling out the least hint against you.

One thing you are pleased to fix on me, as what you are sure of; that the Examiner had talked after me, when he said Mr. Addison had bridled you in point of party.[1] I do not read one in six of those papers, nor ever knew he had such a passage; and I am so ignorant of this, that I cannot tell what it means: Whether, that Mr. Addison kept you close to a party, or that he hindred you from writing about party. I never talkt or writ to that author in my life,[1] so that he could not have learned it from me. And, in short, I solemnly affirm, that, with relation to every friend I have, I am as innocent, as it is possible for a human creature to be. And, whether you believe me or not, I think, with submission, you ought to act as if you believed me, till you have demonstration to the contrary. I have all the Ministry to be my witnesses, that there is hardly a man of wit of the adverse party, whom I have not been so bold as to recommend often and with earnestness to them. For, I think, principles at present are quite out of the case, and that we dispute wholly about persons. In these last you and I differ; but in the other, I think, we agree: For I have in print professed myself in politics, to be what we formerly called a Whig.

As to the great man whose defence you undertake; though I do not think so well of him as you do, yet I have been the cause of preventing five hundred hard things being said against him.[2]

[1] See Steele's letter of the previous day and notes.
[2] On more than one occasion Swift said as much in the *Journal*. On 6 Jan.

I am sensible I have talked too much when myself is the subject; therefore I conclude with sincere wishes for your health and prosperity, and am, | Sir, | Your, &c.

You cannot but remember, that, in the only thing I ever published with my name, I took care to celebrate you as much as I could, and in as handsome a manner, though it was in a letter to the present Lord Treasurer.[1]

B.M. Add. MS. 39839
Swift to Miss Esther Vanhomrigh

[31 May 1713.][2]

I promised to write to you; and I have let you know that it is impossible for any body to have more acknowledgements at heart for all your kindness and generosity to me. I hope this Journy will restore my Health; I will ride but little every day; and I will write a common Letter to you all, from some of my Stages; but directed to you. I could not get here till ten this night.[3] Pray be merry and eat and walk; and be good. and send me your Commands whatever M^r L—[4] shall think proper to advise you. I have hardly time to put my Pen to Paper; but I would make any Promise. — Pray God

1712/13 he claimed to have 'hindred many a bitter thing' being said against Marlborough. See also *Journal*, 7 Mar. 1710/11 and 25 Jan. 1711/12: 'I am of your opinion, that Lord Marlborough is used too hardly: I have often scratched out passages from papers and pamphlets sent me before they were printed; because I thought them too severe.'

[1] *A Proposal for Correcting, Improving and Ascertaining the English Tongue*, 1712. On p. 37 Swift refers to an 'Author, who hath tried the Force and Compass of our Language with so much Success'. In the context the allusion to Steele would be unmistakable.

[2] We know the date of this letter from Swift's account-book (Forster, No. 509), and from the last letter of the *Journal*, 6 June 1713, where he writes from Chester, 'I am come here after six days, I sett out on Monday last.'

[3] From Swift's account-book it appears that he had spent the day at Kensington.

[4] Erasmus Lewis.

preserve you and make You happy and easy.—and so adieu
bratt—

M^r B's House[1]
11 at night,   Service to Mother
company weighting   and Molkin
who came to take
leave of me.

Address: To Miss Hessy Vanhomrigh
Endorsed: 1st

4804

Erasmus Lewis to Swift

Whitehall Jun. 2. 1713

I hope this will meet you at Chester and that your passage at sea
will be favour'd with as mild weather as your journey by land has
been these two first days. The Division yesterday in the House of
Lords was 64 agt. 54. Proxy's were call'd for and we had, 17 to 13.
This is the greatest victory we ever had, The Duke of Argyll & the
Scotch were against us to a man. Lds Weymouth & Carteret were
with 'em.[2] twas very comical to see the Tory's, who voted with
Ld Treasurer agt. the Dissolution of the Union, under all perplexity's in the world least they sh'd be victorious, and the Scotch who
voted for a bill of Dissolution under agony's least they themselves
sh'd carry the point they pretended to desire.[3] in all the time I have
been conversant in business, I never before observ'd both sides at
the same time acting parts wch they thought contrary to their

---

[1] Swift was evidently spending the night with John Barber before setting out
for Chester on the following morning.
[2] Lady Carteret was a granddaughter of Lord Weymouth.
[3] A tax of sixpence a bushel on all British malt was voted in the spring of
1713. The anger roused in Scotland was so strong that Scottish members at
Westminster combined to demand a repeal of the Union. Oxford, sincerely
believing in the Union, played adroitly to save it, though many Tories had little
love for it. This explains Lewis's account of the division. Exactly what happened
is not clear. In any event the motion for leave to bring in Repeal was defeated in
the Lords and was never introduced into the Commons. See Trevelyan, *England
under Queen Anne*, iii. 241–3.

Interests. let us hear from you sometimes and believe there is nobody with more sincerity yours than.

Endorsed by Swift with receipt date: Jun. 12. 1713 | 1713

4804

The Rev. John Sharpe to Swift

London June 4th 1713

Reverend Sir,

I was commanded by his Excellency Brigadier Hunter Governor of New York[1] to deliver the inclosed with my own hand had I been so happy for his service and my own satisfaction as to have seen you at London, I am persuaded your Influence here might have contributed to create a better opinion of him, amongst some leading men in the Society for the propogation of the Gospel in Foreign parts who have been much imposed on by the clamorous memorials of some indiscreet Missionaries abroad. he has the Just Esteem of two thirds of the Clergy in his Governments and the greatest part of the Layety who have either sense probity or honour, but his Adversaries have made the Churches cause a favourable handle for their repeated complaints which, with the application of their Friends here, makes them very hopefull of success.

I have been twelve years abroad, in the Service of the Church in America: the last ten were in the Station of Chaplain to her Majesties Forces at New York, where I had the opportunity [of] being very near to the several Governours, and assure you that if I had ever observed in him any inclination to weaken the interest of the Church there, I could not in conscience offer to excuse him, but he is better known to you, than that I who am altogether unknown should presume to give his character. What I beg to entreat of you is to recommend me in my endeavours for his service, to the advice and assistance of your Friends, The perplexity of all his affairs at this time claims the good offices of all that wish him well. If, in favour to his Excly you are pleased to honour me with the pardon of this and what return the enclosed may require direct for me to the care of Mr James Douglas Merchant in Fen court, Fen Church street

[1] See p. 335.

362

London. I beg leave to subscribe my self, with great respect |
Revernd Sir | Your most obedient & | most humble Servant |

John Sharpe.

Endorsed by Swift: Jun. 4th 1713.

4804

Robert Hunter to Swift

N York ye 14. March 171⅔

[*Enclosure*]

Quonorough Quaneough Dvradadega Generoghqua aguegon
tehitche nágarcé, Or least you should not have your Iróquoise
dictionary at hand, Brother I honor you and all your tribe tho' that
is to be taken cum grano salis for one of them has done me much
harm. God reward him &c. For that and what besides you want to
know that relates to me I referr you to the bearer Mr Sharp our
Chaplain a very worthy Ingenious conscientious Clergy man I wrote
to you sometime agoe by a merchantship and therein gave you some
hints of my sufferings which are not diminish'd since that time. In
hopes of a better settlement I wish'd for your company untill that
comes I can contribute to nothing but your spleen. Here is the finest
air to live upon in the Universe and if our trees and birds could
speake and our assembly men be silent the finest conversation too.
Fert omnia Tellŭs but not for me, for you must understand, according to the customs of our Countrey the Sachems are of the poorest
of the people. I have gott the wrong side of Sr Polidores[1] office, a
great deal to do and nothing to receive. In a word, and to be serious
at last, I have spent these years of life in such torment and vexation
that nothin in life can ever make amends for it. Tu interim sis laetus
et memor nostrum vale |

RH

Address: To the Revnd | Doctor Jonathan Swift at | London

---

[1] The allusion may be to the part played by Polydore in Otway's play *The Orphan*.

Miss Esther Vanhomrigh to Swift

London June ye 6 1713

S.^r

Now you are good beyond expression in sending me that D.^{r1} voluntary from St Albans,[2] it gives me more happyness than you can imagine or I describe to find that your head is so much better already. I do assure you all my wishes are imployed for the continuance of it. I hope your next will tell me they have been of force. had I the power I want every day I did not add as much to your health till it was quite established as Monday last[3] has done should be stroke out of the Kalendar as useless ones. I believe you little thought to have been teased by me so soon. but when M.^r L:[4] told me if I would write to you that he would take care of my letter, I must need own I had not self denyal enough to for bear writing to you pray why did not you remember me at Dunstable[5] as well as moll Lord what a monster is Moll grown since but nothing of poor Hess except that the marke will be in the same place Davila[6] as you left it. indeed it is not much advanced yett for I have been studying of Rochefoucaut[7] to see if he describes as much self love as I found in my self a Sunday and I find he falls very short of it.

how does Bolinbroke[8] perform you have not kept your promise of

---

[1] The contraction stands for 'Dear'.

[2] A word is erased after 'St. Albans'. The following letter shows that John Barber accompanied Swift as far as St. Albans, and that Swift gave him when returning a letter for Vanessa.

[3] 'last' is written above the line, and 'has done' has a single line struck through it.

[4] Lewis.

[5] On the first night Swift stayed at Dunstable. Thence he sent another letter to Vanessa.

[6] Enrico Caterino Davila (1576–1631), famous as the author of the *Historia delle Guerre Civili di Francia*, 1630, which was translated into English in 1647 by William Aylesbury and Sir Charles Cotterel. A copy of the English translation appears in the sale catalogue of Swift's books, No. 594, marked as annotated by him. Swift mentions Davila in *The Battle of the Books* and quotes from him in the *Examiner*.

[7] Swift was well acquainted with La Rochefoucauld's *Reflexions ou sentences et maximes morales*. Cf. *Poems*, p. 553, n.

[8] The name of Swift's horse.

rideing but a little every day 30 miles I take to be a very great Journey I am very impatient to hear from you at Chester it is impossible to tell you how often I have wished you a cupe of coffee and an orange at your Inn

Endorsed: 1

B.M. Add. MS. 39839

Swift to Mrs. Vanhomrigh

Chester. June 6th 1713

You heard of me from Dunstable by the way of Hessy,[1] I have had a good time since, If Mol's Even so had been there, she would have none left.[2] Now Hessy grumbles that I talk of Moll. I have resolved upon the Direction of my Letter already; for I reckon Hess and Moll are Widows as well as you, or at the least half Widows. D'avila goes off rarely now. I have often wished for a little of your Rats-bane; what I met upon the Road does not deserve the name of Rats bane.[3] I have told Mr Lewis the Circumstances of my Journey, and the Curious may consult him upon it. Who will Hessy get now to chide, or Moll to tell her Storyes, and bring her Sugar plumbs? We never know anything enough till we want it. I design to send Hessy a Letter in print from Ireland, because she cannot read writing hand, except from Mr Partington.[4] I hope you have heard again from the Colonell,[5] and that he is fully cured of his—I don't know what. I forget; It was under cover to Mr Lewis that I writt You from Dunstable; I writt to Hessy by Barber from St Albans. I left London without taking leave of Sr John, I fear a Person of his

---

[1] This is a slip. Swift wrote to Hessy from St. Albans and to Moll from Dunstable. As Dunstable is thirty-two miles from London and Chester 180 he appears to have maintained a steady average over the six days.

[2] Under the same date as this letter in his account-book (Forster, 509) Swift records a payment of 16*s.* 11*d.* to an apothecary. He was not well, Moll's health was delicate; and they probably compared notes.

[3] Ratsbane signified coffee.

[4] Mr. Partington, or Partinton, was executor of the Vanhomrigh estate. He succeeded avoiding a division of the property in the terms of the will of the elder Bartholomew for years. At last Vanessa instituted a lawsuit against him; but he resisted her successfully until her death; and for years thereafter he continued to cause trouble with her executors, Berkeley and Marshall.

[5] Bartholomew who was still in Paris. See p. 341, n. 5.

Civility will never pardon me: I mett no Adventures in all my Travells, onely my Horse once fell under me, for which Reason I will not ride him to Holyhead, I can assure him that.[1] I could not see any marks in the Chimn⟨ey⟩ at Dunstable of the Coffee Hessy spilt there; and I had no Diamond ring about me, to write any of your Names in the Windows. But I saw written, *Dearest Lady Betty Hamilton*,[2] and hard by, Middleton Walker, who⟨m⟩ I take to be an Irish Man-mid-wife, which was a plain omen of her getting a Husband. I hear, Moor the handsom Parson,[3] came over with the A. B. of Dublin. Did not he marry one Mrs Devenish, Ld Lanes-borow[4] [has] been here lately in his way to Ireland, and has gott the good will of all the Folks in our Town: He had something to say to every little boy he met in the Streets. Well, he is the Courteousest Man, and nothing is so fine in the Quality, as to be courteous. Now Moll laughs because I speak wisely, and now Hessy murmurs again. Well, I had a charming handsom Couzen here twenty years ago, I was to see her to night, and, in my conscience she is not handsom at all.[5] I wonder how it comes about, but she is very good neetured, and you know Moll, good Neeture is better than Beauty. I desire you will let me know what Fellows Hessy has got to come to her bed-side in a morning, and when you design to hobble again to Chelsea, if you did not tell me a Lye, as I much suspect. My head is something better, though not so well as I expected by my Journey.—I think I have said enough for a poor weary Traveller; I will conclude without

[1] Letters for Ireland were sent by Holyhead, nearly ninety miles beyond Chester over very rough roads. Passengers usually crossed from Parkgate, near Chester. In his account-book (Forster 509) Swift entered the expense of sending the horse across from Parkgate, as well as the cost of hiring a horse for his servant from London to Chester.

[2] Lady Elizabeth Hamilton, eldest daughter of James, sixth earl of Abercorn, was married in the previous year to William Brownlow, M.P. for Armagh.

[3] The Rev. John Moore, fourth son of the third Earl of Drogheda, was a chaplain to the Earl of Pembroke when Lord Lieutenant. He married a daughter of Sir Charles Porter, who had been Lord Chancellor of Ireland in the reign of William III. She had been previously married to Edward Devenish.

[4] The second Viscount Lanesborough of the first creation.

[5] In the first letter of the *Journal*, 2 Sept. 1710, also written at Chester, Swift observes casually, 'My Cozn Abigail is grown prodigiously old'. Sixteen years later, 23 Nov. 1726, he wrote to a Mrs. Greenvil (should be Greenfield) at Abbey Court, Chester, doubtless the cousin referred to in the *Journal* and in this letter, but that she was in any way akin to Swift is questionable. See further notes upon the letter of 23 Nov. 1726.

Ceremony, and go to bed; and if you cannot guess who is the Writer, consult your Pillow, and the first fine Gentleman you dream of is the Man—so adieu

Address: To Madam Van, at the Sign of the | three Widows, in Pom-roy Alley. | With Care and Speed | Present.

Swift to Charles Ford

[*Fragment*]¹

Chester. June 7, 1713.

If dissolving the Union could be without ill consequence to the Ministry, I should wish for it with all my heart. But I have been too long out of London to judge of politicks.

B.M. Add. MS. 39839

Miss Esther Vanhomrigh to Swift

London June yᵉ 23ᵈ 1713

Here is now three Long, long weeks passed since you wrote to me,² oh happy Dublin that can imploy all your thoughts and happy Mʳˢ Emerson³ that could hear from you the moment you landed. had it not been for her I should be yet⁴ more uneasy than I am, I really believe before you leave Ireland I shall give you just reason to wish I did not kno⟨w⟩ my letters, or at least that I could not write, and I had rather you should wish ⟨so⟩ than intirely forgett me. confess have you once thought of me since you wrote to my mother att chester⁵ which letter I assure you I take very ill, my mother and

¹ On 4 June 1896, at Messrs. Christie's, a Swift letter, described as 'one page 4to', was put up for sale. This brief extract was reprinted from the catalogue by Professor Nichol Smith, *Letters of Swift to Ford*, p. 11. The letter was not sold, and has disappeared. At Chester Swift had received news, perhaps from Ford as well as from Erasmus Lewis (see 2 June), of the motion in the House of Lords on 1 June to bring in a Bill to dissolve the Union with Scotland.

² Swift had arrived in Dublin on Wednesday, 10 June.

³ Not identified.   ⁴ 'yet' written above the line.

⁵ 6 June. 'from' before 'chester' scored out.

I have counted the Molls, and the Hessys, tis true the number is equal, but you talk to Moll, and only say now Hessy grumbles. how can you possibly be so ill natured, to make me either quarrel or grumble when you are at so great a distance, that tis impossible for me to gain by doing so: beside you promised the letter should be directed to me, but ile say no more of that, but keep my temper till we meet. pray have you received the letter I wrote to Chester. I hear you had a very quick passage[1] I hope it was a pleasant one, and that you had no reason to complain of your health, we have had a vast deall of Thunder for this week past I wish you had been here last Thursday I am sure you could have prevented the bills being lost.[2] are not you prodigiously surprised at Sᵣ T.H. and Lord A:[3] lord how much we differ from the Ancients who used to sacrifice every thing for the good of their common wealth. but now our greatest men will at any time give up their country out of a pique. and that for nothing. tis impossible to describe the rejoycings that are amongst the Whigs since that day and I fear the Elections[4] will add to them Lord Treasurer has been extreamly to blame for all his Friends advised him to let it be dropt by consent till next session but he would not, depending on the same success he had in the malt tax. I know youl say what does the slut mean to talk all this stuff to me if I was there I would as live hear it as any thing she would say but to persue me with her nonsense is intolerable ile read no more. will,[5] go to the post Office and see if there be more Letters for me what will this paquett only serve to tease me I can tell you you'll have none from lady Orkney by the post[6] what ever you may by any other carriage

---

[1] Swift had a good passage, reaching Holyhead on the 10th and landing at Dublin on the evening of the same day.

[2] On 18 June the commercial clauses of the Treaty of Peace, establishing trade with France, a project of Bolingbroke, went to a vote, the Ministry was defeated by 194 to 185, and these clauses were cut out from the Treaty. This was a triumph for the Whigs. See Trevelyan, *England under Queen Anne*, iii. 254–8.

[3] Hanmer, at the last moment, came out against the Treaty of Commerce; and Lord Anglesey also opposed it.

[4] Under the Triennial Act Parliament was dissolved. A general election followed in August and September, and a Tory government was again returned.

[5] Swift's then servant, who had taken Patrick's place. The account book for 1711–12 (Forster, 508) has the following entry:

Apr. 8 . 1712 Patrick left me
—— 11 William came.

[6] Probably Lady Orkney was unwilling to trust the post office as a channel of communication.

I have strictly ubsarved your commands as to reading and walking M.͏ Ford can witness the latter for he has paddled with us several nights. (I have a vast deall to tell you about him when I see you) M.͏ Lewis has given me les Dialogues des morts[1] and I am so charmed with them that I am resolved to quit my poste let the consequence be what it will except you will talke to me for I find no conversation upon earth comparable but yours so if you care I should stay do but talke and youl keepe me with pleasure

B.M. Add. MS. 39839

Miss Esther Vanhomrigh to Swift

June London 1713[2]

   Tis unexpressible the concern I am in ever since I heard from M.͏ Lewis that your head is so much out of order who is your physician for god sake dont be persuaded to take many slops satisfy so much as to twll me what[3] medicines you have taken and and do take how did you find yourself whilst a ship boarde I fear tis your vioage has discomposed you and then so much business folowing so immediatly before you had time to recruit twas to much I beg make all the haste imaginable to the Country for I firmly believe that time and rest will do you more good than any thing in the world besides if I talk impertinently I know you have goodness enough to forgive me when you consider how great an ease tis to me to ask these questions thô I know it will be a great while before I can be answered. I am sure I shall think it so oh what would I give to know how you doe at this instant my fortune is to hand your absence was enoogh without this cruill addition. Sure the powers above are envious[4] of your thinking so well which makes them at sometimes strive to interrupt you but I must confine my thoughts or at least stop from telling telling them to you or you'l chide which will still add to my uneasiness I have done all that was possible to hinder my self from writing to you till I heard you were better for fear of breaking my

[1] English translations of Fontenelle's *Nouveaux dialogues des morts* appeared in 1683, 1692, and 1708; but Vanessa may have read the work in the original.
[2] Ball suggests the 27th of the month.
[3] Word obliterated after 'what'.
[4] 'envious' is written above an obliterated word.

promise but twas all in vain for had [I] voued neither to touch pen ink or paper I certainly should have had some other invention therefore I beg you wont be angery with me for doing what is not in my power to avoide, pray make Parvosole write me word what I desire to know for I would not for the world have you hold down your head I am impatient to the last degree to hear how you are I hope I shall soon have you here

Endorsed: 3ᵈ

P.R.O., Dublin¹

Swift to Joshua Dawson

Trim, 29 June 1713.²

Sir,³

Dr. Raymond just now tells me he has received an account that Mr. Browne, your clerk, said the Doctor's warrant⁴ was not signed yet, and that the Lords Justices⁵ designed to consider of it. This gives the Doctor some uneasiness and you the trouble of this letter. I can assure you that the day before I left London I laid the whole matter before my Lord Duke of Ormond in so plain a manner that he immediately complied with it, and I gave his Grace the Bishop of Meath's memorial, which showed how hard it would be not only upon the Doctor, but upon the church of Trim, if that small rectory, only of forty pounds a year, were disposed of any other way.⁶ If any

¹ The originals of the Church Miscellaneous Papers were not saved from the destruction of the Public Record Office, Dublin. A calendar of them has been republished in the latest report of the Deputy Keeper of the Records; but the entry, under No. 59, is less informative and helpful than the text furnished in Ball's edition of the *Correspondence*, ii. 49–50.

² In his account-book (Forster Collection, No. 509) Swift records that he was installed Dean of St. Patrick's on Saturday the 13th, and that he left Dublin for Laracor on Thursday the 25th.

³ For Joshua Dawson see p. 161, n. 3.

⁴ For the text of the Memorial see 5 May 1713.

⁵ Sir Constantine Phipps, the Lord Chancellor, and John Vesey, the Archbishop of Tuam.

⁶ On 13 May Swift had written to Stella asking her to tell Raymond that he could not succeed in getting him the living of Moymet. On 6 June he wrote again to say he hoped 'he may yet have it' (*Journal*, pp. 668, 671). Ball quotes from the Departmental Correspondence then in the P.R.O. of Ireland a curious statement from Secretary Southwell to the Lords Justices 16 May: 'His Grace

difficulty should yet remain, I must make it my request to you to present my duty to my Lord Chancellor, and let him know what I now tell you, and assure him that if it were not for the good of the Church, and that I knew every circumstance of the Bishop's memorial to be true, I would never have moved one step in it, though Dr. Raymond is a gentleman wholly unexceptionable, and very much in my esteem.

My health has been so ill that I was forced to steal away without waiting on my Lord Chancellor or anybody else, and here I am riding for life, but hope to be in town in a week or two. I am, Sir, |
Your most obedient humble servant, |

                                                            J. Swift.

You will consider what it is to keep an honest gentleman in suspense and put him out of pain as soon as you can.

B.M. Add. MS. 39839

Miss Esther Vanhomrigh to Swift

                                          June [30?] London 1713

S.̠

M.̠ Lewis assures me that you are now well, but will not tell me what authority he has for it, I hope he is rightly informed. thô tis not my usual custom, when a thing of consequence is in doubt to fix on what I earnestly wish. but I have already suffered so much by knowing that you were ill, and fearing that you were worse than I hope you have b⟨een⟩ that I will strive to change that thought if possible that I may have a little ease and more that I may not write you a splenetick letter. pray why would not you make paruisole[1] write me word when you did when I beged it so much and if you were able your self how could you be so cruel to defer telling me the

in his last letter wrote to your Lordships to give the living of Moymet, near Trim, to Dr. Dunbar, the blind clergyman, his Grace supposing at that time he had no bread or subsistence. By the last packets Dr. Raymond sends over a certificate that Dunbar has a living. Some inform his Grace that Moymet is a sinecure, others say not. Some tell his Grace that Dr. Raymond has above £200 a year without this, and others say he cannot live if he has it not. His Grace therefore orders me to desire of your Lordships to a strict enquiry into this matter and your answer thereupon, and in the mean time to stop the disposal thereof.'   [1] Parvisol.

thing of the world I wish⟨ed⟩ most to know. if you think I write to
often your only way is to tell me so or at least to write to me again
that I may know you dont quite forgett me for I very much fear that
I never imploy a thought of yours now except when you are reading
my letters which makes me ply you with them (M.ʳ Lewis complains
of you to) if you are very happy it is ill natured of you not to tell me
so except tis what is inconsistent with mi⟨ne⟩ but why dont you tell
me that you know will please me I have often heard you say that you
would willingly suffer a little uneasiness provided it gave another a
vast deall of pleasure pray remember this maxime because it makes
for me this is now the 4ᵗʰ I have now wrote to you the[y] could not
miscarry for the[y] were all under M.ʳ Lewis's cover nor could you
avoid opening them for the same reason. pray what have you don
about the two livings. have you recovered them or no¹ you know I
love law bussiness I have been with Lawyers since I saw you but
have not yett had their answers therefore wont trouble you with
what I have don till I can tell you all pray let me know when you
designe coming over for I must beg you to talke to Mr. P:[artinton]²
and settle some affairs for me pray let me heare from you soon which
will be an unexpressable Joy to her that is allways

Endorsed: 4ᵗʰ

B.M. Add. MS. 39839

Swift to Miss Esther Vanhomrigh

Laracor. Jul. 8ᵗʰ 1713

I stayed but a fortnight in Dublin, very sick, and returned not one
Visit of a hundred that were made me³ but all to the Dean, and none

¹ In addition to the Deanery of St. Patrick's Stearne held the two livings into
which the parish of St. Nicholas Without, Dublin, had been divided. On his
appointment to the Bishopric of Dromore Stearne and the Chapter hastened to
nominate incumbents to the two livings lest the Crown should claim presentation
to them as well as to the Deanery. Swift was much incensed, for he hoped to
present Parnell to one of the livings. See *Journal*, 16 May 1713.
² Cf. Swift to Vanessa, 6 June 1713.
³ Orrery (*Remarks*, pp. 41–42) avers that when Swift came over 'to take
possession of the deanery' he had an unpleasant reception from the rabble.
There is little reason to accept this story. His health was poor, he was little
abroad, and within two weeks he left for Laracor.

to the Doctor; I am riding here for life, and think I am something
better, and hate the Thoughts of Dublin, and prefer a field-bed and
an Earthen floor[1] before the great House there, which they say is
mine:[2] I had your last spleenatick Letter:[3] I told you when I left
England, I would endeavor to forget every thing there, and would
write as seldom as I could. I did indeed design one generall Round
of Letters to my Friends, but my Health has not yet suffered me . . .
I design to pass the greatest part of the time I stay in Ireland here
in the Cabin where I am now writing, neither will I leave the Kingdom till I am sent for, and if they have no further service for me, I
will never see England again: At my first coming I thought I should
have dyed with Discontent, and was horribly melancholy while they
were installing me, but it begins to wear off, and change to Dullness.
My River walk is extremely pretty, and my Canal in great Beauty,
and I see Trout playing in it. I know not any one Thing in Dublin
but Mr Ford is very kind, and writes to me constantly what passes
among You. I find you are likewise a good Politician and I will say
so much to you; that I verily think if the thing you know of had been
published just upon the Peace, the Ministry might have avoided
what hath since happened.[4] But I am now fitter to look after Willows,
and to cutt Hedges than meddle with Affairs of State. I must order
one of the Workmen to drive those Cows out of my Island, and make
up the Ditch again; a Work much more proper for a Country Vicar
than driving out Factions and fencing against them: And I must go
and take my bitter Draughts the Publick hath given me . . . How
does Davila go on?[5] Jonny Clark[6] is chosen Portrieve of our Town
of Trim,[7] and we shall have the Assizes there next week; and fine
doings; and I must go and borrow a Horse to meet the Judges, and

---

[1] When Swift was appointed to Laracor there was no dwelling house attached
to the benefice. He built a humble cottage and cultivated the surrounding
ground. See Landa, *Swift and the Church of Ireland*, pp. 35–41.

[2] Little remains of the deanery built by Stearne. After Swift's death a fire
destroyed all save the basement and a minor part of the floor above. Stearne's
house seems to have been a dull, unpleasing structure (*H.M.C., Rept. 8*, pt. ii,
p. 114).

[3] See previous letter.

[4] The allusion is to *The Four Last Years of the Queen*.

[5] See p. 364, n. 6.

[6] Presumably a man of some means resident in Trim. His will was proved in
the Consistorial Court in 1732.

[7] Trim was the assize town of co. Meath.

Jo Beaumont[1] and all the Boys that can get horses will go too. M[r] Warburton[2] has but a thin School; M[r] Percevall has built up the other side of his House, but People whisper that it is but scurvily built. M[r] Steers is come to live in M[r] Melthorp's House, and tis thought the Widow Melthorp will remove to Dublin.—Nay, if you do not like this sort of News, I have no better. So go to your Dukes and Dutchesses, and leave me to Goodman Bumford,[3] and Patrick Dolan of Clanduggan.—Adieu—

Address: To Miss-Hessy
Endorsed: 3[d]

4804

Erasmus Lewis to Swift

Whitehall | Jul. 9. 1713

We are all running headlong into the greatest confusion imaginable, Sr Thomas Hanmer is gone into the Country this morning, I believe, much discontented, and I am very apprehensive neither Ld Anglesea nor He will continue long with us. I heartily wish you were here, for you might certainly be of great use to Us by yr endeavours to reconcile, and by representing to them the infallible consequences of these Divisions.[4] we had Letters this morning from Ireland, wt is the reason I had none from you? Adieu. I hope yr want of health is not the cause.

Address: To | The Reverend Dr Swift | Dean of St Patricks | at Dublin | Ireland.
Endorsed by Swift: M[r] Lewis about | the Divisions &c | Jul. 9th 1713

[1] A linen draper and general dealer of Trim. Deane Swift describes him as 'a venerable, handsome, grey-headed man, of quick and various abilities'. His slaying tables, for use in the weaving of linen, won him a government award. As early as 1715 he showed signs of mental derangement, and a few years later he became hopelessly mad.

[2] The Rev. Thomas Warburton, Swift's curate at Laracor, kept a school at Trim.

[3] Probably Lawrence Bomford of Clonmahon, in the parish of Laracor, a member of a well-known Meath family, who is said to have died in 1720 at the age of 103.—Ball.

[4] See Vanessa to Swift, 23 June, and notes.

Swift to Charles Ford

Laracor. July. 9. 1713

I am extreamly obliged to you for writing to me so often, but I beg you will suspend or leave it off, when it begins to be too troublesome. I believe I have had your 6 Letters, for 3 came here, and I think I left as many in Dublin. I stayd there no longer than Business forced me. I received no Visits but one day, for I was very ill, and I payd none at all, but stole down here to ride and drink bitter Draughts. I am somewhat better, I thank God, but have still a very disordered[1]

I am tempted to think, that if the Tract[2] I left with Mr L—[3] had been published at the time of the Peace, some ill Consequences might not have happened. Ld T—[4] said both to others and my self, that he did not care whether this Parlmt passt the Commerce or no, and that the next should have the Honor of it. But your Steps are sometimes so odd that I could not account for them while I was among you, much less at this distance, and you change so fast, that whoever is a Month from you is wholly a Stranger to Affairs.[5] I do not at all like the generall Face of them; and if Domvile[6] would tell you the Advice I gave him you would think me a very desponding Person, and Ld Tr would call me the greatest of his four Cowards[7] if he knew it. A Country Vicar must quote Texts. Two men shall be in the Field, the one shall be taken, and the other left; but how soon, or which shall be taken, and which left, is a shuddering Question.[8] If I am called for this Winter, I will come and take what share my Health will permit me, otherwise I will stay where I am, and learn by Habitude to render this Country supportable. Neither shall the Promises I received of a thousand Pounds to pay my debts,[9] draw me over to sollicite, except I am commanded to come. In that Case, I will shew my Courage: though I know the Malice of a victorious Faction would not overlook me. Atqui sciebat quæ sibi barbarus

---

[1] Sentence unfinished; 'head'?

[2] The *Four Last Years of the Queen*. In his letter to Vanessa of 8 July Swift made the same observation.

[3] Erasmus Lewis.   [4] Lord Treasurer.

[5] The Treaty of Commerce. See Vanessa to Swift, 23 June 1713, and note.

[6] William Domvile, M.P. for co. Dublin.

[7] Another of Oxford's four cowards was Lord Dartmouth. Swift to Dartmouth, 8 Aug. 1713.   [8] Oxford or Bolingbroke?

[9] See p. 353, n. 2; and see *Journal*, 23 Apr. 1713.

tortor pararet.[1] I sent the Book to Mrs Barnard,[2] but I never saw your Mother; I was not able to do it. I write this Post to Mr Manley.[3] I am apt to think he is too obnoxious, and too much at mercy at present, to do any thing of that kind, if he were disposed to it. I dare not write more, it is as much as my Head is worth, and that at present is not worth very much; but my Heart is good, and that must answer for the defects of its Superior, as Servants are forced to do sometimes for their Masters.—Sr T. Hanmer positively assured me that he was perfectly satisfied with every Part of the Commerce Treaty, after a full hearing of the Arguments for and against it in the House: So that nothing is strange.

Address, on separate cover: To Charles Ford Esqr | at His Office at Whitehall | London
Postmark: 20 IY

Faulkner 1762

Swift to Archbishop King

Trim, July 16, 1713.

My Lord,

I have been about five Weeks in this Kingdom, but so extremely ill with the Return of an old Disorder in my Head, that I was not able to write to your Grace, I have been the greatest Part of that Time at my Country Parish, riding every Day for my Health. I can tell your Grace nothing from *Dublin* having spent the Days I was there between Business and Physic, and paid no Visits nor received any but one Day; and, I reckon it no great Loss, for I hear they are all Party-mad; and, it is one Felicity of being among Willows, that one is not troubled with Faction. I hope, you have as little of it at the *Bath*;[4] for, I cannot fancy it does well with the Waters. If your Grace goeth to *London* from the *Bath*, I believe, I may have the Honour of waiting on you, although I shall do all in my Power to save the

---

[1] Horace, *Odes*, III. v. 49, 50.
[2] Unidentified. It has been suggested, without much probability, that she was Swift's nurse at the end of his days. See W. Monck Mason, *Cathedral Church of St. Patrick*, 1820, p. 412.
[3] Isaac Manley, Postmaster-General in Ireland.
[4] King had been at Bath since 27 May.

Trouble of such a Journey, which neither my Fortune nor my Health will very well bear. I hope, you feel the good Effects of the Place you are in, and I pray God continue your Life, for the Good of his Church.

The other day, Mr. *Theaker*, Prebendary of *Saggart* and Vicar of *Rathcoole*, dyed;[1] and, it would be a great Mark of Goodness in your Grace, as well as a personal Favour to me, if you would please to dispose of his Livings in Favour of Mr. *Thomas Warburton*,[2] who hath been many Years my Assistant in the Cure of *Laracor*, hath behaved himself altogether unblameably, and is a Gentleman of very good Learning and Sense. If I knew any one more deserving I would not recommend him, neither would I do it however, because I know your Grace hath a great many Dependants; but, that it will be a great Use to me to have a Vicar in one of my Rectories, and upon my Deanery,[3] in whom I can confide. I am told the Livings amount to an Hundred and Twenty Pounds a Year at most; and, it may probably happen in my Way to be able to oblige some Friend of yours in a greater Matter, which I shall very readily do. I am, with the greatest Respect, | My Lord, | Your Grace's most obedient, and | Most humble Servant, |

Jon. Swift.

Rothschild

Swift to Charles Ford

Laracor. July. 30. 1713.

I had both your Letters. I here send you inclosed one to Ld Bol.[4] which you may seal, and get sent to him if it be in the manner you

---

[1] The united parishes of Saggart and Rathcoole lie in the south of co. Dublin. The parishes had been held for over ten years by the Rev. Thomas Theaker, a scholar, 1672, and M.A. of Trinity College. See *Alum. Dub.*, p. 805.

[2] Swift's curate at Laracor, who also conducted a school at Trim. He married in 1716/17 and obtained the living of Magherafelt in the diocese of Armagh, which he held until his death in 1736 (Leslie, *Armagh Clergy*, p. 364). Swift's present application was unsuccessful.

[3] The possessions of the Dean of St. Patrick's included the tithes of Rathcoole and land within that parish as well as in the immediate vicinity.—Ball.

[4] The letter to Bolingbroke appears not to be extant, and the post that Ford sought is not known.

approve. I hope you may succeed, for M^r L— may twenty ways do you good Offices in it; and if you get in, I hope you will prove a Man of Business. I am still riding in the Country, and I thank God, am much better. I am not of your Opinion about coming over till I am called; and called I am not yet, as I think; for though M^r L— tells you the Ministry desire it, it does not so absolutely appear to me.¹ You may be sure I should be glad to come on many Accounts, and because I should hope they would perform their Promises in giving me money to pay my Debts. I alway[s] intended to come in October; but not sooner without sending for. My Service to all Friends.

I am [of] your Opinion about the Chancellor.² I believe he is yet very happy, for his Longings were violent.

I write this Post to M^r L—.³

No address.

4804

Erasmus Lewis to Swift

Whitehall|Jul. 30. 1713.

This day sen'ight the Queen goes to Hampton Court and the Monday following to Windsor. I fancy by that time Mr Bromley will be Secretary of State in the room of my Lord.⁴

Lord Treasurer was abroad this evening for ye 1st time, after a fortnights illness. I hear there came a dozen of Letters from you by the same Post to yr friends here, my Lord Treasurer desires you will make all possible hast over, for we want you extreamly.

Endorsed by Swift: Mr Lewis | July. 30. 1713 | pressing me to come over

¹ In the following letter, written on the same day by Erasmus Lewis to Swift, the latter is urged to 'make all possible hast over, for we want you extreamly'.
² Sir Constantine Phipps, Lord Chancellor of Ireland.
³ Writing to Swift in Jan. 1714–15 the cautious Lewis advised him to hide his papers securely lest they should fall into the hands of enemies. He himself seems to have hidden or destroyed all letters received from Swift. The only letter from Swift to Lewis which survives is that dated 23 July 1737, first printed by Deane Swift in 1765.
⁴ Lewis had served as Under-Secretary of State to Lord Dartmouth. On Dartmouth's promotion to the office of Lord Privy Seal, Bromley was appointed in his room, and Lewis served under him.

Swift to Bishop Atterbury

The Country in Ireland, Aug. 3, 1713.

My Lord,

It is with the greatest pleasure I heard of your Lordship's promotion, I mean that particular promotion, which I believe is agreeable to you, though it does not mend your fortune.[1] There is but one other change I could wish you, because I have heard you prefer it before all the rest; and that likewise is now ready, unless it be thought too soon, and that you are made to wait till another person has used it for a step to cross the water.[2] Though I am here in a way of sinking into utter oblivion, for *hæ latebræ nec dulces, nec, si mihi credis, amœnæ*,[3] yet I shall challenge the continuance of your Lordship's favour, and whenever I come to London, shall with great assurance cross the Park to your Lordship's house at Westminster, as if it were no more than crossing the street at Chelsea.[4] I talked at this threatening rate so often to you about two years past, that you are not now to forget it.

Pray, my Lord, do not let your being made a Bishop hinder you from cultivating the politer studies, which your heart was set upon when you went to govern Christ Church. Providence has made you successor to a person, who, though of a much inferiour genius,[5] turned all his thoughts that way; and, I have been told, with great success, by his countenance to those who deserved. I envy Dr. Freind that he has you for his inspector;[6] and I envy you for having such a person in your district, and whom you love so well. Shall not I have liberty to be sometimes a third among you, though I am an Irish Dean? *Vervecum in patriâ, crassoque sub aëre natus.*[7]

---

[1] The Deanery of Westminster was then linked with the bishopric of Rochester to which Atterbury had recently been appointed.

[2] Henry Compton, Bishop of London since 1675, died 7 July 1713. The bishopric of London has frequently served as a step to Canterbury by way of Lambeth Palace across the Thames.

[3] Horace, *Ep.* i., xvi. 15: 'Hae latebrae dulces, etiam, si credis, amoenae.'

[4] When Swift lodged at Chelsea he was a near neighbour of Atterbury.

[5] Thomas Sprat, Dean of Westminster and Bishop of Rochester, who died 20 May 1713.

[6] Dr. Robert Freind, under whose headmastership, ending with his retirement in 1733, Westminster school prospered.

[7] Juvenal, x. 50.

379

A very disordered head hindered me from writing early to your Lordship, when I first heard of your preferment; and I have reproached myself of ingratitude, when I remembered your kindness in sending me a letter[1] upon the deanery they thought fit to throw me into; to which I am yet a stranger, being forced into the country, in one of my old parishes, to ride about for a little health. I hope to have the honour of asking your Lordship's blessing some time in October. In the mean while, I desire your Lordship to believe me to be, with very great respect and truth, my Lord, your Lordship's most dutiful and most humble servant, |

J. Swift.

4804

Matthew Prior to Swift

Paris the 16 [o.s. 5] Aug. 1713[2]

As I did not expect, my good friend Jonathan, to have received a letter from you at Dublin, so I am sure I did not intend to write One thither to you: but Mr Roseingrave[3] thinks it may do him service, in recommending him to you, if so, I am very glad of it, for I can be of no other use imaginable: I have writ Letters now above 22 years. I have taken towns, destroyed fleets, made treaties, and settled Commerce in Letters, and what of all this? why nothing, but that I have had some subject to write upon: but to write a letter only because Mr Roseingrave has a Mind to carry One in his pockett, to tell you that you are sure of a friendship wch can never do you three pence of good; and wish you well in England very soon, when I dont know when I am likely to be there my self: all this, I say is very absurd for a letter, especially when I have this day written a dozen much more to the purpose. if I had seen your Manuscript,[4] if I had

---

[1] 21 Apr. 1713.

[2] There is also a copy of this letter P.R.O., S.P., 105-28, f. 131ᵛ.

[3] Daniel Roseingrave (1655?-1727) after successive appointments as organist of Winchester and Salisbury Cathedrals crossed to Dublin, where he settled as organist of St. Patrick's and Christchurch Cathedrals. It was probably Thomas Roseingrave, his elder son, whom Prior met in Paris (*D.N.B.*).

[4] *Four Last Years of the Queen.*

received Dr Parnel's poem,[1] if I had any news of Landau[2] being taken, why well and good; but as I know no more than that the Duke of Shrewsbury designs for England within 3 weeks, that I must stay here till some body comes,[3] and then—brings Me necessarily to say, good Mr Dean, that I am like the fellow in the Rehearsal, who did not know whether he was to be merry or serious, or in what way or mood to act his part,[4] one thing only I am assured of, that I love you very well and am most sincerely and faithfully | dear Sir | Your Servant and Brother,

M. Prior.

Lord and Lady Shrewsbry give their service to you. Vanhoumerigh[5] has run terribly here into Debt and being in durance has sent to his Mother upon pecuniary concerns. Adieu, once more what we are doing or what is to become of us, I know not:

Prudens futuri temporis exitum
Caliginosâ nocte premit Deus,
Ridetque—[6]

This is all the Latin and writing I can at present spare you, pray give my service to your Chancellor[7] and be much acquainted with Judge Nutley, and love him very well for my sake adieu. Once more, find out my Cousin Pennefather[8] and Nutley (if he is not too grave for you) and according to the laudable Custom of your Country drink this Louis out for a token of my generosity and your Sobriety. and now, I think I have furnished you out a very pretty letter.

Endorsed by Swift: Mr Prior | Paris. Aug. 16 · 1713

[1] 'On Queen Ann's Peace', the latter part of which was clearly composed after the signing of the Treaty.

[2] Landau was at the time besieged by the French.

[3] Invested with plenipotentiary powers Prior remained in Paris after the departure of Bolingbroke. On his recall he reached England in the latter part of March 1715.

[4] 'I can't guess for my life what humour I'm to be in: whether angry, melancholy, merry, or in love. I don't know what to make on't.' *The Rehearsal*, by George Villiers, Duke of Buckingham, Act I.

[5] Bartholomew Vanhomrigh, still in Paris.

[6] Horace, *Odes*, III. xxix. 29–31.

[7] Sir Constantine Phipps's extreme Toryism excited suspicion of Jacobitism in Ireland. Richard Nutley, Justice of the Queen's Bench in Ireland, also held advanced Tory opinions (Ball, *Judges in Ireland*, ii. 72)

[8] Probably Colonel Matthew Pennefather, Commissary-General of Ireland, who may have been related to Prior through his mother, who was a Kingsmill.

King's Letter-book

Archbishop King to Swift

Bath august 5.th 1713

Revd S^{r}

I have had the favour of yours of the 16. of July and am sorry to find by it that you are not in a good state of health especially that you complain of any disorder in the head for though such are not very mortall yet they make one uneasy in Company or in business and effect not only the body, but the mind, an odd thought came into my mind on reading that you were among Willows imagining that perhaps your mistress had forsaken you and that was the cause of your malady. If that be the case cheer up, the loss may be repaired, and I hope the remedy easy.

I retired here for my health, and hoped to find a recess from faction and business, but now I find that is a happiness reserved for heaven. I have recd just a hundred and three letters, most long ones, and most of them concerning business since I came here and wrote near as many. Judge if this be agreeable to waters drinking.

As to faction tho you had much of it in London and it had its Centre there, yet the out skirts reached here and I believe everywhere else, but I kept my self pretty well out of its reach by conversing with few but the company I brought with me.

I leave this God willing to morrow and go to Chester, and so to Ireland, leaving the parties to struggle for Elections as they please. If I cannot avoid hearing of them in Dublin tis not my fault being hurried to that Place by duty. As to Mr Theakers benefices I have twelve or fourteen letters about them, but shall not dispose of them till I get to Ireland, and will discourse you before I do any thing in that and several other matters.

I intend to go thrô Northampton Shire to recruit my sett with fresh horses, if I can find them,[1] I hope to be at Holyhead about the 23rd instant.

I pray God send us a good meeting in Dublin, where we will study to be as easy as we can in spite of faction and business. I recommend you etc.

W.D.

Dr Swift

[1] On visits to Bath Archbishop King used to travel in his own coach drawn by eight horses.

Erasmus Lewis to Swift

Whitehall | Aug. 6. 1713.

I have so often and in so pressing a manner desired you to come over, that if wt. I have already said has no effect I shall despair of better success by any further arguments, if I were to recapitulate the several reasons you offer to the Contrary & answer 'em separately, I shd grow peevish, wch I have no way to avoid but by telling you in general, 'tis all wrong. you and I have already laid it down for a Maxim that we must serve Ld T— without receiving orders, or particular Instructions, and I doe not yet see a reason for changing that rule, his mind has been communicated more freely to you than any other.[1] but you won't understand it. The *desires* of Great Men are *commands*, at least the onely ones I hope, they ever will be able to use. you have a mind to stay in Ireland till October, and desire me to give my opinion whether you sh'd come sooner. I answer yes. then you bid me consider again that is you w'd have me say that I am of opinion you sh'd stay till October. when Judges w'd have a Jury change their verdict they bid them consider again, when a man is determin'd to marry a woman and his friend advises him against it, he asks his opinion again, and if his friend is so silly as not to alter his advice, he marry's without it. I am as much in the spleen now I am answering yr Letter as you were when you writt it. come over you'l cure your self and me to. Adieu.

Endorsed by Swift: Mr Lewis | Aug—6—1713 | Pressing me to come over | &c.

Rothschild[2]

Swift to Archdeacon Walls

Trim. Aug. 7. 1713.

Sr

I received your Notification relating to one Dorothy and her new Productions, which like other second Parts are seldom so good as the

[1] Lewis may have believed this; but we know that Oxford was far from confiding to Swift all that took place.

[2] Previously in the possession of Sir John Murray. Since 1935 in Lord Rothschild's Library.

first. I shall be in Town I hope by the time appointed, and contribute as far towards making your new Inhabitant a Christian as one of that Sex can be.[1]

You are mistaken in your Conjectures about Mother Midnight,[2] with whom I have not the least Acquaintance, or with her Works of Darkness, and if she tells you she has been with me on a Broomstick, she lyes egegriously, tho by the Moons paleness of late, one would think some such Hecate's have been abroad; and I take their Spight to Diana to be owing to her interfering in their Office.

The old Fellow you are pleased to be so free with, is a very honest Gentleman; though he has not your Faculty of encreasing the Queen's Subjects. He has told no Tales but what he can make good; and I do not doubt but he will do Justice to himself and his Friends; and he has drunk so much Claret of late that it has hardned his Tallow too much for You to melt it.[3]

Since the thoughts of your Girl raised your Fancy, it is but just that her Noise should disturb it. Jo[4] says all your Spight to him arise from your Jealousy, and that you dare not trust him with Dorothy, and truly his poor Wife here is as jealous of him as your self; and has been lately told that the Girl you vapour about very much; resembles him: and that a Fortune teller has foretold she will take after him in never being Father of a Child.

Your melancholy Story of the Cask is not new to me. I have. I have known it very frequent to have empty wooden Vessells stufft with Books.—

Jo bids me say he defyes you, and that his Grease has been melted down long ago. Pray say nothing of Dorothy's Jealosy for if one Jonny Clark[5] of Trim should hear of it, there would be no living for poor Jo. But I promise you one thing, that Jo will stand to nothing he says. Jo says the[6] Women do not like him, because they cannot abide *Ridges* nor *Hills*[7] I can not tell the meaning of this.

---

[1] Swift had apparently been asked by the Archdeacon and his wife to be god-father to one of their daughters. In 1711 he had also been requested to stand godfather to a baby of Mrs. Walls (*Journal to Stella*, pp. 203, 208, 213, 234).

[2] The midwife.

[3] At this time Swift was staying at Trim, probably with his friend Raymond, the rector. In the preceding month he had paid similar visits, and on these occasions the purchase of wine was an item in his accounts (Forster Collection, No. 509).

[4] Joe Beaumont.   [5] See p. 373.

[6] the] that *Ball*.   [7] A play on Beaumont's name.

Postscript in another handwriting: I wish you joy but you have mist of yʳ Rain bow and got a plummet. A: R:[1]

Postscript in Swift's handwriting: Jo says he was never cut out to be a Father: take care he fathers nothing upon you.

Postscript in a third handwriting: Jo: sais Parson upon Dorothy is good old Country dance but wonders you did not fill yʳ bullet mold

T. W.[2]

Address: To Dorothy's young Girl's | Father
Endorsement: Dean Swift | Augᵗ 7ᵗʰ 1713

H.M.C. Report 11

Swift to the Earl of Dartmouth

The Country, August 8, 1713.

My Lord,

The way I take of showing my duty and gratitude to those I owe most of both, is by troubling them as seldom as I can. This made me hitherto contradict the violent inclinations I had to write to your Lordship, which now I can resist no longer, especially since I begin to hold up my head after a long disorder it has suffered by the ill life I led, and the ill company I kept among you. And I am not altogether in jest, for God knows I kept some very ill company every Saturday, worse than any of my neighbouring justices here;[3] but I hope that will be mended at my return. And now, my Lord, you are to know that I will not obey your commands of waiting on you in Staffordshire[4] in my way to London; neither do I think it seasonable or safe for me to be on that side of the Channel while you are on this side the Thames. Your Lordship, who has the honour to be one of my brother cowards[5] (as you know who calls four of us), will pardon me if my heart begins to ache when I look about at Court and cannot find you. Therefore, pray give timely warning to Mr. Lewis and me, that he may trot down to Wales, and I gallop to Holyhead. But, my

[1] Anthony Raymond.
[2] T. Warburton.
[3] Dartmouth, now Lord Keeper of the Privy Seal, had, since the beginning of the year, been admitted to the inner Cabinet dinners.
[4] Sandwell, a seat of the Earls of Dartmouth, is in Staffordshire.
[5] See p. 375, n. 7.

Lord, we, the common people, who have the care of your preferment, are resolved not to take away the seals from you, till we have
given you another, much more easy and honourable, though perhaps
not altogether so rich. And I, who am much older than your Lordship,[1] can assure you, that whenever you change your station your
enemies will be able to produce very few examples in the memory of
man, of a Minister who has served with so much honour and integrity. My Lord, I am preparing myself to come over and demand
the dinner you owe me, and hope to find your Lordship in your
Turret at Windsor. In the mean time I desire you to believe that I
am, with the greatest respect and truth, &c. |

J. Swift.

Robert H. Taylor

Swift to John Grigsby

Mᵣ Grigsby,
    Pray pay to Mᵣ John Barber, my Dividend on Five hundred
Pounds, being all my Stock in the South-Sea Company's Books, for
half a Years Interest due at Midsummer last, and this shall be your
Sufficient Warrant |[2]

Jonath: Swift

London Sept. 15. | 1713.

Rothschild[3]

Swift to Archdeacon Walls

London. Sepᵗʳ 17. 1713.

    Our Sᵗ Mary friends I suppose have told you I got well here;[4] It
is an empty Toun, & I believe I shall go to Windsor for some time.

---

    [1] Lord Dartmouth, born in 1672, was only five years younger than Swift.
    [2] This order, in Swift's hand, previously in the Carew Hunt Collection, is
now in the possession of Robert H. Taylor, 575 North Broadway, Yomkers 3,
N.Y., by whose permission it is here reproduced. A similar order will be found
under the date of 20 July 1714. Grigsby was the accountant of the South Sea
Company.

[For notes 3, 4 see opposite

I protest I am less fond of Engld than ever. The Ldyes tell me they are going to live at Trim, I hope they will pass their Christmas at Dublin. Our Club is strangely broke; the Bishop at Dromore, I here, and none but you and Stoits left.[1] Our Goody Walls my Gossip will dy of the Spleen. Pray write to me when you have Leisure, I care not five pence for yr Dublin news, but of our Friends, and of my own Affairs, and give my service to my Commiss^nr Forbes. You will have D. Shrewsbury[2] soon over with you; and Sr John Stanley his Secr^ty;[3] I have not yet seen the Duke nor Dutchess; for they are at Windsor with the Court. My Service to the Alderman, and Goody & Catharine;[4] & Mr Manly & Lady:[5] I think I know no others. Inclose yr Letters to me under a Cover, which Cover you must direct to Erasmus Lewis Esqr, at Mr Secretary Bromley's Office at Whitehall.[6] My Service to Parnel,[7] I have lazily deferrd this Letter till the Post is going. Pray God bless my little Goddaughter; I hope

---

[1] For previous mention of this club and its card parties see p. 108.

[2] The Duke of Shrewsbury was appointed Lord Lieutenant upon the resignation of the Duke of Ormonde. The appointment had been expected for some time (*Journal*, pp. 483, 517, 523, 558, 569).

[3] Sir John Stanley, Bt., was Commissioner of Customs from 1708 to his death in 1744. He was related to Mary Granville, afterwards the well-known Mrs. Delany.

[4] Alderman Stoyte, who was a Whig, married a Miss Lloyd, and Catherine was her unmarried sister. He lived near the green on which Donnybrook Fair was held.

[5] See p. 244, n. 5.

[6] On appointment as Secretary of State Bromley had become Erasmus Lewis's chief.

[7] See p. 345, n. 1.

---

[3] Formerly in the possession of Sir John Murray. Since 1935 in Lord Rothschild's Library.

[4] Swift set sail from Dublin on Saturday, 29 Aug., and landed at Parkgate (see p. 58, n. 1) on the following Monday. On his way to London he spent four days with one of the Irish judges, Sir Gilbert Dolben, at his seat in Northamptonshire. He stayed also for a night at Chester, Newport in Shropshire, Coventry, and Market Street in Hertfordshire, through which his route lay. On some days he travelled nearly fifty miles, and arrived in London on Tuesday, 9 Sept. For the hire of horses he notes a payment of £2. 10s. As appears from a fragmentary list of letters kept by him that year, Swift on his return to England began another journalistic correspondence with the ladies of St. Mary's. The first of his letters to them was written from Chester on 1 Sept.—Ball.

to breed her up to be good for Something, if her Mother will let me. |
Yrs &c.

Address: To the Rev· | Mʳ Archdeacon Walls | at his house over against | the
Hospital in Queen street | Dublin.¹
Postmark: 17 SE
Frank: C. Ford
Later endorsement: Dean Swift | Sepᵗʳ 17ᵗʰ 1713

4804

Dean Smalridge to Swift

Ch—Ch Sept. 27. 1713.

Mr Dean,²

When You were so kind as to favour the Master of the Temple³ &
Me with yr Company at the Chaplain's table at Kensington, there
dined wth Us One Mr Fiddes⁴ a well-deserving Clergy-Man, whose
Circumstances We told You were not at all suitable to his Merits.
You express'd on that Occasion so generous a concern for Him, &
so great a readiness to do Him any good Offices, wch might lie in
Yr way, that He seems to think He shd be wanting to Himself if he
did not endeavour to cultivate an Interest with One so Willing & so
Able to serve him. He has therefore made repeated instances to Me
that I would remind You of Him, which I should not have hearkened
to, were I not well assur'd that You wd excuse if not thank Me for
furnishing You with an Opportunity of doing a Generous & Good-

---

¹ Before this time Walls had resigned the mastership of the Cathedral school
and become incumbent of Castleknock.

² The 'famous Dr. Smalridge' with whom Swift dined, 28 Dec. 1710 (*Journal*,
p. 142), was Canon of Christ Church, Oxford, 1711; Dean of Carlisle, 1711–13.
He then followed Atterbury as Dean of Christ Church, where he described himself as coming with 'a bucket of water' to quench the fires started by his predecessor. At one time he was credited with the authorship of *A Tale of a Tub*.
In 1714 he was appointed Bishop of Bristol.

³ Thomas Sherlock (1678–1761), for half a century a popular Master of the
Temple. In 1714 he was elected Master of St. Catherine's Hall, Cambridge; and
became involved in the Bangorian controversy. He was successively Bishop of
Bangor, Salisbury, and London.

⁴ Richard Fiddes, a struggling divine and historian. Swift introduced him to
Lord Oxford; and he was appointed to the chaplaincy of the garrison at Hull.
His most notable work was his *Life of Cardinal Wolsey*, 1724, which brought him
into suspicion of popery.

natured thing. You will not I fancy, think a formall Application to Any Great Man in his behalf either proper or requisite; but if You should upon the perusall of One or two of his Sermons, think as well of 'em as I do, & shd in Conversation with my Lord Treasurer express a good Opinion of the Author, One kind word from You, seasonably dropt might determine his fortunes, & give You the satisfaction of having made Him and His Family as happy as they can wish to be. I am |Sʳ | Your most Humble Servant |

Geo: Smalridge.

Address: For | The Reverend the Dean | of St Patricks
Endorsed by Swift: Ld Bp of Bristow | Dr Smalridge | Dec_{br} (*sic*) 27ᵗʰ 1713

Nichols 1779

Swift to Archdeacon Walls

Windsor-Castle, Oct. 1, 1713.

I had just now a letter from you, wherein you mention the design of making me Prolocutor.[1] I will confess to you, there are two reasons why I should comply with it; one is, that I am heartily weary of Courts, and Ministers, and politicks, for several reasons impossible to tell you; and I have a mind to be at home, since the Queen has been pleased that *Ireland* should be my home: the other reason is, that I think somebody educated in *Dublin College* should be Prolocutor; and I hear there are designs of turning it another way. But, if you find it will not do, I hope you will quit the design in proper season. I condole with you for the loss of your companions this winter; and I was always of opinion they should be in town, unless they find their health better at *Trim*.[2]

I am a little disappointed in *Parvisol's*[3] return. I hoped it would have amounted to near five hundred pounds in the tithes: I doubt not the cause, and beg you will have no sort of tenderness for him, further than it regards my interest. As to the land-rents, they are one hundred and seventy-four pounds a year in the country, besides

---

[1] A meeting of the Irish Parliament was to be called in the autumn, and Convocation was to be summoned at the same time. The vacancy in the office of Prolocutor arose from Stearne's elevation to the episcopal bench.

[2] Stella and Rebecca Dingley.

[3] Swift had appointed Parvisol his Proctor to set and let the tithes of the Deanery of St. Patrick's (*Journal*, 16 May 1713).

some small things in town; and I am in no pain about them, because they are sure; nor do I desire him to concern himself about them.

I hoped, and was told, my license would be under six pounds, though all was paid; and I heard, if Lord Chancellor had taken his fees, it would have been eight pounds. Tell Mr. *Fetherston*[1] I have spoken to Baron *Scrope*[2] about his affair, who promiseth to dispatch it with the first opportunity. I am now with some Ministers and Lords, and other company, and withdrawn to a table; and hardly know what I write, they are so loud. My humble service to your *Dorothy*, and Alderman *Stoyte*, his wife, and *Cellarius*;[3] and duty to the Bishop of *Dromore*. Yours,

J.S.

4804

Sir Constantine Phipps to Swift

Dublin 10 Oct 1713

S^r

I had the favour of yor kind Letter of the 22nd of Sept^4 & had sooner acknowledg'd it if I had not been prevented by the constant Hurry we have been in with relation to the City & Parliam^t Affairs.[5]

I heartily congratulate yr safe arrival in London & return you with all the gratitude imaginable my thanks for the great trouble you have given yr self as well on behalf of my son[6] in particular as of this Kingdom in Generall & I am sorry you should venture so far as to burn yr fingers but you know[7] such Misfortunes often happen to

---

[1] Probably the Rev. Thomas Fetherston, who became a prebendary of St. Patrick's Cathedral.

[2] John Scrope, at this time baron of the Court of Exchequer in Scotland (*D.N.B.*).

[3] Catherine, sister of Mrs. Stoyte.

[4] The letter is not forthcoming.

[5] Sir Constantine Phipps was making every endeavour to establish a Tory administration in Ireland. A general election was impending. At the same time the choice of a Lord Mayor of the city of Dublin was at issue; and the Whig Corporation was strongly opposed to Tory influences from the Castle.

[6] Phipps desired for his son William, who was then about to enter Trinity College, Dublin (*Alum. Dub.*, p. 668), 'the place of Register of the Forfeited Estates'. See further Phipps to Swift, 24 Oct. 1713, and 15 Jan. 1713–14.

[7] know] prove *Ball.*

Gentlemen who have a hearty zeal for the Interest of their Friends but this comfort attends them that the burning goes off soon Whereas the Credit & Honour of serving one's friend lasts always.

The Acc^t you sent me of Mr Worseleyes[1] being an Envoy was new & had not reach'd us before yr Letter came I know not how sufficiently to acknowledge the obligations you have laid on me but assure you if you have any Commands of this Side the Water there is no one will be more proud of being honour'd with them than he who is with very great respect | yr most obedient | humble Servt |

Con Phipps

Endorsed by Swift: Ld Chanc^{lr} of Ireld | Oct^{br} 10th 1713

Nichols 1779

Swift to Archdeacon Walls

London, Oct. 13, 1713.

I have two letters of yours to acknowledge—No, I mistake, it is but one; for I answered the former, of *September* twenty-second, some time ago; your other is of the first instant, with an account of your mayor-squabble, which we regard as much here as if you sent us an account of your little son playing at cherry-stones. I told your Lord Chancellor, that the best thing the government there could do would be, never to trouble us with your affairs, but do the best you can; for we will neither support nor regard you. I have received the Lords Justices' representation, just now sent to the Queen.[2] I have said more upon it than any body else would; and I hope my Lord Lieutenant will put a good end to the dispute. I am heartily sorry for poor *Hawley*: and doubt such a shake at his age will not be well recovered. Of your four candidates to succeed him, I dislike all but the first, which is *Bolton*.[3] As to the chair of Prolocutor, I said to you in my former all I thought necessary. I dislike the thing for myself;

[1] Henry, brother of Sir Thomas Worsley, Bt., whose daughter married Lord Carteret. At this time Henry was appointed envoy to the Court of Portugal, and later became governor of the Barbadoes.

[2] Owing to the continuing civic quarrel concerning the election of a new mayor of Dublin the Lords Justices contended that the sitting mayor had the right to remain in office for another year.

[3] Thomas Hawley, Archdeacon of Dublin, died two years later at the age of sixty-eight. Swift favoured as his successor Theophilus Bolton, afterwards Archbishop of Cashel.

but I would keep a wrong man out, and would be glad of an honest excuse to leave Courts and public thoughts: but it would vex me to be proposed, and not succeed.[1]

As for *Williams*, I am an old courtier, and will think of it; but, if we want a singer, and I can get a better, that better one shall be preferred, although my father were competitor.[2]

I have spoken to Baron *Scrope* about Mr. *Fetherston's* affair, and hope to get him a good account of it.[3]

You very artificially bring in your friend, Mrs. *South*:[4] I have spoke to her, and heard from her; and spoke to the Duke of *Ormond*: I will do her what service I can.

My service to Gossip *Doll*, and God bless my goddaughter!

I think you need not inquire about the land-rents of the deanery: they are secure enough; and I believe I shall not trouble Mr. *Parvisol* about them.

There is one farm set for one hundred and twenty pounds a year, another for fifty-four pounds. Rents adjoining to the deanery, about two pounds ten shillings, and duties about eight pounds, or something under; and a small lease of tithes, about four or five pounds; which last I would be glad you would ask *Parvisol* whether it be included among the tithes he has set. You see all the rents together are under two hundred pounds. I forgot five pounds a-year for the verger's house.—Service to *Stoyte* and *Manley*,[5] and duty to Bishop of *Dromore*.

P.R.O., State Papers relating to Ireland[6]

Bishop Ellis to Swift

Dublin Octobr. | 20. 1713

R^d S^r[7]

I have the favor of yrs relating to Garencieres:[8] I thank you for the trouble you have been at: I don't doubt but He will be liket

[1] As Prolocutor of Convocation. See p. 389.

[2] Edward Williams, who had been previously a half vicar, was three years later appointed a Vicar Choral of St. Patrick's Cathedral.—Ball.

[3] See p. 390, n. 1.

[4] She was probably the widow of John South, who was a brother commissioner of Bartholomew Vanhomrigh in the Irish revenue department.—Ball.

[5] See p. 387.

[*For notes 6, 7, 8 see opposite*

very well; having pleased so good Judges. He may be admitted at S[t] Patricks as soon as he comes, by your order to your Subdean. your vacancy is a Vicaridge, ours a Stipendiary; but both together may be worth about 80 a year: if the person you have your eye on, will accept that at present, It wou'd be a service to the Quire to send him over too; and you may if you please give him some allowance from the oeconomy of S[t] Patricks, w[ch] is sometimes don, till a vacancy happens there. I have given your directions to M[r] Worral[1] for a list of the Anthems we have here, w[ch] I shall continue to put him in mind of, till it is don. I think what you propose will be for the honour of both Churches; and ours will readily concur with you in so good a design.

you went away without giving order about supplying your Preaching turns at Xtchurch. you know they have been annext to the station many years: the usage can be traced, at least as far as Queen Elisabeth's Reign, which is a long prescription, whatever opinion you may entertain of it: I suppose scarce any usage the Dean and Chapter of S[t] Patricks, at their admission swore to observe, is of much longer continuance; and the members of that Cathedral think themselves hitherto under the influence of that obligation. I have sent you a President[2] of one of your Predecessors upon a neglect of this kind, who has left behind him the character of a very good Governour[3]

[1] John Worrall had been Dean's vicar at St. Patrick's since 1694 (*Fasti Eccl. Hib.* ii. 85, 206, 208, 417). He also held the position of Vicar Choral in Christchurch Cathedral.   [2] i.e. Precedent.

[3] The reference is to John Worth who held the deanery in the reign of James II.

[6] The original of this letter is now among the State Papers in the Public Record Office. It is probable, as Ball suggests, that the originals of this and several other letters were left by Swift either in the office of Erasmus Lewis or in that of Charles Ford, the Gazetteer, and thence found their way into the official papers.

[7] Welbore Ellis, whose leanings were wholly English, was Bishop of Kildare from 1705 to 1731, when he was translated to the see of Meath. The Deanery of Christchurch Cathedral, Dublin, was held by him *in commendam*. The same choir served both cathedrals; and at stated intervals the dignitaries of St. Patrick's were accustomed to preach in the sister cathedral. Despite Ellis's protest in this letter against neglect of an ancient custom Swift and his chapter, in Dec. 1714, notified him that they proposed to treat the act as 'null and void'. See Landa, *Swift and the Church of Ireland*, pp. 70–73.

[8] John Garencieres was installed as Vicar Choral of St. Patrick's on 11 Jan. following.

And this transaction happen'd, whilst His Grace the present Archbishop of Dublin was a member of that church. you having farther considered of this matter, will, I presume, give such directions in it as have been usual.

All here at present are very busy about elections, some for Parliament, others for convocation. Sᵣ Wᵐ Founds, the Recorder, Mᵣ Burton & Mᵣ Tucker appear for this city.¹ on Saturday night last a mob attackt the Archbishop of Tuam's house & hurt one of the centinels with a brick-bat but upō a reinforcement they soon got off: they were for pulling the old Prelate out of his house for a Whig.² the pretence as well as the thing were somewhat extraordinary. you cou'd not have sent any news to me so acceptable as the Health of the Queen. pray God continue it. I am | Rᵈ Sᵣ | your very humble servant |

W Kildare

I just now got the list of the Anthems from Mᵣ Worral.

Endorsed by Swift: R Bp Kildare

Nichols 1779

Swift to Archdeacon Walls

London, Oct. 20, 1713

Sir,

I writ to you immediately upon receiving your former, as I do now upon your last of the tenth instant. As to the business of being prolocutor, I will tell you the short of my story. Although I have done more service to *Ireland*, and particularly to the Church, than any man of my level, I have never been able to get a good word; and I incurred the displeasure of the Bishops, by being the instrument *sine qua non* of procuring the first-fruits: neither had I credit to be a convocation-man in the meanest diocese of the kingdom, till poor Dean *Synge*, who happened to think well of me, got me to be chosen

¹ The election for the city of Dublin was accompanied with much turbulence. Sir William Fownes, M.P. for the borough of Wicklow, and Benjamin Burton, Dublin banker, had both occupied the mayoral chair. The Recorder of Dublin was John Forster. Tucker was a common councillor. Forster and Burton were Whigs. Fownes and Tucker were their Tory opponents.

² John Vesey, 1638–1716, now of great age, had been Archbishop of Tuam since 1678. It is unlikely that he was a supporter of Whig policy.

for *St. Patrick*'s;[1] so that I think there will be a great change if I am
chosen Prolocutor. And yet, at the same time, I am so very nice,
that I will not think of moving towards *Ireland* till I am actually
chosen. You will say, 'What then must the clergy do for a Prolocutor?' Why, I suppose they may appoint a Vice-Prolocutor, until
my coming over, which may be in ten days.—But this perhaps is not
feasible: if not, you may be sure I shall not so openly declare my
ambition to that post, when I am not sure to carry it; and if I fail,
the comfort of *mecum certasse ferretur* will not perhaps fall to my
share. But I go on too fast; for I find in your next lines, that the
Archbishop says, 'There will be an indispensable necessity that I
should be there at the election.' Why, if the Bishops will all fix it,
so as to give a man time to come over, with all my heart; but, if the
election must be struggled for, I will have nothing to do with it. As
for the Bishops, I have not the least interest with above three in the
kingdom: and, unless the thought strikes the clergy in general, that
I must be their man, nothing can come of it. We always settle a
Speaker here as soon as the writs are issued out for a Parliament; if
you do so for a Prolocutor, a man might have warning in time. But I
should make the foolishest figure in nature, to come over hawking
for an employment I no wise seek or desire, and then fail of it. Pray
communicate the sense of what I say to the Archbishop, to whom I
will write by this post.

As to my private affairs, I am sure they are in good hands; but I
beg you will not have the least regard or tenderness to *Parvisol*,
farther than you shall find he deserves. I am my gossip's very humble
servant; and the like to Mr. *Stoyte*, his lady, and *Catherine*; and Mr.
Manley, and his lady and daughter. I am, | Your obedient humble
servant,

J. Swift.

I wrote lately to Dr. *Synge*; twice in all. I think you should force
the St. *Mary* ladies to town towards *Christmas*. My duty to the
Bishop of *Dromore*. Dr. *Synge* wrote me word a month ago, that
Roseingrave, our organist, was at the point of death. Is he dead or
alive?

---

[1] In July 1707 Swift was elected proctor in the Lower House of Convocation,
through the influence, he believed, of Dr. Samuel Synge, who was then Prolocutor of the Lower House. For the part Swift played in his brief tenure of this
office see Landa, *Swift and the Church of Ireland*, pp. 50–52.

Swift to Archbishop King

London, Oct. 20, 1713.

My Lord,

The Opportunity I had of a Ship was so sudden, that I had not Time to receive your Grace's last Commands, or pay my Respects, which it was my Duty and Inclination to do;[1] and, as for writing, I have always told your Grace that I could not set about it with a good Conscience, until I were provided with Matter enough for your Trouble of Reading. We are outwardly pretty quiet during this Interval of Parliament; but, I will not answer what Seeds are sowing to make the next Spring produce better Fruit. There are several Reasons, impossible for me to tell at this Distance, why I shall not be so good a Correspondent as I have formerly been, but may probably serve to entertain you a Year or two hence: For, the fashion of this World passeth away, and there is nothing of so little Consequence as the greatest Court Secrets, when once the Scene is changed. I said to somebody, when I was last in *Ireland*, who talked to me of the Advantage and Felicity I had in the Familiarity of great Ministers, that it was well enough while it continued a Vanity; but as soon as it ceased to be a Vanity, it began to be a Vexation of Spirit.[2] I have some Thoughts of passing this Winter at the *Bath*, because my Health requireth it, and because I shall then be a pretty equal Distance from the Factions on both Sides the Water; for it is not impossible your Grace may have a warm Winter.

I have had some Letters, particularly from Dr. *Synge*, and Mr. Archdeacon *Walls*, about my being Prolocutor. I have this Post writ my Thoughts upon that Subject to Mr. *Walls*;[3] and to save you the Trouble, have desired him to communicate them to your Grace. Our Elections for the City still continue: I was this afternoon at *Guildhall*. I find three of the old Members [leading], and *Withers*, who is the lowest, tells me he doth not despair of carrying it for himself.

[1] Archbishop King had returned to Dublin only twelve days before 29 Aug. when Swift set sail on the first stage of his return to London, which he reached on 9 Sept.

[2] The rift between Oxford and Bolingbroke was ever widening. A lack of cordial understanding between the two began as early as May 1711, and continued to enlarge. See *Journal*, pp. 334, 389, 568, 593.

[3] The previous letter.

There is Abundance of Artifice (to give it the softest Word) used on both Sides.[1]

I came Yesterday from *Windsor*, where I saw the Queen in very good Health, which she findeth there more than any where else, and I believe will hardly remove until *December*.[2] I believe my Lord Lieutenant will be landed before this Letter cometh to your Hands:[3] He is the finest Gentleman we have, and of an excellent Understanding, and Capacity for Business: If I were with your Grace, I would say more, but leave it to your own Sagacity.

I will only venture to say one Thing relating to *Ireland*, because I believe it will be of Use that your Grace should know it. If your House of Commons should run into any Violences, disagreeable to us here, it will be of the worst Consequences imaginable to that Kingdom: For, I know no Maxim more strongly maintained at present in our Court, than that her Majesty ought to exert her Power to the utmost, upon any Uneasiness given on your Side to herself or her Servants: Neither can I answer, that even the legislative Power here may not take Cognizance of any Thing that may pass among you, in Opposition to the Persons and Principles that are now favoured by the Queen.[4] Perhaps I am gone too far; and therefore shall end without any Ceremony. | Your Grace's, &c.

Direct to me under Cover, to | *Erasmus Lewis*, Esq; at Mr. | Secretary *Bromley*'s Office at | *Whitehall*.

[1] The Treaty of Commerce was the chief question at issue in this election. Among London merchants there was strong opposition to its terms. Sir William Withers had held his seat in the Tory interest since 1707.
[2] During that month Swift stayed at Windsor each week from Saturday to Monday. Probably he drove down with Oxford. (Forster, 509.)
[3] The Duke of Shrewsbury arrived in Dublin on 27 Oct.
[4] The dissensions between Whig and Tory in Ireland had risen to an extreme height, and Archbishop King said that he had never seen the kingdom in so great a ferment except during actual war in the time of James II. Bolingbroke was aware of its condition, and wrote to Prior of 'that distracted nation, who from knowing no distinction but Protestant and Papist are come to be more madly divided about Whig and Tory, High Church and Low, than are this society of lunatics to which you and I belong'; but Shrewsbury appears to have gone to the country under the impression that there was 'no difference but Protestant and Papist' (cf. *Bolingbroke's Letters*, ii. 490, and *Wentworth Papers*, p. 356).— Ball.

Sir Constantine Phipps to Swift

Dublin 24 Octr. 1713
Dear S^r

I am indebted to you for yr kind letters of the 8^th1 & 10th instant &
I very heartily acknowledge the obligation. that of the 8th gave me a
great many melancholy thoughts when I reflected upon the danger
our Constitution is in by the Neglect & supineness of our Friends[2]
& the vigilance & unanimity of our Enemies but I hope the Parliam^t
proving for good will awaken our Friends & unite them more firmly
& make them more active

That part of yr Letter of the 10th wch related to my Son gave me
great satisfaction for tho the Com^rs have heard nothing of it yet I
believed Mr Keightley[3] might bring over full instructions in it but
he is arrived & knows nothing of it so that whatever good intentions
my Ld Treasurer had in relation to my son his Ldsp has forgotten
to give any directions concerning him for with him things are just
as they were when you left Dublin if you will be so kind to put his
Ldsp in mind of it you will be very obliging—

I cannot discharge the pt of a Friend if I omit to let you know that
yr great Neighbour at St Pulchers is very angry with you[4] he accuseth
you for going away without taking yr leave of him & intends in a
little to compell you to reside at yr Deanery. He lays some other
things to yr charge wch you shall know in a little time

We hourly expect my Ld Lieutn^t.[5] The Whigs begin to be sensible
they must expect no great Countenance from him & begin to be a
little down in the mouth since they find Brodrick is not to be their
Speaker.[6] I am wth very great truth | yr most obedient humble | Servt

Twice endorsed by Swift: (1) Ld. Chancell^r Ireld. | Octr 24. 1713
(2) Ld Chanc^llr of Ireld | Octbr. 4th 1713 (*sic*)

[1] The letter of the 8th is not forthcoming.
[2] In writing to Phipps Swift had evidently referred in guarded terms to
Oxford's procrastinating political leadership.
[3] The Right Hon. Thomas Keightley, a Commissioner of the Irish Revenue.
Swift had once met him at Oxford's table (*Journal*, 8 Jan. 1712/13).
[4] Archbishop King. Phipps himself, at this time, was scarcely on friendly
terms with the Archbishop, who favoured the claims of the Dublin Corporation.
[5] Shrewsbury reached Dublin three days later.
[6] Alan Brodrick had been appointed Chief Justice of the Queen's Bench in
Ireland in 1709. He was removed from that position when the Tories came into

Charles Davenant to Swift

Windsor Nov. 3ᵈ 1713.

Sʳ¹

You have the Character of employing in good offices to others the
Honor and Happyness you have of being often with my Lord Treasurer, This use of your Access to Him, is an uncommon Instance of
Generosity, deserving the highest praises, for most commonly Men
are most apt to convert such Advantages to their own single Interest,
without any regard of others, tho in my poor Opinion not so wisely.
Acts of Friendship create Friends even among Strangers that tast
not of em; And in my Experience I hardly ever knew a Man Friendly
in the course of his Proceedings but he was supported in the world,
Ingratitude being the vice, of which the generality of men are most
ashamd to be thought guilty.

My Son & I have reasons to return you our Thanks for what You
have already done of this kind in his Favour, & we beg the continuance of it.²

Ministers of state have such multiplicity of Business, that it is no
wonder if they forget low Individuals and in such a case private
Persons must be beholden to some good naturd Man to put those
in Power in Mind of em, otherwise they may lie forgotten til old Age
overtakes em. Such well disposd Remembrancers, deserve Accesse,
Familiarity, & Interest with Great Men & perhaps they are the most
usefull Servants they can countenance in their Hours of Leisure

I need not tell you that in point of Time he is before all Pretenders
to Foreign Businesse. That his affairs have now depended almost three
years, that in the Interim it has gone very hard with Him & that he
gave a very early Instance of his Zeal to the present Administration.
But what he builds his Hopes most upon is, the promise My Lord
Treasurer was pleasd to make to the Duke of Shrewsbury, just as his
Grace left Windsor, That a provision should be made for Mr
Davenant. We must intreat you to find some lucky moment of repre-

power. He had long occupied the Speaker's chair, and now succeeded in defeat-
ing Sir Richard Levinge the court candidate.

¹ Swift had been long acquainted with Dr. Charles Davenant, the political
economist, who was uncle to Thomas Swift, the 'little parson cousin'.

² Henry Molins Davenant is here alluded to by his father. During the reign
of Queen Anne he served in diplomatic station at Frankfort. Under George I he
acted as envoy extraordinary to the Princess of Italy.

senting to My Lord that the young Man is pressed by a nearer concern than that of making his Fortune, & that lovers can hardly be
perswaded to be as patient as other Men. The Duke has carried his
Mistrisse from him, & will not consent to make him happy till he
sees him in some way of being settled, in which how anxious any
delay must be (Possession depending upon it) he leaves You to Judg,
who have so well studied Mankind, & who know that love is a
Passion, in one of his age, much stronger than Ambition. I beg your
Pardon for this long trouble & am | S^r |
Your most humble & most | obedient servant |

                                                    Charles Davenant.

Endorsed by Swift: D^r D'avenant. | Windsor Novr 3^d 1713

4804

The Duchess of Ormonde to Swift

D^r

I hope yr servant has told you I sent to beg the favour of you to
come hither to night, but since you cou'd not conveniently, I hope
you wont deny me the satisfaction of seeing you to morrow morning,
my L^d joyns wth me in that request & will see no company, but you,
I hope you'l come before ten a clock, because he is to go at that hour
to Windsor I beg your pardon for sending so early, as I have order'd
'em to carry this, but the fear of yr being gon abroad if they went
latter, occasioned that trouble given you by S^r | y^r most sincere & |
most faithfull humble | servant |

                                                    M Ormonde

Nov: the 3^d | 11 a clock at night

Endorsed by Swift: Dutchess Orm | Novr 3^d 1713[1]

---

[1] Ball (vi. 233) conjecturally assigns this letter to 1712; but there appears to
be no good reason for ignoring Swift's endorsement.

P.R.O., State Papers of Ireland

Mr. Justice Nutley to Swift

5 November 1713.

S^r

    I have the honor & favour of y^{rs} of a date too long since to name, it having lain so long unanswer'd:[1] Had you been less complaisant, I could not have been so rude as I have been, for then I myself should not have thought it an excuse to tell you, that I have been studying for an answer, & as it is I fear you will not allow it, for when you see my manner of doing it, you will hardly believe my performance to be the result of labour, but indeed it has cost me many a thought how I should impart to you the pleasure & satisfaction I found in the kind tender you made me of yor friendship, & at last I know no way of doing it, but by bidding you fancy me as great as yor imagination could make me, and then that you heard me say to you; I will do every thing for you wch is in my power. I sincerely thank you for this earnest of yor friendship in so readily offering to comply with my request concerning Mr Williams,[2] if I should judge it for the service of yor Quire. I willingly give up the most advantageous part of the condition, & desire my request may be granted only if it suits with yor just intention of bettering the oeconomy of yor church, & mending the beauty & harmony of the service to be performed in it; but as I understood the favour I was to ask was, that since you have one in yor Quire, who is a good performer, & as I am told, a sober reputable man, whose present stipend is but 15^{ll} p^{an} that you would advance him to be a vicar in a vacancy now in yor church, but since it is so that you keep that promotion for a voice wch you want, I must submit my pretensions, & wait for an oportunity, when they may wth more reason be revived.

    I am most extremely glad to hear that her Majesty & my Lord Treasurer are in so good health: May they long continue so, & like a well built Arch, may that wch is below support what is above, & that wch is highest strengthen & establish that wch is under it.

    I have done myself the honour severall times since our Lord Lieutnt landed[3] to wait upon his Grace, but having never been a Courtier before, It did not come into my mind to consider what an

---

[1] Swift had received Prior's letter, 16 Aug. N.S., too late to enable him to make Judge Nutley's acquaintance before leaving Ireland, 29 Aug. O.S.

[2] See p. 392.

[3] 27 Oct.

awkward figure that man makes at a Levy who has not been re-
com̄ended to the great man in the middle of the Croud. ffor that
reason I cannot but wish that some other great man, by himself or
by his less busy friend would intimate to his Grace that it would be
kind & condescending in him if he would take some notice of
He is   & would be proud to   ¹ Pray, S^r, try how you can
fill up these blanks, & then tell me how you like the whole piece,
when it is altogether. You see, S^r, upon the encouragement you
have given me how great a favour I venture to ask: In return for it
I will at any time save y^{or} blushes, & be y^{or} zealous Advocate whenever I can have an interest.

His Grace the Primate dyed the 2^d just at two o'clock in the
morning.² The poor Exec^{ors} I dare say, strugled hard to save a
quarters rent & it is more than probable, this good man was so much
tortured to make him live, as even Criminall was to make him dye.
I am of opinion that the Deanery of St Patricks is a fine preferment
for a Lord Lieutenants Chaplain to jump into after one or two months
service, & if you can be tempted to part wth y^{or} fine house in Dublin
for an ill contrived one on a Country Bishoprick, I can easily cut out
a scheme for the advancing some eminent worthy active Prelate to
the Primacy, & so three good persons may be promoted at once.

I am much obliged to my friend Mr Prior for his recom̄endation
of me to you. It is placed by that he knew you well, & how good a
friend you can be, but I am surprised that he should know so well
what he desired, & do it before I could think of asking it. I delivered
your com̄ands to my Lord Chancellor, but he had before acknowledged the receipt of yor tres.³

I know I am long, but I will say no worse of my self, & there-
fore I will conclude wth assuring you that I most sincerely am | S^r |
Yo^r most humble | & ffaithful Servt |

R. Nutley

Novr the 5th 1713

¹ Thus, blank spaces in manuscript.
² Archbishop Marsh died in Dublin, and was buried in a vault of St. Patrick's
Cathedral adjoining his library.
³ Thus, for 'letters'.

Sir Constantine Phipps to Swift

Dublin 9 November 1713

Dear S[r]

I had the favour of yo[rs] of the 27 Oct & own wth all the gratitude
in the world that the trouble you have given yo[r] self in my sons
affair[1] & the many other Instances of yo[r] Friendship to so late an
acquaintance are such that I know not in what terms to express my
acknowledgm[t] this I can assure you that yo[r] favours are not betow'd
on an ungratefull pson but on one who when ever he has an opptun-
ity will be glad to shew how great a sense he has of the obligations

I believe the great Affairs in w[ch] my L[d] Treas̄er is engaged puts
matters of so small a moment as my sons out of his mind for the
Warr[t] is not yet come down to the Com[rs] of the Revenue, tis probable
it may be for want of some body to pay the Fees if so & since you
have don me the honour to concern yor self so far in it I desire you
would be so kind to lay out the money & let me know w[ht] it is & I
will order the paym[t] of it to you

Our Elections of Parl[t] men in this Kingdom prove beyond Ex-
pectation for by the nicest calculation can be made we shall have a
Majority of 3 to 2[2] and there is a great Spirit of Loyalty even among
the mob. I am wth very great Sincerity & | respect | yo[r] most obedient
humble Serv[t] | Con Phipps
D[r] Swift

Endorsed by Swift: Chanc[ll] Ire[d]

P.R.O., State Papers of Ireland

Sir John Stanley to Swift

Dublin Castle, November 20 [1713].

Sir,

Though you used to forget me[3] for a year together in the same
town, I have been so careful of your commands at this distance, that

[1] See Phipps's letter to Swift of 24 Oct.
[2] This was an extraordinary miscalculation. On the first trial of strength, the
election of a Speaker, the Tories found themselves in a minority of four, and in
subsequent divisions more immediately affecting the government, the majority
against them was as great as forty-six.—Ball.   *[For note 3 see overleaf.]*

I have got three of your favourites made chaplains to my Lord
Lieutenant as you desired, Dr. Raymond, Mr. Thomas Forbes, and
Mr. Wade.[1] I could not succeed in getting in the whole forty you
named, because his Grace has not in all above a dozen, being unwilling to entertain more than he has a prospect of providing for. We are
got here in the most eating, drinking, wrangling, quarrelsome country that ever I saw. There is no keeping the peace among them. It
were easier to reconcile the Postboy and Flying Post, and I cannot
but think you in the right to hold the deanery of St. Patrick's at
London; I should be glad to hold my Secretary's office there too.
I hear you have been scribbling lately.[2] Send me your works as they
come out, or you shall be summoned to attend your deanery. In the
meantime, I am, | Yours most faithfully. |

J. Stanley.

Deane Swift 1765

Swift to Lord Oxford

November 21, 1713

My Lord,
Your Lordship is the person in the world to whom every body
ought to be silent upon such an occasion as this, which is only to be
supported by the greatest wisdom and strength of mind:[3] wherein,
God knows, the wisest and best of us, who would presume to offer
their thoughts, are far your inferiors. It is true, indeed, that a great
misfortune is apt to weaken the mind, and disturb the understanding. This, indeed, might be some pretence to us to administer our

---

[1] The Rev. Anthony Raymond, Rector of Trim; the Rev. Thomas Forbes,
Rector of Dunboyne; Mr. Wade unidentified.

[2] If the immediate past is meant by 'lately' the allusion must be to *Part of the
Seventh Epistle of the First Book of Horace Imitated*, published 23 Oct. 1713, and
The Importance of the Guardian Consider'd, published on the last day of October.

[3] On 16 Dec. 1712 Peregrine Hyde Osborne, Marquis of Carmarthen, eldest
son of the second Duke of Leeds, married Elizabeth, eldest daughter of Lord
Oxford. She died within the year on the day before Swift wrote this moving,
gravely phrased letter.

---

[3] John Stanley of Grange Gorman, co. Dublin, held several minor govern-
ment posts, and was created a baronet in 1699. He was Commissioner of
Customs from 1708 to his death in 1744. The Duke of Shrewsbury, as Lord
Lieutenant, brought him to Ireland as Chief Secretary.

consolations, if we had been wholly strangers to the person gone. But, my Lord, whoever had the honour to know her, wants a comforter as much as your Lordship; because, though their loss is not so great, yet they have not the same firmness and prudence, to support the want of a friend, a patroness, a benefactor, as you have to support that of a daughter. My Lord, both religion and reason forbid me to have the least concern for that Lady's death, upon her own account, and he must be an ill Christian, or a perfect stranger to her virtues, who would not wish himself, with all submission to God Almighty's will, in her condition. But your Lordship, who hath lost such a daughter, and we, who have lost such a friend, and the world, which hath lost such an example, have, in our several degrees, greater cause to lament, than, perhaps, was ever given by any private person before. For, my Lord, I have sat down to think of every amiable quality that could enter into the composition of a lady, and could not single out one, which she did not possess in as high a perfection as human nature is capable of. But, as to your Lordship's own particular, as it is an unconceivable misfortune to have lost such a daughter, so it is a possession which few can boast of, to have had such a daughter. I have often said to your Lordship, that I never knew any one, by many degrees, so happy in their domestic as you; and I affirm you are so still, though not by so many degrees: From whence it is very obvious, that your Lordship should reflect upon what you have left, and not upon what you have lost.

To say the truth, my Lord, you began to be too happy for a mortal; much more happy than is usual with the dispensations of Providence long to continue. You had been the great instrument of preserving your country from foreign and domestic ruin: You have had the felicity of establishing your family in the greatest lustre, without any obligation to the bounty of your Prince, or any industry of your own: You have triumphed over the violence and treachery of your enemies, by your courage and abilities; and, by the steadiness of your temper, over the inconstancy and caprice of your friends. Perhaps your Lordship has felt too much complacency within yourself, upon this universal success: and God Almighty, who would not disappoint your endeavours for the public, thought fit to punish you with a domestic loss, where he knew your heart was most exposed; and, at the same time, has fulfilled his own wise purposes, by rewarding in a better life, that excellent creature he has taken from you.

I know not, my Lord, why I write this to you, nor hardly what I

am writing. I am sure, it is not from any compliance with form; it
is not from thinking that I can give your Lordship any ease. I think
it was an impulse upon me that I should say something: And whether
I shall send you what I have written, I am yet in doubt, &c.

P.R.O., State Papers of Ireland

Bishop Lindsay to Swift

Nov: 21 1713

S^r

This day Mr Justice Nutley shewed me a letter of yours to him,
wherein I find myself much obliged to you for kind offices done me
to Ld Treasurer by using your endeavours to promote me to a Post,
wch my ambition could never aim at, and I am sure my merits will
never come up to—[1]

I have already received severall favours from that great Lord, but
this last I fear would swell my debt so high that I should never be
able by any future services to discharge it.

I know not who hath represented me to you as an enemy; But if
you will be pleased at any time to hint to me in what I hope I shall
be able to shew the contrary to satisfaction: But had there been any
thing of that kind, I am sure now all enmity ought to cease at least
on my part, and therefore I desire leave to subscribe myself | Your
Friend & | Humble servant |

Tho: Raphoe[2]

Endorsed by Swift: Ld Primate

[1] The post to which Lindsay refers was the primacy vacant by the death of
Narcissus Marsh. Lindsay was one of the two Irish bishops to whom was
addressed Swift's commission, 31 Aug. 1710, charging them to assist him in
soliciting the remission of the First Fruits. At that time Swift was not well disposed to Thomas Lindsay, referring to him slightingly in a letter addressed to
Archbishop King. As late as March 1713 he believed that Lindsay had been a
hindrance to him in the execution of his mission. During the recent political
antagonisms of Ireland, however, King's Whig proclivities had become too
pronounced, and Swift realized that he could not recommend him unreservedly
to Oxford. The Tory principles of Lindsay were as unassailable as those of
Lord Chancellor Phipps; and Swift's influence with the Ministry secured for
him the Archbishopric of Armagh.

[2] Lindsay had been appointed successively Dean of St. Patrick's, Bishop of
Killaloe, and Bishop of Raphoe. The last promotion synchronized with that of
Swift to the deanery of St. Patrick's.

Mr. Justice Nutley to Swift

Dublin, Nov. 21, 1713.

Sir

I can't help telling you that I think you do me great wrong in charging me with being too civil, and with want of plainness in my letters to you.[1] If you will be abundant in your favours to me, how can I forbear thanking you? and if you will call that by a wrong name, that is your fault, and not mine. I hope I shall be able to convince you of your mistake, by putting you in the place of the party obliged; and then I will shew you that I can be as ready (as you are) in doing good offices for a friend, and when I have done them, can treat you as you do me, as if you were the benefactor, and I had received the favour: I am sorry I did not keep a copy of my letter to you, that I might compare it with that which I shall have from you, whenever I shall be so happy as to receive one from you upon that subject; for I am thoroughly persuaded, you will then as much outdo me in civility of expression, as you do now in the power of conferring favours.

By this time I hope, I have satisfied you, that it is fit for me (and I am resolved) to express the sense I have of your friendship in as high a manner as I can, until I have an opportunity of making a better return: but to shew you, that it is as uneasy to me to write civil things, as it can be to you to read them, I will, as often as I can, do you services, that I may not be at the trouble or bear the reproach of being complaisant.

I am so much a philosopher as to know that to be great, is to be, but not to be thought, miserable; and I am of the opinion of those among them, who allow retaliation; and therefore since you have declared your intention of loading me with cares, I will, as far as I can, make you sensible of the hurt you do me by laying a like burthen upon you.

I thank you most sincerely for the clear and full information you have given me of your grand Church affair.[2] It entirely agrees with my judgment; for I do think that what you propose will be the best service that has been done to this Church and kingdom since the Restoration, and the doing it soon will be of great advantage to the

[1] See Nutley's letter 5 Nov. to Swift.
[2] The proposed promotion of Lindsay to the primacy.

407

Queen's affairs at this juncture. For, it has been given out among the party, that the Ministry have an eye toward the *Whigs*, and that, if they now exert themselves, they will soon have an open declaration in their favour: we have a remarkable proof of this; for Mr. *Brodrick* has engaged a considerable number of the Parliament men (many of them not of his party) to promise him their votes for Speaker,[1] by telling them he has the approbation of the Ministry and Lord Lieutenant; and since his Grace has made known her Majesty's pleasure, a new word is given out that the liberties of the people are in the last danger, and that the Crown is attempting the nomination of a Speaker. I own I am no politician; but I think I understand the posture of affairs here, and I am assured that the Church party is so strong, that if anything be done on your side to excite their zeal, and discourage their adversaries, there will be but a short struggle here. But if the *Whigs* are permitted to hope, or what is as bad, to boast of their expectations, and nothing is done, to enable others to confute them, they will, 'tis probable, be able to give trouble to the government; and what is now easy to be effected, will become difficult by delay; and I fear, the want of doing this in time will occasion some uneasiness to the Duke of *Shrewsbury*; for to this is owing the doubtful dispute, who shall be Speaker.

I have shewed your letter to the gentleman chiefly concerned in it:[2] this I did, because I knew it would produce a full expression of his sentiments; and I can assure you, whatever occasion may have been given you to think what you say in your letter, he has a true sense of your friendship to him.[3] I will be guarantee, that according to the power he has, he will be ready to serve you, and that in kind.

My Lord Chancellor will send you his own thanks. I am, most truly and sincerely, | Yours, *&c.*

P.R.O., State Papers of Ireland

John Arbuthnot to Swift

[November 1713.]

Dear Friend[4]

I'm most heartily greivd for the loss of your excellent & worthy freind, & more for the affliction of another.[5] I dont love to irritate

[1] See p. 398, n. 6.   [2] i.e. Bishop Lindsay.
[3] Cf. Lindsay to Swift, 21 Nov. 1713.   *[For notes 4, 5 see opposite.*

a fresh wound else, I would have taken the freedom to have wrote to My Lord. I pity his case with all my heart, for what ever other affliction he has been usd to he is much a stranger to domestick calamitys I have a true sense of his present condition for which I know philosophy & religion are both too weak, & I beleive it is the will of god that it should be so. I have lost six children. If I am not deceivd I beleive I could have been content to have ransomd the lives of every one of them, ev'n at the hard terms of begging their bread. I know My lord has the sentiment of humanity & paternall affection very strong, & I should not love him so well if he had not; therfor my Dear Friend I question not but that yow will upon this occasion do those offices of humanity that are incumbent upon yow upon many accounts, which yow will find will succeed better by turning his thoughts to other objects than by the most rational reflections, upon the present affliction, every body here shares in his greif from her Majesty down to the meanest of his humble servants. My Lady Masham was so much surprisd & greived that we were affraid it would hurt her in her present condition.[1] I am glad I did not know My lady Carmarthen so well as yow, but I know enough to beleive her a most valuable person, I have nothing left to wish for My Lord as a saving in this case but that god would preserve the life of the poor child to be some comfort to him. I beleive it will not be a good way for My Lord to keep up, but to appear as soon as possible again in his business; for I know by Experience, that the best cure is by diverting the thoughts. I hope we may see yow here

[1] Under similar circumstances, on more occasions than one, anxiety was felt for Lady Masham (*Journal, passim*).

4 This is the first letter of a correspondence between friends deeply attached to each other; who, furthermore, held each other's gifts of mind in sincere regard. It is reasonable to suppose that Swift and Arbuthnot became acquainted early in 1711. In a letter written to Arbuthnot in 1734 Swift speaks of 'above five-and-twenty years' acquaintance', which would carry the date back to 1709, a little earlier than is probable. John Arbuthnot, 1667–1735, took his medical degree at St. Andrews. In 1709 he was appointed Physician in Ordinary to the Queen, and he attended her in her last illness. In addition to scientific works he wrote literary and political satires, of which the best known is the *History of John Bull* (1712). Swift wrote of him to Ford, 19 Jan. 1723–4, 'there does not live a better Man'.
5 This letter is evidently a reply to one from Swift to Arbuthnot deploring the death of the Marchioness of Carmarthen.

next Saturday.¹ your freinds remember yow kindly. I am | Dear sir |
Your affectionat Brother | & most humble servant |

Jo: Arbuthnott

Take your opportunity to make my compliments to My Lord. I
am truly sorry for him, & I have the Vanity to think he would be so
for me upon such an occasion.

Swift to Archdeacon Walls

London. Novbr. 26. 1713

Sᵣ²

I have had two Letters from You very lately, the last of the 19ᵗʰ
instant came yesterday. As for those you sent me about the Prolo-
cutorship I reckon them for nothing.³ I would see you all whippt
before I would venture my self in any manner to come over upon
a Fool's Errand; and for what? for a Place I would rather be without,
neither would I take it upon any other score but being chosen freely
by a vast Majority, which would let the world see they thought me
a Man fit to serve the Church, and since they have not chosen me
they shew they do not think me such a Man, and consequently they
and I do not deserve each other.⁴ Your last letter but one was full
of a project of advising our Sᵗ Mary's Friends to come to Toun⁵
wherein I shall not offer to interpose; You think me a very idle
fellow and very wise: However I think if the Black Lady does not
find Amendment in her Health they had better come where Company is stirring and so I told them in a Letter I writt to them three

¹ This reference shows that Swift's week-end visits to Windsor continued.
² Previously in the possession of Sir John Murray. Since 1935 in the library
of Lord Rothschild.   ³ See p. 394.
⁴ The Irish Convocation did not meet till four days later, but it was probably
known beforehand that the choice of the Lower House would fall on Archdeacon Percival (see p. 395). Archbishop King may have used his influence
against Swift; but Swift's absence from Ireland at the time would naturally
militate against him. At this time King took no part in the proceedings of
Convocation as the Crown had appointed Archbishop Vesey President of the
Upper House.   ⁵ See p. 395.

days ago. when by the same Token I forgot to send Mrs Dingley a Bill for 8^11 which I have receivd of hers here on one^1 Branch of her Exchequer money; I will therefore now send one at the end of this Letter, which you will please to tear off, and have conveyd to her. Indeed I could hardly then think of any thing, having just lost a Friend I extreamly loved, the poor Marchioness of Caermarthen, She was but 24 years old,^2 a most excellent Person adorned with all possible good Qualityes. She was Ld Treasurer's eldest daughter, and his Favorite. I have seen him but twice since, the last time was yesterday in the afternoon, and to morrow she will have been dead a Week. He is in great Affliction; and so are 500 others.

As to the School,^3 I did not know I had any Part in the Disposall of it. Yet I asked amongst you when I was in Dublin, and thought I had no Answer. I have no Engagemt. But I tell you one thing, I will Sacrifice in every thing of this kind to Reputation. I take your word and Judgmt, and if it were a Thing not lyable to Censure, I would do it immediatly at your Request (supposing it in my disposall) but I will wait, and have your Person approved by others, both for Your sake and my own; and then Your Recommendation shall have the Preference—But it comes this very moment into my Head, that a little before I left Ireland I saw Mr Dawson with the A. Bp, recommending to his Grace some other Person, & the A. Bp. talked as if it were a Thing of his own, and talked of the Person Dawson recommended, as one that would stand very fair for it;^4 It is somebody that teaches Dawsons Children, I know not his Name. So that I believe you and I are talking of the golden Tooth.^5

Dr Ratcliff^6 and I did 3 weeks ago besett L^d Tr about Mrs South, and he assured us it was done,^7 I made the D. Ormd speak about it lately once or twice, & I spoke to Ld. Tr my self half a dozen

---

^1 one] a *Ball.*

^2 The Marchioness of Carmarthen, six years older than her husband, was twenty-eight at the time of her death.

^3 The Cathedral school in which Walls, as a former master, was interested. His successor as master, Edward Drury, was then appointed to the prebend of Saggart.

^4 Swift must have seen Archbishop King at least once after his return from Bath.

^5 See Brewer, *Dictionary of Phrase and Fable*, 1912, p. 534.

^6 Swift was not an admirer of Radcliffe (*Prose Works, passim*).

^7 See p. 392, n 4.

times | I am my Gossips most humble Servt. . . . .¹ Pray ask the
Bp of Dromore and give him My Duty | I am | Yr | most obedient |
humble Servt |

J: Swift.

Endorsed in a later hand: Dr Swift | Novr 26th 1713

Harvard University (Orrery Transcript)

*Alexander Pope to Swift*²

Binfield. Decr. 8th 1713.

Sir,

Not to trouble you at present with the Recital of all my Obligations to you I shall only mention two Things, which I take particularly well of you; your Desire that I should write to you;—and your Proposal of giving me twenty Guineas to change my Religion, which last you must give me Leave to make the Subject of this Letter.

Sure no Clergyman ever offered so much, out of his own Purse, for the Sake of any Religion. 'Tis almost as many Pieces of Gold, as an Apostle could get of Silver from the Priests of old, on a much more valuable Consideration.

I believe it will be better worth my while to propose a Change of my Faith by Subscription, than a Translation of Homer. And to convince you how well disposed I am to the Reformation, I shall be content, if you can prevail with my Lord Treasurer, and the Ministry, to rise to the same Sum, each of them, on this pious Account, as my Lord Halifax has done on the prophane one.³ I am afraid there is no being at once a Poet, and a good Christian; and I am very much straitned between Two, while the Whigs seem willing to contribute as much to continue me the one, as you would to make me the other. But if you can move every Man in the Government, that has above

---

¹ Three lines have here been scrawled over and are illegible.
² This letter was first printed by Orrery in his *Remarks* (1752), p. 53. Here reprinted from a transcript made by Orrery, now in Harvard College Library. The transcript carries the caption: 'Mr Pope to Dr Swift, in Answer to a | Letter from the Dr persuading Mr Pope to Change his Religion.' The friendship of Pope and Swift was of recent origin, and may have been inspired by the praise of the Tory peace in *Windsor-Forest*, published on 7 Mar. 1713. Cf. Swift's only reference to Pope in the *Journal to Stella*, p. 635.
³ Lord Halifax subscribed for ten sets of the *Iliad*. Swift became an active canvasser for subscriptions. See Nichols, *Lit. Anec.* i. 399–400.

ten Thousand Pounds a Year, to subscribe as much as your self, I shall become a Convert, as most Men do, when the Lords turn[1] it to my Interest. I know they have the Truth of Religion so much at Heart, that they would certainly give more to have one good Subject translated from Popery to the Church of England, than twenty heathenish Authors out of any unknown Tongue into ours. I therefore commission you, Mr Dean, with full Authority to transact this Affair in my Name, and to propose as follows.

First,—That as to the Head of our Church, the Pope, I may engage to renounce his Power, whensoever I shall receive any particular Indulgences from the Head of your Church, the Queen.

As to Communion in one Kind, I shall also promise to change it for Communion in both, as soon as the Ministry will allow me ⌈wherewithal to eat, and to drink.⌉[2]

For Invocations to Saints, mine shall be turned to Dedications to Sinners, when I shall find the Great Ones of this World as willing to do me any Good, as I believe those of the other are.

You see, I shall not be obstinate in the main Points. But there is one Article I must reserve, and which you seemed not unwilling to allow me, Prayer for the Dead. There are People, to whose Souls I wish as well as to my own, and I must crave Leave humbly to lay before them, that tho' the Subscriptions above mentioned will suffice for my self, there are necessary Perquisits, and Additions, which I must demand on the Score of this charitable Article. It is also to be considered, that the greater Part of those, whose Souls I am most concerned for, were unfortunately Heretics, Schismatics, Poets, Painters, or Persons of such Lives, and Manners, as few, or no Churches are willing to save. The Expence will be therefore the greater to make an effectual Provision for the said Souls.

Old Dryden, tho' a Roman Catholick, was a Poet; and 'tis revealed in the Visions of some ancient Saints, that no Poet was ever saved under some Hundreds of Masses. I cannot set his Delivery from Purgatory at less than Fifty Pounds sterling.

Walsh was not only a Socinian, but (what you'll own is harder to be saved) a Whig. He cannot modestly be rated at less than a Hundred.

L'Estrange being a Tory, we compute him but at Twenty Pounds, which I hope no Friend of the Party can deny to give, to keep him

---

[1] Lords turn] Lord turns. Orrery, *Remarks*.
[2] Omitted by Orrery and succeeding editors.

from damning in the next Life, considering they never gave him Sixpence to keep him from starving in this.

All this together amounts to 170 Pounds.

In the next Place, I must desire you to represent, that there are several of my Friends yet living, whom I design, God willing, to outlive, in consideration of Legacies, out of which it is a Doctrine in the Reformed Church that not a Farthing shall be allowed, to save their Souls, who gave them.

There is One,[1] who will dye within these few Months, with one[1] Mr Jervas,[2] who hath grievously offended in making the Likeness of almost all Things in Heaven above, and Earth below. And one Mr Gay, an unhappy Youth, that writes Pastorals during the Time of Divine Service, whose Case is the more deplorable, as he hath miserably lavished away all that Silver he should have reserved for his Soul's Health, in Buttons and Loops for his Coat.[3]

I cannot pretend to have these People honestly saved under some Hundred Pounds, whether you consider the Difficulty of such a Work, or the extreme Love and Tenderness I bear them, which will infallibly make me push this Charity as far as I am able. There is but One more, whose Salvation I insist upon, and then I have done: But indeed it may prove of so much greater Charge than all the rest, that I will only lay the Case before you, and the Ministry, and leave to their Prudence and Generosity what Summ they shall think fit to bestow upon it.

The Person I mean is Dr Swift, a dignified Clergyman, but One who, by his own Confession, has composed more Libels than Sermons. If it be true, what I have heard often affirmed by innocent People, that too much Wit is dangerous to Salvation, this unfortunate Gentleman must certainly be damned to all Eternity. But I hope

---

[1] After each 'one' asterisks appear in the text of this letter as printed in Orrery's *Remarks* as if a name were suppressed.

[2] At this time Pope, believing himself to be artistically gifted, was receiving lessons in painting from Charles Jervas. Swift and Jervas were already well acquainted. For portraits of Swift by Jervas see Sir Frederick Falkiner's essay in *Prose Works*, ed. Temple Scott, xii. 5–18.

[3] John Gay's six pastorals, *The Shepherd's Week*, were evidently composed by this time, whether during divine service or not. They were published in Apr. 1714 with a poetic 'Prologue to the Right Honourable the Lord Viscount Bolingbroke', which did not advance Gay's fortunes with the Whigs. It did contain the lines Pope here alludes to:

> I sold my sheep and lambkins too,
> For silver loops and garment blue.

his long Experience in the World, and frequent Conversation with Great Men, will cause him (as it has some others) to have less and less Wit every Day. Be it as it will, I should not think my own Soul deserved to be saved, if I did not endeavour to save his, for I have all the Obligations in Nature to him. He has brought me into better Company than I cared for, made me merrier, when I was sick, than I had a Mind to be, put me upon making Poems on Purpose that he might alter them, &c. I once thought I could never have discharged my Debt to his Kindness, but have lately been informed, to my un-speakable Comfort, that I have more than paid it all. For Monsieur de Montayne[1] has assured me, that the Person, who receives a Benefit, obliges the Giver; for since the chief Endeavour of one Friend is to do Good to the other, He, who administers both the Matter, and Occasion, is the Man that is Liberal. At this Rate it is impossible Dr Swift should be ever out of my Debt, as matters stand already; and for the future he may expect daily more Obligations from | His most Faithful, Affectionate, | Humble Servant |

A. Pope.

I have finished the Rape of the Lock,[2] but believe I may stay here till Christmas without Hindrance of Busyness.

P.R.O., State Papers of Ireland

Archbishop King to Swift

Dublin dec^r 15/1713

Rev^d S^r[3]

I recd the favour of yours of the 20th of Octr last you may perhaps reckon me an ill correspondent that have delayed my answer so long, but to deal ingenuously with you I have been so little pleased with the noise, bustle & unreasonable transactions here, that I had no heart to communicate to a frend things so uneasy to my self. for 6 weeks we had nothing but tumults, contentions, quarrels calumnys & drinking about elections. our parlement men now met, have had,

---

[1] Montaigne, *Essais*, I. xxviii, De l'amitié. Ed. Armaingaud, Paris, 1924, ii. 205.
[2] The enlarged version of the poem in five cantos, published 4 Mar. 1714.
[3] This letter is printed from the original in the P.R.O., S.P., Ireland, 63/369. There is a copy in Trinity College, Dublin, N.3.4, pp. 230–2. Froude, *English in Ireland*, i. 353, refers to the letter but failed to identify the writer.

as the publick papers will tell, a fair tryall of skill for a majority, the choice of a speaker & chairman for elections tell you who has it. this I assure you is a great disappointment, for the minor party as it proves were assured & declared wth the greatest confidence that they were the greater. & it is strange to me that they are not, considering the government, privy councill, benches, custom house, army, pensioners, officers of all sorts dependents & expectants were all for them.

I expected this before & therefore laboured to the utmost of my power to persuade them to make up the contest wth the city before the parlement sate, for seeing that if it were not quieted before that happened, it wou'd come into parlement, & Gd knows w^t turn it might take there but they turned a deaf ear not only to me but to those of greater authority,[1] & plainly told their mind, that they had a majority, they were sure of the privy council & house of Lds & as to the house of commons they had that in their pocket as I think the expression was, & wou'd be justifyed in all they did. nay they went so far as to brand all that were for compounding & quieting matters, & keeping the parlement from taking cognisance of w^t had pass'd before wth the odious name of whiggs, & as incouragers of the city & others in the refractoryness, factuousness & as some termed it rebellion. I cou'd never pesuade myself that this cou'd be agreable to the ministry on yor side, for I believed that they had business enuf there, without being pestered with memorials, representations & frivolous conteste from this kingdom, & I was farther confirmed in this opinion w^n I saw the reports of the Attorney Genl of England wth w^m the sollicitor gen^l concurred on a long representation from the council here about the city of dublin. That representation was drawn up, w^n I was in the country, & you may assure your self if ever the matter come to be debated in parlement, as I doubt it now will, it will show a different face from w^t it appears to have in that paper. yet as it was, the Attorney & sollicitor gen^l agreed wth me in every point, w^erin I differed from the major part of the council, & as I thought, the council of Englands sending it here was a plain intimation, that it was her majestys pleasure that the affair shou'd be made

[1] Shrewsbury had been counselled to placate the disputants between the Castle and the City, but he was frustrated in every attempt at a settlement by Sir Constantine Phipps's ascendancy over the Irish Privy Council. Shrewsbury was unacquainted with the real situation in Ireland. His best endeavours were unavailing.

up, wch might have bin done w^thout any reflexion on the council, to avoid wch I imagined it was sent in that manner, that the council here might make it their own act & not seem obliged to do it, by any command or determination against them from her Majesty. but this would not be allowed to be the sense of it at all, but a confutation of the Attorney & sollicitors opinion is sent from the Judges[1] here, & the city continues w^thout any settled magistracy[2] or government.

This except the penning the last memoriall all happened before the parlement sate & seemd to be done in confidence of a majority, & may perhaps be excused as a mistake, but since their weakness in the house appeared, Mr Tucker & Sr Wm Fownds have petitioned against the recorder & Alderman Burton for an undue election in the city wch openeth a way to many inquirys, & brings things on the carpet, that had I am sure bin much better let alone. you can be no stranger to the riots mobs & quarrels that happened at the city election, & that one man was killed in it. now w^t shoud tempt them to bring such a matter before a house w^re they knew the majority was against them I can't imagine, they have already spent two days in the examination, & perhaps it may last 2 days more. & I doubt this may produce some smart votes, that may hurt both those that make them & those against w^m they are made.

I find however them all unanimous in professing that they will do every thing, that shall be for her majestys service & the ease of the government here, I wish they may say & hold. I verily believe they will not break on money matters. & the prevailing party pretend that they chiefly endeavoured to appear so by their zeal & forwardness to comply with Her Majestys desires they might have an opportunity to confute the false representations of their enemys & the calumnys wth wch they have loaded them as enemys to the constitution of church & state. but a house of commons is a strange thing & no mortal man can answer for them.

I can't find that they intend any such thing as an impeachment, the most they seem to aim at is to lay a representation of what they call grievances before her majesty.

How the proceedings of the parlement here will relish with you I can't tell, but I can assure you I have not failed to lay before all,

---

[1] The Irish Judges upheld the right of the existing Lord Mayor to hold office for another year. After debate by the Irish Privy Council the opinion was forwarded to London without ratification.

[2] magistracy] magistrates.—*Ball.*

that I have any influence on, the hazard they ran, & the danger of provoking her Majesty, the ministry and parlement there. but I prove too often a prophet wth Cassandra's fate, not to be believed till the event confirmeth w^t I say. I believe I cou'd give 20 instances where it has so happened, but it is the misfortune of mankind to prefer a present humour or view to their true interest.

I have taken your advice in relation to her Grace the Dutchess of Shrewsbury, & find w^t you told me to be true, for wch I return you my thanks.¹

Dean Swift

Endorsed by Swift: A. B Dubl

4804

Swift to Bishop Stearne

London. Dec^br 19. 1713

My Lord

I have two Letters from You to acknowledge, one of the 5th, and tother of the 11th instant. I am very glad it lyes in my way to do any Service to Mr Worrall,² and that his Merits and my Inclinations agree so well. I write this Post to Dr Synge³ to admit him. I am glad Your Lordship thinks of removing your Palace to the old, or some better Place.⁴ I wish I were near enough to give my Approbation, and if you do not chuse till Summer, I shall, God willing, certainly attend You. Your Second Letter is about Dr Marsh,⁵ who is one I allways loved; and have shewn it lately by doing every thing he could

¹ The Duke of Shrewsbury married in 1705 Adelaide, then a widow, daughter of the Marchese Andrea Paleotti of Bologna. Lady Cowper (*Diary*, pp. 8–9) says the Duke was forced into a marriage after an intrigue. She describes the Duchess as possessed of 'a wonderful Art at entertaining and diverting People, though she would sometimes exceed the Bounds of Decency'. See also *Wentworth Papers, passim.* Evidently Swift had addressed a word of caution to King.

² The address shows that Stearne was residing in St. Patrick's Deanery. Apparently he had recommended Swift to confer some favour on Worrall.

³ Dr. Samuel Synge, precentor of St. Patrick's.

⁴ Stearne's predecessor at Dromore had built a new episcopal house.

⁵ Dr. Jeremiah Marsh, Treasurer of St. Patrick's Cathedral; apparently no relation of the late Primate. Stearne had evidently suggested to Swift the promotion of Dr. Marsh to the bishoprics of Kilmore and Ardagh, then vacant. These sees had been united only forty years previously.

desire from a Brother; I should be glad for some Reasons that he
would get a Recommendation from the Ld L^t., or at least he be
named. I cannot say more at this Distance, but assure you, that all
due Care is taken of him. I have had an old Scheam as Your Ldship
may remember, of dividing the Bishoprics of Kilmore and Ardagh;
I advised it many months ago, & repeated it lately; and the Qu— and
M—ry,[1] I suppose are fallen into it. I did likewise lay very earnestly
before proper Persons the Justice and indeed Necessity of chusing
to promote those of the Kingdom, which advice has been hearkened
to, and I hope will be followed. I would say something likewise in
relation to a Friend of your Ldships[2] but I can only venture thus
much, that it was not to be done, and you may easily guess the
Reasons.

I know not who are named among you for the Prefermts; and my
Lord, this is a very nice point to talk of at the distance I am.[3] I know
a Person there better qualifyed perhaps than any that will succeed;
But my Lord, our thoughts here are, that your Kingdom leans too
much one way—and believe me, it can not do so long while the
Qu— and Administration here act upon so very different a foot.
This is more than I care to say. I should be thought a very vile man
if I presumed to recommend to a [Minister] my own Brother if he
were the least disinclined to the present Measures of Her M—y and
Ministry here. Whoever is thought to do so must shake off that
Character, or wait for other Junctures. This, my Lord, I believe you
will find to be true, And I will at once venture a Step further than
perhaps discretion should let me; that I never saw so great a Firmness in the Court, as it there now is, to pursue those Measures, upon
which this Ministry began, whatever some People may pretend to
think to the contrary. And were certain Objections made agst some
Persons we both know, I believe I might have been instrumental to
the Service of some whom I much esteem. Pick what you can out of
all this & believe [me] to be ever &c.

Address: To the Right Reverend the Lord | Bishop of Dromore at his House in
St Kevin's Street | Dublin | Ireland

[1] Ministry.
[2] In this sentence Swift hints that Archbishop King, by the line he had taken
on political issues, had made his promotion to the Primacy impossible.
[3] The Bishopric of Derry was also vacant.

P.R.O., State Papers of Ireland

Sir Gilbert Dolben to Swift

Finedon Dec. 22 1713

Rev^d S^{r1}

I take the liberty on the death of Mr Swords, (late Vicar of St Patricks), to renew my recommendation of Mr Williams to your favor whose singing to the Organ is very much better than to the tossing of a boat.² He is (in musicians language) a ready Sight-man, (& in my poor judgment) both his Voice and manner are Agreable; He has a salary as Supernumerary, which (if he be made Vicar) will be sav'd; He so distinguished himself by his diligence that your predecessor thought fit to give him an Extraordinary gratuity for it. I must not omitt this Opportunity of expressing my thankful acknÒwledgments of your great friendship in pleading my Cause Effectually with Philippus; I doubt not but, in due time I shall find the benefit of having so good an Advocate.³ My Spouse presents her Respectfull Services, & bids me say, If you be disposed to play a Xtmass Gambol with The Lion; He is now mounted on a Tankard Burnishd without and Unctuous within. I hope the mildness of the Weather & passableness of the way & (super omnia) the Heartyness of the Invitation may tempt you to think this as good a place to Spend a month of leisure in, as ev'n Lingerland it self. I am Rev^d S^r, | Your Obligd & | Most humble Servant |

G. Dolben

¹ On his way to London in Sept. 1713 Swift stayed four days with Sir Gilbert Dolben at his seat at Finedon near Wellingborough in Northamptonshire. This estate he inherited through his wife, Anne, eldest daughter of Tanfield Mulso of Finedon. In 1701 he went to Ireland as a third Justice of the Common Pleas, and was created a baronet in 1704. He took no part in the conflict between the Castle and the aldermen of Dublin; and was the only judge on the Irish bench not superseded on the accession of George I. Gifted with a scholarly taste he presented Lord Oxford with a valuable manuscript collection (*Portland MSS.* v. 146). See further Ball, *Judges in Ireland*, ii. 65–66; and *D.N.B.*

² The Rev. Henry Swords, one of the Vicars-Choral, died early in this same month. Edward Williams has been mentioned before (p. 392, n. 2). It may be, as Ball suggests, that Swift 'met Williams when suffering from the effects of the turbulence of the Irish Channel, and was not favourably impressed by him'.

³ Probably a Captain William Phillips, *attaché* of Sir Thomas Hanmer. Dolben was anxious to secure Hanmer's favour. Phillips is frequently mentioned in *The Correspondence of Sir Thomas Hanmer*, ed. Sir Henry Bunbury, 1838.

P.R.O., State Papers of Ireland

Dean Smalridge to Swift

Christ Church, 26 December 1713

Mr Dean,

I should long before this time have acknowledg'd the favour of Your Letter, & the kind offices you were pleas'd at my request to do Mr Fiddis,[1] but that when I receiv'd Yo^{rs} I had some thoughts of quickly going up to town, & there paying my Thanks in Person. These should not have been put off wth my Journey, but that I knew you were not in half so much hast to receive thanks, as You were to deserve 'em. You aim at much better things for Mr Fiddis, than He, I fancy, in his utmost Ambition ever aspir'd to, & altho' I doubt not but Yo^{r} Interest will be able to compass All wch You propose, yet I am confident his Modesty is such, that He will be thankfull even for Less. You was extremely kind in introducing Him to my Lord Treasurer; but I am afraid he would make as awkward a Figure there as your good freind Horace[2] did when He first waited on his Ld M.[3] My Lord has done the poor man a great deal of Honour in admitting Him to be his chaplain, & suffering Him to dedicate a Volume of Sermons to his L^{p}; and I hope He will take care not to disgrace his Patron in either of those Capacitys. I am only afraid least in the overflowings of his Gratitude he should lay his colours on with too liberal an Hand, & use the Trowell instead of the Pencill. But I will take an Opportunity of giving Him a friendly hint how apt his L^{p} will be to wince if strok'd in a clumsy manner, or in a wrong place. If I am not much mistaken in his L^{p} He would choose rather to be treated as He is by John Dunton,[4] than fall into the Hands of Some Dedicators. But such is the Unhappy Lot of some men, that they can

---

[1] See p. 388.

[2] Smalridge doubtless had in mind those lines of Swift's imitation of Horace
I. vii, beginning:

> 'Poor Swift departs, and, what is worse,
> With borrow'd Money in his Purse',

Poems, pp. 173–4. As already mentioned Swift found that on taking possession of his deanery he incurred liability to Stearne; and the expenses of installation were heavy. The poem was published 23 Oct. 1713.

[3] Maecenas.

[4] In *The Publick Spirit of the Whigs* Swift ridiculed John Dunton's pamphlet, *Neck or Nothing*, as 'the shrewdest Piece, and written with the most Spirit' of all attacks on the Ministry.

neither escape Libells, nor Pen-Knifes, nor Panegyricks. But I hope my freind Fiddis will make a discreet Use of the power which is put into his Hands, and will in that respect as well as in others [show][1] himself not altogether unworthy of the favors You have done Him at my instance, whereby You have not more oblig'd Him than you have | S^r | Yor most Humble Servant |

George Smalridge

Ch. Ch. Dec. | 26. 1713.

Address: For | The Reverend Dr. Swift Dean | of St Patricks. to be left | wth Mr Thomas, at the | Lord-Treasurer's in York- | -buildings Westminster
Postmark: 28 DE
Endorsed by Swift: Dr Smalridge

4804

Bishop Lindsay to Swift

Dec: 26th 1713

S^r

Yours of Dec: the 8th I received and have obeyed your commands; But am much troubled to find that the trade of doing ill offices is still continued.[2] As for my part, I can entirely clear myself from either writing or saying any thing to any ones prejudice upon this occasion, and if others have wounded me in the dark, it is no more than they have done before. For Archbishop Tillotson formerly remarked, that if he should hearken to what the Irish Clergy said of one another, there was not a man in the whole country that ought to be preferred.

We are now adjourned for a fortnight and the Commons for 3 weeks.[3] I hear our Ld Lieutenant is not well pleased, that we have

[1] Paper injured.

[2] Shrewsbury recommended for the Primacy an appointment from England, suggesting either the Bishop of Hereford, or Chester, or Dr. Smalridge. At the same time he complained that so little attention was paid to any advice he tendered that he was 'incapable of doing any service under the opinion the two parties have conceived of my small credit at Court' (*H.M.C., Bath MSS.* i. 245).

[3] The second Irish Parliament of Queen Anne's reign adjourned on Christmas Eve, and did not meet again. During this last session Sir Constantine Phipps was in the forefront of all debates, denounced by the Commons, applauded by the Lords. The case for him was set out in a pamphlet entitled *A Long History of a Short Session*, which may have been written by Dr. Delany. The case against him was set out in *The Conduct of the Purse in Ireland*.

adjourned short of them, and I fancy the Queen will not be well pleased that the Commons have had so little regard to the dispatch of publick business as to make so long an Adjournment as three weeks—And indeed they hereby seem to intimate, that if the Ld Ch: is not removed by that time, they will give her Majesty no more money;[1] and indeed some of them doe not stick to say as much, and think it a duty incumbent on the Crown, to turn out that Minister (how innocent soever he be) whom the Commons have addressed against.[2]

I think it is plain to any who know the state of affairs here, that no party hath strength enough directly to oppose a money bill in this Kingdom when the Government thinks fit to exert itself, as to be sure it always will doe upon such occasions—And the halfpay Officers no doubt will readily come in to that supply out of wch they are to receive their pay.

But should all fail, yet the Q: still may make herself easy by disbanding two or three regiments, and striking off some unnecessary Pensions.

Hobs in his Behemoth talks of a height in time as well as place,[3] and if ever there was a height in time here, it is certainly now; For some men seem to carry things higher according to their poor power than they did in England in 41—And they now threaten (and I am pretty well assured have resolved upon it) that if the Ch: is not discarded, they will impeach him before the Lords in England. But if they have no more to say against him, than what their address contains I think they will goe upon no very wise errand.

I question not but that you will receive the votes, Addresses and Representations of both Houses from other hands, and therefore I have not troubled you with them. But if the Parliamᵗ shall continue to sit, you may expect a greater product of that kind—For the Commons have taken upon themselves to be a Court of Judicature, have taken examinations out of the Judges hands about murder wch is treason here, without ever applying to the Government for them and before tryall have voted the Sheriffs and Officers to have done their duty and acquitted themselves well, when possibly the time

[1] The Commons had only voted supplies for three months.

[2] Before adjournment the Commons had voted an address to the Queen beseeching her to remove Phipps from office.

[3] *Behemoth; Or an Epitome of the Civil Wars of England, From 1640, to 1660,* three editions: 1679, 1680, 1682.

may yet come that some may be still hanged for that fact, wch in my poor opinion is intirely destructive of Liberty & the freedom of Elections. I am | Your most Humble servant &c.

Faulkner 1762
Swift to Archbishop King

London, Dec. 31, 1713.

My Lord,

Your Grace's Letter,[1] which I received but last Post, is of an earlier Date than what have since arrived. We have received the Address for removing the Chancellor, and the counter Addresses from the Lords and Convocation; and, you will know, before this reacheth you, our Sentiments of them here. I am at a Loss what to say in this whole Affair. When I writ to you before, I dropt a Word on Purpose for you to take Notice of; that our Court seemed resolved to be very firm in their Resolutions about *Ireland.* I think it impossible for the two Kingdoms to proceed long upon a different Scheme of Politicks. The Controversy with the City I am not Master of: It took its Rise before I ever concerned myself in the Affairs of *Ireland,* further than to be an Instrument of doing some Services to the Kingdom, for which I have been ill requited. But, my Lord, the Question with us here is, whether there was a Necessity, that the other Party should be a Majority? There was put into my Hands a List of your House of Commons, by some who know the Kingdom well: I desired they would (as they often do here) set a Mark on the Names of those who would be for the Ministry, who I found amounted to one hundred and forty-three, which I think comes within an Equality: Twenty Names besides they could not determine upon; so that suppose eight to be of the same Side, there would be a Majority by one: But, besides we reckon, that the first Number, one hundred and forty-three, would easily rise to a great Majority, by the Influence of the Government, if that had been thought fit. This is Demonstration to us; for the Government there hath more Influence than the Court here and, yet our Court carried it for many Years against a natural Majority, and a much greater one. I shall not examine the Reasons

[1] 15 Dec. 1713.

among you for proceeding otherwise, but your Grace will find, that we are determined upon the Conclusion, which is, that *Ireland* must proceed on the same Foot with *England*. I am of Opinion, my Lord, that nothing could do more Hurt to the Whig Party in both King-doms, than their Manner of proceeding in your House of Commons. It will confirm the Crown and Ministry, that there can be no Safety, while those People are able to give Disturbance; and, indeed the Effects it hath already produced here are hardly to be believed: Neither do we here think it worth our while to be opposed and encourage our Enemies only for 70,000*l.* a Year; to supply which, it may not be hard to find other Expedients; and, when there shall be Occasion for a Parliament, we are confident a new one may be called, with a Majority of Men in the Interest of the Queen and Church;[1] for, when the present Majority pretends to regard either, we look upon such Professions to signify no more than if they were penned by my Lord *Wharton*, or Mr. *Molesworth*.[2] I have suffered very much for my Tenderness to some Persons of that Party, which I still preserve; but I believe it will not be long in my Power to serve those who may want it. It would be endless to recount to your Grace the Reproaches that have been made me on Account of your Neigh-bour.[3]

It is but true, my Lord, we do not care to be troubled with the Affairs of *Ireland*; but, there being no War, nor Meeting of Parlia-ment, we have Leisure at present: Besides, we look upon ourselves as touched in the tenderest Part. We know the Whig Party are pre-paring to attack us next Sessions, and their prevailing in *Ireland*, would, we think, be a great Strength and Encouragement to them here: Besides, our Remissness would dishearten our Friends, and make them think, we acted a trimming Game. There are some Things which we much wonder at, as they are represented: The Address for removing the Chancellor is grounded upon two Facts;

[1] Shrewsbury, writing to Bolingbroke, more sagaciously gave it as his opinion that if a new Parliament was chosen 'the humour of the House of Commons would not mend' (*H.M.C., Bath MSS.* i. 243).

[2] Swift in observations upon members of the Irish Privy Council which he submitted to Oxford characterized Robert Molesworth as 'very bad' (*H.M.C., Portland MSS.* v. 211). He was, however, raised to the peerage in 1716 as Viscount Molesworth of Swords in reward for his support of the Hanoverian succession (Lodge, *Peerage of Ireland*, v. 135).

[3] i.e. Stearne, who was still residing in St. Patrick's deanery, had voted against the government.

in the former of which he was only concerned with several others. The Criminal was poor and penitent, and a *Nolle prosequi* was no illegal Thing.[1] As to *Moore*'s Business, the Chancellor's Speech on that Occasion hath been transmitted hither, and seemeth to clear him from the Imputation of prejudging.[2] Another Thing we wonder at, is to find the Commons in their Votes approve the sending for the Guards, by whom a Man was killed. Such a Thing, would they say, look monstrous in *England*.

Your Grace seemeth to think, they would not break on Money Matters; but, we are taught another Opinion, that they will not pass the great Bill until they have Satisfaction about the Chancellor; and what the Consequence of that will be, I suppose, you may guess from what you know by this Time.

My Lord, we can judge no otherwise here than by the Representations made to us. I sincerely look upon your Grace to be Master of as much Wisdom and Sagacity as any Person I have known, and from my particular Respect to you and your great Abilities, shall never presume to censure your Proceedings, until I am fully apprized of the Matter. Your Grace is looked upon here as altogether in the other Party, which I do not allow when it is said to me. I conceive you to follow the Dictates of your Reason and Conscience; and, whoever does that, will, in publick Management, often differ as well from one Side as another.

As to myself, I take *Ireland* to be the worst Place to be in while the Parliament sits, and probably I may think the same of *England* in a Month or two. I have few Obligations (further than personal Friendship and Civilities) to any Party: I have nothing to ask for but a little Money to pay my Debts, which I doubt they never will give me; and wanting Wisdom to judge better, I follow those who I think, are most for preserving the Constitution in Church and State, without examining whether they do so from a Principle of Virtue or of Interest.

---

[1] The first charge against Phipps was that he had caused the prosecution of a bookseller, who had sold a pamphlet, 'impeaching her Majesty's title to the Crown', to be dropped.—Ball.

[2] The second charge against Phipps was that in a speech to the Corporation of Dublin 'he had inflamed and prepossessed the minds of the aldermen' against one Dudley Moore, who was about to be prosecuted for riot on the occasion when Garth's prologue was called for in the Dublin theatre.—Ball.

Swift to the Rev. John Worrall

London. Dec^br 31. 1713.

S^rı

I received last Post, your Letter relating to a Lease to be made to My Ld Abercorn[2] by the Vicars Chorall[3] I desire you will let the Vicars know, that I shall to the utmost resent their presuming to make any Lease without the consent of the Dean and Chapter, which they are bound to have by their own Subscriptions.[4] Let them know further that I am very well instructed in my own Power both from the late Dean, and from Dr Synge; and that I will immediately deprive every Man of them who consents to any Lease[5] without the Approbation aforesaid, and shall think the Church well ridd of such men who to gratify their unreasonable Averice would starve their Successors. I shall write this Post to Dr Synge, to take[6] proper Measures on this Occasion. I desire you will read this Letter to the Vicars, and let them count upon it that I will be as good as my Word. I am | Sr Your most humble Servt |

Jonath: Swift.

Address: For |
          The rev^d Mr John Woorral

---

[1] In the possession of Mr. W. R. Le Fanu, Librarian to the Royal College of Surgeons of England.

[2] James Hamilton, 1656–1734, sixth Earl of Abercorn, succeeded his cousin in the title in 1701. Swift had known him for some years; but he was a Whig and paid him little attention, earning Swift's vexation, who claimed that 'The Whelp owes me all the kind Receptions he has had from the Ministry' (*Journal*, 1 Jan. 1712–13). This may account for the tone of the letter.

[3] As Dean's Vicar Worrall was at the head of the Vicars Choral.

[4] The land which it was proposed to lease was already held by the Earl of Abercorn, and lay behind his Dublin residence which was situated on the western side of St. Stephen's Green. See Mason's *History of St. Patrick's*, p. 97; and *The Georgian Society Records*, ii. 99.—Ball.

[5] A word is scrawled out before 'Lease'.

[6] 'and' scrawled out before 'to take'.

PRINTED IN GREAT BRITAIN
AT THE UNIVERSITY PRESS, OXFORD
BY VIVIAN RIDLER
PRINTER TO THE UNIVERSITY